Index to Collinson's History of Somerset

Edwin Pearce

INDEX

TO

COLLINSON'S HISTORY OF SOMERSET

*EDITED BY THE REV. F. W. WEAVER, M.A., AND THE
REV. E. H. BATES, M.A.*

INCLUDING A
SUPPLEMENTAL INDEX (ALPHABET AND ORDINARY)
TO ALL THE ARMORIAL BEARINGS MENTIONED IN THE WORK,
CONTRIBUTED BY
LT.-COL. J. R. BRAMBLE, F.S.A.

Taunton:

BARNICOTT AND PEARCE, ATHENÆUM PRESS, FORE STREET

1898.

BARNICOTT AND PEARCE

PRINTERS

PREFACE.

THE two following extracts tell us practically all that is known about John Collinson.

1. From Foster's *Alumni Oxonienses*.

> Collinson, John, son of John Collinson, of Bromham, Wilts, cler., B.N.C. matric. 8 April 1775, aged 18 : "The Historian of Somerset," V. of Long Ashton, Somerset 1787 and P.C. Whitchurch ; died 27 Sept. 1793.

2. From *Dictionary of National Biography*, vol. xi, p. 382 [under the signature W. H.]

> Collinson, John (1757 ?—1793), county historian, vicar of Clanfield, Oxfordshire, was instituted to the vicarage of Long Ashton, Somerset, in 1787, and also held the perpetual curacy of Whitchurch in the same county. He died at the Hotwells Bristol on the 27 Sept. 1793 at the age of 36. He published 'The Beauties of British Antiquities selected from the writings of Antiquaries' 1779 8vo. and in 1781 issued proposals for a history of the county of Somerset in one volume folio. The work was finally published in 1791, with the title 'History and Antiquities of the County of Somerset collected from authentick Records and an actual Survey made by the late Mr. Edmund Rack' in 3 vols. 4to. (For account of Rack see Collinson's *Somerset*, i 77). Collinson appears to have largely used and indeed to have appropriated bodily from the Palmer MSS. now in the possession of Sir Alexander Acland Hood, bart., of St. Audries, Somerset. The 'History' was severely criticized in the *Gentleman's Magazine*.
>
> [*Gent. Mag.*, 1793, lxiii, i 148, 236, ii 865 ; Collinson's *Somerset*, ii 299 ; *Hist. MSS. Comm.* 6th Report Introd. p. xiii and 344 ; *Athenæum*, 8 Jan. 1887, p. 65].

The fact that will strike everyone is that Collinson was only thirty-four when the history was published. It seems almost incredible. He was only twenty-four when he issued the proposals for bringing out a history, and within ten years he had gathered, copied, digested, and compiled the three familiar quarto volumes which have made his name a household word in the county of Somerset. It is not surprising to learn that within two more years he was dead. Much original research cannot of course be expected : he took the standard antiquarian and historical works and based his history upon them. That, after the lapse of a century, errors many, derivations comical in their genesis, observations trivial or puerile, remarks telling of an artificial standard of taste and feeling, are scattered over the pages ; this does not detract in the slightest degree from the credit due to a man who first made his way through the enormous mass of details which make up parochial history. The critic of the _Gentleman's Magazine_ may have satisfied himself of Collinson's incompetence, but the Rev. R. W. Eyton could thus write of him,* "It would ill become us to proceed further in our enumeration of authorities for the present work without acknowledging a great obligation to the labours of Collinson, the Somerset historian. His discernment in the matter of Domesday nomenclature, and of the principles which guide those who would seek the modern equivalents of Domesday forms, was as keen as that of the great Anglo–Saxon scholar Kemble. His topographical knowledge was more than adequate to his work. Having adhered to his method with the utmost precision and constancy, he has so much the more enlightened us on the many questions where Domesday identities can only be established by post-Domesday evidences." This is no faint praise. And again there is one point in which Collinson's history becomes of greater value every year. We mean in regard to the many monumental inscriptions swept out of the churches by the besom of Restoration (save the mark !) but happily conserved in his pages. His history is indeed, both for himself and for the ill-treated nobles, squires, knights of the shire, incumbents, _et hoc genus omne_, a '_monumentum ære perennius._'

An index was the one thing wanting to the book, and this has now been ably supplied by Mr. Edwin Pearce. It is hardly an Irishism to say that if Collinson could have had this index before him while he was writing, it would have saved the reader many a doubt as to the rightful spelling of names and places, in which the historian displays a playful irregularity.

The thanks of the Society are due to Lieut.-Col. Bramble, F.S.A., for his excellent ' Armorial Index.'

It should be noted that Vol. I has eighty-four pages under the head of " Bath," after which the numbers begin afresh from page 1. These eighty-four pages are in this Index distinguished as " B " _ex. gra._ B 46. In Vol. II, pages 97 to 104 are numbered 89 to 96, those numbers being used twice over. This error should be corrected. In this Index it is assumed that the correction has been made.

F. W. W.
E. H. B.

* _Domesday Studies in Somerset_, i 10.

CONTENTS

PLATES

ADDENDA.

Berneford, Agnes, married (1) Sir John Argentine, (2) John Nerford, (3) John Maltravers, iii 206.

Blake, Humphrey, buried in Over Stowey church, i 260.

Canning, Letitia, monument in Bath abbey, 1786, B 68.

Cazalet, Peter, monument in Bath abbey, 1788, B 68.

Dallamore, Charity, wife of Walter Wiltshire, i 168.

INDEX

TO

COLLINSON'S HISTORY OF SOMERSET.

A

Abarough, John, owner of land in North Barrow, ii 62; marries Margery Gregory, 63; John of Ditcheat marries Isabel Hannam, 63; Anthony, 63; Hercules, 63; Mary, 63; Agnes, 63.

Abbas Combe (*see* Abbots Combe).

Abbey baths, Bath, position of, B 41; churchyard, 33; green, 33; lane, 33, 58; street, 33.

Abbey House, Glastonbury, ii 262.

Abbeys.—Athelney, i 86. Banwell, iii 566. Bath, B 54. Brewton, i 214. Cleeve, iii 511. Glastonbury, ii 240. Keynsham, 402. Muchelney, iii 134.

Abbodeston, Walter and Robert de, held lands of the abbot of Glastonbury, ii 244.

Abbot, Thomas, inscription in North-Cheriton church, ii 360; Thomas, benefactor to Horsington, 373.

Abbot's Causeway, Mark, i 183.

Abbot's Hill, or Birt's Hill, Pendomer, ii 348.

Abbot's Tithing, Portbury, iii 142.

Abbots Combe, Abbas Combe, or Combe Porter, ii 359; situation, 359; Domesday survey, 359; owned by the abbey of Shaftesbury, 359; granted at the Dissolution to William Sherrington, 359; subsequently owned by Richard Duke, 359; George Sprint, 359; Earl of Uxbridge, 359; Temple-Combe hamlet, 359; granted by Serlo Fitz-Odo to the Knights Templars, 359; afterwards granted to the knights of St. John of Jerusalem, 359; Richard Andrewes and Leonard Chamberlain, 359; Lord Clinton, 359; Richard Duke, 359; Sir William Wogan, 359; chapel ruins, 359; church, 359; bells (5) 359; lands in, called Gadgrove, 373.

Abbots Leigh, iii 152; situation, 152; Leigh Down, 152; limestone rocks, 152; Mineral products, 152; owned by the bishop of Coutances, 153; Robert Fitz-Harding,

Abbots Leigh—*continued*.

153; canons of St. Augustine, Bristol, 153; Paul Bush, bishop of Bristol, 153; the family of Norton, 153; the family of Trenchard, 154; Robert Hippisley, who assumed the name of Trenchard, 154; Manor House, 154; church and its monuments, 154; bells (6), 154; Charles II, concealed here by Sir George Norton, 153; Thomas Gordon, translator of Tacitus, lived here, 154.

Abbotsbury abbey, Dorset, owned Holwell, ii 369. Skilgate, settled on, iii 545.

Abdick, hundred of, i 1; topography, 1; part of the ancient possessions of the Crown, 1; given to Henry de Ortrai, 1; held by William de Montacute, 1; John de Beaufort, 1; Henry de Beaufort, 2; vested in bishops of Bath and Wells, 2; licence granted to bishop of London, 2; owned by the Speke family, 2; Lord North, 2; hundred-court, held at Ilford bridges inn, 2; population, 2.

Abindon, Richard de, and Maud his wife held land in Little Lopen, Drayton, and South Petherton, iii 108.

Abraham, Rev. Mr., incumbent of Carhampton, ii 3; Adam, of Purtington and Wadham college, Oxon, tomb in Winsham churchyard, 480; Atkins, 480.

Abrincis, Gilbert de, drowned at sea, ii 390; Ada de, married Fulke Paganel, 390; Hugh de, 365.

Abyndon, Henry, master of St. Catherine's hospital, Bedminster, ii 283.

Acford, Richard, receives pension from Brewton, i 214.

Ache, ancient name of Oake, iii 273.

Achelai, ancient name of Hurst, iii 2.

Acland family, owners of Curry Rivel, i 27; Fivehead, 40; East Lyng, 85. Bankland,

Aelfred, first sheriff of Bath, B 22.

Aelfric, abbot of Glastonbury, ii 249.

Aelfstan, abbot of Glastonbury, ii 249.

Aelfwithe, Queen, gave Winscombe to the monks of Glastonbury, iii 612.

Aelmer, holder of Cutcombe, ii 5.

Aethelred, King, gave the tithes of Somerton Erleigh to the abbey of Athelney, iii 186.

Agard, Cecily, married Thomas Arthur, iii 178.

Agricultural products of the county, i xv.

Agricultural society, institution of, in 1777, B 79.

Ahmuty, Alice Frideswide, monument in Bath abbey, 1790, B 67.

Ailesford, Lady, owned Puriton, ii 396.

Ailgi, name given to Yellow in Domesday survey, iii 546.

Ailmar held land in Pennard-Minster, iii 478; and Halse, 527, 528.

Ailric held Ash Priors (Aixe), ii 497. Easton-in-Gordano, iii 146. Hiwis (Huish-Champflower), 530.

Ailuert, holder of Beckington, ii 198.

Ailwacre, held Blackford, iii 452.

Ailward, holder of Fiddington, i 241. Stawley, iii 28; Samford-Arundel, 26; Quarum Kitnor, 556.

Aiselle (*see* Ashill).

Aishe family owned Chelvy, ii 317; Richard, 317; Hugh, 317; John owned Chelvy, Midghill, Tickenham, and Compton Bishop, 317; Joan, 317; Mary, 317; John married Isabel Gorges, 317.

Aissecome, ancient name of Ashcombe, iii 468.

Aissecote, ancient name of Ashcot, iii 425.

Aisseford (*see* Ashford).

Aisseforde (*see* Exford).

Akeman street, i 100.

Alabaster quarries, Somerton, iii 182.

Alan-Zouche, Helen, second wife of Nicholas de Sto. Mauro, ii 54.

Albaniaco de, family (*see* Daubeney).

Albemarle, William de, held Middle-Chinnock, ii 328; Geffrey de, 328.

Albert, abbot of Glastonbury, ii 249.

Albin, memorial tablet in Brewton church, i 218.

Albini family (*see* Daubeney).

Albriet held Quarum-Mounceaux, iii 556.

Albyn, Rev. Lancelot, incumbent of Wembdon, iii 104.

Alchorn, Rev. Edward, monument in Bath abbey, 1652, B 67.

Alcombe, vill of Dunster, ii 16; Domesday survey, 16; held by Algar, 16; given by Sir William de Mohun to the priory of Dunster, 16.

Aldebury, Walter, owned Alston, ii 393.

Aldedeford (*see* Alford).

Aldenham, owned by the Wrotham family, iii 64; by Richard de Placetis, who took the name of Wrotham, 65.

Aldham, heir of Baldwin de, owner of Chilterne-Fage, iii 217.

Aldhelm, founder of monastery at Frome, ii 186; founder of Malmesbury abbey, iii 473; chapel erected to his memory at Doulting, 473; church built on site of, 474.

Aldhelm, Athelm, Aldhun or Aldun, abbot of Glastonbury, ii 249. first bishop of Wells, iii 377. owned Wellington, Buckland, and Lydiard, ii 482.

Aldida held Foxcote, iii 349.

Aldred, holder of Fivehead, i 40.

Aldridge, Rev. Joseph, incumbent of North Petherton, iii 74.

Alduin held Shipham, iii 601.

Aldwick manor (*see* Butcombe).

Aldwyn, bishop of Wells, owned Wellington, Buckland, and Lydiard, ii 482.

Alentone, ancient name of Alhampton, iii 471.

Alestan held Barton-David, ii 64. Wick, iii 332; land in Butleigh, 448.

Alexander, dean of Wells, 1180, i 189.

Alfagestone (*see* Alfoxton).

Alfakeston, John de, purchases land from William de Cunteville, i 266.

Alfhilla held lands in Westcombe, iii 466.

Alfi held Durleigh, i 78. Kilmington, iii 39.

Alford (Aldedeford), its situation, ii 58; Alford Well, mineral spring, 58; Domesday survey, 58; owned by Earl Morton and held by Anseger; by Godric T.R.E. 58; owned by the family of Fitzpaine and John Willes, 58; the church (All Saints), its monument and benefactions, 59.

Alford Mineral Spring, i xvii.

Alford family, tombs in Ashill church, i 13; Curry Rivel church, 29; Thomas and Mary, memorial stones in Ashill church, 13; Rev. Samuel, J.P., xlii; Rev. Samuel, incumbent of Curry-Rivel, 27. Rev. Samuel, Richard, Lætitia, Richard, and Marmaduke, monument in Weston-Zoyland church, iii 441. Rev. Thomas, incumbent of Ashill, i 13; Rev. Thomas, J.P., xlii. Rev. Thomas, founded school at Weston-Zoyland, iii 441. Rev. Mr., incumbent of Chard, ii 473.

Alfoxton, i 263; manor in Stringston, Domesday survey, 264; owned by Alured de Ispania and held by Rannulf; by Alwi T.R.E. 264; held by William de Alveston of Philip de Columbers, whose right is disputed by Adam de Cunteville, and the lands subsequently released by Richard de Cunteville to William de Alfoxton, 264; and subsequently owned by the families of Burlond, Ayshe, Popham, and St. Albyn, 264, 265.

Alfoxton, William de, accepts release of lands from Richard de Cunteville, i 264; William, son of John, sells his right to Robert

Almsworthy, ii 21.

Almundesford (*see* Almsford).

Alneto, Alexander de, owned Camely, gave it to St. Peter's church, Bath, ii *125*; inscription in St. Peter's church, 125. Robert de, prior, in England, of the Order of St. John of Jerusalem, iii 97.

Alno or Danno or Dando family, owned Compton-Dando, ii 421; Alexander de, i *xxvi*, *xxviii*, ii 421. Robert de, ii 421; Henry de, owned also lands in Dorset, 421; Fulk de, 421; Gefferey, owned also lands in Ashton, 421; Alexander de, 421.

Alnod held Blackford, iii 452. Broomfield, i 72. Bradney, iii 92. Broadway, i 18. Clapton, ii 73. Holton, iii 453. Ultone, ii 73; Withycombe, 47. Yarlington, i 228.

Alnod, a monk, held land in Pilton, iii 480.

Alownshay hamlet, Kingston, iii 322; church or chapel (demolished), 323.

Alpher, duke, buried at Glastonbury, ii 262.

Alps of Somersetshire, ii 1.

Alresford (*see* Allerford).

Alric held land in Compton-Bishop, iii 582. Doverhay, ii 23. East-Harptree, iii 587. Freshford, i 125. Goldsoncot, iii 510; Grindham, 28; Halsway, 545; Holford, 456; Kilve, 532; Lydiard St. Laurence, 265; Thorn-Coffin, 322.

Alrod, Walter, gives pulpit cloth to South-Brent church, i 200; memorial stone, 200.

Alstan, bishop of Sherborne, leader of the Saxons against the Danes at the battle of Stoke Courcy, i 249.

Alta villa (*see* Hauteville).

Altone, ancient name of Holton, iii 453.

Altremine church, Cornwall, owned by Montacute priory, iii 312.

Aluer, held Seaborough, ii 171.

Aluerd held Charlton-Adam, iii 191. Timberscombe, ii 44.

Alured held Belluton, ii 401, 434. Bradford, iii 243; Chilthorne-Domer, 216. Chinnock, ii 327; Chisselborough, 330; Cloford, 205. Hill-Bishops, iii 254. Iford, i 124. lands in Keynsham Hundred, ii 399. Monksilver, iii 487, 535; Montacute, 311. Pendomer, ii 348; Rodehuish, 2. lands in Taunton, iii 231; Twerton, 347; Wick, in Camerton, 332; Woolavington, 427, 437.

Alured de Lincoln, held Midsummer Norton, ii 150.

Aluric held Ashway, iii 529. Avill, ii 15. land in Badgworth, iii 565. Bathwick, i 120; Bickenhall, 62. Blackmore, iii 579. Bratton, ii 31; Chew Magna, 94; Coleford, 446; Dunster, 7; Farmborough, 424; Holnicot, 41; Keynsham, 402; Lydford, West, 84. Martock, iii 4; Monk-

Aluric—*continued.*

silver, 535; Newton St. Loe, 341; Portishead, 144. Redlinch, i 225. Rodhuish, ii 2. lands added afterwards to Somerton, iii 183; Taunton, 231. Winford, ii 320. Wolley, i 167. Wraxall, iii 155.

Alvera held land in Wellington, ii 482.

Alvered, Nicholas de, held lands in Keynsham Hundred, ii 399.

Alveston, William, held Alfoxton, i 264.

Alviet held Clatworthy, iii 509, and land in Telsford, 363.

Alviet, the priest, held one hide in South Petherton, iii 111.

Alvington, hamlet, Brimpton-D'Evercy, iii 214.

Alwacre, holder of Over-Weare, i 185.

Alwald held Pendomer, ii 348. Swell, i 65.

Alward held land in Angersleigh, iii 241; Blackford, 452. Compton Paunceford, ii 76. Congresbury, iii 585; Dowlish-Wake, 119; East-Lydford, 196; Elborough, 591. Farringdon, ii 61. Gautheney, i 239; Halswell, 80. Holcombe, ii 456. land in Holford, iii 456; Hunstile, 89; Kilton, 531. Lexworthy, i 194. Lidiard and Lega, iii 231; Lopen, 122; Preston-Bermondsey, 223. Puckington, i 56. Seaborough, ii 171. Sevington, iii 123; Stawel, 431; Stoke-Giffard, 602; land in Taunton, 231. Ternoc, i 176. land in Twinney, iii 334; land in Wells, 393; White-Stanton, 126; Wigborough, 110: lands in Worspring, 594.

Alwarditone (*see* Chapel Allerton).

Alwi held Alfoxton, i 264; Charlinch, 238. Chilthorne-Domer, iii 217. Currypool, i 239. Durston, iii 95; East-Bower, 84. Goathurst, i 80. Hill-Farence, iii 256; Huntworth, 71; Hurst, 8. Isle Brewers, i 53. Luckington, ii 446. Malrige, i 244. Michaelchurch, iii 99. Nether-Adbeer, ii 382. Over-Stowey, i 259; Preston-Plucknet, iii 223. Spaxton, i 243; Stringston, 261. Weston-Bampfylde, ii 89. Wolmersdon, iii 71.

Alwin held Cossington, iii 434. Huntspill, ii 390. Lufton (*Luston*, Collinson), iii 321; Sandford-Bret, 543; Stochet, 320; Westrow, 487.

Alwine held Edstone, i 252. Weston-Bampfylde, ii 89.

Alwod held Littleton, ii 148.

Alwold held Alston, ii 393; Cadbury, North, 65; Cadbury, South, 73. Dunkerton, iii 337; land in Ham, 444. Midsummer Norton, ii 150; Maperton, 85; North Cheriton, 360. Pitcombe, i 224. Stratton-on-the-Fosse, ii 458; Wanstraw, 229; Winford, 320.

Alwyn, bishop of Wells, iii 377; effigy in Wells cathedral, 399.

Archdeaconries of the county, i *lii.*

Archer, Margaret, third wife of John de Vernai, and mother of Alexander of Wolmerston, i 254. Patrick, a monk of Bath, who received pension, B 57. Theophilus owned part of Rowberrow, iii 599. Thomas, sheriff, 1718, i *xxxviii.*

Arches, Agnes de (mother of Peter de Falke-berge) founded the nunnery of Nun-Kelling, iii 6.

Archiaco, Adomar de, ii 150. Fulk de married Mabel de Fortibus, iii 462.

Archis, William de, married Beatrix Malet, i 90.

Are (*see* Oare).

Arden, Richard Pepper, J.P., i *xlii.*

Ardern, Peter de, did service of Ralph Daubeney for the manors of Barrington and Chillington, iii 113.

Argentine, Sir John, Knt., married Agnes Berneford, iii 206; Agnes, widow of Sir John, married John Nerford, 206.

Argyle buildings, Bath, B 39, 74.

Aris, William, buried in Farmborough church, ii 425.

Arleston, John, monk of Bath, who received a pension, B 57.

Arms :—

Abarough, ii 63. Acland, i 256. Acton, ii 312; iii 589. Adams, ii 110. Allen, i 119. Ansell, ii 103. Arthur, iii 177, 179; Ash, 163. de Ashton, ii 297; Arundel, 39. Aubemarle, iii 360; Ayshe, 112.

Baber, ii 97; Babington, 450. Bacon, iii 20; Baker, 27; Ballowe, 176. Bampfield, ii 313, 453. Banbury, iii 198. Barbe, i 236. Bardolf, iii 589; Barnard, 463; Basset, 166; Bath abbey, 341; Bath priory, 398; Baudrip, 91; Bave, 166. Bayouse, ii 312. Beauchamp, iii 320. Beckington, ii 438; iii 201, 376, 568. Bennet, iii 336, 350. Berkeley, i 217; iii 143, 166, 590. Biggs, i 173. Bingham, ii 350. Bisse, iii 467. Blanchard, i 139, 140. Blake, ii 498. Blathwaite, i 132. Blewet, or Bluet, iii 29, 260. Blount, i 263. Bole, ii 443. Botetourt, iii 359; Botreaux, 359. Boulting, i 192. Bower, ii 407; Bowyer, 10. Bradford, ii 208. Bradney (Beatrix de), iii 92; Bradney (Simon de), 92. Bragge, ii 77; Branch (or Braunche), 187; Brattone, 31. Brent, i 256, iii 160, 435. Bretesche, ii 315. Brett, iii 127. Brewton monastery, i 214. Brice, iii 121; Brickdale, 454. Bridges, ii 405, 408. Bridgwater town, iii 76; Brito, 544; Brokesby, 261. Brome, ii 339; Brooke, 300. Broughton, i 258; Brown, 135. Bull, 219, ii 151, 192, iii 428. Bubwith, iii 399, 408. Burgess, i 162. Burnel, iii 359. Burton, i 165. Buckland, ii 142. Byam, ii 24. Bykele, iii 15.

Arms—*continued.*

Cabell, ii 193; Camville, ii 358; Cannon, 492. Capell, i 153. Carent, ii 367. Carew, iii 332, 333, 517. Cary of Gotten, i 256, 455; Cary of Putney, 163; Cely, 77. Chaldicote, or Chalcot, iii 21; Champneys, 350; ii 223. Chandos, ii 405. Chapman, iii 345. Chedder, ii 156; iii 176, 575, 576, 577, 589. Cheney, ii 376. Chetle, i 60; Cheyne, 161. Chichester, iii 541, 549; Chipleigh, 260. Choke, ii 300, 311. Churchey, iii 35; Churchill, 581; Clambow, 589. Clarke, ii 99, iii 23, 268, 421; Clavelshey, iii 73; Claville, 260; Clivedon, 167. Clutterbuck, i 149. Codrington, ii 235. Coffin, iii 322. Coker, ii 343. Cole (Coles), iii 163. Collins, ii 99; Colmer, 61. Columbers, iii 264, 551; Compton, ii 443; iii 112; Coney, 95; Cooke, ii 303. Coopey, iii 160. Cork and Orrery, ii 188. Cornish, iii 401; Cornwall, 359. Cotton, i 164. Cottrell, ii 321. Court, i 222, ii 470. Courtney, ii 343, iii 359, 360. Coward, iii 407, 468; Cozens, 416. Crayle, i 149. Crofts, iii 150, 606. Crooke, i 209. Crowther, ii 491. Cuffe, i 77, iii 261.

Darknell, ii 455. Davis, ii 308, iii 165. Dawe, iii 472. Delamere, ii 218, 220. Desmond, iii 261. Dickinson, ii 81, 417. Doble, iii 291. Dodington, or Doddington, ii 373, iii 519, 593. Donne, i 217. Dormer, iii 361. Draper, ii 333. Draycot, i 225; Durston, 202.

Edgell, ii 202. Edward the Confessor, iii 401. Elsworth, ii 45; England, 171. Englowes, iii 159. Erleigh, ii 200.

Fane, ii 394. Farewel, iii 255, 256; Fauconbergh, or Falconbridge, 6. Feckenham, i 141; Fewtrell, 18; Fisher, 165; Fitchet, 94, 224; Fitz-James, 226. Fitz-Nicholas, iii 166. Flower, ii 220. Fluri, or Flory, iii 267; de la Ford, 91; Forest, 402. Fortescue, ii 464, iii 469. Forward, i 162. Foster, ii 436. Fowel, iii 256. Frankland, i 161.

Gambon, i 256. Gatchell, ii 484. Gay, iii 341. Gilbert, i 122. Gifford, iii 373; Glastonbury abbey, 267. Godolphin, i 216. Godwyn, iii 84. Gold, ii 264. Goodden, iii 11. Goodhind, ii 443; Goodman, 98; Gore, 311. Gorges, iii 156, 157, 159; Gould, 219; Gournay, 320, 590. Greville, earl of Warwick, ii 104; Gunning, iii 465; Gunter, 130.

Hales, ii 455. Hall, i 164, iii 407. Hampton, iii 176, 589, 620; Harbin, 206, 261; Harewel, 383. Harington, i 129, ii 130, iii 347. Harptree, iii 590. Hart, ii 99. Hartgill, iii 42. Harvey, ii 59, 121, 308. Hawley, i 115, iii 261. Hayes, iii 406; Healy, 407; Heron, 133; Hewish,

Athelney abbots, list of, i 87, 88; landowners, temp. Ed. I, i *xxvi.* received pension from Dunster, ii 41. gave lands in Ham for the support of lights in the chapel of St. Mary, Bridgwater, iii 84; composition with the hospital of St. John, Bridgwater, 84.

At-Brook or Brook family (*see* Brook).

Athelred granted Ham to the abbey of Athelney, iii 83.

Athelstan, Duke, i 206.

Athelstan, Earl, bestowed mills on Glastonbury abbey, ii 462; buried at Glastonbury, 262.

Athelstan, King, granted Relengen (Ling) to the church of St. Peter, Athelney, i 84; gave the manor of Wrington to duke Athelstan, 206. gave Marksbury to duke Athelm, ii 426; gave Priston to Bath abbey, 430. kept feast at Petherton, iii 107; founded Muchelney abbey, 134.

Athelward, abbot of Athelney, 1016, i 87.

Athelwin, abbot of Athelney, i 87.

Atherstone, hamlet of White Lackington, i 68.

Atherton, John, bishop of Waterford and Lismore, born at Bawdrip, iii 93.

Atiltone (*see* Ilton).

Atkins, Abraham, governor of Bath hospital, B 47.

Atkyns, William, purchased Burgages in Chard without license, ii 474.

Atkys, John, benefaction to Brushford, iii 507.

Aubemarle (*see* D'Aubemarle).

Aubeney (*see* D'Aubeney).

Auberville, Odburuile, or Otberville, Ralph de, owned lands in Newton, iii 63. Robert de, received lands from William the Conqueror, i *xxv.* held lands in Milverton Hundred, iii 13: and in the Hundred of North Petherton, 53; owned Wellisford, 19; Melcombe, 73; land in Ham, 444; Withypool, 558; Sir Hugh de, a daughter of, married Philip de Maunsel, 72.

Aucome (*see* Alcombe).

Audley family owned Otterhampton, i 242. Stanton, ii 16; Puriton, 396. Ayle, iii 546; Blagdon, 569; Stowey, 552; Woolavington, 437; Hugh de, second husband of Margaret de Clare, 148; Joan, married Sir John Touchet, 552. Margaret, second wife of John Luttrell, ii 11. Margaret married Sir Roger Hillary, iii 552. Nicholas de married Joane Martin, ii 84, 132; James succeeded to the Lydford estates: was attainted for treason, 84, 132; Phillippa, wife of Richard Hadley, 48, iii 254.

Audley, James, Lord Audley, son of Nicholas and Joan, Countess of Lincoln, inherited Stowey and other lands formerly belonging to Lord Columbers, married Joan Mortimer, iii 552; Nicholas, lord, married Alice de Beaumont, countess of Buchan, died without issue, 552; Sir John Touchet, Lord

Audley—*continued.*

Audley, succeeded to the title and half the estates of Nicholas, Lord Audley, 552; James Touchet, lord, slain at Bloreheath, 552; John Touchet, lord, 552; James Touchet, lord, executed on Tower hill (1497), 553; John Touchet, lord, received certain of his father's estates: sold the castle and land in Stowey, 553; George Touchet, lord, created earl of Castlehaven: governor of the Netherlands, married Lucy Mervin, 553; Lady Elizabeth owned Ayle, 546.

Audry, corruption of Othery, iii 443.

Auger, Robert, M.P. for Bath, 1396, B 20.

Aula, Warren de, gave Budscombe to Buckland priory, iii 98.

Aulton, Henry de, sheriff, 1262, i *xxxiv.*

Aumari, Gilbert de, ii 156.

Aungel, John, master of St. Catherine's hospital, Bedminster, ii 283.

Aungier, William, i 262.

Aure, John de, sheriff, 1254, i *xxxiv.* William de, ii 33.

Avalon, ancient name of Glastonbury, ii 240, 269; King Arthur and Queen Guinever, buried at, 240, 262.

Avalon, John Mordaunt, earl of, ii 269.

Ave Maria preserved, ii 384.

Avele, Gefferey de, holder of half a knight's fee from John de Mohun, ii 14. Richard held land in Clatworthy, iii 509.

Avena (*see* Avill).

Avenant family held Worle, iii 540; Walter de temp. Ed. I, i *xxix,* iii 540. Richard de, landowner, temp. Ed. I, i *xxix,* iii 540; Alice married Thomas Fitzours, 540; arms, 540.

Avery, John and Thomas, representatives in Parliament of Nether Wear, i 184. William, monument in Bath abbey, 1745, B 67.

Avill, vill of Dunster, Domesday survey, ii 15; owned by William de Mohun and held by Ralph: Aluric T.R.E. 15.

Avon hamlet, iii 614.

Avon river, its course, i *xii, xiii.* made navigable, arrival of first barge, B 28, *see* also ii 400, 431, iii 139, 146, 347.

Avon street, Bath, B 35.

Avury, Mrs. Joan, bequest to Frome, ii 198.

Ax, river, course, i *xiii, xiv, see* also ii 159, 478, iii 417, 571, 608.

Axbridge chace, i *xv.*

Axbridge deanery, taxation of pope Nicholas, ii 245.

Axbridge manor, granted to the bishopric of Bath and Wells, iii 381, 567; rating of, in 1293, 394; accompted for by the bishops in 1329, 394; lands in, granted by Roger Hanam to Robert de Chedder, 576.

Axford's buildings, Bath, B 38.

Axford, John, mayor of Bath, 1696, B 26.

Ayle, a manor in Stogumber, owned by lady Elizabeth Audley, iii 546.

Aylesford, earl of, J.P., i *xli*. Lady, owner of Staye manor, i 40; lady, owner of Isle Abbots, 51.

Aylworth, Mary, grand-daughter of Thomas Montague, and heiress to Cathanger manor, i 41.

Aysh, Thomas, M.P. for Bath, 1583, B 21.

Ayshe, James, of Chagford, owner of Alfoxton, i 264; John, who sells it to Richard Popham, 264. James and Elizabeth, monuments in South Petherton church, iii 112.

Ayshent, John, prior of Taunton, 1475, iii 236.

Azeline, progenitor of the Percival family, ii 137. held Langridge, i 131. Farrington Gournay, ii 137; West-Harptree Gournay, 140; Stone Easton, 154; Bishopworth, 284; Babington, 450; land in Mells, 462. lands in Westcombe, iii 466; Hutton, 590; Elborough, 591. John de assumed the name of de Harptree, ii 137.

Azor held Warley, i 112. Combe St. Nicholas, ii 475.

B

Baalun, William, held lands in Dunkerton, iii 338

Babcary, its situation, ii 60; Domesday survey, 60; owned by Hunfridus (or Humphry): held by Bruno T.R.E. 60; owned by the families of Beauchamp of Hatch, D'Erleigh, Seymour, Bampfylde, and Stawel, 60; hamlets of Stert and Farringdon, 61; land owned by the hospital of St. John, Wells, 61; the church (Holy Cross) and its monuments, 61, 62; benefactions, 62.

Babcary, John of, master of St. Catherine's hospital, Bedminster, ii 283.

Baber, Benjamin, mayor of Bath, 1677, 1687, B 25; Benjamin, mayor of Bath, 1700, B 26. Edward purchased Chew-Magna, ii 95; Edward received Regilbury and other lands from Edward Barnard, 319; Edward conveyed Regilbury to Sir Halswell Tynte, 319; Elizabeth purchased Sutton Court and settled it upon her son, Samuel Jep, 96; and on his death on John Strachey, 96. Florence, daughter of Roger Bourne, benefaction to Charlinch, i 241. Florence, benefaction to Nemnet, ii 320; family owned Norton - Hautville living, 108; monuments in Chew Magna church, 97; arms, 97.

Babington family owned Babington, ii 450; arms, 450; branches seated in Nottinghamshire, Derbyshire, and other counties, 450; Sir John de owned Babington, 450; Gervaise successively bishop of Landaff, Exeter and Worcester, 450. Babington, Sir Jehan de, i *l*. Joan, iii 98. George married Helena Cheyney, i 244. William owned Thurloxton, iii 103; and Middlezoy, 442; and Dulverton, which he sold to John Sydenham, 521.

Babington manor, situation, ii 450; Domesday survey, 450; owned by the bishop of Coutances: held by Azeline, 450; subsequently owned by the Babington family, 450; the Ap-Adam family, 450; the lords Botreaux, 450; the Chedders, 450; the Newtons, 450, 451; Sir Thomas Griffin, 451; Wil-

Babington manor—*continued.*
liam Long, 451; Norton Knatchbull, 451; lands in, owned by Andrew de Sulleny, 445; tithings which had belonged to Kilmersdon Hundred, withdrawn by Richard, earl of Gloucester, 457; church (St. Margaret), 451; mansion owned by Mr. Knatchbull, 451; Middlecote hamlet depopulated, 450.

Bablew or Balhow, a cell to Montacute priory, situated in Tintinhull, owned by John Lyte, iii 309.

Bach, Yvor: story of his abduction of William, earl of Gloucester, iii 147.

Bachcroft, John, monk of Hinton, pensioned, iii 368.

Bache, John, sheriff, 1392, i *xxxv*.

Bachell, William, held half a knight's fee in Culbone, ii 4.

Back street, Bath, B 35.

Backwell, situation, ii 305; Domesday survey, 305; owned by the bishop of Coutances: held by Fulcran and Nigel: Turchil held it T.R.E. 305; divided into two parts, 306. Backwell-Bayouse owned by (1) the Bayouse or Baiocis family, 306, iii 347. (2) Walter Rodney, ii 306; Backwell-Sore, held by the Sor family, 306; who granted land to Richard de Rodney, 306; Elizabeth Wickham conveyed all her right to Sir Walter Rodney, who became lord of the whole manor, 306; the Rodney family, 306, iii 477, 603, 604. FitzJames family, ii 306; Sir John Churchill, 306; Thomas Thynne, 306; Lord Viscount Weymouth, 307; hamlets of West-Town, Farley, Moor-Side, Downside, 307; market (discontinued), 305; fair, 305; church (St. Andrew) and its monuments, 307, 308; bells (5), 307; cross, 308.

Bacon, Catherine, second wife of Sir Henry Waldegrave, ii 117.

Bacon, George, of Harpford, and Mary his wife, William and Joan his wife, monuments in Langford Budville church, iii 20; arms, 20.

Baker—*continued.*
J.P., *xlii.* Samuel owned Aldwick, ii 316. Thomas, mathematician, i 49. Sir William, monument in Bath abbey, 1770, B 67. William, first bishop of Bangor, inscription in Ilton church, i 49. monument in Bath abbey, 1732, B 67. the Rev. Mr., incumbent of Burnet, ii 415; of Marksbury, 427; the Rev. Richard, incumbent of Brislington, 413. the Rev. Nicholas, incumbent of Martock, iii 8; prebendary of Wells, 397. the Rev. Nicholas, buried in Chisselborough church, ii 330. Mr., owner of Upton Noble, i 227.

Baker family owned Samford Arundel, iii 26.

Baker memorial stone in Wedmore church, i 193.

Baker, Thomas Att-Ayshe, owned lands in Curry-Rivel, Langport, and Westover, iii 50.

Bakere, Jo., one of the Commissioners appointed to sell Puckington, i 57.

Baketerpe, Robert de (*see* Bawdrip).

Baland, Nicholas, monk of Hinton, pensioned, iii 368.

Balch, John, trustee of Ilminster grammar school, i 3; Robert Everard, J.P., i *xlii.* owned Stowey, iii 553.

Baldewyne, Richard, vicar of Muchelney, iii 136.

Baldock, Ralph, iii 209.

Baldred, king of Kent, gave Pennard to the abbey of Glastonbury, ii 275; gave Leigh to the abbey of Glastonbury, 465.

Baldwin held one hide in Hardington, ii 453; owned Porlock, 36.

Baldwin, Sir Timothy, Knt., married Ellen, widow of George Norton, iii 153. Winthrop, governor of Bath hospital, B 47.

Bale, Rev. Chaloner, incumbent of Lydford West, ii 84; John, married Alice Gold, and became part owner of Seaborough, 173.

Baliol college, Oxford, held the patronage of Stringston, i 266. and of Timsbury, ii 112.

Ball family owned the site of Barlinch priory, iii 503. Mary, monument in Bath abbey, 1787, B 67; Thomas, monument in Bath abbey, 1786, B 67.

Ballance street, Bath, B 37.

Balmeton wood, boundary of Selwood forest, ii 195.

Baltonsbury, situation, ii 269; river Brew, 269; containing six hamlets, 270; Domesday survey, 269; owned by the abbey of Glastonbury, 269; granted at the dissolution to Edward, duke of Somerset, 269; to John Ryther, 269; a moiety owned by William Hungate, of Saxton, Yorkshire, 269; William St. Loe held lands here, 269; the fee-farm rents of the manor belonged to John Codrington, 269; mill, 269; survey

Baltonsbury—*continued.*
of the manor in the roll of Glastonbury, 270; living is a chapel to Butleigh, 270; church (St. Dunstan) and its monuments, 270, 271; bells (5), 270.

Bampfylde or Baumfilde family owned Babcary, ii 60; Weston-Bampfylde, 89; Road, jointly with the Stawel family, 224; part of Buckland - Dinham, 452; Hemington, 454. Michaelchurch, iii 99; Flax Bourton, 161; Camerton, 331; lands in West-Monkton, 454. Sir Amias married Elizabeth Clifton, ii 90; Catherine, monument in Barrow church, 313. Sir Charles owned Burnham, i 180; Sir Charles Warwick, J.P., *xlii*; patron of Creech St. Michael church, 76. Hardington, ii 453; Hemington, 454, iii 158. Sir Coplestone sided with Charles I: made high sheriff and knight of the shire, married (1) Margaret Bulkeley; (2) Jane Pole, ii 91. owned Bankland, iii 72. Coplestone Warre, J.P., i *xlii.* was of Hestercombe, ii 91. married Mary Knight, of Wolverley, and was seated at Hestercombe house, iii 263; owned Middlezoy, 442. Coplestone Warwick, M.P. for Exeter and Devon, married Gertrude Carew, ii 91; Edward married Elizabeth Wadham, 90. Elizabeth, daughter of Sir John, of Poltimore, married Thomas Moore, of Cheddon Fitzpaine, iii 246. Elizabeth, wife of Henry Fraunceis, ii 90; Hugh married Mary Clifford, 91. John de, landowner in time of Edward I, i *xxvii.* John, M.P. for Tiverton and Devon, married Elizabeth Drake, ii 91; John married Joan Hoxham, 89; John married Agnes de Pederton, 90; and became possessed of Hardington, 453. and of Dunkerton, iii 338. John, M.P. for Devon and Exeter, married (1) Elizabeth Basset; (2) Margaret Warre, ii 91. and became possessed of Hestercombe, iii 263. John, M.P. for Penryn, made baronet in 1642, married Gertrude Coplestone, ii 91; Margaret, 91. Margaretta married John Tyndale, of Bristol, iii 263. Margaret, wife of Sir James Drax, monument in Hardington church, ii 453; Mary, wife of Sir Coventry Carew, 91; Peter, 453. Richard married Elizabeth Wadham, i 48. Richard married a daughter of John Hastings, ii 89; Richard, supposed to have been kidnapped in his childhood, but restored through the intervention of his nurse, married Elizabeth Sydenham, 90; Sir Richard Warwick, knight of the shire of Devon, married Jane Codrington, 91. Sir Richard, Bt., owned Tickenham, iii 165. Thomas married Agnes Coplestone, ii 90; Walter married (1) Grace or Joan Pudsey; (2) Constance Langford, 90; Warwick,

Bampfylde family—*continued.*
sheriff, 1693, i *xxxviii.* Warwick, Colonel, benefaction to Buckland-Dinham, ii 452; to Hemington, 456; William married (1) Margaret St. Maur, 90, 200; (2) Margaret Kirkham, 90; Sir William married Margaret Paunceford, 90; monument in Hardington church, 453; arms, 453.

Banastre family owned Wheathill, iii 450; William, 450.

Banbury, Elizabeth, wife of Thomas, monument in Long-Sutton church, iii 198.

Band, John, J.P., i *xlii.*

Banewell, Thomas de, prior of Woodspring, 1414, iii 595.

Banister, William, owner of Lovington, ii 82; William, held Radstock, 457; Joan married (1) Robert de Alfoxton; (2) Sir John Hill, 457

Bankland (*see* Petherton, North).

Banks, Sir Jacob, gave statue of Queen Anne to Minehead, ii 32.

Banner Down, Bath Easton, i 99.

Banwell, situation, iii 566; Wint-Hill, 566; monastery stood here in the days of King Alfred: destroyed in the Danish wars, 566; manor afterwards owned by Harold, earl of Wessex, 566; Dudoco, bishop of Wells, 566; Domesday survey, 566; owned by Giso, bishop of Wells: Serlo, Ralph, Rohard, Fastrade, Bono, Elwi, and Ordulf held lands here, 566; held by the bishopric of Bath and Wells, 378, 392, 394, 567; Edward, duke of Somerset, 395, 567; Sir William St. Loe, 567; restored to the bishopric, 396, 567; bishop's palace, 567; Banwell park, 567; Tower-Head hamlet, 567; East and West Rolston, anciently Worlestone, 567; formerly the head of a barony, which included Tornoke and Stonen-Halle, held by lady Mary de Courtney: Kewstoke, held by the daughters of Geffrey Vassell, 567; Burton, held by Adam le Iroys, 567; Locking, in which was one yardland held by Worspring priory, 567; Edingworth, held by George de Cantilupe, 567; this manor held by the Percival family, 567; the Wyndham family, 567; the Hon. James Everard Arundel, 567; Woolford's-Hill, or Overshill, owned by the Wyndhams, 567; Mr. Arundel, 567; St. George, chapel at, demolished, 567; Westwick, Knightcot (or Nedcut), and Yarborough hamlets, 567; church (St. Andrew) and its monuments, 567, 568; bells (6), 568; benefactions, 568; cross, 568; spring, 568; fairs, 568. rectory appropriated to the prior and canons of Brewton, i 214.

Banwell moor, i *xv.*

Banwell park, iii 567.

Banys, John, incumbent of the free-chapel of Whitehall, Ilchester, iii 300.

Baptism of Pagans at Aller, iii 188.

Baptist chapel, Bath, в 74.

Barba-Fluta, name given to Richard de Placetis, iii 64.

Barber memorial stone in Creech St. Michael church, i 78.

Barber, William, part owner of Curry Rivel, i 27; of Fivehead, 40.

Barbour's-Mede, owned by Witham priory, ii 233

Barclay, Jacob, monument in Weston church, i 162.

Bardolf, Hugh, sheriff, 1189, i *xxxiii.*

Bardstone, Joan, married John Brook, iii 303.

Bare, Humphrey, benefaction to Brushford, iii 507.

Baret, Thomas, bishop of Knachdune, in Ireland, owner of a moiety of the lordship of Brean, i 179.

Barjew, Rev. Mr., incumbent of Sutton-Bingham, ii 350.

Barker family, memorial stones in Evercreech church, iii 416.

Barker, Mrs. Dorothy, monument in Charlcombe church, i 143.

Barkham, Ezekiel, gift to Wells church, iii 410; Margaret, benefactions to Wells church, 410

Barkley, Andrew, monument in Bath abbey, 1790, в 67.

Barle river, i *xiv*; iii 503, 506, 520, 557.

Barlinch priory, founded by William de Say, iii 503; endowed by Maud de Say, with the rectory of Brompton-Regis, 503; list of priors, 503. owned land T.R.E. i *xxvi.* held the livings of Bradford, iii 244; Hill Farence, 257; Winsford, 556; the tithes of Upton, 555; site granted at the dissolution to Sir John Wallop, 503; sold to the Ball family, 503; Mr. Lucas, 503.

Barloe married Elizabeth Hardwick, ii 96.

Barlow, Ralph, dean of Wells, 1621, i 190.

Barlow, William, bishop of Bath and Wells, 1547, iii 387; offices previously held by, 387; great losses to the See during his time, 387. exchanged Bath-hampton and Claverton, with Edward VI, i 117, 146. granted to Edward, duke of Somerset, Chew-Magna, ii 95; Wellington, 482. Banwell, iii 567; gave up Chedder to Edward VI, 575; other grants to the duke of Somerset, 395, 409, 414, 452.

Barnaby, Isabella, owned Skilgate, iii 545.

Barnard, Edward, purchased the manor of Regilbury, ii 319; conveyed it to Edward Baber, 319; the Rev. Edward, memorial stone in Stowey church, 111. Sarah, daughter of John, was the second wife of Geffrey Strode, 210.

Barnard, Edward, of Downside, married Jane Smythes, iii 463. Joan, their daughter, married William Strode, ii 210. monuments in Shepton-Mallet church, iii 463; arms, 436.

Basings—*continued.*
   borough, ii 46; and Kentsford, iii 492.
John, ii 46; iii 492. Gilbert, ii 46; iii 492.
Simon, ii 46; iii 492. Alianor, wife of (1)
John Hamme; (2) John Williams, who
passed over her right in these lands to Sir
William Bonville, in trust for Richard
Luttrell, ii 46. levied a fine on Kentsford,
iii 492.

Basket, Thomas, monument in Charlton Adam
church, iii 192.

Bason bridge, Burnham, i 179.

Basset family owned Claverton, i 146; monuments in Claverton church, 148. held Saltford, ii 431. monuments in Combe-Monkton church, i 152; Alice, wife of William
Malet, 32. Sir Arthur held Ash-Brittle for
the use of John Blewet, iii 21. Edmund
owned lands in Dundry, ii 105; Edmund,
heirs of, owned land in Winford, 320;
Elizabeth, first wife of John Bampfylde,
91; Eustachia, daughter of Gilbert, married (1) Thomas de Verdon; (2) Richard
de Camville, 356; Gilbert, 356; John,
landowner in time of Edward I, i *xxviii*;
John, sheriff, 1262, i *xxxiv*. Maud, holder
of knight's fee in Hallatrow and Littleton,
ii 148; Philip, witness to a charter granted
by Henry I to Glastonbury abbey, 265;
Ralph held lands of Glastonbury abbey,
245. Richard, justice itinerant in the
reign of Stephen, iii 107. Robert owned
Norton Malreward, ii 109. Roger, landowner in time of Edward I, i *xxviii*; Sir
William, of Bath-hampton, 117. Sir William, of Claverton, ii 109.

Basset, of Winterbourne, a daughter of, married Sir William Arthur, iii 177.

Basset, Philip, sheriff, 1263, i *xxxiv*. Sir William, M.P. for Bath, 1678, 1685, 1688, B 22.

Bastenbergh, Thurstan de, came into England
with the Conqueror, iii 351. Hugh, his
son, was called de Montfort (*see* Montfort).

Batch, hamlet in Lympsham, i 202.

Batchelor, Edward, and Katharine, his wife:
memorial stone in Hemington church, ii
455; benefaction, 455; the Rev. Mr., incumbent of Babington, 451. the Rev.
William, J.P., i *xlii*. the Rev. William,
incumbent of Telsford, iii 363. monuments
in Bathwick church, i 123.

Batcombe, situation, iii 466; river, 466; Port-
way and Walter's-hill, 466; includes Westcombe, Ashcombe, Allam and Spargrove,
466; owned by Glastonbury abbey, 466,
467; Domesday survey, 466; Roger held
land here, which Ulwi held T.R.E. 466;
granted at the dissolution to James Bisse,
467; held by the families of Malte and
Harington, 467; the Bridges family: the
Duke of Chandos, 467; dispute between

Batcombe—*continued.*
   the abbots of Glastonbury and the family
of Sanzaver, 467; Spargrove hamlet,
anciently Spertegrave, 467; owned by the
Sanzaver family, 467; John, earl of
Arundel, 467; John Bisse, 467; Thomas
Coward, 468; church (St. Mary) and
monuments, 468; bells (6), 468; Ashcombe
hamlet, 468; Domesday survey, 468;
owned by the bishop of Coutances: held
by Herluin: Brictric held it T.R.E. 468;
subsequently held by the Arthur family,
468; Westcombe hamlet, Domesday survey, 466; held by Azelin: Alfhilla held it
T.R.E. 466; subsequently held by John
Bisse, 467; and with Batcombe lodge by
Thomas Whitehead, 468.

Bateman, viscount, J.P., i *xli*.

Bath, position of, B 1; early names of, 1, 2;
derivation of its present name, 2; Roman
city, 7; Roman memorial stone, 7; discovery of the Roman baths, 9; Roman remains, 10, 11, 12, 13, 14; Roman evacu-
ation, 15; Danish invasions, 16; captured
by the Saxons, 16; progress under King
Edgar, 17; state in time of William the
Conqueror, 17. eight burgesses in, belonged to Keynsham at the time of Domesday survey, ii 401. purchase of the city, B
18; parliamentary representatives, 1297—
1471, 19—21; 1553—1790, 21—22; city
government, 22; charters of the city, 22;
first aldermen, 23; liberties of the city, 23;
first mayor, 1590, 25; arms of the city, 27;
citizen's oath, 27; destruction by fire, 28.
rating of the bishop's temporalities in, in
1293, iii 394. fairs, B 28; commerce, 28;
arrival of first barge up the Avon, 28;
siege, 31; parochial church, 58; parishes:
(St. James), 72; (St. Michael), 72; (St.
Michael's Conduit), 73; (Walcot), 73; parsonage house, 72; first archdeacon, 72;
philosophical society, 80; titles of dignity, 82

Bath abbey, origin, B 54; foundation, 54;
name in time of King Ecfrid, 54; converted
from monastery to abbey, by King Edgar,
54; curious certificate in, 55; first presi-
dents, 54, 55; annexed by John de Villula,
and governed by priors, 55; dispute about
the ringing of bells, 56; visited by archbishop of Canterbury, 1494, 56. restoration
begun by bishop Oliver King, iii 386. rebuilding, B 56; surrendered to Edward VI,
56; pensions assigned, 57; given to Humphry Colles, 57; sold to Matthew Colthurst,
whose son, Edmund, gave it to the mayor
and citizens of Bath, 57, 58; description of
the buildings, 58; dimensions of the old and
new, 58, 59; restoration, 59; description
of the new, 58, 59; arms in the choir of,
63; monumental inscriptions, 67; bishops

Bawdrip—*continued.*
sequently held by the families of Beaupine and Worston or Wroughton, 91 ; Jefferys Allen, 91 ; Ford manor, held by the Ford family, 91 ; Robert Brent of Cossington, 91 ; chantry and chapel, 91 ; Crandon or Grenedone manor, 92 ; Domesday survey, held by Eldred, 92 ; the Trivet family held lands here, 92 ; divided between the Vernays and Dodingtons, 92 ; manor owned by the duke of Chandos, 92 ; Bradney manor, 92 ; Domesday survey, owned by Walter de Dowai : held by Renewald : Alnod held it T.R.E. 92 ; held by the lords of Castle Cary, 92 ; the de Bradneys, 92 ; Sir William Sturmy, 92 ; William Beaumont, 92 ; Thomas Muttlebury, 92 ; Knolle, hamlet, 92 ; the church given by Robert de Baggedrippe to the church of St. Athelwin of Athelney, 92 ; church (St. Michael) ; monuments, 92, 93 ; bells (4), 92 ; John Atherton, bishop of Waterford and Lismore, born here, 93.

Bayeux, Odo, bishop of, received lands from William the Conqueror, i *xxv.* owned Combe, iii 334 ; joined the barons' rebellion against William Rufus, 299, 334 ; his estates confiscated, and he himself banished the kingdom, 334.

Bayham, lord viscount, M.P. for Bath, 1790, B 22 ; governor of Bath hospital, 47.

Bayley, Mr., increased the stipend of the master of Martock grammar school, iii 11.

Bayley, William, prebendary of Wells, iii 397.

Bayley's brook, Fairfield, i 252.

Baylie, John, incumbent of a guild at Shepton Mallet, iii 465.

Baylie, William, received a pension from Taunton priory, iii 236.

Bayly, Zachary, owned a manor in Burnham, i 181 ; the benefice of Mark, to which he appointed his own curate, 183. owned Martock, which he sold to Henry and John Slade, iii 5 ; memorial in Wheathill church, 450.

Baynard, Elizabeth, of Cliffe-house, monument erected by, in Bishop's Lydiard church, ii 495.

Baynard family owned Blagdon, iii 570 ; Edmund, 570 ; Thomas, benefaction to Blagdon, 570.

Baynard family owned Wanstraw, ii 229 ; vault in Wanstraw church, 229.

Baynham, Margaret, second wife to John de Ken, iii 592.

Baynton, Richard, M.P., 1416, i *xxxi.*

Bayntun family owned Farley Montacute, iii 356.

Bayntun, Sir Edward, patron of Charlinch, i 240. Sir Edward, governor of Bath hospital, B 47. Sir Edward Rolt, J.P., i *xlii.*

Bayntun, Henry, of Spy park, Wilts, married Anne Malet, and became possessed of Enmore, i 92.

Bayntun, Rev. Henry, incumbent of Road and Wolverton, ii 224, 225. Rev. John, incumbent of Charlinch, i 240.

Bayouse family (*see* Baiouse).

Bays, John, gave up the holding of Beer-Crocombe, i 14 ; released to Guy de Brien all his rights to lands in Buckland-St.-Mary, and in the advowson of Wanstrow church, 21

Beach, William, owned Mark, i 183.

Beacon hill, Bath, B 38.

Beacon-house, Dundry, ii 105.

Beacons—Bicknoller, iii 501 ; Doulting, 473. Dundry, ii 105 ; Dunkery, 5. Ilminster, i 3.

Bead roll, ii 18.

Beadon, David, Edward, and Robert, benefactions to Brushford, iii 507.

Beague, John, owned Hollam, iii 524.

Beal, Dr., examination of the water in Sock farm spring, iii 221.

Beal, John, vicar of Yeovil, iii 212.

Bean-bridge, iii 26.

Bearn-back rock, Weston Super Mare, iii 610.

Beatson, Rev., incumbent of Road and Wolverton, ii 225.

Beau Nash (*see* Nash, Richard).

Beauchamp (De Bello Campo) family, of Hatch, i 44, 45. owned Ashington, iii 213. Babcary, ii 60 ; Beauchamp-Stoke, 319 ; Chewstoke, 101. Compton - Dunden, iii 447 ; Dunden-upon-Polden, 213. Hatch-Beauchamp, i 44. Lillisdon, ii 179. Limington, iii 218. Marston Magna, ii 374. Norton, near Kewstoke, iii 596. North Widcombe, ii 118. Shepton-Beauchamp, iii 125 ; Sock-Dennis, 307 ; Stoke-under-Hamden, 315. White Lackington, i 67. arms, iii 320. Alice, daughter of Thomas Beauchamp, earl of Warwick, married (1) John Beauchamp, of Hatch, i 45. (2) Matthew Gournay, ii 139 ; granted North Widcombe to Matthew Gournay, 118. Alice, wife of Sir John Speke, i 67. Cecilia, married (1) Roger Seymour ; (2) Richard Turberville, i 45, iii 125. Eleanor, wife of Sir John Meriet, ii 170, iii 319, 320 ; Hugh de, held land in Chaffcombe, 115. Sir Humphrey de, i *l.* Ida, first wife to John Brent, of Cossington, iii 435. Idonea held a knight's fee in Wanstraw, ii 229. James, monument in Wrington church, i 209 ; John de, landowner in time of Edward I, i *xxviii.* married Cecilia de Fortibus or de Vivonia, ii 118, 150, iii 447, 462. John de, governor of the castles of Carmarthen and Cardigan, i 44 ; Sir John fortified Hatch castle, 45 ; M.P., 1307, 1314, 1316, *xxix.* built the castle at Stoke-under-Hamden, iii 316 ; John, summoned to parliament, obtained

Beauchamp—*continued.*
license to transport wool from England, i
45, iii 319. John married Alice de Beauchamp, i 45, iii 125, 319. John de, commissioner of sewers, i *xii*; Robert de,
baron in time of Henry II, *xxvi*; Robert
went into France with Henry III, 44; Sir
Thomas, of White Lackington, 12, 67.
married Elizabeth Streche, and became
possessed of Samford Arundel, iii 26.
Thomas, M.P., 1399, 1424, i *xxxi*. William
de and Joan, his wife, held Chelworth, ii
420; William de, owned part of Wanstraw,
229.
Beauchamp, Elizabeth, daughter of lord Beauchamp of Powick, married lord Willoughby of Broke, ii 376.
Beauchamp, Alice, daughter of Thomas Beauchamp, earl of Warwick, married John
Beauchamp of Hatch, i 45; Richard, earl
of Warwick, married Elizabeth de Berkeley
and became possessed of Bedminster, ii 282;
Margaret, married John Talbot, earl of
Shrewsbury, 282; Eleanor, married (1)
lord Roos, (2) Edmund Beaufort, duke of
Somerset, 282; Elizabeth, married George
Nevil, lord Latimer, 282.
Beauchamp, Rev., first incumbent of new
church, Frome, ii 194.
Beauchamp, viscount, J.P., i *xli.*
Beaucham-Stoke (*see* Nempnet).
Beaufitz, Thomas de, married the daughter of
William Russell, i 253.
Beaufort, dukes of Somerset (*see* Somerset,
dukes of).
Beaufort, John de, owner of the hundred of
Abdick, i 1; Henry de, owner of the hun-
dred of Abdick, 2.
Beaufort, Henry, dean of Wells, 1397, i 190.
cardinal of St. Eusebius, bishop of Win-
chester, 1405, iii 232; Jane, married Sir
William Stradling, 335. Margaret, married
Thomas Courtney, ii 161.
Beaufort, Elizabeth, dowager duchess of, sister
of Norborne Berkeley, inherited the barony
of Botetourt, iii 280.
Beaufort family owned Curry Rivel, i 26.
Beaufort square, Bath, ß 35.
Beaumond, Stephen, owned Winsford Bosun,
iii 556.
Beaumont, Catherine, wife of (1) John Strecche
(2) Hugh Luttrell, ii 10; Elizabeth, wife of
William Botreaux, 67; Henry, rector of
Trent, 383; Henry, married Elizabeth
Stawel, iii 250; Henry, owned Plaish, 526;
Humphry of Elworthy, 526; Margaret,
married Thomas Keynes, 120; Philip held
also Willet, 525; Sir Thomas, knt. of
Elworthy, 525; William, owned Bradney,
Willet, and Plaish, 92, 525.
Beaumont family owned Leigh Flory, iii 265.

Beaupine family owned North-Petherton, iii
55, and Bawdrip, 91; Agnes, married John
Bluet of Grindham, 55. Thomas de, M.P.
1389, i *xxxi*; held Beer Crocombe, 14;
attached for trespass and procured license
to lop trees in Ilbare Wood, 14.
Beaupré, Maud Fichett, married Henry Strode,
ii 209.
Beauvoir, Rev. Osmund, D.D., monument in
Bath abbey, 1789, ß 67.
Beaver, Rev. George, rector of Trent, ii 383;
J.P., i *xlii.*
Bec, John, of Eresby, granted the advowson of
Brean to Henry de Laci, i 179. owned
Steep-Holmes Island and granted it to
Henry de Laci, iii 609.
Bec-Hellouin abbey, Normandy, owned the
church at Cleeve, iii 512.
Becher, Henry, owned Brean, i 178; Tuxwell,
245. purchased Belluton and Pensford, ii
435.
Bechintone (*see* Beckington).
Beck, Joseph, owned Ford, iii 613.
Beckery, Isle of, ii 265; ruined chapel on, 265.
Beckford, William, J.P., i *xlii.* William, lord
mayor of London, owned Witham, and be-
gan the building of a mansion there, ii 234;
William of Fonthill, 234.
Beckington, its situation, ii 198; Saxon origin,
198; Domesday survey, 198; owned by
Roger Arundel: held by Ailuert T.R.E. 198;
owned by the families of Erleigh, St. Maur,
199; Bampfylde, Ashe, and Methuen, 200;
Seymour's court, 200; the church (St.
Gregory) and its monuments, 200, 201,
202; bells (6), 201; hamlet of Ridge, 202;
benefactions, 202; the living appropriated
to Buckland priory, 200, iii 98. birthplace
of bishop Beckington, iii 384; his bequest
to, iii 385.
Beckington square, Wells, iii 376.
Beckington, Thomas de, bishop of Bath and
Wells, iii 384; birth and education, 384;
chancellor of Oxford University, tutor to
Henry VI, and dean of Arches, 384.
elected bishop of Bath and Wells, iii 384,
ii 198. directed annual payment of pension
to the master of St. John's Hospital, Bath,
ß 43; built portion of Bath priory, 58.
ordination for building vicar's house at
Puriton, ii 397; built the dormitory of
Witham friary, 235. built houses, gate-
ways, and the conduit at Wells, iii 376, 384;
the west cloister of Wells cathedral, 385;
the rector's lodgings at Lincoln college,
Oxford, 385; augmented the vicar's close,
Wells, 403; added to Bubwith's hospital,
Wells, 408; built the bishop's palace, Banwell, 567; device, 385; bequests, 385;
buried in Wells cathedral, 1464, 386; monument, 400. arms, ii 438, iii 376, 568.

Bells, time of ringing, dispute between the convent and mayor of Bath, B 56.

Belltree lane, Bath, B 43.

Belluton or Belgetone, hamlet in Stanton-Drew parish (*see* Stanton-Drew).

Belmont, Bath, B 38.

Belmont, Wraxall, seat of William Turner, iii 155

Belvidere, Bath, B 38.

Belvoir Castle, owned by Robert de Todenei, founder of the Daubeney family, iii 107.

Bemstone or Bempston hundred, i 175. Alston anciently considered part of, ii 393.

Benacre or Binegar (*see* Binegar).

Bendel, Hannah, memorial tablet in Emborow church, ii 136.

Bending, William de, sheriff, 1182, 1183, i *xxxiii.*

Benedict, John, member for Chard, 1300, ii 472.

Benedict, abbot of Athelney, i 47, 87.
Benefactions to Bath abbey, 1608-1769, B 70, 71.
Benet, Dr. Thomas, commissary to cardinal Wolsey, appointed John Norman, prior of Barlinch, iii 503.
Benett, John, monk of Bath, who received pension, B 57.
Bennet, John, prior of Montacute, 1449, iii 313. Philip, M.P. for Bath, 1741, B 22. Philip and Jane, memorial stone in Maperton church, ii 86. Philip, builder of a mansion at Widcombe, i 168; vault in Widcombe church and tomb in Widcombe churchyard, 172. Thomas, prior of Taunton, iii 236. Mr., owned South Brewham, i 221; Rev. Edward and Mary, memorial brasses in South Brewham church, 222. the Rev. Hugh, incumbent of Runnington, iii 25. the Rev., incumbent of Treborough, ii 46.
Bennet family of Steeple Ashton, Thomas, owned also Combe-Hay, iii 336; Thomas, 336; Anne, wife of John Smith of Stony-Littleton: monument in Foxcote church, 350; Mary, married Robert Smith, 336; John, monument in Combe-Hay church, 336; arms, 336, 350.
Bennet street, Bath, B 37.
Bennett, Francis, mayor of Bath, 1773, 1781, B 26. the Rev. Hugh, J.P., xlii, incumbent of Nettlecombe, iii 541; Richard Henry, owned Hurcott, 186.
Bentor manor, ii 158.
Beokery [*sic* Collinson, but it is a misprint for Beckery] isle of, ii 265; ruined chapel on, 265
Beorgret, abbot of Glastonbury, ii 249.
Beorthred, abbot of Glastonbury, 986, ii 250.
Berche, John, sub-prior of Woodspring, iii 595.
Berd, Hugh, part owner of Norton Veel, iii 272.
Bere (*see* Beer Crocombe).
Bere, Gilbert de, commissioner of sewers, 1304, i xii; Sir Gilbert de, M.P., 1312, xxix; Johanna de, prioress of Cannington, 233. John, owned part of Huntspill Mareys, ii 393. the Rev. John, incumbent of Skilgate, iii 545. the Rev., incumbent of Butcombe, ii 316; Richard, owned Haselborough, 332; Thomas, forfeited his estates, 332. William de, M.P., 1311, i xxix. the Rev. Thomas, J.P., i xlii.
Bere mills, Dowlish Wake, iii 119.
Beresford, Rt. Hon. John, J.P., i xlii.
Berewyk, Sir Hugh de, owned Emborow, ii 157; Thomas, 157; Margaret, wife of Ralph Boteler, 157.
Bergersh (*see* Burghersh).
Berghel water, Exmoor, ii 19.
Berghersh, (*see* Burghersh).
Berjew, Rev., incumbent of Bathford, i 112; and Bath-Hampton, 118.
Berkeley Castle, Gloucestershire, owned by William de Berkeley, founder of the Berke-

Berkeley Castle—*continued.*
ley family, iii 275; enlarged by Robert, lord Berkeley, 276; Henry III entertained there by Maurice, lord Berkeley, 277; Edward II murdered there, 279.
Berkeley family, descended from Robert Fitz-Harding, ii 281. of Berkeley Castle, iii 275; royal ancestry, 283. owned Bedminster, ii 281. Brewton, i 215, iii 280. lands in Brockley, ii 121. Charlton house, iii 155. hundred of Hareclive and Bedminster, ii 279; Knolle, 284. Orchard Portman, iii 281; Portbury, 140, 142; Portishead, 144; Pylle, 483; Sock-Dennis, 307; Stoke-Giffard, 279, 280; Steep-Holmes Island, 609; lands in Tickenham, 165; Walton, 170; Winterhead, 602. members of, buried in Keynsham abbey church, ii 403. arms, iii 143.
Berkeley family of Berkeley castle, iii 275-282; Roger, a Saxon nobleman, owned Berkeley castle, and assumed that surname, 275; William de, 275; Roger de, was lord of Berkeley and Dursley: deprived of his estates and title of Berkeley which were bestowed on Robert Fitz-Harding, 275, 276; Alice, daughter of Roger, married Maurice, son of Robert Fitzharding, 276 (*see* also 141); Robert, son of Roger, married Helena, daughter of Robert Fitzharding, lord of Berkeley, 276; Sir Robert Fitzharding, received the barony and lands of Berkeley, 275, 276; was direct ancestor of the Berkeley families, 275; founded the monastery of St. Augustine, Bristol: married Eve de Estmond, 276. owned Bedminster, ii 281 (*see* also iii 141). Helena, daughter of Robert, married Robert, son of Roger, lord Dursley. Maurice, son of Robert, dropped the name of Harding and took that of Berkeley, married Alice, daughter of Roger, lord Dursley, iii 276 (*see* also iii 141, ii 281). Robert, son of Maurice, founded the hospital of St. Catherine, Bedminster, and two chantries, ii 281. forfeited his estates, but received them again; married Juliana de Portlarch, iii 277. Thomas de, brother of Robert, ii 281. married Joan de Somery, iii 277. Maurice, i xxvii, ii 281. married Isabel, daughter to the earl of Cornwall: benefactions to St. Augustine's monastery, Bristol, iii 277; Maurice de, slain in tournament at Kenilworth, 277. Thomas de, fortified his mansion at Bedminster, enlarged the hospital there, ii 281; patron of Minchin Barrow priory, 310. married Joan de Ferrers, iii 277, 278; Sir Thomas, second son of Thomas, ancestor of the Berkeleys of Wymondham, 278. Maurice, summoned to parliament by title of lord Berkeley of

Berkeley family—*continued*.

Berkeley castle, ii 281 ; built a priory on the Flat Holmes, 281. married (1) Eve le Zouch (2) Isabel de Clare. imprisoned for rebellion and his estates confiscated, iii 278 (*see* also iii 143). Sir Maurice, second son of Lord Maurice (*see* under Berkeley of Stoke Gifford). Thomas, restored to his father's estates, iii 278 ; built Beverstone castle, married Margaret Mortimer, 279. founded a chantry and hermitage at Bedminster, and gave lands to St. Catherine's hospital there, ii 281, 282 (*see* also iii 143). Maurice, founded several chantries, ii 282. ancestor of the earls of Berkeley, iii 279 ; Ela, daughter of Maurice, married John Maltravers, 206. Thomas, ii 282 ; Elizabeth, daughter of Thomas, married Richard Beauchamp, earl of Warwick, 282. Jane, married Sir Thomas Stawel, iii 250.

Berkeley, Thomas de, lord of the hundred of Hareclive, gave a license to the trustees of Simon de Meriet, to grant the manor of Ashton-Meriet to St. Peter's priory, Bath, ii 298 (*see* Berkeley).

Berkeley family of Stoke-Gifford, iii 279, 280 ; Sir Maurice, bart., second son of Maurice, lord Berkeley, owned Stoke-Gifford, and lands in Gloucester, Wilts, and Somerset, and the manor and castle of Brimpsfield, 279, 280 ; lands in Milverton, 14. and Kingston Seymour, ii 123. Sir Thomas, son of Sir Maurice, married Catherine, daughter of lord Botetourt, iii 280 (*see* also ii 123). Maurice, married Joan Dinham, iii 280 ; Sir Maurice, knt., son of Sir Thomas, owned also Weley castle : married Helena Montford, 280 ; Catherine, daughter of Sir Maurice, married a son of Maurice, lord Berkeley, 280 ; Sir William, knt., son of Sir Maurice, married Anne Stafford, 280 ; was chief lord of Wigborough, 272 ; Richard, son of Sir William, married Elizabeth Coningsby, 280. Anne, married Thomas Speke, i 67 ; Sir Maurice, was of Brewton (*see* Berkeley of Brewton). Sir John, ancestor of Norborne Berkeley, iii 280 ; Norborne, claimed the barony of Botetourt : with him the name of Berkeley became extinct in this branch, 280 ; Elizabeth, sister of Norborne, married the duke of Beaufort, 280.

Berkeley family, of Brewton, i 215-218. iii 280, 281 ; Sir Maurice, second son of Richard Berkeley of Stoke Gifford, was of Brewton, 280 ; married (1) Catherine Blount (2) Elizabeth Sandys, 280 ; was mesne lord of Foxcote, 349. held the chapel of Pitcombe, i 224 (*see* also 215). Elizabeth, married Sir James Perceval, iii 175 ; Sir Henry, son of Sir Maurice, married Margaret Liggon,

Berkeley family—*continued*.

280 ; sold Foxcote, 350 (*see* also i 215). Sir Henry, second son of Sir Henry, was ancestor of the Berkeleys of Yarlington, iii 281. Sir Maurice, married Elizabeth Killigrew, 281. M.P., 1563, i *xxxi* ; 1572, 1601, *xxxii*. Sir Charles, created baron Berkeley and viscount Fitzharding, iii 281, M.P., 1620, i *xxxii*. Charles, second son of Sir Charles created baron Berkeley of Rathdown, viscount Fitzharding, baron Botetourt, and earl of Falmouth, iii 281. M.P., 1640, B 21 (*see* also i 215). Maurice, baron Berkeley and viscount Fitzharding, iii 281 ; John, third son of Sir Charles, baron Berkeley, died without issue, 281 ; Sir John, brother of Sir Charles, created lord Berkeley of Stratton, 281 (*see* also i 215). monuments in Brewton church, 216-218.

Berkeley family of Pylle, iii 281, 282 ; Sir Edward, third son of Sir Henry Berkeley of Brewton, married Margaret Holland, built the manor-house of Pylle, 281, 282 ; Edward, married Philippa Speke, 282 ; Edward, married Elizabeth Ryves, 282 ; Maurice, 282 ; William, took the name and inherited the estates of the Portman family, 282 (*see* also Portman) ; married Anne Seymour, 282 ; Edward, second son of William, inherited the Berkeley property : married Anne Ryves, 282 ; Letitia, daughter of William, held for life the Berkeley estates and mansion house at Pylle, married Sir John Burland, 282.

Berkeley family of Beverstone, owned Barrow Gournay, ii 309 ; Thomas de and Margaret, 309. Eleanor, daughter of Sir John, married Richard Poynings, iii 246.

Berkeley, John, of Arlingham, held land in Wanstraw, ii 229.

Berkeley, Lady Catherine, of Over, owned the manor of Ham and Ham Burci, iii 445 ; Sir John, married Alice de Ashton, 445.

Berkeley, John, of Tickenham, held the manor of Brytton, and lands in Mark and Burnham iii, 165 ; Cecilia, wife of James Ash, 165 ; Lady Cecilia, legatee under the will of John Luttrell, 500.

Berkeley, Robert de, married Alice de Gant, and assumed the title of Were, i 185 ; Maurice, who took the title of Gant, 185 ; Eva, who married Thomas de Harptree, who adopted the name of Gournay, 185.

Berkeley, Alice, daughter of James, lord Berkeley, married Richard Arthur of Clapton, iii 178 ; Gilbert, bishop of Bath and Wells, 1559 - 1581 ; buried in Wells cathedral, 387, 400. Henry, M.P., 1586, 1587, 1626, i *xxxii*, *xxxvii* ; Sir Henry, sheriff, 1587, *xxxvii* ; John de, M.P., 1390, 1393, *xxxi* ; Sir John de, sheriff, 1390, 1394, *xxxv* ; William, sheriff, 1477, 1478, *xxxvi*.

Berkley, situation, ii 202 ; Oldford, hamlet in, 202 ; Domesday survey, 202 ; owned by Roger Arundel, held by Toui, T.R.E. 202 ; subsequently owned by the families of Fayroke, Newborough, and Carent, 202 ; church of Fayroke annexed to benefice of, 204 ; church (St. Mary) and its monuments, 204.

Berkley, Alexander de, writer of the sixteenth century, entered into order of St. Benedict, and afterwards became a Franciscan, ii 204.

Berkley, Ralph de, holder of Tatwick, i 154.

Berkrolls, Sir Roger, married a daughter and co-heir of Pagan de Turberville, iii 335 ; Sir Laurence, 335 ; Wentlian, married Sir Edward Stradling, 335.

Berlegh, Roger de, M.P. for Bath, 1357, 1360, B 20

Bermondsey abbey, Surrey, owned land in Somerset in time of Edward I, i *xxvii.* cluniac abbey, ii 80 ; owned King-Weston, 80 ; part of the tithes of Charleton-Horethorne, 356. a pension from Chilthorne Domer church, iii 217 ; Stone, 221 ; a manor in Preston, 223 ; Inglishcombe church, 340 ; register of charters and muniments compiled by William de Preston, 223.

Bermyngham Fulk de, owner of Merrifield manor, i 47.

Bernaby, Simon, held Skilgate, iii 545.

Bernard, held South-Cadbury, ii 73 ; North-Cheriton, 360.

Bernard, Cannanvell, memorial stone in Pitney church, iii 131.

Bernard, James, J.P., i *xliii.* erected a monument in Stanton Drew church, ii 435. owned Clatworthy, iii 509 ; married Elizabeth Carew, and became possessed of Crocombe, 516 ; Elizabeth, his wife, monument in Crowcombe church, 517.

Bernard, Mr., married the heiress of John Fisher, and became possessed of Somerton, iii 186 ; John, his son, succeeded to a third of that estate, 186 ; a sister of John married Mr. Gill, who became possessed of the other two-thirds, 186.

Bernersworth, held by William Russell of William de Dodeton, i 253.

Berneville, Sir John de, M.P., 1318, i *xxix.*

Berrill, John, M.P. for Bath, 1335, B 19.

Berrow, situation, i 201 ; Domesday survey, 201 ; owned by Walter de Douai, and held by Ralph : by Elsi, T.R.E. 201 ; granted by King William Rufus to the abbey of Glastonbury, 201 ; afterwards owned by Edward, duke of Somerset, 201 ; William Whitchurch and the Stanley family, 202 ; church (St. Mary) and its monuments, 202 ; bells (5), 202.

Berry, Amos, rector of Trent, ii 383 ; memorial stone in Trent church, 386

Berry, Peter, owned land in the manor of Glastonbury, ii 259.

Berthwald, abbot of Glastonbury : archbishop of Canterbury, ii 249. received Andredesey from King Kenewalch, iii 605.

Bertie, Bridgett, wife of John, lord Poulett, ii 167.

Bertone (*see* Barton David).

Bertran, holder of Fivehead manor, i 40.

Berve (*see* Berrow).

Berwald, abbot of Glastonbury, ii 249.

Berwick, hundred of, containing Berwick and Chilton-Cantelo, ii 323.

Berwick, situation, ii 337 ; hamlet of Stoford, 337 ; owned successively by the families of Courteney, Cantilupe, and de Hastings (created earls of Pembroke), 337 ; Reginald Grey, of Ruthen, 338 ; Richard, earl of Arundel, as of his wife's dowry, 338 ; the Nevils, 338 ; the Rogers family held it of the earl of Somerset, 338 ; the Symes family, 338 ; John Newman, 338 ; Elizabeth, widow of John Holland, earl of Kent, held two knights' fees here, owned afterwards by John Rogers, 338 ; church (St. Mary Magdalen) and its monuments, 338 ; bells (5), 338 ; Chilton-Cantelo, anciently held of the manor of, 339. lands in, owned by the guilds of Shepton Mallet, granted to John Horner, iii 465.

Besam, Nicholas, received a pension from Taunton priory, iii 236.

Besborough, earl of, J.P., i *xli.*

Besilles, Matthew de, landowner in time of Edward I, i *xxviii.* styled Batilon, owned Brompton Regis : was ancestor to the Besilles of Besilles-Leigh, iii 503 ; Elizabeth, his widow, held Brompton in dower, 504 ; Geffrey, owned also Radcot, Oxon, 504 ; Sir Thomas, knt., 504 ; John, 504 ; Peter, uncle to John, 504 ; Sir William founded a poor house at Brompton-Regis, 504 ; Elizabeth, daughter of Sir William, married Sir Richard Eliot, 504.

Best, Mr. de, patron of the living of Backwell, ii 307.

Besylis, William, held part of a knight's fee in Bower, iii 85 ; the fourth part of a knight's fee in Chilton, 89.

Betham, tithing of Combe St. Nicholas, ii 475.

Bethune, Mr., purchased land in Wanstraw, ii 229 ; the Rev., incumbent of Wanstraw, 229. owned a manor in Muchelney, iii 136.

Bettesworth, Mr., receives moiety of Brewton manor, i 215.

Beveridge, William, nominated to the bishopric of Bath and Wells, and declined it, iii 390.

Beverstone castle, built by Thomas, lord Berkeley, iii 279.

Beverton hill, iii 509.

Bevial, owned by St. John's priory, Wells, iii 408.

Bevine, John, i *xl.*

Binfords, the seat of Joan Jeane, i 72.

Bingham, Alice, married Tristeram Storke, ii 385; monument in Trent church, 385.

Bingham family descended from Roger Buissel, owned Sutton-Bingham, ii 350; Sir John, 350; Sylvester, 350; Gefferey, 350; Augustine, 350; William, 350; Ralph, 350; Sir Ralph, knt., 350; Sir William, 350; Margaret, married Ralph, lord Bisset, and conveyed to him the manor of Sutton-Bingham, 350; other branches of the family had seats in Dorset, Warwickshire, Kent, Herts and Notts, 350; arms, 350.

Binham hamlet, Old-Cleeve, iii 511.

Birch, Mr., owned Chedder-Fitzwalter, iii 576.

Birchanger hamlet, Monksilver, iii 534.

Bird, Samuel, benefaction to Wiveliscombe, ii 491.

Bird, Thomas, prior of Barlinch, 1524, iii 503.

Bird, William, prior of Bath, 1499-1525, B 56; began the rebuilding of the monastery: ruined by chemical experiments and building, 56; arms on monks' lodgings, 64; chapel and supposed burial place, 64.

Birds, notable miracle about, ii 273.

Birds of the county, i *xvii.*

Birke, Alexander, i *xl*; William, *xl.*

Birlaunde, Richard de, presented to Porlock church, by Herbert de Marisco, ii 37.

Birth, prolific, i 13.

Birth, extraordinary, i 53.

Birt's hill, or Abbot's hill, Pendomer, ii 348.

Bishop, Ambrose, mayor of Bath, 1743, B 26.

Bishop, James, owned Worle, iii 615.

Bishop, the Rev. John, J.P., D.D., i *xliii.* incumbent of Doulting, iii 474. of East Cranmore, ii 210; of Holcombe, 456; of Mells, 464. of Stoke-Lane, iii 484. of Whatley, ii 231. prebendary of Wells, iii 397.

Bishop, Samuel, subscribed to the charity school at Chew-Stoke, ii 102.

Bishop, the Rev., incumbent of Wedmore, i 191. the Rev. Mr., incumbent of Abbotscombe, ii 359; Rev. Mr., incumbent of West-Coker, 344.

Bishops of Wells, iii 377-379; of Bath and Wells, 379-390. interred in Bath abbey, B 67. in Wells cathedral, iii 399, 401. mandate respecting the baths, B 40.

Bishops' palaces: Banwell, iii 567. Chew Magna, ii 95, 489. Claverton, i 146, ii 489. Evercreech, ii 489; iii 414; Twiverton, ii 489. Wells, iii 403. Wiveliscombe, ii 489. Wookey, iii 421.

Bishops' parks: Evercreech, iii 414; Banwell, 567.

Bishops-Chew (*see* Chew Magna).

Bishops-Huish (*see* Huish-Episcopi).

Bishops-Hull (*see* Hill-Bishops).

Bishops-Lydiard (*see* Lydiard-Episcopi).

Bishops-Sutton, tithing of Chew Magna, ii 95.

Bishops-well, spring Yatton, iii 616.

Bishopston, ancient name of Montacute, iii 311; lands in, owned by the Brook family, 303.

Bishopston, tithing, Montacute, iii 314.

Bishopworth hamlet (*see* Bedminster).

Biss, James and John, owners of Norton-Hautville, ii 108; James, who sells the estates to James Ford, 108.

Biss, of Spargrove, quibble on the window of Bath abbey, B 59 (*see* Bisse).

Bisse family, owned Widcombe and Lyncombe, i 171. West Chelworth, ii 420. Edward, attends the consecration of Wick chapel, i 219. George and Mary his wife, inscription in Martock church, iii 10; James, held the advowson of Inglishcombe, 340; the manor of Batcombe, 467; benefaction to Croscombe, 470; memorial in Croscombe church 470. John, owned Belluton and Pensford, ii 435. Peglinch, Shascombe, East-Wick, Whiteoxmead, lands in Woodborough, Wellow, and Camerton, iii 328; manors of Spargrove and Westcombe, 467; Philip, benefaction to Wadham college, Oxford, 467; inscription in Batcombe church, 467; arms, 467.

Bisset family owned Sutton-Bingham, through marriage of Ralph, lord Bisset, with Margaret de Bingham, ii 350. Manser, owned Yarnfield: bestowed it on his leper's hospital at Maiden Bradley, iii 41.

Bitewode, boundary of Selwood forest, ii 195.

Bittercliff, owned by Sir John Davie, iii 554.

Bittiscombe hamlet, in Upton, held by the Bratton family, iii 554; Thomas Bratton held it of James Luttrell, 555; chapel formerly stood here, 555.

Bitton, John, who marries Hawise de Fourneaux, i 263.

Bitton or Button, William de, two bishops of Bath and Wells of this name (*see* Button).

Blachedone (*see* Blagdon).

Black Alms, Bath, founded by the sisters Bimbury, B 44.

Black Nore, i *xii.*

Blackdown hill, i *xiv,* 58; iii 26, 374.

Blackdown or Blagdon manor (*see* Pitminster).

Blackford, situation, iii 452; Domesday survey, 452. owned by the abbots of Glastonbury, ii 243. iii 452; held by Ailwacre: Alnod held it T.R.E.: Turstin Fitz-Rolf owned land here: held by Alward, 452. subsequently passed to the bishopric of Bath and Wells, ii 252. iii 452; the duke of Somerset, 452; land here was held by the barons Moels and Lovel, 452; Nicholas de Seymour, 452; land called "The Estalle" held of Hamo de Blackford, 452; "Wythele" held of Thomas de Courtney, 452; "Bricestenement" held under Sir John d'Acton,

Blackford—*continued.*
and the heir of James de Wylton, 452;
Thistlesham, held of the earl of Salisbury,
452; these estates inherited by the families
of Bampfylde and Stawel, 452; church (St.
Michael) 453; bells (3), 453.

Blackford, hamlet of Wedmore, once the property of the bishop of Bath: owned by
the feoffees of Bruton hospital, i 187; mineral spring, 187. rating of, in 1293, iii 394;
report in 1329, 394; granted to Edward,
duke of Somerset, 395.

Blackford or Tivington, vill of Selworthy, ii 41.

Blackford, Hamo de, held land in Blackford, iii
452.

Blackford, William, sheriff, 1711, i *xxxviii.*
William, owned Kentsford, iii 493.

Blackford, memorial brasses in Dunster church,
ii 18.

Blackfriars, London, property in, given by
Richard Huish for the endowment of a
hospital at Taunton and scholarship at Oxford or Cambridge, iii 238.

Blackindone, Wilhelma de, prioress of Cannington, i 233.

Blackland, iii 467.

Blackmore forest, Dorset: Holwell, Buckshaw,
and Woodbridge, situated in, but subject to
the jurisdiction of Somerset, ii 369, 370.

Blackmore green, owned by the bishopric of
Bath and Wells, iii 579.

Blackmore hamlet (*see* Churchill).

Blackmore, Henry, granted Skilgate to Abbotsbury abbey, iii 545.

Blackmore, Richard, benefaction to West-Buckland parish, ii 486.

Black-rock, iii 608.

Blacker's hill, Chilcompton, ii 127.

Blackwell, Hugh, receives pension from Brewton, i 214.

Bladney hamlet, Wookey, iii 421.

Bladud, supposed discoverer of Bath waters, B 5.

Bladud's buildings, Bath, B 39.

Blagden, the Rev., inscription in Hardington
church, ii 348.

Blagdon, situation, iii 569; springs, 569; includes part of Rickford, Bathe, Elwick,
and part of Aldwick, 569; Domesday survey, owned by Serlo de Burci: Almar held
it T.R.E. 569; subsequently owned by the
Martin family, 569; the Columbers and
Audley families, 569; Robert Vere, earl of
Oxford, 569; the Hollands, earls of Huntingdon, 569; the earls of Derby, 569;
Edmund Baynard, 570; the Gorges, of
Eye, co. Hereford, 570; Henry Hardy,
570; Captain Reed, 570; Thomas Keedwell, 570; John Billingsley, 570; Flaxley
abbey owned land in Blagdon, 570; church
(St. Andrew) and its monuments, 570;
bells (5), 570; benefactions, 570.

Blagdon or Blackdown (*see* Pitminster).

Blagrave, Anthony, married Mary Gore, and
became possessed of Barrow-Gournay, ii
309; John, inherited Barrow-Gournay,
309; John, owned land in Dundry, 106.
John, owned Failands, iii 155.

Blaithwayt, William, M.P. for Bath, 1690,
1695, 1698, 1701, 1702, 1705, 1708, B 22
(*see* Blathwaite).

Blake, Edith, of Langport, married Sir Edward
Phelips, iii 315.

Blake, Humphry, owned Tuxwell, i 245;
memorial stone in Asholt church, 238;
Nathaniel, memorial stone in Asholt church,
238.

Blake, Mr., of Minehead, owned Cooksley, iii
555.

Blake, Rev., incumbent of Stockland-Bristol, i
248.

Blake, Robert, admiral, born at Bridgwater, iii
82; career of, 82, 83. M.P., 1653, i *xxxii.*
besieged and captured Taunton castle, iii
229; buried in Westminster abbey, 83.

Blake, Robert, monument in Ash-Priors church,
ii 498.

Blake memorial stone in Charlinch church, i
241.

Blakebergh, boundary of Exmoor perambulation, 1298, ii 19.

Blanchard family, owners of St. Katherine's
manor, i 138; monuments in St. Katherine's church, 139, 140; arms, 139, 140;
Elizabeth, wife of James Walters, 138;
Quirina, wife of Thomas Parry, 138;
monuments in St. Katherine's church,
139.

Blanchard, James, monument in Bath abbey,
1690, B 67.

Blanchard, Thomas, of North Wraxall, i 107.

Blanchard, married Thomas Strode, ii 210.

Bland family, held land in Exton, iii 526.

Bland, John le, owned Low Ham, iii 445; John,
445.

Blandford, Jonas, owned Catash, ii 51.

Blandon, John and Elizabeth, monument in
Banwell church, iii 568.

Blaney's, lord, daughter, wife of John Miller, i
105.

Blanketings, manufacture of, at Dulverton, iii
520.

Blatch bridge, Frome, ii 185.

Blatchwell spring, iii 39.

Blathwaite family owned Porlock, ii 37;
William of Dirham, owned Porlock, 37.
the royalties of Lansdowne, i 159; disputed
the ownership of that manor with William
Oliver, 160; owned Langridge, 132; incumbent of Langridge, 132; arms, 132.

Blaunchsale or White Hall, hospital, Ilchester,
iii 300; converted into a nunnery, 300;
a free chapel, 300, 301.

Bleadon, situation, iii 571 ; river Ax, 571 ;
Domesday survey, 571 ; owned by bishop
of Winchester : Saulf held one hide, 571 ;
held by the bishopric, and at the reformation settled on the dean and chapter of
Winchester, 571 ; sometime residence of
the Rev. Meric Casaubon, 572 ; church
(St. Peter) and monument, 571 ; bells (5),
571.

Bleadon, Mr., owned the manor of Glastonbury,
ii 259.

Blencowe, William, prebendary of Wells, iii 397.

Bletchly, Sarah, monument in Wellow church,
iii 329.

Blewet family (*see* Bluet).

Blobole, Water, tomb in Pointington church,
ii 377.

Blois, Henry de, abbot of Glastonbury, ii 250 ;
rebuilt many of the manor houses and
buildings belonging to the abbey, 251 ;
gifts to the abbey, 251 ; contention with
Roger de la Mere, respecting Mells, 462.
created bishop of Winchester, 1129, iii
231 ; was a great benefactor to Taunton
priory, 235 ; in his time, the manor of Camerton was restored to Glastonbury by the
Cotele family, 330.

Blome, John, procured license to search at Glastonbury for the body of Joseph of Arimathea, ii 262.

Bloodstone, found at Filton, ii 440.

Bloomberg, baron, married Elizabeth Dickinson, widow of Sir Edward Shires, ii 417.

Blount, Catherine, daughter of lord Mountjoy,
married Sir Maurice Berkeley, i 215.

Blount, Isabel, owned Brimpton D'Evercy, iii
214.

Blount, Elizabeth, first wife of Sir Hugh Paulet,
ii 167.

Blount, Sir John, who married Elizabeth Fourneaux, i 262 ; Alice, who married (1) Sir
Richard Stafford (2) Sir Richard Stury,
262 ; William, 262 ; Maud, 262.

Bloynes, Edward, owned Norton-Ferrers, iii 37.

Blue Coat Charity, Bath, founded by Robert
Nelson, B 50.

Bluet or Blewet family owned Almsworthy, ii
21. Ashbrittle, iii 21 ; Grindham, 29.
Hinton Blewet, ii 144, 145. Holcombe,
iii 275 ; North Petherton, 55 ; Lottisham,
24. Lydiard-Pincherton, ii 494. Sydenham, iii 24 ; Thorn-Coffin, 322 ; West-
Melcombe, 73. Wanstraw, ii 229. members of, buried in North-Petherton church,
iii 74 ; arms, 29 ; Catherine, daughter of
Sir Roger, married Richard Warre, 262 ;
Elizabeth, married Thomas de Rodney,
603. John, owned Hinton Blewet, ii 144 ;
John, owned Wanstraw, 229. John, owned
Clayhill, iii 89 ; John, of Grindham, married Agnes Beaupine, and inherited the

Bluet or Blewet family—*continued.*
estate of North Petherton, 55 ; John, married Margery Hogshaw, and became possessed of Clevedon, and rents in Tickenham,
Langford, and Kingston-Seymour, 167 (*see*
also i 223). John, of Holcombe, married
Elizabeth Portman, iii 275 ; John, conveyed
Ashbrittle to Sir John Chichester, 21. Nicholas, i xl. Nicholas, owned Almsworthy, ii
21. Nicholas, of Lottisham, married Agnes de Sydenham, became possessed of
Sydenham, iii 24. Walter, M.P., 1368,
1373, 1377, i xxx. Walter, owned part of
Lydiard-Pincherton, ii 494. Sir Walter,
married Christian de Grindham, and became possessed of Grindham, iii 29.

Blund, John le, married Constance de Wrotham,
iii 55, 64. Susanna, heiress to Cathanger, i 41

Blundell, John, incumbent of Broomfield, i 72.
Thomas, married Emma Montague, ii 88.

Blunt family held Bathford, i 112. Alice,
daughter of Sir John, married (1) Sir
Richard Stafford, (2) Sir Richard Storey,
iii 213, 532. Edmund, held Bath Easton, i
107 ; Bath Hampton, 117 ; Swainswick,
153. Sir John, knt., married Elizabeth de
Fourneaux, and became possessed of Ashington, iii 213 ; and of Kilve, 532. Simon,
held Bath Easton, i 107, and Bathampton,
117.

Blyhe, Simon, married Alice Warmwell, iii 206.

Boarden bridge, ii 346.

Boat Stall lane, Bath, B 32.

Bobbett, memorial stone in Creech St. Michael
church, i 78.

Bochelande (*see* Buckland St. Mary).

Bochelcot, owned by Buckland priory, iii 98.

Bodden tithing, Shepton-Mallet, iii 460.

Bode, Thomas, received a pension from Keynsham abbey, ii 403.

Bodell, William, bailiff of Taunton, iii 228.

Bodicombe or Budecumbe family owned Butcombe, ii 313.

Boduchelei (*see* Butleigh).

Bohun, Humphrey de, married Eleanor de
Braose, iii 80 ; Humphrey de, owned land
in Foxcote, 349 ; Humphrey de, married
Maud de Sarisberi, 366 ; Humphrey de,
witness to a deed between John Marshall
and Hugh de Ralegh, 536. Joan, sister of
Sir Alan Plugenet, owned Haselborough, ii
332 ; Margaret, wife of Hugh de Courtney,
160. Muriel de, gave lands in Sherborne
and Primesley to Buckland priory, iii 98.
Robert, held knight's fee from the Mohun
family, ii 14.

Boissier, John Lewis, governor of Bath hospital,
B 48 ; Peter, governor of Bath hospital, 48.

Bole, Elizabeth, married John Holbeach, ii 441 ;
Nicholas de, part owner of Ubley, sold it
to Nicholas Huscarle, 156 ; arms, 443.

Bolebec, Osborne de, iii 41.

Boleville, Nicholas de, M.P., 1343, i *xxx.*

Bolewil, Nicholas de, ii 265.

Boleworth, owned by John Roche, iii 547; John Catar, 547.

Bollo, holder of Hatch Beauchamp, i 44.

Bolsover, baron (*see* Cavendish).

Bolter, Roger, married Alice de Sydenham, iii 522.

Bolton, duke of, J.P., i *xli.*

Bond family owned Brean, i 178.

Bond, Sir George, lord mayor of London, born at Trull, iii 293; Dionysia, his daughter, married Sir Henry Winston, 293; the duke of Marlborough was descended from this family, 293.

Bond, James, master of St. Catherine's hospital, Bedminster, ii 283.

Bond, John, master of Taunton-school; distinguished scholar and author, iii 239; monument in church of St. Mary Magdalen, Taunton, 239, 240.

Bond, Richard, last incumbent of the fraternity at Croscombe, iii 470.

Bond street, Bath, B 37.

Bondland, custom of tenure in Taunton manor, iii 233.

Bondmen, explanation of the term, i 5.

Bones, gigantic, i 189, iii 370.

Boniton, Margaret, wife of Sir Thomas Paulet, ii 167.

Bonner family: Henry, Mary, Elizabeth, monument in Combe St. Nicholas church, ii 476, 477.

Bono, held land in Banwell, iii 566.

Bonstone, hamlet of Fiddington, i 241.

Bonus, Marcus Fisicus, prior of Montacute, iii 312.

Bonville family owned Beer, i 235, iii 90. Chewton-Mendip, ii 116. East-Lydford, iii 196; Idstock, 90. Lillisdon, ii 179. Limington, iii 219. Merriot, ii 170; Porlock, 37. Puckington, i 56. Sock-Dennis, iii 307. Thurlbeer, ii 182. Catherine, married (1) Sir John Cobham, (2) John Wyke, of Ninehead, iii 267. Cecily, married Thomas Grey, marquis of Dorset, i 56, ii 170; Cecily, married Henry Grey, duke of Suffolk, 37; Elizabeth, married Thomas West, lord de la Warre, 413. John, landowner in time of Edward I, i *xxviii.* Sir John owned Chewton-Mendip, ii 116. Sir John held East Lydford, iii 196; Nicholas, constable of Taunton castle, 227; held Sock-Dennis, 307; married Hawise de Pyne, 521; conveyed all his rights in Dulverton to Taunton priory, 521; Sir Nicholas de, patron of Blanchsale, 300. Sir Thomas, married Margaret Meriet, and became possessed of Merriot manor, ii 170, Lopen, iii 122. Sir Thomas, married Cecily

Bonville family—*continued.*

Streche, iii 26. William, M.P., 1366, 1383, 1384, i *xxx*, 1386, 1392, 1394, 1398, *xxxi*; Sir William, sheriff, 1380, 1381, *xxxv.* received lands in trust for Richard Luttrell, ii 46. held land in Stapleton and Martock, iii 7; held Limington, 219. married Elizabeth Harington, i 56, ii 170. owned Chewton - Mendip, 116; was summoned to Parliament by the title of lord Bonville of Chewton, 116. was keeper of Petherton park, iii 62, 492; one of the lords of Mendip, 375. assisted in the destruction of Stoke Courcy fortress, i 251. killed at the battle of St. Albans, ii 116; tomb in Chewton Mendip church, 119. William, lord Harington, married Catherine Nevil, i 56, ii 170; owned Porlock, 37. killed at Wakefield, i 56.

Bonville, William, lord (*see* Bonville family).

Books on Bath waters, B 83, 84.

Booles, John, benefaction to Otterford, iii 284.

Boomer or West-Melcomb (*see* North Petherton)

Booth, lady, benefaction to Bath abbey, B 71.

Boothby, Sir William, bart., monument in Bath abbey, 1787, B 67.

Bord, William, owned Uphill, iii 610.

Bordarii, the, i 5, 106.

Bordesley, passed from the De Tort family to the Raleighs, iii 537.

Borefordescote-Wyke, Richard of, master of St. Catherine's hospital, Bedminster, ii 283.

Boringdon, John Parker, baron, J.P., i *xlii.* owned Buckland, iii 99.

Borough, tithing of Wedmore, i 188.

Borough walls, Bath, B 32.

Borough - bank, chapel formerly standing at, demolished, ii 429.

Boroughbridge, hamlet of East Ling, i 84; situation, 85; origin of its name, 85; ancient chapel, 85; garrisoned by Goring, 85; stone bridge and by whom repaired, 86; width of the river, 86.

Bosanquet, Jacob, monument in Bath abbey, 1767, B 67.

Boscawen, Hugh, married Margaret, daughter of Theophilus, earl of Lincoln, baron Clinton, iii 469; Bridget, their daughter, married Hugh Fortescue, 469.

Bosco family, tenants in South Cadbury, ii 73. held Exton, iii 527. Edward de, ii 314. Joan, daughter of Richard, married Sir Ralph Perceval, iii 165, 174.

Boscome, Alestan, held land in Chilthorne, iii 217.

Bosintune (*see* Bossington).

Bossington, hamlet of Porlock, ii 37; Domesday survey, 37; owned by the abbots of Athelney T.R.E., held by Radulfus de Limesi, 37; Talbot de Hethfield, Henry de Glasten,

F

Bossington—*continued.*
John Whyton, Walter Paunsfort, John Syd-
enham, Sir Thomas Acland, 38 (*see* also iii
215).
Bossington point, Porlock, ii 35.
Bostock, John, owned part of the manor of
Ash-Priors, ii 498.
Bostock, Richard, M.D., monument in Bath
abbey, 1747, B 67.
Boteburne, given by the countess of Leicester
to Buckland priory, iii 96.
Boteler family owned Brean, i 178, 197; Avicia
held Bath Easton, 107. John, lawsuit with
Richard Choke, ii 434; Sir John owned
Emborow, 135; John, granted the lake in
Emborow to the monks of Charterhouse
Hinton, 158; James, earl of Ormond (*see*
Ormond); Margaret, of Overley, married
(1) Warine de Ralege (2) John de Bretesche,
314. Margaret, of Badminton, married John
Arthur, iii 178. Ralph, ii 135; married
Margaret Berewyk, 157.
Botetourt, baron, title conferred on Charles Berk-
eley of Brewton, iii 281; barony claimed by
Norborne Berkeley, 280; descended to
Elizabeth, duchess dowager of Beaufort, 280
Botetourt, Catherine, married Sir Thomas
Berkeley of Stoke, iii 280.
Boteville (*see* Botville).
Botiler (*see* Boteler).
Botreaux chantry, B 70, iii 199, 200.
Botreaux family, owned Aller and Aller-Moor,
iii 188. Babington, ii 450; Cadbury-North,
66. Cricket St. Thomas, iii 116; lands
in Holton, 453. lands in Kilmersdon, ii
446; Luckington and Walton, 447; Publow, 428; Rodden, 226. Shipham, iii
601; Winterhead, 602. Wollard, ii 423.
Yeovilton, iii 199. Elizabeth, received
lands from Sir William de Palton, ii
152; Gefferey, 66; Hamon, 66. Sir John,
married Hawise Newmarch, iii 338. Margaret, married Sir Robert Hungerford, ii
67, 226, iii 343, 355. Reginald, ii 66. monument in Aller church, iii 189. William
de, land owner temp. Ed. I, i *xxviii.* William de, married the heiress of Moels, ii
66; owned North Cadbury, 66, and land
in Kilmersdon, 446. William de, witness
to a deed, iii 536. William, married Elizabeth Daubeney, ii 66, 67, iii 108; Sir
William, knt., 66. married Elizabeth St.
Lo, and became possessed of Yeovilton,
and Aller, iii 199, and of Newton St. Lo,
iii 343; held a fair, and the advowson of
the church in Barrington, 113. William, ii
66, iii 199. William, gave Yeovilton to the
priors of Bath for the foundation of a chantry there, ii 67, iii 199, 200. held Cricket St.
Thomas, iii 116. married Elizabeth Beaumont, ii 67; buried at North Cadbury, 67.

Botville family, owned Langham manor, ii 25.
William, held land in Langford and Welles-
ford, iii 19.
Boucher, Eleanor, gift to Castle Cary church,
ii 58.
Boudon, John, remitted to Elias Spelly his right
in Kingston Seymour, ii 123; Sir John de,
married Joan de Wengham, 123.
Bough-Hayes, iii 306.
Boulting family, owned West Theal, i 188;
monument in Wedmore church, 192.
Boundslane, Chard, ii 471.
Bourbache, held of the heir of John Wyke, by
William de Palton, ii 456.
Bourchier, Anne, daughter of Edward, earl of
Bath, married Sir Christopher Wrey, ii 392;
Cecily, married Thomas Peyton, 391;
Dorothy, married Thomas Grey, son of the
earl of Stamford, owned land in Huntspill
Cogan, 392; Mary, married Hugh Wyatt,
391. John, sheriff, 1519, i *xxxvii.* Sir
John, married Elizabeth Hungerford, iii
356 (*see* also Bath, earls of, and Fitzwarren,
earls).
Bourchier, Henry, earl of Essex, owned Bed-
minster, ii 282.
Bourchier, William, earl of Ewe (*see* Ewe, earl
of), ii 391.
Boure Ashton, hamlet in Long Ashton, ii 304.
Bourne, Gilbert, bishop of Bath and Wells, 1554-9,
and lord president of Wales, iii 387; benefactions to bishop's close and Bubwith's hospital, 387, 408; deprived of his bishopric,
387; received a grant of Banwell and lands
in Axbridge, Worle, and Churchill, 567;
ceded Yatton to the crown, 617.
Bourne, Roger, owned Gautheney, i 240;
Thomas, last male heir, 240; Anne, daugh-
ter of John Malet, wife of Roger, monu-
ment in Charlinch church, 241.
Bourton manor, Wick, iii 612; owned by the
Percevals, 612; the Vanhams, 612; Mrs.
Yate, 612; the Rev. Mr. Somerville, 612.
Bourton-Combe, Flax-Bourton, iii 161.
Bourwardesleye, William de, iii 402.
Bovett, Rev. Dr., incumbent of Ninehead
church, iii 268.
Bovett, Richard, J.P., i *xliii.*
Bowachyn, William, monk of Bath, received
pension, B 57.
Bowden, hamlet of Henstridge, ii 364.
Bowditch, Roman encampment at Chew Magna,
ii 96.
Bowdler, John, governor of Bath hospital, B 47;
Thomas, governor of Bath hospital, 47.
Bowen, Rev. John, J.P., i *xliii.*
Bowen, Rev. Mr., incumbent of Bishop's-Lydi-
ard, ii 495.
Bower, Edmund, purchased King-Weston from
Sir John Smyth, ii 81. John, owned Id-
stock, iii 90.

Bower, Cecily, tablet in St. Cuthbert's church, Wells, iii 407 ; arms, 407.

Bower-Henton, hamlet, Martock, iii 2 ; name of Newton given to part of, 3.

Bower, West and East (*see* Bridgwater).

Bowerman, Henry, monk of Hinton, pensioned, iii 368.

Bowerman, James, held Isle-Brewers rectory, i 54.

Bowerman, William, benefaction to Wiveliscombe, ii 491. to Wookey, iii 421.

Bowes, Matilda, married Thomas Whalesborough, iii 538.

Bowet, Henry, bishop of Bath and Wells, 1401-1407, translated to York, iii 383, 384.

Bowhall, hamlet of Staple Fitzpaine, i 58.

Bowles, John, benefaction to Keynsham, ii 410.

Bowles, Rev. Mr., incumbent of Brean, i 179.

Bowlish, hamlet, Shepton-Mallet, iii 460.

Bowring, Alice, married William Pike, iii 7.

Bowser, Catherine, last prioress of Buckland, iii 98.

Bowyer or Bures family, owned Preston-Bowyer, iii 16 ; John de, held Milverton, 14. John, owned Beer, i 235 ; Edmund, 235.

Bowyer, Rev. George, incumbent of White Lackington, i 69.

Bowyer, Rev. Mr., of Martock, donation to the living of East-Lambrook, ii 469. monument in Martock church, iii 10 ; arms, 10.

Boyce, John, mayor of Bath, 1656, B 25.

Boyce or Bosco family (*see* Bosco).

Boyd, Mary, monument in Bath Abbey, 1762, B 67.

Boyse (*see* Bosco).

Bozun, Robert, married Joan, daughter of John de Sydenham and widow of Richard Cave, iii 87. William, received lands in Heathfield and Ford from John de Bretesche, ii 315

Bracey, John, abbot of Muchelney, iii 135.

Bracton (*see* Bratton).

Bradenei, Simon de, sold lands in Huntspill, iii 101

Bradenstoke priory, Wilts, owned land in Somerset temp. Ed. I, i *xxvii.* prior exchanged Chedder church for Chilcompton with the bishop of Bath and Wells, ii 129 ; received lands in Kington St. Michael from Sir Thomas Delamere, 218 ; owned an estate at Lypiat, 447.

Bradeston, Philip, the heirs of, held the reversion of an estate in Clatworthy, iii 509.

Bradewei (*see* Broadway).

Bradford, situation, iii 243 ; river Tone, bridges, 243 ; Domesday survey, 243 ; owned by the bishop of Winchester, held of him by Eduin, T.R.E., 243 ; given at the conquest to the earl of Morton : held by Alured, 243 ; subsequently held by John de Montacute, 244 ; Meriet family, 244, 259 ; the Warres of Hestercombe, 244, 262 ; Sir Thomas de Camoys, 244 ; Simon de Meriet, 244 ; John

Bradford—*continued.*
Parker, 244 ; Edward Clarke and William Doble Burridge, 244 ; the prior of Montacute had an estate here, 244 ; Hele, and Stoford, hamlets, 244 ; Forde, owned by William de Forde, 244 ; Roger de Vernay, 244 ; church (St. Giles), 244 ; bells (5), 244 ; chantry, 244.

Bradford, Joan, daughter of Robert : wife of John Godwyn, iii 84.

Bradford, John de, vicar of Long Ashton, 1340, ii 299 ; John de, abbot of Keynsham, 1348, 402.

Bradford, Mr., joint owner of East-Cranmore, ii 208.

Bradford, William de, held the fourth part of a knight's fee in Tickenham, iii 165.

Bradford's-bridge, hamlet of Marston Bigot, ii 216.

Bradford's-bridge, Frome, ii 185.

Bradley, situation, ii 271 ; Domesday survey, 271 ; owned by the abbot of Glastonbury, 271 ; held by Roger : Winegod held it T.R.E. 271 ; subsequently owned by Mr. Keate, 271 ; living, a chapel to East-Pennard, 271 ; chapel, 271.

Bradley, Mr., of Mells, owned Tothill, iii 476. John, incumbent of Knolle chapel, ii 287.

Bradney, Joachim de, held land in Slape and Donwere, iii 85 ; owned Bradney, 92. Simon de, M.P., 1346, i *xxx.* held also lands in Bridgwater, Currypool, Sanford and Bawdrip, iii 92 ; monument in Bawdrip church, 93 ; Beatrix de, 92 ; arms, 92.

Bradney hamlet (*see* Bawdrip).

Bradon, South, position, i 15 ; owned by earl Morton, and held by Drogo or Drew, 15 ; Domesday survey, 15 ; division of the manor, 15 ; church, demolished (St. Mary Magdalene), 16 ; inhabitants attend Puckington church, 16 ; hamlet of North Bradon, 16 ; parish of Goose Bradon, now depopulated, 16 ; origin of its name, 16 ; held by the Warre family, 16.

Bradston, Joan, owned Samford Arundel, iii 26 ; Elizabeth, married Sir John Streche, 26.

Brag-church, Henford, iii 207.

Bragg, John, J.P., i *xliii.* owned Wayford, ii 175 ; Mrs. Elizabeth, benefaction to Wayford, 175 ; Mr., part-owner of Castle Cary, sold it to lord Holland, 56. Margaret, married John Prowse, iii 583.

Bragge, William, monument in Compton-Pauncefor church, ii 77.

Braham, John, inscription in Wells cathedral, iii 401.

Braibroc, Robert de, owned Horsington, ii 371.

Brailsford, Matthew, dean of Wells, 1713, i 190.

Bramic, Braunc or Branuc gave Downhead to the abbot of Glastonbury, iii 475.

Bramora, Geffrey de, holder of Brymore, i 233.

Brampton, Devon, granted to Cleeve abbey, iii 511.

Bramston, Diana, monument in Bath abbey, B 64, 67.

Branch or Braunche family: William, married Joan Fitz-Bernard, and became owner of Frome, ii 187; landowner temp. Ed. I, i *xxvii.* Nicholas, ii 187. landowner temp. Ed. I, i *xxvii.* Andrew, owned also lands in Nunney, ii 218; Sir Andrew granted land to Robert Adymot, 187; Thomas, 187; Alianor, wife of Richard Winslade, 187; memorial tablet in Dundry church, 106.

Brandon, Frances, wife of Henry Grey, marquis of Dorset, i 56.

Brandy-street, vill of Selworthy, ii 41.

Braose, William de, landowner temp. Ed. I, i *xxviii.* lord of Brecknock, Radnor, and Abergavenny, iii 80; married Graecia Briwere, and became possessed of the castle, manor, and borough of Bridgwater, and the manors of Haygrove and Odcombe, 80; William, his son, massacred by Llewellyn, prince of Wales, 80, ii 324. his four daughters were his co-heiresses, iii 80; Maud, married Roger de Mortimer, 80, ii 324. Eve, married William de Cantilupe, iii 80; Eleanor, married Humphrey de Bohun, 80; Isabel, married (1) David, son of Llewellyn, prince of Wales, (2) Peter Fitzherbert, 80. Reginald de, married Grecia Briwere, i 54 [*v.* footnote.]

Brass mills, Weston, i 156. Keynsham, ii 400.

Brathwaite, John, governor of Bath hospital, B 47.

Bratone (*see* Bratton).

Bratton family held Bratton, ii 31, 32; iii 555. Henry de, ii 32; John de, held Culbone, 3, 4, 32; John de, held half a knight's fee from John de Mohun, 15. Nicholas, i *xl.* Peter owned Culbone, ii 3, 32; gave lands in Sparkhay to Dunster priory, 17; Robert held a knight's fee from Sir William de Mohun, 14; Simon, of Culbone, 4, 32; Thomas de, landowner temp. Ed. 1, i *xxvii.* Thomas, ii 32; held half a knight's fee in Timberscombe, 44. held Bittelscombe and Bratton, and lands in Wichanger, Wydon, Allerford, and Puriton, iii 555.

Bratton, hamlet of Minehead, ii 31; Domesday survey, 31; owned by William de Mohun, and held by Roger and Aluric, 31; owned by the family of Bratton, 31, 32; iii 555. Peter Lord King, ii 32.

Bratton hill, i *xiv*; ii 27.

Bratton-Seymour, iii 36; situation, 36; Domesday survey, 36; owned by Walter de Dowai: Gerard held it of him: Elsi held it T.R.E. 36; subsequently held by the Lovels, 36; the St. Maurs, 36; the Zou-

Bratton-Seymour—*continued.* ches, 36; one moiety held by the Dyer family, 36; the other held by Jerom Dibben, 36; the monks of Brewton held land there, 36; afterwards, one moiety held by Mr. Warner, 36; the other by Mr. Chilwell, 36; church (Holy Trinity), 36; bells (3), 36.

Braunche (*see* Branch).

Bray, Ralph, sheriff, 1215, i *xxiii.* Sir Ralph de, knt., witness to a deed of gift from Anastatia Croc to Sir Thomas Trivet iii 101; William de, the service of, granted by Anastatia Croc to Sir Thomas Trivet, 101.

Braybrook, Joan, married Sir Thomas Brook, afterwards created lord Cobham, iii 303.

Brean, situation, i 177; Brean Down, 177; owned by Walter de Dowai, 177; Domesday survey, 178; held by Merlesuain T.R.E. 178; owned by the families of Grandison, Boteler, Elizabeth, wife of William de Montacute, Wykham, lords Say and Sele, Becher, Bond, Cann, Thomas Master, 178; place from which the Guy Briens take their name, 179; the church, 179 (*see* also ii 392).

Brean, John, bequest to Chew Stoke, ii 102; subscribes to the charity school, 102.

Brean-Down, i *xii,* 177, iii 608.

Breant, Normandy, granted to Sir Walter Hungerford, iii 354.

Brecon, Elizabeth, widow of Reginald de Brecon, owned Elm, ii 206. held Skilgate, iii 545.

Bremmesmore, lands in, given by the countess of Leicester to Buckland priory, iii 96.

Brendon-Hill, i *xiv,* iii 502, 505, 525.

Brenetour, Peter le, M.P. for Bath, 1299, B 19; 1313, B 19.

Brenne, Robert, lord of a parcel of Brene, i 179.

Brent-cum-Wrington hundred, i 195; owned by the abbots of Glastonbury, Edward, duke of Somerset, and Sir Charles Kemeys Tynte, 195.

Brent-East, early records, i 195, 196; Domesday survey, 196; manor owned by abbey of Glastonbury, 196; held by Roger, Ralph, Alfric, and Godwin, T.R.E. 196; held by families of Bythemore and Percival, 196; granted to the duke of Somerset, afterwards owned by the city of London, the Whitmore family, Arthur Green Wollers, and Robert Mackrath, 196; hamlets of Edingworth, Rook's-Bridge, and North-Yeo, 197; mansion house built by abbot Selwood, 197; church (St. Mary) and its monuments, 198; damaged by lightning, 198.

Brent-South, situation, i 199; owned by the abbots of Glastonbury, and held by the family of St. Barb, 199; owned by the Brent family, duke of Somerset, Mr. Slade, and Mr. Hales, 199; church (St. Michael)

Brent-South—*continued.*
　and its monuments, 200; benefactions, 200,
　201; curious carvings on the bench ends,
　201. land here granted to the poor of
　Wells, iii 411.
Brent church, exempted from episcopal author-
　ity, ii 241.
Brent, Falk de, who marries Margaret de Red-
　vers *née* FitzGerald, i 251; fortifies and
　garrisons Stoke Courcy manor house, 251;
　exiled, 251; sells Fenne to William Russell,
　253; warder of Nicholas FitzMartin, ii 132.
Brent family of Cossington, iii 434, 435, 436;
　owned Cossington, 434; East Bagborough,
　242; Compton-Pauncefoot, Godwyn's-
　Bower, and West-Bagborough, 436; Dun-
　were and Slap, 85. lands in South Brent,
　i 199. Wheatley, ii 231. Robert de, re-
　ceived Cossington from Jordan Ridel, 1254,
　iii 434, 435; Millicent, widow of Robert,
　married Raymond Malet, 435; Robert de,
　married Isabella de Montacute, 435. land-
　owner temp. Ed. I, i *xxviii*; M.P. 1298, *xxix*;
　arms, *l.* the service of, granted by Anas-
　tatia Croc to Sir Thomas Trivet, iii 101;
　Sir Robert, married Claricia de Ford, and
　became possessed of Ford, 91, 435; John,
　son of Sir Robert, progenitor of the Fords
　of Charing, 435; Havysia, married Hugh
　de Popham, 435; Joan, married Thomas
　Denebaud, 435; Robert, son of Sir Robert,
　married Elizabeth Denebaud, 435; John,
　married Joan le Eyre, 435; John, married
　(1) Ida Beauchamp (2) Joan Latimer, 435;
　Joan, married (1) Thomas Horsey (2)
　Thomas Tretheke, 435; Sir Robert, mar-
　ried Jane Harewell, 435; John, half-brother
　of Sir Robert, succeeded to Cossington
　after a law-suit with Joan, his half-sister,
　436. owned Cathanger, i 41. Eleanor,
　married John Verney, i 254, iii 436. Robert,
　landowner in time of Henry VII, i *xl.*
　married Margaret Malet, iii 436. Robert,
　married Joan Malet, i 91. John, married
　Maud Pauncefort, ii 77. owned also God-
　wyn's Bower, Bagborough, Dunwere, Slap,
　and East-Bower, iii 84, 85; Compton-Paunce-
　ford and Pauanceford Hill, 436; monumental
　brass in Cossington church, 437. William,
　ii 77. married a daughter of lord Stourton,
　iii 436. Richard, ii 77, iii 436. Anne, only
　child of Richard, married lord Thomas
　Poulett, ii 77, iii 436. the estate passed to
　her daughter, Elizabeth Hoby, iii 436;
　John, second son of John and Maud Paunce-
　fort, married (1) a daughter of Thomas
　Godwyn (2) Mary Culpeper, 436; Stephen,
　of Dorchester, 436; John, son of Stephen,
　purchased Cossington, Ford, and Godwyn's
　Bower on the death of Elizabeth Hoby,
　436; John, married (1) Winifred Arundel

Brent family of Cossington—*continued.*
　(2) Mary Ludlow, died without issue, 1692,
　436; Hodges, grandson of Anne, daughter
　of Stephen, declared heir to the Cossington
　estates, 436.
Brent, Elizabeth, married Henry de Strode, ii
　209.
Brent, Mary, daughter of John Brent, of Wim-
　borne, wife of John Yerbury, ii 211.
Brent, Margareta, daughter of the Rev. Charles,
　a descendant of the Brents, of Cossington,
　married Samuel Coopey: monument in
　Wraxall church, iii 160; Mr., owned Hut-
　ton, and bequeaths it to his nephew, Samuel
　Coopey, who took the name of Brent, 590;
　Humphrey Coopey, 591; Charles Coopey,
　591.
Brent Knowle, i *xiv*, 195.
Brentmarsh, i *xv*, 195.
Brent, the river, its course, i *xiii.*
Brentemerse (*see* East Brent).
Breose or Braose (*see* Braose).
Brereton, William, governor of Bath hospital,
　b 47.
Bresmar, held Kilve, iii 532.
Bret or Brito family owned Whitestanton, iii
　127; Thorncombe, 501; Sandford-Bret,
　543; arms, 127, 128. Adam le, M.P., 1330,
　1335, i *xxix*; Adam le, landowner temp.
　Ed. I, *xxix.* Alice and Annora held
　lands in Trent, ii 381. Ansgerius, des-
　cendant of Ansger de Montagud, gave
　Preston to Bermondsey priory, iii 223;
　Edmund, called de Sandford, 543; Henry
　sold Whitestanton to Sir Abraham Elton,
　127. John le, M.P., 1337, i *xxx*; John,
　sheriff, 1579, *xxxvii.* John, holder of a
　knight's fee from John de Mohun, ii 14.
　John, of Sandford-Bret, iii 543. Lucia,
　married Hugh de Valletort, i 239. Marga-
　ret, wife of John Bret, monument in
　Whitestanton church, iii 127; Margaret,
　married John de Raleigh, 537; Maud, mar-
　ried John de St. Quintin, 543; Maud, mar-
　ried (1) Gerard, (2) Robert de Ouvre; great
　benefactress to Woodspring priory, 543;
　Ralph, married Agnes Warmwell, 206;
　Richard, called Brito, concerned in the
　murder of Thomas à Becket, 543; Richard,
　abbot of Cleeve, 1315, 512; Richard, one
　of the translators of the Bible, 127; Roger
　held land in Long-Sutton, 197; Roger gave
　Upcott to Taunton priory, 235. Simon held
　half a knight's fee from Sir William de
　Mohun, ii 14. Simon, ancestor to the
　Brets, of Thorncombe, iii 543; Simon,
　married a daughter of Thurloe, 543;
　Walter, founder of the Bretts, of White-
　stanton, 127. Walter, baron in time of
　Henry II, i *xxvi*; landowner temp. Ed. I,
　xxviii. Walter, held Trent, of the castle

Bridgwater: sea-port and market town, iii 75; ancient names, 75; situation, 75; river Parret, 75; Dunbal isle, 75; bridge, 75; quay, 75; markets, 75; fairs, 75; town government, 76; arms, 76; Domesday survey: owned by Walscin or Walter de Dowai: Merlesuain held it T.R.E. 78; subsequently owned by the Paganel or Paynel family, 78; William de Briwere, and William, his son: William de Braose, and William, his son, 78, 80; the castle and a third of the manor passed to the Mortimer family, earls of March, 80; Richard, duke of York, 80; the borough of Bridgwater, and manor of Haygrove, passed to the de Cantilupe family, 80; the lords Zouch, of Harringworth, 81; part of this estate given to Giles, lord D'Aubney, 81; the earls of Bridgwater, 81; castle and borough for some time held by the Queens of England, 81; castle and manor granted by Charles I to the Whitmore family, 81, 82; who sold it to the Harvey family, 82; the castle leased to Edmund Wyndham, 82; principal manor owned by the Trivet family, 82; the Pyms, 82; the family of Hales, 82; the corporation holds a manor, 82; castle field, 77; hospital, 78—80; priory, 80; birthplace of Admiral Blake, 82; Ham, village in the parish of Bridgwater, land in, owned by Wigfruth, in the time of Brithric, king of the West Saxons, description, 83; a manse there given to Ceolward by King Edwi, 83; Athelred granted the whole territory to the abbey of Athelney, 83, 235; Domesday survey, 83; manor subsequently belonged to Lady Tynte, 84; hamlets, Bower, West and East, 84; Domesday survey, 84; (1) owned by Walter de Dowai, held by Rademer: Saric held it T.R.E., when it belonged to Melecome (Melcumb); (2) owned by Alured de Ispania: Alwi held it T.R.E.: land in Peret (Petherton), belonged to this manor, 84; the family of Godwyn subsequently owned lands in Bower, and gave it the name of Godwyn's-Bower, 84; the Brent family, 84; John Horsey was lord of East and West Bower, temp. Ed. III, 85; Thomas Mychell, William Besylis, and John Walyngford held the fourth of a knight's fee here, formerly held by Robert Chilton, 85; Coker family owned lands here, 85; Philip Cave held lands in North Bower, 87; Dunweer, owned by Geffrey Cocus or Cook, and his descendants, 85; the Bradney family, 85; the Chichesters, 85; family of de Donwere held lands here, temp. Henry II and Richard I, 85; Philip Cave had lands here, 87; Horsey: Domesday survey, 85; owned by Walter de

Bridgwater—*continued.*
  Dowai: held by Rademer, 85; by Elward T.R.E. 85; subsequently owned by the Horsey family, 85; Sir John Stawel, 85; chapel here, demolished, 86; Pignes, Pegens, or Horsey-Pignes, 86; Domesday survey, held by John the Porter: Brictric held it T.R.E. 86; owned subsequently by the Horsey family, 86; mother-church to Chilton, supposed to have been here, 86; Sydenham, 86; held T.R.E. by Cheping: given at the Conquest to Roger Arundel, 86; owned by the Sydenhams, 86, 87; the Caves, 87; the Percevals, 87; Mr. Bull, 87; George Bubb Doddington, 87; manor house, rebuilt by Thomas Perceval, 87; church (St. Mary), 87, 88; chantries: St. George's, B.V.M., Trinity, 88; chapel of St. Saviour, built by William Pole, 88.
Bridgwater castle, description, iii 76; built by William Briwere, 78; subsequently owned by William de Braose, and William, his son, 80; the Mortimers, earls of March, 80; Richard, duke of York, 80; held for some time by the queens of England, 81; the Whitmores, 81, 82; the Harveys, 82; leased to Edmund Wyndham, 82; besieged and nearly destroyed by the Parliamentary army, 76, 77; old gatehouse converted into a mansion, 77; Giles, lord Daubeny, constable of, 109; Edmund Wyndham, governor, 492.
Bridgwater hospital, founded by William Briwere, iii 78; endowment and regulations, 79; list of masters, 79; suppressed, and the site granted to Humphrey Colles, 80; owned Wembdon church, 103.
Bridgwater priory of Grey Friars: founded by William Briwere, iii 80; held land in, and the church of, Northover, 306; bishop Beckington's bequest to, 385; site granted at the dissolution to Emanuel Lukar, 80.
Bridgwater, Henry, lord D'Aubeny created earl of: died without issue, iii 81, 109; title revived by James I: John Egerton, baron of Ellesmere, and viscount Brackley, created earl of, 81; John, second earl of, 81; John, third earl of, 81; Scroop, created marquis of Brackley and duke of, 81; John, duke of, 81; Francis, duke of, 81. monument in South Petherton church, iii 112.
Bridgwater, John, rector of Porlock, ii 40; master of St. Catherine's hospital, Bedminster, 283.
Bridmanston, Sire Stephen de, i *l.*
Bridport, Giles de, dean of Wells, 1253, i 189; Thomas de, sheriff, 1361, 1362, 1363, *xxxv.* Richard de, vicar of Wembdon, iii 103.
Bridwell, hamlet in West-Coker, ii 344.
Brien (*see* Bryan).
Brigg street or Beggar street, Wells, iii 408.

Brigge, John, abbot of Athelney, 1410, i 87.

Bright, Richard Meyler, J.P., i *xliii.*

Brimpsfield castle and manor forfeited by John de Maltravers, granted to Sir Maurice Berkley, iii 279.

Brimpton, John de, abbot of Glastonbury, 1335, ii 255.

Brimpton-D'Evercy, situation, iii 214; Alvington, hamlet, 214; Domesday survey, 214; owned by Roger de Curcelle, 214; held by Herbert: Seulf held it T.R.E. 214; subsequently held of the Fourneaux by the family of D'Evercy, 214; the Glamorgan family, 214; Sir Nicholas Glamorgan held it of Isabel Blount, 214; the Sydenhams, 214, 215; Mr. Penny, 215; the Fanes, 215; John Fane, earl of Westmoreland, 215; manor house, 215; chantry, 215; church (S. Andrew) and its monuments, 215, 216; bells (2) 215; cross, 216; yew-tree, 216; church owned by Montacute priory, 312.

Brin, Hawise de, married Robert Stradling, iii 335.

Brindsey hamlet, iii 584.

Brinscombe, hamlet of Overweare, i 184.

Brintsfield bridge, Weston-Zoyland, iii 440.

Brionis, Baldwin de (*see* Exeter).

Brislington, situation, ii 411; owned by Robert Fitz-Hamon, 411; Robert, earl of Gloucester, and William, his son, 411; prince John, 411; the de la Warres, 411, 412; the Wests, lords de la Warre, 412, 413; the Laceys, 413; the Langtons, 413; William Gore-Langton, 413; chapel of St. Anne, demolished, 413; church (St. Luke), 413; bells (5), 413; benefactions, 413; church and chapel of St. Anne, granted to Sir John St. Loe, 403.

Brismar held Freshford, i 125. Luxborough, ii 25; Farrington Gournay, 137; Haselborough, 331.

Brisnod held Trent, ii 380. and lands afterwards added to the manor of Somerton, iii 183.

Bristive held land in Stringston, i 261.

Bristol, Harding the Dane governor of, iii 275. messuages in, owned by Witham priory, ii 233. lands in, owned by John Arthur, iii 178.

Bristol chamber, patrons of Stockland-Bristol, i 248. held Rowberrow, iii 599. mayor and corporation held Burnet in trust for the Redmaids' hospital, ii 415. held Congresbury, iii 585; and Wick, 611. port of, allowed one hogshead of wine annually to Mendip miners digging on soil belonging to Witham priory, ii 234.

Bristol, abbey of St. Augustine (subsequently the cathedral), founded by Robert Fitzharding, lord of Berkeley, 1146, who was buried there, iii 276; Robert and Thomas,

Bristol, abbey of St. Augustine—*continued.* lords Berkeley, also buried there, 276; enriched by Maurice, lord Berkeley, who was buried there, 277; Thomas, lord Berkeley, buried there, 278; owned the church of Pawlet, 102; of Portbury, 143; the manor of Abbot's-Leigh, 153; lands in Beggeridge, 327; bishop Beckington's bequest to, 599.

Bristol castle, built by Robert, earl of Gloucester, iii 146; Giles, lord Daubeny, constable of, 109; Sir William Arthur, constable of, 177; Robert, bishop of Wells imprisoned in, 379.

Bristol, dean and chapter of, patrons of Drayton, i 39; Fivehead, 42; Isle Abbots, 51; Swell, 66; Bath-Ford, 112; Overweare, 186. Merriot, ii 170. Portbury, iii 142.

Bristol, John Digby, earl of, owned Portbury priors, iii 142; Clevedon, 168; married Beatrice, daughter of Charles Walcot, and widow of Sir John Dyve, 336; George Digby, earl of: their son, 336.

Bristow, Alexander, monk of Bath, who received pension, B 57.

Bristow, William, prior of Dunster, 1411, ii 17.

Bristuin, held one hide in Ash, iii 6.

Bristward, held Merriot, ii 169.

Britanny, earl of, married Amice, daughter of Robert Fitz-Hamon, ii 411.

Britashe family (*see* Bretesche).

Britell, held two hides and a half in the hundred of Milverton, iii 13.

Brithelm, bishop of Wells, 958, iii 377; effigy in Wells cathedral, 399; adjoined Street to the jurisdiction of Glastonbury, 423. owned Wellington Buckland and Lydiard, ii 482.

Brithric, king of the West Saxons, gave lands in Ham to Wigfruth, iii 83.

Brithwin, abbot of Glastonbury, and afterwards bishop of Wells, ii 250; owned Wellington, Buckland, and Lydiard, 482. bishop of Wells, iii 378; died, 1013, 378; effigy in Wells cathedral, 399.

Britnod, held Pen, iii 44, and Weston, 172.

Brito or Brett family (*see* Brett).

Briton, Thomas le, married a daughter of Henry Lovel, and became possessed of a fourth of the manor of Weston-in-Gordano, iii 172; received another fourth from William Fitzwalter, 172; conveyed both shares to Gefferey Maundeville, 172.

Briton, William, chief justice of the forest of Winford, ii 315.

Britte, Richard and Margaret, owned Lud-Huish, iii 541.

Brittin, William, benefaction to Wells, iii 411.

Brittle, Richard, forester of Petherton park, iii 62

Britty, hamlet of Curland, i 23.

Briweham (*see* North-Brewham).

Briwerne abbey, Oxford, held a manor in Priddy, iii 418.

G

Briwetone (*see* Brewton).

Brixi, held Burnham, i 180; Stoke-Courcy, 249.

Broad-cloth manufacture, Bath-Wick, i 120.

Broad-lodge, Newton Regis, built by Sir Thomas Wrothe, iii 62.

Broad-Marston (*see* Marston Magna).

Broad-street, Bath, B 38.

Broad-street conduit, Bath, B 51.

Broadfield down, i xiv, ii 321.

Broadfield, tithing of Wrington, i 207.

Broadmead brook, Camely, ii 125.

Broadmead, Mrs. Elizabeth, remarkable case of longevity, iii 293.

Broadrep family (*see* Baudrip).

Broadway, origin of its name, i 16; forest of Neroche, 16; the tithings divided into two, of Broadway and Capland, 18; position, 18; manufactures, 18; Domesday survey, 18; owned by the earl of Morton and the L'Orti family, 18; licence for a market granted, 18; held by Hugh Brook, 18; owned by the Speke family and Henry William Portman, 18; church (St. Aldhelm), 18; bells (5), 18; monuments in the church, 18, 19; cross, 19; yew tree, 19; almshouse, 19.

Broadwell down, Wrington, i 206, 207.

Brocas, Mary, monument in Bath abbey, 1775, B 67; Thomas, monument in Bath abbey, 1750, 67.

Brochelie (*see* Brockley).

Brock street, Bath, B 36.

Brockley, its situation, ii 120; Brockley Combe, 120; lead mines and columnar stone quarries, 120; yew tree, 120; Domesday survey, 120; held by Eldred, 120; owned by Peter de Sancta Cruce, 120; the families of Ashton, Berkley, Harvey and Pigott, 121; the church (St. Nicholas) and its monuments, 121; bell (1), 121; Richard Durban's benefaction, 121.

Brockley Combe, ii 120.

Brockman, Margaret, of Witham, first wife of Sir Richard Warre, knt., iii 261.

Brockwell, hamlet of Wotton-Courtney, ii 49.

Broctune or Brokton (*see* Bratton-Seymour).

Brodhome, John, owner of Lillisdon, granted a moiety to Richard Stapleton, ii 179.

Brodripp, Jane, of London, first wife of Anthony Wickham, ii 373.

Broke family held Lympsham, i 203. Clutton, ii 104.

Broke, Elizabeth, grand-daughter of Thomas Montague, and heiress to Cathanger, i 41; afterwards married Robert Palmer, 41; Jane, married John Walshe, 41.

Broke, Matthias, last incumbent of St. John Baptist's chapel, Ilminster, i 7.

Broke, Thomas, abbot of Muchelney, iii 135.

Broke, Thomas, and Alice, his wife, inscription on a window in Pilton church, iii 482.

Broke, lord, of Beauchamp court, title conferred on Sir Fulk Greville, 1620, ii 376; Francis, lord, inherited estates formerly belonging to Sir George Strode, 339.

Broke, Willoughby, lord, received from Henry VII John Zouche's manor and castle of Cary, ii 55

Brokenbere, William de, M.P. for Bath, 1311, 1312, B 19.

Brokenbergh, William de, M.P. for Bath, 1316, 1318, 1321, 1322, 1324, 1326, 1327, 1328, 1330, B 19; 1343, B 20.

Brome, Theophilus, monument in Chilton-Cantelo church, ii 339; arms, 339; legend, 340.

Bromere priory, Hants, held a pension from Stanton Drew church, ii 435, and a cell and a manor at Portbury, called Portbury-priors, iii 142 (*see* Brymore).

Bromesburgh, William de, M.P. for Bath, 1332, B 19.

Bromley, Henry, created lord Montford: married the heiress of the Wyndham family, and became possessed of part of the manor of Trent, ii 381. Roger, owned land in Aller, Allermore, and Combe, iii 188.

Brompton, Andrew de, held half a knight's fee at Walton in Gordano, iii 170.

Brompton-Ralph, situation, iii 505; Brendon hill, 505; Burton hamlet, 505; Rooksnest hamlet, 505; owned by the abbots of Glastonbury, 505; given at the conquest to Sir William de Mohun, 505; Domesday survey, 505; held by Turgis: Brictric held it T.R.E. 505; held under the Mohuns, by the family of Fitz-Urse, 505; Thomas de Tymmeworth held a third of a knight's fee, 505; Adam de Bagtrepe and Ralph Fitzurse held two parts of a knight's fee, 505; whole manor held by Ralph Fitz-Urse, 505; the Fulfords, 505, 506; Sir John Palton, 506; the Willingtons, 505; the Lacys, 506; the Rich family, 506; Mrs. Margaret Hay, 506; Sir William Yea, 506; land in, held by Walter Meriet, 259; church (St. Mary), 506; bells (4), 506.

Brompton-Regis, situation, iii 502; Brendon hills, 502; tumuli, Wiveliscombe-Burrow, Leather Burrow and Cutcombe - Burrow, 502; Haddon-hill, 502; Hadborough, 502; hamlet of Hartford, 502; Bury or Brompton-Bury, 502; Bury-Castle, 502; Domesday survey, 502; held by the King: Ghida held it T.R.E. 502; earl Morton held one hide in Prestetune, 502; subsequently held by the de Say family, 503; the Bucklands, 503; the Besilles, 503, 504; the Eliots, 504; the Fettiplaces, 504; the Cheekes, 504; Sir Henry Wallop, 504; Lady Acland, 504; market and fairs, 504; Barlinch priory, founded by William de Say, 503; church (St. Mary) and its monuments, 504; bells (4), 504; poor-house, 504.

Brook family of Ashton-Philips, ii 297; John, serjeant-at-law, married Jane A'Merryck, and became possessed of the manor of Ashton-Philips, 297; Sir Christopher Wroughton enfeoffed him of his estates, 133; Thomas, 297; Hugh, 297; monument in Long Ashton church, 300. held Broadway, i 18. Elizabeth, married Giles Walwyn, ii 297; Frances, married William Clarke, 297; Susan, married Hugh Halswell, 297; Alice, married Thomas Vatchell, 297.

Brook, de la Brooke, Broke or At-Brooke family, of Brook, iii 302, 304. part owners of Welton, ii 151; Stone-Easton, 154; Ubley, 156. owners of Sock-Dennis, iii 307; Luston, 321; Stony-Littleton, 327; of lands in Wellow, Peglinch, Hassage, Woodborough, Shascombe and Camely, 327; Milton, 405; Badgworth, 565; residence at Brook's court, 304; William de, landowner temp. Ed. I, 302; Henry de la, married Nichola Gonvile, 302; Henry, 302; John de la held also lands in Sock-Dennis, Bishopston and Kingston, married Joan Bardstone, 303; Sir Thomas, knt., married Constance Markensfeld, 303. commissioner of sewers, i xii. owned Chilcompton, ii 128; land in Hinton-Blewet, 144; Thorn-Falcon, 182; Ubley, 156; Aldwick, 315. Bagborough-West, Luston and Brooke-Ivelchester, iii 242. Sir Thomas, married Joan, daughter of Simon Hanape, and widow of Robert Chedder, 303, ii 128, 145. M.P., 1386, 1391, 1392, 1394, 1396, 1397, 1398, 1402, 1403, 1407, 1408, 1413, i xxxi. Joan, widow of Sir Thomas, died seized of twenty manors in Somerset, ii 128, 145, iii 303; Sir Thomas, married Joan Braybrook, 303; created lord Cobham, 303 (*see* under that title). Thomas, M.P., 1417, 1422, 1426, i xxxi; Edward, M.P., 1441, xxxi. Elizabeth, married John St. Maur, ii 199, iii 303. Joan, married John Carent, ii 367, iii 303. Elizabeth, daughter of George Brook, lord Cobham, second wife to William Parr, marquis of Northampton, iii 303 (*see* Cobham, earls of).

Brook, Charles, vicar of Caverly, benefaction to Wincaunton, iii 35.

Brook-Lavington, hamlet of Cadbury, North, ii 65.

Brook, Mr., of Bath, owned part of the manor at Glastonbury, ii 259.

Brooke-Ivelchester, seat of the Brooke family, iii 242, 302.

Brooke, David, lessee of Norton-Malreward, ii 109.

Brooke, Major William, governor of Bath hospital, B 47.

Brookes, Rev., owner of land in Hinton-Blewet, ii 144; patron and incumbent, 145.

Brookman, monuments in Bathwick church, i 122.

Brooking, Alice, first wife of George Speke, i 68.

Brook's court, residence of the Brook family, iii 304.

Broome, John, owned Wigborough, iii 111.

Broomfield, situation, i 71; favourable to the growth of timber, its flora, 72; Domesday survey, 72; held by William de Mohun: Alnod, T.R.E. 72; owned successively by the Montacute, Lynde, de Crocumbe, and Biccombe families, 72; Hugh Smyth, of Long Ashton, 72; Edward Morgan, whose sons sell the manor to Andrew Crosse and William Towill, 72; Towill sells his part to Hugh Halswell, from whom it came to the Tynte family, 72; Binfords, the seat of John Jeane, 72; the church, 72; bells (5), 72; the monuments, 73; yew trees and cross, 73; Towil charity, 73. tithes belonged to Buckland priory, iii 98.

Broomhill hamlet, Lopen, iii 121.

Broughton hamlet, Stoke St. Mary, iii 291.

Broughton, Joan, wife of William de Vernai, i 254.

Broughton, Rev. Thomas, incumbent of Corston, iii 346; of Twiverton, 348.

Browford hamlet (*see* Exton).

Brown, Anne Catharina, tomb in Corfe churchyard, iii 249. Anne, second wife of John Poulett, ii 167. Charles, memorial stone in Brewton church, i 217; Colonel Edward, monument in North Stoke church, 135. Elizabeth, wife of Robert Hunt, monument in Compton Paunceford church, ii 77. Francis John, governor of Bath hospital, B 47. Rev. James, incumbent of Portishead, iii 145; of Kingston, 263; Joseph, owned Street, 424. Nicholas, monument in Bath abbey, 1762, B 67. Richard, benefactor to Wedmore, i 193. Thomas, prior of Dunster, 1499, ii 17. Valentine, owner of Curland, i 23, ii 181. William Frederick, prebendary of Wells, iii 397; Mr., stone in Charlton-Mackarell church, 194. Mr., of Street, owned land in Godney, ii 272.

Brown, hamlet of Treborough, ii 46.

Browne, Anne, wife of John Miller, i 105; arms, 105. Barbara, married (1) Sir Edward Mostyn, (2) Edward Gore, of Kiddington, Oxon, ii 311. George and Robert, clerks of the castle, town and lordship of Taunton, and gatekeeper of the castle: succeeded in these offices by John, their brother, iii 228. James, monument in Bath abbey, 1788, B 67.

Browne, John, monk of Bath, who received pension, B 57. John, received a pension from Keynsham abbey, ii 403. Joseph, sheriff, 1717, i xxxviii. Simon, born at Shepton-Mallet, iii 461. Mr., of Limestreet, London, owned Pensford, ii 429.

Bruce family owned Castle Cary, disposed of it to William Ettricke and Mr. Player, ii 55.

Brucheford (*see* Brushford).

Brudeport, John, M.P. for Bath, 1333, B 19.

Bruer, Alice, wife of (1) Reginald de Mohun, (2) William Paganel, ii 8; contributes the marble for twelve years to Salisbury cathedral, 8.

Bruerne, Oxford, abbots of, received three marks from Bedminster manor, ii 283.

Bruges or Bridge, hamlet of South-Petherton, iii 108.

Bruges, Sir Thomas, married Jane Sydenham, of Orchard, iii 489.

Brugia, Brugie, Brugge, Brugge-Walter and Burgh-Walter (*see* Bridgwater).

Bruke house, boundary of Selwood forest, ii 195.

Brumetone (*see* Brewton).

Brumpton manor, in Milverton, Preston-Bowyer and Torrells-Preston, formerly included in, iii 15.

Brunantun (*see* Brompton-Ralph).

Brune, Mary, daughter of Sir George Farewel, monument in Hill-Bishops church, erected by her daughter, Bridget Fowel, iii 256.

Brune or Brown (*see* Brown).

Brunetone (*see* Brompton-Regis).

Bruno held Babcary, ii 60.

Brunswick place, Bath, B 37.

Brus, Robert de, landowner temp. Ed. I, i *xxvii*; owner of Staple Fitzpaine, 58; John, 58; Beatrix marries Robert Burnell, who receives manor of Staple, 58.

Brushford, situation, iii 506; river Barle, 506; hamlets of Knightcot, 506; and Langridge, where was formerly a chapel: a fair held there, 506; Domesday survey, 506; owned by the earl of Morton, held by Malger: Ordulf held it T.R.E. 507; owned by the Warre family, 261; manor subsequently owned by lady Acland, 507; church (St. Nicholas) and monument, 507; bells (5), 507; benefactions, 507.

Brutasche, one of the boundaries of Glaston Twelve Hides, ii 237.

Bruton, John de, abbot of Muchelney, iii 135.

Bryan, Brien or Brian family took their name from Brean manor, i 179; owned White-Lackington, 67; Bathford, 112. Elizabeth, wife of Hugh Courtney le Fitz, ii 161. Elizabeth, wife of Robert Lovel, i 107. Sir Francis, knt., held certain lands jointly with Matthew Colthurst, iii 236. Sir Guy de, commissioner of sewers, i *xii.* owned Kingston, Somerton-Erleigh and Somerton-Randolph, iii 185; Guy de, 185. held Beer-Crocombe, i 14; and lands in Buckland St. Mary, 21. Joan, daughter of Sir Guy, wife of Sir John Dinham, ii 362. Joan, wife of Sir William, iii 475. Maud, wife of Nicholas Fitz-Martin, ii 132;

Bryan, Brien or Brian family—*continued.*
Margaret, wife of John de Erleigh, 199. Philip, M.P., 1385, i *xxxi.* Philippa, wife of (1) John Devereux, (2) Henry le Scroop, i 107. inherited the estates of her cousin, Guy de Bryan, iii 185. William, owned Bath-Easton, i 106. Sir William, of Shockerwick, held Downhead, iii 475.

Bryan, Rev., incumbent of Otterhampton, i 243.

Bryanston, seat of William Berkeley Portman, iii 282.

Bryant family, patrons of the living of Withiel-Flory, iii 295; James and Jane, monument in Withiel-Flory church, 296. Robert, owned Ashill manor, i 12. Rev., incumbent of Wotton Courtney, ii 49.

Bryce, Robert, last incumbent of Compton-Paunceford chantry, received a pension, ii 77

Brytton, held by John Berkely, of the bishops of Bath and Wells, iii 165.

Brymore, in Cannington, held by Geffrey de Bramora, Odo, son of Durand de Derleigh, William Fitchet, and the Pym family, i 233.

Brymore (Bromere), Hants, prior of, landowner temp. Ed. I, i *xxvii* (*see* Bromere).

Brynsmede, William, received a pension from Taunton priory, iii 236.

Brywham, William de, iii 37.

Bubb, Jeremias, married Mary Dodington, iii 519; George, their son, owned Dodington, and assumed the name of Dodington, 519.

Bubwith, Nicholas, bishop of Bath and Wells, 1408—1424, built an almshouse, iii 384; the library over the cathedral cloisters, 384; a chapel, and the north-west tower to the cathedral, 384, 398, 399; arms, 399; he purchased Loxton and granted it to the heirs of Latimer and Grenham, 597.

Bubwith's hospital, Wells, iii 408; increased by bishops Beckington and Bourne, 408; bishop Still, 388, 408; bishop Willes, 408; description of buildings, 408; arms in chapel window, 408.

Buchan, Alice de Beaumont, countess of, whose daughter Elizabeth married Nicholas, lord Audley, iii 552.

Buck, lady Anne, monument in Bath abbey, 1764, B 67.

Buck, William, memorial stone in church of Weston, near Bath, i 165.

Buckham, Walter, owned North Parret, ii 335.

Buckham-Weston [*sic* in Collinson for Buckhorn-Weston], Dorset, lands in, owned by Stavordale priory, iii 33.

Buckingham, Henry Stafford, duke of, owned Yarlington, i 228. Bedminster, ii 282. Martock, iii 5. Edward, duke of, owned Bedminster, ii 282; was attainted, 282.

Buckingham, Walter Giffard, first earl of, related to William the Conqueror, iii 41; owned Yarnfield, 41; Walter, earl of, 41.

Buckingham, marquis of, J.P., i *xli*; marquis of, joint owner of Durborough, 252.

Buckinghamshire, earl of, J.P., i *xli*.

Buckinghamshire, lands in, owned by Sir John Vere, passed to the Luttrells, of Dunster, iii 500.

Buckland family, of Hemington, took their name from Buckland Dinham, ii 452; owned Hemington, 454; Richard, conveyed Hemington to the Bampfield family, 454. Agnes and Walter de, built the market cross at Shepton-Mallet, iii 460; John de, constable of Taunton castle, 227; William de, married Maud de Say, and became possessed of Brompton-Regis, 503.

Buckland family, of West-Harptree-Tilly, ii 141; John, 141; Ralph, a celebrated Puritan, became a Roman Catholic, published several books: supposed to have had some connection with the gunpowder plot, 141, 142; Charles, married Bridget Reliffe, 143; John, benefaction to West Harptree, 143; Mrs. Mary, benefaction to West Harptree, 143; family monument in West Harptree church, 143.

Buckland, John, M.P., 1654, 1656, 1659, i *xxxii*.

Buckland, Mary, of Stanley, held lands in Martock, iii 8.

Buckland-Dinham, situation, ii 451; springs, 451; formerly had a market, a fair, and large manufacture of woollen cloth, 451; a market-cross and town-house, where assizes were held, 451; ancient prosperity, mainly owing to the Denham family, 451; their house here entirely destroyed, 451; Domesday survey, 451; Donno held it T.R.E. 451; subsequently owned by the Dinham family, 452; held in moieties, 452; John, lord Zouch, and Seymour held a moiety, 452; Sir William Compton, knt., held a fourth, which his descendants sold to Webb, and he to Hodges, 452; John, earl of Bath, sold a fourth to Thomas Bamfeilde, 452; manor jointly vested in the families of Bamfeilde and Hodges, 452; Sir Charles Bampfylde and Henry Strachey, 452; church (St. Michael) and its monuments, 452; bells (5), 452; chantry, 452; benefactions, 452; hamlet of Murtree, 452.

Buckland St. Mary, Saxon origin of name, i 20; position, 20; tithings and hamlets of Buckland, Westcomb and Dommet, 20; evidences of warlike action, 20; owned by Isaac Elton, 20; Domesday survey, 20, 21; owned by the Meriet family, 21; licence granted to Thomas de Merleberge to amortize certain lands, 21; the church, 21; cross, 21; yew tree, 21. three farms near, belonged to the hundred of Martock, iii 2.

Buckland-Sororum priory, iii 96; founded by William de Erleigh, for canons of the order

Buckland-Sororum priory—*continued*.
of St. Augustine, 96; these canons removed and their houses and lands here given to a priory of sisters hospitallers of the order of St. John of Jerusalem, 96; account of the order, 96, 97; endowment by the countess of Leicester, 96, and Henry IV, 97; William de Erleigh and others, 98. hospital landowner, temp. Ed. I, i *xxvi*. the rectory of Beckington appropriated to the priory, ii 200; owned Kilmersdon church, 447. chapels at Newton Regis and Newton Comitis, iii 70; at Huntworth and Sheerston, 72; owned Bankland, 72; Thurloxton chapel, 103; church of Tolland, 292; dissolved in 1539, 98; preceptors, 98, 99; priory and manor subsequently owned by the Halley or Hawley family, 99; the Bakers, 99; the Parker family, 99; John Parker, baron Boringdon, 99.

Buckland-West, situation, ii 485; hamlets of Ham, Stert, and Chilson, 485; common land and springs, 486; Rugging mill, 486; owned by the bishops of Wells, 486; church (St. Mary), 486; bells (5), 486; benefactions, 486.

Buckler, Beatrice, married Thomas de Dodeton, iii 518.

Buckler, William, J.P., i *xliii*.

Buckshaw, hamlet, (*see* Holwell).

Budcaleth (*see* Butleigh).

Budd, William, benefaction to Crewkerne, ii 164.

Buddecle or Boduchelei (*see* Butleigh).

Budecale (*see* Butleigh).

Budecleg (*see* Butleigh).

Budecumbe family owned Butcombe, ii 313.

Budell, Richard, M.P. for Bath, 1376, 1377, 1378, 1383, 1384, B 20.

Budicome (*see* Butcombe).

Budley (Butleigh), owned by the abbots of Glastonbury, ii 243.

Budscombe, owned by the priory of Buckland, iii 98.

Buissel, Roger, held Sutton-Bingham, ii 349; progenitor of the Bingham family, 350.

Bulbeke, Robert, owned lands in Kingston-Seymour, ii 123; tomb in Kingston-Seymour churchyard, 124.

Bulford, hamlet in Staple Fitzpaine, i 58.

Bulkeley, Margaret, first wife of Sir Coplestone Bampfylde, ii 91.

Bull family held Norton Canonicorum, a manor in Midsummer Norton, ii 151; buried in Midsummer Norton church, 151; arms, 192; monument in Frome church, 192; Edward of Wellow, buried in Stanton-Drew church, 437. George, bishop of St. David's, sometime vicar of Easton-in-Gordano, iii 152; born at Wells, 411; Henry, last incumbent of St. Andrew's chantry,

Burleston, William, owned the manor of High-church, ii 454, and Falkland, 455.

Burley, John, last incumbent of chantry of St. Andrew, Frome, and receives pension, ii 194.

Burlington street, Bath, B 37.

Burlond, Robert de, who purchased certain lands from William de Alfoxton, i 264; Thomas, 264; Christina, who settled Alfoxton on James Ayshe of Chagford, 264.

Burne, boundary of Glaston Twelve Hides, ii 237, 238.

Burnel family owned Upton Noble, i 227. Sparkford, ii 87; Camely, 125; Compton Dando, 422, and Over Badgworth, iii 565. Robert, bishop of Bath and Wells, lord chancellor and lord treasurer of England, owned Compton-Dando, ii 422. bishop of Wells from 1274 to 1292: added a great hall to the bishop's palace, iii 382. obtained parliamentary representation for Bath, B 19. appropriated the church of Stanton-Drew to the bishopric, ii 435; owned an estate in Kilmersdon, 446. appropriated the church of Wembdon to St. John's hospital, Bridg-water, iii 103; held land in Sock-Dennis, 307; buried in Wells Cathedral, 399. Philip, nephew of the bishop, inherited Compton-Dando, married Maud, daughter of Richard, earl of Arundel, ii 422. Robert, landowner temp. Ed. 1, i *xxvii*; married Beatrix de Brus: owned Staple, 58; William, dean of Wells, 1292, 189. Edward, son of Philip, inherited Compton-Dando, 1293, ii 422; died without issue, 422; Maud, sister of Edward, was his heir, married John de Handlo, 422; owned North Cheriton, 360; Nicholas, her son, created lord Burnel, 422. owned Compton-Durville, iii 110. Hugh, ii 422; Edward, 422; Margery, married Edmund Hunger-ford, 422, iii 354. Cecilia, married Stephen Laundey, iii 518.

Burnet, situation, ii 415; river Chew, 415; held by the wife of Ulward, 415; by Robert Fitz-Hamon, as of the honour of Gloucester, 415; abbey of Tewkesbury, 415; at the dissolution granted to John Cutte and Richard Roberts, 415; William Cutte, and John, his son, 415; John Whit-son, who gave it in trust for the endowment of the Redmaids' hospital in Bristol, 415; held by Samuel Day under the mayor and corporation of Bristol, as feofees of that trust, 415; house occupied by Samuel Day, 415; church (St. Michael) and its monu-ments, 415, 416.

Burnetone (*see* Brompton-Ralph).

Burnham, situation, i 179; hamlets of Watch-field, Paradise, Eddy Mead, Huish juxta Highbridge, 179, 180; Domesday survey,

Burnham—*continued.*
180; held by Walter de Dowai: Brixi T.R.E. 180; Rademer, 180; Robert de Mucegros, 180; John Tregoz, 180, ii 420. the families of Grandison, Wickham, Say and Sele, and Sir Charles Bampfylde, i 180; manors owned by the dean and chapter of Wells, and Zachary Bayly, 181; pension paid to bishop of Bath and Wells by the church, 181; the church, dedicated to St. Andrew, by Bishop Drokensford, who issued an indulgence of forty days, 181; the priory, 181; the church (St. Andrew) and its monuments, 181, 182; bells (5), 181; benefactions to the parish, 181. John Berke-ley owned land here, iii 165.

Burning of the hill, iii 374.

Burridge family, of Lyme, owners of Thorn Falcon, ii 182.

Burridge, William Doble, held land in Brad-ford, iii 244; owned Stoke-House, 291; owned West-Oldmixon, 591.

Burrington, situation, i 203; hamlets of Lang-ford, Link, Havyat Green, Rickford, 203; originally part of Wrington, 204; owned by the Pulteney family, 204; Langford court, the church, and its monuments, 204, 205; cross, 205; yew tree, 205; tithing of Wrington, 207.

Burrow, hamlet in Wotton Courtney, ii 49.

Burrow, hamlet in Kingsbury, ii 469.

Burrow, Rev. John, incumbent of Bradford, iii 244.

Burt, Rev. Mr., incumbent of Odcombe, ii 325.

Burtle, hamlet in Chilton, iii 433.

Burtle-Moor, iii 423.

Burton, Dorset, lands in, owned by the Carent family, ii 367.

Burton, hamlet in Brompton-Ralph, iii 505.

Burton, hamlet in Kew Stoke, iii 596; held of the barony of Worleston, by Adam le Iroys, 567, 596; of the crown, by Thomas de Lyons, 596.

Burton, hamlet in Stoke Courcy, i 249.

Burton, lands in, owned by Muchelney abbey, iii 135.

Burton, Rev. Henry, monument in Weston church, i 165. memorial inscriptions in Clutton church, ii 104.

Burton, Margaret, second wife to Sir Thomas Stawel, iii 250.

Burton street, Bath, B 37.

Burton-Pinsent, in Curry-Rivel, seat of the earl of Chatham: description, i 24; monument, 25.

Burtynghburg, boundary of Selwood forest, ii 195

Burwalls, Long-Ashton, Roman encampment, ii 289; land bestowed by Alexander de Alneto on St. Catherine's hospital, Bedmin-ster, 290. boundary of Portbury hundred, iii 139.

Burwold, bishop of Wells, iii 377; effigy in Wells cathedral, 399. owned Wellington, Buckland, and Lydiard, ii 482.

Bury or Brompton Bury, iii 502; owned by Sir John Wallop, 503.

Bury castle, built on site of ancient Roman works, iii 502; inhabited by the Besilles family, 502.

Bury, Kingsmill, owned Chatley-house, ii 225.

Bury, Richard de, dean of Wells, 1332, i 189.

Bury, Thomas, governor of Bath hospital, B 47.

Bury, Thomas, prior of Barlinch, 1430—1456, iii 503.

Buryhale, John, M.P. for Bath, 1336, B 19.

Busby, Dr. Richard, master of Westminster school, some time prebendary of Cudworth, iii 118; gift to the old almshouse at Wells, 411. Anne, his daughter, married Sir Charles Kemys Tynte, i 80, ii 317. monument in Bath abbey, 1751, B 67.

Buschell, John, the service of, granted by Anastatia Croke to Sir Thomas Trivet, iii 101.

Bush family, owned the manor of Butcombe, which passed to William Mann on his marriage with the widow of Sir John Bush, ii 315; tomb in Barton S. David church, 65.

Bush, John, owned Fryenborough, ii 425; John, conveyed it to Matthew Smyth, 425.

Bush, John, of Regell, benefaction to Winford. Edward, benefaction to Winford, ii 322.

Bush, John, mayor of Bath, 1675, B 25; 1697, 1703, 26.

Bush, John, incumbent of Weston in Gordano, iii 174.

Bush, Joseph, mayor of Bath, 1684, B 25.

Bush, Paul, first bishop of Bristol, owned Abbots-Leigh, iii 153; owned Rowberrow, 599.

Bush, Samuel, mayor of Bath, 1755, 1763, B 26.

Bush, William, gift to Wobourne's almshouse, Yeovil, 1474, iii 210.

Bush, William, mayor of Bath, 1680, 1692, B 25; 1704, 26; William, mayor of Bath, 1722, 1739, 26.

Bushell, Edward, senior, mayor of Bath, 1681, 1693, B 25; Edward, junior, mayor of Bath, 1708, 26; Hester, monument in Bath abbey, 1671, 67; Thomas, mayor of Bath, 1718, 26; Tobias, monument in Bath abbey, 1664, 67.

Bussa, Gilbert de, prior of Montacute, 1266, iii 312.

Bussex, hamlet in Weston-Zoyland, iii 440.

Bussex rhine, Weston-Zoyland, iii 440.

Butcombe, situation, ii 313; included Butcombe, 313; Thrubwell, 314; and Aldwick, 315; owned by the bishop of Coutances, 313; Domesday survey, 313; held by Fulcran: Elward held it T.R.E. 313; owned successively by the Bodicombe family, 313; the Mohuns, 313; the De Percevals, 313,

Butcombe—*continued.*

314; Evan Lloyd and Thomas Salisbury, 314; held by the service of half a knight's fee of John le Sor, 314; the Clevedon family held land here, 315; as also the abbots of Flaxley, 315; hospital of St. John, in Redcliff - pit, Bristol, held a manor here which passed to George Owen, 315; the Bush family, 315; the Manns, 315; the Plaisters, 315; John Curtis, 315; John Savery, 315; lands in, granted to Sir Anthony Kingston, 319; Thrubwell, manor partly in Butcombe and partly in Nemnet, 314; owned by the Bretesche family, 314; the Percevals, 314, 315; the Clevedon family held lands here, 315; Aldwick manor lies in Blagdon and Butcombe, 315; Domesday survey, 315; owned by Serlo de Burci, held by Walter: Almar held it T.R.E. 315; subsequently held by the Martin family, 315; Sir Thomas Brook, 315; Thomas de Chedder, 315; the duke of Exeter, 315; the Newtons, 315, 316; Sir Giles Capel, 316; Samuel Baker, 316; manor house, 315; church (St. Michael) and its monuments, 316; bells (3), 316; cross, 316.

Butcombe, name assumed by Robert Perceval, iii 173.

Bute, earl of, J.P., i *xli.*

Butleigh, situation, iii 448; Butleigh-Wootton, 448; ancient names, 448; Domesday survey, 448. boundary of Glaston Twelve Hides, ii 238. owned by the abbots of Glastonbury, iii 448, ii 243. Turstin, Roger, the earl of Morton, and Alestan, held lands there, iii 448; subsequently owned by the duke of Somerset, 448; Sir Edward Peacham, 448; John Robinson, 448; Henry Billingsley, 448; Christopher Simcocks, 448; the Right Hon. James Grenville, 449; church (St. Benedict) and monuments 449; bells (5), 449. church exempted from episcopal authority by king Ina's charter to Glastonbury, ii 241; Baltonsbury living, a chaplaincy to, 270.

Butleigh-Wootton, hamlet in Butleigh, iii 448.

Butler family owned Emborow, ii 135; descended from John Boteler or Botiler, 135; John, 135. owned Pen, iii 44. Ralph, ii 135; William, married Theophila Newton, 136; Sir John, married Sylvestra Guise, 136.

Butler, John, altar-piece in Martock church, erected at the expense of, iii 9.

Butler, Margaret, of Oldacres, Durham, first wife to John Sydenham, of Dulverton, iii 523.

Butler, Rev. Mr., incumbent of North Barrow, ii 63; patron and incumbent of Chew Stoke, 101; patron and incumbent of Norton Malreward, 109.

Butolf held Witham, ii 232.

C

Camville, Canvill or de Campvilla family owned Charleton Horethorne, ii 356; Gerard de, gave two parts of the tithe there to the abbey of Bermondsey, 356; Richard de, founded Combe abbey (Warwick): granted the church of Charlton in perpetual alms to the church of St. Mary, Kenilworth, in a deed witnessed to by many members of the family, 356; Gerard de, married Nicola de la Hay: banished, but reinstated, 356; Richard married Eustachia Bassett, relict of Thomas Verdon, 356; Idonea married William de Longespee, and conveyed the family estates to him, 356, 357, iii 367. arms, ii 358.

Cancia, John de, abbot of Glastonbury, ii 253.

Candel manor, given to the monks of Athelney, in exchange for Montacute, iii 311.

Candell, John, held half a knight's fee in Stowey, ii 110.

Candetone (*see* Cannington).

Candos family held Preston-Bowyer, and bestowed it on Goldclive priory, iii 16; bestowed Monksilver on Goldclive priory, 535. Robert de held Puriton, ii 396; held lands of the abbot of Glastonbury, 244. held Woolavington, iii 437; and Stowey, 550; founded the priory of Goldclive at Caerleon, 550. Walter, ii 244, 396; Maud, married Philip de Columbers, 396, iii 437, 551. granted the manor of Fairfield to Martin, the son of Goidslan, to be held by knight's service, i 252. Isabella, augmented the endowment of Goldclive priory, iii 550. Egelina, first wife of Henry de Erleigh, ii 199.

Canford manor, paid six quarters of salt to Witham priory, ii 233.

Cangi, the, i *xxiii*, 231, iii 420.

Cangick giants, remains of, i 189.

Cann family owned Brean, i 178; William, 178; Sir Robert, 178; Elizabeth, married Thomas Master, 178.

Cann, Sir William, benefaction to Brislington, ii 414.

Cannard's grave, iii 459.

Cannington hundred, situation, i 231; held successively by the families of Walrond, Fitzpain, Poynings, Percy, and Sir Francis Rogers, 231.

Cannington, supposed residence of the Cangi, i 231; situation, 231; Domesday survey, 232; ancient demesne of the crown, 232; small part held by Robert: Semar held it T.R.E. 232; the church held by Erchenger, 232; held by Walter de Courcy, 232; Robert, who founds a priory of Benedictine nuns, 232; after its suppression the lands were granted to Edward Rogers and subsequently became the property of Thomas, lord Clifford of Chudleigh, 233; manors of Radway-Fitzpaine, 233; Brymore, 233;

Cannington—*continued.*
Beer, 235; hamlets of Combwick, 234; Perdham or Petherham, 234; Salthay, 235; West Chilton, 235; the church (St. Mary) and its monuments, 235, 236; bells (5), 235; benefactions, 236, 237. lands here held by Idstock chantry, iii 90.

Cannington, prioress of, landowner temp. Ed. I i *xxvi*.

Cannon, Simon, and Jane, his wife: Mary, wife of John Southby: Robert: tablets in Fitzhead church, ii 492; arms, 492.

Canon-Leigh, Devon, abbess and nuns of, held the rectory of Samford Arundel, iii 26.

Cantelupe or Cantilupe family owned the hundred of Brewton, i 211. manor of Donniford, iii 491. Alexander de, bestowed the hundred and the market of Brewton on the priory of Brewton, i 211. William de, owned the manor of Berwick, married Eve, daughter of Walter Mareschal, earl of Pembroke, ii 337. became possessed of the borough of Bridgwater and the out manor of Haygrove, iii 80; inherited half the estates of Sir William de Courtney, 615. George, held a moiety of Edingworth, East Brent, died without issue, i 197, ii 337; iii 80, 567. Millicent, married (1) John de Montalt, (2) Ivo le Zouch, ii 337. inherited part of the manor of Bridgwater, iii 80, 81. Joan, married Henry de Hastings, ii 337, iii 80.

Cantelupe family of Chilton-Cantelo, ii 339; Richard, 339; John, 339; Emma, married Walter Parker, 339.

Cantlow, John, prior of Bath, 1489-1499, great benefactor, B 56; arms in monks' lodgings, 58. gave the east window in Katherine church, i 140; founded a small chapel dedicated to St. Mary Magdalen at Widcombe, 172; supposed builder of the lunatic hospital at Widcombe, 174.

Cantocheheve (*see* East Quantockshead).

Cantocheve (*see* St. Audries).

Cantoesheved-minor (*see* St. Audries).

Canvill (*see* Camville).

Canytone (*see* Cannington).

Capel, Dorothy, daughter of William Capel, lord mayor of London, first wife to John Zouch, ii 55.

Capel, Margaret, wife of Anthony Stocker, ii 130.

Capel family owned Ubley, ii 156; Thorn Falcon, 182. an estate in Christon, iii 578; part of Shipham, 601; Yatton, 617. Sir Giles married Isabel Newton, and became possessed of Ubley, ii 156; of Aldwick, 316. of Angers-Leigh, iii 241, 588. Sir Henry, ii 156, iii 241. owned Wrington, i 207. Sir Arthur, ii 156, iii 241; owned Wellow, 326. Arthur, Lord Capel, ii 156. sold an estate in Christon to Francis Vaughan, iii 578. Elizabeth, daughter of

Capel family—*continued.*
　Arthur, married Sir Ralph Hopton, ii 234.
Capel, earl of Essex, owned Bathwick, i
　121 ; sold Bathwick and the Ubley estates
　to William Pulteney, 121, ii 156.
Capell family owned Swainswick, i 153 ;
　memorial tablets in Swainswick church,
　155.
Capeland, land in, held by Walter Meriet, iii
　259.
Capenor court (*see* Portishead).
Capenor family held Capenor court, iii 145.
Capper, Silvestra, second wife to George Lutt-
　rell, and afterwards married to Sir Edmund
　Story and Gyles Penny, ii 12.
Cappes, Robert, sheriff, 1444, i *xxxvi.* Eliza-
　beth, widow of Robert, held Stawel, ii 379.
Caprarius, John, prior of Montacute, iii 313.
Capton (*see* Stogumber).
Carantacus, a British saint, from whom Car-
　hampton probably derived its name, ii 2.
Cardiff castle, built by Robert, earl of Glouces-
　ter, iii 146.
Cardon, John, representative to parliament of
　Lower Weare, i 184.
Carent's court, seat of the Carent family, ii 366.
Carent or Carwent family owned Berkley and
　Fayroke, ii 203 ; Toomer, 366 ; Adbeer and
　Hummer, 383. Kingston Pitney and lands
　in Hunteleghe Marsh, iii 207. Owen de
　owned land in Caerwent, ii 366 ; Alexander
　de conveyed lands in Newent to William de
　Fauconberge, 366 ; John, 367 ; William,
　367 ; William owned manors of Kington
　and West Marsh, and lands in Hinton St.
　George and Dorsetshire, 367 ; William,
　lord of Great Wishford, Wilts, 367 ; Sir
　William, married Alice Toomer, and became
　possessed of Toomer, 366, 367 ; monument
　in Henstridge church, 368 ; William, mar-
　ried Margaret Stourton, 367 ; John, mar-
　ried Joan Brook, 367, iii 303. William,
　M.P. for Somerset, 1423, 1450, i *xxxi.*
　sheriff of Somerset and Dorset, 1427, 1440,
　ii 367, i *xxxv, xxxvi.* married Catherine,
　widow of John Sturton, iii 201. Alice,
　daughter of William, married John New-
　burgh, ii 203 ; John, M.P. for Dorset, and
　sheriff of Somerset, 1459, 367, i *xxxvi.*
　William, added to the buildings of Toomer
　court, owned also lands in Henstridge,
　Whitchurch, Venn, Milborne, and Poin-
　tington, ii 367 ; John, 367 ; William, 367,
　i *xl.* John, ii 367 ; Sir William, K.B.,
　sheriff, 1522, 367, i *xxxvii.* William, ii 367 ;
　chapel in Henstridge church, burial place
　of the Toomer and Carent families, 368 ;
　arms, 367 ; last representatives, 367.
Carent, Nicholas, dean of Wells, 1446, i 190.
Carentone received customary rent from Oare,
　ii 33 ; Allerford, 41.

Carentone (*see* Carhampton).
Carew, Dorothy, married John Stawel, iii 250.
　Edward, sheriff, 1494, i *xxxvi.* Sir Coven-
　try, married Mary Bampfylde, ii 91 ; Ger-
　trude, wife of Sir Coplestone W. Bampfylde,
　91. Sir John, sheriff, 1507, i *xxxvi.* Sir
　Nicholas, married Margaret Dinham, ii
　362 ; Sir Peter, received a grant of the
　house and site of the monastery at Glaston-
　bury, Wearyall park and other lands, 259.
　Peter held the manor of Priddy, iii 418.
　Sir William, sheriff, 1501, i *xxxvi.* Mr.,
　benefactor to the poor of Keynsham, ii
　409.
Carew family of Camerton and Crowcombe, iii
　331-333, 516, 517 ; John, married a daugh-
　ter of William Kelly, and became possessed
　of Camerton, 331 ; monuments in Camer-
　ton church, 332, 333 ; arms, 332, 333 ;
　Thomas, sold Camerton to Philip Stephens,
　331 ; owned Clatworthy, Tripp, and Synder-
　combe, 509, 510 ; afterwards inherited
　Crowcombe, 517 ; Thomas, of Crowcombe,
　married Elizabeth Biccombe, 516, 517 ;
　Sir John, married Elizabeth Southcot, 516 ;
　Thomas, married Margery Wyndham, 516 ;
　Elizabeth, benefactor to Crowcombe and
　Studley, 517 ; Thomas Carew, of Camerton,
　succeeded to the Crowcombe estate : mar-
　ried Mary Heatley, 517 ; Thomas, married
　Elizabeth Sandford, 517 ; Thomas, married
　(1) Mary Drewe, of Grange (2) Mary
　Horne ; built the family mansion at Crow-
　combe, and founded a school in that place,
　517 ; Elizabeth, married James Bernard,
　517 ; monuments in Crowcombe church,
　516, 517.
Carey, Alice, wife of John de Vernai, i 254.
　Elizabeth, married John Mordaunt, ii 269.
　Elizabeth, a sister of Buckland priory,
　married Thomas Speed, iii 98.
Carhampton hundred, ii 1.
Carhampton manor, situation, ii 2 ; origin of
　name, 2 ; Domesday survey, 2 ; owned by
　William de Mohun, 2 ; Luttrell family, 2,
　iii 500. Eastbury manor, ii 2 ; hamlet of
　Rodhuish, 2 ; church (S. John Baptist) and
　its monuments, 3 ; bells (4), 3.
Cari (*see* Castle Cary).
Carle held Chelworth T.R.E. ii 419.
Carlile family held Locking, iii 597. Henry,
　memorial stone in Spaxton church, i 246.
Carlisle, earl of, J.P., i *xli.*
Carlton, John de, dean of Wells, 1350, i 189.
Carmarthen, marquess of, J.P., i *xli* ; patron of
　Yarlington, 229 ; owned Yarlington, and
　sold it to John Rogers, 229.
Carme, ancient name of Quarum-Mounceaux,
　iii 556.
Carmichael, William, archbishop of Dublin,
　memorial stone in Weston church, i 165.

Carne, Joan, brass tablet in Withycombe church, ii 48.

Carnedd, or pile of stones on Duncorne-hill, iii 337.

Carnicut or Creedlingcot (*see* Camerton).

Carnwell conduit, Bath, в 73.

Carr, John, of Bristol, owned the chief manor at Congresbury: bestowed it on the hospital for Orphans founded by him at Bristol, iii 585.

Carr, Robert, earl of Somerset, 1614, i *xlviii*.

Carre, William, owned the site of Woodspring priory, and the manors of Woodspring and Locking, iii 595; Edward, 595; Anne, married William Yonge, 595.

Carru, John, married a daughter of John de Sydenham, iii 86, 87.

Carter, Mr., stone in Charlton-Mackarell church, iii 194.

Carter, Robert, benefaction to Wedmore, i 193.

Carter, William, benefaction to Keynsham, ii 409.

Carter, William and Rose, memorial stones in Bathwick church, i 123.

Cartere, Thomas, M.P. for Dunster, 1361, ii 15.

Carteret, baron, J.P., i *xlii*.

Cartwright, William, lines on Sir Bevil Grenville, i 158, 159.

Carucate, explanation of the term, i 5.

Carved bench ends in South Brent church, i 201. screen in Norton Fitzwarren church, iii 272.

Carverwell, William, incumbent of chantry at West-Monkton, iii 456.

Carwent (*see* Carent).

Cary, barony of, owned by the Lovel family, iii 172.

Cary family, of Gotton, iii 455; John, 455; arms, 455.

Cary, Louise and Robert, monument in Weston church, i 163; Sir Thomas de, sheriff, 1344—1351, *xxxiv*. owned Elm, ii 206; Thomasine de, 206.

Cary, river: its course, i *xiii*, ii 60, iii 182, 191, 192.

Cary-Fitzpaine, situation, iii 192; Domesday survey, 192; owned by Roger Arundel: held by Robert, 192; subsequently owned by the Fitzpaine family, 192; the Grey family, 193; by Robert, lord Poynings, 246.

Caryll, John, part owner of Evercreech park, iii 414.

Casaubon, Meric, rector of Bleadon, iii 572.

Casberd, Rev. Dr., incumbent of Portbury, iii 143; John, incumbent of Tickenham, 165.

Caslake, Stogumber, land in, granted by Oliver Hewish to Sir Edward Stradling, iii 546; anciently spelt Carslake, 547.

Caslo, holder of Bagley, i 187.

Castello, bishop Adrian de, iii 386; birthplace, 386; sent to England by pope Innocent

Castello, bishop Adrian de—*continued.*
VIII, 386; bishop of Hereford, 386; cardinal, 386; bishop of Bath and Wells, 1504—1518, 386; deprived of all his offices, 386. ordination of Dunster vicarage, ii 17.

Castle or Fenny Castle hamlet, Wookey, iii 421; castle formerly standing at, 421.

Castle Cary, its situation, ii 51; Domesday survey, 51; owned by Walter de Dowai: held by Elsi T.R.E. 51; owned by the families of Perceval, 52, 53; Lovel, 53, 54; St. Maur, 54; Zouche, 55, i 224. Robert Willoughby, lord Broke, ii 55; Edward, first duke of Somerset, 55; Bruce, 55; Ettricke, 55; Player, 55; Mrs. Powell, 56; Bragg, 56; lord Holland, 56; Benjamin Collins, 56; Richard Colt Hoare, 56; the manor house, the hiding place of King Charles II, 56; hamlets of Dummer, Clanvill, Cockhill, 56; Thorne, 56; markets and fairs, 56; the church (All Saints), 56; bells (6), 56; monuments, 57; benefactions, 57, 58. the lords of the barony owned also Bawdrip, iii 91; Bradney, 92; Cricket St. Thomas, 116.

Castle-field, Bridgwater, scene of Monmouth's encampment before Sedgmoor, iii 77.

Castle-house, Nunney, ii 217.

Castlehaven, earldom of, conferred on George Touchet, lord Audley, who married Lucy Mervin, iii 553; Mervin, earl of, sold Stowey to Angel Grey, 553.

Castleman, Henry, memorial stone in Wedmore church, i 192.

Castles: Bridgwater, iii 76; Brompton Bury, 502. Cary, ii 52, 53; Dunster, 13. Enmore, i 94. Farley, iii 357; Fenny, 421; Inglish-Combe, 340; Langport, 132. Midford, i 136. Montacute, iii 311. Nunney, ii 216. Portishead Point, i *xlvi*, iii 144; Richmont, 587, 589; Somerton, 182. Stoke Courcy, i 251. Stowey, iii 550; Taunton, 227; Torweston, 544; Walton, 169.

Castlin, John, receives pension from Brewton abbey, i 214.

Casualty hospital, Bath, в 50.

Caswell tithing, Portbury, iii 142; the Arthurs, of Clapton, held an estate here under the Berkeleys, *see* note, 142.

Catacombs: Nemnet, ii 319. West Camel, iii 189.

Catar, John, owned Vexford and Ripenhole, iii 547.

Catash hundred: its situation, ii 51; origin of its name, 51; held by Richard de Cumpton, John Holland, earl of Huntingdon, John Holland, duke of Exeter, Burghe family, and Jonas Blandford, 51.

Catcot: anciently Caldecote and Cadecote, iii 432; situation, 432; Catcot-Burtle, 432; held of the abbot of Glastonbury by Roger

Catcot—*continued*.
de Curcelle, 432; Walter de Cadecote, 432; the Stawel family, 432; Robert Dodington, 432; Sir Henry Newton held it of Charles Waldegrave, 432; the duke of Chandos, 432; Sir John Henniker, 432; moors, 432; chantry: deed respecting, 432; church, 432; bells (2), 432.

Catcot-Burtle, iii 432.

Catesby, Elizabeth, daughter of Sir William, of Ashby-Legers, Northamptonshire, married Roger Wake, iii 168.

Catford, Joan, married Roger Sydenham, iii 522.

Cathanger manor: position, i 40; owned by Wadel, 40; given to Muchelney abbey, 40, iii 135. Domesday survey, i 40; held by William de Wrotham, 41, iii 63. Richard de Wrotham, i 41; the Scoland family, 41; Thomas Montague, 41; Mary Aylworth, 41; Elizabeth Broke, 41; Robert Palmer, 41; John Brent, 41; John Walshe, builds the manor house, 42; Geo. Salisbury, 42; Hugh Pyme [Pyne], 42; the Wyndham family, 42; Edmund Elliot, 42; description of the manor house, 42. Taunton priory owned tenements here which were granted to Humphrey Colles at the dissolution, iii 285; manor was situated in Fivehead parish, but was considered a member of the manor of Newton, 70.

Cathedraticks, explanation of, iii 586.

Catherall family, patrons of the living of Inglishcombe, iii 340.

Catherine place, Bath, B 37.

"Cato," published by Mr. Trenchard and Thomas Gordon, iii 154.

Cattle, ancient price of, ii 476.

Caulfield, Margaret, wife of John Miller, i 104.

Causeways, i 183, iii 442.

Cavardo, Guy de Rupe de, married Sybill de Fortibus, iii 462.

Cave, Thomas, married Isolda de Marisco, iii 87; Richard Cuffe or Cave, their son, married Joan de Sydenham, and became possessor of the manor of Sydenham, 87; Philip, married Catherine Tilly, and became possessed of the manors of Moorland and Willy; owned also estates in Wembdon, Bridgwater, Bawdrip, North-Petherton, Dunweer, North-Bower, Woolmersdon, and Netherham, 87; William, 87; John, died without issue, 87; Alice, daughter of William, married Thomas Perceval, 87.

Cavendish, Sir William, married Elizabeth Barloe (*née* Hardwick), ii 96; Charles received the greater part of his mother's estates, 96; William, afterwards lord Ogle, viscount Mansfield, baron Bolsover, and earl of Newcastle, 96.

Cavendish, Lord George, J.P., i *xlii*; Lord John, J.P., *xlii*.

Caverns, ii 35, iii 418, 587.

Cavill, William, one of the first aldermen of Bath, B 23.

Cayford (*see* Keyford).

Ceder (*see* Chedder).

Cedre (*see* Chedder).

Cedwalla enriched the abbey of Glastonbury, ii 241; confirmed the gift of Leigh to the abbey, 465.

Celeworde (*see* Chelwood).

Cellewert (*see* Chelwood).

Celric held T.R.E. Curry Mallet, i 32. Chipstaple, iii 508. part of Drayton, i 38.

Celric, King, enriched the abbey of Glastonbury, ii 241.

Celtic monuments, ii 433.

Cely, Celey or Ceely, memorial stones in Creech St. Michael church, i 77, 78.

Cengille, abbot of Glastonbury, ii 249.

Ceolseberge (*see* Chisselborough).

Ceolward held a manse in Ham, iii 83.

Ceolwlph enriched the abbey of Glastonbury, ii 241.

Ceptone, name given to Chilton in Domesday survey, iii 433.

Cerd, Simon de (*see* Chard).

Cerdesling (*see* Charlinch).

Cerdic, a Saxon general, ii 471.

Cerdre (*see* Chard).

Cerlecume (*see* Charlcombe).

Cerletune (*see* Charlton-Adam).

Cerne, John, M.P. for Bath, 1379, B 20. William de, sheriff, 1260, 1261, i *xxxiv*.

Cernel, tithes of, owned by Montacute priory, iii 312.

Cerney, Gloucestershire, lands in, owned by Walter de Meriet, iii 259.

Cerric held Syndercombe T.R.E. iii 510.

Cestreton, Bardolph de, married Joan de Stawel, iii 250; curious deed respecting the baptism of their son, iii 431.

Chaces: Axbridge, Chedder, Filwood, i *xv*.

Chadd, Humphry, sheriff, 1259, i *xxxiv*.

Chaffcombe, formerly Caffecome, iii 115; situation, 115; hamlet of Libnash, 115; Domesday survey, owned by the bishop of Coutances: held by Ralph, 115; subsequently part of the honour of Gloucester, 115; Hugh de Beauchamp held a moiety, 115; Ralph de Stocklinch held the other moiety, 115; John Denbaud held this manor of the abbot of Ford, and lands here of Sir John Rodney, 116; the Poulet family subsequently owned it, 116; Mrs. Mallard holds another manor here, 116; church (St. Michael) and its monuments, 116; Sir Amias Paulet, knt., buried here, 116; bells (3), 116.

Chaffey, tombs in White Lackington churchyard, i 69.

Chaffin family, owners of Ston-Easton minor, ii 158.

Chafie, John, incumbent of Somerton, iii 186.

Chafin, William, incumbent of St. Mary Magdalen's church, Taunton, iii 237.

Chair, monastic, ii 81.

Chaivert (*see* Keyford).

Chaldicote or Chalcot family, of Quarrelston and East-Whiteway, in Dorset, owned Ashbrittle, iii 21 ; arms, 21.

Chalengelondemen, tenants of the lords of South Brent, i 197.

Chalwell, ii 157.

Chamberlain, Leonard, owned land in Abbot's Combe, ii 359.

Chamberlain, Margaret, married Edward Wyndham, iii 492.

Chamberlain street, Wells, iii 375.

Chamberlaine, John, monk of Hinton, pensioned, iii 368.

Chamberline, Walter, fair at Lopen granted to, iii 122.

Chambers, Humphrey, rector of Claverton, one of the assembly of divines appointed by parliament to sit at Westminster, i 147; grants licence to eat flesh to William Bassett, 147; memorial stone in Claverton church, 149.

Champflower or de Campo-Florido family held Wick, i 218, 219. and Huish-Champflower, iii 530. Thomas de, held a knight's fee from Sir William de Mohun, ii 14, i 218. Lucas or Luke de, held a knight's fee from the Mohun family, ii 14, i 218. Henry de, sheriff, 1236, i *xxxiv* ; owned Wick, 219; Elena, 219; John de, 219; William de, landowner temp. Ed. I, i *xxvii*. Baldwin de, lord of the manor of Ash, iii 6; Margaret married Thomas de Orchard, 488.

Champion, Edward, benefaction to Chilton, iii 434.

Champion, Stephen and William, benefactions to Wedmore, i 193.

Champneys, Henry, i *xl.* married Joan Paine, and became possessed of Orchardley, ii 223 ; memorial plate in Frome church, 192. Thomas, i *xl* ; John, sheriff, 1695, *xxxviii*. Dorothy, wife of Robert Smith, monument in Foxcote church, iii 350; arms, 350; William, married Margaret Sydenham, 522; Jane, married Humphry Sydenham, 522. Richard, sheriff, 1728, i *xxxviii*. Sir Thomas, created a baronet by George III, ii 223. sheriff, 1775, i *xxxix* ; J.P., *xlii*. Richard, and Sarah, his wife, monument in Orchardley church, ii 222 ; arms, 223.

Champneys, Sir John, lord mayor of London: birthplace, ii 96.

Chancellor, Charles, benefaction to Stanton-Drew, ii 438.

Chancellor, Matthew, said to have discovered a miraculous spring at Glastonbury, ii 266.

Chandefeld, William de, the service of, granted to Woodspring priory, iii 594.

Chandfeld or Chaldfield, Wilts, lands in, granted to Woodspring priory, iii 543, 594.

Chandos buildings, Bath, B 33.

Chandos, Baron, title conferred on Sir John Bridges, ii 404.

Chandos, duke of, descended from the Bridge family, ii 405. J.P., i *xli*. rebuilt St. John's hospital, Bath, in 1728, B 43. lord of the borough of Wedmore, i 188; and of the manor of Wedmore, 191. owned Huntspill-de-la-Hay, ii 393; a mansion at Keynsham, 403 ; the manor of Saltford, 431. Crandon, iii 92; part of Twiverton manor, 348 ; sold Catcot to Sir John Henniker, 432 ; owned Batcombe, 467; Stoke-Giffard, 605. sold Compton Martin to John Heniker, ii 133.

Chandos family, owners of Compton Martin, ii 133 ; patrons of Compton Martin, 134 ; benefaction to Compton Martin, 134.

Chantries :—

Aller, iii 188. Ashton-Phillips, ii 296, 297. Bath, B 70. Bawdrip, iii 93. Bedminster, ii 281, 282. Bradford, iii 244 ; Bridgwater, 88 ; Brimpton D'Evercy, 215. Buckland Dinham, ii 452.

Catcot, iii 432. Chard, ii 474. Charlton-Adam, iii 191. Charleton-Horethorne, ii 358. Charleton-Mackerel, iii 193 ; Chedder, 577 ; Combe-Flory, 248. Compton Paunceford, ii 77.

East-Coker, ii 341.

Farley, iii 354. Frome, ii 193, 194.

Hestercombe, iii 258 ; Hill-Farence, 257. Holwell, ii 371. Hutton, iii 591.

Idstock, iii 90. Ile Brewers, i 55 ; Ilminster, 7, iii 114.

Kilve, iii 533.

Limington, iii 218. Long-Ashton, ii 291. Martock, iii 8. Merriot, ii 171.

Nettlecombe, iii 538 ; Newton, 65. North-Barrow, ii 63. North-Petherton, iii 74. Norton Hautville, ii 108 ; Nunney, 221. Pensford, ii 429; Portbury, 281, iii 143. Rowdon, iii 537.

South Petherton, iii 111 ; Speckington, 200 ; Stavordale, 34 ; Stoke-under-Hamden, 316. Swell, i 66.

Taunton, iii 238. Trent, ii 382.

Wells (Cathedral), iii 402 ; Wells (St. Cuthbert's church), 408. Wembdon, ii 343, iii 104. Whitchurch, ii 444 ; Witham, 235 ; Wiveliscombe, 490. Woolavington, iii 438.

Yeovil, iii 208.

Chapel court, B 33, 43 ; row, 35.

Chapels :—

Adbeer in Trent (demolished), ii 382. Alhampton (demolished), iii 472 ; Alownshay (demolished), 323. Atherstone in White Lackington, i 68.

Cheverel, John, sheriff, 1471, 1472, i *xxxvi.*

Chew hundred, ii 93 ; John de Bretesche held lands in, 314. granted to Edward, duke of Somerset, iii 395.

Chew, river : course, i *xiv,* ii 93, 400, 415, 428, 429, 432.

Chew Magna : its situation, ii 94 ; Tun bridge, 94 ; Port bridge, 94 ; Sprat's bridge, 94 ; Domesday survey, 94 ; owned by bishop of the diocese, 94, iii 392. held by Richard, Rohard, Aluric, Uluric, and Stefan, ii 94. rating in 1293, iii 394 ; in king's hand, 1329, 394. alienated by bishop Barlow to Edward, duke of Somerset, reverts to the crown, granted to lord Lumley, who sells it to Sir Francis Popham and Edward Baber, ii 95 ; Edward Popham sells to Richard Summers, 95 ; tithings of North Elm, Knoll, Stone, and Bishop's Sutton, 95 ; hamlets of Sutton Wick, North Wick, and Sutton North, *alias* Knighton Sutton or Sutton Militis, 95 ; produces a bolus called ruddle, 96 ; Roman encampment called Bow-ditch, 96 ; birthplace of ·Sir John Champneys, lord mayor of London, 96 ; the church appropriated by bishop Ralph de Salopia, 96 ; the church and its monuments, 97—100 ; bells (6), 97 ; benefactions, 100.

Chew Stoke : its situation, ii 101 ; Domesday survey, 101 ; owned by Gilbert Fitz-Turold, held by Osbern, Edric, T.R.E. 101 ; owned by the lords Beauchamp of Hatch, the St. Loe's, and John Savery, 101 ; hamlets of Walley and St. Cross, 101 ; stone quarries, 101 ; the church (St. Andrew), 101 ; memorial stones, 102 ; benefactions, 102 ; old parsonage-house, 103.

Chewton hundred, ii 115 ; John de Bretesche held lands in, 314.

Chewton, John, earl Waldegrave, viscount, owned Radstock, ii 458.

Chewton-Keynsham, formerly a member of the manor of Keynsham, ii 405 ; annexed to that abbey, 405 ; granted to John St. Lo, 403 ; owned after the dissolution by Clarke, 405 ; the Popham family, 405 ; Thomas Lediard, 405.

Chewton-Mendip, its situation, ii 115 ; lead mines, 115 ; owned by queen Editha, 116 ; Domesday survey, 116 ; owned by the families of Martel, Reginald Fitz-Peter, Vivonia, Fitz-Reginald, Fitz-Roger, Bonville, 116 ; disputes between the tenants of Chewton and the prior of Greenoar, 116 ; the minery court, 117 ; owned by the family of Waldegrave, 117, 118 ; Sacrafield rents, 118 ; hamlet of North Widcombe, 118 ; the church (St. Mary Magdalen), early notice, 118, 119 ; bells (5), 119 ; monuments, 119 ; yew trees, 119 ; free school,

Chewton-Mendip—*continued.*

119 ; fair, 120 ; lands here were held of the heir of John Wyke, by William Palton, 456.

Cheyne or Cheyney family owned Norton-Hautville, ii 107 ; founded a chantry there, 108 ; held Purtington, 479. monuments in church of Weston, near Bath, i 161, 162. Cecilia, widow of Sir William, owned Thurlbeer, ii 182, and Sevington, iii 123. Edmund, sheriff, 1369, i *xxxv.* Edmund of Norton-Hautville, ii 107 ; Edward, alienated the property of Norton Hautville, 107. John, sheriff, 1454, i *xxxvi.* Robert, married Egelina, the widow of John de Wick, and became owner of Norton Hautville, ii 107 ; Sir William, of Norton Hautville, 107.

Cheyney family owned Spaxton, i 244. Radstock, ii 457. Ludhuish, iii 541 ; Agnes, of Pinhoe, married Edward Stawel, 250. Anne, married Robert Hussey, i 244 ; Elizabeth, married William Clopton, 244 ; Helena, married George Babington, 244 ; John, married Elizabeth Hill and became possessed of Spaxton, 244, and Radstock, ii 457. John, left four daughters, i 244, ii 457, 458. Mabel, married Edward Waldegrave : inherited the Spaxton estates, i 244. Margaret (*née* Kirkham), second wife of William Baumfylde, ii 90. Nicholas, M.P., 1308, i *xxix.*

Chichester family owned Begarn-Huish, iii 541. Henry, J.P., i *xliii.* Henry, owns Northover, iii 306. John Hody, J.P., i *xliii.* Sir John, held Ashbrittle for the use of John Blewit, iii 21 ; Urith, married John Trevelyan, 539.

Chichester, Seffride, bishop of, buried at Glastonbury, ii 262.

Chicke, Rev. John, monument in Charlinch church, i 241.

Chidiock or Chidiok family owned Chisselborough, ii 330. held Kingston, iii 323. John de, sheriff, 1312-1313, i *xxxiv* ; John, sheriff, 1447, i *xxxvi.*

Chigwell, Essex, owned by the Wrotham family iii 64.

Chilcomb, owned by Buckland priory, iii 98.

Chilcompton : its situation, ii 126 ; variation of soil, 126 ; stone quarries, 127 ; coal mines, 127 ; at Stockhill, 127 ; Old Down common, 127 ; Roman encampment at Blacker's Hill, 127 ; the Fairy Slatts, 128 ; Domesday survey, 128 ; owned by the bishop of Coutance, 128 ; held by Edric, T.R.E. 128 ; owned by the families of Percy, Broke, Chedder, Michelden, Seward, 128 ; Stocker, and lord Weymouth, 129 ; the manor house, 129 ; Park Field, 129 ; ancient house owned by the family of Werret, 129 ; Gilbert de Percy grants this church for the foundation of a prebend in Wells cathedral,

Chilcompton—*continued.*
afterwards exchanged with the prior and convent of Bradenstoke, for Chedder, 129; the church (St. John the Baptist) and its monuments, 129, 130; bells (6), 129; Werret's benefactions, 130; yew tree, 131.

Chilcot, hamlet in Wells, iii 405.

Child, Elizabeth, of Stanford, married John de l'Orti, and received from him the manors of Stoke-Trister, Bayford, and Cucklington, which she released to Sir John de Molyns, iii 50.

Child, Charles, mayor of Bath, 1709, B 26. Robert, owned Shepton Beauchamp, iii 125; his widow owned Southarp manor, 109. his daughter married the earl of Westmoreland and conveyed to him the estate of Norton-under-Hamden, ii 334. William, mayor of Bath, 1669, B 25; William, monument in Bath abbey, 1675, 68.

Childes-Chauntery, Witham, ii 235.

Chillington, branch of the manor of South-Petherton, iii 114; situation, 114; Domesday survey: owned by Roger de Curcelle: held by Anschitil: Godric held it T.R.E. 114; held with Barrington by the Daubeneys, 113, 114; Thomas, lord Wentworth, 114; land in, given for the maintenance of three chantry priests at Ilminster, 114; passed to Henry Simson, 114; Rev. Mr. Notley, 114; church (St. James), 114; bells (2), 114; yew tree, 114.

Chillington-down, iii 114, 117.

Chillwell, Mr., owned land in Bratton-Seymour, iii 36.

Chilson, hamlet in West-Buckland, ii 485.

Chilthorne, Alicia de, expelled from Whitehall nunnery, iii 300.

Chilthorne - Domer, iii 216; situation, 216; Domesday survey, 216, 217; divided in two parts, and owned by earl of Morton, and held by Alured: Brictuin and Alwi held it T.R.E. 216, 217; another part of the manor owned by William de Ow: held by Warner: Alestan Boscome held it T.R.E. 217; manor subsequently owned by the family of Domer or Dommere, 217; Fage, 217; Sydenhams held it of the earl of Devon, 215, 217; the Hawker family, 217. land here given to Thomas, bishop of Exeter, who bestowed it with the church on Brewton priory, ii 366, iii 217. by Witham priory, ii 233. by William Brocas, iii 221.

Chilthorne-Fage or Vagg held by the Fage family, iii 217; of the heir of Baldwin de Aldham, 217; of the heir of Sir John de St. Clair, 217; church (St. Mary) and its monuments, 217, 218; bells (2), 217; rectory held by Brewton priory, 214; part of the tithes owned by Montacute priory, 312.

Chilton, Devon, owned by the Luttrell family, iii 500.

Chilton, iii 88; situation, 88; common, near river Parret, 88; anciently a hundred: includes East-Chilton, West-Chilton or Chilton-Trivet, Idstoke-Inverne and Hunstile, 88; East Chilton: Domesday survey, 88; owned by Roger de Curcelle: held by Anschitil: Levegar held it T.R.E. 88; subsequently owned by the de Chilton family, 89; Thomas Mychell, William Besyls, and John Walyngford held the fourth part of a knight's fee, 89; held by the de Wigberes, 89; de Horseys, 89; division of Chilton Trinitatis, 88; Hunstile manor: Domesday survey, 89; held by John, the porter: Alward held it T.R.E. 89; land here formerly belonged to Sumertone, 89; manor subsequently owned by the Chiltons, 89; de Wigberes, 89; Cogans, of Huntspill, 89; Bourchiers, lords Fitzwarren, 89; West-Chilton or Chilton Trivet: Domesday survey, 89; owned by Roger de Curcelle: Anschitil held it: Mereswet held it T.R.E. 89; subsequently owned by the Trivets of Durborough, 89; John de Compton, 89; Elizabeth Tryvet held it of Sir Robert Poynings, knt., 89.

Chilton or Chilton-upon-Poldon, iii 433; origin of name, 433; situation, 433; Burtle, hamlet in, 433; called in Domesday "Ceptone," 433; held under the abbot of Glastonbury, by Roger de Curcelle, 433; subsequently the Mitchels held it of the Strangways, 433, 434; lady Tynte, 434; church and monument, 434; bells (2), 434; Champion's benefaction, 434.

Chilton family owned Chilton, and lands in South Petherton and Pitney, iii 89; a daughter of Peter de married Wimond de Raleigh, 537; Robert, held part of a knight's fee in Bower, 85.

Chilton Cantelo, ii 339; situation, 339; bridge, 339; held of the manor of Berwick by a younger branch of the family of Cantilupe, 339; John de Cantelo, 339; Walter Parker, 339; Wadham family, 339; Parham family, 339; Richard Parham held a moiety of the manor from Sir John Rogers, knt., 339; the family of Strode of Parnham, 339; the countess of Hertford, 339; earl of Northumberland, 339; J. Goodford, of Yeovil, 339; church (St. James) and its monuments, 339; bells (3), 339; legend of Brome's head, 340; a member of the hundred of Houndsborough, Berwick, and Coker: formerly in Berwick hundred, 323.

Chilton-Trivet (*see* Chilton).

Chilvetune (*see* Kilton).

Chimney money, i *li.*

Christmas custom at West Hatch, ii 180.

Christon, situation, iii 578; owned by Ywein de Chricheston, 578; held of the barony of Martin, 578; jointly held by William Donvile and John Howel, 578; Hugh and John de Draicote held the fourth part of a knight's fee, 578; Hugh D'Ovile held another fourth, 578; William de Pulteney another fourth, 578; the Pokeswell family held a fourth, 578, which passed to the Strodes, 578; the Wykes family held a fourth of · lord Stanley, 578; the whole manor subsequently owned by John Payne, 578; the Vaughans, 578; lady Smith, 578; held jointly by Sir John Hugh Smith, John Gore, and Edward Gore, 578; an estate here held by the Chedder family, 578; the Newtons and Capels, 578; the Vaughans, 578; lady Anne Smyth, 578; church and monument, 578; bells (3), 578.

Christopher, Mrs. Ann, memorial stone in Bathwick church, i 124.

Christy, Thomas, prior of Bath, 1333-1340, B 56.

Chubb, Matthew, benefaction to Crewkerne, ii 164.

Chubbeworth, Robert de, held land in Chubbeworth, iii 601.

Chubbeworth (*see* Shobworth).

Chudleigh, Sir Richard, married Mary Wadham, i 48.

Chudley, John, married Elizabeth Speke, i 68.

Church cross, Long Ashton, ii 304.

Church house, Long Ashton, ii 292.

Church land, Evercreech, iii 416.

Church street, Bath, B 33.

Church of Yatton strewed with grass on Whitsunday, iii 620.

Churches dedicated to St. Michael, generally on elevated ground, instances of, i 76.

Churches, subjected to Glastonbury, exempted from episcopal authority, ii 241.

Churches, now demolished: Berwick, in Widcombe, i 171; Earnshill, 31. Estham, ii 160. Goose-Bradon, i 16. Ilchester: St. Andrew, St. John Baptist, St. Michael, St. Mary Major, S. Mary Minor, St. Peter, iii 301; Milverton, 16. Norton Hautville, ii 108. Shockerwick, in Bathford, i 112. Sock-Dennis, iii 308. South Bradon, i 16. Spargrove, iii 468. Standerwick, ii 228. Walton-in-Gordano, iii 171. West Dowlish, i 38; Woodwick in Freshford, 125.

Churchey, James, monument in Wincaunton church, iii 35; Thomas, married (1) Sarah Wadman, (2) Dorothy Mogg: monument in Wincaunton church, 35; Thomas, benefaction to Somerton, 187.

Churchill, Charles, monument in Bath abbey, 1745, B 68. Henrietta, wife of Sir Charles Waldegrave, ii 117; Sir John, master of the Rolls, owned Backwell, 306. and

Churchill—*continued.*

Churchill, iii 580; effigies in Churchill church, 581; John, of Mintern, married Sarah Winston, 293; Winston, 293; John, duke of Marlborough, 293.

Churchill or Courcelle, Roger de (*see* Corcelle).

Churchill, situation, iii 579; here Mendip hills begin to rise, 579; Doleberry castle: encampment, 579; Lower-Langford hamlet, 579; owned by Roger de Curcelle, 580; Blackmore hamlet: Domesday survey, owned by Roger de Curcelle: held by Anschitil: Aluric held it T.R.E. 579; subsequently owned by the bishopric of Bath and Wells, 579; Blackmore Green, 579; belongs to the benefice of Filton *alias* Whitchurch, 579; details of, 579; Stock hamlet, 579; Smeath's moor, 580. at the Conquest formed part of the manor of Banwell, 580; subsequently owned by the Cogans, 580; the Fitzwarrens, 580; David Swian, 580; the St. Loes, 580; the Jennyns family, 580; Sir John Churchill, 580; John Stoke, 580; William Whitchurch, 580; John Gibbons held a moiety which passed to David Peloquin, 580; Nathaniel Elias Cosserat, 580; the Saunders family held the other moiety, 580; which was mortgaged to John Elbridge, 580; and sold in moieties, 580; one moiety owned by the Woolnoughs, 580; Sir John Hugh Smyth, 580; the other moiety owned by Mrs. Anne Hort, 580; Henry Muggleworth, 580; Samuel Newnham, 580; Peter Kington, 580; church (St. John the Baptist) and monuments, 581; bells (5), 581; benefactions, 581, 582; yew tree, 582.

Churchland, tithing of Wedmore, i 188.

Churchset, iii 230.

Churchwardens and their duties, i 89.

Churchyard, smallest in the kingdom, i 143.

Churi (*see* Curry Rivel).

Chyke, John, memorial brass in Sparkford church, ii 87.

Chynne, John, last incumbent of St. Mary's chantry, Aller, iii 188.

Cibewrde (*see* Shobworth).

Ciceter, Peter de, dean of Wells, 1220, i 189.

Cilemetone (*see* Kilmington).

Cilletone (*see* Chillington).

Cilterne (*see* Chilthorne-Domer).

Cilve or Culve (*see* Kilve).

Cipestaple (*see* Chipstaple).

Circus lane, Bath, B 37.

Cirencester abbey, Gloucestershire: held land in Somerset, temp. Ed. I, i *xxvi.* owned West Woodlands, ii 188; received a pension from Frome church, 191; owned the benefice of Marston-Bigot, 215; property in Milborne Port, 353. benefice of Wellow, iii 328.

Clatworthy—*continued.*

sham, 509; and John Jacob, 509; the other moiety held by the Arundel family, 509; the whole manor owned by Baldwin Malet, 509; Thomas Carew, 509; James Bernard, 509; Ford abbey held lands here, 510; Tripp manor, 510; held by the Carews, 510; Syndercombe manor: Domesday survey, 510; owned by Turstin Fitz-Rolf: held by Hugh: Cerric held it T.R.E. 510; subsequently held by the Carew family, 510; church (St. Mary), 510; bells (4), 510; church-house, 510.

Clause, Mary, second wife to John Walshe, i 42.

Clavel (*see* Claville).

Clavelshay family took their name from Clavelshay, iii 73; Cuthbert: Richard: John, of Curry Rivel, 73; arms, 73.

Clavelshay or Classy farm, North-Petherton, iii 72.

Clavering, Elizabeth, monument in Bath abbey, 1763, B 68.

Claverham (*see* Yatton).

Claverton, situation, i 145; Claverton down, 145; Domesday survey, 145; held by Hugoline; Suain held it T.R.E. 145. sold by Hugo *cum barba* to John de Villula, iii 351. who sold it to Bath abbey, i 146; retaken from the abbey and annexed to the bishopric, 146; charter of free warren granted to William Button, 146; made a liberty, 146; exchanged by William Barlow, 146, iii 395. granted by Edward VI to Matthew Colthurst, and held successively by the families of Hungerford, Estcourt, Basset, Holder, William Skrine, Ralph Allen, who bequeathed it to Mrs. Gertrude Warburton, afterwards the wife of the Rev. Martin Stafford Smith, i 146; the manor houses, i 146, iii 383. the church and its monuments, i 147-150; bells (3), 147; rectors from the time of queen Elizabeth, i 147. rating in 1293, iii 394; in 1329, 394.

Claverton street, Bath, B 34.

Claville, Grace, daughter of Joseph, second wife to William Knoyle, ii 378. Margaret, of Clavelshay, iii 73. Roger de, married Joan de Deaudon, ii 494, iii 496; Thomas, of Clavelshay, gave lands there to Jordan le King, 72.

Clayhanger tithing, Combe St. Nicholas, ii 475.

Clay-hill, iii 51.

Clayhill, hamlet in Chilton, iii 89, 90.

Clayton, John, owner of East Ling, who sells the same to John Tynbury, i 85; receives site on which Athelney abbey is built, 88.

Cleeve abbey (Cistercian), founded by William de Romara, iii 511; possessions, 511; list of abbots, 512; site granted at the dissolution to Robert, earl of Sussex, 512; ruins, 512. Abbot, a landowner, temp. Ed. I, i

Cleeve abbey—*continued.*

xxvi. held Washford, iii 91. held half a knight's fee from John de Mohun, ii 15. John Brent, steward, iii 436; chantry founded by Gilbert de le Waleis, 438.

Cleeve-Toot hill, iii 616.

Clemens, of Alexandria: supposed allusion to Wookey Hole, iii 420.

Clement, Samuel, monument in Bath-Easton church, i 110. William, monk of Bath, received pension, B 57.

Clement, Rev., incumbent of South-Brent, i 200. Mr., benefaction to Bath abbey, B 71; William, master of St. John's hospital, 1683, 43.

Clements, William, monument in Bath abbey, B 61, 68.

Clendon, Rev. John, incumbent of Upton, iii 555.

Clerby, Madelina de, first wife to Richard de Placetis, iii 64.

Clerk, John, received a pension from Montacute priory, iii 313; John, bishop of Bath and Wells, 1523—1540, poisoned in Germany, buried in the church of the Minories, London, 387. Peter, M.P. for Chard, ii 472; Thomas and Margery, his sister, had a lease of Elm, 207.

Clerke or Clarke, Christopher and William, of Minchin-Barrow (*see* Clarke).

Clerke, William, master of St. Catherine's hospital, Bedminster, ii 287; William (son of Robert), and Richard, granted land in Stanton Drew to Richard Choke, 434.

Cleve, hamlet in Yatton, iii 618.

Clevedon, situation, iii 166; rocks, 166; Wake's tower, 166; lead mines, 166; lapis calaminaris, 166; Domesday survey, 167; owned by Matthew de Moretania: held by Ildebert: John [the Dane] held it T.R.E. 167; subsequently held of the honour of Gloucester by the de Clivedon family, 167; Thomas Hogshaw, 167; John Blanc, 167; Sir Thomas Lovel, 167; the Wake family, 167; in moieties by Sir Humphrey Stanley and Sir James Parker, John Crocker and John Dudley, 168; restored to the Wake family, 168; passed to the Digbys, earls of Bristol, 168; the Elton family, 168; manor-house, 168; church (St. Andrew) and its monuments, 168, 169; benefactions, 169.

Clevedon, Clivedon, or Clyvedon family held Milton Clevedon, i 222. lands in Thrubwell and Butcombe, ii 315. Penselwood, iii 44; Clevedon, 167; Thorn-Coffin, 322; William de, held Clevedon, 167; Matthew de, obtains suit against Richard Ken, 167, 592. Elizabeth, held land in Wanstraw, ii 229. John, landowner temp. Ed. I, i *xxviii*; M.P., 1326, *xxix*; commissioner of sewers, *xii.* held land in Rodden, ii 226; in Wanstraw, 229; Sir John, held land in Oakhampton, 489.

K

Clevedon, Clivedon, or Clyvedon family—*contd.*
Clevedon, iii 167; witness to a deed by
Matilda Falconbridge, 259. Edward, M.P.,
1354, i *xxx*; Matthew de, M.P., 1360, 1362,
1369, *xxx*; held the bailiwick of Neroche
forest, 17; was guardian to the children of
Ralph de Vernai, 253. keeper of Selwood
forest, 1345, ii 195. Clevedon, iii 167.
Edmund de, owned land in Wanstraw, ii
229. owned Clevedon, iii 167. Emma de,
married Edmund Hogshaw, i 223. held
land in Wanstraw, ii 229. conveyed Clivedon to Edmund Hogshaw, iii 167; Richard
and Alexander de, lived at Clivedon, but
were not in the direct line of descent, 167.

Clewer, hamlet of Wedmore, i 188; situation,
188; given by St. Wilfrid to the abbey of
Glastonbury, 188; Domesday survey, 188;
owned by the bishop of Coutance, 188; held
by Fulcran and Nigell; Turchill held it
T.R.E. 188. the families of the Percivals,
iii 173; the Chedders, 576, and lord Weymouth, i 188. lands here were granted by
John de Wyke to John de Edyndon, iii
618.

Clifford, Alice, second wife to Sir Walter Rodney, iii 603. lady Anne, erected a monument to Samuel Daniel, ii 201; Maud,
daughter of Sir Walter, married William
de Longespee, 357; Mary, wife of Hugh
Bampfylde, 91. Richard, bishop of Worcester, previously elected to the see of Bath
and Wells, iii 383; Rosamond, mother of
William Longespee, earl of Salisbury,
367.

Clifford, lord, of Chudleigh, owner of land formerly belonging to the priory of Cannington,
i 233; vault in Cannington church, 236.

Cliffords' house, Beckington, ii 200.

Clift, Matthew, mayor of Bath, 1657, B 25.

Clifton family owned Stone-Easton, ii 154.
held Barrington, and land in the forest of
Neroche, iii 113. Elizabeth, wife of Sir
Amias Baumfilde, ii 90. Gervase, landowner temp. Ed. I, i *xxvii*. held a knight's
fee in Stone Easton, ii 154. Ignatius de,
landowner temp. Ed. I, i *xxvii*. held a
knight's fee in Stone Easton, ii 154. Sir
John, sheriff, 1586, i *xxxvii*. Sir John, of
Barrington, iii 113. William, owned the
rectory and advowson of Curry Rivel, i 27.
William, of Barrington, iii 113.

Clink, hamlet in Frome, ii 186.

Clinton, lord, owned Temple-combe, ii 359.
Margaret, daughter of Theophilus, earl of
Lincoln, and baron Clinton, married Hugh
Boscawen, iii 469; title conferred on Hugh
Fortescue, 469.

Clivedon or Clevedon family (*see* Clevedon).

Cliveham (*see* Claverham).

Cliveware (*see* Clewer).

Clock, astronomical, erected at Glastonbury by
Peter Lightfoot, ii 254. removed to Wells,
iii 399.

Cloford, situation, ii 205; Domesday survey, 205;
owned by the earl of Morton: held by Alured, 205; the Flory family, 205; the Horner
family, 205; Leighton manor, 205; Holwell hamlet, 205; Postlebury wood, 205;
part of Hill-house liberty, included in this
parish, 206; church appropriated to Keynsham abbey, 205; church (St. Mary) and
monuments, 206; bells (2), 206. a moiety
of the tithes owned by Montacute priory,
iii 312.

Cloisters in monasteries, ii 250.

Clootwick, Jane, monument in Bath abbey,
1786, B 68.

Cloppecote, Robert de, prior of Bath, 1303—
1332, B 55.

Clopton, William, married Elizabeth Cheyney,
i 244.

Cloptone (*see* Clapton, in Cadbury, South).

Cloptone, Adam de, iii 140.

Close, Rev. H. J., governor of Bath hospital, B
48.

Close-hall, Wells, iii 403.

Closewell, bequeathed by John Buckland to
West Harptree parish, ii 143.

Closworth, ii 346; situation, 346; river Ivel,
346; Boarden-bridge, 346; Netherton and
Weston hamlets, 346; Domesday survey,
346; owned by earl Morton, 346; Montacute priory, 346, iii 311. granted at the
dissolution to Sir Richard Morison, ii 346,
327; passed to Stephen Hales, 346; the
Portman family, 346; church (All Saints)
and monuments, 347; bells (5), 347.

Cloth manufacture, Ilminster, i 2; Broadway,
18. Pensford, ii 429; Winsham, 478.
Dulverton, iii 520.

Clothier, John, incumbent of Limington, iii 219.

Clotune (*see* Clapton-in-Gordano).

Clotworthy, Philip and Margaret de, held land
in Clatworthy, iii 509.

Cloutsham, William, held half a knight's fee in
Timberscombe, ii 44. William, married the
heiress of John Lambrook, and became
possessed of land in Clatworthy, iii 509.

Clutone (*see* Clutton).

Clutterbuck, John, monument in Claverton
church, i 149.

Clutton, its situation, ii 103; coal mines, 103;
Domesday survey, 103; owned by the
bishop of Coutance, 103; held by William,
by Turchel, T.R.E. 103; owned by the
families of Greyville (or Grevile), Stafford,
Willoughby, Broke, and earl of Warwick,
103, 104; church (St. Augustine) and monuments, 104; bells (5), 104.

Clyffe, John, received a pension from Witham
priory, ii 234.

Clyfford, Sir Jehan de, i *l.*

Clyfton, Sir Ignatius de, held Easton-in-Gordano, iii 148.

Clyne, Thomas, held half a knight's fee in
Quarum-Mounceaux, iii 556.

Clyve, Robert de, abbot of Cleeve, 1321, iii 512.

Clyvedon family (*see* Clevedon).

Cnut, king, gave Sevington-Abbots to Athelney
abbey, iii 124.

Coal mines, i *xvi.* Strachey's observations on,
ii 145-148; Chilcompton, 127; Clutton,
103; Farrington-Gournay, 137; Haygrove,
423; High-Littleton, 145; Mells, 462;
Midsummer Norton, 149. Nailsea, iii 162.
Queen-Charleton, ii 417; Radstock, 458.
Rodford, iii 331. Timsbury, ii 111.

Coarme (*see* Quarum-Kitnor).

Coat, hamlet in Martock, iii 2.

Coates, Peter, owned Stanton-Drew, ii 434;
trustee for Mrs. Lyde's benefaction, 437.

Cobb, Ann, monument in Newton - St. - Lo
church, iii 344; Christian, daughter of Sir
George, married Paul Methuen, 246.

Cobham, Sir John, knt., held Yeovilton, iii 199;
married Catherine Bonville, 267; Catharine,
his widow, married John Wyke, 267.

Cobham, Reginald, lord, keeper of Selwood
forest, 1403, ii 195. Reginald, lord of Ster-
burg, married Eleanor, widow of Sir John
Fitzalan, iii 207; Joan, heiress of, owned
Winsford, 556.

Cobham, Sir Thomas Brook, created lord Cobham by Henry VI, iii 303; married Joan
Braybrook, 303; Edward, lord, son of
Thomas, owned the manors of Ivelchester,
Luston, Sewardswicke and Grubbeswick,
and lands in Sevenhampton, Brook-Monta-
cute and Chard, 303; John, lord, married
Margaret Neville, 303; Thomas, lord, married Dorothy Heydon, 303; George, lord,
303; William, lord, son of George, 303,
304; Henry, lord, attainted, and his estates
forfeited, 304; William, restored in blood,
but only allowed to use the title by the
king's special grace, 304; John Brook, of
Hekington, lord, 304.

Cock and Gorepit, hamlets in Stoke Courcy,
owned by John Acland, i 252.

Cock or le Cok, Thomas, prior of Taunton,
1346, iii 235.

Cock lane, Bath, B 32.

Cocke, John, owned Ford and Woodborough,
iii 613; John, of Churchill, 613.

Cockeram, John, received a pension from Taunton priory, iii 236.

Cockerell, Samuel, owned land in Huntspill-
Cogan, ii 392; Luke, sold his estate there,
392.

Cockhill, hamlet in Castle-Cary, ii 56.

Cocklake, hamlet in Wedmore, i 188.

Cocklate (*see* Cocklake).

Cockmill, iii 478.

Cocks family held West Chelworth, ii 420.

Cocks family of Wraxall, owned land in Dundry, ii 105.

Cockswell, John, owned West-Chelworth, ii 420.

Cockwell-Croft or Close, bequeathed by Mary
Buckland to West-Harptree parish, ii 143.

Cockworthy, Avice, married John Trevelyan,
iii 539.

Cocre or Coker family (*see* Coker).

Cocus (*see* Cook).

Codington, William de, married Agnes de
Orchard, iii 489.

Codrington family owned Flax-Bourton, iii 161;
Tickenham, 165; held Hutton through a
marriage with the Still family, 590. Jane,
wife of John, monument in Witham church,
ii 235. John, M.P. for Bath, 1710, 1713,
1714, 1722, 1734, B 22. owned property in
Baltonsbury, ii 269. John, married Elizabeth Gorges, and became possessed of the
manors of Wraxall, Nailsea, Bourton and
Tickenham, iii 158; gift to Wraxall church,
161; Elizabeth, wife of John, monument in
Wraxall church, 159. Jane, daughter of
John, married Sir Richard Warwick Bampfylde, ii 91. inherited her father's property,
iii 158. Sir William, J.P., i *xlii.*

Codsend, hamlet in Cutcombe, ii 6.

Coel, king, buried at Glastonbury, ii 262.
statue in front of town hall, Bath, B 32.

Coffin, Robert, held Thorn-Coffin, iii 322; arms,
322.

Coffine, Elizabeth, wife of John Wyke, monument in Crewkerne church, ii 163.

Coffins, Mr., benefaction to Crewkerne, ii 164.

Cogan family owned Huntspill, ii 390, 391;
Alston, 393, and Churchill, iii 580. Sir
Milo, knt., married Christian Paganel and
became possessed of Huntspill, ii 390;
William, 390; John, 390. landowner temp.
Ed. I, i *xxvii.* benefaction to Shepton
Beauchamp, iii 126. Sir John, knt., ii 390;
buried at Huntspill, 391; Thomas, 391;
Richard, 391, *xl*; married Mary Wigbere
and became possessed of Wigborough, 391;
Sir William, knt., 391, 393. sheriff, 1378,
i *xxxv.* John, ii 391; Elizabeth, married
(1) Sir Fulke Fitzwarren (2) Sir Hugh
Courtney, 391. Gilbert, married a daughter of Sir John Percival, iii 174. Isabella,
prioress of Minchin-Barrow, 1511, ii 311.

Cogges, a messuage and lands in, held by William de Gardino, iii 186.

Cogswell, John, mayor of Bath, 1745, B 26.

Cogyn, Thomas, of St. John's hospital, Bridgwater, subscribed to the supremacy, iii 79.

Coiners, notorious asylum of, ii 194.

Coit, a huge, ii 432.

Cok or le Cock, Thomas, prior of Taunton,
1346, iii 235.

Coke family owned Portbury, iii 142 ; and Portishead, 144 ; Sir Edward, lord chief justice of England, 142 ; Thomas, created baron Lovel, and afterwards viscount Coke and earl of Leicester : married Margaret Tufton, 142 ; Edward, 142 ; Thomas Wenman, sold Portbury to James Gordon, 142.

Coke, Robert, prior of Woodspring, iii 595.

Coke, Walter, prior of Taunton, iii 235.

Coke's-mead, Taunton, owned by Walter Meriet, iii 259.

Coker-East, situation, ii 340 ; Roman remains, 340 ; Domesday survey, 340 ; held by the king : Ghida held it T.R.E. 340 ; part of the manor granted to the abbey of St. Stephen, at Caen, 341 ; the residue owned by the families of Courteney and Mandeville, 341 ; heirs of John and Clement de Montalt held property here, 341 ; manor sold to Bartholomew Trevilian, 341 ; Symes family, 341 ; William Hellyar, 341 ; seat of Mr. Hellyar, 341 ; chantry, 342 ; lands belonging to, granted to Edward Nevil, 342 ; church (St. Michael) and its monuments, 342, 343 ; bells (8), 342 ; almshouse, 343 ; old mansion, 343 ; Nash-house, 343 ; Coker family, 343.

Coker-North, hamlet in East Coker, ii 340 ; owned by the bishop of Exeter, 342 ; chapel, owned by Edward Nevil, 342 ; mansion, 343.

Coker-West, situation, ii 344 ; hamlets of Fontenoy and Bridwell, 344 ; the abbey of St. Stephen, at Caen, owned land here, 344 ; convent established here by the monks of Caen, 344 ; granted, at the dissolution of alien priories, to the priory of Montacute, 344 ; manor owned by the Courteney family, 344 ; Henry William Portman, 344 ; church (St. Martin) and monuments, 344, 345 ; bells (6), 344 ; almshouse, 346 ; benefactions, 346.

Coker or Cocre family owned Coker, ii 343. lands in Bower, iii 85 ; and Worle, 615 ; a branch of, lived at Lydiard St. Laurence, 266. Robert, de, ii 343 ; Matthias, founded a chantry at Wembdon, 343, iii 104. Richard, gave lands to Brewton priory, ii 343 ; Matthias, 343. Matthew, sheriff, 1408, 1417, i *xxxv.* John, of West Coker, ii 343. John, married Hawise Malet, i 91. Bartholomew, of Coker, ii 343 ; Elizabeth, married John Seymour, of Wolf-hall, Wilts, 343 ; William, of Rolston and Bower, married Elizabeth Norris of Pentelyn, 344. held the reversion of Oake after the death of Sir John Trivet, iii 273. Robert, of Bower, married the daughter of John Wallys, of Worle, ii 344. sheriff, 1422, i *xxxv.* John, ancestor of the Cokers, of Mapouder, Dorset, ii 344 ; Bridget, of Ma-

Coker or Cocre family—*continued.*
pouder, married Thomas Hussey, 385. Susanna, of Mapouder, married Nathaniel Farewell, iii 38. the Rev. John, author of a " Survey of Dorchester," ii 344.

Coker, Robert, vicar of Long Ashton, ii 299.

Coker, Berwick and Houndsborough hundred, ii 323.

Colbey, Mrs., benefaction to Lydiard St. Laurence, iii 266.

Colborne, Benjamin, governor of Bath hospital, B 48 ; William, governor of Bath hospital, 48.

Cold Harbour, hamlet in Dundry, ii 105.

Cold Hinton (*see* Hinton-Blewet).

Cole, John, iii 210.

Cole, Richard, sheriff, 1646, i *xxxviii.* owned a manor in Nailsea, iii 162 ; married Ann Hopton, 162 ; Dorothy, wife of Alexander Popham ; Ann, wife of William Collins ; William ; monuments in Nailsea church, 162, 163 ; arms, 163.

Cole, Rev. Potter, governor of Bath hospital, B 48.

Cole, Thomas, incumbent of Dulverton, iii 524.

Coleford, hamlet in Kilmersdon, ii 446.

Colefree land, Kingston Seymour : occupiers of had a lawsuit with the assessors of Yatton, ii 124.

Cole-house, Kenn, owned by Mr. Willoughby, iii 593.

Coles, Elizabeth, wife of John Coles, and daughter of Humphrey Windham : benefactions to Wiveliscombe, ii 491. John, sheriff, 1625, i *xxxviii.* Mr., benefaction to Kingston, iii 264. Rev., incumbent of Durleigh, i 79 ; Rev., incumbent of Lympsham, 203. Thomas, sheriff, 1747, i *xxxix.* William, monument in Norton St. Philips church, iii 371.

Coleshill, Sir John, owned Lopen, iii 122 ; and Sevington, 123.

Coleshull, Richard de, sheriff, 1274, 1275, 1276, 1277, i *xxxiv.*

Coley hamlet, iii 587.

Colford, William de, M.P., 1341, i *xxx.* Mary, of Bromfield, married (1) Alexander Webber, (2) Oliver Galhampton : inscription in Oake church, iii 273 ; Thomas, of Bromfield, married Elizabeth Sydenham, 523.

Colgrin, held Bath-hampton, i 117.

Coliberti, tenants in free socage, i 106.

Collard, Joan, wife of Lancelot St. Albyn, i 265.

College close, Wells, iii 403.

College lane, Wells, iii 383.

College of priests, founded at Wells by bishop Erghum, iii 383, 402 ; Stoke under Hamden, 316.

Colles, Humphrey, owned Blagdon, Barton, Middlecot, and lands in Orchard, Trull, Pitminster, and Corfe, rectories and advow-

Colles—*continued.*
sons of three last-mentioned places, and tenements in Cathanger : was seated at Barton, iii 285. sheriff, 1557, i *xxvii*. received letters patent from Henry VIII, granting him the abbey, etc. of Bath, B 57. received the manor of Combe-Monkton, i 151. the site of Dunster priory, ii 17. lands in Martock, iii 8 ; the hospital of St. John, Bridgwater, and lands called Small-croft, 80 ; held the rectory and advowson of Corfe, 249 ; purchased Bridghampton cum Speckington, 200. Elizabeth, daughter of Humphrey, married Thomas Malet, i 92. John, married Anne Thynne, iii 285 ; John, married Elizabeth Wyndham, 275, 285, ii 490. sheriff of Somerset, 1578, i *xxvii*, 1597, 1617, *xxxviii*. purchased Honibere for the children of Sir Thomas Palmer, iii 534 ; Anne, daughter and co-heir of John, married Sir William Portman, 275, 285 ; Elizabeth, married John Coventry, 285 ; to whom she conveyed the Barton estate, 285 ; Margaret, married Sir Gerard Napier, 285.

Colley, lands in, owned by Sir John Newton, iii 588

Colleys-green, iii 478.

Collibee, George, mayor of Bath, 1691, B 25 ; William, mayor of Bath, 1719, 26 ; Edward Bushell, mayor of Bath, 1756, 1765, 1775, 26 ; 1785, 27.

Collins, held Bath-ford, i 112. Ann, wife of William, monument in Nailsea church, iii 163. Benjamin, of Salisbury, purchased lands in Castle Cary, ii 56 ; Daniel, monument in Castle Cary church, 57. John, sheriff, i *xliii* ; John, sheriff, 1757, *xxxix* ; John, seat at Hatch Beauchamp, 43, 44. John, owned Lillesdon, ii 179 ; John, erected a monument to Mr. Joel Smith, 477. John Rawe, J.P., i *xliii* ; Mary, widow of Thomas, monument in South Stoke church, 137. Samuel, memorial stone in Maperton church, ii 86 ; Major Samuel, monument in Chew Magna church, 99.

Collinson, Rev., incumbent of King Weston, ii 81 ; Rev. John, of Bromham, incumbent of Road and Wolverton, 225 ; John, vicar of Long Ashton, 299 ; and vicar of Filton, alias Whitchurch, 442. Septimus, incumbent of West-Dowlish, i 38. of Dowlish-Wake, iii 120.

Colliton, Mr., owned Trent, ii 381.

Collyngborn, William, sheriff, 1475, 1476, i *xxxvi*

Colman, John le, M.P. for Bath, 1337, B 19.

Colmady, Warwick, owned a manor at North Curry, ii 179.

Colmer, Rev. John, benefaction to Babcary, ii 62 ; monuments in Babcary church, 61, 62.

Colmstoke, Richard de, prior of Taunton, 1325, iii 235 ; Ralph de, prior of Taunton, 1331—1338, 235.

Colo held Nunney, ii 218. land in Woodspring, iii 594.

Colston, Edward, purchased Beer, and appropriated it to the support of his school at Bristol, i 235. purchased Lydford-West, and devised it to Mrs. Mary Edwards, ii 84 ; benefactions to Kew - Stoke, 102. granted Locking to his school at Bristol, iii 597. name assumed by Alexander Ready, ii 84 ; Mrs., widow of Alexander, held the patronage of Lydford West, 84. Mrs., of Broughton, owned part of the manor of Clapton-in-Gordano, iii 178.

Colsuain, held one hide in Winford, ii 320.

Colthurst, Matthew, owned Claverton, i 146 ; Combe - Monkton, 151. purchased Bath abbey, B 57. held with Sir Francis Brian, the site of Taunton priory and its appurtenances, lands in Taunton, Hill-Bishops, Staplegrove, Ruishton, Trull, Corfe, Pitminster, Hill-Farence, Norton, Kingston and Cheddon, iii 236 ; owned the site of Hinton priory, 369. Edmund, son of Matthew, sold Claverton to Edward Hungerford, i 146. gave the Abbey church to the mayor and citizens of Bath, B 58 ; sold the Abbey house and park, 58. sold Hinton priory, iii 369. Richard, incumbent of Claverton, i 147.

Colthurst or Cultura (*see* Cultura).

Colton, hamlet in Nettlecombe, iii 541.

Columbers family, of Nether-Stowey, iii 551 ; held lands in Heathfield, 253, 254 ; in Woolavington, 438 ; owned Blagdon, 569, and Puriton, ii 396. Philip de, iii 551. baron in time of Henry II, i *xxvi* ; owned land in Goathurst, 80 ; Spaxton, 243 ; dispute with Adam de Cunteville, concerning his right to the manor of Alfoxton, 264 ; owned a knight's fee in Otterhampton, 242. held half a knight's fee from John de Mohun, ii 14 ; married Maud de Candos, and became possessed of Puriton and other estates, 396, iii 437. Philip, married Cecilia de Vernai, iii 551, i 253, iii 437. lady Cecilia, wife of Philip, granted her lands in Hill-Farence, to Maud de Vernai, her daughter, iii 257; William, of Woolavington, 437, 551 ; Henry, 551 ; Sir Philip, knt., owned Stowey, Honibere, and Woolavington, 551 ; Philip, died without issue, 551. John de, landowner temp. Ed. I, i *xxvii*; owned Fiddington, and procured a charter of free-warren there, 241. married Alice de Pencester, iii 551 ; his lands were confiscated, but afterwards restored to him, 551; John, 551; Stephen, 551; Joan, daughter of John, married Sir Geffrey de Stawel, 250 ; Sir Ralph, witness to a deed, 101 ; Philip, or William de, married Alianor Martin, died without issue, 551, ii 84, 132, iii 218.

Commons and Moors—*continued.*
moor, i *xv*; Staple Fitzpaine, 58. Stoley's
Green, ii 180. Vagg Common, iii 132;
Walton-in-Gordano, 169. Warmoor, i *xv*;
West-Moor, *xv*, ii 469. West-Sedgmoor,
i *xv*; Weston-Moor, *xv*, iii 440. Westwall,
i *xv*; Winterhay Green, Ilminster, 6.

Compe, John, M.P. for Bath, 1376, B 20.

Compton, in Berkshire, owned by the bishopric
of Bath and Wells, iii 394.

Compton, in Midsummer Norton, ii 151.

Compton-Bishop or Episcopi, iii 582; situation,
582; includes the hamlets of Cross, Dun-
net, Ratley, and Wiventon, 582; anciently
written "Contune," 582; Domesday survey, 582; owned by Walter de Dowai, 582;
held by Ralph: Elwacre held it T.R.E.
582; Alric held one hide T.R.E. 582; subsequently owned by the bishop of Bath and
Wells, 582. John Aishe, ii 317. the Prowse
family, iii 582; Sir John Mordaunt, 583;
rating in 1293, 394; in manu Regis, 394, 395;
church (St. Andrew) and monuments, 583;
bells (6), 583; benefactions, 583; cross, 583.

Compton-Dando, situation, ii 421; river Chew,
421; Domesday survey, 421; held by Mat-
hildis, of earl Eustace: Ulnod held it
T.R.E. 421; afterwards owned by the
family of de Alno, 421; Burnel, 422; de
Handlo, created lords Burnel, 422; Hungerford, 422; Smyth, 422; Popham, 422;
Bath priory held land here, 422; Severys-
wyke or Sewardswick manor, held by
Thomas de Ryvere, of Thomas de Lyons,
422; Grubbeswyke, held by Emma, wife of
Richard de la Ryvere, 422; these lands
subsequently held by Richard Priour, of
Widcombe, 422; Edward Brooke, iind Cobham, 423; George Young, 423; Mrs. Popham, 423; Wollard hamlet, partly in this
parish, owned formerly by the lords Botreaux and Hungerford, 423; Wansdike,
423; church (St. Mary) and monuments,
423; bells (5), 423; benefactions, 423.

Compton-Dunden, situation, iii 446; Dunden-
Beacon, 446; Compton-street, 447; hamlet
of Littleton, 447; Compton, anciently included with Walton, 447; Dunden, owned
by Glastonbury abbey: Domesday survey,
447; held by Roger de Curcelle: Algar
held it T.R.E. 447; subsequently held by
the family of Malet, 447; of de Vivonne,
447; of Beauchamp of Hatch, 447; of
Meriet, 447; of Seymour, 447; Humphry
Stafford, 447; the Strangways family, 447;
the earl of Ilchester, 447; market and fair,
447; Littleton manor, held by the Fitchets,
447; the Hills, of Spaxton, 447; John
Lyde, 447; church (St. Andrew), 447;
bells (5), 447; dungeon-house, 448; Sir
John Strangways' benefaction, 448.

Compton-Durville, South Petherton, iii 106, 110.

Compton-East, tithing, Pilton, iii 480.

Compton-Episcopi (*see* Compton-Bishops).

Compton-Martin, its situation, ii 131; Domesday survey, 131; owned by Serlo de Burci,
part held by Richard: Euvacre held it
T.R.E. 131; owned by the families of Martin, of Tours, 132; Wake, 132, iii 119.
Keynes, ii 132; Chandos and John Heniker,
133; tithing of Moreton, 133; Bigfield mansion, 133; church (St. Michael), monuments, 134; benefactions, bells (6) 134;
Nemnet, a chapel to, 320; Wulfric, the hermit, born at, 331.

Compton-Paunceford, situation, ii 76; Domesday survey, 76; owned by Turstin Fitz-
Rolf, and held by Goisfrid: Alward T.R.E.
76; owned by the families of Pauncefoot,
76. John Brent, iii 436. Thomas, lord
Paulet, Giles Hoby, and John Hunt, ii 76,
77; chantry founded by one of the Pauncefoot family, 77; church (St. Mary) and
monuments, 77; bells (3), 77.

Compton-street, iii 447.

Compton-West, iii 480.

Compton family owned Barrow Gournay, ii 309.
Exton, iii 527; arms, 112, ii 443. John, of
West Chilton, iii 89. monument in Beckington church, ii 201. Sir William, sheriff,
1513, i *xxxvii*. owned part of Buckland-
Dinham, ii 452; Peter, owned Barrow-
Gournay, 309; his widow, Anne, married
William, earl of Pembroke, 309; Francis,
owned Barrow-Gournay, 309; Sir Henry,
owned Elm, 207; Barrow-Gournay, 309;
sold Buckland-Dinham to — Webb, 452.
Henry, monument in South-Petherton
church, iii 112. William, lord Compton,
sold Barrow-Gournay to William Clarke,
ii 309. Elizabeth, married Walter Rodney,
iii 604. Joan, wife of Richard Compton,
monument in Trent church, ii 385.

Condidin, British king, B 16.

Conditt, Mr., owned Holford, iii 457.

Conduits: Bath, B 29, 31. Ilminster, i 2.
Wells, iii 376, 384.

Coney, Bicknell, governor of Bath hospital, B
48. patron of the living of Batcombe, iii
468; Thomas, incumbent of Batcombe,
468; monuments in Chedzoy church, 94;
arms, 95.

Confessional, curious, ii 162.

Congar, saint, iii 584.

Congresbury, situation, iii 584; river Yow, 584;
bridge, 584; Yowwood or Highwood hamlet, 584; Brindsey hamlet, 584; cross, 584;
market and fair, 584; legend of St. Congar,
584; part of the manor bestowed by king
Ina on the monks of Sherborne, 584;
another part granted by Edward the Confessor to the bishopric of Wells, 378, 584;

Congresbury—*continued.*
  chief part held by the crown, 584 ; Domesday survey, 584 ; owned by the king, earl
  Harold held it T.R.E. 584 ; Alward, Ordric,
  and Ordulf held lands here T.R.E. 585 ;
  Maurice, bishop of London, held the
  church : bishop Giso held one hide, Serlo
  de Burci and Gislebert Fitz-Turold held
  another hide, 585 ; chief manor granted
  by king John to the bishopric of Bath and
  Wells, 381, 585 ; disafforested by Henry
  III, 585 ; rating in 1293, 394 ; in manu regis
  1329, 394 ; ceded to the crown by bishop
  Bourne, 396 ; subsequently held by Francis,
  earl of Huntington, 585 ; Richard and
  George Owen, 585 ; John Carr, 585 ; the
  mayor and corporation of Bristol, for the
  use of John Carr's orphanage, 585 ; dean's
  manor : held by the dean and chapter of
  Wells, 585 ; Highwood manor owned by
  Mrs. Richardson, 585 ; church (St. Andrew),
  586 ; bells (5), 586 ; yew-tree, 586 ; cross,
  586 ; East and West Dolemoors : curious
  custom respecting, 586.
Congresbury-Rodney, owned by the Rodneys, of
  Rodney-Stoke, ii 306, iii 603.
Conibeer, memorial stone in Monksilver churchyard, iii 535.
Coningsby, Elizabeth, wife of Richard Berkeley,
  of Stoke, iii 280.
Conmail, British king, B 16.
Conqueror's-mead, tumulus, at Marston-Bigot,
  ii 214.
Conquest or Conquest-farm, Bishop's-Lydiard,
  discovery of Roman coins at, ii 493.
Constabulo, Robert de, owned Crowcombe, iii
  514 ; Robert, 514 ; Simon, took the name
  of Fitz-Robert (*see* under Fitz-Robert).
Constantine, Anne, John, and Philippa, monu-
  ments in Norton-under-Hamden church, ii
  335.
Constentine, Ilbert de, and Triphena, his wife,
  iii 66.
Conteville, Hugh de, landowner temp. Ed. I, i
  xxvii ; Richard de, landowner temp. Ed. I,
  xxvii ; held a knight's fee in Allerton, 176.
  held a knight's fee in Bawdrip, iii 91 ; held
  knights' fees in Cricket-St.-Thomas, 116.
Contitone (*see* Chilcompton).
Contone (*see* Chilcompton).
Contone (*see* Compton-Martin).
Contune (*see* Compton-Bishop).
Conway, Sir Hugh, married Elizabeth Courtney,
  and became possessed of Hemington, ii 454.
Conway, Francis Seymour, created baron, 1702,
  iii 282. Right Hon. Henry Seymour, J.P.,
  i *xliii.*
Cook or Cocus, Geffrey, owned Dunweer, iii 85.
Cook, Ann, monument in Claverton church, i
  149 ; Joseph, benefaction to Spaxton, 246 ;
  Thomas, married Lucy, daughter of John

Cook—*continued.*
  Walshe, 41. William, M.P. for Bath,
  1301, 1313, B 19 ; William, M.P. for Bath,
  1383, 1388, 20. the Rev. Mr., benefaction
  to Nether-Stowey, iii 554.
Cooke, Elizabeth, married John Selleck, ii 437.
Cooke, Richard, vicar of Long-Ashton, ii 299.
Cooke, Richard, married Sarah Cox and became
  possessed of land in Gatcombe, ii 302 ;
  Joseph, his son, sold his property in Gat-
  combe to Richard Grimsted, 302.
Cooke, Rev. Mr., of Thorncombe, benefaction to
  Martock, iii 8.
Cooke, Samuel, incumbent of Hornblotton, iii
  476.
Cooke, William, of Catcot : decree respecting,
  iii 432.
Cooksley, hamlet in Upton, owned by Mr.
  Blake, iii 555.
Cookson, Elizabeth, benefaction to Crewkerne,
  ii 164.
Coomb, William, subscribed towards the char-
  ity-school at Chew-Stoke, ii 102.
Coombe, Richard, benefaction to Frome alms-
  house, ii 196.
Coombe, or Coombes, Richard, of Earnshill, i
  31 ; owned Donyat, 36 ; Mrs. Ann, widow
  of Richard, holds Earnshill, 31, and Donyat,
  36 [*see* also Combe].
Coombes, Rev. Ralph, memorial inscription in
  Wotton Courtney church, ii 50.
Cooper, Edward, prebendary of Wells, iii 397.
Cooper, John, ancestor of the Coopers, earls of
  Shaftesbury, memorial in Beckington
  church, ii 201.
Cooper, Sir John, bart., owned Stanton-Drew,
  ii 434 ; Sir Anthony Ashley, his son and
  heir, 434.
Cooper, Mr., of Salisbury, owned South-Stoke,
  i 136.
Cooper, Rev. Dr., governor of Bath hospital, B
  48.
Cooper monuments in Freshford church, i 126.
Cooper, Richard, benefaction to Babcary, ii 62.
Cooper, Thomas, bishop of Winchester, 1584,
  author of " The Chronicle and Thesaurus,"
  iii 232.
Coopey, Margaret, wife of the Rev. Samuel
  Coopey, and daughter of the Rev. Charles
  Brent : monument in Wraxall church, iii
  160 ; Samuel, owned Hutton : assumed the
  name of Brent, 590 ; Humphrey, also took
  the name of Brent, 591.
Cope, Richard, prebendary of Wells, iii 397.
Cope, description of the, ii 251.
Copeland, East, charter of free warren in, pro-
  cured by Sir John Meriet, ii 297.
Coplestone family owned Hemington, ii 454.
  held West Newton or Newton Hawise of the
  abbey of Athelney, iii 70. Agnes, wife of
  Thomas Baumfilde, ii 90 ; Gertrude, wife

Coplestone—*continued.*
of John Baumfilde, 91 ; Humphrey, conveyed Hemington to the Bampfield family, 454. John de, sheriff, 1385, i *xxv.*

Copley, Eleanor, daughter of Sir Roger, second wife to Thomas West, lord de la Warre, ii 413.

Copper, found at Crowcombe, iii 514 ; at Hutton, 590.

Coquus, surname given to Ansger (the cook), iii 533.

Corbet, Maud, married Sir John Esterling, iii 335

Corbyn, Robert, owned land in Longload tithing, iii 11.

Corcelle, or Curcelle, Roger de, received many grants of land from William the Conqueror, i *xxv.* ownership of Churchill ascribed to, iii 580. owned Ashford, i 46. Ashington, iii 212 ; Ashway, 529. Bagley, i 187. Barrington, iii 113. Barton-David, ii 64. Blackmore, iii 579. Brewham, i 220 ; Brewton, 213. Brimpton-D'Evercy, iii 214 ; Catcot, 432. Charlinch, i 238. land in Chedder, iii 575 ; Chillington, 114 ; Chilton, 88, 89 ; Chilton-upon-Polden, 433 ; Clayhill, 90. Coleford, ii 446. Curry-Mallet, i 31 ; Currypool, 239. Croscombe, iii 469. Dover-hay, ii 23. Dunden, iii 447. Earnshill, i 30 ; East-Brent, 196. Edington, iii 433. Edingworth, i 197 ; Enmore, 89. Exton, iii 527 ; Farley-Montfort, 351. Freshford, i 125 ; Gautheney, 239. Goldsoncot, iii 510 (*see* note). Holcombe, ii 456. Holford, iii 456 ; Holme, 524. Holnicot, ii 40. Idstock, iii 90 ; Kilve, 532. Lexworthy, i 95. Limington, iii 218 ; Long-Sutton, 197 ; Oake, 273. land in Otterhampton, i 242. Peglinch, iii 327. Perdham, i 234. Pixton, iii 523. Radlet, i 245. Sandford-Bret, iii 543 ; Shipham, 600 ; South-Petherton, 107. Standerwick, ii 228. Stoney-Littleton, iii 326. Stringston, i 261 ; Shurton, 252. Thorn-Coffin, iii 322 ; Weacombe, 497 ; Whiteoxmead, 327 ; Woolston, 501 ; Worth, 188. land in Witham, ii 232. Hugh de, landowner in time of Henry II, i *xxvi.*

Coreville, owned by Hugh Perceval, iii 173.

Corewall or Corewill, hamlet in the parish of Holford, belonged anciently to Newton, iii 70, 457 ; spring, 457 ; owned by the de Coriwell family, 457.

Corfe, situation, iii 249 ; Blackdown hill, 249 ; part of the 54 hides of Taunton, and held as parcel of that manor, 249, 235 ; lands in, held by Sir Francis Brian, and Matthew Colthurst, 236 ; lands granted to Humphrey Colles, 285 ; a chapelry to St. Mary Magdalen's church, Taunton, in the gift of Goodenough Earle, 249 ; church and monument, 249 ; bells (4), 249.

Corfe, Robert, granted Skilgate to Abbotsbury abbey, iii 545.

Corfe-Castle, Dorset, Robert Fitzpaine, governor of, iii 245.

Coriscomb, John, master of St. Catherine's hospital, Bedminster, ii 283.

Coristone, ancient name of Croscombe, iii 480.

Coriwell family held Corewill, iii 457 ; Hugh de, 457.

Cork and Orrery, John, earl of, purchased Frome-Branch and Vallis manors, ii 188 ; Hamilton, 188 ; Edmund, 188 ; monuments in Frome church, 192 ; Charles, earl of, inventor of the Orrery, 215 (*see* note). earl of, J.P., i *xli.* owned Marston-Bigot, and built a mansion there, ii 214, 215.

Cormailes, John de, sheriff, 1278—1283, i *xxxiv.*

Corn street, Bath, B 35, 74.

Cornesyete, boundary of Exmoor perambulation, 1298, ii 19.

Cornewail, lady Elizabeth, i 262 ; Sir Brian, 262.

Cornhall, Maud de, married William de Wrotham, iii 64 ; Reginald de, receiver of Customs, 64.

Cornish, Margaret, benefaction to Taunton, iii 240.

Cornish, Susanna, monument in Bath abbey, 1750, B 68.

Cornish, Thomas, master of St. John's hospital, 1483, B 43. Thomas, bishop of Tyne, prior of St. John's hospital, Wells, 1462—1497, iii 408 ; monument in Wells cathedral, 400.

Cornish, Thomas, incumbent of Heathfield, iii 254.

Cornish, William, incumbent of Pawlet, iii 102.

Cornua-Ammonis, found at Keynsham, ii 401 ; Marston Magna, 374. Corston, iii 345.

Cornwall buildings, Bath, B 39.

Cornwall, duchy of, owns Laverton, ii 211. Milton in Martock, iii 6 ; Inglishcombe, 340 ; Shepton-Mallet, 462. Stratton-on-the-Fosse, ii 459. Stoke-sub-Hamdon, iii 320.

Cornwall, dukedom of, conferred on the eldest son of Edward III, i 33.

Cornwall, earldom of, held by the earls of Morton, iii 311. Edmund, earl of, granted Monks-Ham to the monks of Witham, ii 216. Isabel, daughter of Edmund, married Maurice de Berkeley, iii 277 ; Reginald, earl of, witness to a deed between John Marshall and Hugh de Raleigh, 536 ; Richard, earl of, granted lands to Cleeve abbey, 511.

Cornwallis, earl of, J.P., i *xli.*

Corpe, John, incumbent of Wayford, ii 175.

Corscombe (*see* Croscombe).

Corsley, hamlet in Lydiard-St.-Laurence, owned by the Malets, iii 265.

L

Corston or Coston, situation, iii 345; quarries, 345; Domesday survey, 345; owned by Bath abbey, 345; subsequently owned by the St. Lo family, 345; the Inge family, 346; Richard Fitz James, 346; Roger Norman, 346; John Storke, 346; the heirs of Thomas Inge, 346; Harington, 346; Joseph Langton, 346; William Gore Langton, 346; church (All Saints) and its monuments, 346, 347; bells (2), 346.

Corton, Henry, member for Chard, ii 472.

Corton-Ash, tree at Corton-Dinham, ii 361.

Corton-Dinham, situation, ii 361; Roman coins found at, 361; Domesday survey, 361; held by the king: subsequently by the Dinham or Dinant family, 361; divided between the heirs of four daughters of Sir John Dinham, who had married respectively Sir Nicholas Carew, Thomas Arundel, of Lanherne, Lord Fitzwarren, and John, lord Zouche, 362; the manor ultimately owned by Henry William Portman, 362; market and fair, 361; Witcombe hamlet, 362; church (St. Andrew) and monuments, 363; bells (5), 363.

Cory, Roger, master of St. John's hospital, Bridgwater, iii 79.

Coryat, George, rector of Odcombe, ii 325; Thomas, an account of his travels and eccentricities, ii 325, 326.

Coscob, Richard, prior of Muchelney, iii 136.

Cosham, John de, prior of Brewton, 1418, i 214.

Cosinton, Ansketil de, held lands of the abbot of Glastonbury, ii 244.

Cosserat, Nathaniel Elias, governor of Bath hospital, B 48. owned a moiety of Churchill manor, iii 580.

Cossington, situation, iii 434; moors, 434; Domesday survey, 434; owned by the abbots of Glastonbury: held by Walter: Alwin held it T.R.E. 434; subsequently owned by Gilbert, marshal of England, 434; Ridel family, 434; Sir Baldwin Malet, 434; Brent family, 434, 435, 436; Hodges, 436; Robert West, 436; Sir John Gresham, 437; Benjamin Allen, 437; church (St. Mary) and monuments, 437; bells (5), 437; lands here were held by the Woolavington family, 438.

Coster, Thomas, M.P. for Bristol, married Astrea Smyth, ii 293.

Coston (*see* Corston).

Cosyn, William, dean of Wells, 1498, i 190.

Cosyn, Thomas, master of St. Catherine's hospital, Bedminster, ii 283.

Cotarii, the, i 106.

Cotele, Sir Robert, knt., received Camerton from Herlewin, abbot of Glastonbury, iii 330; family subsequently restored this manor to the abbey, but continued as tenants under the abbots, 330; Richard de,

Cotele—*continued.*
330, ii 245. Sir William, knt., iii 330. landowner temp. Ed. I, i *xxviii*. Elias, iii 330, i *l.* held land in Whiteoxmead, iii 327; and in Corscombe, 469.

Cotell (*see* Cotele).

Cothay, Joan de, married William de Sydenham, iii 86.

Cothelstone, situation, iii 249; owned by the Stawel family, 249-252; church and its monuments, 252; bells (6), 252.

Cotbelstone-park, iii 252.

Cottel (*see* Cotele).

Cotterel, or Cottrell, John, of Winford, monument in Winford church, ii 321; benefaction to Winford, 322. Jane, of Winford, married Samuel Gorges, iii 158. Katharine, wife of Tristram, ii 321; Robert, purchased Barrow-Gournay, 309; his daughter, the wife of — Hazel, succeeded to it, 309.

Cotthay, in Kittisford, iii 24; owned by the Every family, 24; divided between the families of Leigh and Henley, 24; lands here held by the Sydenham family, 215.

Cottington, Elizabeth, wife of Thomas Walton, ii 271.

Cottle's lane, Bath, B 37.

Cotton, George, owned Curland, i 23. Currylode, ii 181; lands in Dundry, 105. monuments in church of Weston, near Bath, i 164.

Cotton mills, Keynsham, ii 400.

Cotys, John, M.P. for Bath, 1446, B 21.

Coumbe, Sir John, held land in Bawdrip, tenements in Walpulle, and lands in Washford, iii 91; John, his son, married Emmalina Partiche, 91.

Council, William, benefaction to Wookey, iii 422

Counsel, John, of Mark, benefaction to Mark, i 183; William, of Castle, benefaction to Wedmore, 193; memorial stones in Wedmore church, 192.

Counsell, William, monument in Marksbury church, ii 428. William and Mary, benefactions to Puxton, iii 599.

Counties, why disjointed and mixed with others, ii 370.

Courcelle (*see* Corcelle).

Courcy, Richard de, i 250; Robert, founded the nunnery at Cannington, 250, 232; Richard, a baron of Yorkshire, 251; William, 251; Alice, married Warine Fitz-Gerold, 251.

Court, Alexander. monument in Stoke Gregory church, ii 181; Amy, married James Strode, 210; Edward, monument in Stoke-Gregory church, 181. John, M.P. for Bath, 1587, B 21; recorder of Bath, 23. Lydia, inscription in Rodden church, ii 227; Margaret, monument in Stoke-Gregory church, 181; Thomas, monument in Huish-Episcopi church, 470; arms, 470. memorial tablet in South-Brewham church, i 221.

Coutances—*continued.*
　iii 362. Timsbury, ii 111; West-Harptree-
　Gournay, 140. Weston, iii 171; Weston-
　in-Gordano, 141; Weston-super-Mare, 610.
　Winford, ii 320. Winscombe, iii 613;
　Winterhead, 601. Withycombe, ii 47.
　Wraxall, iii 141, 155.
Covent-Orchard, belonging to Keynsham abbey,
　leased to John Panter, ii 403.
Coventry, Thomas, lord, married Elizabeth
　Aldersey, iii 285; John, his son, married
　Elizabeth Colles: owned Barton, and built
　a mansion there, 285. Sir John, founded a
　hospital at Wiveliscombe, ii 492.
Coventry-Bulkeley, the Hon. J. B., held Wive-
　liscombe, ii 489; and Fitzhead, 489.
Coventry and Litchfield, Walter, bishop of,
　owned the manor of Norton, ii 351.
Coveston, Geffrey de, held lands of Glastonbury
　abbey, ii 244.
Cow castle, Exmoor, ii 20.
Coward, Elizabeth, monument in Bath abbey,
　1764, B 68; Leonard, mayor of Bath, 1782,
　26, 1787, 1789, 27; Leonard, governor of
　Bath hospital, 48; Leonard, monument in
　Bath abbey, 1764, 68. Thomas, and Mary,
　his wife, monument in Batcombe church,
　iii 468. Thomas, sheriff, 1771, i *xxxix*;
　J.P., *xliii*; trustee of Saxey charity, 212.
　owned Spargrove, ii 220, iii 468; William
　and Bridget, monuments in St. Cuthbert's
　church, Wells, 407; arms, 407.
Cowdray, Ann, wife of Richard, was heir to the
　manor of Buckshaw, ii 369; William, 370;
　Avice, widow of William, married Morgan
　Kidwelly, 370.
Cowlands, Ottery St. Mary, belonged to Mine-
　head, ii 29.
Cowper, Rebecca, monument in Bath abbey,
　1762, B 68.
Cowshuish tithing, Kingston, iii 258.
Cox-bridge, Ilminster, i 3.
Cox, Francis, of Gatcombe, ii 302. Mary, of
　Crewkerne, married Humphry Sydenham,
　iii 523. Mr., founder of charity school at
　Exford, ii 21; Rachel, of Gatcombe, mar-
　ried James Sparrow, 302; Sarah, of Gat-
　combe, married Richard Cooke, 302; monu-
　ment in Long-Ashton church, 303; Thomas,
　subscribed towards the charity school at
　Chew-Stoke, 102; Thomas, benefaction to
　the poor of Keynsham, 410; Thomas, and
　Joan, his wife, monument in Stanton-Prior
　church, 440; William, purchased Gat-
　combe from Sir Nicholas Halswell, 302;
　William, buried in Stanton-Drew church,
　437; Rev., incumbent of Exford, 21.
Coxe, Charles, governor of Bath hospital, B 48.
　John, memorial tablet in Widcombe chapel,
　i 173. John, married the daughter of Pres-
　ton Hippisley, and became owner of his

Coxe—*continued.*
　estates: was ancestor of the Hippisley
　Coxes, ii 155, 158; Henry Hippisley, 155.
　sheriff, 1789, i *xxxix*; J.P., *xliii.* owned
　Camely, ii 125; Emborow, 136; Stone-
　Easton, 155, 158. Charles Hippisley, J.P.,
　i *xliii*; Richard Hippisley, M.P., 1768,
　1774, 1780, *xxxiii.* owned Tothill, iii 476.
　Richard, memorial stone in Writhlington
　church, ii 460.
Coxeter, Mary, wife of Thomas, monument in
　Writhlington church, ii 460.
Coxley, hamlet in Wells, owned by the bishopric
　of Wells, iii 396, 405.
Coxwell, Barbara, married John Holbeach, ii
　441.
Cozens family, memorials in Evercreech church,
　iii 416; arms, 416. Richard, bequest to
　Castle Cary, ii 58.
Crabb family, memorial stones in White-Lack-
　ington church, i 69.
Crabbe family, held land in Donniford, iii 491;
　John, 491.
Cracroft, Anne, married Dr. John Langhorn, iii
　570.
Cradock, or Caradoc family, descended from
　Howell ap-Grono, lord of Newton, iii 588;
　Cradock-ap-Howell-ap-Grono, 588; Sir
　William, knt., married Jane Wogan, 588;
　William, married Catherine Delamere, 588;
　John, married Joan Dee, 588; Robert, mar-
　ried Margery Sherborne, 588; John married
　Nesta Russell, 588; John, inherited the
　Welsh estates, married Margaret Moythye,
　588; Sir Richard, took the name of Newton
　(*see* Newton).
Craft-Warre, hamlet in Hinton-St.-George, ii
　166. owned by the Denbaud family, iii
　259; passed to the Warres, 259; held by
　the Warres of the Poulet family, 260, 261.
Crandon (*see* Bawdrip).
Cranes at East Cranmore, ii 207.
Crang, Mr., assisted in purchasing Timsbury
　out of Chancery, ii 112; Rev. James,
　memorial stone in Timsbury church, 113.
Cranmore-East, situation, ii 207; origin of
　name, 207; Merehead and Mere-Mead, 207;
　given by Ælphege to the monks of Glaston-
　bury, 207, 208; Domesday survey, 208;
　owned by the abbot: held by Harding, who
　held it T.R.E. 208; alienated by William
　Rufus, but restored in 1101, 208; ceded to
　the bishopric of Bath and Wells, 208, 252;
　alienated from bishopric and granted to
　Edward, duke of Somerset, 208, iii 395;
　restored to the bishopric, 396. moiety
　owned by the Horner family, ii 208; the
　other moiety owned successively by the
　Bradford family, 208; John Moore, 208;
　Mrs. Mary Jones, 208; manor-house, called
　"Cross-house," passed into the Bradford

Cranmore-East—*continued.*
estate, 208; enclosure of Mendip, 208; Rough-ditch boundary, 209; church (St. James): a chapel of ease to Doulting, 209; monuments, 209. report in 1329, iii 394.

Cranmore-West, situation, ii 209; monks of Glastonbury had possessions here, 209; manor owned by the Strode family, 209, 210; South-hill, seat of John Strode, 209; church, a chapel of ease to Doulting, 210.

Crapnel, hamlet in Dinder, iii 412.

Craucumbe (*see* Crocumbe).

Crawecumbe (*see* Crowcombe).

Cray, William, benefaction to Compton-Bishop, iii 583.

Crayle, Elizabeth, monument in Claverton church, i 149.

Creech-Heathfield, hamlet in Creech St. Michael, i 74.

Creech-hill, iii 477.

Creech St. Michael, evidence of being on the sea coast, i 74; situation, 74; hamlets, 74; Domesday survey, 74; one part owned by Robert, earl of Morton, 74; held by Gunnild T.R.E. 74; the other part held by earl Moriton and Turstin: Sirewold held it T.R.E. 75; given to Montacute priory, 75; seized by Henry I and by him restored to the priory, 75; owned successively by the Wyat family, Edward Hastings, Lawrence Radford, Robert Cuffe, the Keyts of Gloucestershire, and William Hussey, 75, 76; church (St. Michael), 76; bells (5), 76; vicar's emoluments, 76; monuments in the church, 77, 78; yew trees, 78; Mrs. Anne Seager's benefaction, 78. lands here were held by the Wrotham family, iii 64-67.

Creed, Cary, owned Lovington, ii 83; bequest to Castle Cary, 58; monuments in Castle Cary church, 57.

Creedlingcot or Carnicut (*see* Camerton).

Creedy, Elizabeth, wife of Sir John Paulet, ii 166.

Creighton, Robert, dean of Wells, 1660, i 190. bishop of Wells, 1670—1672, iii 389; figure in the west window of Wells cathedral, 399; monument in Wells cathedral, 400.

Creyghton, Robert, chanter of Wells cathedral, benefactions to Wells, iii 410.

Crescy, Jane, married Sir John de Rodney, iii 603.

Crese, William, received a pension from Montacute priory, iii 313.

Crespigny, Claude Champion, governor of Bath hospital, B 48.

Creswick family owned Langford manor, i 204.

Creswicke, Samuel, dean of Wells, 1739, i 190.

Crewkerne, its situation, ii 159; hamlets of Clapton, Hewish, Woolmiston, Furland, Rowndham and Laymore, 159; rivers

Crewkerne—*continued.*
Ax and Parret, 159; market and fair, 159; Domesday survey, 160; held by Eddeva T.R.E. 160; Estham manor, owned by earl Morton, and held by Turstin, 160; owned by the families of Redvers, Courtney, Sir Humphrey Stafford, George, duke of Clarence, John Arundell, Sir Amias Paulett, and John, earl Poulett, 160, 161; church and land belonging to the abbey of St. Stephen, of Caen, and the Domesday survey, 162; church and its monuments, 162, 163, 164; benefactions, 164; Ranahill, with chapel of St. Ranus, 165; lands here formed part of the dowry of Margaret de Ralege, 314.

Crewkerne family, ii 165; John, married Margaret Malet, i 91. William de, abbot of Muchelney, iii 135.

Creyk, Walter de, owned Shockerwicke, i 112.

Cribbe, John, received a pension from Montacute priory, iii 313.

Crice (*see* Creech-St.-Michael).

Crichel-Gouis, Dorset, part of the endowment of the chantry at South-Petherton, founded by Giles, lord Daubeney, iii 109.

Cricket Malherbe, position, i 22; Domesday survey, 22; Drogo held it of earl Morton, 22; owned by the Malherbe family, 22; Dynham family, 22; Drews, of Stanton, 22; Stephen Pitt, 22; church (St. Mary Magdalen), 22; bells (2), 22.

Cricket St. Thomas, situation, iii 116; held of the barony of Castle-Cary, 116; by Richard de Contevyle, 116; Sir Peter Courtney, knt., 116; Margaret, widow of John St. Loe, 116; Sir William Botreaux, knt., 116; the Hungerfords, 116; John Preston, 117; Sir Alexander Hood, 117; mansion, 117; church, 117; bells (2), 117; Ford abbey held an estate here, 117.

Crickham, hamlet in Wedmore, i 188.

Cridland, John, owned Pury-Fitchet, iii 103. Margaret, wife of John Burland, i 257. Thomas, owned Stogumber, iii 548.

Crim-Chard, tithing of Chard, ii 473. owned by the bishopric of Bath and Wells, iii 396.

Crispe, Rebecca, married George Strode, of London, ii 210.

Crispin, Richard, married Arondella Arundel, and became possessed of Samford-Arundel, iii 26; William, 26; Roger, 26; Joan, married Bradston, 26.

Crist, Roger, M.P. for Bath, 1340, B 20.

Croc, Anastatia, widow of Walter: grant of land, houses, and services to Sir Thomas Trivet, iii 101; Gregory, held part of a knight's fee of the bishopric of Wells, 393. John, held a knight's fee from Sir William de Mohun, ii 14. John, the service of, granted to Sir Thomas Trivet, iii 101; William, held part of a knight's fee of the bishopric of Wells, 393.

Crocker, Abraham, governor of Frome charity school, ii 197. John, held land in Clevedon, iii 168.

Crockerne-Pill, hamlet in Easton-in-Gordano, iii 146.

Crockstreet, hamlet in Ilminster, i 4.

Crockstreet, hamlet in Donyat, i 35.

Crocumbe, or Craucumbe family, owned Broomfield, i 72. Godfrey Fitz-Robert took the name of Crocumbe, 515; owned lands in Crowcumbe and Edstone, and gave his manor in Crowcumbe to the nuns of Studley, 515. Simon de, landowner temp. Ed. I, i xxviii. held land in Crowcombe, iii 515; Simon: Thomas: Simon, 515. Isolda, daughter of Simon, married John Biccombe, i 72, iii 515. Wimund de, held land in Beer Crocombe, i 14. his daughter married Simon Fitz-Robert, iii 514.

Croford, hamlet in Wiveliscombe, ii 488.

Croft, Sarah, monument in Bath abbey, 1690, B 68

Crofts, Richard, held the wardship of Sir John Rodney, iii 604; Anne, daughter of Sir James, married Sir John Rodney, 604.

Croke, John, B 31. John, owned Crowcumbe-Studley, iii 515; Sir George, 515.

Crompton, Walter de, M.P. for Bath, 1354, B 20.

Cromwell, Oliver, defaced the ornaments of Castle Cary church, ii 56. letter written by, iii 357

Cromwell, Thomas, dean of Wells, 1537, i 190.

Crook, Charles, governor of Bath hospital, B 48; Simon, governor of Bath hospital, 48; Simon, mayor of Bath, 1778, 26. William, benefaction to Brushford, iii 507.

Crooke, Samuel, monument in Wrington church, i 208.

Crooked lane, Bath, B 37.

Crook's peak, iii 374, 597, 612.

Crooks on horses, a method of conveyance, ii 34.

Croscombe, or Corscombe, situation, iii 469; Croscombe water, 469; market (discontinued), 469; fair, 469; Droop hamlet, 469; the manor formerly a member of Pilton, 469; held by Roger de Curcelle, 469; Elias Cotell held one knight's fee here, 469; passed to the St. Maur family, who held it of the Paltons, 469; held of John, duke of Somerset, by Sir William Palton, 469; the Pomroy family, 469; the Fortescues, 469; earl Clinton, 469; rectorial manor owned by the Rev. Mr. Sampson, 469; church (Blessed Virgin Mary) and its monuments, 469, 470; bells (5), 469; benefactions, 470; guild of St. Anne, 470; cross, 470.

Croscombe water, iii 469.

Cross, John, of Thurloxton, iii 102. Richard, of Broomfield, owned Wick, ii 494. Robert, rector of Spaxton, benefaction to the priory of Cannington, i 233. Thomas, owned land in Bishopworth, ii 284.

Cross, hamlet in Compton-Bishop, iii 582.

Cross, memorial stone in Creech St. Michael church, i 78.

Cross bath, Bath, origin of name, B 41.

Cross house, East-Cranmore, ii 208.

Cross house, Ilminster: the schoolmaster's residence, i 3.

Cross tithing, Portbury, iii 142.

Crosse, Andrew, part owner of Broomfield, i 72. Edward, incumbent of Tolland, iii 292. Richard, J.P., i xliii; Richard, sheriff, 1785, xxxix; William, monument in Staple-Fitzpaine church, 59.

Crosses, original intention of, i 224.

Crosses:—Backwell, ii 308. Banwell, iii 568. Barton-David, ii 65. Bicknoller, iii 502. Bishop's Lydiard, ii 496. Broadway, i 19; Brewton, 211. Brimpton-d'Evercy, iii 216. Broomfield, i 73; Buckland St. Mary, 21; Burrington, 205. Butcombe, ii 316. Chapel-Allerton, i 176; Charlinch, 241. Chew-Magna, ii 100. Compton-Bishop, iii 583; Congresbury, 584, 586; Croscombe, 470; Crowcombe, 514, 517; Ditcheat, 473; Doulting, 475. Drayton, i 39. Dundry, ii 106. East-Pennard, iii 479. Enmore, i 96. Fitzhead, ii 492. Flax-Bourton, iii 161. Hatch-Beauchamp, i 46. Huish-Champflower, iii 530. Long-Ashton, ii 304. Loxton, iii 598. Luckham, ii 24. Mark, i 184. Mere, ii 275; Minehead, 33. Montacute, iii 315; Nettlecombe, 542. Nunney, ii 221. Old-Cleeve, iii 513. Overweare, i 186; Pitcombe, 224. Porlock, ii 34. Portishead, iii 145; Ruishton, 289. Sandford-Orcas, ii 378; Selworthy, 42. Spaxton, i 246. Stalling's cross, Court de Wick, iii 618. Staple-Fitzpaine, i 61. Stavordale, iii 34; Stogumber, 549. Stoke Courcy, i 249; Stringston, 267. Timberscombe, ii 45. Tolland, iii 292. Upton Noble, i 228. Walton-in-Gordano, iii 171. Wedmore, i 194. West-Pennard, ii 276. Wick Champflower, i 220. Wick St. Laurence, iii 496. Widcombe, i 174. Williton, iii 496. Wotton Courtney, ii 50. Wrington, i 206. Wraxall, iii 161; Yatton, 620. [*Pooley,* in "Crosses of Somerset," gives many more].

Crossman, Mr., benefaction to Lympsham, i 203; the Rev. George, LL.D., J.P., xliii. incumbent of West-Monkton, iii 455; incumbent of Blagdon, 570.

Croupes, Sire Richard de, i l.

Crow-lane, Chard, ii 471.

Crowch, William, owned Bathampton, i 117; Wolley, 167. and Beggeridge, iii 327. Walter, alienated Bathampton to Thomas Popham, i 117.

Crowcombe, situation, iii 513; Quantock hills, 513; formerly a borough, 514; market (discontinued), 514; fair, 514; springs,

Crowcombe—*continued.*

514; copper ore found here, 514; hamlets of Larford, Flexpool, Leigh, Water and Triscombe, 514; granted by Gueda to the church of St. Swithin, at Winchester, 514; bestowed at the Conquest on the earl of Morton, 514; Domesday survey, 514; held by the de Constabulo family, 514; Simon Fitz-Robert, 514; Godfrey, who took the name of Crocombe, 515; Crowcombe-Studley, a moiety of the manor of Crowcombe, granted to the nuns of Studley, passed at the dissolution to the Croke family, 515; the Kingsmills, 515; Crowcombe-Bickham, held by the Crocumbe family, 515; the Biccombes, 516; the Carews, 516; James Bernard, 516; park, 516; church (Holy Ghost) and its monuments, 516, 517; bells (5), 516; cross, 514, 517; schools, 517.

Crowcombe court, built by Thomas Carew, iii 516

Crowle, David, monument in Bath abbey, 1757, B 68.

Crowmer, Nicholas, sheriff, 1482, 1483, i *xxxvi.*

Crowther, William, memorial stone in Wiveliscombe church, ii 491; arms, 491.

Crowthorne family, held Sutton-Crowthorne, ii 88

Crucerne, Saxon name of Crewkerne, ii 159.

Crucifix, ii 251.

Crybbe, Richard, received a pension from St. John's hospital, Bridgwater, iii 80. Thomas, last incumbent of North-Barrow chantry, received a pension, ii 63.

Cryche, Robert, prior of Montacute, iii 313; William, prior of Montacute, 313.

Cryklade, Elizabeth, held Buckshaw, ii 369.

Cucking-stool at Shepton-Mallet, iii 460.

Cucklington, situation, iii 51; held with Stoke-Trister, 51; Domesday survey, 51; owned by the earl of Morton: Leuin and Suain held it T.R.E. 51; Clay-hill, 51; springs, 51; markets and fair (discontinued), 51; church (St. Lawrence) and its monuments, 51, 52; bells (5), 51.

Cudmore, Margaret, married William Sydenham, iii 522.

Cudworth, situation, iii 117; Chillington down, 117; Upper and Lower Were, 117; Domesday survey, 117; owned by Roger Arundel: held by Odo: subsequently owned by the families of Wake, 117; Keynes, 117; Speke, 117; lord North, 117; lands here owned by Muchelney abbey, 117; passed to the Buller family, 117; church (St. Michael), 117; bells (2), 117; Dr. Richard Busby, sometime prebendary of Cudworth, 118; Knoll St. Giles, formerly a member of this manor, 118.

Cudworth, Dr. Ralph, rector of Aller, and of North-Cadbury, author of the "Intellectual System," iii 189.

Cuffe, Anne, first wife to Francis Warre, iii 262. Henry, i 76; Robert, owned Creech St. Michael, 76; monument in Creech St. Michael church, 77, 78.

Culbone, situation, ii 3; Domesday survey, 3; held by Drogo, 3; held by Osmund T.R.E. 3; granted to Geffrey, bishop of Coutance, 3; owned successively by William de Kytenore, the Bratton family, 3; Walter Pauncefote, William Bachell, and lord King, 4; church and its romantic situation, 4.

Culliford, Robert, monument in Bath abbey, 1616, B 68.

Cullum, hamlet in Wick, iii 612.

Culme, John, governor of Bath hospital, B 48.

Culpeper, a daughter of Mr., married William Dickinson, ii 417. Mary, second wife to John Brent, of Cossington, iii 436.

Cultura (or Colthurst), Henry de, baron in time of Henry II, i *xxvi.* held Orchardley, ii 222; Robert de, 222; Ralph de, 222; Henry de, transferred his estate in Orchardley to Sir Henry de Merlaund, knt., 222.

Culverhays field, Inglishcombe, iii 340.

Culwel, Ann, wife of John Miller, i 103.

Cuman, abbot of Glastonbury, ii 249.

Cumbe family held Combe-Flory, iii 247; Baldwin de, 247; Robert de, owed service to Andrew Luttrell, 498.

Cumberland, his royal highness, Henry, duke of, J.P., i *xli.*

Cumbert, abbot of Glastonbury, ii 249.

Cume (*see* Combe-Monkton).

Cume, Martin de la, the service of, granted to Woodspring priory, iii 594.

Cummidge (*see* Combwich).

Cumpton, Richard de, held Catash, ii 51.

Cunditt, Mr., owned Kilve, iii 532; John, Joanna, Susannah, monument in Kilve church, 533.

Cunliffe, Margaret, monument in Bath abbey, 1759, B 68. Mary, memorial tablet in church of Weston, near Bath, i 161.

Cunteville, Adam de, owned Stringston, married Amelia de Stringstone, i 262; disputes the right of Philip de Columbers to the manor of Alfoxton, 264. owned Dodington, iii 518. Hugh (also called Hugh Thurloe), i 262, iii 518. Richard, released Alfoxton to William de Alfoxton, i 264; William de, son of Adam, granted land to John de Alfakeston, 266; sold land to William Russell, 253. took the name of Dodeton (*see* Dodington or Dodeton family).

Cuntone (*see* Compton-Paunceford).

Curci, William de, baron in time of Henry II, i *xxvi.* held knight's fee from Sir William de Mohun, ii 14 (*see* Courcy).

Curi (*see* Curry-Mallet).

Curiepol (*see* Currypool).

Curious certificate from Bath abbey, B 55.

Curious presentments at Seaborough court, ii 173

Curland, position, i 23; hamlet of Britty, 23; famous for scythe stones, 23; originally a member of Staple-Fitzpaine, 23; owned by Thomas Reve and George Cotton, 23; Valentine Brown, 23; Robert Howse, 23; John Dorchester and William Powell, 23; Henry Seymour, 23; church, 23.

Curle, Walter, bishop of Winchester, 1632, in whose time the manor of Taunton was alienated from the bishopric of Winchester, iii 233.

Curlond, lands in, held by the Orchard family, iii 489.

Curlwood green (*see* Currylode).

Currer, Sarah, monument in Bath abbey, 1759, B 68.

Currylode, hamlet in Stoke Gregory, ii 180; partly owned by the abbot of Athelney, 181; Thomas Reve, George Cotton, and Valentine Brown, 181.

Curry Mallet, position of, i 31; principal products, 31; common right in West Sedgmoor, 31; Domesday survey, 31; held by Roger de Corcelle, 31; Brictric and Celric held it T.R.E. 31, 32; the Malet family, 32; the Pointz family, 33; received licence for market, 33; owned by the Gournay family, 33; part of the duchy of Cornwall, 33; the church (St. James), 33; monuments, 34. Shipham was held by this barony, iii 601.

Curry moor, i *xv*, ii 177.

Curry, North, its situation, ii 177; common rights on West Sedgmoor, Stanmoor, Warmoor, and West Wall, 177; market and fair, 177; Roman remains, 178; Domesday survey, 178; held by earl Herald T.R.E.: bishop Maurice held the church, 178; Ansger held one hide of earl Morton, 178; granted by Richard I to the church of St. Andrew in Wells, and settled by bishop Reginald on the canons, 178, iii 380. tithings of Knap, Lillisdon, Wrantage, Hillend, Newport and Moordon, ii 178; church (SS. Peter and Paul) and its monuments, 179; bells (5), 179; hundred of, 177.

Currypool manor, Charlinch, i 239; Domesday survey, 239; held by Roger de Curcelle: Alwi T.R.E. 239; the earl of Egmont, 239. lands here were owned by the de Bradney family, iii 92.

Curry-Rivel, position, i 23; hamlets of Hambridge, Heal and Wick, 23; nature of the soil, 24; remarkable oak tree near the Angel inn, 24; Burton Pynsent, the seat of the earl of Chatham, 24; Pynsent monument, 25; Domesday survey, 25; owned by Crown till reign of Richard I, 26; granted to Richard Revel, 26; owned by the family of L'Orti, 26, ii 335. of Mon-

Curry-Rivel—*continued.*

tacute, i 26; of Beaufort, 26; bishop of Bath and Wells, 26; alienated to bishop of London, 26; reverts to the Crown, 26; granted to duke of Norfolk, 26; owned by Henry, lord Strange, 26; Thomas Snagge and Jeffery Morley, 26; yearly rent paid to dean and chapter of Wells, 26; Roger Forte, lord of the manor, 27; owned by the Acland family and William Barber, 27; value of the church, 27; appropriated by bishop Erghum to Bysham priory, 27; church (St. Andrew) and its monuments, 27—30; bells (5), 27; benefactions, 30. Thomas Att-Ayshe Baker owned lands here, iii 50.

Curthose, Robert, duke of Normandy, i 75.

Curtis, John and Agnes, of Chew, benefaction to Chew-Magna, ii 100.

Curtis, John, owned Butcombe, ii 315; his son sold that manor to John Savery, 315.

Curtis memorial inscriptions in Chewton-Mendip church, ii 119.

Curtis, Mr., of Milborne - Port, part owner of North Brewham, i 221.

Curtis, Rev. John Adey, governor of Bath hospital, B 48.

Customs, ancient, ii 180, iii 586.

Cutcombe, situation, ii 5; Watercombe vale, 5; Dunkery beacon, 5; Domesday survey, 5; held by Ælmer T.R.E. 5; owned by William de Mohun, thence called Cutcombe Mohun, 6: Philippa, wife of Edward, duke of York, Richard lord le Strange, of Knocking, who sells his right to Alexander Hody and others, 6; Cutcombe Raleigh, owned by the families of Raleigh, Dodisham, John Gilbert, of Wollavington, Roger Pym, of Brymore, Sir Thomas Hales and Sir Philip Hales, 6; hamlets of Ludwell bridge and Codsend, 6; Oaktrow, 6; church (St. Lawrence), [St. John (*Ecton*),] 7; bells (5), 7; charity school, founded by Richard Elsworth, 7. rectory and presentation held anciently by Brewton priory, i 214. lands in Cutcombe-Raleigh were owned by Nettlecombe chantry, iii 538.

Cutcombe-burrow, tumulus, iii 502.

Cutler, Elizabeth, first wife to Sir William Portman, iii 275. John, owned Norton-Hautville, ii 108.

Cutley hamlet, iii 258.

Cutte, John, mayor of Bristol, owned Burnet, ii 415; monument in Burnet church, 415; William, 415; John, sold Burnet to John Whitson, 415.

Cuttlesham, Stavordale priory owned lands in, iii 33.

Cygenils, king of Wessex, founded the church of Winchester, iii 229.

Cynric granted Lamyat to Glastonbury abbey, iii 477.

D

Dabridgecourt, Mary, wife of Reginald Pym, i 234.

Daccomb, Sir Thomas, sheriff, 1398, i *xxxv*.

Dacre, Lennard, lord, owned Marston-Magna, ii 374.

Dacres, Ralph, held half a knight's fee from Sir William de Mohun, ii 14.

Dacus or Dennis family (*see* Dennis).

D'Albini (*see* Daubeney).

Dale, Henry, part-owner of lands in Yeovilton, Limington, and of Eastern and Western farms, iii 219.

Dale, Valentine, dean of Wells, 1574, i 190.

Dalton, Nathaniel, sheriff, 1787, i *xxxix*; J.P., *xliii*.

Dammeston, Edon de, held knights' fees in Timberscombe, ii 44.

D'Amorie or de Aumari family owned Winford, ii 320; Gilbert, 320; Nicholas, 320; Richard, 320; Richard owned Ubley, 156. Richard held the bailiwick of Neroche forest, i 17. keeper of Selwood forest, 1337, ii 195; granted Ubley to Matthew Peche, 156.

Dando or Danno family (*see* Alno).

Dandoe, Thomas, subscribed to the charity school at Chew-Stoke, ii 102.

Danegeld, i *l*.

Danes: invasions of Somerset, i *xxiv*. defeat at Porlock, ii 35. depredations at Somerton, iii 182; St. Decumans, 487; used Steep-Holmes island as a harbour, 609; baptism of Guthrun at Aller, 188; bones discovered in Knap-Dane field, Nettlecombe, 535.

Daniel, prior of Montacute, iii 312.

Daniel, Samuel, poet and historian, born at Taunton, iii 239. monument in Beckington church, ii 201. Samuel, J.P., *xliii*.

Dannay family, owned land in North-Cheriton, ii 360. Nicholas, held Mudford Torry, iii 221; Sir John, 221; Emma, 221.

Danvers, Daniel, memorial stone in Weston (near Bath) church, i 165; John, married Joan Malet, 91. Susan, first wife to Walter, lord Hungerford, iii 356.

Danvers, lord, part owner of Brean, i 178.

Darch, Rev. William, J.P., i *xliii*; Thomas, J.P., *xliii*; Thomas, junr., J.P., *xliii*. Thomas and Sarah, memorial tablet in Luxborough church, ii 26.

Darell, Catherine, monument in Bath abbey, 1774, B 68. Elizabeth, held the lease of the chapel of Stoke-under-Hamden, iii 133. Sir Francis, sheriff, 1535, i *xxxvii*. George, owned land in Bridgwater, iii 266. John, monument in Bath abbey, 1768, B 68.

Darknel, Adolphus, and Sarah, his wife, stone in Hemington church, ii 455.

Darnett, Sir Thomas, iii 209.

Darsel, hamlet in Shepton-Mallet, iii 460.

Dart, Rev. Philip, incumbent of Stratton-on-the-Fosse, ii 459.

Dartmouth, earl of, J.P., i *xli*.

Daubeney, D'Albini, Albini or de Albaniaco family, descended from Robert de Todenei, who came into England with the Conqueror, iii 107; owned the manor and hundred of South Petherton, 107; held Barrington, 113; Chillington, 114. an estate in Kilmersdon, ii 446. William, son of Robert de Todenei, assumed the name of Albani, iii 107; Ralph de, son of William, progenitor of the Daubeneys, of South Petherton, 107; married the mother of Everard de Ross, 108; Philip de, governor of the castles of Ludlow, Bridgnorth and Devizes: keeper of the forests of Melksham and Chippenham, 108; Ralph de, owned South Petherton, Barrington and Chillington, 108, 113, 114; Philip de, died without male issue, 108. he owned an estate in Kilmersdon, ii 446. Elias de, owned Petherton, Barrington, Chillington and Bruges, iii 108. owned Dummer [Dommet, in Buckland S. Mary], ii 366; and an estate in Kilmersdon, 446. a landowner temp. Ed. I, i *xxviii*. Ralph, wrote his name D'Aubeney, iii 108; married (1) Catherine de Thwenge, (2) Alice, daughter of lord Montacute, 108; Elizabeth, daughter of Ralph, married lord William Botreaux, 108, ii 66; rebuilt the church of North Cadbury, and procured a licence, 1427, to erect a collegiate church and establish a perpetual college, 67. Sir Giles, knt., owned South-Petherton, Barrington, Donyat, Chillington and Southarp, iii 108. M.P., 1383, 1384, i *xxx*. John, iii 108; Sir Giles, 108. M.P., 1424, 1428, i *xxxi*; sheriff, 1425, *xxxv*. William, obtained charter for a fair at South Petherton, iii 109; married Alice Sturton, 201; Giles, lord Daubeney, 109. Giles, sheriff, 1474, 1475, 1480, 1481, i *xxxvi*. owned Isle Brewers manor, i 54. Rodden and Flintford, ii 226; Long-Ashton, 292; Stanton-Drew, 434. owned Wincaunton, iii 33; forester of North-Petherton, 62; other offices and honours held by, 81, 109; owned land in Bridgwater, manors of Wincaunton, North and South Barrow and Marsh, 81; married Elizabeth Arundel, 81, 109; defended Taunton against the Cornish rebels, under Perkin Warbeck, 109, 228; buried in Westminster abbey, 109; Cecily, married John Bourchier, lord Fitzwarren, 109,

M

Daubeney, D'Albini, Albini or de Albaniaco family—*continued.*
ii 391. Henry, created earl of Bridgwater, iii 109. conveyed Long - Ashton to Sir Thomas Arundel, ii 292. also manor and hundred of South Petherton, iii 109; Mary, 1442, brass in South Petherton church, 112. James, sheriff, 1488, i *xxxvi*. Sir John, constable of Taunton castle, iii 227.

Daubeny, Rev. Mr., incumbent of Hardington, ii 348.

D'Audele, James, held knight's fee from John de Mohun, ii 14.

Dauncey family, monuments in Kenton Mande-ville church, ii 79, 80.

Davie, Sir John, owned Bittercliff, iii 554; Welch, benefaction to Wincaunton parish, 35. Sir William, married a daughter of George Stedman, and became owner of lands in Midsummer Norton, ii 158.

Davies, Mary, benefaction to Crewkerne, ii 164; Rev. Mr., incumbent of Saltford, 431. Thomas, governor of Bath hospital, B 48. Thomas, memorial stone in Wedmore church, i 192.

Davis, Rev. George, incumbent of Ruishton, iii 289. Peter, restored Godney chapel, ii 273; Rev. Richard, memorial in Compton-Dando church, 423; William, owned land in Priston, in right of his wife, a daughter of William Jenkins, 430. Rev. Mr., incumbent of Ilchester, iii 302.

Davis, Rice, resided at Tickenham court, married Dorothy Rodney, iii 165, 604; set up a claim to the estate of Dinder, 413. monument in Backwell church, ii 308.

Davis monuments in Bathwick church, i 122.

Davise, Robert, benefaction to Yatton, iii 620.

Davison, John, owned Freshford, i 125.

Daw, John, benefaction to Bishop's-Lydiard, ii 496.

Dawbeney, Edward, i *xl*; George, J.P., *xliii*; James, *xl*.

Dawe, Hill, J.P., i *xliii.* owner of Ditcheat, iii 472.

Dawe and Tipper, fair at Lopen granted to, iii 122.

Dawson, William, governor of Bath hospital, B 48.

Day, Samuel, J.P., i *xliii.* Samuel, held Bur-net, ii 415; monument in Burnet church, 416; Mary, wife of George Phelps, 416; John, memorial stone in Burnet church, 416.

Day, Philip, monument in Ditcheat church, iii 473.

Day, William, dean of Windsor, bishop of Win-chester, 1595, iii 232.

Day, William, surgeon, B 50.

Deacon, Mary, monument in Writhlington church, ii 460.

Dean, Mrs. Ann, benefaction to South-Brent, i 201; to Lympsham, 203.

Deane, hamlet in Lydiard-St.-Lawrence, iii 265.

Deaneries of the county, i *lii.*

Dean's manor, Congresbury, held by the dean and chapter of Wells, iii 585.

Deaudon, Sir Hamelyn de, married Aubrea de Punchardon, and became possessed of Lydiard-Pincherton, ii 494, iii 496. Thomas, ii 494, iii 496. Joan, married Roger de Claville, ii 494, iii 496. Mabilia, married Sir Baldwin Malet, i 90, ii 494, iii 496.

Debenham, lands in, purchased by lady Eliza-beth Luttrell, iii 500.

Dechair, Rev. Dr., governor of Bath hospital, B 48.

Decoys, iii 417, 592, 606.

Dee, Joan, married John Cradock, iii 588.

Deeke monument in Timsbury church, ii 113.

Deenmeed, John, M.P. for Bath, 1341, B 20.

Deering family inherited estates in Kent, for-merly belonging to the Brents, iii 435.

Deering, Nicholas, married Elizabeth West, ii 413.

Dehaney, Philip, governor of Bath hospital, B 48.

Delahay family held land in Huntspill-de-la-Hay, ii 393.

Delalind, Sir Thomas, sheriff, 1516, i *xxxvii*; George, sheriff, 1550, *xxxvii.*

Delalynde, a daughter of Walter, married Robert Delingrige, iii 547.

Delamere family, branches of, seated in Wilts, Oxford, Hereford and Somerset, ii 218.

De la Mere or Delamere family, of Nunney, ii 218; arms, 220; Nicholas, lord of Nunney, time of Henry III, 218; Nicholas, 218; Elias, projector of the castle, 218; Sir Thomas, gave lands in Kington St. Michael to Bradenstoke abbey, 218; Sir Peter, 218; Richard, sold lands in Nunney to Andrew Braunche, of Frome, 218; Sir John, knt., 218; John, sheriff of the county, finished the castle with the aid of his brother, Jaques, 218; Philip, 218; Sir Elias, knt., sheriff of Wilts, died without issue, 218; Eleanor, daughter of Philip, inherited all the family estates in Somerset, married William Paulet, 218; monuments in Nun-ney church, 219, 220. Hugh, iii 101. John, gave lands to the chantry of St. John, Frome, ii 194. Nicholas, landowner temp. Ed. I, i *xxviii*. Petronilla, wife of Andrew Luttrell, iii 498. Roger, contention with Glastonbury abbey as to the ownership of Mells, ii 462. Stephen, landowner temp. Ed. I, i *xxix.*

Delamere, Catharine, married William Cradock, iii 588.

Delawarr, earls, owned land in Shepton-Mallet, iii 462.

Donecan held land in Bishopston (Montacute), iii 311.

Doniet (*see* Donyat).

Donington, Margaret, married (1) Sir Thomas Kitson, (2) Sir Richard Long, (3) John, earl of Bath, ii 391.

Donisthorpe, George, J.P., i *xliii.*

Donne, John, J.P., i *xliii*; John, monument in Brewton church, 217.

Donniford hamlet (*see* St. Decumans).

Donnington church, Lincoln, belonged to Buckland priory, iii 98.

Donno held Buckland Dinham, ii 451.

Donvile (*see* D'Ovile).

Donwere (*see* Dunweer).

Donyat, position, i 35 ; products, 35; hamlets of Widney and Crock street, 35; labourers' wages, 35; labourers' club, 35; the revel, 35; almshouses founded by John Dunster, 35; Domesday survey, 36; owned by Robert, earl of Morton, and held by Drogo, 36; Adulfus, Sawin and Dunstan held it T.R.E. 36; Montacute family, 36. Sir Giles D'Aubeney, iii 108. Pole family, i 36; reverts to the Crown, and granted to Edward, earl of Hertford, 36; lord Lovel, 36; Richard Coombes, 36; church (Blessed Virgin Mary), 36; bells (4), 37; monuments, 37; the lords of this place held West-Dowlish, 37.

Dorchester, John, owned Curland, i 23; alienated the same to William Powell, 23.

Dore, Ann, tomb in Weston churchyard, i 166.

Dormitory in monasteries, ii 251.

Dorset, marquis of, owned Martock, iii 5; Langport, 132; Limington, 219; one of the lords of Mendip, 375 (*see* also Somerset, dukes of).

Dorset, duke of, J.P., i *xli.*

Dorset, manors situated in, but under the civil jurisdiction of Somerset, ii 369, 370.

Dossels, a manure carriage, ii 34.

Dossie, Mr., joint owner of the manor of Moor, in Mark, i 183.

Dotin, John, bachelor of physic, canon of Exeter, master of Exeter college, to which he was a great benefactor, buried at Kingsdon, iii 195.

Doughton, John, bequest to Flax-Bourton, iii 161.

Doulting, situation, iii 473; beacon, 473; St. Aldhelm's well, 473; St. Aldhelm's chapel, 473; Domesday survey, 473; owned by the abbey of Glastonbury, 473, 474, ii 243. Roger, held land here, iii 474; the bishop of Bath had estates here, 474; manor owned after the dissolution by John Malte, 474; the Horner family, 474; Prestleigh hamlet, owned by the St. Mawrs, 474; John, lord Stawel, 474; the Horner family, 474; chapel once stood here, 474; hamlets

Doulting—*continued.*
of Farncombe, Rodden, Newman-Street, Chelinch and Waterlip, 474 : freestone-quarries, 474; church (St. Aldhelm), 474; bells (6), 475; cross, 475; benefaction, 475. East-Cranmore church, a chapel-of-ease to, ii 209. rating in 1293, iii 394.

Doulting quarries, iii 474; stone used in the building of Wells cathedral, 398.

Douse, Geffrey de la, prior of Montacute, 1292, iii 312.

Douseborough castle, Stringston, i 261.

Dovell, William, last abbot of Cleeve, 1510, pensioned, iii 512.

Dover, —, first husband to Isabell Brewer, i 54.

Dover-castle, governors of : Bartholomew, lord Burghesh, iii 352; William de Wrotham, 64.

Dover-hay, hamlet in Luckham, ii 22; Domesday survey, 23; owned by Roger de Curcelle : held by Alric : Eddeve held it T.R.E. 23; church (now demolished), 23.

D'Ovile or Donvile, William de, owned part of the manor of Christon, iii 578; Hugh, 578; held also land in Uphill, 609.

Dowai, Walter de, received lands from William the Conqueror, i *xxv.* Walter de, took the name of de Baunton, ii 390. Julian, married William de Paganel, iii 78. Walter and his successors owned Almsford, ii 59; Alston, 393. Badgworth, iii 565; Bawdrip, 91. Berrow, i 201; Biddisham, 176. Bradney, iii 92; Bratton-Seymour, 36. Brean, i 177. Bridgwater, iii 78. Burnham, i 180. Castle-Cary, ii 51. Chapel-Allerton, i 175. Compton-Bishop, iii 582. Downend, ii 396; Huntspill, 390. Horsey, iii 85; Melcombe, 74; Milton, in Martock, 5; North-Petherton, 53. Over-Weare, i 185. Pawlet, iii 100. Sparkford, ii 87. Stretchill, iii 101; Walpole, 101; Wembdon, 103; West-Bower, 84. West-Harptree-Tilly, ii 140. Wincaunton, iii 32; Worle, 614.

Dowlas manufacture : Bickenhall, i 61. Wincaunton, iii 32; South Petherton, 106; Lopen, 122.

Dowlish Wake or East Dowlish, situation, iii 118; Bere-Mills, 119; springs, 119; Domesday survey, owned by the bishop of Coutances : Alward held it T.R.E.: William de Moncels held land here, 119; subsequently held by the families of Wake, 119; Keynes, who held it of the countess of Warren, 119, 120; Speke, 120; the prior of Farley had an estate here, 120; mansion of J. Hanning, 120; church (St. Andrew) and its monuments, 120.

Dowlish West, position, i 37; hamlets of Moolham and Oxenford, 37; fossils, 37; held by lords of Donyat, 37; owned by the families of Wake, 37; Keines, 37; Speke, 38; church (St. John Baptist), demolished, 38.

Durland, owned by the Hills, of Hounsdon, iii 196.

Durleigh, situation, i 78; owned chiefly by Sir Philip Hales and Sir Charles Kemeys Tynte, 78; Domesday survey, held by Ansger: by Alsi T.R.E. 78; lands here owned by St. John's hospital, Bridgwater, 79; John Smyth, 79; Hugh Smyth, 79; manor house, 79; church, 79; bells (4), 79. lands here held by the Whitmores, iii 81; the Harveys, 82.

Durnford, William, owned Hardington-Wytenine, iii 6.

Duroys manufacture, i 18.

Dursley, lord of, title retained by Roger, lord of Berkeley, after he had forfeited his title and estates of Berkeley, iii 276; Alice, his daughter, married Maurice, son of lord Berkeley, 276; Robert, son and heir of lord Dursley, married Helena, daughter of lord Berkeley, 276.

Durston, situation, iii 95; Domesday survey, 95; owned by Roger Arundel: held by Richard: by Alwi T.R.E. 95; afterwards by the Erleighs, 95; the St. Maurs, 96; the Stawels, 96; Mr. Portman, 96; Henry Seymour, 96; church, 99; tithes belonged to Buckland priory, 98; William Dennis held lands here, 63; priory of Buckland-Sororum (*see* Buckland).

Durston, Joseph, monument in Berrow church, i 202.

Durville family owned Compton-Durville, iii 110; Eustace de, attainted, 110.

Dyble, John, priest of Wells, pensioned, iii 409.

Dyer family owned Street, iii 424. memorial stone in Katherine church, i 140; in Wedmore church, 193. Alexander and Catherine, monument in Glastonbury church, ii 264. Edward, M.P., 1589, 1593, i *xxxii.* Sir Edward, knt., owned Stawel, iii 431; Frances, married Sir John Stawel, 251; James, 33; Jane, married Maurice de Rodney, 604.

Dyer family—*continued.*

Jane and Ralph, memorial stone in Burnet church, ii 416; John, master of St. Catherine's hospital, Bedminster, 283. John, owned land in Barrow-Common, iii 33; John, owned land in Bratton Seymour, 36; John, inscription in High-Ham church, 446; Laurence, 36; Margaret, memorial stone in Street church, 424; Thomas, held Greinton, 428. Sir Thomas, sheriff, 1559, i *xxxvii.* Sir Thomas, knt., one of the commission for the survey of churches, chapels, etc., in Somersetshire, ii 286. Sir Thomas, knt., commissioner for the survey of Stoke-under-Hamden chapel, iii 318; Sir Thomas, knt., held Othery, 443.

Dyke, Edward, sheriff, 1727, i *xxxviii;* George, J.P., *xliii.* Joan, monument in Brompton-Regis church, iii 504. John, founder of charity-school at Bishop's-Lydiard, ii 496. Thomas, sheriff, 1697, i *xxxviii.* benefaction to Kingston, iii 264.

Dyker, John, i *xl.*

Dykere, Richard le, member for Chard, ii 472.

Dymock, Elizabeth, monument in Hornblotton church, iii 476; Elizabeth and Thomas, gifts to Evercreech church, 416.

Dynant (*see* Dinham).

Dyngley, Etheldred (*see* Malte).

Dyngley (or Dobson), Joanna, i 128.

Dynham (*see* Dinham).

Dytte, John, received a pension from St. John's hospital, Wells, iii 409.

Dyve, Sir John, knt., of Bromham, married Beatrice Walcot, iii 336; Beatrice, widow of Sir John, married the earl of Bristol, 336; Sir Lewis, knt., owned Combe-Hay, married Howard Strangways, 336; Francis, 336; Lewis, 336; John, 336; Grace, married George Hussey, to whom she conveyed the manor of Combe-Hay, 336; inscription in Combe-Hay church, 336.

E

Eagles, Thomas, married Charlotte Tyndale, iii 263.

Ealdbright, Clito, defeated by Ina, at Taunton, iii 229.

Earle, William, married a daughter of Smart Goodenough, and became possessed of Blagdon, Burton and other estates in Pitminster, iii 285. benefaction to West-Harptree, ii 144. Goodenough, J.P., i *xliii.* owned West-Harptree Tilly, ii 142. patron of Corfe, iii 249; succeeded to the Pitminster estates, 285; patron of Trull, 294. monument in West-Harptree church, ii 143.

Earnshill: Domesday survey, i 30; owned by Roger de Corcelle, 30; held by Ulward and Girard, 30; Living held it T.R.E. 30; Muchelney abbey, 31; the earl of Hertford, 31; the Jennings family, 31; Mrs. Coombe, 31; church (now demolished), 31.

Earnshill, West, owned by Muchelney abbey, iii 135.

Earthquakes, ii 262, 265, iii 95.

Eason, John, J.P., i *xliii.*

East-Bagborough (*see* Bagborough).

East, Mrs. Mary, benefaction to Bath abbey, B 71.

East-Camel (*see* Camel Queens).

Edgar, king—*continued.*
bury abbey, ii 242 ; buried at Glastonbury, 262. gave High - Ham to Glastonbury abbey, iii 444 ; gave Wheat-hill to Glastonbury abbey, 450 ; gave Puddimore-Milton to Glastonbury abbey, 451 ; confirms grant of Blackford to Glastonbury abbey, 452.

Edgar, Robert, received a pension from Athelney, i 88.

Edgarley, hamlet in Glastonbury, ii 265 ; chapel converted into a barn, 265.

Edgeberry or Edgeborough, hamlet in North-Petherton, iii 54 ; owned by Osbert and William Dacus or Dennis, 63, 74.

Edgeborough (*see* Edgeberry).

Edgecombe, Margaret, wife of Sir William St. Maur, ii 200.

Edgecut, hamlet in Exford, ii 21.

Edgell, James, Harry, and Elizabeth, monument in Beckington church, ii 202. Harry, J.P., i *xliii.* seat at Standerwick, ii 227 ; owned Standerwick, 228.

Edington, situation, iii 433 ; moors, 433 ; river Brew, 433 ; Edington-Burtle, 433 ; Roman remains, 433 ; held under Glastonbury abbey by Roger de Curcelle, 433 ; William Fitz-Gefferey, 433 ; Edington family, 433 ; Michael Marshall, 433 ; Robert Hull, 433 ; earl Waldegrave, 433 ; church, 433 ; bells (2), 433 ; Henry de Woolavington held lands here, 438.

Edington family held Edington, iii 433 ; Gilbert de, 433.

Edington-Burtle, hamlet in Edington, iii 433.

Edingworth, hamlet in East Brent, i 197 ; Domesday survey, 197 ; held by Roger : by Edric T.R.E. : George de Cantilupe, 197, iii 567. the Zouch family, Richard, earl of Warwick, John Boteller, James Hyet, Henry, earl of Rutland, the Jennys family, Wadham Wyndham, and James Everard Arundel, i 197, iii 598.

Edistone (*see* Edingworth).

Edith, queen, held Bath, B 17. Chewton-Mendip, ii 116 ; Luckham, 22. Martock, iii 3. Selworthy, ii 40 ; Stoke Pero, 43 ; Puriton, 396. Twiverton, iii 347.

Edmar held Dinnington, iii 121.

Edmer held Chinnock, ii 327. and Camerton, iii 330.

Edmond, John, abbot of Glastonbury (*sic* Collinson, but an error : John Edmond was *not* abbot of Glastonbury), benefactor to Brewton free grammar school, i 212.

Edmond, Nicholas, owned Charleton - Horethorne, ii 358.

Edmor held land in Taunton, iii 231.

Edmund, king, rebuilt Glastonbury abbey, and established Dunstan there, ii 242 ; rebuilt the town of Glastonbury, 262 ; buried at Glastonbury, 262. gave Kingston, in Tintinhull hundred, to Glastonbury abbey, iii 323.

Edmund-Ironside, buried at Glastonbury, ii 262.

Edmundesworde (*see* Edingworth).

Edols, Richard, married Ann Emery, monument in Felton church, ii 444.

Edred held Plainsfield T.R.E. i 259.

Edric held Allerford, ii 41 ; Barrow, 309 ; Bishopworth, 284 ; Chew-Stoke, 101 ; Chilcompton, 128. Edingworth, i 197. Farmborough, ii 423 ; Oare, 33 ; Rodden, 226. land in Tickenham, iii 164 ; Tunley, 331 ; Wells, 393. land in Weston, near Bath, i 160.

Edstone, hamlet in Stoke Courcy, i 252 ; Domesday survey, 252 ; owned by Roger, and held by Anschitil : by Alwine T.R.E. 252 ; owned by Sir James Langham, 252.

Edui held West Harptree Gournay, ii 140.

Eduin held Isle-Abbots, i 50 ; Otterhampton, 242. Bradford, iii 243 ; Exton, 526 ; Goldsoncot, 510.

Edward held Walpole, iii 101 ; and Telsford, 362.

Edward, duke of Somerset (*see* Somerset).

Edward the Confessor's charter to Giso, bishop of Wells, iii 390, 391.

Edwards, Elizabeth, of Lyme Regis, married Thomas Napier, monument in Tintinhull church, iii 309.

Edwards, Mary, owned Lydford-West, ii 84 ; Sophia, wife of Alexander Ready, 84.

Edwards, Thomas, of Bristol, benefaction to Charlton-Musgrave, iii 38 ; owned land in Clapton-in-Gordano, 178.

Edwards' memorial stone in Wedmore church, i 193.

Edwaye, Edward, monk of Bath, who received pension, B 57.

Edwi, king, gave a manse in Ham to Ceolward, iii 83 ; held land in Dunkerton, 337.

Edwinetone (*see* Edington).

Edwold held Brown, ii 46. and Stretchill, iii 101.

Edwy granted Blackford to Glastonbury abbey, iii 452.

Edyndone, John de, owned Elm, ii 206. received the manor of Wyke [in Yatton], from John de Wyke, iii 618.

Effingham, earl of, J.P., i *xli.*

Eford, Amos, stone in Martock church, iii 11.

Eford (*see* Iford).

Eford-juxta-Taunton, land in, held by John Fag, of the bishop of Winchester, iii 217.

Egelnoth, abbot of Glastonbury, banished to Normandy, ii 250.

Egelward, abbot of Glastonbury, ii 249, 250.

Egerton, Mrs. Anne, received a moiety of the manor of Brewton, i 215.

Egerton, John, baron of Ellesmere, and viscount Brackley, created earl of Bridgwater (*see* Bridgwater).

Egerton monument in East-Brent church, i 198.

Eggesworth, John of, master of St. Catherine's hospital, Bedminster, ii 283.

Eggford, hamlet in Frome, ii 186 ; partly in Whatley parish, 230 ; house in which Mrs. Elizabeth Rowe lived, 230.

Egmont, earl of, J.P., i *xli* ; owner of Asholt, 237 ; Andersfield, 71 ; Charlinch, 239 ; Currypool, 239 ; Enmore, 92 ; Lexworthy, 95 ; Plainsfield, 260 ; Spaxton, 244 ; Stoke-Courcy, 252 ; Friar's manor, Over Stowey, 259. descended from Ralph Perceval, iii 174

Egremont, Charles William, earl of, sold Witham manor to Mr. Beckford, ii 234. owned Orchard-Wyndham, iii 490. George, second earl of, J.P., i *xli* ; owned a field in Ashill, 10 ; Beer Crocombe, 14 ; Ilton, 47. Lux-borough, ii 25. Merrifield, i 48. Orchard-Portman, iii 274 ; Orchard-Wyndham, 491 ; Pen, 44. South-Bradon, i 15. Trudox-hill, ii 217.

Elborough, in Hutton, iii 591 ; owned by Glas-tonbury abbey : given at the Conquest to the bishop of Coutances, 591 ; Domesday survey, 591 ; held by Azelin : Alward held it T.R.E. 591 ; owned by Joseph Daniel Matthews, 591.

Elbridge, John, owned Buckshaw, ii 370. owned a moiety of the manor of Churchill, iii 580.

Eldeva held Horsington, ii 371.

Eldred held T.R.E. Kingston-Seymour, ii 122. and Hill Bishops, iii 254. (Domesday) Brock-ley, ii 120. Crandon, iii 92 ; Kilve, 532.

Eleanor, wife of Prince Edward, owned the hundred of Somerton, iii 181.

Eleanora, prioress of Cannington, 1499 and 1502, i 233.

Elegy on two children drowned at South Pether-ton, iii 106.

Elfeth, bishop of Wells, iii 377. owned Wel-lington, Buckland and Lydiard, ii 482.

Eliot, Richard, married Elizabeth Besilles, iii 504.

Elizabeth, queen, granted the manor of Ilmin-ster to Edward Seymour, i 6. incorporated Minehead, ii 27.

Elizabeth de Sancta Cruce (*see* Sancta Cruce).

Ellerhaye, land in, owned by Newton chapel, iii 65.

Ellesmere, John Egerton, baron, created earl of Bridgwater, iii 81.

Elletson, Roger Hope, monument in Bath abbey, 1775, B 68.

Elliot, Beata, gave £100 to Fivehead church, i 42 (*see* Elyott).

Elliot, Benjamin and Robert, rectors of Trent, ii 383.

Elliot, Edmund, owned Cathanger, i 42.

Ellis, Rev. John, LL.B., monument in Bath abbey, 1785, B 68. Philip, tablet in Bath-ford church, i 114.

Ellis, Welbore, J.P., i *xliii*. owned Charter-house-on-Mendip, ii 235.

Ellyot, William, incumbent of the chapel of Whitehall, iii 300.

Ellys, Thomas, last incumbent of Norton-Hauteville chantry, received a pension, ii 108.

Elm, situation, ii 206 ; hamlet of Little Elm, 206 ; Murder-Combe, 206 ; Roman encamp-ment (Tedbury), 206 ; Roman coins, 206 ; owned by Sir Thomas de Cary, 206 ; John de Edyndone, 206 ; Elizabeth de Brecon owned a moiety, 206 ; John Panys, 207 ; Thomas Clerk held it on lease, 207 ; subse-quently owned by Humphry Stafford, earl of Devon, 207 ; Henry, lord Compton, 207 ; Spencer, 207 ; Robert Webb : Alex-ander Chocke, 207 ; Thomas Hodges, 207 ; Henry Strachey, 207 ; church (St. Mary) and monument, 207 ; bells (3), 207.

Elm-trees, Hatch Beauchamp, i 46. Northover, iii 306 ; Wheathill, tree growing in the church, 450.

Elmar held Walton, ii 447. and land in Mud-ford, iii 220.

Elmer held Wheathill, iii 450 ; and land in Shepton-Mallet and Croscombe, 480.

Elmer, John, bishop Beckington's bequest to, iii 385.

Elnod held West-Quantockshead, iii 496.

Elphege, prior of Glastonbury, and first abbot of Bath, B 54. born at Weston, i 166.

Elphege, bishop of Wells (*see* Elfeth).

Elric held land in Moreton, ii 133.

Elsi held Berrow, i 201. Castle Cary, ii 51. Wincaunton, iii 32 ; Bratton-Seymour, 36. owned Winsham, but was compelled by bishop Giso to restore it to the see of Wells, ii 478.

Elston, lands in, formerly owned by the guilds of Shepton-Mallet, granted to John Horner, iii 465.

Elston-Combe chapel, demolished, iii 207.

Elsworth, Richard, of Timberscombe, founded the charity school at Cutcombe, ii 7.

Elsworth, Richard, of Bickham, gave an altar piece to Timberscombe church, and founded a charity school there, ii 45.

Elton, Abraham, sheriff, 1791, i *xxxix* ; J.P., *xliii* ; Rev. Abraham, J.P., *xliii*. Sir Abraham, owned Winford, ii 321. White-stanton, iii 127 ; Clevedon, 168 ; benefaction to Clevedon church, 169. Sir Abraham Isaac, J.P., i *xliii*. owned Clevedon, iii 168. Edward, sheriff, 1780, i *xxxix* ; J.P., *xliii* ; Isaac, J.P., *xliii* ; owned Buckland St. Mary, 20. Winford, ii 321. White-Stan-ton, iii 127.

Elwacre held Sparkford, ii 87 ; West-Harptree Tilly, 140 ; Huntspill, 390. Milton in Martock, iii 5 ; Compton-Bishop, 582.

Elward held Horsey, iii 85.

Elwi held land in Banwell, iii 566.

Elwick, vill of Blagdon, depopulated, iii 569.

Elworthe, William de, held knights' fees from Sir William de Mohun, ii 13. held Elworthy, iii 525 ; John de, of Elworthy, 525. landowner temp. Ed. I, i *xxviii*.

Elworthy, situation, iii 525 ; Brendon-hill, 525 ; spring, 525 ; tower on Willet-hill, 525 ; Willet hamlet, 525 ; Domesday survey, 525 ; owned by William de Mohun : held by Dudiman : Dunne held it T.R.E. 525 ; subsequently held by the de Elworthe family, 525 ; Thomas de Tymmeworth, Richard de la Pleshe, and James de Torte held lands here, 525 ; manor held by Walter Meriet, 525, 259 ; Sir William Palton, 525, ii 456. the Beaumonts, iii 525 ; Rev. Bickham Escot, 526 ; church (St. Martin), 526 ; bells (4), 526 ; lands here were owned by Nettlecombe chantry, 538.

Ely green, hamlet in Over-Stowey, i 259.

Ely, John, builder of the market-cross at Brewton, i 211 ; last abbot of Brewton, received a pension, 214.

Ely, Nicholas de, bishop of Winchester, 1268, a benefactor to Taunton priory, iii 232.

Elyott family, inscriptions in Fivehead church, i 43.

Emanuel college, Cambridge, patrons of North Cadbury, ii 68. held manor and advowson of Aller, iii 188 ; patrons of Winsford, 557.

Emborough, Richard de, landowner temp. Ed. I, i *xxviii*. owned Emborow : granted it to Alexander de Mountfort, ii 157.

Emborow, its situation, ii 134 ; coal mines and stone quarries, 134 ; tithings of Emborow, Dolton and Ashwick, 134 ; Emborow and Leachmore pond, 135 ; occupied by the Romans and Saxons, 135 ; Domesday survey, 135 ; owned by the bishop of Coutance, and held by Robert, 135 ; owned by the families of Trewithose, Hugh le Dispencer, William Tracy, Henry Tracy, Botiler (or Boteler), 135 ; Hippesley and Coxe, 136 ; church (St. Mary) and its monuments, 136 ; bells (2), 136 ; manors of Emborow and Whittenhull, 157 ; lake, 158.

Emborow pond, ii 135.

Emery, Isaac, Thomas, Charity ; Ann, wife of Richard Edols, monument in Whitchurch church, ii 444.

Emmeberwe, Sir Richard de (*see* Emborough).

Emorice, Richard de, memorial acrostic in South Barrow church, ii 64.

Enderby, Walter, sheriff, 1493, i *xxxvi*.

Endeston (*see* Yeanston).

Endistone (*see* Edingworth).

Enfield, Middlesex, seat of Hugh de Placetis, iii 64 ; Thomas Durant owned lands there, and built the house called " Durants," 65 ;

Enfield, Middlesex—*continued.* the Wrothe or Wrotham family held lands there, 65, 66 ; Wrothe-place, seat of John Wrothe, 66.

Enfield, John de, the wardship of, held by John Wrothe, iii 66.

Engaine or Engayne, Richard de, held lands in Buckingham and Huntingdon, iii 615 ; Richard, of Blatherwick, 615 ; Vitalis owned Worle, 615. received part of the estates of Robert de Courteney, ii 337. Henry and John, grant Worle to Woodspring priory, iii 594, 615.

Engeler, held land in Tickenham, iii 164.

England, John, monument in Merriot church, ii 171 ; Thomas, incumbent of Haselborough, 333. Rev. Mr., owned land in Twiverton, iii 348.

Englowes, arms emblazoned on window of Wraxall church, iii 159.

Enmore, situation, i 89 ; owned by Roger de Curcelle, 89 ; Domesday survey, 89 ; held by Goisfrid : by Algar T.R.E. 89 ; owned by the Malet family, 90 ; Sir John Hull, 91 ; John, earl of Rochester, 92 ; Henry Bayntun, 92 ; James Smyth, of St. Audries, 92 ; earl of Egmont, 92 ; Enmore castle, 94 ; manor of Lexworthy, 94 ; church (St. Michael) and its monuments, 95, 96 ; bells (5), 95.

Enulf, earl, gave Ditcheat to Glastonbury abbey, iii 471 ; gave Hornblotton to Glastonbury abbey, 476.

Enys, Dorothy, monument in Bath abbey, 1784, B 68 ; Maria, monument in Bath abbey, 1784, 68.

Epse or Episbury (*see* Pisbury).

Erchenger held the church of Cannington, i 232.

Erghum, Gilbert and Agnes, parents of bishop Erghum, and of Agnes Robas, iii 402 ; Ralph, bishop of Salisbury, translated to Bath and Wells, 1388, 383 ; gifts to Wells cathedral, 383 ; founded a chantry-chapel at Wells, 383 ; fortified the bishop's palace, 383 ; buried in Wells cathedral, 383, 399. appropriated the church of Curry Rivel to the priory of Bysham, i 27.

Erington, Gerard, purchased Stanton - Prior : conveyed the same to William Rosewell, ii 439.

Erle, Thomas, married Elizabeth Wyndham, iii 495.

Erlebald held Witham, ii 232.

Erlebold held part of Brewham manor, i 220.

Erlega family (*see* Erleigh).

Erleigh or Somerton-Erle (*see* Somerton).

Erleigh, Erlega or d'Erleigh family of Beckington, ii 198, 199, 200 ; held Babcary, 60 ; Beckington, 198, 199. North - Petherton, iii 54 ; Durston, 95 ; Michaelchurch, 99 ;

Erleigh, Erlega or d'Erleigh family—*continued.*
Somerton-Erle, 185 ; members buried in
North-Petherton church, 74. arms, ii 200 ;
John de, paid for the scutage of his lands in
Somerset, 198. held North-Petherton, iii 54.
William de, founder of Buckland priory,
ii 199. baron in time of Henry II, i *xxvi.*
appropriated Kilmersdon church to Buckland priory, ii 447. gave the chapels at
Newton - Regis and Newton - Comitis to
Buckland priory, iii 70 ; owned Mansel,
72 ; founded and endowed the priory of
Buckland-Sororum, 96, 98 ; gave the chapel
of Thurloxton to Buckland priory, 103 ;
confirmed the grant of the tithes of Somerton-Erleigh to Athelney-abbey, 186 ; Mabil,
daughter of William, married Philip Arbalistarius, 72. John de, son of William, held
the hundred of North-Petherton, ii 199 ;
William paid scutage for lands in Berkshire
and Somersetshire, 199 ; John, 199 ; Henry,
married (1) Egelina de Candos, (2) Claricia,
199. granted chapel at Michaelchurch and
lands in Ridene to the abbey of Athelney,
iii 99. Philip, married Rosa de Marisco, ii 199 ; a daughter of Philip married
Richard de Acton, 199 ; Maud, widow of
Philip, married Sir Geffrey de Wroxall,
199 ; Sir John, 199. sheriff, 1291, 1314,
1325, i *xxxiv* ; M.P., 1308, 1313, 1329,
1330, 1331, 1332, *xxix.* Roland, ii 199 ;
John, 199 ; Catherine, prioress of Buckland,
199 ; Elizabeth, wife of Sir John Stafford,
199 ; Alice, wife of Sir Nicholas Poines,
199 ; John, attended the Black Prince into
Spain, was taken prisoner and forced to sell
many of his estates to pay ransom, married
Margaret de Brien, 199. sold Somerton
Erle to Richard Brice, iii 185. Richard,
ii 199 ; Philip, 199 ; Sir John, married
Isabel Pavely, 199 ; his daughter and heir,
married (1) John St. Maur, (2) Sir Walter
Sondes, (3) Sir William Cheney, 199.
Ernebold held Yarnfield T.R.E., iii 41.
Erneis held lands in Brewton, i 213. in Wells,
iii 392 ; in Evercreech, 414 ; held Down-
head, 475.
Ernele, Walter, monument in Bath abbey, B 62,
68.
Erneshull, John de, rector of Goose Bradon,
i 16.
Escape from a cannon shot, i 146.
Escott, hamlet in Stogumber, iii 546.
Escott, Rev. Bickham, J.P., i *xliii.* incum-
bent of Kittisford, iii 24 ; patron of Heath-
field, 254 ; patron and incumbent of Bromp-
ton-Ralph, 506 ; owned Elworthy, 526 ; held
Hartrow, 547 ; Rev. Bickham, Sarah, his
wife, and James, their son, monument in
Kittisford church, 24.
Esgar held Worle, iii 614.

Espek, Richard le (afterwards Speke), held
three knights' fees of Robert Fitz - Roy,
i 67 ; his grandson, Richard, father of Sir
William, married Alice Gervois, 67 ; William, married Julian de Valletort, John,
altered the name to L'Espek, and married
Constance de Esse, 67 ; William, abbrevi-
ated the name to Speke, 67 ; John, married
Joan Keynes, 67 (*see* Speke).
Esquire, his daily stipend, iii 277.
Esse, Constance de, wife of John l'Espek, i 67.
Henry de, canon of Sarum, received a pen-
sion from the benefice of Hemington, ii 455.
Matthew, landowner temp. Ed. I, i *xxvii* ;
juror for perambulation of Neroche forest,
17.
Essecote, Baldwin de, held land of Glastonbury
abbey, ii 245.
Esseleg, Walter de (*see* Ashley).
Essentone (*see* Ashington).
Essex, Henry Bourchier, earl of, owned Bed-
minster, ii 282.
Essex, earls of, Capel, owned Bathwick, i 121.
Essex, earls of, Mandeville, held Keinton-Mande-
ville, ii 79 (*see* Mandeville).
Essexe, George and Margery, monument in
Huish-Episcopi church, ii 470 ; arms, 470.
Estables, Roger, iii 63, 64.
Estalle, the, part of Blackford, in Whitley
hundred, held of Hamo de Blackford,
iii 452.
Estan held Otterhampton, i 242 ; Radlet, 245 ;
Tuxwell, 245.
Estcote, land in, held by Walter Meriet,
iii 259.
Estcourt family owned Claverton, i 146. Sir
Thomas, M.P. for Bath, 1695, B 22.
Esterling, Sir William le, founder of the Strad-
ling family, iii 334 ; owned the castle and
manor of St. Donat's, Glamorganshire,
335 ; Sir John, married Maud Corbet, 335 ;
Sir Maurice, married Cecily de Say, 335.
Sir Robert wrote his name Stradling (*see*
Stradling).
Estham manor, ii 160 ; owned by earl Morton,
and held by Turstin : by Goduin T.R.E.
160 ; Domesday survey, 160.
Estmond, Eve de, niece of William the Con-
queror, married Robert Fitzharding, lord of
Berkeley, iii 276, 283.
Estoket or Stoket (*see* Stoke under Hamden).
Eston, Gilbert de, abbot of Keynsham, ii 402.
John de, gift to Woodspring priory, iii 594.
Estone (*see* Bath-Easton).
Estre, Richard del, baron in time of Henry II,
i *xxvi* ; owned Asholt, 237. and Stoke-
Trister, iii 50. Robert del, sheriff, 1272,
i *xxxiv.*
Estrecholte, lands and tenements in, granted by
Anastatia Croc to Sir Thomas Trivet,
iii 101.

Estredolmore, land in, granted by Alice de Ouvre to Woodspring priory, iii 594.

Estrepe, lands in, owned by Stavordale priory, iii 33.

Est-Wall, lands in, held by John Stourton, iii 405.

Est-wick (*see* Eastwick).

Estwood, lands in, owned by Sir John Newton, iii 588.

Etenberge, owned by Montacute priory, iii 311.

Ethelard, king of Wessex, bestowed the town of Taunton upon the bishops of Winchester, iii 229.

Ethelbald, king, gave Bradley to the monks of Glastonbury, ii 271. held the palace and castle at Somerton, iii 182.

Ethelmar or Adomar, son of Hugh, earl of March, bishop of Winchester, 1260, iii 232.

Ethelmund granted Huntspill to the church of Glastonbury, ii 390.

Ethelstan, duke, granted Weston (near Foxcote) to Glastonbury abbey, iii 349.

Ethelwyn, bishop of Wells, owned Wellington, Buckland and Lydiard, ii 482. removed from his bishopric, iii 378 ; effigy in Wells cathedral, 399.

Eton college owned Monkton manor, in Stoke Courcy, i 252; patrons of Stoke Courcy, 257. of Wotton-Courtney, ii 49.

Etone, Walter de, prior of Stavordale, iii 33.

Ettricke, William, part owner of Castle-Cary, ii 55; Mrs. Ettricke, of London, bequeathed that estate to Mrs. Powell, 56.

Eurard held Lexworthy, i 94. land in Ditcheat, iii 472.

Euroac held Worspring, iii 594.

Eustace, earl, held four hides in Belluton, ii 401; owned Compton-Dando, 421.

Eustace, earl of Bulloigne (*see* Bulloigne).

Euvacre held Compton-Martin, ii 131.

Evans, John, incumbent of Beckington, ii 200.

Evans, Lewis, incumbent of Knoll, iii 118.

Eve, Anne, monument in Charlcombe church, i 144.

Eveleigh, John, monument in Chard church, ii 474.

Evelton chapel, purchased by the trustees of Ilminster grammar school, i 4.

Evelyn, Mrs., monument in Yarlington church, i 229.

Everard family owned Luxborough, ii 25; held lands in Carhampton and Dunster, 19; effigy in Dunster churchyard, 19.

Everard, John, of Huntspill, witness to a deed, ii 394. Mrs. Joan, monument in Stockland-Bristol church, i 248; Mrs., owned Otterhampton, 242; Edmund, landowner temp. Ed. I, *xxviii*; Edmund, M.P., 1305, 1312, *xxix*, 1352, *xxx*; Robert, sheriff, 1719, *xxxviii*. owned Stowey, iii 553. William, sheriff, 1258, 1259, i *xxxiv*. held a fourth part of a knight's fee from John de Mohun, ii 14.

Evercreech, situation, iii 413; hamlets of Chesterblade and Stoney-Stratton, 413; Bagbury, Southwood and Pecking Mill, 414; Roman encampment on Small-down hill, 413; common, 414; salt spring, 414; Domesday survey, 414; owned by the bishop of Wells: Erneis, Macharius and Ildebert held land of him, 414; granted by Edward VI to the duke of Somerset, 414, 395, 396; owned by lord Grey, 414, 444; sold off in parcels, 414; rating in 1293 amongst the bishop's temporalities, 394; manor house rebuilt by bishop Ralph de Salopia, 383; Stoney-Stratton and Bagbury manors held under Glastonbury abbey by the Stawel family, 415; church (St. Peter) and its monuments, 415; benefactions, 416; bells (6), 415; Evercreech-park, 414; old park of the bishops of Bath and Wells, 414; courthouse erected by bishop Ralph de Salopia, 414; mansion built by Sir Ralph Hopton, 414; estate sold to John Caryll and John Trethery, 414; owned by the Newman family, 415; Thomas Sampson, 415.

Evercriche, John de, prior of Witham, ii 234.

Evercy family held Brimpton d'Evercy, iii 214; Sir John de, knt., 214; Peter, 214. landowner temp. Ed. I, i *xxvii*; M.P., 1316, *xxix*. Anne, married Sir John Glamorgan, iii 214; owned by dame Isabel, 214; Amice, married — Glamorgan, 214.

Evered, John, owned Athelney abbey, i 88. Robert, J.P., i *xliii*.

Evereux, the earl of, married Mabil, daughter of William, earl of Gloucester, iii 148; Almaric, their son, died without issue, 148.

Every, John, of Cothay, married Anne Williams, iii 24; Ann, married John Leigh, 24; Barbara, married Sir Robert Henley, 24; John, left his estates to the eldest sons of his sisters, Barbara and Ann, 24; arms, 24; the Everys, of Chard, a branch of the family, 24; Mary, married William Raymond, 302.

Every, Sir Simon, bart., of Chard, ii 475; a great royalist, 475; married the daughter of Sir Henry Leigh, of Egginton, Derby, and became possessed of that estate, 475.

Evett, Elizabeth, monument in Whitchurch church, ii 442.

Ewacre held Uphill, iii 609.

Ewe, William de, joined the rebellion against William Rufus, besieged Ivelchester, iii 299.

Ewe, William Bourchier, earl of, married Anne, daughter of Thomas of Woodstock, duke of Gloucester, ii 391.

Ewyas, Harold de, owned Chelworth, ii 419; John de, lord Sudley, 419; Robert de, owned Chelworth, 419; Sibil de, married Robert de Tregoz, 419.

Ex river, its course, i *xiv*, iii 520, 526.

Excursions of the Glastonbury abbots, i 183.

Excecestre, Baldwin de (*see* Exeter).

Exeter, Baldwin de, received land from William the Conqueror, i *xxv.* formerly called de Brionis, was sheriff of Devon, and owned Hemington, ii 454. owned land in Apley, iii 28 ; and in Mudford, 220.

Exeter, bishop of, owned two knights' fees held by Richard de Raddon, ii 226 ; owned North-Coker, 342 ; Thomas, bishop of, received lands in Chilthorne - Domer from John de Dommere, 366. bestowed these lands on Brewton priory, iii 217.

Exeter castle : Ralph de Gorges, governor of, iii 156.

Exeter, John de Holland, earl of Huntingdon, created duke of, owned Haselborough, married Anne, daughter of Edmund, earl of Stafford, ii 333 ; Henry, duke of, married Anne, daughter of Richard, duke of York, was attainted, and lost his estates, 333. forfeited Blagdon to the Crown, iii 569.

Exeter, Henry, marquis of, owned Portbury Priors, lost his life for treasonable correspondence with cardinal Pole, iii 142.

Exford, its situation, ii 19 ; ancient remains, 20 ; Symonsbath, 20 ; Sadler's stone, 20 ; owned by William de Mohun : held by Domno and Sarpo T.R.E., 20, 21 ; Domesday survey, 20 ; Monkham manor, owned by the Cistercian abbey of Neth, 21 ; Almsworthy manor, 21 ; hamlets of Edgecut and Lower-Mill, 21 ; church (St. Mary Magdalen), 21 ; bells (4), 21 ; charity school, 21 ; remains of iron works, 21.

Exmoor forest, i *xv.* description, ii 19, 20. survey in the reign of Edward I, iii 57, 58 ; foresters of, held the greater part of Withypool T.R.E. 558. bailiwick held by William de Placetis, ii 20 ; afterwards by

Exmoor forest—*continued*.
family of Peche and Sir Thomas Acland, 20.

Exon, Thomas, incumbent of Creech St. Michael, i 76. incumbent of Exton, iii 527.

Expeditation of dogs, i 207.

Exton, situation, iii 526 ; river Ex, 526 ; Bridgetown, 526 ; Domesday survey, 526 ; owned by Geffrey, bishop of Coutances : held by Drogo : Eduin held it T.R.E. 526 ; subsequently owned by the de Wrothams, 526 ; divided between the families of Placey, Scoland, Picot, and Bland, 526 ; the manor united and held successively by Compton, Rolles, Boyce, Wyndham, and Hole, 527 ; church (St. Peter), 527 ; bells (4), 527 ; Browford hamlet : Domesday survey, 527 ; owned by Roger de Curcelle : held by William : Ulwin and Almar held it T.R.E. 527 ; subsequently held by William de Holne, 527 ; lands here belonged to Thomas Durant, 65 ; lands held by the Luttrells, 492. manor held by James, earl of Ormond, ii 392 ; James, earl of Wiltshire, 392.

Exton, Philip de and Henry de, priors of St. John's hospital, Wells, iii 408.

Exwater, boundary of Exmoor perambulation, 1298, ii 19.

Eynsham, William, one of the jury to decide position of the city pillory, B 31.

Eyre, Bridget, tablet in Writhlington church, ii 460 ; Bridget, married John Salmon, 460. Joan le, married John Brent, of Cossington, to whom she conveyed a manor in Middlezoy, iii 435. Rev. Thomas, LL.D., J.P., i *xliii.* prebendary of Wells, iii 397. Samuel, governor of Bath hospital, B 48.

Eyton, John, one of the jury to decide position of the city pillory, B 31.

F

Fabri, Henry, M.P. for Chard, ii 472.

Faderwin, Robert, incumbent of Weston-in-Gordano, iii 174.

Fage, John, held land in Chiltern-Fage and in Elford, iii 217 ; John and Catherine held Chilthorn-Fage and Chilthorne-Domer, 217 ; Marmaduke and Alice, 217 ; Thomas, 217.

Failand family owned Fayland, iii 155.

Fair-close, Stavordale, iii 34.

Fairfield, hamlet in Stoke Courcy, i 252 ; granted by Maud de Candos to Martin, the son of Goidslan, called Martin de Ferefelle, to be held by knights' service, 252 ; granted by Philip de Columbers to William Russell, 253 ; owned by the family of Vernai, 253, ii 393. Palmer, i 254, 255, iii 257. Acland, i 255 ; chapel and its arms, 256.

Fairhill, Rev. Robert, inscription in Fivehead church, i 43.

Fair maids of Fosscot, monument in Norton St. Philip's church, iii 371.

Fairs :—
Ashill, i 12.

Backwell, ii 305. Banwell, iii 568 ; Binegar, 412. Bishop's Lydiard, ii 493, 494. Bridgwater, iii 75. Broadway, i 18. Brompton-Regis, iii 504. Broomfield, i 72. Buckland-Dinham (discontinued), ii 451. Buckland St. Mary, i 20.

Camel-Queens, ii 75, 76 ; Castle Cary, 56 ; Chard, 472 ; Charleton-Horethorne, 357. Chedder, iii 572. Chewton-Mendip, ii 120 ; Chisselborough, 330 ; Corton-Dinham, 361 ; Crewkerne, 159. Croscombe,

Farnaby, Thomas, author, kept a school at Martock, iii 11.

Farncombe, hamlet in Doulting, iii 474.

Farnham, memorial tablets in Staple Fitz-paine church, i 60, 61.

Farr, Samuel, M.D., J.P., i *xliii*; analysis of Ashill medicinal spring by, 10, 11, 12.

Farringdon, hamlet in Babcary, ii 61; Domesday survey, 61; held by Hugh and Schelin: Alward and Bricstoward held it T.R.E. 61; owned by the lords of Babcary, 61.

Farringdon, lands in, held by William de Gardino, iii 186.

Farrington-Gournay, situation, ii 137; coalmine, 137; Domesday survey, 137; owned by the bishop of Coutances, 137; held by Azelin: Brismar T.R.E. 137; the families of Harpetre, Gournay, Ap-Adam, and Gournay, and the Prince of Wales, 137, 138, 139; church (St. John Baptist) and its monuments, 139, 140.

Farsy, Ranulf de, owned Road, ii 223.

Farthing, John, incumbent of Fitzhead, ii 492. the Rev. John, monument in Crowcombe church, iii 517.

Farthing, *alias* Ley, William, held a part of the manor of Lambrooks-Hatch, in Milverton, iii 18.

Farway, Joan, married Walter Stawel, iii 250.

Farwell, Rev. John, minister of Laverton, ii 212.

Fastrade held lands in Wells, iii 392, 393; and in Banwell, 566.

Fauconberge, Falkeberge or Falconbridge family owned Milton, iii 5, 6. and Hardington, ii 348. Peter de, son of Agnes de Arches, iii 6; William, 6; Stephen, 6; Walter, married Agnes Fitz-Simon, 6; Peter de, 6; Walter de, married Agnes de Brus, 6; Peter de, 6. landowner temp. Ed. I, i *xxvii*. Maud gave the manor of Hardington-Wytenine to William de Durnford, iii 6; Peter de, last of his name to own Milton, in Martock, 6; held also lands in Ash, 6. Sir William de, M.P., 1318, 1324, 1328, i *xxix*, 1344, *xxx*. Maud or Matilda, wife of Sir William de Falconberge, and sister of Robert de Mandeville, released all her rights in Coker to Hugh de Courtney, ii 341. Deed witnessed by Matthew la Warre and others, iii 259.

Fawconer, John, of West-Marsh, released his rights in Kingston and Huntleghe-Marsh to William de Carent, iii 207.

Fayland, in Wraxall, iii 155.

Fayroke family owned Berkley, ii 203.

Fayroke manor, ii 203; village depopulated: benefice annexed to Berkeley, 203, 204; seat of the Carent family, 203, 366.

Fear, James, subscribed to the charity-school at Chew-Stoke, ii 102.

Feckenham family, memorial stones in Kelweston [Kelston] church, i 130; and in Katherine churchyard, 141.

Felde, Nicholas de la, prior of Witham, ii 234.

Felton, hamlet in Winford, ii 320; owned by the Rodney family, 306, 320.

Fenhampton tithing, Norton-Fitzwarren, iii 271; held by John de Stapleton of Walter Meriet, iii 272.

Fenn, Ann, memorial stone in Brewton church, i 217; John, memorial stone in Kelweston church, 130. William, monument in Long-Ashton, ii 303.

Fenne, held by William Russell under Falk de Brent, i 253.

Fenny Castle or Castle, hamlet in Wookey, iii 421; castle formerly standing there, 421.

Fenwick, Jane, monument in Bath abbey, 1769, B 68.

Ferefelle, Martin de, held the manor of Fairfield of Maud de Candos, for knights' service, i 252.

Ferenberge (*see* Farmborough).

Ferenton, Robert de, received half of one knight's fee from William de Harpetre, ii 137.

Ferentone (*see* Farrington-Gournay).

Fermor, Richard and Anne, held Mudford, iii 221; John and Maud, 221; ancestors to the earls of Pomfret, 221.

Fermor, Rev. John Shirley, governor of Bath hospital, B 48.

Fern (afterwards Bramston), Diana, monument in Bath abbey, B 64.

Ferneberge family owned Farmborough, ii 424; William de, gave lands there to Keynsham abbey, 424.

Feron family (*see* Ferun).

Ferrers family, lords Ferrers, of Chartley, iii 40, 41. John de, landowner temp. Ed. I, i *xxviii*. married Hawise de Mucegros, and became possessed of Charlton-Musgrave, iii 37; and Norton-Ferrers, 40; Robert de, fought at Cressy, 40; Robert de, lord of Wem and Oversley, 40; John, married Elizabeth, daughter of the earl of Stafford, 40; Robert, married Margaret Despencer, 40. Edmund, woodward of Selwood forest, 1436, ii 195. William de, last of the male line owning Charlton and Norton, iii 40; Anne, his daughter, married Walter Devereux, and conveyed Norton and Charlton to him: he took the title of lord Ferrers, of Chartley, 40; John Devereux, lord, 41; Walter Devereux, lord, sold Norton-Ferrers to lord Stourton, 41.

Ferrers, Joan de, daughter of William, earl of Derby, married Thomas, lord Berkeley, iii 278

Ferrers, Sybill de, daughter of William Marshall, earl of Pembroke. Maud de, married (1) Simon de Kyme, (2) William de Vivonne, iii 462.

Fitzwarren, Bourchier, family, lords Fitzwarren, ii 391, iii 110, 271. William Bourchier, married Thomasina Hankford, and became possessed of Huntspill-Cogan and other manors, ii 391. created lord Fitzwarren, owned Norton-Fitzwarren, iii 271. Fulke, second lord, married Elizabeth Dinham, ii 362, 391. appointed Wigborough to be held in trust for the accumulation of dowries for his daughters, Jane and Elizabeth : owned also Huntspill, Novington, Norton-Fitzwarren, and lands in Pitney and Taunton, iii 111, 271. John, third lord, married Cecily Daubney, ii 391, iii 109. was created earl of Bath (*see* Bath, earls of). John, lord, died in his father's life-time, ii 391 : Walter, lord, 362.

Fitz-wido (*see* Fitz-Odo).

Fitz-William, Robert, held Ashington, iii 213 ; and Kilve, 532 ; Reginald, his son, 213 ; Joan, daughter of Robert, married Henry de Furnellis, to whom she conveyed Ashington and Kilve, 213.

Fitz-Williams, William, dean of Wells, 1540, i 190.

Fivehead, situation, i 40 ; quarry, 40 ; right of common on West-Sedgmoor, 40 ; manors of Fivehead, Staye and Cathanger, 40 ; Fivehead manor, owned by Roger de Churchill, 40 ; Domesday survey, 40 ; held by Bertran : Aldred T.R.E. 40 ; became the property of Muchelney abbey, 40 ; granted to Edward, earl of Hertford, iii 136. held by Thomas and Michael Henneage, i 40 ; owned by Mrs. Maria Acland, Thomas Chapple, and William Barber, 40 ; the church, 42. formerly held by Muchelney abbey, iii 135. inscriptions in the church, i 43 ; Beata Elliot's gift of £100, 42.

Fivehead or Fitzhead (*see* Fitzhead).

Flambard, Rannulf, held Woodwick, i 125.

Flat-Holmes island, iii 609 ; farm-house, 609 ; light-house, 609.

Flax cultivated at Stocklinch Ottersey, i 63 ; at Stocklinch St. Magdalen, 64. at Fitzhead, ii 492. at Samford Arundel, iii 25.

Flax-Bourton, "Hamleta de Burton," iii 161 ; lands here held by the abbey of Flaxley, 161 ; houses belonging to John Gore and James Sparrow, 161 ; Bourton-Combe, 161 ; Stancombe-spring, 161 ; a member of the manor of Wraxall, 161 ; passed through the families of de Wrockshale, Moreville, Gorges, Codrington and Bampfylde, 161 ; church, 161 ; saints' bell, 161 ; yew-tree, 161 ; cross, 161 ; John Doughton's benefaction, 161.

Flaxley abbey, Gloucestershire, owned land temp. Ed. I, i *xxvi*. in Regil, ii 321. in Flax-Bourton, iii 161 ; in Blagdon, 570.

Fleet, William, brass tablet in Selworthy church, ii 42.

Fleming, Erchenbald le, iii 543.

Fletcher, Thomas, monk of Hinton, pensioned, iii 368.

Flete, Robert, i 262.

Flexpool, hamlet in Crowcombe, iii 514.

Flintford manor, sold by Sir John Choke to Giles, lord Daubeney, ii 226.

Flood, Luke, monument in Bath abbey, 1768, B 68 ; Anne, monument in Bath abbey, 1774, 68.

Flora of the county, i *xvii—xxii.*

Flory, Flury or Fluri family held Cloford and Postbury, ii 205. Pyleigh or Leigh-Flory, in Lydeard St. Lawrence, iii 265 ; Ninehead-Flory, 267 ; Withiel-Flory, 295 ; arms, 267 ; Hugh de, held Combe-Flory, 247 ; Ranulf, son of Hugh, 247 ; held Ninehead-Flory, 267 ; Hugh de, 267 ; gave land in Hestercombe to Taunton priory, 235. Giles de, ii 205. Upton-Noble, held of the heirs of, i 227. John, ii 205 ; John, 205 ; Richard, founded a chantry in Cloford church, 205 ; Thomas, 205 ; John, held lands in Orchard-leigh, 205 ; John, 205. John, sheriff, 1418, i *xxxv.*

Flower family : Edward, married the heiress of Samborne, ii 220 ; Mawdley, Edward, Sarah and Edward, monuments in Nunney church, 220 ; arms, 220 ; memorials in Saltford church, 431. in Norton St. Philips church, iii 371.

Floyer family held Moorlinch, iii 429 ; Katherine, daughter of William, second wife to Humphry Sydenham, 523.

Floyre, Thomasine, daughter of John le, married Thomas Stawel, iii 250.

Fodindone (*see* Farringdon, in Babcary).

Folcheran held Claverham, iii 617.

Folcran held five hides in Winford, ii 320.

Folioth, Roger, held lands of the abbey of Glastonbury, ii 244.

Folkland (*see* Falkland).

Fontenoy, hamlet in West-Coker, ii 344.

Fonthill - Gifford, Wilts, land in, owned by Witham priory, ii 233.

Fonticuli (*see* Wells).

Forbes, Mr., owner of a field at East-Coker, in which Roman remains were discovered, ii 340.

Ford, abbey of, landowner temp. Ed. I, i *xxvii.* owned an estate in Winsham, ii 478. Chaffcombe, iii 116 ; Cricket-St.-Thomas, 117 ; Clatworthy, 510.

Ford (*see* Otterford).

Ford, Kent, lands in, owned by Richard de Placetis, iii 65.

Ford, hamlet in Bawdrip, iii 91.

Ford, in Bradford, owned by William de Forde, iii 244 ; Roger de Vernay, 244.

Ford, hamlet in Norton Fitzwarren, iii 271.

Ford, hamlet in Wellington, ii 485.

Ford, hamlet in Wiveliscombe, ii 488.

Ford or Foord juxta Winscombe, iii 613.

Ford family owned Ford, in Bawdrip, iii 91. Freshford, i 126. Otterford, iii 283.

Ford, monument in Broadway church, i 18.

Ford, Sir Adam, of Ford in Bawdrip, iii 91 ; founded a chantry at Ford, 91 ; arms, 91. Agnes, third wife of William de Vernai, i 253. Claricia, of Ford, married Robert Brent, iii 91, 435. Edmund bought the manor and advowson of Swainswick from William Schawe and Thomas Norton, i 153 ; monument in Swainswick church, 154. Edward, incumbent of Midsummer Norton, ii 151. Eleanor, 1732, Frances, 1745, monuments in Bath abbey, B 68. James, owned Norton Hautville, ii 108. John, owned Hadspen house, i 224. John, mayor of Bath, 1661, B 25. John, sheriff, 1781, i *xxxix*. Mary, 1749, Priscilla, 1743, monuments in Bath abbey, B 68. Richard, J.P., i *xliii*. Richard, mayor of Bath, 1713, 1730, B 26 ; Richard, monument in Bath abbey, 1733, 68. Richard, incumbent of Charlton-Mackarell, iii 193. Roger de, sheriff, 1222, 1225, i *xxxiii*. Thomas de, M.P. for Bath, 1332, B 19. M.P. for the county, 1340, i *xxx*. William, sold Norton Hauteville to the Rev. Nathaniel Ingelo, ii 108. William de, of Ford, granted the manor to Roger de Vernay, iii 244.

Ford's description of the procession to St. Mary's conduit, Bath, B 29.

Forde, Roger, abbot of Glastonbury, killed at the bishop of Rochester's palace, Bromley, buried in Westminster abbey, ii 253.

Fordham, John, dean of Wells, 1378, i 190.

Forest, John, dean of Wells, 1425, i 190. monument in Wells cathedral, iii 400.

Forester, John, held half a knight's fee in Stoke Pero, ii 43. Roger le, gave lands in Bathwick to Wherwell nunnery, i 121.

Foresters of the county, i 16, iii 55.

Forests : Exmoor, i *xv*, iii 57, 58. Keynsham, ii 399. Mendip, i *xv*, ii 233, iii 58, 373, 375. Neroche, i *xv*, 10, 16, iii 57, 113. North-Petherton, i *xv*, iii 53, 59. Selwood, i *xv*, ii 194, 233, iii 56. Winford, ii 320.

Forests, perambulations of, i 16, 63, ii 19, 195, iii 56—59, 373.

Forshefe park, ii 195.

Forster, Elizabeth, widow of William, married William, lord Stawel, iii 251. Richard, vicar of Long-Ashton, ii 299 ; buried in Long-Ashton church, 301.

Forte, Roger, lord of the manor of Curry Rivel, i 27.

Fortescue, Elizabeth, of Filleigh, married George Horner, of Mells, ii 463 ; monu-

Fortescue, Elizabeth, of Filleigh—*continued*. ment in Mells church, 464 ; arms, 464 ; Grace, married Sir Halswell Tynte, bart., 317. Hugh, owned Croscombe, married Bridget Boscawen, iii 469 ; Hugh, created earl Clinton, dismembered the manor of Croscombe, 469.

Fortibus or Vivonia, William de, owned lands in Somerset and Dorset, second husband to Maud de Kyme, ii 150. owned Shepton-Mallet, iii 462. Joan, married Reginald Fitz-Peter, ii 150, iii 462. Cecilia, married John de Beauchamp, ii 118, 150, iii 462 ; Mabil, married Fulk de Archiaco, 462 ; Sybil, married Guy de Rupe de Cavardo [*recte* Canardo], 462.

Forton tithing, Chard, ii 473.

Forward, Mrs. Isabella, memorial tablet in Weston church, i 162.

Fosarius, Girard, held lands in Ham, iii 444.

Fosscot, fair maids of, monument in Norton St. Philip's church, iii 371.

Fosscot (*see* Foxcote).

Fosse road (*see* Roman fosse road).

Fosse street, Bath, B 39.

Fossils, found at : Ilminster, i 3 ; West-Dowlish, 37 ; Fivehead, 40 ; Hatch-Beauchamp, 44 ; Stocklinch Ottersey, 63 ; Stocklinch St. Magdalen, 64 ; Swell, 65 ; Bath-Easton, 99 ; Combe-Monkton, 151 ; Weston, 156 ; Wolley, 167. Timsbury, ii 111 ; Marston-Magna, 374 ; Saltford, 431. Kingsdon, iii 195 ; Corston, 345.

Fosstoke (*see* Norton St. Philips).

Foster, Aaron, incumbent of Mudford, iii 222 ; and of East Pennard, 479 ; Edward, incumbent of Compton-Bishop, 583. Rev. Mr., incumbent of Bradley, ii 271. the Right Hon. John, J.P., i *xliii*. Sir Michael, judge of the court of King's Bench, married Martha Lyde, monument in Stanton-Drew church, ii 436 ; arms, 436.

Foston, William of, master (1349) of St. Catherine's hospital, Bedminster, ii 283.

Fountain buildings, Bath, B 38.

Founteyne and Newdigate, owned Wanstraw-Rogers, ii 229.

Fourneaux, Furneaux or de Furnellis family owned Merridge, i 245. Pury-Furneaux, iii 103 ; Ashington, 213 ; Brimpton D'Evercy, 214 ; Holford, 456 ; and Kilve, 532 ; Henry de, married Joan Fitz-William, and became possessed of Ashington and Kilve, 213 ; Matthew, 213. Sir Matthew de, commissioner of sewers, i *xii* ; landowner temp. Ed. I, *xxvii* ; sheriff, 1305, 1315, *xxxiv*. married Maud de Ralegh, iii 213. Catharine de, married Thomas Roche, i 263. Hawise de, married John Button or Bitton, ii 209, i 263 ; Simon de, M.P., 1328, *xxix*, 1345, *xxx* ; purchased Stringston from

Fourneaux, Furneaux or de Furnellis family--*con.* William Fichet, 262 ; married Alice de Umfraville, 262, iii 213 ; founded and endowed a chantry at Kilve, 532, 533.' Elizabeth, married Sir John Blount, and founded a chantry in the abbey of Athelney, i 262, iii 213, 532 ; Alice, who married (1) Sir Richard Stafford, (2) Sir Richard Storey, 213. Walter, second son of Sir Matthew, held one knight's fee in Holford of John de Mohun, ii 14, iii 213, 457 ; Margaret, sister of Sir Simon, married Sir Humphrey Langland, 213.

Fowel, Bridget, daughter of Mary Brune, erected a monument in Hill - Bishop's church, iii 256 ; arms, 256.

Fowell, Richard Bridgen, monument in Bath abbey, 1783, B 68.

Fownes, Henry, married Margaret Luttrell, and assumed the name of Luttrell, ii 13. Thomas, prebendary of Wells, iii 396.

Fox, Richard, bishop of Bath and Wells, 1492— 1494, iii 386 ; translated to Durham, 1494— 1502, 386 ; to Winchester, 1502—1528, founded the free school at Taunton, 232, 239.

Fox, Stephen, married Elizabeth Horner, and became possessed of the manors of Chinnock and West-Chinnock, ii 329. created baron of Redlinch, i 226 ; viscount Stavordale, iii 34. and earl of Ilchester, ii 329, iii 305. Henry Thomas, i 226, ii 329. Right Hon. Charles James, J.P., i *xliii.*

Foxcote family held Foxcote, iii 349 ; Herbert de, 349 ; William de, 349.

Foxcote or Fosscot, situation, iii 349 ; rivulet and bridge, 349 ; formerly called " Westone," 349 ; owned by Glastonbury abbey, but alienated before the Conquest, 349 ; Domesday survey, 349 ; owned by the bishop of Coutances : held by William de Muncellis : by Aldida T.R.E. 349 ; subsequently held by the Foxcote family, 349 ; held under the Berkeleys, 349 ; by the Giffards, 349 ; the Kingstons, 350 ; the Orange family, 350 ; the Smiths, 350 ; Sir John Hugh Smyth, 350 ; church (St. James) and its monuments, 350 ; bells (2), 350.

Fraine, Joseph, governor of Bath hospital, B 48.

Frampton family held Farley, iii 356 ; Joan, married Sir Thomas Stawel, 250. Mary, monument in Bath abbey, 1698, B 68.

Frampton monument, Bath, B 62.

Franca-Quercu, Milo de, gave lands in Lopen to the knights of St. John of Jerusalem, iii 122.

Franceys, William, sheriff, 1623, i *xxxviii.*

Francis, prior of Montacute, 1384, iii 313.

Francis, Sewall, M.P. for Bath, 1383, 1386, B 20. John, sheriff, 1595, i *xxxviii* ; William, sheriff, 1731, *xxxix.*

Francis, Ann and Joseph, inscriptions in Elm church, ii 207.

Frank of Trent, benefactor to Oriel college, Oxford, ii 382.

Frank, Elizabeth, wife of John Sydenham, iii 522

Frankland, Sir Charles Henry, monument in Weston church, i 161.

Frankleyn, John, consented to the uniting of Freshford and Woodwick, i 125.

Franklin, Samuel, J.P., i *xliii.*

Fraternities or guilds (*see* Guilds).

Fraunceis family owned Combe-Flory, iii 248 ; Lydiard St. Laurence, 266 ; and land in Donniford, 491. Henry, married Elizabeth Baumfilde, ii 90. John, of Donniford, iii 491. William, sheriff, 1707, i *xxxviii.*

Freame, Joseph Osgood, governor of Bath hospital, B 48.

Free, Rev. Dr., incumbent of East Coker, ii 342.

Free or Phreas (*see* Phreas).

Free schools (*see* Schools).

Free warren charters, ii 298.
[Obtained by every owner of land who wished to enjoy sporting rights on his own ground. Notices of them (71) will be found in the accounts of the different parishes and manors.]

Free-bench, custom of, ii 446.

Freeman, Francis, part owner of Norton Malreward, ii 109 ; Mary, benefaction to Queen's-Charleton parish, 418. Thomas Edwards, governor of Bath hospital, B 48.

Freemanors hundred, held by John, lord Stourton, iii 207.

Freestone quarries, Hamden - hill, iii 310 ; Doulting, 474.

Freethorn, Gefferey de, held North-Cheriton of Richard le Moels, ii 360.

Freke, Frances, married Sir George Norton, iii 152 ; Robert, owned the site of Montacute priory, 313. Sarah, first wife of Humphrey Mildmay, ii 75. Thomas, Philip, William, Thomas, of Bristol, benefactions to Preston, iii 224.

French, Thomas, owned a moiety of the manor of Buckshaw, ii 370.

Freshford, situation, i 124 ; hamlets of Shaston, Shrubs, Pipards, Park-corner, Shitten lane, Iford, i 124 ; Woodwick parish united with Freshford, 125 ; Domesday survey, 125 ; held by Alric and Robert : Domne and Brismar held it T.R.E. 125 ; given to the Carthusian abbey at Hinton, 125, iii 368. afterwards owned by Anthony Stringer, John Cheeke, John Davison, and the Ford, Ash, and Methuen families, i 125, 126 ; church (St. Peter) and its monuments, 126 ; bells (4), 126 ; Iford held by Alured : Teodric held it T.R.E. 124 ; Woodwick held by Rannulf : a monk of Bath held it T.R.E. 125.

Friar's manor, Over-Stowey, i 259.

Friaries: Ivelchester, iii 301; Taunton, 236. Witham, ii 234.

Friary-green, hamlet in Hinton-Charterhouse, iii 366.

Fridogitha or Frithogitha, queen, gave Brompton-Ralph to Glastonbury abbey, iii 505; persuaded king Ethelard to give Taunton to See of Winchester, 229.

Friend, James, memorial stone in Creech St. Michael church, i 78.

Friggle street, hamlet in Frome, ii 186.

Friseham church and hundred, Devon, owned by Montacute priory, iii 312.

Frog lane, Bath, B 37, 74.

Frome, Richard de, held lands in Pen, iii 44; William de, 44; Reginald de, held also lands in Compton-Pounceford and South Cadbury, 44. M.P., 1321, i xxix; John, sheriff, 1402, xxxv. Nicholas de, abbot of Glastonbury, 1420, ii 255.

Frome, its situation, ii 185; bridges, 185; markets and fairs, 185; cloth manufacture, 185, 186; statistics, 186; hamlets of Tytherington, Roddenbury hill, Friggle street, Little Keyford, Eggford, Oldford and Clink, 186; tithings of Town, West Woodlands and East Woodlands, 186; early records, 186; monastery founded by Aldhelm, bishop of Sherborne, 186; Domesday survey, 187; "Terra Regis," 187; owned by the families of Fitz Bernard, Branch (or Braunche), Winslade, Leversege, 187, 188; Thynne, lord Weymouth, 188; Seaman and earl of Cork and Orrery, 188; Vallis house, 188; Domesday survey, 191; the church (St. John), endowments in, held by Reinbald, 191; its monuments, 192, 193; endowments and benefactions, 193, 194, 196, 197, 198; Woodlands new church, 194; Selwood forest and its keepers, 195; lepers house, 196; almshouse, 196; charity school, 197.

Frome river: its course, i xiv, ii 195, 212, 222, iii 351, 362.

Fromond, Geoffrey, abbot of Glastonbury, granted a pension to Richard Saint-Barbe, i 199. benefactions to the abbey, began the building of the great hall and chapter-house, ii 254; procured a charter of free-warren for Mells, 463.

Fromund (*see* Fromond).

Froster, Rev. Thomas, murdered in Cameley, ii 157.

Frowd, Joseph, owned part of the liberty of Hinton and Norton, iii 365; married Ellen Robinson, owned part of the manor of Hinton, and the site of the priory, 369; owned Norton-St.-Philips, 371.

Frowde, Sir Philip, monument in Bath abbey, 1674, B 68.

Fry memorial stones in Drayton churchyard, i 39; in Brewton church, 218; in Cannington church, 236.

Fry, Peter, the heirs of, owned part of Barton, iii 613. Thomas, benefaction to Ubley, ii 157.

Frye, John, last incumbent of the chantry of St. Catherine, Frome, received a pension, ii 194. Robert, monk of Hinton, received a pension, iii 368.

Fulcran held Clewer, i 188. lands in Kingston-Seymour, ii 122; Backwell, 305.

Fulcuin held Sparkford, ii 87. Badgworth, iii 565.

Fulford family owned Brompton Ralph, iii 505, 506; members of, buried in North-Petherton church, 74. Thomas, sheriff, 1485, i xxxvi. Fulford, —, of Fulford, married a daughter of Sir Ralph Fitz-Urse, and became possessed of a manor in Williton, iii 488; and Brompton-Ralph, 505; William, 506; Humphry, 506; Florence, widow of Humphry, married lord Fitzwarren, 506; Sir John, 506; Sir Thomas, 506; Sir Francis, sold Brompton-Ralph to William Lacy, 506. Thomas, married Joan Malet, i 93.

Fulford, Thomas, master of St. Catherine's hospital, Bedminster, 1425, ii 283.

Fulgeriis, Ernulph de, married Maud de Vernai, i 253.

Fuller, Elizabeth, wife of John Acland, i 256.

Fuller's earth found at Mells, ii 462.

Fullerton, Sir James, owned part of the manor of Wellington, ii 482; granted it to feofees in trust for Sir Francis Popham, 482.

Fulling mill, Bath, B 33.

Furland, hamlet in Crewkerne, ii 159.

Furneaux (*see* Fourneaux).

Furnell family, lords of Lexworthy, i 95.

Furnellis (*see* Fourneaux).

Fuscot (*see* Foxcote).

Fust, Sir Edward, of Hill-court, married Elizabeth Mohun, and became possessed of the manor of Capenor-court, iii 145; Sir John, 145; vault and banners in Portishead church, 145.

Fychet, John, chaplain of Limington, iii 218.

Fydeok, held of the bishops of Winchester by William Tanfield, iii 242.

Fyndern, William, sheriff, 1426, i xxxv.

Fynes (*see* Fiennes).

Fysher, Robert, received a pension from St. John's hospital, Bridgwater, iii 80.

Fyshour, corruption of Fitz-Urse, iii 487.

Fytch or Fytche, Henry, rector of Lydiard-St.-Lawrence, married Dorothy Gatchell, and became possessed of part of the lease of Clavelshay, iii 73; Anne, married Henry William Berkeley Portman, 282.

G

Gloucester, earldom—*continued.*
Clapton, 177; Claverham, 617; Dinnington, 121; East-Lydford, 196. Holcombe, ii 456. Hutton, iii 590. Publow, ii 428. land in Tickenham, iii 165; Wellow, 326; Weston-super-Mare, 611; Winterhead, 601.
Gloucester, earls of, iii 146—148; Robert Fitz-Hamon, created earl by William Rufus, 146; owned Easton-in-Gordano, 146; was chief lord of all Glamorganshire, 147; Mabel, his eldest daughter, married Robert Mellent, 146. he owned Radstock, ii 457. Robert Mellent, married Mabel Fitz-Hamon, and received the title and estates, iii 146; built Bristol and Cardiff castles, and founded the abbey of Margam : a great benefactor to monasteries, 146. owned Bedminster, ii 280. and Brislington, 411; William Mellent, chief lord of all Glamorganshire, founded Keynsham abbey, which he endowed with the manor and hundred of Keynsham, 402; and Filton, 441; appointed Prince John, his heir, 411. legend of his abduction by Yvor Bach, iii 147; granted lands in Easton, Weston and Clapton to Peter de Marisco, 147; munificence to monasteries, 147; married Hawise, daughter of Robert, earl of Leicester, 148; had three daughters : Mabil, married to the earl of Evereux, 148; Amice, married to Richard de Clare, 148. and Isabel, married to Prince John, afterwards King of England, ii 411. he was buried in Keynsham abbey, iii 147, ii 403. Gilbert de Clare, son of Amice Mellent and Richard de Clare, succeeded to the estates : was first earl of Gloucester and Hertford, married Isabel, daughter of the earl of Pembroke, iii 148. owned Thrubwell, ii 315; founded a cell at Publow, 428. Richard de Clare, general, ambassador, and counsellor to Henry III, inscription on tomb at Tewkesbury, iii 148. he withdrew the tithings of Radstock, Babington, Hardington and Holcombe, which had formerly belonged to the hundred of Kilmersdon, ii 457. Gilbert de Clare, surnamed the Red, iii 148. landowner temp. Ed. I, i *xxviii.* married (1) Alice de March, (2) Joan of Acres, daughter of Edward I, gave up all his manors in England and Wales, but received them again of the king, iii 148. Gilbert de Clare, owned Hallatrow and Littleton, ii 148. was slain at the battle of Bannockburn, iii 148; his estates divided between his sisters, Eleanor, wife of Hugh Despenser, Margaret, wife firstly of Piers de Gaveston, and then of Hugh de Audley; and Elizabeth, wife of John de Burgh, and then of Sir Roger D'Amori, the last of whom inherited Easton-in-Gordano, 148.

Gloucester, earls of—*continued.*
Thomas le Despenser, owned Brislington, ii 412; Radstock, 457.
Gloucester street, Bath, B 37.
Glove manufacture, Yeovil, iii 204.
Glover, Thomas, benefactions to Somerton, iii 187; Sir Stephen, conveyed Ford to Sir Reginald Stourton, 613.
Goathill, situation, ii 363; lord Digby's park, 363; springs, 363; Domesday survey, 363; owned by the earl of Morton : held by Hunfrid : Godric held it T.R.E. 363; owned by the de Montacute family, 363; Thomas Montague, earl of Salisbury, 363; Richard Neville, earl of Salisbury, 363; John, marquis of Montacute, 364; the Stoner family, 364; divided : held by Baggart, Long, North and Hannam, 364; the whole manor vested in John Hannam, 364; owned by Henry, lord Digby, 364; church (St. Peter), 364.
Goathill mineral spring, i *xvii,* ii 363.
Goathurst, i 79; hamlet of Andersfield, 79; fine chestnut-trees in Halswell park, 79; origin of name, 79; Domesday survey, 80; owned by Alured (de Ispania) : held by Walter and Ansger : by Alwi T.R.E. 80; one knight's fee held by Hugh, son of Malger de Gaherste, 80; owned by the Poulet family, 80, iii 74. the Tynte and Jeane families, i 80; Halswell manor held by Wido, of Roger Arundel : Alward held it T.R.E. 80; mansion house of the Tynte family rebuilt in 1689, 80; building given by Sir Charles Tynte for use of the poor, 83; church (St. Edward) and its monuments, 83; bells (6), 83.
Gobrigge, Surrey, lands in, held by Richard de Placetis, iii 65.
Goda held Skilgate, iii 544.
Goddard, James, benefaction to Wellington parish, ii 484. Rev., incumbent of Drayton, i 39. of Barrow, ii 311.
Goddinge (*see* Goodwin).
Godebold received land from William the Conqueror, i *xxv.* held Quarum-Mounceaux, iii 556.
Godelege manor (*see* Gautheney).
Godelege, John de, dean of Wells, and commissioner of sewers, i *xii*; Richard de, landowner temp. Ed. I, *xxvii*; owned Gautheney, 240.
Godelney (*see* Gautheney).
Godely, Hameline de, granted Knap, in North Curry, to the dean and chapter of Wells, ii 178.
Godeman held Credlingcot, iii 331.
Godescal held Stawel, iii 431.
Godeve held one hide in Mells, ii 462.
Godfrey, bishop of Bath, interred in Bath abbey, 1135, B 67, iii 379.

Q

Golfyse, Johanna, prioress of Cannington, 1440, i 233.

Gollop, Thomas, of Strode, purchased Holwell from the family of Hanham, but reconveyed it to them, ii 369.

Golwege, Thomas, vicar of Chewton, official decree respecting the chaplains of Paulton and Farrington, ii 153.

Gondulph, William, grant to Adam de Cloptone, iii 140.

Gonnil held Claverham T.R.E., iii 617.

Gonning, Joan, married Edward Strode, of Downside, memorial stone in Shepton Mallett church, iii 465.

Gonuerd held Timsbury, ii 112.

Gonvile, Nichola, married Henry de la Brook, iii 302.

Gooch, John, prebendary of Wells, iii 397; Matilda, daughter of Sir Thomas, married Paul Cobb Methuen, 246.

Good, Joseph, incumbent of East-Lambrook, ii 469; William, of Middle Chinnock, author of "Ecclesiæ Anglicanæ Trophæa," 329.

Goodden, Hannah, wife of John Rice, of Coate, iii 10; John, benefactor to Martock, 11; Robert, of Compton-house, Dorset, owned large estates in Martock, 11. J.P., i *xliii*; John Culliford, J.P., *xliii*; Wyndham, J.P., *xliii*. arms, iii 11.

Goodenough, Smart, sheriff, 1699, i *xxxviii*. owned Blagdon, iii 285; his daughter married William Earle, 285.

Goodfellow, Charles, monument in Bath abbey, 1728, B 68.

Goodford, John, of Yeovil, owned Chilton-Cantelo, ii 339. John Old, sheriff, 1774, i *xxxix*; J.P., *xliii*; trustee of the Saxey charity, Brewton, 212.

Goodhind, Richard and Anne, monument in Whitchurch church, ii 443; arms, 443.

Goodman, Gabriel, monument in Chew Magna church, ii 98; owned Kilmersdon, 447; Mary, wife of William Hilliard, Sarah, wife of James Twyford, monuments in Kilmersdon church, 447, 448.

Goodman, John, dean of Wells, 1548, i 190.

Goodricke, Right Hon. Sir John, J.P., i *xlii*.

Goodson, Thomas, subscribed to the charity school at Chew Stoke, ii 102.

Goodwin family owned Stawel, iii 431.

Goodwin, Robert, owned Portbury-Priors, iii 142; Margaret, of Portbury, married John Wake, 168; Henry, owned Prior's-Wood, 142; and Charlton-house, 155.

Goodwin, Rev. John, monument in Lydiard-St.-Lawrence church, iii 266.

Goodwin or Goddinge, William, owned Puriton, ii 396.

Goodwyn, Thomas Wyndham, incumbent of Angers-Leigh, iii 241.

Goolle, John, brother of St. John's hospital, Bridgwater, subscribed to the supremacy, 1534, iii 79, 80.

Goose Bradon, a depopulated parish, i 16.

Gordein (*see* Gardino).

Gordon, George, monument in Bath abbey, 1779, B 68.

Gordon, James, J.P., i *xliii*; James, junr., J.P., *xliii*. owned Portbury and Portbury-Priors, iii 142; Portishead, 144.

Gordon, Thomas, translator of Tacitus: was secretary to Mr. Trenchard, and after his death married his widow, iii 154.

Gordwent, Edward, benefaction to Wells, iii 409.

Gore family, ii 311; arms, 311, 312; William, son of John, of Gilston, Herts, owned Barrow, 311; married Ruth Tibbot, 309; Mary, married Anthony Blagrave, 309; Sir Thomas, knt., married Philippa Tooker, 311; William, 311; William, who died without issue, 311; Edward, of Flax-Bourton, married Arabella Smyth, and became possessed of the third of the manor of Long-Ashton, 294; succeeded to the Barrow estate, 311; monument in Barrow church, 312; Mrs. Arabella, gift of candlesticks to Long-Ashton church, 304; monument in Barrow church, 312. John, son of Edward, J.P., i *xliii*. inherited the Long-Ashton estate and sold it to Sir Jarrit Smyth, ii 294; sold Charterhouse-on-Mendip, 235; owned Barrow-Court, 311. house at Flax-Bourton, iii 161; owned land in Christon, 578. Edward, of Kiddington, J.P., i *xliii*; owned Gautheney, 240. land in Bedminster and Long-Ashton, ii 282; Bishopworth, 284; inherited one third of the manor of Long-Ashton from his aunt, Ann Smyth, 294; married Barbara, daughter of Sir George Browne and widow of Sir Edward Mostyn, 311; part owner of Filton manor, 441. of Christon, iii 578. William Gore Langton: John: Charles, ii 311.

Gore, John, purchased the manor of Ilminster, 1684, i 6.

Gore, Sir William, married Anne, daughter of lord viscount Charlemont and widow of Sir Paul Harris, iii 69.

Gore, Mr., steward to lord Stourton, owned the hundred of Andersfield, i 71. held the bailiwick of the hundred of Williton-Freemanors, iii 485.

Gorepit manor, Stoke Courcy, i 252.

Gorewell, Dorset, belonged to the Wake family, iii 119.

Gorge (*see* Gorges).

Gorges family, of Wraxall, iii 156—158. owned Hill-house, ii 206. Charlton-house, iii 155; Wraxall and Nailsea, 156; Flax-Bourton,

Gournay family—*continued.*
son of Thomas and Eva, also assumed the name of Gournay, 185. lord of Harptree, Farrington, Inglishcombe, and Overweare, married Hawisa de Longchamp, and founded the hospital of Gaunt or Billeswicke, Bristol, ii 138, 309, iii 100, 340. Anselm, married Sibella de Vivonne, i 185. granted Farrington - Gournay to his son Thomas, ii 138; owned Barrow-Gournay, 309. granted Inglishcombe to his son Thomas, iii 340. John de, eldest son of Anselm, married Olivia Lovel, of Castle Cary, ii 53, 309, 138; Elizabeth, daughter of John, married John Ap-Adam, 138, 309; with her the elder branch of the family became extinct, 139. Robert, the second son of Anselm and Sibella de Gournay, succeeded to Overweare, i 185; Anselm, of Overweare, exempted from payment of customs, 184; Thomas, of Overweare, 185; Joan, daughter of Thomas, married George de la More, 185. Thomas de, youngest son of Anselm and Sibylla de Gournay, was lord of Farrington, Inglishcombe, and West-Harptree, ii 139, iii 340. landowner temp. Ed. I, i *xxviii, l.* Sir Thomas, had charge of Edward II after his deposition, and was accessory to his murder: escaped to Spain: was executed at sea and his estates confiscated and annexed to the duchy of Cornwall, ii 139, iii 279, 319, 320, 340, 587; Joan, daughter of Thomas, married Walter de Cadicot, 588. Thomas de, succeeded, held, under Royal grant, Farrington, Inglishcombe and West-Harptree, ii 139; effigy in Farrington-Gournay church, 140; John, of Knolle, 139; granted land in Knolle to Bristol priory, 284; George, 139; Thomas, son of Thomas, died without issue, 139; Sir Matthew, brother of Thomas, succeeded to the estates, 139; married (1) Alice Beauchamp, (2) Philippa, sister of lord Talbot, 139; was a great warrior, 139. held Swainswick, i 153. North - Widcombe, ii 118; Moreton, 133; Stawel, as part of his manor of Curry-Malet, 379. Telsford, iii 363; Shipham, 601; Stoke-under-Hamden, 320; inscription on his monument in Stoke-under-Hamden church, 320; arms, 320.
Gournay Slade, hamlet in Binegar, iii 412.
Gournay street, Cannington, the residence of the Michel family, i 232.
Gowdies farm, Weston, near Bath, i 159.
Grabbarrows tumulus, iii 487.
Grabbist hill, ii 48.
Grabham, Mr., benefaction to Taunton, iii 240.
Grafton, duke of, J.P., i *xli.*
Graham, William, dean of Wells, 1704, i 190.
Grain, price of, in 1317, ii 286.

Grainton, Hugh de, held lands of Glastonbury abbey, ii 244.
Graintone (*see* Greinton).
Grainville, Richard and Constantia de, founders of Neth Cistercian abbey, ii 21.
Grammar schools (*see* Schools).
Granado, Bernadine de, owned Middlezoy, iii 442.
Grand parade, Bath, B 34.
Grandison family owned Brean, i 178; Burnham, 180. John de, bishop of Exeter, had property in Pointington, ii 375. Otto de, went on an embassy to the pope, iii 245. William de, married Sibyll de Tregoz, ii 420.
Grandy, Juliana de, prioress of Minchin-Barrow, ii 311; William, purchased the site of the manor of Buckshaw, 370; William, sold the same to John Elbridge, 370.
Grant, Duncan, monument in Bath abbey, 1788, B 68.
Grant monument in West - Pennard church, ii 276.
Grantley, baron, J.P., i *xlii.*
Granville, Sir John, earl of Bath, B 83; Charles, earl of Bath, 83; Henry William, earl of Bath, 83.
Gratley, Walter de, prior of Taunton, 1361, iii 235.
Graunt, John, abbot of Keynsham, ii 402. Rev. Mr., incumbent of Stawley, iii 29.
Graves, Richard, incumbent of Claverton, i 146; owned Combe - Monkton, 151; monument in Claverton church, 148. Rev. Richard, incumbent of Kilmersdon, ii 447.
Gray, Robert, founder of an almshouse at Taunton, iii 238; monument in Taunton church, 238.
Graylake, hamlet in Middlezoy, iii 442.
Graylake's or Grilleck's Foss, iii 442.
Great-Bedwin, bishop Beckington's bequest to, iii 385.
Great Pulteney street, Bath, B 39.
Great - Wishford, Wilts, owned by William Carent, ii 367.
Green, John, benefaction to Wincaunton parish, iii 35.
Green, Rev., incumbent of Kelweston, i 129.
Greenaleigh, Minehead, ii 26.
Greenfield, Henry, one of the founders of Ilminster grammar school, i 3.
Greenham (*see* Grindham).
Greenly, Edward, governor of Bath hospital, B 48.
Greenoar, prior of, and the tenants of Chewton, dispute between, ii 116.
Greenslade, John, benefaction to Wellington parish, ii 484.
Greenway, hamlet in Thurlbeer, ii 183.
Gregg, Rev. Jonathan, J.P., i *xliv.*

H

Hallatrow—*continued.*
Sore, 148 ; the Rodneys, 148, 306, iii 603. the abbot of Keynsham and Sir Walter Romesey and Maud Basset, ii 148 ; Jacob Mogg and William Gore-Langton, 148.

Hallerhawes, rents in, owned by Christopher Simcox, iii 448.

Hallet, Edward, sheriff, 1741, i *xxix.*

Hallett, memorial stones in White Lackington church, i 69.

Halley, William, owned the priory and manor of Buckland, iii 99 ; owned Halse, 528.

Halliday, Edmund Trowbridge, J.P., i *xliv* ; John, J.P., *xliv* ; John, sheriff, 1746, *xxxix.*

Halse, anciently Halse-Priors, iii 527 ; situation, 527 ; Northay hamlet, 527 ; owned by the bishop of Winchester : held by Ailmar T.R.E. : granted at the Conquest to Roger Arundel, 527 ; subsequently owned by the hospital of St. John of Jerusalem, 98, 528 ; Alexander Popham and William Halley, 528 ; the Halley family, 528 ; Mr. Prior, 528 ; church (St. James), 528 ; benefactions, 528 ; bells (5), 528.

Halse, Walter, constable of Taunton castle, iii 228.

Halsey family owned Halsway, iii 545.

Halsway, iii 545 ; held T.R.E., and at the Conquest by Alric, 545 ; subsequently by the family of Halsey, 545 ; Stradling, 335, 546 ; Cade, 546 ; mansion and ruined chapel, 546.

Halswell : Domesday survey, i 80 ; owned by the Halswell family, the Tynte family, John Johnson, who assumed the name of Kemeys Tynte, 80 ; description of the house, 80, 81 ; Arthur Young's description, 81, 82, 83.

Halswell, Hugh, present at consecration of Wick Champflower chapel, i 219. Richard, married Catherine Gatecombe, and became possessed of Gatcomb, ii 302. Sir Nicholas, committed John Gilbert *alias* Gogulmere, for attempting to preach naked in North-Petherton church, i 266. sold Gatcomb to William Cox, ii 302. joined in the purchase of Honibere for the children of Sir Thomas Palmer, iii 534 ; Grace, wife of Robert, inscription in Portishead church, 145 ; Mary, wife of Christopher Simcocks, 449. Elizabeth, wife of Lancelot St. Albyn, i 265 ; Hugh, part owner of Broomfield, 72. married Susan Brook, owned land in Ashton - Philips, ii 297 ; Thomas, conveyed his manor in Ashton-Philips to Sir Hugh Smyth, knt., 297 ; Jane, married John Tynte, 317, i 80 ; whose son, Sir Charles Kemeys Tynte, married Anne Busby, and bequeathed Halswell to his wife, 80 ; remainder to his sister's daughter, who married John Johnson, who assumed the name of Kemeys-Tynte, 80.

Halywell, Jane, wife of John Trevelyan, iii 539.

Ham or High-Ham (*see* High-Ham).

Ham, in Bridgwater, iii 83 ; owned by Wigfruth and Ceolward, 83 ; granted to Athelney abbey, 83 ; Domesday survey, 83 ; hospital of St. John, Bridgwater, had certain rights here, 84 ; owned by lady Tynte, 84.

Ham, in Combe-St.-Nicholas, ii 475.

Ham, in Creech-St.-Michael, i 74.

Ham, or Monk's Ham, Marston-Bigot, ii 216 ; owned by the monks of Witham, 216 ; William, lord Stourton, 216 ; Sir John Thynne, 216.

Ham, in Pilton, iii 480.

Ham, in West-Buckland, ii 485.

Ham and Wemberham manor, in Yatton, iii 618 ; owned by John Pigott, 618.

Ham-Burci, hamlet in High-Ham, iii 444, 445.

Ham Gate, Bath, B 33, 34.

Ham-Green, Portbury, iii 142.

Ham-Hill, iii 444.

Hambridge, hamlet in Curry Rivel, i 23.

Hambridge, or Henbridge, hamlet in East-Pennard, iii 478.

Hamden Hill, i *xiv*, ii 334, iii 310.

Hame, Nicholas, received King-Weston from Henry VIII, ii 81.

Hamelden, Laurence de, M.P., 1307, i *xxix.* held land in Midsummer Norton, ii 150.

Hamelyn, John, sheriff, 1373, i *xxxv.*

Hamilton, Rev. James Arch., D.D., governor of Bath hospital, B 48.

Hamilton, Thomas, tomb in Bishop's-Lydiard churchyard, ii 496.

Hamintone, held one hide in Hardington, ii 453.

Hamlyn, Alexander, i *xl.*

Hamlyn, Robert, last abbot of Athelney, 1539, i 88 ; surrendered the monastery to Henry VIII, and received a yearly pension and the prebend of Long-Sutton, 88.

Hamme, Peter de, landowner temp. Ed. I, i *xxix* ; appointed deputy forester by Sabina Peche, 16, ii 19, iii 56. witness to a deed of Richard de Placetis, iii 65 ; held the bailiwick of Williton freemanors, 485 ; owned land in Low-Ham, 445 ; Peter, 445. Geffery de, chaplain to the hamlet of Atherstone, i 68. John, married Alianor Basings, ii 46.

Hammet, Sir Benjamin, J.P., i *xlii.* seat at Sherford, iii 294 ; gift to Wilton church, 294.

Hampton, owned by the bishopric of Bath and Wells, iii 394 ; ceded to Edward VI, 395.

Hampton, John de, M.P. for Bath, 1327, B 19 ; Robert, 1328, 1331, B 19.

Hampton, Richard, iii 588 ; Philip, married Alice de Cadicott, 588 ; owned Downhead and Stoke, 185 ; Richard, of East-Harptree, married Egelina Neville, 588 ; Sir

R

Hampton—*continued.*
Thomas, married Julian Stillington, 588 ;
Lucy, married Thomas Newton, 588 ;
Catherine, wife of Richard Perceval, monument in Weston-in-Gordano church, 174.

Hampton or Hanton family (*see* Hanton).

Hampton cliffs, Bathford, i 111.

Hampton-down, Bath-hampton, i 116.

Hamstreet, hamlet in Baltonsbury, ii 270.

Hanam, Roger, son of Thomas, granted lands to Robert de Chedder, iii 575, 576 ; Simon, 576 ; Joan, daughter of [Hanape, iii 303], married (1) Robert Chedder, 576, (2) Sir Thomas Brooke, 303.

Hancock, Philip, part owner of Lydiard-St.-Laurence, iii 266.

Handlo, John de, owned Upton Noble, i 227. John de, married Maud Burnel, and became possessed of Compton-Dando, ii 422 : Nicholas, his son, created lord Burnel (*see* Burnel) ; John de, married Maud Lovel, owned land in North Cheriton, 360.

Hanging-chapel, Langport, iii 133.

Hanging lands, Lyncombe, i 169.

Hanham, Ismayn, second wife to John de Raleigh, iii 537. James, married Mary Watkins, and became possessed of the manors of Holwell and Buckshaw, ii 369, 370 ; William, part - purchaser of the manor of Barrow Gournay, ii 309.

Hankford, Sir Richard, married Elizabeth Fitz-warren, of Huntspill, ii 391. owned Wigborough, iii 110 ; Norton-Fitzwarren, 271 ; and half a knight's fee in Quarum-Mounceaux, 556. Thomasine, married William Bourchier, lord Fitzwarren, ii 391, iii 110, 271. Elizabeth, ii 391, iii 110 ; Christian, married Robert Warre, 260.

Hannam family owned land in Goathill, ii 364 ; John, became owner of the whole manor, 364 ; Alice, of Evercreech, wife of Richard Walton, tomb in Baltonsbury church, ii 270, 271 ; Isabel, wife of John Abarough, of Ditcheat, 63.

Hanning family, tombs in White Lackington churchyard, i 69.

Hanning, John, J.P., i *xliv.* mansion at Dowlish-Wake, iii 120. William, J.P., i *xliv.*

Hanton or Hampton family, iii 565 ; William de, married Agnes de Mariscis, 565 ; William, owned Badgworth, 565 ; William, 565.

Hantone (*see* Bath-hampton).

Hantone (*see* Hinton-Blewet).

Hantone (*see* Hinton-St.-George).

Hantone (*see* Hinton-Charterhouse).

Hazlegrove, hamlet in Queens-Camel, ii 74.

Harbin, Anne, second wife of Baldwin Malet, i 94.

Harbin, John, of Weeke and Newton, married Bridget Drewry, iii 209 ; Robert, married Gertrude Stocker, 209 ; John, married (1)

Harbin—*continued.*
Isabella Pert, (2) Elizabeth Strode, 209 ; Robert, 209 ; William, married Elizabeth Wyndham, 209, ii 387. John, William and Wyndham, iii 209. Wyndham, J.P., i *xliv.* owned Sutton - Bingham, ii 350. Newton - Sermonville, iii 206 ; erected a monument in Yeovil church, 209.

Harbin, Margaret, second wife to Francis Warre, iii 262.

Harbord family, buried at Midsummer Norton ii 151.

Harbour, Samuel Alford, J.P., i *xliv.*

Harcourt, James, benefaction to South-Petherton, iii 113.

Harding, son of a king of Denmark, fought at Hastings : was governor of Bristol and owned great estates in Somerset and Gloucester, married Lyveda, and was ancestor to the Berkeley family, iii 275, 283. owned Capland, i 15 ; Dishcove, 215. East Cranmore, ii 208 ; wrested Mells from the abbot of Glastonbury, but was compelled to restore it, 462. owned Portbury, iii 141 ; Robert, his son, was called Fitzharding (*see* Fitzharding).

Harding, John, sheriff, 1752, i *xxxix.*

Hardington, in Kilmersdon hundred, ii 453 ; Domesday survey, 453 ; owned by the bishop of Coutances : held by Ralph : Baldwin held one hide, pertaining to Hemington, 453 ; subsequently owned by the Hardington family, 453 ; the heirs of John le Sore, 453 ; John de Pederton, 453 ; the Bampfyldes, 453 ; manor-house, 453 ; church and monument, 453 ; tithings withdrawn by Richard, earl of Gloucester, 457.

Hardington, or Hardington-Mandeville, ii 347 ; Domesday survey, 347 ; held by the king : Gunnild held it T.R.E. 347 ; subsequently held of the barony of Marshwood, and held by the Mandeville family, 347 ; Alexander Luttrell, 348 ; passed to the families of Fauconbergh, Wadham, and Strangeways, 348 ; the earl of Ilchester, 348 ; church and its monuments, 348 ; bells (5), 348 ; chapel converted into a weaving-shop, 348.

Hardington, William and Alexander, held Hardington, ii 453.

Hardington-Wytenine, owned by William de Durnford, iii 6.

Hardintone (*see* Hardington).

Hardistone Point, Porlock, ii 35.

Hardwick, Elizabeth, wife of (1) Barloe (2) Sir William Cavendish (3) Sir William St. Loe (4) George, earl of Shrewsbury, ii 96 ; bestowed the greater part of her estates on her second son, Charles Cavendish, 96.

Hardwicke, earl of, J.P., i *xli.*

Hardy, Henry, owned Blagdon, iii 570.

Hare, Anne, married Sir John Sydenham, iii 216. William, tomb in Staple Fitz-paine church-yard, i 61.

Hare, Richard le, held part of a knight's fee in Clayhill, iii 90.

Hare-cliff, ii 279, 439.

Hare-lane, ii 279, 439.

Hareclive and Bedminster hundred, ii 279; situation, 279; derivation of name, 279, 439; owned by the Crown: Osbert Giffard held a fifth: Turstin a sixth, 279; subsequently held by the Fitz-Hardings and the Berkeleys, 279; the lords of the manor of Bedminster, 279; parishes contained in, 280; John de Bretesche held land here, 314.

Hareclive, Gilbert, gave lands to Minchin-Bar-row priory, ii 310.

Harecourt, Richard, i 54.

Harepath, Long-Sutton, iii 197.

Haretre, Richard de, released his rights in Vex-ford and Ripenhole to John Catar, iii 547.

Harewell, Jane, of Wotton, married Sir Robert Brent, of Cossington, iii 435.

Harewell, John, bishop of Bath and Wells, 1368—1386, iii 383; built the south-west tower of Wells cathedral, glazed the west window, and gave two large bells and many costly gifts, 383; buried in Wells cathedral, 383, 401; arms, 383; appropriated Win-caunton rectory to Stavordale priory, 34.

Harewell, John, held Beer Crocombe, i 14; married Anne Middleton, 14; Elizabeth, married (1) Anthony Raleigh, (2) Leonard Rede, 14.

Harford bridge, Langton Budville, iii 19.

Harington family held Kelweston, i 128. Cors-ton, iii 346; Batcombe, 467. John, mar-ried Etheldred Malte, and became possessed of Kelweston, i 128; annexed the great tithes to Weston church, 160; memorial tablet in Weston church, 166; Sir John, built the old Roman house at Kelweston, 128; rebuilt by Sir Cæsar Hawkins, 128; monuments in Kelweston church, 129, 130; vault in the churchyard, 131; arms, 129; benefactions, 131; Sir John, translator of Ariosto's "Orlando Furioso," 128; James, author of "Oceana," 128; Phœbe, monu-ment in Weston church, 163; John, sheriff, 1591, xxxvii; John, M.P., 1642, 1654, 1656, xxxii; Rev. John, D.D., J.P., xliv. Henry, physician, B 46; governor of Bath hospital, 48.

Harington, Robert, lord, married Isabel de Loring, and became possessed of Porlock, ii 37. Elizabeth, married William, lord Bonville, i 56, ii 170. was cousin to John Luttrell, iii 500. William Bonville, lord, ii 37. married Catherine Neville, i 56, ii 170; founded a chantry at Porlock, 39. Cecilia, married Thomas Grey, i 56, ii 170.

Harington, Henry, prebendary of Wells, iii 396.

Harington place, Bath, B 38.

Harleigh, Malcoline de, landowner temp. Ed. I, i xxix; one of the king's commissioners for the perambulations of forests, 16, ii 19, iii 58.

Harlequin row, Bath, B 39, 74.

Harley place, Bath, B 37.

Harley, Right Hon. Thomas, J.P., i xliv.

Harling, Thomas, incumbent of Yeovil, iii 209.

Harnam, owned by the Hill family, of Houns-don, iii 196.

Harneys, David, chaplain of Idstock chantry, iii 90.

Harold, earl of Wessex, subsequently king of England, attack on Porlock, ii 35, 36; held North Curry, 178; despoiled the church of Wells, 497, iii 378; banished bishop Giso, 378. gave Wedmore to bishop Giso, i 189. owned Lullington, ii 212; Henstridge, 365; Ash-Priors, 497. Preston, iii 15; Stawley, 28; Old-Cleeve, 511; Dulverton, 521; Capton, in Stogum-ber, 546; Banwell, 566.

Harold, John, gift to William Woburne's alms-house at Yeovil, iii 210. John, received a pension from Brewton, i 214.

Harper, Archibald, benefaction to Wells, iii 411.

Harper, William Francis, and Robert le: the heirs of, held land in Camerton, iii 331.

Harpetre or Harptree family, owned Farring-ton-Gournay, ii 137; John, son of Azelin de Percival, assumed the name of de Harp-etre, owned Farrington and Harptree, 137, iii 587. William, gave half a knight's fee to Robert de Ferenton, ii 137; owned Rod-den, 226. garrisoned Richmont castle against king Stephen, iii 589. John, ii 137; John, 138; William, fined for trespassing in Henry II's forests in Dorsetshire: gave 100 marks to make his peace with Richard I, married Maud Orescuilz or Orcas, 138; and became possessed of Sandford-Orcas, 378; Pagan, 138; William, 138. Thomas, married Eva de Gorniaco, or Gournay, or Gaunt, sister of Maurice de Berkeley, i 185, ii 138; became possessed of Barrow-Gour-nay, 309. owned Inglishcombe, iii 340. Robert, assumed the name of Gournay, i 185. was summoned to Bristol to march into Wales: founded the hospital of Gaunts or Billeswyke, Bristol, married Hawisa de Longchamp, ii 138, 309, iii 340.

Harptree-East, situation, iii 587; hamlets of Coley and Shrole, 587; Sherborne farm, 587; mines of lapis calaminaris, 587; Lamb-Hill cavern, 587; Domesday survey, 587; owned by Geffrey, bishop of Coutances: held by Azelin Gouel de Percheval: Alric and Uluric held it T.R.E. 587; subsequently owned by the Percevals, 587; Harptrees,

Harptree-East—*continued.*
587; Gournays, 587; Walter de Cadicot, 588; Hamptons, 588; Newtons, 588; Scroopes, 589; Richmont castle, 589; Eastwood house, 589; church (St. Laurence) and its monuments, 589, 590; bells (5), 589; school house, 590.

Harptree-West, its situation, ii 140; Pileswell spring, 140; hamlet of Down Edge, 140; manors of West-Harptree Gournay, and West Harptree Tilly, 140; Domesday survey, 140; owned by the bishop of Coutance and Walter de Dowai, and held by Azelin, and Ralph, 140; by Edui and Eluvacre, T.R.E. 140; owned by the families of Tylly or Tilly, Rodney, Raynon or Roynon, John, lord Russell, Buckland, 141; and Goodenough Earl, 142; ordination of the vicarage, 1344, 142; church (St. Mary) and its monuments, 143; bells (5), 143; benefactions, 143, 144; yew trees, 144; West Harptree Gournay, 140; Domesday survey, 140; owned by the bishop of Coutances and held by Azelin: by Edui T.R.E. 140; owned by the Prince of Wales, 140; West Harptree Tilly, 140; Domesday survey, 140; owned by Walter de Dowai and held by Ralph, by Eluvacre T.R.E. 140; owned by the families of Tylly or Tilly, Rodney, Raynon or Roynon, John, lord Russell, Buckland, 141; and Goodenough Earl, 142.

Harptree (*see* Harptree, East and West).

Harptree family (*see* Harpetre).

Harpetrev (*see* Harptree, East and West).

Harris, Rt. Hon. Sir James, J.P., i *xlii*; John, dean of Wells, 1736, 190. Sir Paul, married Anne, daughter of viscount Charlemont, iii 69; Raphe, name carved on screen in Norton Fitzwarren church, 272. Rev., benefaction to Burnham, i 181. Wilmot, married John Trevelyan, iii 539.

Harrison, Benjamin, governor of Bath hospital, b 48. Thomas, owned the borough of Wellington, ii 482.

Harrison family, held the house and demesnes of Weacombe, iii 497; Alexander, built the chancel of St. Audries' church, 497; Ames, repaired it, 497.

Hart, Sir Richard, second husband to Elizabeth Pinnel, ii 98; William, 98, 99. Jane, wife of Robert Wrothe, iii 67.

Harte, Richard, received a pension from Brewton abbey, i 214.

Hartford, hamlet in Brompton-Regis, iii 502.

Hartgill family owned Kilmington, iii 40. Edward, sheriff, 1479, 1480, i *xxxvi*. William, one of the commission for the survey of churches, chapels, etc., at the time of the Reformation, ii 286. William and John, assassinated by lord Stourton, iii 40, 41;

Hartgill family—*continued.*
memorial stones in ·Kilmington church, 41, 42; John, Ferdinando, John, 42; Hartgill and Willoughby owned Norton-Ferrers, 41; arms, 42.

Hartland point, Porlock, ii 35.

Hartrow, in Stogumber, iii 546; Domesday survey, 546; owned by William de Mohun: held by Roger: Ulwold held it T.R.E. 546; held of the Mohuns, by the Hartrow family, 547; the Laceys, 547; the family of Rich, 547; the Rev. Bickham Escott, 547; mansion, 547; chapel, demolished, 547.

Hartsbridge, in Lamyat, iii 477.

Harvey, Edmund, erected a monument in South Brewham church to the memory of Edmund Hussey, i 222.

Harvey family, of Bridgwater, iii 82; Henry, owned the manor and castle of Bridgwater, and land in Haygrove, Durleigh, Chilton and North-Petherton, 82. Henry, M.P., 1653, i *xxxii.* leased the castle to Edmund Wyndham, iii 82; John, 82; Francis, 82; John, 82; Robert, M.D., 82.

Harvey family, of Brockley, ii 121; Humphry, 121; Nicholas, 121; Judith, memorial stone in Brockley church, 121; Elizabeth, monument in Backwell church, 308.

Harvey, Margaret, wife of Sir Amias Paulet, ii 167.

Harvey, Mercy, monument in Alford church, ii 59.

Harvey, Mr., endowed a hospital at Chard, ii 472.

Harvye, John, i *xl.*

Haseberge or Haselberge, name assumed by William Fitzwalter, of Haselborough, ii 331; William de, 331. baron in time of Henry II, i *xxvi.* William de, ii 332; Richard, joined the rebellion against king John, and was hanged at Sherborne, 332.

Hasecumbe (*see* Hestercombe).

Haselborough, situation, ii 331; river Parret, 331; bridge, 331; Wulfric the hermit, 1146, 331; Domesday survey, 331; Brismar held it T.R.E. and at Conquest, 331; William Fitz-Walter, whose successors took the name of de Haseberge, 331, 332; Marshall family, 332; Alan Plugenet, 332; Joan de Bohun, 332; Richard de la Bere and Thomas, his son, 332; Ingelram de Ghisnes, 332; John de Holland, 332; the earl of Huntingdon, 332; dukes of Exeter, 333; earls of Derby, 333; Portman family, 333; market, 332; church (St. Michael) and its monuments, 333; bells (5), 333.

Haselshaw, Walter de, dean of Wells, 1295, i 189. bishop of Bath and Wells, 1302—1311, iii 382; author of several statutes, 382; buried in Wells cathedral, 382, 399; ordination respecting the vicarage of Wemb-

Herlewin, abbot of Glastonbury, built a new church there, and gave rich ornaments, ii 250; petition for East-Cranmore, 208; procured the restoration of Mells to the abbey of Glastonbury, 462. granted Camerton to Sir Robert de Cotele, iii 330.

Herluin held Ashcombe, iii 468; Clapton, 177; Winterhead, 601.

Hermitages: Clarelewe, ii 428; Rownham, 296; St. Wulfric, in Haselborough, 331.

Herne, William, prior of Keynsham, subscribed to the supremacy, 1534, ii 402.

Heron or Hairun, John, married Emma de Placetis, iii 56, 96; and became possessed of a third of the manor of Newton, 69; John, 69; Hugh, 69; Margaret sold her share of the manor of Newton, with the advowson of the chantry to Hugh Garton, 69. Joanna, wife of John Dynham, i 22. Edward, owned part of the site of St. Catherine's hospital, Bedminster, ii 282.

Heron or Herne family, monument in Langport church, iii 133; arms, 133.

Heron hill, Donyat, i 35.

Herpetrev (*see* West-Harptree).

Herte, John, abbot of Athelney, 1525, i 87.

Hertford, Robert de, M.P. for Bath, 1314, B 19.

Hertford, Richard de Clare, earl of, married Amice, daughter of William, earl of Gloucester, who at her father's death inherited his honour and estates, iii 148; Gilbert de, their first son, earl of Gloucester and Hertford (*see* Gloucester, earls of).

Herun or Heyron, Adam, owned land in Ashton, ii 290. John, i *xl*.

Hervey, Edward, married Frances Luttrell, ii 13.

Hesding, Ernulph de, received land from William the Conqueror, i *xxv*; owned land in Weston, 160. Rodden and Tickenham, ii 226, iii 164. and land in the hundred of Portbury, iii 140.

Hestelshagh (*see* Haselshaw).

Hestercombe manor, Kingston, seat of the Warre family, of Coplestone Warre Bampfylde, iii 258; Domesday survey, 258; owned by Glastonbury abbey T.R.E.: granted at the Conquest to the bishop of Coutances: held of him by William, 258; subsequently owned by the Mohuns, 258; the Flory family, who gave lands here to Taunton priory, 235, 258; held by the Meriet family of the bishops of Winchester, 258, 259; the la Warre family, 259—263; the Bampfyldes, 263.

Hethfield, Talbot de, held Bossington, ii 38.

Hethmore, Glastonbury, ii 268.

Hetling Court, Bath, B 33, 43.

Hewardswyke, granted to Ivelchester, iii 299.

Hewis, ancient name of Huish-Champflower, iii 457.

Hewis, ancient name of Begarn-Huish, iii 540.

Hewis family (*see* Hewish).

Hewish, Huish or Hywis family of Linch and Donniford, iii 491; owned Newton-Hawise, 70; Sheerston, 72; descended from John de Hywis, 491; arms, 492; dispute with the Stradling family, 546; Richard de, owned Lud-Hewish, 541; Elizabeth, married John Dodington, 518; Oliver, gave lands at Linch to his son, Richard, 491; granted all his rights in Halsway, Donniford, Watchet, and other places, to Sir Edward Stradling, 546; Joan, second wife to Simon de Raleigh, 538; Richard, of Holnicot, ancestor of the Staynings family, 491; Oliver, escheator of Somerset, 491; James, of London, 491; Richard, founder of a hospital at Taunton, 237; and of scholarships at Oxford and Cambridge, 238; buried in St. Mary Magdalen's church, Taunton, 237; Roland, 491. William, of Donniford, ii 201, iii 491. Alexander, one of the editors of the Polyglot Bible: inscription in Beckington church, ii 201, iii 491; William, married Dorothy Sydenham, 522; George, benefactor to Chipstaple, 508; William, sold Donniford to Sir William Wyndham, 491.

Hewish, or Lud-Hewish, owned by the Hewish family, iii 491.

Hewish, hamlet in Yatton, iii 618.

Hewishe, granted to James Bisse, iii 467.

Hewish's charity, Taunton, founded by Richard Hewish, iii 237, 491.

Hext, George, owned Low-Ham, iii 445. Sir Edward, sheriff, 1608, i *xxxviii*. founded an almshouse at Somerton, iii 182; bought the manor of Somerton, 185; and Aller, 188; built a mansion and chapel at Low-Ham, 445; monument, 445; Elizabeth, married (1) Sir Ralph Killigrew (2) Sir John Stawel, 185, 251, 445.

Hey, Gefferey le, M.P. for Bath, 1311, B 19.

Heydon, Benjamin, dean of Wells, 1602, i 190. Dorothy, wife of Thomas Brook, lord Cobham, iii 303.

Heynes, Thomas, vicar of Long-Ashton, ii 299.

Heyron (*see* Herun).

Heytesbury, Maud, married Sir Giles Hungerford, iii 353.

Heywood family, monuments in Claverton church, i 148, 149.

Hickes family, owned Dinder, iii 413; Robert, 413.

Hickes, Adrian, benefaction to Wells, iii 410. Rev. Robert Adams, monument in Bath abbey, 1788, B 68.

Hickman, Edward, benefaction to Wellington parish, ii 484.

Hicks, Walter, mayor of Bath, 1683, B 25; 1695, 1705, 26; John, mayor of Bath, 1723, 26; Thomas, governor of Bath hospital, 48.

Hicks, Mr., of Stocklinch Ottersey, inventor of a horse-hoe, i 63.

Hide, Laurence, received part of the property of the guild of St. Anne, Croscombe, iii 470.

Hide, explanation of term, i 5.

Hidone, Osbert, and Geffrey de, gave Middleton to Taunton priory, iii 235.

Hiet, memorial tablet in Brewton church, i 218.

High Cross Conduit, Bath, B 31.

High street, Bath, B 29. Brewton, i 211. Wells, iii 375.

High-Church, in Hemington, ii 454; original parish church of Hemington stood here, 454; held by Thomas Flory, 454; owned by William Burleston, 454; William le Prous, 454; Hugh Courtney, earl of Devon, 454; one house only remaining, owned by Mr. Hill, 454.

High-hall farm-house, Mark, i 183.

High-Ham, situation, iii 444; owned by Glastonbury abbey, 444; Domesday survey, 444; held by Robert de Otberville, Serlo de Burci and Girard Fosarius: Leuric, Alwold, and Almar T.R.E. 444; manor granted at the dissolution to John, lord Grey, 444; owned by the Rolle family, 444; Thomas Galton, 444; hamlets of Beer, Henly, and Hays, 444; church (St. Andrew) and its monuments, 446; bells (5), 446; school, 446; hospital, 446; Low-Ham or Nether-Ham (*see* Low-Ham).

High-Littleton, situation, ii 145; hamlet of Hallatrow, 145, 148; coal mines, 145; Strachey's observations on the strata of coal mines, 145—148; Domesday survey, 148; owned by the bishop of Coutances and held by Roger and Ralph, Alwod T.R.E. 148; owned by the families of Gournay and Clare, Keynsham abbey, Jacob Mogg, and William Gore-Langton, 148; church (Holy Trinity) and its monuments, 149; bells (3), 149.

Highbridge, hamlet in Huntspill, ii 389; fairs, 390.

Higher-Odcombe, hamlet in Odcombe, ii 324.

Higher and Lower South-Town, hamlets in West-Pennard, ii 275.

Highmore, land in, belonged to Newton chapel, iii 65.

Highridge common, iii 140.

High-Ridge, hamlet in Dundry, ii 105.

Highwood, in Congresbury, iii 584, 585.

Higson, Rev., incumbent of Bath-Easton, i 108.

Hiley, Rev. Haviland John, monument in Saltford church, ii 431.

Hill, Charles, married Margaretta Tyndale, iii 263. Christian, monument in Haselborough church, ii 333. Grace, wife of Humphry Sydenham, iii 523. Joan, first wife of Sir Nicholas Wadham, i 48; Joan, wife of Sir John Malet, 91. Langley, governor

Hill—*continued.*
of Bath hospital, B 48. Margaret, first wife of Hugh Luttrell, ii 11. the Rev. Montrich, monument in West Camel church, iii 190. the Rev., incumbent of Chilton-Cantelo, ii 339: incumbent of Hardington, 453; owned High-Church manor house, 454; Richard, married Margaret Strode, of Parnham, widow of Thomas Luttrell, 12; Rev. Stephen, monument in Hemington church, 455; Thomas, subscriber to the charity school at Chew-Stoke, 102; W., churchwarden of Keynsham, 1685, 410. William, prebendary of Wells, iii 397.

Hill family, of Hounsdon and Spaxton, i 244, ii 457, iii 196. owned Asholt, i 237; Fiddington, 241. Radstock, ii 457. East-Lydford, iii 196; Poundisford, 287; Littleton, 447; Ludhuish, 541; and Radington, 542. Sir John, knt., married Joan Banister, widow of Robert de Alfoxton, and became possessed of Radstock, ii 457. held East-Lydford, Harnam, Pury-Fitchet, Asholt, Postridge, Durland, iii 196; land in Taunton, 233; lands in Wellsleigh, 405; and Wheathill, 450. Sir Robert, M.P., 1414, 1415, 1416, i xxxi; sheriff, 1409, 1419, 1421, 1422, xxxv; married Isabel Fichet, and became possessed of Spaxton, 244, ii 457, iii 196; bailiff and feodary of Taunton, 228. John, i 244, ii 457, iii 196; held Radington in right of Cicely, his wife, 542. John, married Margaret Rodney, i 244, ii 457, iii 196, 542. Genovefa, daughter of John, married Sir William Say, i 244, ii 457. dying without issue, the estates passed to her aunt Elizabeth, who married John Cheyney, of Pinhoe, i 244, ii 457.

Hill or Hyla (*see* Hyla).

Hill, hamlet in East-Pennard, iii 478.

Hill street, Bath, B 37.

Hill-Bishops or Bishop's-Hull, situation, iii 254; river Tone, 254; tithings of Hill-Bishops, Fidick, and Rumwell, 254; Domesday survey, 254; held of the bishops of Winchester by the earl of Morton: Alured held it of him: Eldred T.R.E. 254; parcel of the 54 hides of Taunton, 254; vested in the bishopric of Winchester, 255; Sir Francis Brian and Matthew Colthurst held lands here, 236; church and its monuments, 255, 256; bells (5), 255; Upcott, hamlet in, 256.

Hill-Farence, situation, iii 256; Domesday survey, 256; held by Alured de Ispania, and of him by Walter: Alwi T.R.E. 256; owned by the families of Ferun, 256; Vernai, 256, 257; Palmer, 257; Acland, 257; Allarford, hamlet in, 257; owned by the Allarford family, jointly by William de Vernai and Robert de Staunton, 257; held

S

Hordeghe, Argentine, gave lands to the chantry of St. John, Frome, ii 194.
Horsley-chapel, founded by John Horsey, iii 195.
Horstenstone (*see* Horsington).
Hart, Anne, owned a moiety of the manor of Churchill, iii 580.
Hart bridge, Ilminster, i 3.
Horton family, of Chatley-house, Wolverton, owned Road, ii 224; Edward, monument in Wolverton church, 225.
Horton, hamlet in Ilminster, i 4.
Horton, William, mayor of Bath, 1731, B 26; John, mayor of Bath, 1764, 1771, 26; 1790, 1791, 27; governor of Bath hospital, 48.
Horton mineral springs, i xvii.
Horwood common, iii 32. mineral spring, i xvii, iii 32.
Harwood, hamlet in Horsington, ii 372.
Hosatus (*see* Osatus and Hosett).
Hosed, William, held Tatwick, i 154.
Hosett or Hosatus family, held Charlecombe, i 141, 142; William, held Charlcombe, 141; agreement with convent of Bath, 141, 142; William, 142; Walter, a subscriber and witness to John de Villula's charter, removing the episcopal see to Bath, 142; Walkeline, 142. holder of half a knight's fee of the bishopric of Bath and Wells, iii 393. William, i 142. holder of part of a knight's fee of the bishopric of Bath and Wells, iii 393.
Hosiery manufacture, Brewton, i 213.
Hoskins, Henry, married Catherine Gold and became part owner of Seaborough, ii 173. Thomas, J.P., i xliv. William, M.P. for Bath, 1450, 1454, B 21. William, J.P. i xliv.
Hoskyns, Thomas, seat at North-Parret, ii 336; William and Joan, monument in Haselborough church, 333; arms, 333.
Hospitallers of St. John of Jerusalem, iii 96, 97, 98; sisterhood established at Buckland priory, 96 (*see* also St. John of Jerusalem).
Hospitals: Bath, i 42 — 50. Bedminster (St. Catherine's), ii 281—283. Brewton, i 211. Bridgwater (St. John's), iii 78—80. Chard, ii 472. Cleeve, iii 510. Frome, ii 196; Glastonbury, 262, 263. High-Ham, iii 446. Holloway, i 174. Ivelchester, iii 300, 301; Langport (for poor lepers), 132, 133. Lansdown, i 156. Maiden-Bradley (leprous women), iii 41; Taunton (lepers), 236; Taunton (county hospital), 240. Wellington, ii 483. Wells, iii 408, 409; West-Monkton, 456. Wiveliscombe, ii 492. Yeovil, iii 209.
Hot bath, Bath, B 42.
Hot and cross baths, Bath, B 33.
Hotchkin, Thomas, J.P., i xliv.
Hottune (*see* Hutton).
Hough, Daniel, married Senobia Malet, i 93.
Houlton family held Farley, iii 356; Joseph, 356; held Telsford, 363.

Houndmoor, hamlet in Milverton, iii 15.
Houndsborough, Berwick and Coker hundred, ii 323; formerly three distinct hundreds: now united in one, 323; ancient distribution of parishes, 323; derivation of names, 323; Houndsborough-cross, 323; Houndston farm, 323; owned by Glastonbury abbey, 323; Robert, earl of Morton, 323; Montacute priory, 323, iii 311.
Houndsborough-cross, ii 323.
Houndston, in Odcombe, ii 323, 325; owned by the earl of Morton: held by Aneger, 325; Roger de Petford held half a knight's fee of John de Mohun, 325.
Houndstreet or Hunstreet, hamlet in Marksbury parish, ii 426.
Houseden (*see* Houndston).
Housten, Sir Patrick, monument in Bath abbey, 1785, B 68.
Hove, Isabel, held part of a knight's fee in Clayhill, iii 90.
How, John, ancestor to the lords Chedworth, buried in Stawley church, iii 29; bequest to that and other churches, 29; benefaction to Radington, 542. to Luxborough, ii 26.
Howard, Anne, wife of Sir Edmund Gorges, iii 157; monument in Wraxall church, 158, 159; John, duke of Norfolk, held Farley, 355. Thomas, created viscount Bindon, ii 203; lord William, owned Thurlbeer, and sold it to Sir William Portman, 183.
Howe family, owned Huntspill-de-la-Hay, ii 393.
Howe, Grobham, founded an almshouse at Bishop's Lydiard, ii 496. William, J.P., i xliv; Right Hon. Sir William, J.P., xlii.
Howe, viscount, J.P., i xli.
Howel, John, part owner of Christon, iii 578.
Howse, Elizabeth, monument in Bath abbey, 1787, B 69; Henry, governor of Bath hospital, B 48; Henry Edward, governor of Bath hospital, B 48. Robert, owned Curland, i 23. Samuel, governor of Bath hospital, B 48.
Hoxham, Joan, wife of John Baumfilde, ii 89.
Hubba, Danish leader, plundered Somerton, iii 182.
Hubert held Kingston, iii 323.
Hubert, William, held land in Keynsham hundred, ii 399.
Huckmore, Jane, second wife of George Speke, i 68.
Hudleston family, monuments in Kelweston church, i 130; benefaction to the parish, 131; Rev. William, married Mary Burland, 257.
Hudson, Henry, monument in Bath abbey, 1789, B 69.
Huet, co-founder of Wobourne's almshouse, Yeovil, iii 209, 211.

Hugh held land in Ashway, iii 529. Farringdon, ii 61. Fiddington, i 241. Hinton-Blewet, ii 144. Plainsfield, i 259. Preston, iii 223. Tuxwell, i 245. land in Taunton, iii 231; in Yeovil, 204.

Hugh, the interpreter, held a house in Bath-Easton, B 17.

Hugh, abbot of Cleeve, iii 512.

Hugh, bishop of Lincoln, first prior of Witham, ii 234.

Hugh, prior of Montacute, iii 312.

Hughes, admiral Robert, monument in Bath abbey, 1774, B 69. the Rev. Edward, re-built the chancel of the church of Stratton-on-the-Fosse, ii 459; Rev., incumbent of South Barrow, 63.

Hugo held Bath-hampton, i 117. Rodehuish, ii 2.

Hugo-cum-Barba held Claverton, sold the same to John de Villula, i 146.

Hugoline, William, the Conqueror's interpreter, held Claverton, i 145; Warley, 112.

Huish or Hewish family (*see* Hewish).

Huish-Champflower, situation, iii 530; Domesday survey, 530; owned by Roger Arundel: Ailric held it T.R.E. 530; held of the Mohuns by the family of de Campo-Florido or Champflower, 530; the Verney family, 530; the Walshe family, 530; John Nethewaye, 530; John Norman, 530; Sir John Trevelyan, 530; church and monument, 530; bells (5), 530; cross, 530.

Huish-Episcopi, ii 470; situation, 470; rivers Ivel and Parret, 470; bridge, 470; hamlets of Combe, Pisbury, and part of Wearne, 470; manor owned by the bishopric, 470; village of Pisbury, formerly written Epse or Episbury, 470; Domesday survey, 470; held by Ralph de Limesi: Ulward held it T.R.E. 470; church (St. Mary) and its monuments, 470, 471. rating in 1293, iii 394; ceded to the king, 1548, 395; restored to the bishopric, 396.

Huish-juxta-Highbridge, hamlet in Burnham, i 180. granted by Sir John Luttrell to Richard Luttrell, iii 492; reverted to Sir James Luttrell, 493.

Hull, division of Taunton, iii 233; "recognition money," paid to the bishops of Winchester, 233.

Hull, Dorset, owned by the Wake family, iii 119.

Hull family, owned Ashill, i 12; White-Lack-ington, 67.

Hull, Catherine, daughter of Sir Robert, married Sir Robert Latimer, iii 321. Edward, M.P., 1446, i *xxxi*; sheriff, 1438, *xxxv*, 1443, 1448, *xxxvi*; Henry, M.P., 1466, *xxxi*; Sir John, married Eleanor Malet, owned Enmore, 91. Robert, held Edington, iii 433; Sir Robert, owned Stoket, 321; Walter de, canon of Wells, founder of the Vicar's close, Wells, 403.

Hulle, Alianore, owned Ashton-Lions, ii 291.

Hulle-Ferun (*see* Hill-Farence).

Hultemore, Glastonbury, ii 268.

Hummer, hamlet in Trent, ii 380; owned by Montacute priory, 382, iii 312. the Carents, ii 383; the Wadhams, 383.

Humphrey held land in Cameley, ii 125; Moreton, 133.

Humphrey, the chamberlain, received land from William the Conqueror, i *xxv*. owned Babcary, ii 60. Holton, iii 453.

Humphrys, James, part owner of the liberty of Hinton and Norton, iii 365; married Margaret Robinson, and became possessed of part of the manor of Hinton-Charterhouse, and the site of the priory, 369; owned Norton-Philips, 371.

Humphreys, Richard, monument in Butcombe church, ii 316.

Humylyte, John, monk of Bath, who received pension, B 57.

Hun, earl of Somerset, i *xlvii*.

Hundred pence, meaning of, iii 230.

Hundreds, why disjointed into parcels, ii 370.

Hundreds and liberties of the county, i *li*; Abdick and Bulston, 1; Andersfield, 71; Bath-Forum, 97; Bemstone, 175; Brent-cum-Wrington, 195; Brewton, 211; Cannington, 231. Carhampton, ii 1; Catash, 51: Chew, 93; Chewton, 115; Cranmore (Liberty), 207; Crewkerne, 159. Easton and Amrill (Liberty), i 97. Frome, ii 185, 211; Glaston-Twelve-Hides, 237. Hampton and Claverton (Liberty), i 97. Hare-clive and Bedminster, ii 279; Hill-House (Liberty), 205, iii 475; Hinton and Norton (Liberty), 365. Horethorne, ii 351; Houndsborough, Berwick and Coker, 323; Huntspill-cum-Puriton, 389; Keynsham, 399; Kilmersdon, 445; Kingsbury-East, 467; Kingsbury-West, 481. Martock, iii 1. Mells and Leigh (Liberty), ii 461. Milverton, iii 13. North Curry, ii 177. North-Petherton, iii 53; Norton-Ferrers, 31; Pitney, 129; Portbury, 139; Somerton, 181; South-Petherton, 105; Stone and Yeovil, 203; Taunton-Dean, 225; Tintinhull, 297; Wellow, 325; Wells-Forum, 373; Whitley, 423; Whitstone, 459; Williton-Freemanors, 485; Winterstoke, 559. Witham Friary (Liberty), ii 232.

Hunecote (*see* Holnicot).

Hunecroft, rent in, owned by Montacute priory, iii 312.

Hunfrid held one hide in Goathill, ii 363. Pitney, iii 129.

Hunfridus (*see* Humphrey).

Hungate, William, owned Baltonsbury, ii 269.

Hungerford family, iii 352—356; originally seated at Hungerford, Berks, 353; owned Aller, 188. Bath-hampton, i 117; Claver-

Hungerford family—*continued.*

ton, 146. Cricket-St.-Thomas, iii 116 ; Farley, 352—356 ; the site of Hinton priory, 369 ; land in Holton, 453. in Kilmersdon, ii 446 ; Lydford - West, 84 ; Maperton, 85 ; Pensford, 428 ; Publow, 428 ; Road, 224 ; Standerwick, 228. Telsford, iii 363 ; the hundred of Wellow, 325, 326, 327, 328. Wollard, ii 423. monuments in the chapel of Farley castle, iii 358—361 ; Sir Giles, married Maud Heytesbury, 353 ; Sir Walter, married Elizabeth Fitz - John, 353. Thomas de, M.P., 1340, i *xxx*, 1388, 1389, 1390, *xxxi*. son of Sir Walter, purchased Wellow, Farley, and other large estates, iii 352 ; fortified his mansion at Farley : married Joan Hussey, 353 ; monument in the chapel of Farley-castle, 358 ; Rodolph : Thomas : John : Sir Walter, 353. John, M.P. for Bath, 1338, B 20. Joan, widow of Thomas, held Farley in dower, founded a chantry there, iii 353 ; her will, 353 ; buried in the chapel of Farley-castle, 353. Sir Walter, son of Sir Thomas, M.P., 1408, i *xxxi* ; sheriff, 1413, *xxxv*. married Catherine Peveril, and became possessed of Wotton Courtney, ii 49 ; was lord of Heytesbury, and made a highway through the marsh at Standerwick, 228 ; keeper of Selwood forest, 195. held property in Normandy, served in the French wars, and filled important offices, founded two chantries at Farley, was buried in Salisbury cathedral, iii 353, ; Sir Robert : Sir Edmund, 354 ; Elizabeth, wife of Sir Philip Courtney, 355 ; Margaret, wife of Sir Walter Rodney, 355, 604 ; Sir Edmund, second son of Sir Walter, married Margery Burnel, 354. owned Compton-Dando, ii 422 ; Sir John : Sir Anthony : John : Thomas, 422 ; Sir Robert, eldest son of Walter, married Margaret de Botreaux, and became owner of Cadbury - North, 67 ; of Newton St. Lo, iii 343 ; and Shipham, 601 ; fought in France, buried in Salisbury cathedral, 355. Philippa, wife of Thomas St. Maur, ii 199. Sir Robert, imprisoned in France, fought with the Lancastrians, was attainted and beheaded, buried in Salisbury cathedral, iii 355 ; married Eleanor, daughter of lord Moulins, 355 ; Sir Thomas : Sir Walter : Leonard : Frideswide, 355 ; Frideswide, became a nun, 355. released all her rights in Rodden and Standerwick, and lands in Stockland and Camley to Sir Richard Choke, ii 226. Sir Thomas, fought first with the Yorkists, and afterwards with the Lancastrians, was beheaded at Salisbury, iii 355 ; he married Anne Percy, 356. Mary, only child, mar-

Hungerford family—*continued.*

ried Edward, lord Hastings, ii 67. and conveyed to her husband eighty - seven manors, lying in Somerset, Wilts, Devon, Cornwall, Warwick, Oxford and Buckingham, iii 356 ; Walter, lord, second son of Sir Robert, succeeded to Farley manor on the removal of the attainder of the late lord, 355, 356 ; married Jane Bulstrode, 356 ; Sir Edward, 356. Elizabeth, first wife of John Bourchier, earl of Bath, ii 391, iii 356. John, i *xl* ; William, *xl*. Sir Edward, of Heytesbury, son of lord Walter, married Jane, daughter of lord Zouch, iii 356 ; Walter, lord, married (1) Susan Danvers, (2) Alice, daughter of lord Sandys, (3) Elizabeth Hussey : was attainted for treason, and beheaded, 356 ; Sir William : Walter : Sir Edward : Mary, 356 ; Sir William, of Farley, 356 ; Sir Walter, second son of lord Walter, buried in the chapel of Farley-castle, with his son, Edward, 356 ; Lucy, daughter of Sir Walter, married Sir Anthony Hungerford, of Black-Borton, 356 ; Sir Edward, third son of Sir Walter, succeeded to the Farley estates, 356 ; Mary, daughter of lord Walter, married Thomas Shaa, 356 ; monument in the chapel of Farley-castle, 360. Sir Edward, M.P., 1625, B 21. Giles and Ursula, monuments in Wellow church, iii 329 ; Frances, wife of Sir William Wyndham, 490 ; Sir Edward, descended from Sir Anthony and Lucy Hungerford, owned Farley, 356 ; married Margaret Hollyday [Halliday, 356, note *e*], 356 ; monument in the chapel of Farley-castle, 358, 359 ; Sir Edward, knt., dissipated his estates : sold Farley to the Bayntun family, 356. sold Lydford to Edward Colston, ii 84. sold his property in Hinton-Charterhouse to Walter Robinson, iii 369.

Hungerford, Sir Anthony, of Black Borton, married Lucy Hungerford, of Farley, iii 356 ; Anthony, memorial stone in Hinton-Charterhouse church, 369.

Hungerford arms in Monks' lodgings, Bath, B 58. in the chapel of Farley - castle, iii 358—361.

Hunlavington (*see* Woolavington).

Hunstile, in Chilton, iii 88 ; Domesday survey, 89 ; owned by the Wigbere family, 89, 110 ; the Cogans, 89 ; the Bourchiers, lords Fitzwarren, 89, 111, 271.

Hunt, Dodington, J.P., i *xliv*. Dorrington, of Pitcombe, owned Sandford-Orcas, ii 378 ; Elizabeth, wife of William Bragge, 77 ; monument in Compton-Paunceford church, 77. Mr., married Mary Latch, who, after his death, married Mr. Plumly, iii 582. John, M.P., 1659, 1698, i *xxxii*, 1699, 1700,

Hunt—*continued.*

xxxiii; John, J.P., *xliv*; John, trustee of the Saxey charity, 212; the Rev. John, LL.D., J.P., *xliv*. incumbent of Kingston-alias-Pitney, iii 207; John and Katherine, monument in Yeovilton church, 201. John, owned Compton-Paunceford, ii 77. and Speckington-cum-Bridghampton, iii 200. Rev. Mr., incumbent of Compton-Paunceford, ii 77. Ralph, M.P. for Bath, 1417, 1422, 1423, B 21. a member of the Hunt family married Sir William Lacy, iii 506.

Hunt monuments in Compton-Paunceford church, ii 77; in Hinton-Blewet church, 145; in Saltford church, 431. in Yeovilton church, iii 201.

Hunteleghe or Huntley Marsh (*see* Marsh).

Huntersweye, ii 195.

Huntham *cum* Slough, ii 179.

Huntingdon, earls of, owned Stocklinch Ostricer, iii 115; Tickenham, 165; Stone, with the hundred of Catash, 203; Wheathill, 450. John Holland, earl of, held Catash, ii 51; Lydford-West, 84; Haselborough, 332; was attainted, but his estates subsequently restored to him, 332. owned Blagdon, iii 569. Richard de Holland, earl of, owned Haselborough, ii 332; John de Holland, earl of Huntingdon, and duke of Exeter, held Catash hundred, 51; Haselborough, 332. Henry, earl of Huntingdon, and duke of Exeter, forfeited Blagdon, iii 569. George Hastings, earl of, ii 67; owned Wotton-Courtney, 49; Publow, 428; Maperton, 85. Kilmington, iii 40; Aller, Aller Moor, and Combe, 188; Newton-St.-Lo, 343; Wellow, 326. Francis Hastings, earl of, married Catherine Pole, ii 67. owned Somerton, iii 185; and the chief manor of Congresbury, 585. Henry Hastings, earl of, sold Kilmersdon and Walton to John Spencer, ii 446. sold part of the Aller estates to Roger Bromely and Christopher Southowse, iii 188. gave advowson of North Cadbury to Emmanuel college, ii 68. earl of, J.P., i *xli*.

Huntleghe-Marsh or Marsh, in Yeovil, iii 207; owned by the Huntley family, 207; John Fawconer, released all his rights therein to William de Carent, 207; chapel (demolished), 207.

Huntleghe, Thomas, held lands in Adbeer, ii 383.

Huntley family held Marsh or Huntleghe-Marsh, iii 207; John de, 207.

Huntley, John, i *xl*.

Huntminster, ancient manor in Hemington, ii 455; held by William le Prouz, 455; depopulated, 455.

Huntsgate-Mill, hamlet in Wotton-Courtney, ii 49.

Huntspill, ii 389; rivers Brew and Parret, 389; farm of Pill's Mouth, 389; bridge, 389; market (discontinued) and fairs, 390; owned by Glastonbury abbey, 390; at the Conquest conferred on Walter de Dowai, whose son took the name of de Baunton, 390; Domesday survey, 390; Elwacre and Alwin T.R.E. 390. Huntspill-Cogan, owned by the Paganel family, 390; the Cogans, 390; the Fitzwarrens, 391; the Bourchiers, lords Fitzwarren, and earls of Bath, 391, iii 271. lord Stamford and Sir Bourchier Wrey, ii 392; James Grove, 392; William Arnold, 392; the Cockerells, 392. Huntspill-Mareys, 392; owned by the de Marisco or Mareys family, 392; the earls of Ormond, 392; James, earl of Wiltshire, 392; the Beecher family, 392; Thomas Ansel, 393; the Henlys, 393; part of the manor owned by Eleanor Maundrel and John Bere, 393; Richard Gould, 393. Huntspill-de-la-Hay, 393; Delhayes grange, 393; owned by Sir William Cogan, 393; the Delahays, 393; the Howes, 393; the Rodneys, 393; the duke of Chandos, 393. Huntspill Verney, 393; owned by the Verney family, 393; the Palmers, 393; John Acland, 393. Alston or Alliston, 393; Domesday survey, 393; owned by Walter de Dowai: held by Rademer, 393; Alwold T.R.E. 393; held of the Cogan family by the de Mariscos, 393; owned by Thomas de Drokensford, 393; John de Storteforde, 393; Walter Aldebury, 393; Robert Chedder, 393; the families of Newton and Griffin, 393; Henry Walrond, 393; Thomas White, 393; Thomas Jeane, 393; Sir Raymund de Sully held lands here, 394. Withy, ancient manor of Glastonbury abbey, 394; church (All Saints) and its monuments, 394, 395; benefactions, 395, 396.

Huntworth, in North-Petherton, iii 71; Domesday survey, 71; owned by Alured de Ispania: Alwi held it T.R.E. 71; subsequently owned by Jordan Ruffus, 71; the de Kentisbury family, 71; the Pophams, 71; the Portman family, 72; chapel belonged to Buckland priory, 72, 98.

Huntyngdon, Thomasine, received a pension from Buckland priory, iii 98.

Huntyngeye lake, in North Petherton, iii 59.

Hurcot, hamlet in Ilton, i 46.

Hurcott or Hurdecote, Somerton, owned by lord Grey, iii 186; Richard Henry Bennett, 186.

Hurman, John, benefaction to Ashcot, iii 426.

Hurne, William, incumbent of a guild at Shepton-Mallet, iii 465.

Hursi (*see* Horsey).

Hurst, Robert, enquiry into miracle worked at St. John's well, Wembdon, iii 104.

Hurst, hamlet in Martock, iii 2; name of New-ton given to part of, 3; anciently written Achelai, 8; Domesday survey, 8; owned by Alured de Ispania: Alwi held it T.R.E. 8.

Huscarl held Street, in Winsham, ii 479.

Huscarle, Nicholas, purchased Ubley, and granted it to Sir Thomas de Acton, ii 156.

Huse, Ralph, held lands of the abbot of Glastonbury, ii 244.

Husee, Hussy or Osatus family, lords of Bath-Easton, i 106; Shockerwick, 112. Walter, held one knight's fee of the bishopric of Wells, iii 393.

Husee, Henry, dean of Wells, 1302, i 189. monument in Wells cathedral, iii 401. James, M.P., 1341, i xxx.

Husei's court, Shockerwick, i 112.

Husey, James, M.P. for Bath, 1334, 1337, 1338, B 19; 1339, 1340, 1341, B 20.

Huson, Richard, rector of Claverton, i 147; memorial stones in Claverton church, 149.

Hussey, Edmund and Anne, memorials in South-Brewham church, i 222. Gefferey, holder of a knight's fee from Sir William de Mohun, ii 14. George, married Grace Dyve, and became possessed of Combe-Hay, iii 336; John, last incumbent of Bradford chantry, 244. Ralph, holder of knight's fees from Sir William de Mohun, ii 14. Robert, married Anne Cheyney, i 244. Thomas, owned Norton Hautville, ii 107; sold the estates to John Cutler, 108; Thomas, monument in Trent church, 385; William, owned Crewkerne rectorial manor, 162. William, owned Creech-St.-Michael, i 76; William, J.P., xliv.

Hussy, Elizabeth, daughter of John, lord Hussy, third wife to Walter, lord Hunger-ford, iii 356.

Hussy, Joan, daughter of Sir Edmund, second wife to Thomas, lord Hungerford, iii 353.

Hutchings, Rev. George, J.P., i xliv; Charles, J.P., xliv.

Hutchines, John, benefaction to Wiveliscombe, ii 491.

Hutchins, Rev. George, incumbent of Goathill, ii 364.

Hutchins, Charles and John, owned Sandford-Orcas, ii 378; John and Elizabeth (Medly-cott), his wife, monument in Sandford-Orcas church, 378.

Hutchinson, —, of Bath, owned land in Hinton-Blewet, ii 144. Edmund, monument in Bath abbey, 1791, B 69. Rt. Hon. John Hely, J.P., i xliv.

Hutton, situation, iii 590; copper, lapis-calam-inaris and yellow-ochre, found here, 590; owned by Glastonbury abbey, 590; given at the Conquest to Geffery, bishop of Cou-

Hutton—*continued.*

tances, 590; Domesday survey, 590; held by Azelin, 590; subsequently held of the earls of Gloucester by the Waleys family, 590; Sir Hugh de Langlond held lands here, 590; the Paynes, 590; the Stills, 590; the Codringtons, 590; the Brents, 590; the Coopeys, who took the name of Brent, 590, 591. Elborough, ancient vill, 591; owned by Glastonbury abbey, but granted at the Conquest to the bishop of Coutances, 591; Domesday survey, 591; held by Azelin: Alward held it T.R.E. 591; held by Joseph Daniel Matthews, 591. Oldmixon, 591; held of the Arthur family by the Wykes, 591; the Oldmixons, 591; Thomas Symons and William Doble Burridge, 591; church (St. Mary) and its monuments, 591; bells (5), 591; chantry, 591.

Huxham or Huckesham, East - Pennard, iii 478.

Huysh (*see* Hewish).

Hwatelei, William de, held lands of Glaston-bury abbey, ii 244.

Hycinge village, granted to Ivelchester, iii 299.

Hyde, Laurence, holder of the chantries of St. Andrews and St. John the Baptist, Frome, ii 194.

Hyde, tithing in Montacute, iii 314.

Hydon Grange, Temple-Hydon or Charterhouse Hydon, ii 236; owned by Witham priory, 236; granted to Robert May, 236.

Hydon, Margaret, wife of Josce Dinant, ii 362, [or, *Oliver* Dinant, according to iii 330].

Hyet, James, owned Edingworth, i 197. Joan, wife of John Arthur, of Clapton, iii 178.

Hygden, Richard, chaplain of the chantry at Catcot, iii 432; decree respecting, 432.

Hygecok, John, one of the jury to decide position of the city pillory, B 31.

Hyla or Hill, John de, holder of part of a knight's fee of the bishop of Bath and Wells, iii 393.

Hylbere, Joan, received pension from Buckland priory, iii 98.

Hylle, Robert, abbot of Athelney, 1457, i 87.

Hylle, Robert, steward of court to decide the position of the city pillory, Bath, B 31.

Hyndford, Cecily, wife of John St. Albyn, i 265.

Hypocaust, Roman, B 9, i 111.

Hywet, John, one of the jury to decide position of the city pillory, B 31.

Hywis, John de, of Linch, progenitor of the Hewish family, iii 491.

Hywish, Elizabeth, wife of John Dodington, iii 518.

Hywish, John, abbot of Athelney, and preben-dary of Long-Sutton, 1391, i 87.

I

Inge or Ynge, Hugh, chancellor of Ireland, born at Shepton-Mallet, 1460, iii 461.

Ingelo, Rev. Nathaniel, owned Norton Hautville, ii 108.

Ingelramn held Rodden, ii 226.

Ingepen, Ricarda, wife of Sir Thomas Fichet, i 244.

Inger, John, last incumbent of Trinity chantry, Bridgwater, iii 88.

Inglefeld, Francis, one of the commissioners appointed to sell Puckington, i 57.

Inglisbatch, hamlet in Inglishcombe, iii 340.

Inglishcombe, situation, iii 339 ; derivation of name, 339 ; Wansdike, 339 ; Round-Barrow or Barrow-hill tumulus, 339 ; Domesday survey, 339 ; owned by the bishop of Coutances : held by Nigel, 339 ; owned by the Harptree family, who took the name of Gournay, 340 ; the duchy of Cornwall, 340 ; castle demolished, 340 ; Culverhays-field, 340 ; Inglishbatch hamlet, 340 ; church and its monuments, 341 ; bells (5), 341.

Ingolsthorp, Isabel, daughter of Sir Edmund, married John, marquis of Montacute, ii 364.

Ingram, Esther, second wife of Sir Francis Wyndham, ii 387.

Inguar, Danish leader, plundered Somerton, iii 182.

Ingulfus, holder of Cathanger manor, i 40.

Inigo Jones, design for town hall, Bath, B 32.

Inman, Rev. George, incumbent of Burrington, i 204 ; family memorial stones in Burrington church, 205. incumbent of Withycombe, ii 48. incumbent of Rowberrow, iii 600.

Inrek, i 84.

Inundation at Kingston Seymour, ii 122.

Inweans, Ralph, held half a knight's fee in Knoll, and land in North-Stoke, iii 118.

Inyn, Sir John, knt., of Inyn's court, Bedminster, ii 284 ; owned Ashton-Theynes, 295 ; William, 295 ; left one daughter, who married (1) Robert Bowring, (2) John Kekewich, 295 ; Isabel, daughter of Sir John, married John Kenn, 295.

Inyn's court, Bishopworth, ii 284 ; arms on window, 284.

Ireland, James, sheriff, 1782, i *xxxix* ; J.P., *xliv* ; Rev. Thomas, D.D., J.P., *xliv*. prebendary of Wells, iii 396.

Ireson, Nathaniel, benefaction to Wincaunton church, iii 35.

Irford, John de, prior of Bath, 1346, B 56.

Irish, George, benefaction to Banwell, iii 568.

Irnham, owned by Andrew Luttrell, iii 498.

Iron forge (supposed) at Bickenhall, i 62. at Exford, ii 21.

Iroys, Adam le, held Burton, iii 567, 596 ; Philip, 596.

Isaac, Baptist, vicar of Henstridge, married (1) Mary Weston, (2) Jenny Wright, ii 368 ; monument in Henstridge church, 368.

Isabel's mill, Bath, B 57.

Iscbalis or Iscalis, Roman name of Ivelchester, i *xxiii*, iii 298.

Isham, Susanna, monument in Bath abbey, 1726, B 69.

Isle of Nobles, Athelney, i 86.

Isle, Robert de, abbot of Athelney, 1325, i 87. William de, held the chief manor in Wanstraw, ii 229.

Isle-Abbots, derivation of its name, i 50 ; situation, 50 ; right of common in Neroche forest, and on West Sedgmoor, 50 : owned by the abbots of Muchelney, 50 ; Domesday survey, 50 ; held by Goduin and Eduin T.R.E. 50 ; Portman family, 51 ; earl of Hertford, 51 ; Pryme [Prynne] family, 51 ; lady Aylesford and Mr. Pine, 51 ; church (St. Mary), 51 ; appropriated to Muchelney abbey, but now in patronage of dean and chapter of Bristol, 51 ; inscriptions in the church, 51, 52 ; bells (5), 51.

Isle-Brewers, situation, i 52 ; rights on Ilemoor, 52 ; revel, 53 ; the village divided by William the Conqueror, 53 ; and given to Robert, earl of Morton, and Alured de Ispania, 53 ; Domesday survey, 53 ; held by Ansger and Richard, 53 ; Ulnod and Alwi T.R.E. 53 ; forfeited by William, earl of Morton's son, and held by the Crown, 53 ; held by William Torel, who was fined for neglecting to make proper enquiry respecting the death of Alured de Aneville, 53 ; held by the Briwere or Brewer family, 53 ; de Mohun family, 54 ; Thomas de Merleberghe, 54 ; Henry de Haddon, 54 ; William Fitzwarren, 54 ; John Chideock, 54 ; Catherine Stafford and Margaret Stourton, 54 ; Giles Daubeny, 54 ; Laurence Wyther, 54 ; the Walronds, 54 ; David Robert Mitchel, 54 ; James Bowerman, 54 ; the church appropriated to William Brewer's hospital of St. John, Bridgwater, 54 ; chantry founded by Thomas de Merleberge, 55 ; church (All Saints), 54 ; bells (4), 54.

Ispania, Alured de, received land from William the Conqueror, i *xxv* ; owned Alfoxton, 264. Denesmodeswelle, iii 183 ; Dodington, 518 ; East-Bower, 84. Goathurst, i 80. Hill-Farence, iii 256 ; Huntworth, 71 ; Hurst (Achelai), in Martock, 8. Isle-Brewers, i 53. Luckington, ii 446. Merridge, i 244. Monksilver, iii 534 ; Mounceaux castle, 529. Otterhampton, i 242 ; Over Stowey, 259 ; Plainsfield, 259. Preston-Plucknet, iii 223. Radlet, i 245 ; Spaxton, 243. Stawley, iii 28. Stringston, i 261. Wolmersdon, iii 71.

J

Joyce, Mrs. Mary, benefaction to the abbey, Bath, B 71.

Joyner, David, abbot of Cleeve, 1438, iii 512.

Jubbe family, of Jubbe's court, seat at Faylands, iii 155.

Judde, Thomas, conveyed Ford to John Mawdley, iii 613.

Juliers, Elizabeth, countess of Kent, owned land in Somerton-Randolf, iii 185.

Julius Vitalis, monumental stone, B 7, 8.

Jumieges, abbot of, held Chewton Mendip church, ii 116, 118.

Justices of the Peace for Somerset, 1787, i *xl.*

K

Kally-hill, hamlet in Wookey, iii 421.

Karnicke, Thomas, dean of Wells, 1413, i 190.

Katherine, situation, i 138; Holt down, 138; owned by the monks of Bath, 138; description of Katherine's court in time of Henry VIII, 138; given to John Malte and Etheldred Malte (or Dyngley), 138; owned by the Blanchards, James Walters, 138; Thomas Parry, 139; the church and its monuments, 139, 140, 141; bells (4), 139.

Katherine-hill, Frome, where was a small cell of nuns, ii 187.

Katherine lands (*see* Catherine).

Kaynes, Robert, received license to grant lands to a chaplain in Frome, ii 193.

Kayton, Richard, released his right to Standerwick to William, lord Botreaux, ii 228.

Keate, Mrs., wife of the Rev. Mr. Wightwick, ii 65; Thomas, monument in Huish Episcopi church, 470, 471; Rev. Mr., incumbent of Laverton, 211; Rev. Mr., owned Bradley, 271. Rev. William, married Anne Burland, i 257. prebendary of Wells, iii 397; incumbent of Wookey, 421.

Keedwell, Thomas, owned Blagdon, iii 570.

Keene, Francis, constable of Taunton castle, iii 228.

Keines family, owned West - Dowlish, i 37; John de, 37; Thomas, 37; John, 37; John, 37; John, 37; Joan, married John Speke, 38.

Kellaway, Lora, second wife of Sir Amias Paulet, ii 167.

Kelleway, John, married Joan Tregarthin, i 48; Joan, widow of John, married John Wadham, of Edge, 48.

Kelly, John, held Alhampton, iii 472. John, married Joan Paulton, ii 112; Joan, wife of John, owned part of the Paulton estates, 152; owned lands in Holcombe, 456. lands in Camerton, iii 330, 331; Thomas, 331; Edith, wife of Humphry Calwodelegh, 331; William, 331; Margaret, wife of Michael Kelly, 331; a daughter of William married John Carew, 331.

Kelly, Michael, married Margaret Kelly, iii 331.

Kelston round-hill, Kelweston, i 127.

Kelveston (*see* Kelweston).

Kelway, Giles, i 3. Robert, one of the commissioners for the survey of churches,

Kelway—*continued.*
chapels, etc., in Somerset, at the time of the Reformation, ii 286.

Kelweston [Kelston], situation, i 127; Combesbrook, 127; Henstridge-hill, 127; owned by the abbey of Shaftesbury, and charter of free warren procured by abbess Mabel Gifford, 127; granted by Henry VIII to John Malte and Etheldred Malte (or Dyngley), who married John Harington, 128; Cæsar Hawkins, 128; the Harington family, 128; church (St. Nicholas) and its monuments, 129, 130, 131; bells (4), 129; benefactions to the parish, 131.

Kemeys, Jane, daughter of Sir Charles, married Sir John Tynte, ii 317.

Kemish, Sarah, wife of Walter, inscription in Portbury church, iii 143; arms, 143.

Kemp, William, rector of Puddimore-Milton, iii 451.

Kempe, Thomas, married Amy Moyle, ii 81; Thomas, succeeded to the King Weston estates, and sold them to Matthew Smyth, 81.

Kemys, Roger, owned lands in Swainswick, i 153. Roger, married Alice Arthur, of Bishopworth, iii 178; Mrs. —, owned Naish-house and Dunhills, 179.

Kencot cross, Long-Ashton, ii 304.

Kencot, hamlet in Long-Ashton, ii 291, 304.

Ken (*see* Kenn).

Kene, Hugh, granted Skilgate to Abbotsbury abbey, iii 545.

Kenewalch, king of Wessex, enriched Glastonbury abbey, ii 241; granted Mere, Godney and Westhay to the abbey, 272. granted Andredsey to the abbey, iii 605.

Kenilworth, St. Mary's church at, received from Richard de Camville the church of Charleton-Horethorne, ii 356.

Kenn, situation, iii 592; Ken-moor, 592; river, 592; Domesday survey, 592; owned by the bishop of Coutances, 592; subsequently held of the bishop of Bath by the Ken family, 592; the earls Poulett, 593; Colehouse, owned by Mr. Willoughby, 593; church and its monuments, 593; bell (1), 593.

Kenn or Ken family, of Kenn, iii 592. held lands in Kingston Seymour, ii 123; owned Inyn's court, Bishopworth, 284. Court de

Kenn or Ken family, of Kenn—*continued.*
Wick, iii 268; Yatton, 617; arms, 169, 592; John, de, held two knights' fees of the bishops of Bath and Wells, 592. Richard de, landowner temp. Ed. I, i *xxviii.* married Joan de Wengham, ii 122. suit with Matthew de Clevedon, iii 167, 592; Sir Richard, knt., 592; Sir John de, knt., 592; John de, 592; John de, 592. Robert, held lands in Kingston Seymour, ii 123. was of Kenn, iii 592. John, ii 123. arms of, iii 592; John, 592. married Isabel Inyn, ii 295. John de, married (1) — May, (2) Margaret Baynham, iii 592; Thomas, second son of John, married a daughter of — Speke, 592; John, third son of John, was of Clevedon, 592; monument in Clevedon church, 168; Edmund, of Hutton, married — Strode, 592. John, grandson of John and Isabel Inyn, owned Ashton-Theynes, ii 295. Christopher, sheriff, 1575, i *xxxvii.* owned lands in Kingston Seymour, ii 123; Inyn's court, 284; sold Ashton Theynes to William Clerk, 295. owned Walton-in-Gordano, iii 170; owned Kenn, 592; Florence, widow of Christopher, married Sir Nicholas Stalling, 592; Margaret, married William Guise, 593. Elizabeth, wife of John Poulett, ii 167, 284, iii 170, 593; Elizabeth, third wife of James Perceval, 175; Joan, daughter of John, wife of Sir James Perceval, 175; a daughter of Ken, of Ken, married Sir Thomas Arthur, 178; monument to Christopher and dame Florence in Kenn church, 593.
Kenn, Thomas, bishop of Bath and Wells, 1684—1691, iii 389; descended from the Kenns, of Kenn-court, 389; education: offices held by, 389; created bishop, 389; was a zealous Anti-Papist: imprisoned in the tower for opposition to the declaration of indulgence, 390; on the accession of William III, gave up his bishopric and retired to Longleat, 390; author of several works, 390; buried at Frome, 390, ii 193.
Kenn moor, i *xv,* iii 592.
Kennard moor, i *xv.*
Kenne, Hugh, held lands in Ash and Witcombe, iii 6; Agnes, 6; William, 6; Anthony, 7.
Kenning, Rev. Robert, monument in Kelweston church, i 130; benefactions to the parish, 130, 131.
Kent, Ambrose, D.D., J.P., i *xliv.* incumbent of Berkley, ii 204; Anne, wife of Nathaniel Kent, inscription in Berkley church, 204; Rev. Thomas, memorial inscription in Clutton church, 104.
Kent, earls of, tenants of Queens Camel, ii 74. John de Woodstock, earl of, held Somerton, Kingsbury and East - Camel, iii 184; Thomas Holland, earl of, married Joan the

Kent, earls of—*continued.*
fair, grand-daughter of Edward I, 281; Joan, widow of Thomas, married Edward the Black Prince, 282; Elizabeth Juliers, countess of, owned land in Somerton Randolf, 185. Elizabeth, widow of John Holland, earl of, held two knights' fees in Berwick, ii 338.
Kentisbury family, owned Huntworth, iii 71; Walter de, married Julyan Ruffus, and so became possessed of that estate, 71; Sir Walter, knt., 71; Sir Stephen, 71; Joan, married (1) Sir John Trivet, (2) Sir Hugh de Popham, to whom she brought the estate, 71.
Kenton-Mandevill, its situation, ii 78: stone quarries, 78; Domesday survey, 78; owned by earl Morton, and held by Malger, 78; owned by the family of Mandeville, 79; church (St. Mary Magdalen) and its monuments, 79, 80; bells (3), 79.
Kentsford, hamlet in St. Decumans, iii 492; owned by John de Mohun, 492; held by the Basings family, 492; the Luttrells, 492; the Wyndhams, 492; William Blackford, 493.
Kentwine, king, enriched Glastonbury abbey, ii 241; consented to the grant of Leigh to the abbey, 465. granted West-Monkton to the abbey, iii 454. buried at Glastonbury, ii 262.
Kenulph, king, gave Houndsborough to Tican, abbot of Glastonbury, ii 323.
Kenyon, Rt. Hon. Sir Lloyd, J.P., i *xlii.*
Keredic, a British king, ii 2.
Kersey cloth manufacture, Dunster, ii 16.
Kew-Stoke, situation, iii 593; Worle-hill, 593; St. Kew, 593; Milton hamlet, 593; Swallow-cliff, 594; Woodspring or Worspring priory, 594 — 596; Norton hamlet, 596; Sand hamlet, 596; Burton hamlet, held by the Iroys family, 596; by Thomas de Lyons, 596; church (St. Paul), 596; bells (5), 596; the daughters of Geffrey Vassell held half a knight's fee here, 567.
Kew street, iii 593.
Keyford or Cayford, in Frome, ii 189; Domesday survey, 189; owned by Turstin Fitz-Rolf: held by Norman: Leuedai held it T.R.E. 189; subsequently owned by William Polayn, 189; the Twyniho or Twiney family, 189, iii 328. curious petition concerning Ankarette Twyniho, ii 189.
Keylle, Sir Richard, held the fifth part of a knight's fee in Tickenham, iii 165.
Keyna, the virgin, legend of, ii 400, 401.
Keynes family, owned Compton Martin, ii 132. Cudworth, iii 117; East and West Dowlish, 119; arms, 120; monuments in Dowlish-Wake church, 120; John de, married Isabel Wake, and became possessed of

Kittisford : situation, iii 24 ; river Tone, 24 ; Domesday survey, 24 ; owned by Roger Arundel : held by William : Osmund Stramun held it T.R.E. 24 ; successively owned by the families of de Kittisford, 24 ; Sydenham, 24, 86 ; Blewet, 24 ; Thomas Langdon, 24 ; Cotthay, seat of the Every family, 24 ; church (St. Nicholas) and monument, 24 ; bells (3), 24.

Kittisford family, owned Kittisford, iii 24 ; the daughter of John de, married John de Sydenham, 24, 86.

Knap, hamlet in North Curry, ii 178 ; granted by Hameline de Godely to the dean and chapter of Wells, 178.

Knap-Dane, Nettlecombe, discovery of human bones at, iii 535.

Knatchbull, Charles, J.P., i *xliv.* Mrs., owned Stoke-Lane, iii 484. Norton, owned Babington, ii 451 ; mansion at Babington, 451.

Knevett, Sir William, owned Hemington, ii 454.

Knight, Mary, of Wolverley, wife of Coplestone Warre Bampfylde, iii 263 ; Robert, owned Sutton-Mallet, 430 ; Robert, his son, 430 ; the Rev. Samuel, incumbent of Withiel-Flory, 295. Thomas and Elizabeth, monument in Closworth church, ii 347.

Knight, William, bishop of Bath and Wells, 1541—1547, iii 387 ; other honours held by, 387 ; act, settling the right of election of the bishops of Bath and Wells, 387 ; buried in Wells cathedral, 387 ; he built the market-cross, Wells, 376 ; and erected the pulpit in the cathedral, 399 ; arms, 399.

Knight banneret, his pay, iii 279.

Knight Templar's tomb in Porlock church, ii 38.

Knights of St. John of Jerusalem (*see* St. John of Jerusalem).

Knights of the shire, i *xxxix.*

Knights'-Leigh (*see* Angers-Leigh).

Knightcot or Nedcut, hamlet in Banwell, iii 567.

Knightcot, hamlet in Brushford, iii 506.

Knighton, hamlet in Stoke Courcy, i 249.

Knighton-Sutton (*see* Sutton, North).

Knoll, in Chew-Magna, ii 95.

Knoll, in Selworthy, ii 41.

Knoll, in Shepton-Montacute, iii 45.

Knoll or Knowle-St.-Giles, situation, iii 118 ; formerly a member of the manor of Cudworth, 118 ; owned by the family of L'Orti, 118 ; held by lord William de Parys, 118 ; Ralph Inweans, 118 ; Sir Amias Poulett, from whom it descended to

Knoll or Knowle-St.-Giles—*continued.* lord Poulett, 118 ; church (St. Giles), 118 ; bells (2), 118.

Knoll, Edward de la, dean of Wells, 1256, i 189.

Knolle, in Bawdrip, iii 92.

Knolle, in Bedminster, ii 284 ; Domesday survey, 284 ; held by Osbern Giffard : Alnod held it T.R.E. 284 ; subsequently held of the Berkeley family by the Gournays, 284 ; land granted by John de Gournay to St. Augustine's priory, Bristol, 284 ; Ravenswell fountain, 284 ; chapel (demolished), 284 ; report of at time of Reformation, 287.

Knott, Rev. James, incumbent of White-Stanton, iii 127.

Knowell, Alice, wife of John Portman, i 62.

Knowle, in Long-Sutton, iii 197 ; held of Athelney abbey by the families of Middleney, 198 ; L'Orti, 198 ; Gunter, 198, 130 ; chapel to Long-Sutton, 198.

Knowle-St.-Giles (*see* Knoll-St.-Giles).

Knowles, John, memorial inscription in West Hatch church, ii 180.

Knoyle, William, i *xl* ; sheriff, 1492, *xxxvi.* William, married (1) Filip Morgane, (2) Grace Clavel, monument in Sandford-Orcas church, ii 378 ; arms, 378.

Knyfton, Rev. George, incumbent of St. Decumans, iii 493.

Knypnton, Rev. George, incumbent of Timberscombe, ii 45.

Kylbeck, Bartholomew, owned land in Wanstraw, ii 229.

Kyme, Maud de, landowner temp. Ed. I, i *xxix.* married William de Vivonia or Fortibus, ii 150, iii 462 ; Simon, 462.

Kymer, the Rev. William, incumbent of Stoke-Giffard, iii 606 ; of Winscombe, 614.

Kymer inscriptions in Buckland St. Mary church, i 21.

Kymrydge, Richard, received a pension from St. John's hospital, Bridgwater, iii 80.

Kynegilsus, king, i 86.

Kynge, Richard le, held lands in Withypool, iii 558.

Kyngton, Thomas, one of the jury to decide the position of the city pillory, B 31.

Kyngessecke, ii 195.

Kynnyard moor, Glastonbury, ii 268.

Kyte, John, examination by the Commissioners for the survey of Stoke - under - Hamden chapel, iii 318, 319.

Kytenore (*see* Culbone).

Kytenore, William de, owned Culbone, ii 3. Quarum-Kitnor, iii 556.

L

Langton—*continued.*
Joseph, M.P. for Bath, 1690, B 22. Joseph, sheriff, 1735, i *xxxix.* monuments in New-ton-St.-Lo church, iii 343, 344 ; Anne, mar-ried (1) Robert Langton, (2) Sir George Cobb, 344 ; Joseph, owned Corston, 346 ; his daughter married William Gore Lang-ton, to whom she conveyed that estate, 346. William Gore, J.P., i *xliv.* governor of Bath hospital, B 48. part owner of Hallatrow and Littleton, ii 148 ; owned North Wotton, 276 ; Brislington, 413 ; Stanton-Prior, 439. Wellow, iii 326 ; New-ton-St.-Lo, 343 ; Corston, 346 ; land in Twiverton, 348 ; Pilton, 481.

Langton, Thomas, bishop of Winchester, re-paired Taunton castle, iii 227, 232.

Lanporth borough, included with Somerton in the Domesday survey, iii 183 [v. Langport.]

Lansdown, battle, 1643, between the Royalist and Parliamentary forces, description, i 156—158.

Lansdown family, seat at Woodborough, iii 326. Richard, J.P., i *xliv.* Richard and Doro-thy, monument in Wellow church, iii 329.

Lansdown hill, i *xiv.*

Lansdown, marquis of, J.P., i *xli.*

Lansdown place, Bath, B 37, 74 ; street, 38.

Lantocai (*see* Leigh).

Lanyard, John, owned lands in the parish of Winford, ii 321.

Lapis calaminaris mines at Chewton Mendip, ii 115. Shipham, iii 600 ; description, 600 ; miner's wages, 600 ; found also at Clevedon, 166 ; Mendip, 374 ; Priddy, 418 ; East-Harptree, 587 ; Hutton, 590 ; Rowberrow, 599.

Lapis hæmatites found at Filton, ii 440.

Lapley, Mr., memorial stone in Charlton-Mackarell church, iii 194.

Larbeck, Henry, incumbent of Trinity chantry, Aller, iii 188.

Larder, John, married Anne Stork, of Trent, ii 385.

Larford, hamlet in Crocombe, iii 514.

Latch, John, sheriff, 1627, i *xxxviii.* John, monument in Churchill church, iii 581 ; John, son of Thomas, benefaction to Churchill, 581 ; Mary, wife of (1) Mr. Hunt, (2) Mr. Plumly, benefaction to Churchill, 582.

Latcham, hamlet in Wedmore, i 188.

Latchem, Richard, benefaction to Wedmore, i 193.

Latimer, Edward, of West-Chelworth, ii 420 ; Elizabeth, wife of — Gryffin, 420. Joan, second wife of John Brent, of Cossington, iii 435. Nicholas, sheriff, 1453, i *xxxvi* ; Sir Nicholas, sheriff, 1460, 1471, *xxxvi.* Sir Robert, knt., owned Kingston, iii 185 ; Sir Robert, married Catherine Hull, and

Latimer—*continued.*
became possessed of Stoket, 321. Sir Thomas, knt., of Braybrock, held West-Chelworth, ii 420. William [Latymer], sheriff, 1374, 1375, 1380, i *xxxv.* an heir of, owned part of the manor of Loxton, iii 597.

Latimer, George Nevil, lord Latimer, married Elizabeth Beauchamp, ii 282.

Laud, William, bishop of Bath and Wells, 1626, iii 389 ; previously bishop of St. David's, 389 ; promoted to London, 389 ; to Canterbury, 389.

Laundey, Cecilia, owned Bickenhall, i 62. Stephen, married Cecilia Burnel, iii 518 ; Maud, wife of Thomas de Dodeton, 518.

Laura place, Bath, B 39.

Lavatory in monasteries, ii 250.

Laverley, hamlet in West Pennard, ii 275.

Laverswell, ii 76.

Laverton, situation, ii 211 ; remarkable trees, 211 ; river and bridge, 211 ; Domesday survey, 211 ; owned by William de Ow : held by Herbert, 211 ; held of the earl of Norfolk by the Panes family, 211 ; passed to the Moignes, 211 ; the Gournays, 211 ; attached to the duchy of Cornwall, 211 ; church (St. Bartholomew) and its monu-ments, 211 ; bells (3), 211.

Laverton, Geffrey de, held Shepton-Mallet, iii 462.

Law suit between the assessors of Yatton and the occupiers of Colefree land in Kingston-Seymour, ii 124.

Laws for Mendip lead mines, iii 374.

Lay, Mr., patron of Broadway, i 18.

Layard, Rev. Dr., incumbent of Kew-Stoke, iii 596 ; incumbent of Worle, 615.

Laycock nunnery, Wilts, founded by Ela, coun-tess of Salisbury, iii 184.

Laycocke, Hugh, monk of Hinton, pensioned, iii 368.

Laymore, hamlet in Crewkerne, ii 159.

Lazar's hospital, Bath, B 42.

Le Brode Mersche, lands in, granted by Anas-tatia Croc to Sir Thomas Trivet, iii 101.

Le Galley, Glastonbury, ii 259.

Le Heye, lands in, granted by Alice de Ouvre to Woodspring priory, iii 594.

Le Sor (*see* Sor).

Leach family, patrons of Sutton Montis, ii 88.

Leach, Rev. James, incumbent of Lovington, ii 83.

Leachmore pond, Emborow, ii 135.

Lead-miners laws, iii 374.

Lead-mines, Chewton-Mendip, ii 115 ; Brockley, 120 ; Mells, 462. Abbots Leigh, iii 152 ; Clevedon, 166 ; Mendip, 374 ; Priddy, 418 ; Lamb-hill, East-Harptree, 587 ; Rowberrow, 599.

Leake, James, mayor of Bath, 1783, B 27.

Lilstock, situation, iii 533 ; tithing of Honibere, 533 ; Domesday survey, 533 ; owned by Ansger Coquus : Bricsic held it T.R.E. 533 ; subsequently held of the owners of Stoke-Courcy castle, 534 ; part of the demesnes of the lords of Stowey, 534 ; owned by the Luttrells, 534 ; Sir Thomas Palmer, 534 ; again by the Luttrells, 534 ; Honibere, purchased by Nicholas Halswell, and John Colles, for the children of Sir Thomas Palmer, 534 ; Lilstock, owned by earl Temple, 534 ; Honibere court, 534 ; church (St. Andrew) 534 ; bells (4), 534.

Limebridge wood, Tickenham, owned by the Berkeley family, iii 164 ; attached to the manor of Portbury, 164.

Limeshest, Henry, grant to Woodspring priory, iii 594.

Limesi, Ralph de, received lands from William the Conqueror, i *xxv* ; owned Combwick, 234. part of Luckham, ii 22 ; Bossington, 37 ; Selworthy, 40 ; Allerford, 41 ; Treborough, 45 ; Pisbury, 470. Aller, iii 188. Alan, Gerard, John, Hugh de, holders of Selworthy, ii 40.

Limington, situation, iii 218 ; river Ivel, 218 ; tithings of Limington and Draycot, 218 : Domesday survey, 218 ; owned by Glastonbury abbey, 218 ; Roger de Curcelle, 218 ; Saulf held it T.R.E. 218 ; subsequently held of the Beauchamps, of Hatch, by the Fitz-Bernards, 218 ; the Gyverneys, 218 ; Henry Power, 218 ; William de Shareshull, 219 ; the Bonvilles, 219 ; the marquis of Dorset, 219 ; the manor, lands in Yeovilton, and Eastern and Western farms, held by William and Thomas Rosewell, William Smithe and Henry Dale, 219 ; Draycot hamlet, 219 ; chantry founded and endowed by Sir Richard Gyverney, 218 ; church (St. Mary) and its monuments, 219, 220 ; bells (4), 219 ; arms carved on pews, 219 ; cardinal Wolsey rector here, 219, 220 ; lands here granted to Sir Michael Stanhope, 301.

Limpet for marking linen, found at Minehead, ii 29.

Linch, owned by the Hewish family, iii 491.

Lincoln, Alured de, sheriff, 1169, 1170, 1171, 1172, 1173, 1174, i *xxxiii.* sometimes called Nichole, ii 150 ; owned Midsummer Norton, 150 ; held lands of the abbot of Glastonbury, 244. Margaret, his sister, married Roger Fitz-Pain, iii 245.

Lincoln, Richard, monk of Bath, received pension, B 57.

Lincoln college, Oxford, rectors' lodgings, built by bishop Beckington, iii 385.

Lincoln, Henry Lacy, earl of, owned Henstridge, ii 365. and Steep-Holmes island, iii 609.

Lincoln, William de Romara, earl of, iii 511.

Lincoln taxation of 1292, i 212.

Lincume (*see* Lyncombe).

Lind, Hugh de la, M.P. for Bath, 1391, 1392, 1397, B 20.

Lindsey, Rev., patron of Chew-Magna, ii 96.

Liney, hamlet in Weston-Zoyland, iii 440.

Ling-East, situation, i 84 ; hamlets of West-Ling, Outwood and Boroughbridge, 84 ; granted by king Athelstan to the church of Athelney, 84 ; Domesday survey, 85 ; owned successively by John Clayton, John and William Tynbury, Thomas Leigh, George Grenville, Sir Thomas Wroth, Palmer family, Acland family, 85 ; abbey of Athelney, 86 ; list of abbots, 87 ; church (St. Bartholomew), 89 ; bells (5), 89.

Ling, lands in, granted to Athelney abbey by Richard de Newton, iii 70.

Link, hamlet in Burrington, i 203.

Lintmore, lands in, owned by Richard de Placetis (afterwards de Wrotham, iii 65.

Lions family, owned Ashton-Lions, ii 290 ; Nicholas de, Reeve of Bristol, 290 ; William de, bought lands from Agnes de Alno and William de Ashton, 290 ; Adam, 290 ; Thomas, 291 ; Edmund de, granted Stokeleigh to St. Augustine's abbey, Bristol : had also lands in the hamlet of Kencot, 291 ; held the lease of the manor of the parsonage of Ashton and advowson of the vicarage, 298 ; William, 291 ; Thomas, enclosed a park, 291.

Lisborn [or Lisburn], John, lord, married the youngest daughter of John, earl of Rochester, i 92. owned Sutton Mallet, iii 430.

Lisle family held Lympsham, i 203. Badgworth, iii 565 ; Amicia, countess, owned Winsford, 556 ; Joan, viscountess, monument in Wells cathedral, 401 ; John, lord, married Joan de Chedder, 576. lord, owner of land in Midsummer-Norton, ii 151.

Lisley, arms of, ii 443.

Lister, Martha, monument in Bath abbey, 1725, B 69.

Lisuns, Osbert de, held land of the abbot of Glastonbury, ii 244.

Lisures, Warine de, sheriff, 1154, 1156, 1158, 1160, 1161, i *xxxiii.*

Liteltone (*see* High-Littleton).

Little Chipley, iii 18.

Little Elm, hamlet in Elm, ii 206.

Little Keyford, hamlet in Frome, ii 186.

Little Lopen, iii 108.

Little Pennard, iii 478.

Little-Stratton, iii 108.

Little Weston, hamlet in Weston Bampfylde, ii 89.

Littleton manor, Compton-Dunden, iii 447 ; held by the Fytchet family, 447 ; the Hills, 196, 447 ; John Lyde, 447.

Littleton, tithing of Dundry, ii 105.

Littleton, Wiltshire, residence of the de Stanton family, of Stanton-Drew, ii 434.

Littleton, Wibert de, dean of Wells, 1334, i 189.

Litton, situation, iii 416; Sherborne hamlet, 416; Domesday survey, 416; owned by the bishopric of Wells, 378, 392, 416; church (St. Mary), 417; bells (5), 417.

Litune (*see* Litton).

Liversedge (*see* Leversedge).

Living held Earnshill, i 30.

Liward held Ilminster, i 5; Combwick, 234.

Llewellen's, Martin, lines on Sir Bevil Grenville, i 159.

Llewellin [or Luellin], Henry, founded an almshouse at Wells, iii 408; monument in St. Cuthbert's church, Wells, 406; arms, 406.

Lloyd, Dorothy, second wife of Anthony Wickham, ii 373. Catherine, of Place Iscoyd, wife of Thomas Perceval, iii 176. Evan, of Llaneminick, married Anne Perceval, ii 314, iii 176. Evan, monument in Bath abbey, 1728, B 69. Anne, widow of Evan Lloyd, married Thomas Salisbury, ii 314; John, master of St. Catherine's chapel, Bedminster, 283. John, last incumbent of the Fraternity at Banwell, iii 568. John, governor of Bath hospital, B 48. Maurice, J.P., i *xliv*. Sibylla, erected a monument to the Holbeach family in Whitchurch church, ii 442.

Lloyd, William, owned Ford, iii 613; Harford, bequeathed Ford to Joseph Beck, 613.

Load, North, i 188.

Load or Long-load, hamlet in Martock, iii 2; chapel, 2; Peter de Fauconbergh held lands here, 6; account of it, 11.

Load-Bridge, iii 3.

Lochetone (*see* Lufton).

Lock's brook, Weston, i 156.

Lock's lane, Bath, B 32.

Locke, John, birthplace in Wrington, i 209.

Locke, George, monument in Frome church, ii 192; Susannah, monument in Frome church, 192; benefaction to Frome almshouse, 196.

Locke, tombs in Burnham churchyard, i 181,182,

Locket, Rev. Timothy, inscription in West-Monkton church, iii 455.

Locking, situation, iii 596; held under the Courtneys by Geffrey Gibwyne, 596; granted to Woodspring priory, 567, 594, 597; owned after the dissolution by William St. Loe, 596; Thomas Clarke, 596; the Norris family, 597; the Carliles, 597; the Plomleys, 597; Edward Colston, who granted it to his school at Bristol, 597; church (St. Augustin), 597; bells (4), 597.

Lockingcroft, lands in, granted to Woodspring priory by Henry de Pendeney, iii 594.

Lockit, the Rev. Henry, monument in Crowcombe church, iii 517.

Lockyer, Thomas, owned Maperton, ii 85. Charlton-Mackarel, iii 193; Yeovilton, 200; house at Ilchester, 298.

Locumbe (*see* Luckham).

Locumbe, Symon de, held lands in Wileford, iii 256.

Lod-Hywish, Richard de, landowner temp. Ed. I, i *xxviii*. formerly named de Hywis, iii 541; Bartholomew, 541; Andrew, 541; Margaret, wife of Richard de Cottelle, 541.

Loder tithes, owned partly by Montacute priory, iii 312.

Loderford (*see* Lotterford).

Lodres, Richard, married Sarah de Raleigh, iii 537.

Logwor, holder of lands which were subsequently called Montacute: buried at Glastonbury: name preserved on the pyramids there, iii 310, 311.

Logworsborough (*see* Montacute).

Lokeyerd, John, holder of half a knight's fee in Quarum-Mounceaux, iii 556.

Loligtone (*see* Lullington).

Lolochesberie (*see* Luxborough).

London, bishop of [Richard Hill, 1489], purchased Abdick hundred, i 2; and Curry-Rivel, 26. Maurice, bishop of, held the church of St. Andrew, Ivelchester, iii 301. Robert [Lowth], lord bishop of, J.P., i *xli*.

London, city of, owned East-Brent, i 196.

London, hospital of St. Catherine, bishop Beckington's bequest to, iii 385.

London, the Minories or Bath place: John Clerk, bishop of Bath and Wells, buried in the church, iii 387; ceded by the bishop to Edward VI, 395.

London, hamlet in Old Cleeve, iii 511; granted to Robert, earl of Sussex, 512.

London, Hildebrand de, sheriff, 1333, 1334, 1336, i *xxxiv*. Richard de, holder of half a knight's fee from the Mohun family, ii 14. Walter de, dean of Wells, 1335, i 189.

Long, Anne, wife of William Oxenham, i 256. Elizabeth, builder of the church at Babington, 1750, ii 451; Henry, whom Sir Christopher Wroughton enfeoffed in his estates, 133; Sir Henry, married Eleanor, the widow of Edward Leversege, 188. sheriff, 1538, i *xxxvii*. Sir James Tylney, bart., governor of Bath hospital, B 48; John, prior, received pension, 57. John, owned East-End, Stoke, iii 484. Lislebon, M.P., 1656, i *xxxii*. Mr., part-owner of Goathill, ii 364. Sir Philip Parker, owned Weston, i 160; Mr., incumbent of Freshford, 126. Sir Richard, married Margaret Donington, ii 391. Robert, M.P., 1654, 1656, i *xxxii*. Robert, held land in Compton, ii 151; Robert, monument in Stanton-Prior church, 440. Walter, M.P. for Bath, 1627, B 21; governor of Bath hospital, 48.

Long—*continued.*
owned the manor of Muchelney, iii 136;
Peglinch, 328; Shascombe, 328; Hassage,
328; Chedder-Hanham, 576. Sir Walter,
M.P. for Bath, 1681, B 22; William, mayor
of Bath, 1715, 26. married Elizabeth
Wroth, i 256, iii 69. owned Babington,
ii 451.

Long or Lunget family held lands in Uphill,
iii 609; Philip le, 609.

Long-Acre, hamlet in Middlezoy, iii 442.

Long-Ashton, situation, ii 288; river Avon, 288;
Rownam ferry, 288, 296; Roman remains,
288, 289; manors included in, 289; Domesday survey, 289; owned by Gefferey, bishop of
Coutances, held by Roger and Wido, 289;
passed to the Crown, and was divided, 290;
church house, 292; church (All Saints) and
its monuments, 299—303; bells (6), 299;
benefactions, 303, 304; crosses, 304; court
for Hareclive hundred held here, 279.
rating in 1293, iii 394. Ashton - Dando or
Ashton-Lions, ii 290; owned by Adam de
Heyron, 290; families of de Alno, 290;
de Lions, 290; Alianore Hulle, 291; Choke,
291, 292; the Daubeneys, 292; Sir Thomas
Arundel, 292; the Smyths, 292-294; one-
third held by the Gore family, 294; the remainder by the Smyth family, 294; Ashton-
court and park, 294; Ashton-Theynes, 295;
owned by the le Theyne family, 295; John
Power, 295; the Inyn family, 295; the
Kenns, 295; the Clerks, 296; Sir Hugh
Smyth, under whom it became blended
with Ashton-Lions, 296; an estate here
held by the Wyttington family, 296;
passed to John Tovey, 296; to the descendants of Obadiah Webb and Mr.
Richardson, 296; hermitage and chapel
formerly standing here, 296; Ashton-
Philips, owned by the Aston family, 296;
a moiety held successively by John Teysant,
and John, his son, Robert Poyntz of Iron-
Acton, Roger Lyveden, Thomas Wythiford
and Richard A'Merryck, 296; the other
moiety owned by the Westons, 296; Roger
Lyveden, 296; divided:—one half passing
to the Wymbush family, 296; the Seymours, 296; Richard A'Merryck, 296; the
other half passed by Agnes Lyvedon to the
Wythiford family, 297; to Richard A'Merryck, who thus became owner of the whole
manor, 297; passed to the Brook family,
297; divided between the four daughters of
Hugh Brook, who married Giles Walwyn,
William Clarke, Hugh Halswell, and
Thomas Vatchell, and was by their heirs
sold to the Smyth family, 297; lower court,
297; chapel, 297; Ashton-Meriet, 297;
owned by the de Ashton family, 297; the
Meriet family, 297, 298; Bath priory, 298;

Long-Ashton—*continued.*
held by Edmund de Lyons, 298; the Choke
family and John Chapman, 298; Marmaduke and Alexander Mauncel, 298; after
the dissolution granted to John Smyth, 298;
chapel, 298; parsonage, with old hall where
the abbots' courts were held, 299; Gatcomb, seat of the de Gatcombe family, 302;
Yanleigh hamlet, supposed Roman remains
at, 304.

Long-Auler, hamlet in Creech St. Michael, i 74.

Long-Sutton, situation, iii 197; river Yeo, 197;
manor of Knowle, 197, 198; Kingsmoor,
197; fair, 197; granted by king Alfred to
Athelney abbey, 197; Domesday survey,
197; held by Athelney abbey, Roger Brito
and Roger de Corcelle, 197; manor subsequently owned by the countess of Northampton, 197; manor of Sutton-Damer,
197; church (Holy Trinity) and its monuments, 198; bells (5), 198.

Longbridge, hospital at, founded by Maurice de
Berkeley, iii 276.

Longeland, John de, sheriff, 1365—1368, i *xxxv.*

Longespee, William de, son of Rosamund Clifford, and Henry II, created earl of Salisbury (*see* under Salisbury). William de,
son of the earl of Salisbury, married
Idonea de Camville, and became possessed
of Charleton-Horethorne and Henstridge,
ii 357; William, married Maud Clifford,
357; Margaret, married Henry de Lacy,
357.

Longevity, remarkable cases of, ii 414, iii 293.

Longford, Mr., part-owner of Hatherley, ii 86.

Longleat, sold with Lullington, to Sir John
Thynne, ii 212. place of bishop Kenn's
retirement and death, iii 390.

Longleat priory, owned Lullington, ii 212;
property in Nunney, 219; land in Rodden,
227; Luckington and Walton, 447.

Longman, heiress of, wife of Peregrine Palmer,
i 255.

Lopen, situation, iii 121; Broomhill hamlet,
121; Domesday survey, owned by the earl
of Morton, one parcel held by Gerard:
Alward held it T.R.E.: the other held by
Harding Fitz-Alnod: Tovi held it T.R.E.
122; Lopen-Magna, held by the Lopen
family of the Malets, 122; by John Wake,
under the Meriet family, 122; by Humphry Stafford, earl of Devon, under Sir John
Coleshill, 122; the Pouletts, 122; fair and
market, 122; Lopen-Parva, 122; Lopen-
abbis or temple, 122; owned by the preceptory of Temple-Combe, 122; by the
hospitalers of St. John, 122; held by the
master, of Hugh Lovel, 122; dowlas
manufacture, 122; church (All Saints),
122; bells (2), 122.

Lore, Sir Peter Van, owned Greinton, iii 428.

Loring, Sir Nigele or Neale, owner of Porlock, ii 37; Isabel, wife of Robert, lord Harington, 37; Margery, wife of (1) Thomas Peyner, and (2) Thomas Poynings, 37.

L'Orti, Ortiaco or Urtiaco family, owned Abdick and Bulston hundreds, i 1; Broadway, 18; Curry Rivel, 26; Swell, 65. North-Parret, ii 335. Stoke-Trister, Bayford and Cucklington, iii 50; Knoll, 118; Knowle, 198; Pitney, 130; Langport, 132. Henry de, married Sabina Revel, and became possessed of Curry Rivel, i 26. Stoke-Trister, Bayford and Cucklington, iii 50; held Pitney, 130; lady Sabina, 11, 118. Sir Henry de, procured a charter of free-warren in Curry Rivel, i 26, iii 50, 130. Sir Henry de, i 26, iii 50, 130. Walter, confirmed the endowment of the chantry at Swell, i 66; John, 26, iii 130; granted Stoke-Trister, Bayford and Cucklington to Elizabeth Child, whom he married, 50; released all her rights in Stoke-Trister, Bayford and Cucklington to Sir John de Molyns, 50; Elizabeth, married (1) Sir Ralph de Middleney, (2) Sir Robert de Ashton, 130, 445. Maud, owned North-Parret, ii 335. Richard, iii 118.

Lorty, Hugh, descendant of the de L'Orti family, iii 130.

Loscomb, Thomas, inscription on bell in Trent church, ii 384.

Lotingar, Richard, holder of a knight's fee of the bishopric of Wells, iii 393.

Lotisham-Green or Lotsham, Ditcheat, iii 471; owned by the Lotisham family, 472; Mr. Taunton, 472.

Lotterel, Thomas, owned Milton in Martock, iii 6.

Lotterford or Loderford, hamlet in North Cheriton, ii 360; owned by the abbots of Glastonbury, 243.

Lottisham, William, married Mary Warre, and became possessed of Milverton, Chipley, Tolland, iii 15; and Lovelinch, 15, 261; Elizabeth, wife of Edward Clarke, 15, 261; monument in Ninehead church, 269; arms, 269. Oliver, monument in West Lydford church, ii 85.

Loughborough, baron, J.P., i *xlii.*

Lovel (*see* Upton Noble).

Lovel, baron, of Holkham, title conferred on Thomas Coke, 1728, iii 142. held Donyat, i 36

Lovel [Lovall] family, of Castle Cary, ii 53, 54. owned Beer-Crocombe, i 14; Chapel Allerton, 176; Milton-Clevedon, 222; Pitcombe, 224; Redlinch, 225; Upton Noble, 227. Barrow, North and South, ii 62, 63; North Cheriton, 360. Bawdrip, iii 91; Wincaunton, 32; Bratton-Seymour, 36; Cricket-St. Thomas, 116; Lopen Parva, 122; Weston, 172; Camerton, 331. descended from William de Perceval, ii 53, iii 172. arms, ii 54 (*see* also Lovell family).

Lovel or Lupellus, name given to William de Perceval, who married Auberie de Mellent, ii 52, iii 172; Waleran, his son, succeeded to his Norman estates, and took the name of Yvery, 172. Ralph, second son of William, bore the name of Lovel, ii 53, iii 172. married a daughter of Henry de Newmarch, iii 172. Henry, ii 53, iii 172. gave one hundred marks for licence to implead Robert de Lovington for lands in Dishcove, Bratton and Brewton, i 215. Richard, great-grandson of William de Perceval, and progenitor of the Lovels of Castle Cary, ii 53, iii 172. his four sisters married respectively, Walter de Esseleg, Thomas le Briton, Matthew Wake, and William Fitz-Walter, iii 172. Henry, ii 53; Richard, 53; Henry, 53; Hugh, lord, 53; Olivia, wife of John de Gournay, 53, 138, 309; Richard, summoned to parliament, married Muriel Douglas, 54. founded Stavordale priory, iii 33. James, ii 54; Richard, last male heir of this house, 54; Muriel, married Nicholas St. Maur, 54; Maud, widow of John, married John de Handlo, lord Burnell, 360; Elizabeth, wife of John, lord Dinham, 362.

Lovel, James, part-holder of a knight's fee in Wanstraw, ii 229; Thomas, of Wanstraw, 229. married Joan Hogshaw, iii 167. Sir Thomas, ii 229. owned Clevedon, iii 167; Agnes, married Sir Thomas Wake, 167.

Lovel, Robert, married Elizabeth Bryen, i 107. Elizabeth, his wife, held Somerton and other estates, iii 186: held Downhead, 475.

Lovel, Eleanor, of Harling, wife of Edward Waldegrave, ii 117.

Lovel, John and Mary, monument in Portishead church, iii 145.

Lovel, Rev. Dr., incumbent of Chapel-Allerton, i 176.

Lovel, Thomas, sub-dean of Wells, buried in Wells cathedral, iii 399.

Lovell, Dr. Edmund, memorial stone in Pitney church, iii 131. Rev. Edmund, LL.D., J.P., i *xliv.* archdeacon of Bath, a 72, iii 396; prebendary of Wells, 397; incumbent of St. Cuthbert's church, 405. George, J.P., i *xliv.*

Lovell, Edward and Eleanor, monument in Bawdrip church, iii 93.

Lovelinch, owned by the Warre family, iii 15, 261; by William Lottisham, 261; by the Clarke family, 261.

Loveney, Walter de, landowner temp. Ed. I, i *xxviii*; sheriff, 1292, 1293, *xxxiv*; one of the Neroche perambulation jury, i 17.

Loverlay, rent in, owned by Montacute priory, iii 312.

Loveshate, Henry, sold lands in Woodborough to Woodspring priory, iii 595.

Loviare, Peter, prior of Woodspring, 1414, iii 595.

Lovington, its situation, ii 82 ; Domesday survey, 82 ; owned by Serlo de Burci, 82 ; owned by the families of Fitz-Martin, William de Lovington, William Banister, Rodney, 82, iii 603. Smyth, Cary Creed and William Pew and John Tidcombe, ii 83 ; the church (St. Thomas à Becket) and its benefactions, 82.

Lovington, Robert de, impleaded by Henry Lovel for lands in Dishcove, Bratton and Brewton, i 215. William, holder of half a knight's fee in Lovington, ii 82.

Low-Ham or Nether-Ham, iii 444 ; owned by Sir Richard de Wrotham, 445 ; the le Blands, 445 ; Gefferey de Wroxall, 445 ; the de Hamme family, 445 ; the le Vernour family, 445 ; Ralph de Middleney, 445 ; the Berkeleys, 445 ; the Hext family, 445 ; Sir Ralph Killigrew, 445 ; the lords Stawel, 445 ; the Phelips family, 446 ; the Mildmays, 446 ; mansion, 445 ; chapel, 445 ; monument, 445 ; date of construction, 445.

Lowder, John, governor of Bath hospital, B 48.

Lowe, George, rector of Claverton, i 147.

Lower-Asholt, hamlet in Asholt, i 237.

Lower Charles street, Bath, B 35.

Lower-court, manor house, Ashton-Phillips, ii 297 ; chapel, 297.

Lower-East-Hayes, Bath, B 74.

Lower-Langford, hamlet in Churchill, iii 579.

Lower Leigh, hamlet in Street, iii 424.

Lower Mill, hamlet in Exford, ii 21.

Lower-Odcombe, hamlet in Odcombe, ii 324.

Lower Shepton, hamlet in Shepton-Montacute, iii 45.

Lower-Somerton or Somerton-Erleigh (*see* Somerton).

Lower Stoughton, hamlet in Wedmore, i 188.

Lower Town, Minehead, ii 26.

Lower Weare, hamlet in Over Weare, formerly a place of greater importance, having sent members to parliament, and having a market and fair, with other privileges, i 184.

Lowfeild, Thomas, governor of Bath hospital, B 48.

Lowring hospital, founded by Maurice de Berkeley, iii 276.

Lowther, Catherine, monument in Bath abbey, 1764, B 69 ; Henry, monument in Bath abbey, 1744, 69.

Loxley wood, iii 426.

Loxton, situation, iii 597 ; Crook's-Peek (*sic*), 597 ; Domesday survey, 597 ; owned by Eustace, earl of Bulloigne : Ulveva held it T.R.E. 597 ; subsequently held by Osbert de Bath and William Weyland, 597 ; purchased by Nicholas Bubwith, and granted to the heirs of Latimer and Grenham, 597 ; the Dodingtons, 598 ; the Right Hon. Earl Temple, 598 ; church (St. Andrew), 598 ; bells (3), 598 ; benefactions, 598 ; cross, 598.

Lubbon, hamlet in Baltonsbury, ii 270.

Lucan, Philip, married a daughter of Matthew Wake, and became possessed of a fourth of the manor of Weston-in-Gordano, iii 172.

Lucas, Mr., owned the site of Barlinch priory, iii 503 ; Penelope, daughter of Charles, lord Lucas, married Isaac Selfe, of Beanacre, 246 ; Sarah, wife of Alexander Webber, 23. Stuckley, J.P., i *xliv.*

Luccombe, Joan, daughter of Ralph, married John Orchard, iii 489 ; arms, 491.

Luccombe, John de, owned Luckham, ii 23 ; and Selworthy, 40 ; Hugh, 23 ; John, 23 ; Hugh, 23 ; John, 23 ; Elizabeth, wife of Oliver de St. John, 23 ; Richard de (or Luckam), gave pension to abbot of Athelney from land in Selworthy, ii 42.

Luccombe, Robert de, part owner of Ubley, which he sold to Nicholas Huscarle, ii 156.

Luckham, its situation, ii 22 ; hamlets of West Luckham, Horner and Dover-hay, 22 ; Domesday survey, 22 ; owned by Ralph de Limesi, and Odo, son of Gamelin, 22 ; his undertenant, Vitalis : held by queen Eddida, and Fitel T.R.E. 22 ; owned successively by Sir Baldric de Nonington, Robert de Pudele (whose successors assumed the name of Luccombe), 22 ; the families of St. John and Arundel, and Frederick Thomas Wentworth, 23 ; the church (St. Mary) and its monuments, 23, 24 ; bells (5), 23 ; cross, 24.

Luckington, hamlet in Kilmersdon, ii 446 ; Domesday survey, 446 ; owned by Alured de Ispania : by Alwi T.R.E. 446 ; subsequently held by the Botreaux family, 447.

Luco, Godfrey de, prior of Stoke-Courcy, 1328, i 250.

Lucy, Godfrey de, bishop of Winchester, 1189, iii 232.

Luda, Thomas, married a daughter of Henry de Bikeley, owned Holwell, which he granted to the abbey of Abbotsbury, ii 369.

Ludgate, Simon de, married Maud de Sancto Mauro, widow of Walter de Wengham, ii 122 ; Laurence, 123.

Ludhuish, in Nettlecombe, iii 541 ; owned by the Hewis or Huish family, 541 ; Richard Britte, 541 ; Philip de Wellesleigh, 541 ; the families of Hill, Say, Cheyney and Waldegrave, 541 ; Sir John Trevelyan, 541.

Ludlow castle, Philip de Albini, governor of, iii 108.

Ludlow, earl of, J.P., i *xli.*

Ludlow, Edward, and Maud, his wife, purchased Horsington, ii 372 ; Robert, conveyed that manor and Horsington marsh to Matthew Smyth, 372. Mary, second wife of John Brent, of Cossington, iii 436.

Ludney, hamlet in Kingston, iii 322.

Ludwell, Edward, M.P. for Bath, 1553, B 21.

Luxborough, situation, ii 24; hamlet of Pool-town, 24; Domesday survey, 25; owned by William des Mohun, and held by Ran-nulf and Nigel: by two thanes and Bris-mar T.R.E. 25; owned successively by the Everard family, Sir John Wyndham, and earl of Egremont, 25; Langham manor, 25; church (St. Mary) and its monuments, 26; bells (4), 26. rectory formerly held by the priory of Brewton, i 214.

Luxborough, Maurice de, holder of knight's fee in Luxborough Pyket, ii 25.

Luxstone, Rev. Mr., incumbent of Ash-Priors, ii 498.

Luxton, Rev. Laurence Head, incumbent of St. James' church, Taunton, iii 239.

Luytone, Walter de, witness to the charter for the fair at St. Michael de Torre, Glaston-bury, ii 265.

Lychefield, Margaret, monument in Bath abbey, B 69; Thomas, monument in Bath abbey, B 69; embalmed relics, B 65.

Lyd, Muriel de, wife of Gefferey de Wrotham, iii 63.

Lyde, in Yeovil, owned by the families of Fitz-paine and Poynings, iii 207; William Tan-ner, 207.

Lyde family, of Bristol and Stanton-Drew, monuments in Stanton-Drew church, ii 435, 436; James, who married Martha Pope, 435, 436; Mary, wife of Thomas Provis, 436; James, Michael, Sarah, and Esther, 436; Anna Maria, wife of Lyonel, 436; Benjamin and William, 436; Martha, wife of Sir Michael Foster, 436; Elizabeth, wife of John Adams, 436; Elizabeth, relict of James, 436; arms, 436; Cornelius, buried in St. James' church, Bristol, 436; benefactions, 437, 438.

Lyde, John, held Littleton, iii 447. Sir Lionel, J.P., i *xlii*; Roger, sheriff, 1755, *xxxix*. Roger, married Anne Langley, monument in Chelworth church, ii 420, 421; William, married Sarah Jones, 99.

Lyde-spring and rivulet, iii 370.

Lyddon, Hugh, woodward of Taunton, iii 228.

Lydford, memorial stone in Nunney church, ii 221.

Lydford-East, situation, iii 196; river Brew, 196; Roman Fosse road, 196; Domesday survey, 196; held of Glastonbury abbey by Roger: Alward held it T.R.E. 196; subsequently held of the honour of Glou-cester, by Sir John Bonville, 196; the Hills, 196; Richard Mawdley, 196; Rev. Mr. Ryall, 196; church and its monument, 196; bells (2), 196.

Lydford-West, its situation, ii 83; fairs and market, 83; Domesday survey, 84; held by Aluric: by Brictric T.R.E. 84; owned by the families of Martin, Columbers, Audley

Lydford-West—*continued.*
and John Holland, 84; the abbey of St. Mary des Graces, 84; the families of Stan-ley, Hungerford, Edward Colston, Alexan-der Ready, who assumed the name of Cols-ton, 84; church and its monuments, 84, 85; bells (5), 84; benefaction, 85.

Lydiard-Episcopi or Bishops'-Lydiard, situa-tion, ii 493; market and fairs, 494; Con-quest farm, 493; discovery of Roman coins, 493; granted to Asser, 481, 493; and after-wards to the bishopric of Wells, 482, 493; Domesday survey, 493, 494; passed to the Crown, 1548, 494; held by John Leth-bridge, 494; Sandhill park, 494; Lydiard Pincherton hamlet, 494; Week manor, owned by Richard Cross, 494; church (St. Mary) and its monuments, 495; cross, 496; benefactions, almshouse, and free-school, 496. rating in 1293, iii 394.

Lydiard-Pincherton or Punchardon hamlet, ii 494; held by Hugh de Punchardon, and William, his son, 494; Sir Hamelyn de Deaudon, 494; Mabil Malet, 494; Thomas de Pin held half a knight's fee of John de Mohun, 494; the Malet family, 494; leased to William Ronyon and John Wadham, 494; granted to Walter Bluet, William Montague, and John Wadham, junr., 494; vested in lord Fitzwarren, Sir Amice Pou-let, and Sir Nicholas Wadham, 494; owned by lady Acland, 494.

Lydiard St. Lawrence, situation, iii 265; springs, 265; hamlets of Westowe, Holford, Corsley, Nethercot, Pyleigh or Leigh-Flory, Chipleigh, Deane, Hockham, West-Leigh, and Tarr, 265; discovery of Roman coins, 265; fair, 265; Domesday survey, 265; held by William de Mohun: Alric held it T.R.E. 265; subsequently held of the Fraunceis family, 266; by Elizabeth Whiteley, 266; John Seymour, 266; owned by Edward, duke of Somerset, 266; the Sellecke family, 266; the Hancocks, 266; a branch of the Coker family settled here, 266; Taunton priory held an estate here, 231, 235, 266; church (St. Laurence) and its monuments, 266; bells (5), 266.

Lye, hamlet in Wrington, i 206.

Lyewelyn, Thomas, holder of Katherine, i 138.

Lyffe, Alice de, daughter of Maud de Ouvre, confirmed her mother's donations to Wood-spring priory, iii 543.

Lyffe, Godfrey, i 91; Geffrey, married Julian Valletort, and became owner of Charlinch, 239; Richard, 91; was of Currypool, mar-ried Margery Stawel, 239; Amice, second wife of Sir Baldwin Malet, 91, 239; Joan, wife of Walter Tilly, 239.

Lygon, Margaret, wife of Sir Henry Berkeley, i 215.

Lym, Simon de, incumbent of St. Mary Magdalen's church, Taunton, iii 237; bishop Haselshaw's ordination, respecting, 237.

Lymington, Wallop, lord, married a daughter of the Blewett family, iii 262.

Lympsham, situation, i 202; Hobb's boat ferry, 202; owned by Glastonbury abbey, 202; duke of Somerset, 203; Alexander Popham, 203; church (St. Christopher), 203; bells (5), 203; benefactions, 203.

Lynch, West, vill in Selworthy, ii 41.

Lyncombe (*see* Widcombe).

Lyncombe barracks or barrows, ii 439.

Lynde family, owned Broomfield, i 72; Alexander de la, landowner temp. Ed. I, *xxvii*. Alexander and Elias de la, held Dinnington, iii 121. George, commissioner for the survey of churches, ii 286. John de la, landowner temp. Ed. I, i *xxvii*; John de la, held Broomfield, 72. John de la, held Sock-Dennis, iii 307. Walter, of Broomfield, i 72.

Lyne, Edward, J.P., i *xliv*. Edward, M.D., owned royalties in the manor and hundred of Keynsham, ii 405.

Lynewraye, Francis, memorial stone in South Brewham church, i 222.

Lyons, Edward de, M.P., 1336, i *xxx*; Thomas de, landowner temp. Ed. I, *xxviii*.

Lyons family, of Ashton, held the manor of the parsonage of Ashton, ii 298; built the church there, 299; monuments in the church, 301, 302, 303; arms, 299; Edmund de, held the manor of the parsonage of Ashton, 298; Thomas, founder of Long-Ashton church: tombs formerly standing there, 301, 302; Thomas, owned Sewardswick, 422. Burton and Milton, iii 596.

Lyons family, of Lyons' court, Filton, ii 441; arms, 441; distinct from the family of Ashton, 441; owned property at Bishopworth, 284; arms, 443; David de, 441; David,

Lyons family, of Lyons' court, Filton—*contd.* Robert, Stephen, Ralph, Thomas, and Nicholas de, 441; Richard de, 441; Edith, wife of Richard Holbeach, 441.

Lyons-court, Filton, ii 441; mansion, 441; held by the Lyons family of the abbots of Keynsham, 441; the Holbeach family, 441; Francis Adams, 442.

Lyon's-cross, Long-Ashton, ii 304.

Lypemen or retailers of the market, b 32.

Lypiat, hamlet in Kilmersdon, ii 447; granted by the family of Lypiat to Bradenstoke priory, Wilts, 447.

Lyrpole, John, last incumbent of the chantry of St. John, Frome, ii 194.

Lysons, Daniel, physician, b 46; governor of Bath hospital, 48.

Lyte family, owned Lyte's-Cary, iii 193; mansion, 193; arms, 193; monuments in Charlton Mackerel church, 194. Alice, wife of John St. Albyn, i 265; Henry, J.P., *xliv*; John, *xl*. John, married Edith Horsey, iii 193; John, owned Northover, 306; John, owned Bablew in Tintinhull, 309; Margaret, wife of Richard Dodington, 518; Nicholas and Elizabeth, 210. Thomas, i *xl*. Thomas, married an heiress of the Drew family, iii 193; William, owned Northover, 306.

Lytes Cary, manor in Charlton Mackarell, iii 193; owned by the Lyte family, 193; mansion, 193.

Lytton, procured with Combe St. Nicholas, by bishop Giso, of Wells, ii 475 (*see* Litton).

Lytton, Richard Warburton, governor of Bath hospital, b 48.

Lyveden, Roger, of Bristol, owned property in Ashton-Philips, ii 296; Isabella, his widow, afterwards held it in jointure, 296; Jane, wife of Richard Wymbush, 297; Agnes, wife of John Wythiford, 297.

M

Macdonald, Arch., J.P., i *xliv*.

Macharius held land in Evercreech, iii 414.

Macie, David, Eliza and Richard, memorial stones in Weston church, i 162, 163; John, benefaction to the poor of Weston, 166. John, sheriff, 1753, i *xxxix*.

Mackay, Barbara, wife of John Miller, i 104.

Mackenzie, Right Hon. James Stuart, J.P., i *xliv*.

Mackinnon, John, who carried off the Pretender at the battle of Culloden, died in Bath, and memorial tablet in Bathwick church, i 123.

Mackrath, Robert, owned East-Brent, i 196. and Chedzoy, iii 93.

Maddox, Isaac, dean of Wells, 1733, i 190.

Maden, colonel Martin, monument in Bath abbey, 1756, b 69.

Madox family, owned Norton-Ferrers, iii 41; John: Jane: Cecilia: Richard, monument in Kilmington church, 42.

Madox, William, sheriff, 1741, i *xxxix*.

Maggott, Alexander, last incumbent of Twing's chantry, Taunton, iii 238.

Maggs, Thomas, benefaction to Pensford, ii 429.

Magnaville, Geffrey de, constable of the tower, ii 79; William, who allowed the name to be corrupted into Mandeville, married Margaret, daughter of Eudo, 79; Geffrey, appointed constable of the tower, and received title of earl of Essex, 79; William, 79 (*see* also Mandeville).

Maiden Bradley, prior of, landowner temp. Ed. I,
i *xxvii.*

Maidenbrook, hamlet in Cheddon - Fitzpaine,
iii 245 ; lands in, owned by St. John's hospital, Bridgwater, 246.

Main-Down hill race course, ii 487.

Maine, Agnes, epitaph in Broadway churchyard,
i 19.

Mainers, Tirrel de, iii 367.

Mainfrid held Quarum-Kitnor, iii 556.

Malbanc, William de, iii 457 ; Joan, wife of John
Warre, 261.

Malet or Mallet family, owned Curry-Mallet,
i 32 ; land in Puckington, 56 ; Enmore,
90—92 ; St. Audries, 92, iii 496. Wolley
(Devon), i 92, 93 ; Pightley, 245. Lydiard-
Pincherton, ii 494. Ashington, iii 213 ;
Nethercot and Corsley, 265 ; Oake, 273 ;
Sutton-Mallet, 430 ; Dunden, 447 ; Shepton-Mallet, 462 ; West - Quantockshead,
496 ; Shipham, 601. memorial window in
Bath abbey, B 59. tombs in Curry-Mallet
church, i 34. effigies in Shepton-Mallet
church, iii 463. the family arms, i 94 ;
William, distinguished himself at the battle
of Hastings, and was deputed to bury the
body of Harold, 32 ; sheriff of Yorkshire,
32. Robert, great chamberlain of England, disinherited and banished the kingdom by Henry I, 32, iii 462. he held land
of Glastonbury abbey, ii 244. Gilbert, inherited the Somersetshire estates, i 90 ;
Beatrix, married William de Archis, 90 ;
William, baron in time of Henry II, *xxvi* ;
paid Danegeld, 32 ; held Cricket-Malherbe,
22 ; Curry Mallet, 32. lands of Glastonbury abbey, ii 244. Shepton Mallet, iii 462 ;
Wood Advent, 540. William, resided at
Curry, and became sheriff of the county,
i 32. forfeited his estates for rebellion against
king John, iii 447, 462. last in the male
line of this branch of the family, i 90.
Mabel, daughter of William, married Sir
Hugh de Vivonne, iii 462. Helewise, married Sir Hugh Poinz, i 32.

Malet family, of Enmore : William, banish'ed
the kingdom by Henry I, i 90 ; Hugh,
assumed the name of Fitchet, 90 ; Baldwin,
reassumed the name of Malet, and resided
at Enmore, married Emma de Neville, 90 ;
Sir William, married Sarah Sylley, 90. received land in Mudford from Henry de
Modiford, iii 220. Sir William, i 90 ;
sheriff, 1211, 1212, 1213, *xxxiii* ; Sir Baldwin, married Mabilia Deaudon, 90 ; landowner temp. Ed. I, *xxvii.* owned Lydiard-
Pincherton, ii 494. West-Quantockshead,
iii 496 ; owned one knight's fee in Cossington, 434. Sir John, married Sybil de St.
Clare, i 91 ; Sir Baldwin, married Hawise
Ralegh, 91. settled Oake, for life, on

Malet family, of Enmore—*continued.*
Sir John Trivet, reversionary to William
Coker, iii 273 ; held the wardship of John
Luttrell, 499. Sir John, married Elizabeth
Kingston, i 91 ; Sir Baldwin, married (1)
Elizabeth Trivet, (2) Amice Lyffe, 91 ; Sir
John, married Joan Hill, 91 ; on his death,
was succeeded by his daughter, Eleanor,
91 ; Eleanor, married Sir John Hull, 91 ;
on the death of their son, Edward, the
estate reverted to Hugh Malet, son of Sir
Baldwin and Amice Lyffe, 91 ; Sir Hugh,
married Joan Ronyon, 91. leased Lydiard-
Pincherton to John Wadham and others :
granted it to Walter Bluet and others, for
the use of Thomas Malet, his son, and
Joan, his wife, ii 494. owned Sutton-Mallet, iii 430. Thomas, i *xl* ; married Joan
Wadham, 91, ii 494. William, married
Alice Young, of Bristol, i 91. and became
possessed of Easton-in-Gordano, iii 149.
vested the manor of Lydiard-Pincherton in
lord Fitzwarren and others, ii 494. sold
West - Quantockshead to his brother, Sir
Baldwin, of St. Audries, iii 496 ; held Sutton-Mallet of Sir Giles Strangeways, 430 ;
owned Oake, 273. Hugh, married Isabel
Michel, i 91 ; Richard, married Elizabeth
Luttrell, of Dunster, 92 ; Thomas, married
Elizabeth Colles, 92 ; sheriff, 1576, *xxxvii* ;
Sir John, married Mary Popham, 92 ;
sheriff, 1601, *xxxviii* ; John, married the
daughter of Sir John Tracy, 92. M.P. for
Bath, 1623, B 21. John, married Unton,
the daughter of Francis, lord Hawley, i 92,
iii 262. Elizabeth, his daughter, married
John Wilmot, earl of Rochester, and conveyed to him the manor of Enmore, i 92,
iii 262, 430.

Malet family, of St. Audries : Baldwin, second
son of Thomas Malet, of Currypool, and
Joan Wadham, was solicitor to Henry VIII,
married (1) Joan Tacle, (2) Anne Hatch, of
Wolley, i 92, iii 496 ; owned West-Quan-
tockshead, 496 ; and Weacombe, 497 ;
owned Clatworthy, which he sold to
Thomas Carent, 509. John, his second
son, succeeded to the Wolley estates, i 92 ;
Michael, married a daughter of — Stawel,
92 ; was ancestor to the Malets of St.
Audries, 92 ; Richard, of St. Audries, mar-
ried Joane Warre, 93 ; Arthur, 93, iii 496.
Michael, married Catherine Alley, i 93 ;
Richard, 93 ; Gawen, married Cecily Alley,
93 ; Alley, in whom the line of Michael
Malet, of St. Audries, became extinct, 93 ;
Thomas, of Wolley, grandson of John, of
St. Audries, succeeded, 93 ; was judge of
King's Bench, 93 ; married Jane Mills, 93.
surrendered the office of clerk of the castle,
town and lordship of Taunton, iii 228. in-

Manasse, the wife of, held lands in Wells,
iii 393.

Manby [Manley], Rev. H. Churley, incumbent
of Sanford-Arundel, iii 26; of Hawkridge,
529; of Withypool, 558.

Manchester, duke of, J.P., i *xli*.

Mandate of the bishop of Bath and Wells
respecting the baths, в 40.

Mandeville or de Magna Villa family owned
Kenton Mandevill, ii 79; lands in Coker,
341; Hardington, 347. Geffrey de, baron
in time of Henry II, i *xxvi*. owned Kenton Mandeville, ii 79; Hardington, 347;
William de, of Hardington, 347; Robert
de, of Hardington, 347; Robert de, held
one knight's fee in East and West Coker,
with the hundred of Coker, 341; John,
owned land in Coker, which his widow,
Clemence, held in dower, 341; Robert, of
Hardington, 347; John, of Hardington,
347; of East-Coker, 341. Geffrey, landowner temp. Ed. I, i *xxvii*. Robert de, enfeoffed Alexander Luttrell with the Hardington estate, ii 347, 348; Robert, of Coker,
was outlawed, 341; Maud, sister of Robert,
released to Hugh Courtney all her rights in
Coker, 341.

Mangonesse found at East-Harptree, iii 587.

Manheve (*see* Minehead).

Maniple, ii 251.

Mann, William, married the widow of John
Bush, and became possessed of the manor
of Butcombe, ii 315; Francis, sold Butcombe to Richard Plaister, 315.

Manners, Eleanor, daughter of lord Roos, and
second wife of John, earl of Bath, ii 391.

Manningham, Thomas, M.D., governor of Bath
hospital, в 49.

Manno, holder of Oaktrow, ii 6.

Manny, Anne, daughter of lord Manny, married
John, lord Hastings, ii 337.

Mannyngford, Roger, sheriff, 1372, i *xxxv*.

Manor houses: Abbots'-Leigh, iii 154. Ashton-
Philips, ii 296, 297; Backwell, 307. Barrington, iii 113. Barrow, ii 311; Beckington (Seymour's Court), 200. Brimpton
d'Evercy, iii 215. Butcombe, ii 315; Cadbury, 68; Castle-Cary, 56. Cathanger, i 42;
Charlinch, 240. Chilcompton, ii 129. Clapton, iii 179. Claverton, i 146. Claverham,
iii 617; Clevedon, 168; Crowcombe, 516;
Dodington, 519. Donyat, i 35. Downhead,
iii 476. Durleigh, i 79. East-Cranmore
(Cross House), ii 208; Glastonbury (Sharpham Park), 255, 259, 268. Halswell, i 80.
Hardington, ii 453; High Church, 454.
Hinton, iii 369. Langridge, i 132. Marksbury, ii 427; Mere, 273. Montacute, iii 314;
Nailsea, 162. Nemnet, ii 319. Orchard,
iii 491; Pilton, 481. Porlock (Worthy),
ii 37. Pylle, iii 483; Rowdon, 537. Stan-

Manor houses—*continued.*
ton-Drew, ii 434. Stowey, iii 553. Sutton
Court, ii 96. Swainswick, i 153; Swell, 65.
Sydenham, iii 86.

Manors belonging to the bishopric of Bath and
Wells, iii 394, 395, 396.

Mansel, North-Petherton, iii 72; granted by
William de Erleigh to Philip Arbalistarius,
whose descendants took the name of Mansel, 72; subsequently owned by the Bacon
family, 72; seat of John Slade, 72.

Mansel or Maunsel, name assumed by Philip
Arbalistarius, who married a daughter of
Sir Hugh de Auberville, iii 72; family held
Mansel for twenty generations, 72; arms, 72.

Mansewer, Henry, owned land in Bishopworth,
ii 284.

Mansfield, earl of, J.P., i *xli*.

Mansfield, viscount (*see* Cavendish).

Manston, John, founded a chantry in Wells
cathedral, iii 402.

Manworth, lands in, held by the Sydenham
family, iii 215.

Maperton: its situation, ii 85; Domesday survey, 85; owned by Turstin FitzRolf: held
by Goisfrid: by Alwold T.R.E. 85; owned
by the families of Newmarch, Moels (*see*
p. 66), Courtney, Huntingdon, Hungerford,
Thomas Lockyer and Mary Smith, 85;
hamlets of Clapton, Hatherley and Slatter-
ford [Latterford], 86; church (SS. Peter
and Paul) and its monuments, 86; bells (3),
86.

Maplet, Anne, monument in Bath abbey, 1670,
в 69; John, M.D., monument in Bath
abbey, 1670, 69.

Marble found at Vobster-Tor, Mells, ii 462.

Marble, James, monk of Hinton, pensioned,
iii 368.

March, Alice de, daughter of Guy, earl of An-
goulême, married Gilbert de Clare, earl of
Gloucester, was divorced from him, iii 148.

March, Richard, chaplain to lord Berkeley,
iii 143.

March, Mortimer family, earls of, owned Odcombe, ii 324. Milverton, iii 14; Park house
and lands in Newton and Exton, 61;
Bridgwater castle and a third of that manor,
80; the manor of Easton in Gordano, 149;
land in Newhall, 457; were foresters of
Petherton, Exmore, Neroche and Selwood,
61; Roger, owned Milverton, 14; was
forester of Petherton, Exmore, Neroche,
Mendip and Selwood, and custodian of the
warren of Somerton: owned Park house
and lands in Newton and Exton—which
lands and offices passed to his descendants,
61; owned Bridgwater castle and a third of
the manor, 80; Edmund, married Philippa,
daughter of Lionel, duke of Clarence, 14,
80; became possessed of Easton-in-Gor-

Marston-Moat, ii 214.

Marston-Parva, ii 374; owned by the de Hastings family, 337; John, earl of Pembroke, 338.

Martel family owned Chewton-Mendip, ii 116; Geffrey, 116; John, 116; Ivo, 116; William, 116; Roger, 116; Joan, who married Reginald Fitz-Peter, 116.

Martenesey, in Mere, ii 274.

Martin family held Brown, ii 46; Compton-Martin, 132; Seaborough, 174; Lydford West, 84; Aldwick, 315; Nemnet, 319. Pylle, iii 483; Blagdon, 569; Christon, 578; Uphill, 609; effigies in Blagdon church, 570. Adam, tomb in Crewkerne, ii 164; Adam, monument in Seaborough church, 174; Adam and Elizabeth, monument in Hinton St. George church, 168. Alianor, married Philip de Columbers, iii 551. Eleanor, wife of William Columbers, ii 84; inherited part of the estates of Sir William Martin, 132. Gerard, J.P., i *xliv.* Gerard, owned East - Pennard, iii 479; monuments in East-Pennard church, 479; benefaction, 479. Hugh, built a house at Seaborough, ii 173; Joan, wife of Nicholas de Audley, 84, 132. John, M.P. for Bath, 1394, B 20. Nicholas, married Margaret Wadham, i 48. Richard, married Margaret Gold, and became part-owner of Seaborough, ii 173; Robert, ancestor of the Martins, of Seaborough, 132. Robert, sheriff, 1358, i *xxxiv.* Thomas, monument in Baltonsbury church, ii 271; William procured a charter for a market at Lydford-West, 83; and a charter of free-warren, 84; Sir William, married Eleanor Mohun, 132; held half a knight's fee in Morton, 133; and in Bigfold, 133; a fourth of a knight's fee in Beauchampstoke, 319. held Hornblotton, iii 476; held Blagdon, 569; was known also as "Fitzmartin," 569. William, who left his estates to the families of Columbers and Audley, ii 132. William, sheriff, 1490, i *xxxvi*; Sir William, sheriff, 1501, *xxxvi (see* Fitzmartin).

Martindale, Isaac, gift to Wraxall church, iii 161.

Martinseye, lands in, granted by Anastatia Croc to Sir Thomas Trivet, iii 101.

Martin-street, hamlet in Baltonsbury, ii 270.

Martyne, Joan, i 256.

Martoc, John, monument in Banwell church, iii 568.

Martock: situation, iii 2; market, 2; column, 2; tithings of Martock, Hurst, Bower-Henton, Milton, Witcombe, Ash, Coat, Stapleton and Load, 2; includes also three farms near Buckland St. Mary, 2; natural productions, 3; rivers Parret and Yeo, 3; bridges, 3; belonged to Edith, queen of Edward the Confessor, 3; Domesday sur-

Martock—*continued.*
vey, 3; held by the king: two and a half hides held by Ansger and Aluric, 4; subsequently owned by the earls of Bulloigne, 4; the de Fieules family, 4; the de Montacutes, 4; John Beaufort, marquis of Dorset, and his descendants, 5; Henry Stafford, duke of Buckingham, 5; lord Monteagle, 5; the Strodes, of Burrington [Barrington], and Zachary Bayly, who sold part of the manor to various tenants, and the remainder to Henry and John Slade, of Ash, 5; George Slade, 5; mansion of the Fieules and Montacute families: ruined: bridge over moat still remaining, 5; the Mertok family held lands here, 5; as also did Muchelney abbey, 135; manor of Milton - Falconbridge, 5, 6; Stapleton, 7; Ash, Ash-Bulleyn or Pyke's-Ash, 6; Domesday survey, 6; owned by the earls of Bouloigne: held by Ansger: by Bristuin T.R.E. 6; subsequently held of Baldwin de Champflower by the de Camme family, 6; Peter de Fauconbergh, 6; Richard Pavely and Hugh Pike released their rights here to Hugh Kenne, 6; the Kennes, 7; the Pyke family, 7; James Leigh or Reynolds, 7; Napier family of Tintinhull, 7; Hurst tithing, in Domesday "Achelai," 8; owned by Alured: held by Alwi T.R.E. 8; "Prior's-Lands," owned by the priory of St. Michael's Mount, 8; granted to Sion abbey, 8; subsequently owned by Humphry Colles, 8; Mary Buckland, 8; the vicars choral of Wells held several estates here, 9; church (All Saints) and its monuments, 8, 9, 10; bells (5), 9; chantry, 8; benefactions, 9—11; grammar-school, 11; Thomas Farnaby, author, lived here, 11; Longload tithing, 11; river Yeo, 11; Sabina de Urtiaco gave all her lands here to Robert Corbyn, 11; subsequently held with the manor of Martock, 11; chapel, 11; bells (2), 11; benefactions, 12.

Martock hundred: situation, iii 1; derivation of name, 1, 2; oak-trees, 1, 2; owned by the lords of the manor of Martock, 2.

Marwood (*see* Malreward).

Marwood, James Benedictus, seat at Winsham, ii 478.

Masberry-castle, ii 209.

Mascol, John, benefaction to Stoke-Courcy, i 258.

Masham, lady Damaris, monument in Bath abbey, 1708, B 69.

Mashie, William, one of the Camely murderers, ii 157.

Mason, Emanuel, memorial stone in Brewton church, i 217. Robert, monument in Bath abbey, 1664, B 69. William, held land in Hornblotton, iii 476.

Master, Thomas, owned Brean, i 178.

z

Meriet family of Merriot—*continued.*
from John de Mohun, 15; owned Ashton-
Meriet, 298. land in Milverton, iii 15;
Combe-Flory, 247; Fenhampton, 272;
Hestercombe, 259; Elworthy and Willet,
525; benefactor to Taunton priory, 247;
founded a house of Carmelites at Taunton,
236. died without issue, ii 170; Simon,
nephew of Walter, owned Meriot, 170.
Ashton-Meriet, which his trustees granted
to the priory of St. Peter at Bath, 298.
held Bradford, iii 244; founded a chantry
at Combe-Flory, 248; monument in Combe-
Flory church, 248. Sir John, knt., of
Merriot, married Eleanor Beauchamp, of
Hatch, ii 170. inherited the estates of
John de Beauchamp, i 45; was commissioner of sewers, *xii*. held Marston-Magna,
ii 374. Hestercombe, iii 259; Stoke-under-
Hamden, 319. John de, owned also Lopen,
Stratton and Marston Magna, ii 170; Sir
John, knt., of Merriot, 170; George, died
without issue, 170; Margaret, wife of Sir
Thomas Bonville, 170, iii 122. Elizabeth,
wife of Humphrey Stafford, ii 170, iii 122.
Meriet family, of Ashton Meriet, ii 297. and
Combe Flory, iii 247; and Hestercombe,
259. Sir John, knt., received Ashton-
Meriet from William de Ashton, ii 297.
founded a chantry at Hestercombe, iii 258.
Elizabeth, wife of John, ii 297; John, 298;
sold Long-Ashton to his uncle Walter, 298.
Walter, son of John, owned Combe-Flory,
Hestercombe, land at Cerney, Coke's mead
in Taunton, land at Wyke, Bykely, Pil-
leigh, Wydecombe, and Estcote, Elworthy
and Plashe, Brompton - Rauf, Capeland,
Long-Ashton and Bradford, iii 259; Walter,
owned also Merriot (*see* Meriets of Merriot),
Simon (*see* Meriets of Merriot), John, 259;
Sir John, 259; Elizabeth, daughter and
heir of John, married John la Warre, to
whom she conveyed the manor of Hestercombe, 259.
Meriet manor (*see* Merriot).
Merlaund, Henry de, landowner temp. Ed. I,
i *xxvii*. owned Orchardley, ii 222; Henry
de, 222; Henry, 222; Joan de, held
Orchardley in dower, 223; John de, last of
his name to possess that manor, 223.
Merleberge (Marlborough), Alured de, held
Chelworth, ii 419. lands in Newton, iii 63.
Thomas de, granted licence to amortize
lands in Buckland St. Mary, i 21; lord of
the manor of Isle-Brewers, 54; founder of
a chantry at Isle-Brewers, 55.
Merlesuain held Brean, i 178. Bawdrip, iii 91;
Bridgwater, 78; Over - Stratton, 107;
Stockland, Quantockshead, Huish-Champ-
flower, Bagborough and Newhall, 457.
Merlinge (*see* Moorlinch).

Merridge, hamlet of Spaxton, i 244; owned by
Alured de Ispania, and held by Rannulf and
Alwi, 244; owned by the Fichets, and by
them conveyed to the family of Fourneaux,
245.
Merrifield manor, owned by John de Ilminster,
i 47; de Beauchamp family, 47; Fulk de
Bermyngham, 47; Popham family, 47;
Wadham family, 48; Wyndham family,
who pull down the manor house, and build
farm house and alms house, 48; Egremont
family, 48.
Merriot : situation, ii 169; Domesday survey,
169; owned by the earl of Morton (whose
tenant was Dodeman) and Harding Fitz-
Alnod, 169; by Lewin, Bristward and
Goduin T.R.E. 169; owned by the families
of de Meriet, 169, 170; Bonville, Thomas
Gray, marquis of Dorset, Henry, duke of
Suffolk, William Rice and Henry Rodbard,
170; chantry founded by the Meriets, 171;
church (All Saints) and its monuments,
171; bells (5), 171; benefactions, 171.
church belonged to Muchelney abbey,
iii 135.
Merry, John, J.P., i *xliv.*
Mershton, John de, M.P., 1346, 1348, 1350,
i *xxx.* John de, M.P. for Bath, 1346, 1347,
1355, B 20.
Mersitone (*see* Marston Bigot).
Merston, Matilda de, prioress of Cannington,
1317, i 232.
Merstone (*see* Marston Magna).
Mertok family held lands in Martock, iii 5;
Roger : William : Stephen, 5; Peter, out-
lawed for felony, 5.
Merton, Eleanor, wife of Sir Matthew Stawel,
iii 250. William de, dean of Wells, 1236,
i 189.
Merton priory, Surrey, received four marks
from Martock church, iii 8. canons, owned
Norton Canonicorum, ii 151.
Mervin, Lucy, wife of George, earl of Castle-
haven, iii 553.
Meschin, William, baron in time of Henry II,
i *xxvi*, 251.
Meschines, William, lord of Coupland, i 185;
Ranulf, earl of Chester, 185.
Messiter, Rev. John, incumbent of Bratton-
Seymour, iii 36.
Messletre, Thomas de, M.P. for Bath, 1297,
B 19.
Metford, Richard, bishop of Salisbury, granted
an indulgence to the benefactors of Lang-
port hospital, iii 133.
Metford, Walter, dean of Wells, 1413, i 190.
Methuen family owned the Beckington estates,
ii 200. Cheddon-Fitzpaine and Withey,
iii 246. Freshford, i 126. Paul, married
Grace Ashe, ii 200; John, 200; John, lord
chancellor of Ireland, inherited the Becking-

Milverton Wick, hamlet in Milverton, iii 15.

Milverton, John de, a great opponent of Wickliff, iii 18.

Minchin-Barrow (*see* Barrow-Minchin).

Minehead : its situation, ii 26 ; Upper Town, 26 ; Lower or Middle Town, 26 ; Quay Town, 26 ; number of houses, and population in 1705 and 1783, 27 ; Domesday survey, 27 ; owned by William de Mohun, and held by Algar T.R.E. 27 ; owned by the families of Mohun and Luttrell, 27, iii 500. John Fownes Luttrell, ii 27 ; incorporated and endowed by queen Elizabeth, 27 ; a statute for recovering the port obtained from William III by the Luttrell family, and by them the harbour is improved, 27 ; large fishing connection, 27 ; account of its trade and imports, 1745—1778, 28, 29 ; purchase of freehold estate in Ottery St. Mary parish, 29 ; limpets for marking linen, curious process, 29, 30 ; fish of the coast, 30 ; market and fair, 30 ; woollen manufacture, 30 ; Quirck's almshouse, 30, 31 ; bequests by Col. Alexander Luttrell, Joan Moggridge and George Sullivan, 31 ; hamlets of Bratton, Periton and Hindon, 31 ; the church and its monuments, 32, 33 ; bells (5), 32 ; statue to queen Anne, 32 ; cross, 33. advowson held by the prior and canons of Brewton, i 214.

Minehead point, i *xi,* ii 26.

Mineheved (*see* Minehead).

Mineral products of the county, i *xv, xvi.*

Mineral springs (*see* Springs).

Minery court, Chewton-Mendip, ii 117.

Minifie, Rev. James, J.P., i *xliv* ; incumbent of Goathurst, 83. Rev. James, incumbent of Norton-Fitzwarren, iii 272 ; Rev. James, incumbent of Staplegrove, 290 ; monument in Staplegrove church, 290 ; arms, 290.

Minories, in St. Botolph's, London, ceded by the bishop of Bath and Wells to Edward VI, iii 395.

Minsterland in Milverton, estate granted to the church, iii 16.

Mintern, Martha, benefaction to Crewkerne, ii 164

Misiers, Lovis Chevalier de, monument in Middlezoy church, iii 443.

Missingham, Robert de, prior of Taunton, 1339, iii 235.

Mist, Grace (*neé* Lydford), memorial monument in Weston Bampfylde church, ii 92.

Misterton : its situation, ii 165 ; attached to the manor of Crewkerne, 165 ; the church (St. Leonard), 165 ; bells (2), 165.

Mitchel, David Robert, owned Isle-Brewers, i 54 ; Sir Bartholomew, sheriff, 1617, *xxxviii* ; Sir Bartholomew, benefaction to Cannington, 237. Bartholomew, heir to Tristram Mitchel, iii 434 ; Thomas, held Chilton, 433 ; Tristram, 434.

Mitchell, Bridget, wife of (1) Thomas Flower, (2) William Eyre, ii 460. Charles, brass plate in South Brewham church, i 222. Rev. Mr., incumbent of Witham-Friary, ii 234.

Modbury vale, ii 461.

Modeslie (*see* Mudgley).

Modiford family held Mudford, iii 220 ; Henry de, granted land to William Malet, 220 ; arms, 220.

Mody's tenement, Ilminster, i 3.

Moeles, John de, M.P., 1333, i *xxix.*

Moels family owned Cadbury - North, ii 66 ; Cadbury-South, 73 ; Maperton, 85 ; Staeth, 181 ; North - Cheriton, 360. Dunkerton, iii 338 ; land in Blackford, 452 ; land in Holton, 453. Nicholas de, married Hawise de Newmarch, widow of John de Botreaux, and in her right possessed the barony of Newmarch and the lands belonging to it, 338. Roger de, landowner temp. Ed. I, i *xxvii.* owned Cadbury, ii 66 ; served in the Welsh wars, 1277, 66 ; appointed governor of Llanbadarn-Vawr, 66 ; married Alice de Preux, 66 ; held a manor in Wanstraw, 229 ; half a knight's fee in Hemington, 454. John de, landowner temp. Ed. I, i *xxviii.* married the daughter of lord Grey of Ruthyn, and sat in the parliament of Edward I, ii 66 ; owned land in Wanstraw, 229 ; Nicholas de, served in the Scottish wars, 1311 : sat in parliament : married Margaret Courtney, 66 ; Muriel, wife of Thomas Courtney, 66 ; Isabel, wife of Sir William de Botreaux, 66.

Moffat, Elizabeth, monument in Bath abbey, 1791, B 69.

Mogg family owned Stone-Easton Minor, ii 158. Dorothy, second wife of Thomas Churchey, iii 35. George, J.P., i *xlv* ; Jacob, J.P., *xlv.* assisted in purchasing Timsbury out of Chancery, ii 112 ; owned lands in Farrington-Gournay, 137 ; coal-mines, 145 ; part-owner of Hallatrow and Littleton, 148. John, sheriff, 1703, i *xxxviii* ; John, memorial tablet in Wick - Champflower chapel, 219. John, monument in Farrington-Gournay church, ii 140 ; Rev. Thomas and Catharine, his wife, tablet in Stowel church, 379 ; Rev. Thomas, incumbent of High-Littleton, 149.

Moggridge, Joan, bequest to Minehead, ii 31 ; William, vicar of Minehead, 32 ; monument in Porlock church, 39. Mary, benefaction to North-Petherton, iii 74 ; Robert, benefaction to Taunton, 240.

Mohun family of Dunster, ii 7, 8, 9 ; fees belonging to, in time of Henry II, 13, 14 ; Edward III, 14 ; endowments to Dunster priory, 16, 17 ; tomb in Dunster church, 18. owned Badialton, iii 22. Brewton, i 213 ;

Monke, Alice, wife of John Malet, i 93.

Monks' library, Bath : MSS. in, в 66.

Monks' lodgings, Bath, arms in, в 58.

Monks' mill, Bath, в 33, 57.

Monks'-Ham or Ham, Marston-Bigot, ii 216; owned by the monks of Witham, 216, 233; granted at the Dissolution to William, lord Stourton, 216; sold to Sir John Thynne, 216.

Monkham manor, Exford, ii 21.

Monksilver : anciently Silver, Selure and Selvere : situation, iii 534; includes the hamlets of Woodford and Birchanger, 534; owned by Alured de Ispania, 534; Domesday survey, 535; held by Richard : Aluric held it T.R.E. 535; subsequently owned by the de Candos family, 535; the priory of Goldclive, 535, 550; the collegiate church of Windsor, 535; church (All Saints), 535; bells (4), 535.

Monkton, Ninehead-Monks or East-Ninehead, iii 267; owned by Taunton priory, 268.

Monkton, owned by Glastonbury abbey, ii 243.

Monkton manor, Stoke-Courcy, i 252; owned by Eton college, 252.

Monkton-Combe (*see* Combe-Monkton).

Monkton-West : situation, iii 454; river Tone, 454; bridge, 454; Bath-pool, 454; owned by Glastonbury abbey, 454; Domesday survey, 454; Walchel, bishop of Winchester, Roger and Serlo held lands here, 454; owned after the Dissolution by the Powlet family, 454; John Quick, 454; the Warre family, 454, 262; the Bampfyldes, 454; "Court-house," seat of Matthew Brickdale, 454; Gotton hamlet, owned by the families of Cary and Musgrave, 455; Walford, owned by the families of Sellick and Sandford, 455; church (St. Augustine) and its monuments, 455; bells (6), 455; chantries, 456; yew-trees, 456; hospital, 456; Taunton priory owned lands in West-Monkton, 235; lands in, owned by the Wrotham family, 64; Thomas Durant, 65; the Wrothe family, 66, 67.

Monmouth street, Bath, в 35, 74.

Monmouth's rebellion, iii 234; engagement with king's troops at Norton-St.-Philips, 372; at Weston Zoyland, 440; duke proclaimed king at Taunton, 234; encampment at Bridgwater, 77; battle of Sedgmoor, 77; taken and beheaded, 78; general Kirke's barbarities, 234; "The Bloody Assize," 234.

Montacute : situation, iii 309; Montacute or St. Michael's hill, 309; Hedgecock hill and Hamden hill, 310; Roman remains, 310; freestone quarries, 310; formerly a borough and market-town, 310; ancient names, 310, 311; Domesday survey, 311; owned by the earl of Morton : Athelney abbey held it T.R.E. 311; Alured, Drogo, Bretel and

Montacute—*continued.*

Donecan held lands here, 311; subsequently owned by Montacute priory, 311—313; the Phelips family, 313, 314; Montagu family held lands here, 314; manor house, 314; tithings of Bishopston, Hyde, Widcombe and Thorn, 314; leather trade, 314; church (St. Catherine) and its monuments, 314, 315; bells (5), 314; cross, 315; Roman road, 315.

Montacute castle, built by Robert, earl of Morton, iii 311; ruins, converted into a chapel, by Reginald, prior of Montacute, 312.

Montacute hill, i *xiv*, iii 309.

Montacute priory, iii 311—313; founded by William, earl of Morton : possessions, 311, 312; privileges, 313; list of priors, 312, 313; site granted after the Dissolution to Sir William Petre, 313; Robert Freke, 313; Phelips family, 313; dissolution, 313. the priors owned land temp. Ed. I, i *xxvi*; Creech St. Michael, 75. the church and manor of Hunesberge, ii 323; Odcombe church, 325; manor and church of East-Chinnock, 327; a pension from Chisselborough church, 330; land in West-Coker, 344; Closworth, 346; a pension from the church of Marston-Magna, 374; Adbeer and Hummer, 382. land in Mudford, iii 222; in Bradford, 244; a pension from Norton-Fitzwarren church, 272; the hundred of Tintinhull, 297; a revenue from Ivelchester church, 301; Tintinhull manor, 308; the tithes and a pension from Camerton church, 331, 332.

Montacute, Robert de, prior of Montacute, 1460, iii 313.

Montacute, John, marquis of, owned Goathill : married Elizabeth Ingolsthorp, ii 364; killed at Barnet, 364; Ann, his daughter, married Sir William Stoner, 364.

Montacute (*see* Sutton-Montis).

Montacute family (*see* Montague).

Montagud, Ansger de, held Preston-Bermondsey : was progenitor of the Brett family, iii 223.

Montague or Montacute family owned Shepton-Montacute, iii 45; and lands in Montacute, 311; derived their name from Montagu in Normandy, 314; arms, 49. owned also Curry Rivel, i 26; Donyat, 36; Broomfield, 72; Yarlington, 228. Sutton-Montis, ii 88; Thurlbeer, 182; Chisselborough, 330; Norton-under-Hamden, 334; Goathill, 363; Horsington, 371; East - Chelworth, 420. Chedzoy, iii 93; Slow, 190; Thorn-Coffin, 322. Drogo or Drew de, a follower of the Conqueror, held Sutton - Montis, ii 88; Thurlbeer, 182. Shepton-Montacute, iii 45; was castellan of Montacute castle, 311; William de, 45; Richard de, 45. Drogo or

Moore memorial stone in Creech St. Michael church, i 78.

Moorland, hamlet in North-Petherton, iii 72; owned successively by the families of Tilly, Cave, Bythemore and Perceval, 72, 87.

Moorlands, hamlet in Stoke Gregory, ii 180; owned by the families of Tilly and Perceval, 181.

Moorlinch : situation, iii 429; ancient names, 429; spring, 429; fair (discontinued), 429; owned by Glastonbury abbey, 429; cell to Glastonbury, 429; one of " The Seven Sisters," 429; manor vested in the families of Floyer and Rolle, 429; church (St. Mary) and its monuments, 429; bells (6), 429; Mrs. Dodd's benefaction, 429. church exempted from episcopal authority by Ina's charter to Glastonbury, ii 241.

Moors (*see* Commons and Moors).

Moorside, hamlet in Backwell, ii 307.

Mora family (*see* More).

Moravian chapel, Bath, B 74.

Mordaunt, Elizabeth, wife of John Rodney, iii 604. John, created viscount Avalon, 1659, married Elizabeth Carey, ii 269. Sir John, J.P., i *xlii.* owned Badgworth, iii 565; married a daughter of Thomas Prowse, and became possessed of Compton-Bishop, 583, ii 203.

More, Mora or Bythemore family owned Over-Weare, i 185; one knight's fee in Allerton, 176; East-Brent, 196. Sandford - Orcas, ii 378. Moorland, iii 72; a manor in Nailsea, 162. George de la, married Joan de Gournay, i 185; William, 185; arms, 185; John, 186; Roger, 186; John, 186; Alice, wife of David Perceval, 186, iii 87.

More, John, part-owner of Ash-Priors, ii 498.

More, John, of St. John's hospital, Bridgwater, subscribed to the supremacy, 1534, iii 79.

More, Sir Thomas, sheriff, 1532, i *xxxvii.*

More, Walter, abbot of Glastonbury, 1456, ii 255.

Moremen, tenants of the lords of South-Brent, i 197.

Moreshead, in Cannington, iii 302.

Moretaine, Matthew de, received land from William the Conqueror, i *xxv.* owned Chelvy, ii 316. held Clevedon, iii 167.

Moreton tithing of Compton Martin, ii 133; Domesday survey, 133; owned by Serlo de Burci : held by Godric, Elric, Richard and Humphrey, 133; owned by the families of Martin, Sancta Cruce, Mushrom, Gournay, Staunton, Newburgh, Turges, Turberville, Fitz James, Sir Christopher Wroughton, Henry Longe, John Brook, earl of Hertford, and Sir George Morton, 133.

Moreville family owned Flax-Bourton, iii 161; Eudo de, married the heiress of Richard de Wrokeshale, and became possessed of

Moreville family—*continued.*
Wraxall, Bourton and Nailsea, 156 : John de, 156; Elena, wife of Ralph de Gorges, 156.

Morgan, —, married Giles Dodington, iii 598.

Morgan family owned West-Chelworth, ii 420. Easton-in-Gordano, iii 149, 150; monuments in Easton-in-Gordano church, 150.

Morgan, Rev. Charles, married Jane Moore, ii 345. monument in High Ham church, iii 446. Edward, of Lanternan, married a daughter of Hugh Smyth, i 72, ii 292, 293. his sons sold that manor to Andrew Crosse and William Towill, i 72. Elizabeth, benefaction to Shepton - Beauchamp, iii 126. Francis, J.P., i *xlv.* Francis, trustee to Frances Coombe, iii 465. James, benefaction to Stoke-Courcy, i 258. Rev. Nathaniel, governor of Bath hospital, B 49; master of the public grammar school, Bath, 51. incumbent of Charlcombe, i 142. of Clutton, ii 104. prebendary of Wells, iii 397. Richard, sheriff, 1689, i *xxxviii.* Richard, and Mary his wife, monuments in Easton-in-Gordano church, iii 150; trustee to Sturmy's bequest, 151. Richard, mayor of Bath, 1712, 1733, B 26. Thomas Wilkins inherited Easton-in-Gordano from Richard Morgan, and assumed the name of Morgan, iii 150. sheriff, 1776, i *xxxix*; J.P., *xlv.*

Morgane, Fillip, first wife of William Knoyle, ii 378.

Morgane, Mary, of Maperton (daughter of Christopher Brett), monument in White-Stanton church, iii 127; arms, 128.

Morice, Richard de, memorial acrostic in South-Barrow church, ii 64; Walter, M.P. for Dunster, 1361, 15.

Morley family, memorial inscriptions in Wotton Courtney church, ii 50.

Morley, Fulk, purchased the abbey-house, etc., Bath, B 58. Jeffery owned Curry Rivel, i 26; John, J.P., *xlv.*

Morres, Margaret, second wife of Lord Chief Justice Choke, ii 292.

Morris, Daniel, benefactions to Bath abbey, B 71. Elizabeth, wife of John Burland, i 257. Francis held the tithes of Filton, ii 441. John, J.P., i *xlv.* John, governor of Bath hospital, B 48; Thomas, monument in Bath abbey, 1763, 69.

Morrison, Elizabeth, monument in Bath abbey, 1738, B 69.

Morryce, Robert, holder of a pension in Wedmore, i 191.

Mors, John, received a pension from Bridgwater hospital, iii 80.

Morse, Thomas, benefaction to Banwell, iii 568; to Compton-Bishop, 583.

Morson, Sir Richard, received at the Dissolution East-Chinnock and other lands belong-

Morson, Sir Richard—*continued.*
　ing to Montacute priory, ii 327 : sold East-
　Chinnock to Stephen Hales, 327 ; sold
　Closworth to Stephen Hales, 346.

Mortimer, Edward Horlock, J.P., i *xlv* ; Joseph,
　J.P., *xlv.*

Mortimer, John, the daughter of, married Wil-
　liam Wrothe, iii 67. Elizabeth, sister of
　Sir John Mortimer, first wife of Thomas
　West, lord de la Warre, ii 412.

Mortimer, Ralph de, received lands from Wil-
　liam the Conqueror, i *xxv.* was ancestor
　of the earls of March : owned Walton-in-
　Gordano, iii 170. Roger de, married Maud
　de Braose, ii 324. and became possessed
　of a third part of the manor of Bridgwater,
　iii 80. William, inherited his mother's
　estates, married Hawise de Muscegros,
　ii 324, 379, iii 80. Edward (or Edmund ?),
　lord Mortimer, ii 324, iii 80 ; Roger : Sir
　Edmund : Roger, earls of March (*see*
　March). Agnes, wife of Laurence de Has-
　tings, afterwards earl of Pembroke, ii 337.
　Joan, first wife of James, lord Audley,
　iii 552 ; Margaret, first wife of Thomas, lord
　Berkeley, 143, 279 ; Anne, wife of Richard,
　earl of Cambridge, 14, 149 ; her son,
　Richard, duke of York, succeeded to the
　estates of the earls of March, 149.

Morton, Sir George, owned Moreton, ii 133 ;
　John de, held half a knight's fee in demesne
　in Moreton, 133. Richard, sheriff, 1481,
　1482, i *xxxvi* ; Thomas, sheriff, 1566,
　xxxvii.

Morton, Matthew Ducie, owned Winford, ii 321.

Morton, Robert, earl of, received land from
　William the Conqueror, i *xxv* ; was brother
　to William the Conqueror, married Maud
　Montgomery, daughter of the earl of
　Shrewsbury, 75. built Montacute castle,
　iii 311 ; joined the rebellion against William
　Rufus, 299. he owned Alford, ii 58. Ap-
　ley, iii 28 ; Ash-Brittle, 21. Ashill, i 12 ;
　Bickinhall, 62. Bradford, iii 243. lands in
　Brewton, i 213. Brushford, iii 507 ; land
　in Butleigh, 448 ; Charlton-Musgrave, 37 ;
　Chilthorne-Domer, 216. Chisselborough,
　ii 330 ; Cloford, 205 ; Closworth, 346.
　Creech-St.-Michael, i 74. Creedlingcot,
　iii 331. Crewkerne, ii 160. Crowcombe,
　iii 514 ; Cucklington, 51 ; Ditcheat, 472.
　Donyat, i 36. Draycot, iii 219. East-Chin-
　nock, ii 327 ; Estham, 160 ; Goathill, 363.
　Grindham, iii 28 ; Hill - Bishops, 254.
　Houndsborough, ii 323. Ilton, i 47 ; Isle-
　Brewers, 53. Kenton - Mandevill, ii 78.
　Kingston, iii 323 ; Lopen, 122 ; Luston,
　321. Marston-Magna, ii 374 ; Merriot,
　169 ; land in Milborne-Port, 353. Monta-
　cute, iii 311. Nether-Adbeer, ii 382 ; North
　Curry, 178 ; North-Parret, 335. Norton-

Morton, Robert, earl of—*continued.*
　Fitzwarren, iii 271. Norton-under-Ham-
　den, ii 334 ; Odcombe, 324 ; Pendomer,
　348. Pointington, ii 375. Preston, iii 15 ;
　Prestetune, 502. Redlinch, i 225. Seving-
　ton, iii 123 ; Shepton-Beauchamp, 125 ;
　Shepton-Montacute, 45 ; Sock-Dennis, 307.
　South Bradon, i 15 ; Staple Fitzpaine, 58.
　Stoke, iii 484 ; Stoke-Trister, 49 ; Stoke-
　under-Hamden, 315 ; Stochet, 320 ; Stone
　and Stock, 221. Sutton-Montis, ii 88.
　Swell, i 65. Taunton, iii 231. Thorn-
　Falcon, ii 181. Thorn-St.-Margaret, iii 27.
　Thurlbeer, ii 182. Tintinhull, iii 308. Trent,
　ii 380. Wellisford, iii 19 ; White-Stanton,
　126. Yarlington, i 228. land in Yeovil,
　iii 205 ; William, earl of, built and endowed
　the priory of Montacute, 311. on which he
　bestowed Creech, i 75. Houndsborough,
　ii 323 ; East-Chinnock, 327 ; Closworth,
　346. rebelled against Henry I, and was
　deprived of his estates, i 75.

Morton, Robert, owned Pitney, iii 130.

Morton-Brett, John, M.D., monument in Bath
　abbey, 1769, B 67.

Mortone (*see* Moreton).

Mortray, hamlet in Buckland-Dinham, ii 452.

Mortray or Murtree, hamlet in Buckland-Din-
　ham, ii 452.

Moryce, William, one of the commission for the
　survey of churches and chapels in Somer-
　set at the time of the Reformation, ii 286.

Moryson (*see* Morison).

Moss, Charles, bishop of Bath and Wells,
　iii 390, 396 ; Charles, subdean of Wells,
　396 ; Charles, prebendary of Wells, 397 ;
　Rev. Charles, patron of the living of Yatton,
　619. John, of Wells, part-owner of the
　manor of Glastonbury, ii 259.

Mostyn, Sir Edward, knt., married Barbara
　Browne, ii 311 ; Barbara, his widow, mar-
　ried Edward Gore, of Kiddington, 311.
　Margaret, wife of John Malet, i 93.

Moulins, Eleanor, daughter of William, lord
　Moulins, married Sir Robert Hungerford,
　iii 355.

Mounceaux or Mountsey castle, held by Alured
　de Ispania, iii 529.

Mounceaux family took their name from
　Mounceaux castle, iii 529. Agnes de, land-
　owner temp. Ed. I, i *xxviii* ; William de,
　landowner temp. Ed. I, *xxix.*

Mountague, James, bishop of Bath and Wells,
　1608, a descendant of the Mountagus, earls
　of Salisbury, and son of Sir Edward Moun-
　tagu of Boughton, iii 388 ; repaired the
　palaces of Wells and Banwell, the cathe-
　dral of Wells, and the abbey of Bath, 381,
　388 ; translated to Winchester, 1616, 388,
　232 ; buried in the abbey church, Bath,
　388. altar tomb, B 60, 69 ; arms, 60 ; bene-

Mountague, James—*continued.*
faction to the abbey, 70; he placed an inscription over the windows of the abbey, 59.

Mount-Edgcumbe, viscount, J.P., i *xli.*

Mount-Sydenham, Dulverton, iii 520.

Mountery - street, Wells : college for priests founded by bishop Erghum, iii 383, 402.

Mountfort, Alexander de, owned Emborow, ii 157. sire Jehan de, i *l.* Henry de, held Radstock, ii 457 ; Reginald de, held Radstock and Wellow, 457.

Mountsey, lands in, held by the Sydenham family, iii 215.

Mountsey-castle (*see* Mounceaux).

Mountstuart, viscount, J.P., i *xli.*

Moutray, John, monument in Bath abbey, 1785, B 69.

Mowbray arms, iii 159.

Mowcroft, Edward, master of St. Catherine's hospital, Bedminster, ii 283.

Moyle, Sir Thomas, purchased King-Weston, ii 81 ; Catherine, wife of Sir Thomas Finch, 81 ; Amy, wife of Thomas Kempe, 81.

Moyses held Telsford, iii 362.

Moysey, Abel, J.P., i *xlv.* M.P. for Bath, 1774, 1775, 1780, 1784, B 22 ; governor of Bath hospital, 48. Abel, monument in Newton-St.-Lo church, 1780, iii 344, 345.

Moythye, Margaret, wife of John Cradock, iii 588.

Mucan, abbot of Glastonbury, ii 249.

Mucegros (*see* Muscegros).

Mucheldenne, Roger de, iii 439.

Muchelney, or the Great Island, iii 134 ; rivers Parret and Ivel, 134 ; includes the village of Muchelney (in which stands the abbey), the hamlets of Thorney, and Muchelney-Ham, 134 ; Domesday survey, 134 ; owned by the abbey, 134 ; granted at the Dissolution to Edward, earl of Hertford, 136 ; subsequently owned by Walter Long, 136 ; another manor owned by — Bethune, esq., 136 ; church (SS. Peter and Paul), 137 ; bells (5), 137 ; bishop Haselshaw's ordination of the vicarage, 136.

Muchelney abbey, iii 134 ; Benedictine, founded by Athelstan, 134 ; Domesday survey, 134 ; possessions, 135 ; abbots held some lands of Richard Revel and Margaret Tabuel, temp. Henry II, 135 ; revenues in Muchelney, temp. Ed. I, 135 ; list of abbots, 135 ; at the Dissolution, the monastery and its lands granted to Edward, earl of Hertford, 136 ; the abbey buildings, 136.

Muchelney abbots, list of, iii 135. received land from William the Conqueror, i *xxv* ; abbot, a baron in time of Henry II, *xxvi* ; a landowner, temp. Ed. I, *xxvi.* possessions, iii 135, owned Cathanger, i 40. Chipstaple, iii 508 ; lands in Cudworth, 117 ; Downhead, 190. Drayton, i 38, 39 ; Earns-

Muchelney abbots—*continued.*
hill, 31 ; Fivehead, 40 ; Ilminster, which they received from king Ina : extract from Domesday-book : value of their possessions there in 1293, 5 ; Isle-Abbots, 50. a revenue from St. John's church, Ivelchester, iii 301. Middleney, i 39. tithes of Somerton, iii 186. Thorney island, ii 469. lands in Twinney, iii 328. in Wanstraw, ii 229. West-Camel, iii 190.

Mud brook, Bath, B 23.

Mudford : situation, iii 220 ; river Yeo and bridge, 220 ; Mudford-street, West-Mudford and Upper-Mudford, 220 ; Domesday survey : (1) held by Warmund, of Ulward, 220 ; (2) held by Dodeman of Baldwin de Execestre : Wnulf held it T.R.E. 220 : (3) held by Rainald of Serlo de Burci : Elmar held it T.R.E. 220 ; Stane or Stone manor, held by Sareb T.R.E. 220; subsequently the chief manor was held by the de Modiford family, 220 ; William Malet held land here, 220 ; land held by Baldwin de Exeter passed to the Courtney family, 221 ; Mudford-Torry, 221 ; Stone manor, 220 ; Socke or Old-Stock, 221, 222 ; Hinton and East-Lane hamlets, 222 ; Wood court, 222 ; church (St. Mary) and its monuments, 222 ; bells (5), 222 ; Montacute priory held lands here, 222, 312. the Windsore family held lands here, ii 383.

Mudford street, Mudford, iii 220.

Mudford-Torry, iii 221 ; held by the Plugenets under the de Romsey family, 221 ; the Dannay family, 221 ; William Brocas, 221 ; the Fermor family, 221 ; the Raymond family, 221.

Mudgley, hamlet of Wedmore, formerly belonged to church of Wells, i 187, iii 378. spring of petrifying quality, i 187.

Muggleworth family owned Charlton-House, iii 155 ; Henry, owned a moiety of the manor of Churchill, 580 ; his widow married Samuel Newnham, 580.

Mulborn, purchased by William Russell from William Marshall, i 253.

Muleborn, Sir William de, M.P., 1322, 1325, i *xxix.*

Mulgrave, baron, J.P., i *xlii.* Constantine, lord, governor of Bath hospital, B 48.

Multon, Mary, wife of an ancestor of Sir Thomas Beauchamp, i 12. Thomas de, married Maud de Vaux, and became possessed of Sevington, iii 123. Thomas de, landowner temp. Ed. I, i *xxviii.* Thomas de, owned also lands in Pynhoe, Devon, iii 123. owned Ashill manor, and obtained a grant of markets and fairs, i 12 ; owned White-Lackington, 67.

Mulverton, John, M.P. for Bath, 1362, 1373, B 20 ; William, M.P. for Bath, 1361, 20.

N

Neale, Jacob, memorial stone in Bathwick church, i 123.

Neapoli, Garner de, prior in England of the Order of St. John of Jerusalem, iii 96; established the sisters of that order in Buckland priory, 96.

Neath, abbot of, landowner temp. Ed. I, i *xxvi*.

Necham, Alexander, on Bath waters, b 6.

Nedcut or Knightcot, hamlet in Banwell, iii 567.

Neell, Elizabeth, inscription in Newton St. Lo church, iii 344.

Neile, Richard, translated from the See of Durham to that of Winchester, 1628, iii 233.

Nelson, Robert, founder of Blue Coat charity, b 50.

Nemnet, ii 318; situation, 318; West-town and Whitling street hamlets, 318; formerly an appendage of Regilbury manor, and held by the families of Martin and Perceval of the abbot of Flaxley, 319; granted at the Dissolution to Sir Anthony Kingston, 319; passed successively to Edward Barnard: the Baber family: the Tynte family, 319; manor house, called Regilbury-house, 319; Fairyfield tumulus, 318, 319; Beauchamstoke, 319; owned by the Beauchampfamily, 319; part held by Robert de Walton, 319; William Martin, 319; Peter de Sancta Cruce, 319; the heir of John de Leycester, 319; Philip le Walleis, 319; Thomas Ive, 319; Mr. Page, 319; living, a chapel to Compton-Martin, 320; church (St. Mary), 320; bells (5), 320; benefaction, 320.

Nerford, John, married Agnes, widow of Sir John Argentine, iii 206; Agnes, his widow, married John Maltravers, 206.

Neroch castle, i 16, 20.

Neroch forest, i *xv*, 10; claim of Beer-Crowcombe, 14; situation, 16; foresters, 16; perambulation temp. Ed. I, 16, 17, iii 57. Curry-Rivel right of commonage on, i 24.

Nesfeld, John, recovered the presentation to the prebend of Timberscombe, ii 45.

Neth Cistercian abbey owned Monkham manor, Exford, ii 21 (*see* Neath).

Nether-Adbeer, hamlet in Trent, ii 382, 383.

Nether-Badgworth, iii 565.

Nether-Ham (*see* Low-Ham).

Nether-Stowey: situation, iii 550; market, 550; fair, 550; market-cross, 550; castle and church of St. Michael (demolished), 550; Domesday survey, 550; owned by Ralph de Pomerei, held by Beatrix: Almer held it T.R.E. 550; subsequently held by the de Candos family, 550, 551; the de Columbers family, 551; the lords Audley, 552, 553; George, lord Audley, created earl of Castlehaven, 553; the Greys, 553; Edward Top, 553; Robert Everard, 553; Robert

Nether-Stowey—*continued.*
Everard Balch, 553; the Castle, Red-deer park, and farm of Rowbear, owned by Edward Walker, 553; church (St. Mary) and its monuments, 553; bells (6), 553; benefactions, 554; John Hodges' benefaction, 302. Puriton annexed, ii 396. lords of, owned Lilstock, iii 534.

Nether-Weare (*see* Lower-Weare).

Nethercot, hamlet in Lydiard St. Laurence, iii 265; owned by the Malet family, 265.

Netherton, hamlet in Closworth, ii 346.

Nettlecombe: situation, iii 535; Raleigh's down, 535; Knap-Dane, 535; Domesday survey, 535; held by the king, 535; Goduin held it T.R.E. 535; subsequently held under the Marshals of England by the de Raleigh family, 536, 537, 538; Thomas de Whalesborough, 538; the Trevelyans, 539; mansion, 540; chantry, 538; church (St. Mary) and its monuments, 541; bells (3), 541; cross, 542. Wood-Advent hamlet, 540; anciently held of the manor of Compton-Dunden, 540; by the de Wode family: the Avenants, 540; Thomas Fitzours, 540; the Raleighs, 540; Trevelyans, 540. Begarn-Huish hamlet, 540; Domesday survey, 540; owned by Ralph Paganel, 540; Agnes de Gaunt, 540; the Luttrells, 541; the Chichesters, 541; the Luttrells again, 541; the Wyndhams, 541. Ludhuish, 541; held by the Hewish family, 541; Richard de Cottelle, 541; Richard Britte, 541; Philip de Wellesleigh, 541; the families of Hill, Say, Cheyney and Waldegrave, 541; Sir John Trevelyan, 541. Colton hamlet, 541.

Nevil or Neville, Catherine, sister of Buckland priory, married the vicar of Ling, iii 98. Edward, owned Bedminster, ii 282; Edward, owned lands at North Coker, 342; Frances, wife of Sir Edward Waldegrave, 117; Francis, master of St. Catherine's hospital, Bedminster, 283; George, lord Latimer, married Elizabeth Beauchamp, 282; Sir Henry, owned Bedminster, 282. Sir John, iii 300. Sir John and Sir Ralph, lords paramount of the manor of Berwick, ii 338; Anne, daughter of Ralph, earl of Westmoreland, married Sir Fulk-Greville, 376. Catherine, wife of William, lord Harington, i 56, ii 170. Edmund, received the manor of Bathwick from Philip and Mary, i 121. Egelina, wife of Richard Hampton, iii 588. Elizabeth, daughter of Richard, lord Latimer, married Edward, son of lord Willoughby de Broke, ii 376. Hugh, married Joan Fitzgerald, i 251. Isabel, daughter of Richard, earl of Warwick, married George, duke of Clarence, iii 185. John de, landowner temp. Ed. I, i *xxvii*; John de, held one knight's fee in Asholt, 237. John, earl

O

Odcombe : situation, ii 324 ; includes the hamlets of Higher and Lower Odcombe, Woodhouse, and Westbury, 324 ; owned by the earl of Morton : held by Ansger : Edmer held it T.R.E. 324 ; subsequently held of the honour of Oakhampton, 324 ; owned by the Briwere family, 324, iii 80. the Braose family, ii 324, iii 80. the Mortimers, earls of March, ii 324, iii 80. the house of York, ii 324 ; lord Zouch, of Harringworth, 324, iii 81. held by queen Margaret, in dower, ii 324 ; reverted to the Crown, and was granted to the duke of Northumberland, the earl of Hertford, and others, 325 ; dispersed among freeholders and tenants, 325 ; Houndston, 325 ; church (SS. Peter and Paul) and its monuments, 325 ; Thomas Coryat, author, and Humphrey Hody, divine, natives of this place, 325, 326 ; John, earl of Pembroke, owned this manor (temp. Rich. II), 338. church, owned by Montacute priory, iii 312.

Odcombe, Nicholas de, M.P., 1327, i *xxix*.

Odd-Down, iii 325.

Odingseles, John, owner of land in Aller, iii 188.

Odo, bishop of Bayeux, holder of Combe Hay, iii 334.

Odo, holder of Cudworth, iii 117.

Odo Flandrensis, part - holder of Timsbury, ii 112.

Odo, son of Gamelin, owner of Luckham, ii 22.

Offa, king, captured Bath, b 16 ; re-edified the monastery of Osric, b 16, 54. sanctioned the grant of Huntspill to Glastonbury abbey, ii 390.

Offre (*see* Ouvre).

Ogisus held Clatworthy, iii 509 ; Sandford-Bret, 543.

Oglander, Sir John, of Nunwell, owned Stringston, i 263 ; William, 263 ; J.P., *xlii*. owned land in Seaborough, ii 173. Pury-Furneaux, iii 103.

Ogle, John, monument in Bath abbey, 1738, b 69.

Ogle, lord (*see* Cavendish).

Oil mills, Creech, i 74.

Okle, Joan, wife of John Strode, of Shepton-Mallet, ii 209.

Old chapel mansion, Weston, i 156.

Old-Chard, tithing in Chard, ii 472. owned by the bishopric of Bath and Wells, iii 396.

Old-Cleeve : situation, iii 510 ; cliffs abounding with alabaster, 510 ; includes Chapel-Cleeve, Washford (in which stand the ruins of the abbey), Bilbrook, and Goldsoncot, 510 ; Roadwater, Leighland (where is a chapel), Leigh, London, and Binham, 511 ; Domesday survey, 511 ; held by the king : earl Harold held it T.R.E. 511 ; subsequently held by the de Romara family,

Old-Cleeve—*continued.*

511 ; the abbots of Cleeve, 511 ; granted at the Dissolution to Robert, earl of Sussex, 512 ; owned subsequently by Sir James Langham, 512 ; abbey (*see* Cleeve abbey) ; church (St. Andrew) and its monuments, 513 ; bells (4), 513 ; cross, 513.

Old-Down common, Chilcompton, ii 127, 128.

Old-Down inn, Stone-Easton, ii 153.

Old-Moor, Pawlet, iii 102.

Old-Stock (*see* Sock).

Oldbury manor, held of Taunton priory by William Tanfield, iii 242.

Olderworth, i 84.

Oldford, hamlet in Frome, ii 186 ; contained houses belonging to Rodden parish, 225 ; and to Standerwick parish, 227.

Oldmixon or Oldmixton, in Hutton, iii 591 ; held of the Arthur family by the Wykes, 591, 267 ; the Oldmixon family, 591 ; East-Oldmixon, held by Thomas Symons, 591 ; West-Oldmixon, held by William Doble Burridge, 591.

Oldmixon family held Oldmixon, iii 591 ; John, author of a " History of England," " Life of Queen Anne," etc., 591.

Oldway, hamlet in Wellington, ii 485.

Oldwood, hamlet in Wedmore, i 187.

Oliver, Jordan, sheriff, 1240, i *xxxiv* ; Robert, incumbent of Holy Cross chantry, Ilminster, 7 ; William, lord of the hundred of Bath Forum, 98 ; William, whose claim to the manor of Weston was contested by William Blathwaite, 160 ; memorial tablet in Weston church, 165. William, governor of Bath hospital, b 49 ; William, M.D., monument in Bath abbey, 1716, 69.

Onewyn, John, owner of Inyn's court, Bedminster, ii 284.

Onslow, baron, J.P., i *xlii*. Elizabeth, first wife of Sir Francis Wyndham, ii 387.

Opecedre, ancient name of Upper - Chedder, iii 575.

Opetone (*see* Upton Noble).

Opie, William, benefaction to Whitchurch, ii 444.

Opopille, Norman spelling of Uphill, iii 609.

Oram, Mary, tablet in Bath-hampton church, i 119.

Orange grove, Bath, b 34.

Orange, James, of Marston-Bigot, owned Foxcote, iii 350 ; Humphrey sold it to Robert Smith, 350 ; Joanna, monument in Foxcote church, 350 ; arms, 350.

Oratory, the, Porlock, ii 37.

Oratory in Wraxall church porch, iii 158.

Orcas (*see* Orescuilz).

Orchard family, of Orchard-Portman, iii 274 ; Baldwyn de, 274 ; Emerick de, 274. James de, landowner temp. Ed. I, i *xxviii*, iii 274 ; William, 274. owned Bickenhall, i 62.

P

Pen, Penzelwood or Pen-Selwood—*continued.*
bells (3), 44 ; suit between Matthew de
Clievedon and Richard Ken, respecting a
knight's fee here, 167.

Pen-Mill, hamlet in Yeovil, iii 207.

Pen-Pits, Pen-Selwood : supposed origin of,
iii 43.

Penburi, ii 195.

Pence, John, prior of Stavordale, iii 34.

Pencester, Alice de, wife of John de Columbers,
iii 551.

Pendeney, Henry de, grants to Woodspring
priory, iii 594.

Pendomer : situation, ii 348 ; Birt's Hill or
Abbot's Hill, 348 ; Domesday survey, 348 ;
owned by the earl of Morton : held by
Alured : Alwald held it T.R.E. 348 ; subsequently owned by the Domer or Dummer
family, 349 ; earl Poulett, 349 ; church and
its monuments, 349 ; bells (2), 349.

Pengeardmunster (*see* Pennard, East).

Penheved, iii 197.

Pennard, East, iii 478 ; hamlets included in,
478 ; owned by the abbots of Glastonbury,
478 ; Domesday survey, 478 ; one hide held
by Serlo : Ailmar held it T.R.E. 478 ;
granted at the dissolution to William Paulet,
earl of Wiltshire, 479 ; the Smith family,
479 ; Gerard Martin, 479 ; church (All
Saints) and monuments, 479 ; bells (5), 479 ;
cross, 479 ; benefaction, 479. the church
of Bradley was a chapel to this place,
ii 271.

Pennard, West, ii 275 ; included in the Norman
survey under Pennarminstre or East-Pennard, 275 ; owned by Glastonbury abbey,
275 ; granted at the dissolution to the duke
of Somerset, 275 ; hamlets of East-street,
New Town, Laverley, Higher and Lower
South Town, Sticklings and Woodlands,
275 ; church (St. Nicholas) and its monuments, 275, 276 ; bells (5), 276 ; yew-tree,
276 ; cross, 276 ; charity school, 276.
East-street farm was granted as endowment
of a benefaction to the poor of Wells,
iii 410.

Penne, ii 195.

Pennington, hon. lady, monument in Bath
abbey, 1738, B 69. Thomas, recast one of
the bells of Trent church, ii 384.

Penny, Gyles, married Silvestra Story, widow
of Thomas Luttrell, ii 12. the Rev. Henry,
incumbent of Christon, iii 578 ; of Shipham,
602 ; Mr., owned Brimpton-D'Evercy, 215 ;
Richard, married Alice Warmwell, 206 ;
Thomas, monument in Charlton-Musgrave
church, 38.

Penny-pound, Weston-Zoyland : scene of Royalist encampment after the battle of Langport,
iii 440 ; scene of an action during Monmouth's rebellion, 440 ; story respecting, 440.

Penrhyn, baron, J.P., i *xlii.*

Penruddock, Charles, owned Clapton, ii 86.

Penselwood (*see* Pen).

Pensford : situation, ii 429 ; sometimes called
Publow-Saint-Thomas, 429 ; river Chew
and bridge, 429 ; market, 429 ; formerly a
seat of the clothing-trade, 429 ; " Browne
of London owned it " (Leland) 429 ; derivation of name, 429 ; church (St. Thomas
of Canterbury), 429 ; chapel at Borough-
bank : demolished, 429 ; chantry, founded
by a member of the St. Loe family, 429 ;
benefactions, 429 ; held of the honour of
Gloucester by the St. Loe family, 428 ;
owned by James, earl of Ormond, 392 ; by
James, earl of Wiltshire, 392 ; by John
Bisse, 435 ; by Henry Becher, 435.

Penton, Rev. John, governor of Bath hospital,
B 49.

Peper, Nicholas, prior of Taunton, 1513-1523,
iii 236.

Peppin, Arscott Bickford, J.P., i *xlv.* seat at
Dulverton, iii 524 ; Elizabeth, wife of
Humphry Sydenham, 523.

Perambulation of forests, i 16 ; of Neroche, 16,
17, 63, iii 57. Exmoor, ii 19, iii 57. Selwood, ii 195, iii 56 ; North-Petherton, 59 ;
Mendip, 58, 373.

Perce, Gerebert de, holder of knight's fee from
Sir William de Mohun, ii 14 (*see* Percy).

Percehaye, Gonilda, wife of John Atwood,
iii 260 ; arms, 260.

Percepier or Parsley-Piert, prolific, ii 400.

Perceval family, of Weston-in-Gordano, iii 172
—176 ; arms, 176 ; descended from Ascelin
Gouel de Percheval, who was also ancestor
of the Lovels of Castle Cary, 172, ii 137 ;
owned Butcombe, 313, 314. Bourton,
iii 612 ; Capenor court, 145. Castle Cary,
ii 52 ; Chelvy, 317. Clewer, i 188 ; East-
Brent, 196. Eastbury, ii 2. Edingworth,
iii 567. Moorlands, ii 181, iii 72 ; a manor
in Nailsea, 162. Nemnet, ii 319. an estate
in Tickenham, iii 165 ; Weston-in-Gordano,
172 — 176. patrons of Exford, ii 21.
Robert de, a follower of the Conqueror, 52 ;
Ascelin, surnamed Lupus, held Castle Cary,
52 ; Farrington - Gournay, 137 ; Stone-
Easton, 154 ; Stawel, 379. East-Harptree,
iii 587 ; Weston-in-Gordano, 172 ; married
Isabel, daughter of William, earl of Bret-
euil, 172. John de, of Harptree, took the
name of Gournay, ii 52 ; William Gouel de,
surnamed Lupellus, converted into Lovel,
which name he assumed, 52 ; waged war
against Stephen, and erected fortifications
at Cary, 52 ; surrendered to Stephen, 52 ;
again attacked Stephen, and defended the
castle against Henry de Tracey, 52. married Auberie, daughter of Robert, earl of
Mellent, iii 172. Ralph, second son of

Perceval family, of Weston-in-Gordano—*con.*
William, took the name of Lovel (*see* Lovel). Waleran, succeeded to the estates in Normandy, and took the name of Yvery, iii 172; Sir Richard, youngest son of William, owned Weston-in-Gordano, Stawel, Eastbury in Carhampton, and Butcombe, 173, ii 313. married a daughter of William de Mohun, iii 173, ii 313. fought with Richard I in the Holy Land, iii 173; arms, 173; monument in Weston church, destroyed in the civil wars, 173. Richard, landowner temp. Ed. I, i *xxviii.* fought in Palestine: was buried at Weston, iii 173; Robert, surnamed de Butcombe, settled in Ireland: was progenitor of the lords Perceval there, 173; Hugh, held Walton and Coreville, 173; John, held Weston: was sometimes called de Walton, and sometimes de Perceval, 173. bestowed land in Butcombe on the abbey of Thame, Oxfordshire, in a deed witnessed by Hugh, his brother, and others, ii 313, 314. Sir Roger, landowner temp. Ed. I, i *xxvii.* held Weston: married Joan de Bretesche, iii 173. was progenitor of the earls of Egmont, ii 315. Richard, incumbent of Exford, iii 173; Sir John, held Eastbury in Carhampton, Butcombe, Thrubwell and Clewer: through his marriage with Millicent de St. Maur, he became possessed of a moiety of the manor of Weston, which had belonged to Henry Lovel, 173; John de, 173; Sir Walter, married Alice de Acton, 173: Sir Ralph, married Elizabeth de Wyke, through whom he obtained the other moiety of Weston, which had been alienated from his family, 174; Sir John, 174; Richard, married Agnes Arthur, 174; Ralph, lineal ancestor to the earl of Egmont, 174; Sir Ralph, held Weston: married Joan Bosco or Boyce, 174; and became possessed of Tickenham, 165; Richard, held Weston: married Catherine Hampton, 174; monument in Weston church, 174, 176; Sir John, held Weston: married Joan Chedder, 174; his daughter married Gilbert Cogan, 174. Sir James, i *xl.* held Weston, iii 174; restored the church and improved the manor house, 174, 175; married Joan Ken, 175; buried in Weston church, 175. was trustee for Richard Harvey, ii 121. Edmund, of Weston, married (1) Isabel de Mareis, (2) Elizabeth Panthuit, iii 175; James, of Weston, married (1) Mary Gorges, (2) a daughter of — Luttrell, of Dunster, (3) Elizabeth Ken, (4) Elizabeth Marshall, (5) Elizabeth Berkeley, 175; James, held Weston, Thrubwell, Butcombe, Stoke-Bishop, Eastbury, Bridcot, Weston - Capenor, 175; married Alice

Perceval family, of Weston-in-Gordano—*con.*
Chester, 175; Thomas, son and heir of James, 175; an ardent Royalist: his house ransacked by the Parliamentary army, 175; married Catherine Lloyd, 176; Anne, sole daughter and heir of Thomas, married (1) Evan Lloyd, (2) Thomas Salisbury, 176, ii 314. she was the last of this branch of the Perceval family, and cutting off an old entail, she sold the whole estate, iii 176, ii 314.

Perceval, George, of Nailsea, sold that estate to Richard Cole, iii 162.

Perceval, Sir John, and Catherine, of Bourton, sold that estate to William Vanham, 1658, iii 612.

Perceval, Thomas, of Tickenham and Roulston, married Alice Cave, who conveyed to him Sydenham and other estates: he rebuilt the manor house there, iii 87; David, married Alice More or Bythemore, of Nailsea, 87. and became owner of Mark, i 186. George, lord of Sydenham, Moorland, Willy and other estates: sold Nailsea, iii 87; Richard, sold Sydenham to Mr. Bull, 87.

Perci (*see* Percy).

Percival, lord, owned Priston, ii 430.

Percy family owned Stoke Courcy, i 252. Chilcompton, ii 128. lands in Charlton Mackarell, iii 193; Anne, daughter of Henry, earl of Northumberland, married Thomas, lord Hungerford, 356. Gerbert de, sheriff, 1163, 1164, 1165, i *xxxiii.* Gilbert de, granted the church of Chilcompton to the bishop of Bath and Wells for the foundation of a prebend, ii 129. Gilbert de, iii 63; Sir Henry, married Eleanor Poynings, and became possessed of Cheddon - Fitzpaine, 246; he afterwards became earl of Northumberland, 246. William de, married Joan Brewer, i 54, ii 324.

Perdham, hamlet of Cannington, i 234; Domesday survey, 234; owned by Roger de Curcelle, and held by Anschitil: Godwin held it T.R.E. 234; owned by the families of Tilly and Horsey, 235.

Peret, North, ancient name for Petherton, North, iii 54.

Periam, Elizabeth, relict of John Periam, and daughter of John Southey: monument in Bishop's Lydiard church, ii 495; arms, 495. John, J.P., i *xlv*; John, sheriff, 1737, *xxxix.* John, owned Ash-Priors, ii 498. John: Sarah: William: Elizabeth: Rebecca: and Zachariah: memorial stones in Milverton church, iii 17.

Periton, Adam de, iii 101.

Periton, hamlet in Minehead, ii 31.

Perkin Warbeck, defeated at Taunton by Giles, lord Daubeney, iii 109.

Perkins, John, J.P., i *xlv.* Rev. Mr., incumbent of Kingsbury, ii 468.

Perman, George, one of the first aldermen of Bath, B 23.

Pero (*see* Piro).

Perrat, Thomas, monument in Weston-Zoyland church, iii 441.

Perredeham (*see* Perdham).

Perrot, Emma, wife of Sir Richard Newton, iii 588. George, subscriber to the charity school at Chew-Stoke, ii 102.

Perrow, hamlet in Wedmore, i 188.

Perrow or Piro (*see* Piro).

Perry family, memorial inscriptions in Chew-Stoke church, ii 102. tomb in Pitcombe churchyard, i 224; James, sheriff, 1756, *xxxix*. John, of Gerbeston, benefaction to Wiveliscombe, ii 491; John, of Perry, benefaction to Wellington, 485; John, bequest to Chew-Stoke, 102; subscription towards the charity school at Chew-Stoke, 102; monument in West-Coker church, 345. William, governor of Bath hospital, B 49.

Perry, hamlet in Mark, i 182.

Perry-Furneaux (*see* Pury-Furneaux).

Perry-street, hamlet in Chard, ii 473.

Persons, William, receiver of a pension from Taunton priory, iii 236.

Pert, Isabella, first wife of John Harbin, iii 209.

Pery, Isabella, common scold at Seaborough, ii 173.

Pester, John, prior of Witham, ii 234.

Petenie (*see* Pitney).

Peter, bishop, held Kilmersdon, ii 445.

Peter, prior of Bath, 1159—1175, B 55.

Peter, prior of Montacute, iii 312.

Peter, prior of St. John's hospital, Southover, 1228, iii 408.

Peter, William, prebendary of Wells, iii 396.

Peter street, Bath, B 35.

Peter's tithing, Portbury, iii 142.

Peterborough, John, lord bishop of, governor of Bath hospital, B 49.

Peterborough, John, earl of, ii 269; his second son, John, created viscount Avalon, married Elizabeth Carey, 269; Charles, third earl of, 269; Charles, earl of Peterborough and Monmouth, and viscount Avalon, 269.

Peters, Martha, widow of James, owned Worle, iii 615; Arthur, owned land in Worle, 615; Mr. —, owned Yatton, 617.

Petherton bridge, Martock, iii 3.

Petherton, North : hundred, iii 53; river Parret, 53; lands in, held by Walscin de Douai, John the usher, Ansger the cook, Robert de Auberville, and the church of Petherton, 53; royal forest and park, 53; the royalty of the hundred with the manor of North Petherton, owned by Henry de Erleigh and his descendants, 53; included the hundred town, borough of Bridgwater, and eight other parishes, 53.

Petherton, North : situation, iii 54; river Parret, 54; includes North Petherton, Petherton park, North Newton, West Newton, Wolmersdon, Huntworth, Moorland, Bankland, Sheerston, Tuckerton, Mansel, Clavelshay, Boomer, Melcomb-Paulet, Road, Faringdon, and Edgeborough, 54; North Petherton town, 54; market and fair, 54; ancient importance, 54; Domesday survey, 54; held by the king, 54; by king Edward T.R.E. 54; subsequently owned by the de Erleigh family, 54; the Beaupine family, 55; the Bluets, 55; Edward, earl of Hertford, 55; John, duke of Northumberland, 55; Sir Thomas Wroth, 55; John Slade, 55; Petherton park, 55—62; Newton-Forester, Newton-Placey or Newton-Wrothe, 62—70; Newton-Comitis, 70; Wolmersdon and Huntworth, 71; Moorland, Farington, Sheerston and Tuckerton, 72; Bankland, formerly a manor owned by the Preceptory of Buckland, 72; owned by Sir Copleston Bampfylde, 72; Sir Thomas Wrothe, 72; the Acland family, 72; Clavelshay farm, 72; held by the de Claville family, Jordan le King, 72; Walter Clopton, and Henry Hache, 73; the abbot of Athelney owned Pecchy's place, and lands in East and West Clavelleslegh, 73; manor subsequently owned by the Portman family, 73: held by the Gatchells, 73; jointly by the families of Popham and Fytch, 73; Boomer or West-Melcombe, 73; owned by the Blewets: held by the Whiting family, 73; owned by lady Tynte, 73; Melcombe-Paulet, 73; Domesday survey, 73; owned by the Reyney family, 74; the Pouletts, 74; Road, 74; Domesday survey, 74; owned by John Jeane, 74; Edgeberry or Edgeborough, 74; anciently owned by Osbert and William Dennis, 74; Taunton priory held an estate here, 74, 235; Bridgwater hospital held lands here, 79; the rectory and chapels belonged to Buckland priory, 74; to which a pension of four marks was paid annually, 98; church (St. Mary) and its monuments, 74; chantry, 74; benefaction, 74.

Petherton, South, hundred : situation, iii 105; river Parret, 105; divided into three parts, 105; held as a parcel of the manor of its name by the Crown, 105; the lords Daubeny, 105; and lord Arundel, 105.

Petherton, South : situation, iii 105; river Parret and bridge, 105; Roman fosse road, 105; Roman remains at Jailer's mill, Watergore, and Wigborough, 106, 107; seat of the Saxon kings, 107; "Ina's house," 107; Town-tithing, Southarp, Over-Stratton and Compton-Durville, 106; market and fair, 106; dowlas manufacture, 106; Domesday

Pine, John, M.P., 1653, i *xxxii*; Mr. —, the only freeholder in the parish of Curry Mallet, 31 ; Mr. —, part-owner of Isle-Abbots, 51.

Pinkesmoor, ceded by the bishop of Bath and Wells to Edward VI, iii 395, 409.

Pinkham, Robert, benefaction to Brushford, iii 507.

Pinnel, Henry, married Elizabeth Jones, ii 98 ; Henry, 98, 99.

Pinnell, Henry, rector of Trent, married Elizabeth Prattenton : monument in Trent church, ii 385.

Pinney, Azariah, monument in Wayford church, ii 175 ; John, patron of Wayford, 175 ; John Frederick, monument in Wayford church, 175.

Pinny, John, J.P., i *xlv*.

Pipards, hamlet in Freshford, i 124.

Pipards, hamlet in Hinton-Charterhouse, iii 366.

Pipe held lands in Winscombe, iii 613.

Pipe, Thomas, abbot of Muchelney, 1463, iii 135.

Pipeminstre (*see* Pitminster).

Pipe-clay found at Mells, ii 462.

Pipon, Thomas, monument in Bath abbey, 1735, B 69.

Pippesmenstre (*see* Pitminster).

Piro, Gilbert, owner of Stoke Pero, ii 43.

Piro, William de, sold land to William Russell, i 253.

Pisbury, hamlet in Huish - Episcopi, ii 470 ; Domesday survey, 470 ; owned by Ralph de Limesi : held by Ulward T.R.E. 470.

Pitcairn, Rev. Mr., incumbent of Inglishcombe, iii 341.

Pitcher, Richard, benefaction to Bath abbey, B 71.

Pitcombe : situation, i 223 ; Hadspen-house, 223, 277 ; Domesday survey, 224 ; held by Turstin Fitz-Rolf : by Alwold T.R.E. 224 ; attached to the manor of Castle Cary, and owned by the families of Lovel, St. Maur, Zouche and Richard Colt Hoare, 224 ; church (St. Leonard), 224 ; bells (3), 224 ; benefaction by Mrs. Susannah King, 224 ; stone cross, 224.

Pitcott manor, Stratton, ii 458, 459 ; Domesday survey, 459 ; held by Edmund : Iadulf held it T.R.E. 459.

Pitminster : situation, iii 284 ; includes Blagdon, Leigh, Fulford, Trendle and Duddlestone, 284 ; Domesday survey, 284 ; owned by the bishopric of Winchester, 284 ; held by Stigand, 284 ; Blagdon or Blackdown, 284, 571 ; Domesday survey, 284, 285 ; owned by the bishop : Saulf held ten hides, 285 ; passed to Taunton priory, 285 ; the Colles family, 285 ; John Coventry, 285 ; Smart Goodenough, 285 ; the Earle family, 285 ; Priors-park wood, 285 ; residences of William Hawker,

Pitminster—*continued.*

Thomas Welman and John Mallack, 285 ; Poundisford and Trendle, 285 ; chapels, 285 ; church (St. Andrew and St. Mary) and its monuments, 285, 286, 287 ; lands here were held by Sir Francis Brian and Matthew Colthurst, 236.

Pitney, Anne, benefaction to Lamyat, iii 477.

Pitney : hundred, iii 129 ; situation, 129 ; rivers Ivel and Parret, 129 ; includes Langport and two other parishes, 129.

Pitney : situation, iii 129 ; includes Pitney, Wearn and Beer hamlet, 129 ; Pitney-Lorti, 130 ; Domesday survey, 129 ; held by the Crown, 129 ; Hunfrid held half-a-hide, 129 ; subsequently owned by the L'Orti family, 130 ; Sir Ralph de Middleney, 130 ; Sir Robert de Ashton, 130 ; Phillippa Tiptot, 130 ; a moiety held by Elizabeth Andrew, 130 ; another moiety held by Elizabeth Gunter, 130 ; the whole manor held by the Gunter family, 130 ; Robert Morton, 130 ; the Popham family, 130 ; John Pyne, 130 ; Pitney - Wearn, Wearn or Wearn - Plucknet, 130, 131 ; Domesday survey, 131 ; owned by Robert de Auberville, 131 ; William de Wrotham, 131 ; the Plugenet family, 131 ; Henry Haddon, 131 ; the Fitzwarrens, 131, 111 ; the Chidiocks, 131 ; the earls of Northampton, 131 ; church (St. John Baptist) and its monuments, 131 ; bells (4), 131 ; the Chilton family held lands here, 89 ; the Orchard family held lands here, 489.

Pitt, Abigail, of Hartley Wespall, wife of Ralph, lord Stawel, of Somerton, iii 251. Amy, wife of James Strode, ii 210. John, sub-prior, who received a pension, B 57. Samuel, sheriff, 1704, i *xxxviii* ; Stephen, owned Cricket-Malherbe, 22. William, of Dorset, owned North-Parret, ii 336. William, M.P. for Bath, 1761, B 22. Rt. Hon. William, J.P., i *xlv* ; William, earl of Chatham, mansion of Burton Pynsent, 24, 25 ; monument erected to, 25.

Pitt, Ann, monument in Curry Rivel church, i 28.

Pittard, Gideon : Frances : John : Rose and Eleanor (wife of Samuel Noake): memorial stone in Trent church, ii 386.

Pitts, Jane, daughter of — Huckmore, second wife of George Speke, i 68.

Pixton, in Dulverton, iii 523 ; Domesday survey, 524 ; owned by Roger de Curcelle : held by Brictric T.R.E. 524 ; subsequently owned by the de Pixton family, 524 ; lady Acland, 523.

Pixton or Peekstone, Mary, wife of John de Sydenham, iii 86, 521.

Placetis, Placey, or Plessy family, of Newton and North-Petherton, iii 64, 65 ; held land

Portbury, iii 141; situation, 141; evidences of a Roman city here, 141; Roman road, 141; Domesday survey, 141; owned by Geffery, bishop of Coutances: Goduin held it T.R.E. 141; subsequently owned by the Fitz-hardings, lords Berkeley, 141, 142; the Coke family, 142; James Gordon, 142; market and fair, 141; Portbury priors, 142; list of tithings, 142; church (St. Mary), 142, 143; bells (6), 143; chantries, 143; yew-trees, 143; benefaction, 144; fair, 144. John de Bretesche held land here, ii 314.

Portbury-Priors, iii 142; owned by Bromere priory, 142; granted at the dissolution to Henry, marquis of Exeter, 142; passed to Robert Goodwin, 142; the earl of Bristol, 142; James Gordon, 142; the priory, 142; Prior's Wood, owned by Henry Goodwin, 142.

Porter, Catherine, monument in Bath abbey, 1779, B 69. Edith, wife of John Portman, i 62: Else, wife of John Miller, 104. John, prior of Barlinch, 1430, iii 503. Nicholas, M.P. for Bath, 1338, B 20. Richard, held the custody of Ivelchester gaol, iii 300.

Porteshe (*see* Portishead).

Portishead: situation, iii 144; formerly a harbour, 144; rocks, 144; market-boats, 144; Portishead-point, 144; Welly-spring, 144; Domesday survey, 144; owned by the bishop of Coutances: held by William: Aluric held it T.R.E. 144; subsequently held by the same lords as Portbury, 144; church and its monuments, 145; cross, 145; Capenor court: owned by the Capenor family, 145; held by the Percevals, 145; Richard Chocke, 145; the Mohuns of Fleet, 145; the Fust family, 145.

Portishead Point, i xii; weekly payment to the governor of, xlvi. fort at, demolished, iii 144.

Portland, duke of, J.P., i xli.

Portlarch, Juliana de, wife of Robert, lord Berkeley, iii 277.

Portloc (*see* Porlock).

Popt Locan, Saxon name of Porlock, ii 35.

Portman family, of Orchard-Portman, iii 274, 275, 282. owned also Broadway, i 18; Isle Abbots, 51; Puckington, 56, 57; Staple Fitzpaine, 59; Bickenhall, 62. East-Chinnock, ii 327, 328; Haselborough, 333; Closworth, 346. Clavelshay, iii 73; Thurloxton, 103. Thomas, landowner temp. Ed. I, i xxviii, iii 274; William de, was of Taunton, and gave lands to the priory there, 274; Walter, son of William, married Christian Orchard, and became possessed of Orchard—thence called Orchard-Portman, 274; was one of those in whom the estates of Simon de Raleigh were vested, 538. John, of Bickenhall, married Edith

Portman family—*continued.*

Porter, i 62; John, of Bickenhall, married Alice Knowell, 62; William, owned part of the manor of Bickenhall, 62. Sir William, knight, of Orchard, iii 275. purchased land at Thurlbeer, ii 183; restored the tithes, 183. one of the commissioners of enquiry into the estates of cardinal Wolsey, iii 261; lord chief justice of England, 275; monument in St. Dunstan's church, London, 275. Henry, sheriff, 1569, i xxxvii; purchased Puckington, 56, 57. East-Chinnock, ii 328; lands in Pilton and Syckedon, 1557, 277; Closworth, 346. Thurloxton, iii 103; Joan, wife of Sir John Wyndham, 490. Sir John, bart., sheriff, 1607, i xxxviii; married Anne Gifford, iii 275. Grace and Elizabeth, daughters of Sir John: monument in West-Coker church, ii 344. Hugh, sheriff, 1590, i xxxvii; 1600, xxxviii; M.P., 1597, xxxii. Sir Henry, eldest son of Sir John, owned Orchard, married Anne, daughter of William, earl of Derby: left no issue, iii 275. Joan, wife of George Speke, i 68, iii 275; Anne, wife of Sir Edward Seymour, of Bury-Pomeroy, 275; Elizabeth, wife of John Bluet, of Holcombe, 275; Sir William, second son of Sir John, owned Orchard, married Anne Colles, of Barton, 275, 285. Sir William, M.P., 1679, 1681, i xxxii. married (1) Elizabeth Cutler, (2) Elizabeth Southcote, (3) Mary Holman: left no issue, iii 275; devised Orchard Portman and other great estates to Henry Seymour, his cousin, who took the name of Portman, 275, ii 328. he sold Holford and Kilve to Sir John Rogers, iii 457, 532; Henry Seymour, took the name and arms of Portman, 275, ii 328. married (1) Penelope Haslewood (2) Meliora Fitch: died without issue, iii 275; his estates passed to William Berkeley, of Pill, 275, ii 328. Henry, M.P., 1708, i xxxiii. William Berkeley, inherited Orchard and East-Chinnock, and took the name of Portman, iii 275, 282, ii 328. married Anne Seymour, of Bury Pomeroy, iii 282; Henry William Berkeley, eldest son of William, inherited the Portman estates, and married Anne Fytche, 282, ii 328. M.P., 1741, i xxxiii; sheriff, 1750, xxxix; J.P., xlv. Edward, second son of William, took the Berkeley estates, married Anne Ryves, iii 282. J.P., i xlv. Laetitia, daughter of William, held the mansion at Pylle, and the Berkeley estates there, iii 282; married Sir John Burland, knt., 282, i 257. Henry William Berkeley, son of Henry William, owned the Portman and Pylle estates: married Anne Wyndham, iii 283, ii 328. J.P., i xlv. governor of Bath hospital, B 49. trustee of the Saxey charity,

Preceptories : Buckland, iii 96. Temple Combe, ii 359.

Preen, Thomas, memorial stone in Somerton church, iii 186.

Preist, Mrs., benefaction to Blagdon, iii 570.

Presentments, curious, ii 173.

Prestleigh or Presteleye, hamlet in Doulting, iii 474; owned by the St. Maurs : John, lord Stawel : Thomas Horner, 474; a chapel formerly stood here, 474; Stavordale priory owned lands in, 33.

Preston family held Preston-Plucknet, iii 223; Thomas de, 223; William de, 223; John de, 223; John de, gave a lease of lands in Preston-Plucknet to Felicia Warmewell, 223; William de, monk of Bermondsey, compiled a register of the charters and muniments of that abbey, 223.

Preston, John, held Cricket-St.-Thomas and lands in Knoll and Hill, iii 116, 117. John, M.P., 1654, i *xxxii*.

Preston, hamlet in Stogumber, iii 546.

Preston : situation, iii 222; includes Preston-Plucknet and Preston-Bermondsey, 222; springs, 222.

Preston-Plucknet : Domesday survey, iii 223; held by Alured de Ispania : Hugh held it of him : Alwi held it T.R.E. 223; subsequently owned by the Plugenet or Plucknet family, 223; held of them by the de Preston family, 223; a lease held by Felicia Warmewell, 223; manor subsequently owned by the earl of Westmoreland, 223.

Preston-Bermondsey : Domesday survey, iii 223; held by Ansger de Montagud, 223; Alward held it T.R.E. 223; given by Ansgerius Brito to Bermondsey priory, 223; subsequently owned by John Wills, 223; church, 224; bells (4), 224; benefactions, 224; charity school, 224.

Preston-abbey, old mansion at Preston, iii 224.

Preston-Bowyer and Torrell's-Preston, in Milverton, iii 15; formerly part of the manor of Brumpton : now included in the hundred of Williton-freemanors, 15; Domesday survey, 15; held by earl Morton : Robert held one hide : earl Harold formerly held it, 15; successively owned by the families of Bowyer, 16; and Candos, 16; Goldclive priory, 16, 550; the church of Windsor, 16; Torrel's-Preston was held by the Torrel family, 16; Taunton priory held an estate here, 16; " Minster-land," belonged to the church, 16.

Preux, Alice de, wife of Roger de Moels, ii 66.

Price, Elevedale, monument in Bath abbey, 1764, B 69. Hugh, prior of Barlinch, 1320, iii 503. Rev. —, incumbent of Cannington, i 235. Rev. —, incumbent of Merriot, ii 170; Rev. —, incumbent of Stanton

Price family—*continued.*
Drew, 435. Rev. Thomas, incumbent of Fivehead, i 42; of Swell, 66. Rev. William, incumbent of St. Audries, iii 497. William, first common clerk of Bath, B 23.

Priddy : situation, iii 418; spring, 418; lead and lapis calaminaris mines, 418; fair, 418; held at the Conquest with Westbury by the bishopric of Wells, 418, 396; subsequently divided, 418; a manor here granted by William de Fifehead to the abbey of Briwerne, 418; a manor called Pridy granted to Peter Carew, 418; living, a chaplaincy to Westbury, 418; church (St. Lawrence), 418; bells (3), 418; Plummer's benefaction, 418. advowson owned by Brewton priory, i 214.

Prideaux, Catherine, first wife of John Speke, i 68. Humphry, governor of Bath hospital, B 49.

Priest Row, Wells, iii 375, 408.

Prigg, Samuel, part owner of Norton-Malreward, ii 109; Samuel, memorial stone in Stanton-Drew church, 435.

Prigge, Rev., bequest to Frome, ii 198.

Primate of Ireland, governor of Bath hospital, B 49.

Primesley, land in, owned by Buckland priory, iii 98.

Prince of Wales, owner and patron of Curry-Malet, i 33. of Farringdon Gournay, ii 139; West-Harptree, 140; Welton, 151; Stratton, 459.

Princes buildings, Bath, B 37.

Princess street, Bath, B 35.

Pringle, Margaret, monument in Bath abbey, 1728, B 70.

Prior, George, J.P., i *xlv*. John, M.P. for Bath, 1346, B 20. Rev. John, incumbent of Monksilver, iii 535; Mr., owned Halse, 528.

Prior park, Widcombe, i 169.

Priories : Barlinch, iii 503. Barrow, ii 309—311. Bath, i 54—57. Brewton, i 214. Buckland-Sororum, iii 96—99. Burnham, i 181; Cannington, 232. Chewton, ii 118; Dunster, 16; Frome, 186. Hinton, iii 367—369; Ivelchester, 300; Montacute, 311—313; Portbury, 142; Stavordale, 33, 34; Steep-Holmes, 609. Stoke-Courcy, i 250. Taunton, iii 234—236. Witham, ii 232—234. Woodspring, iii 594; Wells, 408. Yeanston, ii 365.

Priors of Bath, B 54, 55, 56.

Priors-Lands, estate in Martock parish, iii 8; owned by the priory of St. Michael's Mount, Cornwall, 8; the abbey of Sion, Middlesex, 8; Humphry Colles, 8; Mary Buckland and her descendants, 8.

Prior's park, Bath, B 58.

Prior's park wood, Blagdon, iii 285.

Priors' wood, Portbury, iii 142.

Priour, Richard, of Widcombe, married Thomasia de la Ryvere, and became possessed of Sewardswick, ii 422, 423.

Prison, the city, Bath, B 52. county, at Ivelchester, iii 300.

Priston : situation, ii 430 ; Prissbarrow hill, 430 ; granted by Athelstan to Bath abbey, 430 ; Domesday survey, 430 ; subsequently owned by lord Perceval, 430 ; William Jenkins, 430 ; William Davis and Miss Jenkins, 430 ; church (St. Luke), 430, 431 ; bells (5), 430 ; yew-tree, 431.

Privates-Brigg, i 84.

Privetes-Moreshed, i 84.

Proctor family held Angers-Leigh, iii 241 ; tomb in Ruishton churchyard, 289 ; John, 1621, 289. John, sheriff, 1732, i *xxxix*. John and Thomas, memorial stone in West-Coker church, ii 345.

Prosser, Mr., part owner of Kingston Seymour, ii 124. William, J.P., i *xlv*.

Prous, William le, held a third of a knight's fee in Hemington, ii 454 ; and the manor of Huntminster, 455.

Provis, Thomas, married Mary Lyde, ii 436. William, sheriff, 1767, i *xxxix* ; J.P., *xlv*. governor of Bath hospital, B 49. trustee of the Saxey charity, i 212.

Prowde, Francis, married Mary Webber : inscription in Oake church, iii 274.

Prowse, Abigail, ii 203. George, J.P., i *xlv*. George Bragge, owned Wigden, iii 207 ; James, monument in Norton - Fitzwarren church, 272 ; John, prior of Taunton, 1492-1513, 236. John, of Compton-Bishop, married Anne Newborough, ii 203, iii 583. John, married Margaret Bragg, iii 583 ; monument in Compton-Bishop church, 583. John, M.P., 1708, i *xxxiii* ; J.P., *xlv* ; Rev. John, J.P., *xlv*. incumbent of Camerton, iii 332 ; prebendary of Wells, 396. Thomas, M.P., 1741, 1747, 1754, 1761, i *xxxiii*. a daughter of Thomas married Sir John Mordaunt, iii 583, ii 203. another daughter married the Rev. John Methuen Rogers, ii 203.

Prowse family held Compton-Bishop, iii 582. inscription in Berkeley church, ii 203.

Prynne family owned Isle-Abbots, i 51. Pilton, iii 481. Gilbert, owned Mere, ii 273. Thomas, memorial stone in Swainswick church, i 155 ; William, the celebrated lawyer, born at Swainswick, 1600, 155. M.P. for Bath, 1660, 1661, B 21. confined in Dunster castle, ii 13.

Publow : situation, ii 428 ; river Chew, 428 ; derivation of name, 428 ; Wansdike, 428 ; held of the honour of Gloucester, 428 ; hermitage founded by Gilbert de Clare, 428 ; held successively by the families of St. Loe, 428, iii 343. Botreaux, ii 428 ;

Publow—*continued.*
Hungerford, 428 ; the earls of Huntingdon, 428 ; Sir Henry Becher, knt., 428 ; Mrs. Popham, 428 ; church (All Saints), 429 ; bells (6), 429.

Publow-St.-Thomas (*see* Pensford).

Puchelege (*see* Peglinch).

Puckerel, Robert de, sheriff, 1166, 1167, 1168, i *xxxiii*.

Puckington, origin of name, i 55 ; situation, 55 ; rights of common on Westmoor and West Sedgmoor, 55 ; commons of Horsemoor and Puddimore, 55 ; Domesday survey, 55 ; owned by Roger de Churchill, 55 ; held by William, 55 ; Leving and Alward held it T.R.E. 55, 56 ; owned by the families of Mallet, Bonvil and Grey, 56 ; confiscated to the Crown and purchased by Henry Portman, 56 ; reply to commissioners' warrant, 56, 57 ; the inhabitants of South Bradon attend this church, 16 ; church (St. Andrew), 57 ; bells (5), 57.

Pucklechurch manor, Gloucestershire, granted to the bishopric of Wells, ii 252. accompted for in 1329, iii 394 ; ceded to the king, 395.

Puddimore common, Puckington, i 55.

Puddimore-Milton, iii 451 ; anciently Mideltone, 451 ; Fosse-road, 451 ; Domesday survey, 451 ; owned by the abbots of Glastonbury, 451 ; granted at the dissolution to John Malte, 451 ; owned by the Horner family, 451 ; church (St. Peter), 451 ; bells (3), 451.

Pudele, Robert de, married Margery Nonington, ii 22 ; his successors assumed the name of Luccombe, 22.

Pudsey, Grace (or Joan), first wife of Walter Baumfilde, ii 90. Richard, i *xxxix* ; Sir Richard, sheriff, 1498, *xxxvi*.

Pukerel, Robert, held lands of the abbot of Glastonbury, ii 244. held one knight's fee of the bishopric of Wells, iii 393.

Pulpit, curious, at Charlcombe, i 143.

Pulsford, Lucas, owned part of the manor of Glastonbury, ii 259.

Pulteney bridge, Bath, B 39.

Pulteney family, owners of Bathwick, i 121 ; Burrington, 204 ; Wrington, 207 ; memorial tablet in Curry Mallet church, 34 ; William, patron of Bath-Wick, 122 ; Wolley, 167 ; and Burrington, 204. built a bridge over the Avon, B 39. earl of Bath, B 83. owner of Ubley, ii 156.

Pulton, Thomas, master of St. John's hospital, Bridgwater, iii 79.

Pump room, Bath, B 40.

Punchardon, Hugh de, holder of half a knight's fee from the Mohun family, ii 14 ; owned Lydiard - Pincherton, 494 ; William de, holder of two knights' fees from Sir William de Mohun, 14 ; owned Lydiard-Pincherton, 494. West-Quantoxhead, iii 496. Aubrea

Punchardon family—*continued.*

de, married Sir Hamelyn de Deaudon, ii 494, iii 496. arms, ii 494.

Purcel, Rev. Robert, incumbent of Mere, ii 274.

Pureton, Adam de, iii 101.

Puriton : situation, ii 396 ; owned by St. Peter at Rome, 396 ; Domesday survey, 396 ; held by queen Eddid T.R.E. 396 ; subsequently annexed to the barony of Stowey, 396 ; held by Robert and Walter de Candos, 396 ; the family of Columbers, 396 ; Audley, 396 ; William Goodwin, 396 ; the earl of Hertford, 396 ; the Finch family, 396 ; lady Ailesford, 396. lands here were held by Thomas Bratton, iii 555. Downend, hamlet in, ii 396 ; owned by Walter de Dowai, 396 ; Domesday survey, 396 ; held by Algar T.R.E. 396 ; subsequently passed with Puriton, 396 ; church (St. Michael), 397 ; bells (5), 397 ; paid a pension to Goldclive priory, 397 ; bishop Beckington's ordination for the building of the vicar's house, 397 ; inscription in the church, 397.

Purlewent, William, iii 465.

Purlivent, Rev. Samuel, memorial stone in Stanton-Prior church, ii 440.

Purnell family, memorials in Saltford church, ii 431.

Purtington manor, Winsham, ii 479 ; owned by the Mohun family, 479 ; held by the Cheynes, 479 ; spring, 479. estate here purchased by the trustees of Ilminster grammar school, i 4.

Pury or Perry-Furneaux, in Wembdon, iii 103 ; owned by the Furneaux family, 103, 213 ; Sir William Oglander, 103.

Pury-Fitchett, in Wembdon, owned by the Fitchett family, iii 103 ; John Cridland, 103 ; the Hills of Hounsdon, 196.

Pusey, the hon. Philip, governor of Bath hospital, в 49.

Puteney, Sir Walter de, M.P., 1347, i *xxx.* William de, held land in Uphill, iii 609.

Putsham, hamlet in Kilve, iii 532.

Putt, Rev. William, J.P., i *xlv.*

Putte, Gilbert de la, verdurer of Exmoor forest, ii 19 ; holder of a knight's fee in Luxborough-Kyne, 25.

Puxton : situation, iii 598 ; anciently a member of the barony of Banwell, and held of the bishops of Bath and Wells, 598 ; held by the families of St. Loe and Jennyns, 598 ; Wadham Windham, 598 ; the hon. James Everard Arundel, 598 ; church (St. Saviour), 599 ; bells (2), 599 ; benefactions, 599. the church (a chapelry attached to Banwell) belonged to the priors and canons of Brewton, i 214.

Pycoteston, Stephen de, prior of Taunton, 1315— 1325, iii 235.

Pye, Mary, wife of George Speke, i 68. Sir Robert, M.P., 1620, 1623, в 21. Rev. —, incumbent of Stawel, ii 379.

Pye-hill, hamlet in East Pennard, iii 478.

Pyke, Dorothea, daughter of John, married(1) John Pitts, (2) James Meacham, ii 477 ; memorial stone in Combe-St.-Nicholas church, 477.

Pyke or Pike family owned Pyke's-Ash, iii 7 ; Hugh, released his rights in Ash and Witcombe to Hugh Kenne, 6 ; William, owned Ash, married Alice Bowring, 7 ; Robert, owned lands in Witcombe and Milton, 7 ; Thomas, married Mary Stawel, 7 ; rumours of a son called Stephen, 7 ; Elizabeth, married James Leigh or Reynolds, who dissipated the estate, 7.

Pyke's Ash or Ash-Bulleyn, Martock, iii 6 ; Domesday survey, 6 ; owned by the earl of Morton : held by Ansger, 6 ; Bristuin held it T.R.E. 6 ; subsequently owned by the earls of Bulloigne, 6 ; the Camme family, 6 ; Peter de Fauconbergh held one yardland of the earl of Sarum, 6 ; Richard Pavely, 6 ; the Kenne family, 6 ; the Pyke family, 7 ; James Leigh or Reynolds, 7 ; the Napier family, 7.

Pyle, William de la, founder of Fairfield chapel, i 256.

Pyleigh or Leigh-Flory, iii 265 ; owned by the Flory family, 265 ; the Meriets, 265 ; the Beauchamps, 265.

Pylle : situation, iii 483 ; Street, hamlet in, 483 ; Fosse road, 483 ; Roman remains, 483 ; at the Conquest included with Pilton, and held of the abbots of Glastonbury by Serlo de Burci, 480, 483 ; subsequently held by the families of Martin and Fitzwarren, 483 ; owned by the Berkeley family, 483, 282 ; Letitia, lady Burland, 282 ; Henry William Berkeley Portman, 282, 483 ; manor house, built by Sir Edward Berkeley, 282, 483 ; church (St. Thomas à Becket), 483 ; bells (5), 483.

Pym, Anne, of Oxford, wife of Sir John Smyth, ii 294.

Pym family, of Brymore, i 233. owned also Langham, ii 25 ; Stoke Pero, 43. a manor in Bridgwater, iii 82. Elias, i 233 ; William, 233 ; John, 233 ; Roger, 233 ; landowner temp. Ed. I, *xxvii* ; Elias, 233 ; Philip, parson of Kentisbury, who conveyed his rights to Philip, son of Henry, 233 ; Philip, married Emmota de Camelis, 233 ; William, 233 ; Elias, held estates in Dulverton and Brumpton-Regis, 233 ; Roger, married Joan Trivet, 234. and became possessed of the principal manor in Bridgwater, iii 82. Philip, i 234, iii 82. Roger, married Joan Gilbert, i 234, ii 6, iii 439. Alexander, i *xl* ; married Thomasia Stainings, 234. owned Woolavington, iii 439.

Pym family, of Brymore—*continued*.
Reginald, i 234; married Mary Dabridge-court, 234. land in Newton, iii 70; owned Hawkridge and Exton, 529. Erasmus, i 234, iii 529. Mary, wife of Edward Arthur, iii 178. John, M.P. for Tavistock, married Anna Hooker, i 234; Charles, made a baronet, 234, iii 82. Mary, wife of Sir Thomas Hales, i 234, iii 82.

Pyme (*see* Pyne).

Pympell, Stephen de, dean of Wells, 1361, i 190.

Pyncombe, Mr., the trustees of: donation to the living of East-Lambrook, ii 469.

Pyne family owned Barton-David, ii 65. Cathanger, i 42; tomb in Curry-Mallet church, 34. in Charlton-Mackarel church, iii 194. Arthur, of Cathanger, i 42; Christabella, wife of Sir Edmund Wyndham, 42, iii 492.

Pyne family—*continued*.
Hugh, of Cathanger, married Mabel Staverton, i 42, 43; John and Juliana, 34; John, J.P., *xlv*. owner of Pitney, iii 130. William, J.P., i *xlv*.

Pyne, Thomas, of Dulverton, iii 521; Hawise, his widow, married Nicholas de Bonville, 521.

Pynsent, Sir William, sheriff, 1742, i *xxxix*; memorial column at Burton-Pynsent, 25.

Pyntenay, land in, held by lord Fitzwarren, iii 271.

Pyper, Granville, monument in Bath abbey, 1717, B 70.

Pyrland, seat of Sir William Yea, iii 289.

Pyrmanne, John, i *xl*.

Pytte, John, last incumbent of the chantry of the Virgin Mary, Taunton, iii 238.

Q

Quakers' meeting house, Bath, B 74. Ilminster, i 2.

Quantoc, Matthew, a resident in Norton-under-Hamden, ii 334; his daughter married John Constantine, rector of Norton-under-Hamden, 335.

Quantock, Matthew, jun., J.P., i *xlv*.

Quantock hills, i *xiv*, iii 496, 497, 501, 531.

Quantockshead (*see* St. Audries and Quantockshead, East).

Quantockshead, East: situation, iii 497; Domesday survey, 497; owned by the Paganel family, 498; the Gaunt family held land here, 498; the Luttrells, 498, 499, 500; church (St. Mary) and its monument, 501; bells (4), 501; benefaction, 501.

Quarles monument in Chewton-Mendip church, ii 119.

Quarries: Ilminster, i 3; Curry Rivel, 24; West Dowlish, 37; Fivehead, 40; Combe-Monkton, 151; Weston, 156. Norton-under-Hamden, ii 334. Kingsdon, iii 195.

Quartz crystals found at Abbot's Leigh, iii 152.

Quarum-Kitnor, in Winsford, iii 556; owned by William de Mohun: held by Mainfrid: Ailward held it T.R.E. 556; sometimes called Beggar-Quarme, 556; held by William de Kytenore, 556; the Sydenham family held lands here, 215.

Quarum - Mounceaux, in Winsford, iii 556; Domesday survey, 556; held by Godebold: Albriet held it T.R.E. 556; subsequently held by the de Mounceaux family, 556; Richard Hankeford, William Dodisham, John Vycory, Thomas Clyne, and John Lokeyerd held half a knight's fee here, 556.

Quay town, Minehead, ii 26.

Queen Anne and the Baths, B 40.

Queen Anne's bounty, granted to East Lambrook, ii 469. Martock, iii 8; Load, 12.

Queen Anne's wishing well, South Cadbury, ii 73.

Queen's bath, Bath, B 33, 40.

Queen Elizabeth: gift to Martock choir, iii 9.

Queen-Charleton, ii 417; situation, 417; coal found here, 417; great road from Bristol to Bath lay through, 417; fair, 417; formerly part of the manor of Keynsham, 417; bestowed on the abbey of Keynsham, 417; given at the Dissolution to Catherine Parr, from whom it obtained its name, 417; tithes of hay and corn, and messuage called the Sextery, given to Sir William Herbert, 417; subsequently this manor owned by the Pophams, 417; Vickris Dickinson, 417; abbots' court-house: old gateway still remaining, 417; church (St. Margaret), 418; bells (4), 418; benefactions, 418.

Queen-street, Bath, B 37; parade, 36; square, 35, 74.

Queen-street, Wells, iii 375.

Queens of England held the castle and borough of Bridgwater, and a share of the patronage of St. John's hospital there, iii 81.

Quick, John, owned land in West-Monkton, iii 454; Richard, benefaction to Brushford, 507.

Quicke, Rev. Nutcombe, incumbent of Ashbrittle, iii 22.

Quiet-street, Bath, B 38.

Quin, James, monument in Bath abbey, 1766, B 60, 70.

Quirck, Robert, bequest to Minehead, ii 31; almshouses, 30; family memorial stones and tablets in Minehead church, 31, 32, 33.

R

Rabayne, Elias de, sheriff, 1251—1254, i *xxxiv.*

Race-course, Main-down hill, Wiveliscombe, ii 487.

Rachiche castle, i 16. [Castle Neroche].

Rack, Edmund : birthplace, B 77 ; early life, 77 ; contributed to the " Monthly Ledger," under the title of " Eusebius," 78 ; settled at Bath, 78 ; published Caspipina's letters and Mentor's letters, 78 ; contributed to the " Farmer's Magazine," 79 ; instituted the agricultural society, 79 ; illness, 80 ; attempted to establish a philosophical society, 80 ; misfortune, 81 ; published a volume of letters, essays and poems, 81 ; contributed towards the history of the county, 81 ; popularity of Mentor's letters, 82 ; his death, 82.

Radcliff, Sir John, married Elizabeth, daughter of lord Fitzwarren, ii 362.

Radcliffe, Elizabeth, wife of Thomas Banbury, iii 198. Rev. Richard, incumbent of Holwell, ii 370. Rev. Arthur, J.P., i *xlv.*

Radcot manor, Oxford, owned by the Besilles family, iii 504.

Raddon family of Rodden, ii 226 ; Walter de, 226 ; Richard de, sheriff of Somerset and Dorset, 226, i *xxxiii.*

Radeflote (*see* Radlet).

Radehewis (*see* Rodhuish).

Radelinge (*see* Redlinch).

Rademer, holder of part of Burnham, i 180. Alston, ii 393. West-Bower, iii 84 ; Horsey, 85 ; Pawlet, 100 ; Walpole, 101.

Radeneye, boundary of Selwood forest, ii 195.

Radenville, Kent, lands in, owned by the Wrotham family, iii 64.

Radestoke, William de, M.P. for Bath, 1414, B 21.

Radeston, Robert de, M.P., 1338, 1339, i *xxx.*

Radford, Lawrence, owner of Creech St. Michael, conveyed it to Robert Cuffe, i 76.

Radingetune (*see* Radington).

Radington or Redington : situation, iii 542 ; Domesday survey, 542 ; owned by Roger Arundel : held by Robert, 542 ; subsequently held by the de Radington family, 542 ; the Hills of Spaxton, 542 ; John Hill held it of John Hywysh, 542 ; church (St. Michael), 542 ; bells (4), 542 ; benefactions, 542.

Radington family held Radington, iii 542 ; Sir John, 542 ; married Margery de Sydenham, 521. John, M.P., 1378, i *xxx.* Sir Baldwin, married Maud Durant, iii 529, 542 ; Maud, widow of Sir Baldwin, married Sir Thomas Wroth, 529 ; Sir William, 542.

Radlet, hamlet in Spaxton, i 245 ; Domesday survey, 245 ; owned by Roger de Curcelle

Radlet, hamlet in Spaxton—*continued.* and Alured de Ispania, 245 ; held by Robert and Herbert, 245 ; Godric and Estan held it T.R.E. 245 (*see* Tuxwell).

Radlich (*see* Redlinch).

Radlis, Eustace de, holder of Redlinch, i 225.

Radstock : situation, ii 457 ; Roman Fosse-road, 457 ; owned by Robert Fitz-Hamon, earl of Gloucester, and held of that honour, 457 ; tithings, which had belonged of old to Kilmersdon hundred, withdrawn therefrom by Richard, earl of Gloucester, 457 ; held by the Mountfort family, 457 ; Philip de Wellesleigh, 457 ; William Banister, 457 ; the Hills, 457 ; the Cheyneys, 457 ; the Waldegrave family, 458 ; John, earl Waldegrave, viscount Chewton, 458 ; Bath priory received a pension of four marks yearly from the benefice, 458 ; church (St. Nicholas, 458 ; coalworks, 458.

Radston, boundary of Exmoor perambulation, 1298, ii 19.

Radway-Fitzpaine, hamlet in Cannington, i 233. owned by Robert, lord Poynings, iii 246.

Rainald, held Beer Crocombe, i 14. Charlton-Musgrave, iii 37 ; and lands in Mudiford, 220.

Raines, Thomas, benefaction to Wedmore, i 193.

Rakynton, lands in, owned by Stavordale priory, iii 33.

Raleghe (*see* Raleigh).

Raleigh family held Nettlecombe, iii 536, 537, 538 ; Wood-Advent, 540. Cutcombe Raleigh, ii 6. monument in Nettlecombe church, iii 541 ; arms, 541 ; Hugh de, of Raleigh, held Nettlecombe of John Marshall, 536 ; conveyed it to Warine de Raleigh in a deed attested by Richard and William de Raleigh, 536 ; Richard de, ancestor of the Raleighs of Raleigh and of Warwickshire, 536. holder of Allerford, ii 41. Warine de, held Nettlecombe, iii 536 ; Ralph de, forfeited his estates, 536 ; Warine de, recovered Nettlecombe from William de Briwere, 536. Warine, of Nettlecombe, 1242, married Margaret Boteler, who, on his decease, married John de Bretesche, ii 314. gift to lady Hawise de Raleigh, attested by Gervase and Wimond de Raleigh, iii 537 ; Wimond, married a daughter of Peter de Chilton and was progenitor of Sir Walter Raleigh, 537 ; Warine de, eldest son of Warine, was of Nettlecombe, 537 ; Reginald de, 537 ; Maud de, wife of Sir Matthew de Furneaux, 213, 537 ; Sarah de, wife of Richard Lodres, 537. Simon de, landowner temp. Ed. I, i *xxvii.* brother of Warine succeeded to Nettlecombe, iii 537 ;

Redlinch—*continued.*
of Ilchester, to whom it gave the title of baron, 226; the mansion house, 227; church, 227.

Red-Lake, iii 479.

Redmaids hospital, Bristol, owned Burnet, ii 415.

Redman, Timothy, memorial stone in Walton church, iii 425.

Redmere, Alice, wife of John de Sydenham, iii 87.

Redvers or Rivers family owned Porlock, ii 36; Crewkerne, 160. Worle, iii 615. were barons of Oakhampton and earls of Devon, ii 36, 454; Baldwin de, owned Porlock, 36; was sometimes called de Execestre (*see* Execestre); Richard, created earl of Devon, owned Hemington, 454. Baldwin, married Margaret Fitz-gerald, i 251. Baldwin, married Alice de Dol, ii 160; Richard, 160; William, surnamed de Vernon, gave the manor of Crewkerne to Robert de Courtney, 160; Mary, wife of Robert de Courtney, 160.

Redwaine, Edward, sheriff, 1484, i *xxxvi.*

Reece, Rev. Evan, curate of Mark, i 183.

Reed, captain, owned Blagdon, iii 570. James, J.P., i *xlv.* John, mayor of Bath, 1674, B 25.

Reeve, Mary, monument in Bath abbey, 1664, B 70. Thomas, owned lands in Dundry, ii 105.

Reeves, William, part owner of the manor of Glastonbury, ii 259.

Refectory in monasteries, ii 251.

Regil, manor in Winford: situation, ii 321; Domesday survey, 321; owned by Serlo de Burci: held by Guntard: Walter held one hide and one virgate, 321; part of the manor subsequently owned by the abbey of Flaxley, 321; the heir of Herbert de St. Quentin held the moiety of a fee of Hugh le Dispenser, 321.

Regilbury manor: village of Nemnet an appendage of, ii 319; abbot of Flaxley, chief lord, 319; granted at the Dissolution to Anthony Kingston, 319.

Regilbury house, Nemnet, ii 319.

Reginald Fitz-Joceline (*see* Fitz-Joceline).

Reginald, precentor of Wells, holder of a knight's fee of the bishopric of Bath and Wells, iii 393.

Reginald, prior of Montacute, iii 312; enlarged the monastery, and converted the ruins of the castle into a chapel, 312.

Reginald, prior of Woodspring, 1317, purchased land in Woodborough, iii 595.

Registers, curious extracts from, i 147, 218, ii 221.

Reigni, Reigny, Reyney or Raygny family owned Sheerston, iii 72; Melcombe-Paulet, 74; Donniford, 491; Ela de, married (1) Simon

Reigni, Reigny, Reyney or Raygny family—*con.*
de Raleigh, who held in her right Wrenchester castle, in Glamorganshire, Michaelstowe, Llantwyd and Lancarvon: (2) Sir Henry de Gamorges, 537. Elizabeth, wife of Sir John Paulet, ii 166. John de, landowner temp. Ed. I, i *xxvii;* juror for the perambulation of Neroche, 17; William de, owner of Asholt, 237.

Reinbald, chancellor to king Edward the Confessor, dean of the prebendal college at Cirencester, and holder of the church of Frome, ii 191; held the church of Milborne-Port, 353. one hide in Road, iii 74.

Relengen (*see* East Ling).

Reliffe, Bridget, wife of Charles Buckland, tomb in West Harptree church, ii 143.

"Reliquiæ Gethinianæ," written by Grace, wife of Sir Richard Gethin, iii 153, 154.

Remar, Thomas, M.P. for Bath, 1419, B 21.

Remberyg, Richard, of St. Thomas' hospital, Bridgwater, subscribed to the supremacy, 1534, iii 79.

Remmesbury, Walter de, first minister of Kilve chantry, 1332, iii 533.

Rendall, name sometimes given to Somerton-Randolf, iii 186.

Renewald held Bawdrip, iii 91; Bradney, 92; Stretchill, 101.

Reve, Thomas, owned Curland, i 23. Curry-lode, ii 181.

Revel or Rivel family owned Curry-Rivel, i 26; Richard, baron in time of Henry II, *xxvi;* received the grant of Curry-Rivel, 26. owned also Stoke-Trister, iii 50; Langport, 132; the abbot of Muchelney held lands of him, 135. Sabina, wife of Henry L'Orti, i 26, iii 50, 130. Mabel, owned North-Parret, ii 335. founded a chantry at Swell, which was afterwards confirmed by Walter de Urtiaco or Orti, and William, bishop of Bath and Wells, i 66.

Revels: Curry Malet, i 31; Donyat, 35; Drayton, 39; Hatch - Beauchamp, 44; Isle-Brewers, 53; Stocklinch St. Magdalen, 64; Wedmore, 188 (*see* Fairs).

Revett or Rivett, Timothy, archdeacon of Bath, present at the consecration of Wick chapel, i 219. benefaction to Wells, iii 410.

Reygners, Avitia de, prioress of Cannington, 1343, i 233.

Reynell, Christian, sold her right in the manor of Newton to John Pym, iii 70.

Reynold, William, monk of Hinton, pensioned, iii 368.

Reynolds, Jane, benefaction to Crewkerne, ii 164. John, rector of Portishead: injunction against Walter Toucker, rector of Weston - in - Gordano, iii 174; Richard, owned Sutton-Mallet, 430; Samuel, benefaction to Taunton, 240.

Rodney family of Rodney-Stoke—*continued*.
ment in Stoke-Giffard church, 606, 607
John : John : Edward : William : George,
his sons, died without issue, and his daughters became his heiresses, 605 ; Anna, wife
of Thomas Bridges, 605. monument in
Keynsham church, ii 407. Catherine,
memorial stone in Stoke-Giffard church,
iii 607.

Rodney, William, monument and inscription in
Huntspill church, ii 394, 395. Sir George
Brydges, created baron Rodney, 1782,
descended from a branch of the Rodneys
of Rodney-Stoke, iii 605.

Rodney-Stoke (*see* Stoke-Giffard).

Roe or Roo, Henry, owned Chedder-Fitzwalter,
iii 576 ; Edmund, monument in Chedder
church, 577 ; arms, 577.

Roebuck, Henry Disney, built Midford castle,
i 136. John, monument in Bath abbey,
1767, B 70.

Roffey, James, monument in Bath abbey, 1769,
B 70 ; benefaction to Bath abbey, 71 ;
Rebecca, monument in Bath abbey, 1765, 70.

Roger, holder of East-Brent, i 196 ; Wrington,
206 ; Durborough, 252 ; Edstone, 252.
Bratton, ii 31 ; Stoke-Pero, 43 ; Hallatrow,
148 ; Bradley, 271 ; Ashton, 289 ; land in
Winford, 320 ; Stanton-Drew, 401 ; Street,
479. Easton-in-Gordano, iii 146 ; Socke,
221 ; East-Lydford, 196 ; Ashcot, 425 ;
land in Compton-Dunden, 425 ; land in
Sutton-Malet, Edington, Chilton, and Catcot, 427 ; Butleigh, 448 ; West-Monkton,
454 ; Batcombe, 466 ; land in Cerletone,
474 ; land in Shepton-Mallet, Croscombe,
480 ; Hartrow, 546 ; land in Chedder, 575 ;
land in Winscombe, 613.

Roger, bishop of Bath and Wells, 1244-1247 :
interred in Bath abbey, B 67.

Rogers family held Porlock, ii 37 ; Sparkford,
87 ; North-Cheriton, 360.

Rogers, Amy, of Cannington, wife of Henry St.
Barbe, monument in Cannington church,
i 236. Andrew and Mary sold Berwick and
Coker to William Symes, ii 338. Elizabeth, married the duke of Richmond,
iii 457 ; sold Kilve to Sir William Portman,
532. Sir Edward, M.P., 1553, 1555, 1557,
1558, 1559, 1563, i *xxxi* ; Edward, sheriff,
1571, *xxxvii* ; Edward, sheriff, 1604,
xxxviii ; Edward, received from Henry
VIII, land formerly belonging to Cannington priory, 233. Edward, owned Porlock,
ii 37 ; Sir Francis owned Porlock, 37 ; Sir
Francis, married Helena Smyth, 293.
George, M.P., 1571, i *xxxii* ; Henry, benefaction to Cannington, 236, 237. to Porlock,
ii 39. Jane, benefaction to Cannington,
i 237 ; John, *xl* ; John, J.P., *xlv* ; John,
purchased Yarlington from the marquis of

Rogers family—*continued*.
Carmarthen, 229 ; owned Upton Noble,
227 ; memorial stone in Upton Noble
church, 228. owned the fourth part of
Wanstraw, ii 229 ; the manor and hundred
of Berwick, and the borough of Stoford,
338. owned Yeovilton, iii 199 ; Holford,
457 ; Kilve, 532. John, ii 338. Sir John,
sheriff, 1521, 1552, i *xxxvii*. one of the
commission for the survey of churches at
the time of the Reformation, ii 286 ; owned
Chilton Cantelo, 339. Sir John, purchased
Kilve, iii 532. Mrs., benefaction to Porlock,
ii 39 ; Rev. Samuel, memorial stone in
Withycombe church, 48.

Rogers, Rev. John Methuen, J.P., i *xlv*. owner
of Berkley, married a daughter of Thomas
Prowse, ii 203 ; owned Rodden, 227.

Roges or Fitz-Roges family owned Porlock,
ii 36. Simon de, landowner temp. Ed. 1,
i *xxvii*. George, presented to the church
of Porlock by Henry Roges, ii 37 ; Simon
de, 37 ; Isabel, widow of Simon, married
Herbert de Marisco, 37.

Rogus, Jordan de, iii 29 ; Julian, married Simon
de Grindham, 29.

Rohard, holder of land in Banwell, iii 566.
Chew Magna, ii 94.

Roicheye, lands in, granted by the countess of
Leicester to Buckland priory, iii 96.

Roisley, Alice, married Adam le Bret, iii 543.

Roland, John, monument in Wells cathedral,
iii 401.

Rolfe, William, abbot of Keynsham, ii 402.

Roliz (*see* Redlinch).

Roll, Francis, M.P., 1656, i *xxxii*.

Rolle family owned Shapwick, iii 427 ; Moorlinch, 429 ; High-Ham, 444 ; Exton, 527 ;
descended from George Rolle, of Steventon,
427 ; whose daughter Margaret married
Richard Wyke, of Ninehead, 268. Elizabeth, wife of Robert Malet, i 93. Judge,
built a mansion at Shapwick, iii 427. Dennis, J.P., i *xlv*. sold Shapwick, iii 427 ;
and High-Ham, 444 ; Edward, incumbent
of Moorlinch, 429. John, J.P., i *xlv*.

Rolleston (*see* Rolston).

Rolston, owned by the Rodney family, iii 477,
603.

Rolston, East and West, hamlets in Banwell,
iii 567.

Rolt, Edward Bayntun, owner of Enmore i 92.
John, incumbent of Road and Wolverton,
ii 225 ; Thomas, benefaction to Horsington,
373.

Roman baths, Bath, B 9, 10.

Roman fosse road, i *xxiii* ; its course and description, 99—103, B 33, ii 445, 457, 458,
479, iii 105, 192, 196, 298, 301, 306, 308,
325, 329, 333, 337, 349, 450, 451, 459, 471,
476, 478, 483.

S

St. Maur family, of Castle Cary—*continued.*
55; John, brother of Richard, and progenitor of a younger branch of the St.
Maur family, 55.

St. Maur family, of Beckington, ii 199, 200;
John, married a daughter of John de
Erleigh, and became owner of Beckington,
199. owned Durston, iii 96; Michaelchurch,
99. John, married Elizabeth Broke, ii 199,
iii 303. Sir Thomas, married Philippa
Hungerford, ii 199; John, married Elizabeth Choke, 199, 200; effigy in Beckington
church, 201; William, married Margaret
Edgecombe, 200; owned Road, 224; Margaret, first wife of William Bampfylde, 90,
200, 224; Anne, wife of Robert Stawel, 200,
224, iii 250.

St. Michael, situation of churches dedicated to,
i 76.

St. Michael extra Muros church, Bath, B 53, 72.

St. Michael intra Muros church, Bath, B 53.

St. Michael's or Michaelchurch: situation, iii 99;
Domesday survey, 99; owned by Ansger:
held by Alwi T.R.E. 99; subsequently held
by the Erleighs, 99; passed to the St.
Maurs, 99; the Bampfyldes, 99; the
Stawels, 99; Edward Seymour and John
Slade, 99; Henry de Erleigh granted the
chapel here, with lands at Ridene and other
properties to the abbey of Athelney, 99;
church, 100; bell (1), 100.

St. Michael's or Montacute hill, i *xiv*, iii 309.

St. Michael's Mount, Cornwall, priory owned an
estate in Martock, iii 8.

St. Patrick, abbot of Glastonbury, ii 249; rebuilt the ruined chapels there, 240, 264.

St. Paulinus, enlarged the abbey of Glastonbury,
ii 241.

St. Peter and St. Paul's parish, Bath, B 54.
church, 53; conduit, 31.

St. Peter's church, Bath, owned Camely, ii 125.

St. Peter's church, Rome, received land from
William the Conqueror, i *xxv*. owned
Puriton, ii 396.

St. Phaganus, abbot of Glastonbury, jointly
with St. Diruvianus, ii 249; rebuilt the oratory of St. Joseph, Glastonbury, and erected
another, to St. Michael, on the Tor hill,
240, 264.

St. Philip the Apostle, sent Joseph of Arimathea,
with the twelve Anchorites, to Britain,
ii 239.

St. Quentin, Anesteise, memorial stone in Hinton St. George church, ii 168. John, married Maud le Bret, iii 543; Walter de and
Sir William de, witnesses to a deed by lady
Margaret de Raleigh, 536, 537.

St. Rayn [Collinson, Ranus], ii 165, iii 126.

St. Sever abbey, Normandy, owned lands in
Yeanston and Henstridge, ii 365.

St. Swithin's church, Walcot, B 73.

St. Swithin's well, Bath, B 31.

St. Thomas' head, i *xii*.

St. Victore, Nicholas de, holder of half a
knight's fee in Hemington, ii 454.

St. Vigore, Nicholas de, holder of the fourth of
a knight's fee in Falkland, ii 455. Thomas
de, sheriff, 1269, 1270, 1271, i *xxxiv*.

St. Walery, John de, sheriff, 1271—1274, i *xxxiv*.

St. Werburgh church, Bath, B 53.

St. White, names of places derived from,
iii 126.

St. Whyte's chapel, formerly standing at Whitchurch, ii 441.

St. Winifrid's chapel, Bath, B 53.

Saints' bells, Brewton, i 216. Portbury, iii 143.

Salignac or Salagniaco (*see* Sulleny).

Salique law: bishop Beckington's treatise in
refutation of, iii 384.

Salisbury, Agnes, daughter of John Walshe,
i 41; George, owner of Cathanger, 42;
Nicholas, who married Agnes Walshe, 41.
Thomas, of Flintshire, married Anne Per-
ceval, widow of Evan Lloyd, ii 314, iii 176.
William, of Barking, gifts to the parish of
East-Chinnock, ii 328.

Salisbury, bishop of, owned Seaborough, ii 171;
Chilcompton, 128.

Salisbury cathedral: members of the Hungerford family buried in, iii 354, 355.

Salisbury, Edward de, received land from William the Conqueror, i *xxv*. Hinton Charterhouse, iii 366; Norton S. Philip, 370.

Salisbury, earl of, J.P., i *xli*.

Salisbury, earls of, owned Hinton-Charterhouse,
iii 366, 367. were tenants of Queen-Camel,
ii 74; owned Goathill, 363. Martock, iii 4;
Langport, 132; Somerton, 183; Thistlesham, 452; Shobworth, 601; Patrick
Devereux, son of Walter de Sarisberi, created earl of Salisbury, 1153, 366; owned
Hinton-Charterhouse, 367; and Norton St.
Philips, 370; was sheriff of Wilts, 366,
367; William Devereux, earl of, sheriff of
Wilts, 367; married Eleanor de Vitrei, 367;
Ela, his daughter and heir married William
de Longespee, or Longsword, natural son
of Henry II, who was created earl of Salisbury, 367; he bestowed his manor of Hatherop on the Carthusian order, and, by will,
left certain moneys for the foundation of a
priory there, 367; he owned Somerton and
founded a nunnery there, 183; was sheriff of
Wilts, Cambridge, Huntingdon, and Somerset, and warden of the Welsh marches,
commander of the fleet, and governor of
the castles of Winchester, Sherborne, and
Porchester, 184; Ela, countess of, surviving
her husband, carried out his bequests, but
founded the Carthusian priory at Hinton
instead of at Hatherop, 367; and granted
to it the liberty of Hinton and Norton,

Seymour family—*continued.*
Webb, J.P., i *xlii* ; William, 6. Sir William, of Shepton - Beauchamp, iii 125. Sir William, buried at Glastonbury abbey, ii 262. lord William, J.P., i *xlii* ; William, duke of Somerset, 1660, *xlix* (*see* Somerset, dukes of).

Seymour, John, lord Zouch, and St. Maur, owned the manor of Buckland Dinham, ii 452. owned the borough of Bridgwater and other estates, iii 81 ; was attainted, 81.

Seymour court, Beckington, ii 200.

Seyncler (*see* St. Clare).

Seyntlowe, Sir John, one of the commission for the survey of churches, chapels, etc., at the time of the Reformation, ii 286.

Shaa, Thomas, married Mary Hungerford, iii 356 ; monument in the chapel of Farley castle, 360.

Shadwell, John, M.D., monument in Bath abbey, 1747, B 70.

Shaftesbury abbey received land from William the Conqueror, i *xxv* ; owned Kelweston, 127. Abbot's Combe, ii 359. Kilmington, iii 39.

Shaftesbury, earl of, owned Pawlet, iii 100. descended from John Cooper, ii 201.

Shaftesbury, John, master of St. John's hospital, 1398, B 43.

Shanks, in Cucklington parish, iii 52.

Shannon, earl of, J.P., i *xli*.

Shapwick : situation, iii 426 ; the moors, 426 ; Loxley-wood, 426 ; ancient names, 426 ; given by Lulla to Glastonbury abbey, 426, ii 242. Domesday survey, iii 426, 427 ; held under the abbot by Roger, Alured and Warmund, 427 ; Sir Walter de Schapewyke held lands here : purchased from him by John de Taunton, 427 ; Abbot's grange, 427 ; manor owned after the Dissolution by Thomas Walton, 427 ; the Rolle family, 427 ; George Templar, 427 ; mansion built by judge Rolle, 427 ; rectorial manor owned by Mrs. Strangways, 427 ; church (Blessed Virgin Mary) and its monuments, 427, 428 ; bells (5), 427 ; benefaction, 428. church exempted from episcopal authority by king Ina's charter, ii 241.

Shapwick, Peter de, chaplain of Woolavington chantry, iii 438.

Shapwick-moor, iii 426 ; act for enclosing, 426.

Shareshull, William de, married Joan Power, iii 219.

Sharp, Edward, Margaret, and Joane Clarke, their daughter : monument in Badialton church, iii 23 ; benefaction to Badialton parish, 23 ; Emmanuel, rector of Badialton, driven from his benefice in the Parliamentary war : recovered it at the restoration, 23.

Sharpham-park : survey taken after the Dissolution, ii 258 ; survey taken in time of

Sharpham-park—*continued.*
abbot Beere, 268 ; manor-house built by abbot Beere, 255 ; birth-place of Henry Fielding, 268 ; Sir Henry Gould, 269.

Shascombe, hamlet in Wellow, iii 328 ; owned by Walter Long, 328 ; lands here were held by John Bisse, 328.

Shaston, hamlet in Freshford, i 124.

Shatwell, Wincaunton, iii 32.

Shaunde, Philibert de, earl of Bath, B 82.

Sheerston, in North-Petherton, iii 72 ; owned by the families of Huish, 72 ; Reigny, 72 ; Poulett, 72 ; chapel belonged to Buckland priory, 72, 98.

Sheid, Mary, monument in Charlcombe church, i 144.

Sheldon, Gilbert, born at Stanton-Prior, ii 440 ; built the Sheldonian theatre, Oxford, 440.

Shells, i 177, ii 389, iii 608.

Shene priory owned the church of Chewton-Mendip, ii 118 ; Paulton chapel, 152.

Sheperton, owned by the Wrotham family, iii 66.

Sheppard, George, subscriber to the charity-school at Chew-Stoke, ii 102.

Shepton, William de, abbot of Muchelney, iii 135.

Shepton-Beauchamp : situation, iii 125 ; springs, 125 ; hamlet of West-Cross, 125 ; Domesday survey, 125 ; owned by the earl of Morton : Algar held it T.R.E. 125 ; subsequently owned by the lords Beauchamp, of Hatch, 125 ; the Seymours, afterwards dukes of Somerset, 125 ; Robert Child, 125 ; church, 125 ; bells (6), 125 ; benefactions, 125, 126 ; ancient house, owned by Thomas Grosvenor, 126.

Shepton-Mallet : situation, iii 459 ; Fosse-road, 459 ; woollen, cloth, and stocking manufacture, 459 ; includes the town tithing, Charlton and Bodden tithing : hamlets of Darsel, Bowlish, and Oakhill, 460 ; market and fair, 460 ; market-cross, 460 ; county Bridewell, 460 ; cucking stool, 460 ; manor owned by the abbots of Glastonbury, 461, ii 243. held by Roger de Curcelle, iii 462 ; the Malet family, 462 ; the Vivonne family, 462 ; Geffrey Laverton and Robert de St. Clare, 462 ; a moiety held by the Beauchamp family, 462 ; the Meriets, 462 ; the Gournays, 462 ; the duchy of Cornwall, 462 ; the other moiety held by the Wests, lords de la Warre, 462, ii 413. Peter Sherston, iii 462 ; church (SS. Peter and Paul) and its monuments, 463, 464, 465 ; bells (8), 463 ; benefactions, 465 ; guilds, 465 ; almshouse, 465 ; school, 465 ; distinguished people born here, 461 ; Charlton manor owned by Levi Ames, 462.

Shepton-Montacute : situation, iii 45 ; includes Upper and Lower Shepton, Knoll, and

Shepton-Montacute—*continued.*
Stoney-Stoke, 45; Domesday survey, 45; owned by the earl of Morton; held of him by Drogo or Drew de Montacute: Toli held it T.R.E.: Robert, son of Wimarc, held Stoney-Stoke T.R.E. 45; manor subsequently owned by the de Montacute family, created earls of Salisbury, 45, 46, 47, 48; Sir Richard de St. Maur, 49; the families of Pole, 49; Dinham, 49; and Berkeley, 49; Edward Phelips, of Montacute, 49; church (St. Peter) and its monuments, 49; bells (3), 49; cross, 49. rectory held by the prior and canons of Brewton, i 214.

Sherall, land in, owned by Sir John Newton, iii 588

Sherborne, Margery, wife of Robert Cradock, iii 588.

Sherborne abbey, held a revenue from St. John's church, Ivelchester, iii 301; land in Congresbury, 584.

Sherborne, bishop Asser of, owned Wellington, Buckland, and Lydiard, ii 481.

Sherborne castle, Ralph de Gorges, governor of, iii 156.

Sherborne farm, East Harptree, iii 587.

Sherborne, hamlet in Litton, iii 416; land in, belonged to Sir John Newton, 588.

Sherborne, Dorset, land in, belonged to Buckland priory, iii 98.

Sherford, hamlet in Wilton, iii 294; seat of Sir Benjamin Hamett, knt., and —. Welman, 294.

Sheriff's order for the execution of the duke of Monmouth's followers, i *xlvii.*

Sheriffs of the county, i *xxxiii.*

Sherington manor, owned by the Hills of Hounsdon, iii 196.

Sherphame park (*see* Sharpham).

Sherrington, lady: gift sermon to Wells church, iii 410. William, owner of Abbot's-Combe, ii 359.

Sherston family owned Charlcombe, i 142; Wolley, 167. William, M.P. for Bath, 1583, 1596, 1600, 1603, 1605, B 21; first mayor of Bath, 23. Arthur, mayor of Bath: monument in Weston church, 1641, i 163; Peter, J.P., *xlv*; sheriff, 1783, *xxxix*. owned the manor of Southover and the site of the priory there, iii 409.

Sherwood, Henry, monument in Bath abbey, 1620, B 70; John, M.D., monument in Bath abbey, 1620, 70; Maria, monument in Bath abbey, 1612, 70.

Sherwood, John Withers, married Elizabeth Jones and became owner of Langford manor, i 204; monument in Barrington church, 204; Robert, tablet in Barrington church, 204.

Sbete, John, last incumbent of the chantry at Trent, ii 382.

Shilling, Norman, its value, i 5.

Shipham: situation, iii 600; lapis-calaminaris mines, 600; fair, 600; Domesday survey, 601; owned by Roger de Curcelle: held by Robert: Alduin held it T.R.E. 601; subsequently held of the barony of Curry Mallet, 601; by the Malherbes, 601, ii 228. Sir Peter Courtney, iii 601; the St. Loes, 601; the Botreaux family, 601; Sir Robert Hungerford, 601; the Chedder family, 601; the families of Newton and Capel, 601; given by bishop Beckington to John Pope and Richard Swan, 601; subsequently held of the dean and chapter of Wells, by William Wesley, 601; church (St. Leonard). 602; bells (5), 602; benefactions, 602; Winterhead hamlet, 601.

Shiplade, hamlet in Bleadon, iii 571.

Shipway, Portbury, iii 142.

Shire family: memorial stones in Buckland St. Mary church, i 21.

Shires, Sir Edward, married Elizabeth Dickinson, ii 417.

Shirley, Thomas, married Elizabeth Gorges and became possesed of North Cheriton, ii 360; and Horsington, 372; Francis, sold all his property in Cheriton and Horsington to Edward Ludlow, 360.

Shirwold-lode, i 84.

Shitten-lane, hamlet in Freshford, i 124.

Shobworth, held by Sir Peter Courtney of the earl of Sarum, iii 601.

Shockerwick, hamlet in Bathford, and gives name to a family, i 112; owned by the Hussey family, 106, 112; Walter de Creyk, 112; the Brien family, 112. held of the bishop of Bath and Wells by Philippa le Scrope, iii 185 (*see* Socherwiche).

Short, John, part-owner of Oare, ii 34. Thomas, mayor of Bath, 1734, B 26.

Shreefe, Margery, wife of William Simcocks, iii 449.

Shrewsbury, Ralph of (*see* Salopia, Ralph de).

Shrewsbury, George, earl of, fourth husband of Elizabeth Hardwick, ii 96; John, earl of, married Margaret Beauchamp, 282.

Shrole, hamlet in East-Harptree, iii 587.

Shrubs, hamlet in Freshford, i 124, 125.

Shurton, hamlet in Stoke Courcy, i 252; Domesday survey, 252; owned by Roger de Curcelle and held by Robert: Sired held it T.R.E. 252.

Shute, Elizabeth, benefaction to Whatley, ii 231; Richard and Philippa, monument in Whatley church, 231; arms, 231; Rev. Henry, endowed a school at Kilmersdon, 447. Thomas, owner of Combe-Monkton, i 151; monuments in Combe - Monkton church, 152.

Shutwood Green, West-Hatch, ii 180.

Sibe, part-holder of Timsbury, ii 112.

Sloo or Slow manor, West-Camel, iii 190 ; owned by the Montagu family, 190.

Slow court, iii 190.

Smaldon hill, Winscombe, iii 614.

Smallcombe hill, Milton Clevedon, i 222.

Small, Hester, gift of sermon to St. Cuthbert's, Wells, iii 410.

Small-Down hill, Evercreech : Roman encampment on, iii 413.

Smallcroft, owned by Humphrey Colles, iii 80.

Smart, John, benefaction to South-Petherton, iii 112. Thomas and Mary, memorial stones in Brewton church, i 217 ; Thomas, benefaction to Brewton, 218.

Smeath moor, i *xv*, iii 580.

Smewin, holder of Standerwick, ii 228. of Farley-Montfort, iii 351.

Smith family, owners of Charlinch, i 239 ; Spaxton, 244. Langham, ii 473. East Pennard, iii 479. memorial stones in Bathwick church, i 123 ; in Kelweston church, 130. in Chew Magna church, ii 98. Agnes, wife of Edmund Rack, B 77. Anne, gift to Frome church, ii 197. Henry, benefaction to Newton-St.-Lo, iii 345 ; Henry, benefaction to Shapwick, 428. Sir Hugh, sheriff, 1613, i *xxxviii* ; Hugh, M.P., 1660, 1678, *xxxii*. Jacob, mayor of Bath, 1788, B 27. Rev. Joel, monument in Combe-St.-Nicholas church, ii 477. John, J.P., i *xlv*. John, owner of Combe-Hay, iii 336 ; John, of Combe-Hay, sold Foxcote to Sir John Hugh Smyth, 350 ; John, owner of Stony-Littleton, 350 ; John and Anne, monument in Foxcote church, 350 ; arms, 350. John, sheriff, 1739, i *xxxix*. John, M.P. for Bath, 1766, 1768, 1774, B 22 ; John, governor of Bath hospital, 49. John Wyldbore, J.P., i *xlv* ; Sir John, M.P., 1685, 1695, *xxxii* ; sheriff, 1690, *xxxviii* ; Sir John, sheriff, 1733, *xxxix* ; Sir John, J.P., *xlii*. Sir John, owner of Langham, ii 473 ; arms, 473 ; Margery, wife of George Strode, 210 ; Mary, third wife of Hodges Strachey, 99 ; Mary, benefaction to Long Ashton, 303. Martha, monument in Widcombe church, i 172 ; Rev. Martin Stafford, 146 ; owner of Prior park, 170. governor of Bath hospital, B 49. incumbent of Uphill, iii 610. Milo, mayor of Bath, 1732, B 26. Milo and Martha, monuments in Widcombe church, i 172. Partridge, owner of a mansion at Pilton and of the rectorial manor there, iii 481. Richard, vicar of Long-Ashton, ii 299. Richard, prior of St. John's hospital, Wells, 1513—1524, iii 409. Robert, sheriff, 1708, i *xxxviii*. Robert : Dorothy : John : memorial tablet Frome church, ii 193. Robert, owner of Combe-Hay, married Mary Bennett : memorial tablet in Combe-Hay church, iii 336 ; Robert and

Smith family—*continued*.

Dorothy, monument in Foxcote church, 350 ; arms, 350 ; Robert, of Frome-Selwood, owned Foxcote, 350 ; Rev. Robert, of Combe-Hay, and Anne, his wife, monument in Foxcote church, 350 ; Robert, whose heirs owned part of Winscombe, 613. Samuel, J.P., i *xlv*. Samuel, married Mary Lockyer and became owner of Maperton, ii 85 ; Thomas, 37. Thomas, J.P., i *xlv* ; Thomas, M.P., 1639, *xxxii*. Thomas, benefaction to Frome almshouse, ii 196 ; Sir Thomas, of Hough, married Mary Smyth, 293. Rev. Thomas, incumbent of Hutton, iii 591 ; William, part-holder of lands in Yeovilton, Eastern-Farm and Western-Farm, 219.

Smithay, lands in, held by the Sydenham family, iii 215.

Smyth and Combe owned Norton-Ferrers, iii 41.

Smyth, Barnabas, rector of Trent, ii 383 ; benefactions to Trent church, 384 ; memorial stone in the churchyard, 388.

Smyth, John le, M.P. for Chard, ii 472.

Smyth family, of Long-Ashton, ii 292-294 ; arms, 294 ; owned the site of St. Catherine's hospital, Bedminster, 282 ; John, of Aylburton, Gloucester, 292 ; Robert, 292 ; John, 292 ; Matthew, married Alice Havard, and was father of John, the purchaser of Long-Ashton, and of a daughter, married to Thomas Phelips, of Montacute, 292 ; John, purchased Long-Ashton, and made his principal seat there, 292 ; mayor of Bristol, 1547 and 1554, married Joan Parr, 292 ; received the manor of Ashton-Meriet at the dissolution, 298. owned Durleigh, i 79. Hugh and Matthew, his children, ii 292 ; Hugh, married Maud Biccombe, of Crowcombe, 292 ; held Filton on lease, 441. Broomfield, i 72 ; Durleigh, 79. his daughter married Edward Morgan, ii 293 ; Matthew, succeeded his brother Hugh, married Jane Tewther, widow of Bartholomew Skerne, 293 ; he purchased the King-Weston estates from Thomas Kempe, 81 ; owned Horsington, 372 ; purchased Compton-Dando, 422 ; owned Fryenburgh manor, 425 ; Hugh and Anne, his children, 293 ; Jane, widow of Matthew, held the capital messuage and demesne of Ashton-Theynes, 295 ; Anne, married George Rodney, 82, 293, iii 413, 604. Sir Hugh, ii 293 ; married Elizabeth Gorges, 293, iii 157. purchased the manor of Ashton Theynes, ii 296 ; owned King Weston, 81 ; held the tithes of Filton, 441 ; benefaction to Filton, 444 ; Thomas : Mary : Helena, his children, 293. Elizabeth, widow of Sir Hugh, married Sir Ferdinand Gorges, ii 293 ; **Mary**, married Sir Thomas Smith, 293 ; Helena,

H ɪ

Smyth family, of Long-Ashton—*continued.*
married Sir Francis Rogers, 293; Thomas, 293; M.P. for Bridgwater, 293; fought on the Royalist side in the civil wars, 293; married Florence Poulett, 293; held the tithes of Filton, 441; owned King Weston, 81; Hugh, Florence, Mary, Helena, Anne, his children, 293; Florence, widow of Thomas, married Thomas Pigott, 293; Hugh, created knight of the bath, 1660, 293; married Anne Ashburnham, 293; monument in Long-Ashton church, 301; sold Compton-Dando and Fryenburgh to Alexander Popham, 422, 425; owned King Weston, 81, owned Christon, iii 578. John: Hugh: Charles: Elizabeth: Florence: Anne, his children, ii 293; Sir John, 293; knight of the shire, 293; married Elizabeth Astry, 293; sold King-Weston to Edmund Bower, 81; monument in Long-Ashton church, 301; benefaction to Long Ashton, 303; John: Hugh: Samuel: Anne: Elizabeth: Astrea: Florence: Arabella, his children, 293, 294; Astrea, married Thomas Coster, 293; Florence, married (1) John Pigott, of Brockley, 121, 294; (2) Sir Jarrit Smyth, 294; Arabella, married Edward Gore, of Flax-Bourton, 294, 311; Sir John, married Anne Pym, 294; leaving no issue the estates passed to his three sisters, Anne, Florence, and Arabella, through whom it came to Sir Jarrit Smyth and Edward Gore, 294; lady Anne, monument in Long-Ashton church, 301; benefaction to Long-Ashton, 304; Sir Jarrit, of Bristol, married Florence Smyth and became owner of a third of the manor of Long-Ashton, 294; purchased another third from John Gore, of Barrow court, 294; John Hugh: Thomas: his children, 294; Sir John Hugh, succeeded to his father's estates in Long-Ashton, 294; married Elizabeth Woolnough, of Puckle-church, 294; owned Bedminster, 282; Bishopworth, 284, 285; Buckshaw, 370. Christon, iii 578; land in Churchill, 580; and Foxcote, 350. was J.P., i *xlii*; and sheriff, 1773, *xxxix.* Thomas, second son of Sir Jarrit, married Jane Whitchurch, ii 294; Hugh: John: Florence; Mary, his children, 294.
Smythe, Thomas, purchased Yarlington from the marquis of Northampton, i 228; alienated it to William Rosewell, 229.
Smythes, Jane, of Wrington, wife of Edward Barnard, iii 463.
Snagge, Thomas, part owner of Curry Rivel, i 26.
Snail-Hill, hamlet in West-Chinnock, ii 329.
Snailes-Meade, Wilts: nunnery founded by Ela, countess of Salisbury, iii 184.
Snell, Sir John, iii 209. William, M.P. for Bath, 1301, B 19.

Snooke, memorial stone in Brewton church, i 218; Wick-Champflower, 219.
Snow, Nicholas, part-owner of Oare and patron of the living, ii 34. Paul George, patron of the living of Martock, iii 8; treasurer of Wells cathedral, 396; prebendary of Wells, 397.
Snowden hill, Chard, i *xiv.*
Snuff mills, Weston, i 156.
Snygg, Thomas, owner of lands in Kingston-Seymour, ii 123.
Soche (*see* Socke).
Soche (*see* Sock Dennis).
Socherwiche, Adam de, i 112. holder of part of a knight's fee of the bishopric of Wells, iii 393 (*see* Shockerwick).
Sock, John de, holder of land in Sock-Dennis, iii 308.
Socke or Old-Stock, Mudford, iii 221; seat of the Raymond family, 221; spring, 221; Domesday survey, 221; held of Roger, by Vitalis: Tochi held it T.R.E. 221; subsequently held by the Courtney family, 222.
Sock-Dennis: situation, iii 307; depopulated, 307; Domesday survey, 307; owned by Robert, earl of Morton, 307; held by the Beauchamps, of Hatch, and under them, by the Dacus family, 307; William de Mohun held lands here, 307; John de Lynde, 307; Robert Burnell, bishop of Bath and Wells, 307; the Bonvilles, 307; the Berkeleys and the Brooks, 307, 303; John de Sock held land here, 308; Phelips family, of Montacute, held the principal farm, 308; Mr. Phipps, 308; Windham's Sock owned by Mr. Windham, 308; White-hall hospital held lands here, 300; manor owned by John, lord Grey, 444.
Sodbury, Adam de, abbot of Glastonbury, procured a market and fair for Wrington, i 206. procured a charter of free-warren for his lands in High Ham, iii 444; obtained a charter for a market and fair at Ditcheat, 472; built part of the manor house and chapel at Pilton, 481. gave many precious ornaments to the abbey, vaulted the body of the church, and caused a curious astronomical clock to be made, ii 254. procured a licence for a market and fair at Middlezoy, iii 442. Richard, M.P. for Bath, 1355, 1357, B 20.
Sodden, William de, woodward of Winford forest, ii 315.
Somaster, William, whose daughter married Sir John Speke, i 67.
Someri, Roger de, witness to a deed by Geffery Luttrell, iii 498.
Somerset, dukes of, i *xlviii*; John Beaufort, 1442, *xlviii.* owned Berwick, ii 338. Croscombe, iii 469. Edmund Beaufort, 1444, married Eleanor Beauchamp, ii 282. killed

Stawel family—*continued.*

was buried in Glastonbury abbey, 250 ; Edward, married Agnes Cheyney, 250 ; Robert, married Anne St. Maur, 250, ii 200. sheriff, 1467, 1468, i *xxxvi, xl.* Elizabeth, married Henry Beaumont, iii 250 ; John, married Dorothy Carew, 250 ; Richard, married lady Alice Poulett, 250 ; Sir John : Thomas, 250. Joan, wife of John Hadley, ii 48, iii 254 ; Thomas, married Thomasine le Floyre, 250 ; Sir John, married Frances Dyer, 251. sold a moiety of Road to Thomas Webbe, ii 224. sheriff, 1574, i *xxxvii.* Sir John, married lady Elizabeth Touchet, iii 251 ; owned West-Bagborough, 242. sheriff, 1596, *xxxviii.* Mary, married Thomas Pike, iii 7. Sir John, K.C.B., sheriff, 1628, *xxxviii.* and deputy-lieutenant for Somerset, married Elizabeth, daughter of Sir Edward Hext, and widow of Sir Joseph Killigrew, iii 251, 185 ; owned Low-Ham, 445 ; imprisoned by parliament for his devotion to the royalist cause, his estates confiscated and his house at Cothelstone demolished, 251 ; monument in Cothelstone church, 253. was M.P., 1625, 1640, 1661, i *xxxii.* Ralph, first lord Stawel, of Somerton, iii 185, 251, 445 ; married (1) Anne Ryves, (2) Abigail Pitt, 251 ; John : William, : Edward : Elizabeth : Catherine, Lucy : Diana, 251 ; John, second lord Stawel, married Margaret, daughter of James, earl of Salisbury, 251 ; owned Horsey, 85 ; Prestleigh, 474 ; was the last member of the family to own Stawel, 431 ; rebuilt the mansion at Low-Ham, 445 ; William, third lord, married Elizabeth Forster, 251 ; William, who died young : Charlotte, 251 ; Edward, fourth lord, married Mary, daughter and heir of Sir Hugh Stewkley, bart. : the hon. Stewkley Stawel died young, 251 ; Mary, 252 ; Mary, married (1) the rt. hon. Henry Bilson Legge, received the title of baroness Stawel of Somerton, to herself, and her heirs male, 252 ; her second husband was the rt. hon. Wills Hill, earl of Hillsborough, 252 ; the hon. Henry Stawel Legge, her son, fifth lord Stawel, owner of Cothelstone, 252. patron of Dunster, ii 17 ; owner and patron of Babcary, 60, 61 ; owner of Wotton Courtney, 49.

Stawell, Thomas, J.P., i *xlv.* house at Withiel-Flory, iii 295 ; owned the chief manor in Withypool, 558. Rev. Thomas, monument in Luckham church, ii 24.

Stawley : situation, iii 28 ; hamlets of Trace-Bridge and Upley or Apley, 28 ; Domesday survey, 28 ; one manor held by Alured de Ispania : earl Harold held it T.R.E. 28 ; the other, held of Alured by Osward and

Stawley—*continued.*

Ailward, 28 ; Stawley subsequently owned by the Poulett family, 28 ; church (St. Michael), 29 ; bells (3), 29 ; benefaction, 29 ; Apley or Upley hamlet, 28 ; Domesday survey, 28 ; owned by earl Morton and Baldwin de Execestre : held by Bretel and Drogo, 28 ; Brismar held it T.R.E. 28 ; Grindham or Greenham manor (*see* Grindham).

Staye manor, owned by lady Aylesford, i 40.

Stayner, Jeffrey, occupier of a tenement assigned to prior Bird, B 57.

Staynings family, monument and brass tablets in Selworthy church, ii 42.

Staynings family, of Holnicot, descended from Richard Hewish, iii 491.

Steel mills, Keynsham, ii 400.

Steep-Holmes island, i *xii,* iii 608 ; retreat of Gildas Badonicus, 608 ; of the Danes, after their defeat at Watchet, 609 ; owned by the Bec family, 609 ; Henry de Laci, earl of Lincoln, 609 ; Berkeleys, one of whom founded a small priory here, 609. James, earl of Ormond, ii 392 ; James, earl of Wiltshire, 392.

Stefan, holder of land in Chew-Magna, ii 94.

Stephen, prior of Taunton, 1175-1189, iii 235.

Stephen, Henry, rector of Trent, ii 383.

Stephens, Anne, wife of Peregrine Palmer, i 255 ; Henry, J.P., *xlv.* owner of Helehouse, South-Petherton, iii 110. James, J.P., i *xlv* ; sheriff, 1786, *xxxix.* governor of Bath hospital, B 49. owner of Camerton, where he had a mansion, iii 331. Philip, sheriff, 1758, i *xxxix.* owner of Camerton, iii 331 ; Richard, incumbent of Nether-Stowey, 553. William, memorial stone in Brockley church, ii 121.

Stephenson, John, sheriff, 1790, i *xxxix.*

Stert, hamlet in Dulverton, owned by Humphry Sydenham, iii 524.

Stert, hamlet in Babcary, ii 61 ; held by John Gilbert, 1456, 61.

Stert or Silver street, hamlet in West-Buckland, ii 485.

Stevens, Richard, incumbent of Kilton, iii 531.

Stevenson, Margery, wife of Humphry Wyndham, ii 490.

Stewart, William, brigadier-general, monument in Bath abbey, 1736, B 70.

Stewkley, Joan, first wife of George Luttrell, ii 12. Mary, wife of lord Stawel, iii 251.

Stewley, hamlet in Curry Mallet, i 31.

Steyning, Edward, i *xl.*

Steyning manor, Stoke Courcy, i 256 ; owned by the Burland family, 256, 257.

Steynings, Charles, M.P., 1654, i *xxxii.* Charles, benefaction to Nether-Stowey, iii 553.

Steynton, John, of Stanton, i *xl.*

Stibbins, Mr., benefactor to Keynsham, ii 409.

Stibbs, captain Bartholomew, monument in Bath abbey, 1735, B 70. Edward, monument in Bath abbey, 1739, 70; John, mayor of Bath, 1685, B 25, 1698, 1707, 26; John, monument in Bath abbey, 1708, 70; John, monument in Bath abbey, 1732, 70.

Sticklepath, hamlet in Combe - St. - Nicholas, ii 475.

Sticklings or Sticklinch, hamlet in West-Pennard, ii 275.

Stigand, abbot of Bath, 1067, B 55.

Still, John, incumbent of a chantry at Combe-Flory, iii 248; Rev. Henry, incumbent of Clapton in Gordano, 179; Samuel, memorial stone in Wraxall church, 159.

Still, John, bishop of Bath and Wells, 1592-1607, iii 388; bequest to Bubwith's hospital, Wells, 388, 408; gift-sermon to Wells church, 410; owned Hutton, 590; monument in Wells cathedral, 400. Nathaniel, sheriff, 1615, i *xxviii.* carried out the bequest of his father, bishop Still, to Bubwith's hospital, iii 388; owned Hutton, 590; monument in Hutton church, 591; his daughter married into the Codrington family, 590.

Stillingfleet, Rev. Robert, D.D., buried in Long-Ashton church, ii 301.

Stillington, Julian, wife of Sir Thomas Hampton, iii 588.

Stillington, Robert, bishop of Bath and Wells, 1465, keeper of the privy seal and chancellor of England, iii 386; a great Yorkist, 386; disgraced and imprisoned at Windsor, 386; buried at Wells, in the chapel he had built there, 386.

Stilvey or Stiveleigh, in Mere, ii 274.

Stocha (*see* Stoke St. Mary).

Stoche (*see* Stoke-Pero, Stoke-Courcy, Stoke-under-Hamden, Stoke Giffard or Stoke Trister).

Stocheland (*see* Stockland-Bristol).

Stock, hamlet in Churchill, iii 579.

Stocker family, owner of Chilcompton, ii 129; monuments in Chilcompton church, 130; owned also Hinton-Blewet, 145; which they sold to William James, of Harptree, 145. Gertrude, wife of Robert Harbin, iii 209. George, John and Katherine, monument in Whitchurch church, ii 443; arms, 443; John, purchaser of Hinton - Blewet, 158; Margaret, wife of John Trethewy, 130; Mary, wife of Benjamin Harrington, 130.

Stockham, hamlet in Bagborough, iii 243.

Stocking manufacture, Shepton-Mallet, iii 459.

Stockland (*see* Stoke-lane).

Stockland-Bristol or Stockland-Gaunts: situation, i 247; Domesday survey, 247; owned by the families of Paganel, Gaunt and Luttrell, 247, iii 498, 540. the hospital of Gaunts or Billeswyke, Bristol, i 247, iii 499.

Stockland-Bristol or Stockland-Gaunts—*contd.* the commonality of Bristol, i 248; the vicar's dues, 248; church and its monuments, 248; bells (4), 248.

Stocklinch, Ralph de, held a moiety of Chaffcombe manor, iii 115.

Stocklinch-Ottersey: situation, i 63; cultivation of hemp and flax, 63; Hicks' horse-hoe, 63; fossils, 63; the perambulation of the forest of Neroche, 63; probable origin of name, 63, iii 115. owned by the Denebaud family, i 63, iii 115. Paulet family, i 63, iii 116. church, i 64; bells (3), 64.

Stocklinch St. Magdalen: situation, i 64; cultivation of hemp and flax, 64; division of the manor, 64; fossils, 64; revel, 64; church, 64; bells (3), 64.

Stockton, Robert, i 262.

Stocks, Staple-Fitzpaine, i 61.

Stockwood, rights in, released by Frideswide, daughter of lord Hungerford, to Sir Richard Choke, ii 226.

Stoford, hamlet in Berwick, ii 337; owned by the de Hastings family, 337.

Stoford, hamlet in Bradford, iii 244.

Stoford, hamlet in Stoke Courcy, i 249.

Stogumber or Stoke-Gomer: situation, iii 545; market, 545; fair, 545; discovery of Roman coins here, 545; owned by the Sydenham family, 548; Thomas Cridland, 548; Barlinch priory held lands here, 548; church (St. Mary) and its monuments, 548, 549; bells (5), 548; cross, 549; almshouse, 549; Halsway, 545, 546; Hartrow, 546; Capton, 546; Domesday survey, 546; held by the king, 546; Ayle or Vellow, held by Thomas Fitchet of lady Elizabeth Audley, 546; Escott, Kingswood, and Preston hamlets, 546; Caslake, 547; Higher and Lower Vexford, 547; Rowdon, 547; Rixton, 547; Combe-Sydenham, 547; held by the Sydenham family under the dean and chapter of Wells, 547; by Sir James Langham, 548.

Stogursey (*see* Stoke Courcy).

Stoke, John, owner of Ubley, which he conveyed to William de Chedder, ii 156. John, owner of Churchill, iii 580.

Stoke house, Stoke St. Mary, iii 291.

Stoke-Bishop, owned by James Perceval, iii 175.

Stoke-Bottom, hamlet in Stoke-lane, iii 484.

Stoke-Courcy: situation, i 249; site of a battle between the Saxons and Danes, 249; hamlets of Week-Fitzpaine (with Burton and Stoford), Shurton, Durborough, Cock, and Edston, Monkton, Knighton, Fairfield, Steyning, 249; styled "the borough and honour of Stoke Courcy," 249; returned to parliament in 1361, John Bakeler and Adam Mareys, 249; market and fairs, 249; Domesday survey, 250; owned by William de Faleise and held by Brixi T.R.E. 250;

Stoke-Courcy—*continued.*

priory founded by William de Faleise, 250; owned by the families of Courcy, who founded the nunnery of Cannington, 250; Warine Fitz - Gerold, 251; Falk de Brent, who garrisoned the manor house, 251; Hugh de Neville, 251; de Walrond, Fitzpaine, Poynings, and Percy, 252; earl of Egmont, 252; church, its monuments and benefactions, 257, 258, 259; yew-trees, 259. lands here belonged to Idstock chantry, iii 90; the lords of the castle were chief lords of Lilstock, 534.

Stoke-Courcy, prior of, a landowner temp. Ed. I, i *xxvi.* patron of Wotton Courtney, ii 49.

Stoke - Giffard or Rodney - Stoke : situation, iii 602; includes part of Draycot hamlet, 602; Domesday survey, 602; held by Alward, 602; subsequently owned by the Dispencer family, 602; the Giffards, 602; the Rodneys, 603, ii 306. Sir Thomas Bridges, iii 605; the representatives of the duke of Chandos, 605; mansion, 605; Nyland or Andredesey, 605; owned by the abbots of Glastonbury, 605; granted at the dissolution to John Malte, 605; Nyland-hill, 606; church (St. Leonard) and its monuments, 606, 607; bells (4), 606; yew-tree, 607.

Stoke-Gomer (*see* Stogumber).

Stoke Gregory : its situation, ii 180; hamlets of Mare Green, Woodhill Green, Currylode (or Curlwood Green), Moorlands, Warmoor, Staeth, 180; owned by the dean and chapter of Wells, 181; church and its monuments, 181; bells (5), 181.

Stoke-Hill, hamlet in Stoke St. Mary, iii 291.

Stoke - in - Blakemore, belonged to the Wake family, iii 119.

Stoke-lane, Stockland, or Stoke St. Michael, iii 484; situation, 484; Stoke-Bottom: East-End, West-End, and the Fishponds, 484; springs, 484; owned by Glastonbury abbey, 484; held by the earl of Morton, 484; subsequently held by Mrs. Knatchbull, 484; East-End owned by John Long, 484; church (St. Nicholas), 484; bell, 484; benefactions, 484; lands here were owned by the guilds at Shepton-Mallet, 465.

Stoke-Lane, hamlet in Yarlington, i 228.

Stoke, North : situation, i 134; hamlet of Swinford, 134; intrenchment on Lansdowne, 134; the manor given by Kenulf to Bath priory, 134; Modbert de Stoke disputed the ownership, 134; owned by the families of Paulet, Bageholte and Yardley, 135; John Hooper, 135; church (St. Martin) and its monuments, 135, 136; yew tree, 136. Ralph Inweans held land here of lord William de Montacute, iii 118.

Stoke, South : situation, i 136; forms part of the hamlet of Midford, 136; bridge, 136;

Stoke, South—*continued.*

Midford castle built by Henry Disney Roebuck, 136; Horsecombe brook, 136; the manor sold by lord Sandwich to Mr. Cooper, of Salisbury, 136; ancient rights of the vicar, 136; church (St. James) and its monuments, 137.

Stoke, East (*see* Stoke under Hamden).

Stoke, West (*see* Stoke under Hamden).

Stoke Pero : its situation, ii 42; hamlet of Wilmotsham, 42; Domesday survey, 43; owned by William de Mohun, and held by Roger : by Eddida T.R.E. 43; owned by Gilbert Piro, 43; John Forster, holder of half a knight's fee, 43; owned by the families of Dodisham and Pym, and Rev. Chancellor Nutcombe, 43; church, 43; bell (1), 43.

Stoke-St.-Mary : situation, iii 291; hamlets of Stoke-Hill and Broughton, 291; vested in the bishopric of Winchester, 291; church and monument, 291; bells (3), 291; Stokehouse, 291; lands here were owned by Taunton priory, 235.

Stoke-St.-Michael (*see* Stoke-Lane or Stockland).

Stoke-Trister, iii 49; hamlet of Bayford, 49; owned by Robert, earl of Morton : held by Bretel 49; Domesday survey, 49, 50; subsequently owned by the de Estre family, 50; Richard Rivel, 50; the de l'Orti family, 50; Sir John de Molyns, 50; William de Montacute, earl of Salisbury, 50; the Fitz-Alans, earls of Arundel, 50; Edward Phelips, 50; church (St. Andrew) and its monument, 51; bells (4), 51.

Stoke-under-Hamden (East and West Stoke), iii 315; Domesday survey, 315; owned by Robert, earl of Morton; held by Robert, 315; subsequently owned by the lords Beauchamp, of Hatch, 315, 316; the Meriets, 319; Sir Thomas de Gournay, 319; the duchy of Cornwall, 320; castle, 316, 320; church and its monuments, 321; bells (5), 321; Estoket or Stoket, 321; owned by the earl of Morton, 321; held by Malger : by Alwin T.R.E. 320; subsequently by Sir Robert Hull, 321; Sir Robert Latimer, 321.

Stoke - under - Hamden castle, built by John Beauchamp, iii 316; chantry founded there by John Beauchamp, 316, 317; survey taken in Edward VI's reign, 318, 319; chantry suppressed, and the lease granted to Mrs. Darrell, 319; ruins of castle and chapel, 320.

Stokeleigh, Long Ashton : Roman encampment at, ii 289; granted to St. Augustine's abbey, Bristol, by Edmund de Lions, 291.

Stokes, Ancilla de, second wife of William de Vernai, i 253.

Stoket or Estoket (*see* Stoke-under-Hamden).

Stokkey family, owners of Porlock, ii 37.

Stole, a monastic garment, ii 251.

Stoley's Green, West Hatch, ii 180.

Stonage, hamlet in Tickenham, iii 164.

Stonchiste, boundary of Exmoor perambulation, 1298, ii 19.

Stone quarries, i *xvi.*

Stone, Charles, mayor of Bath, 1740, 1749, B 26. Rev. Charles, J.P., i *xlv.* Christopher, M.P. for Bath, 1603, 1605, B 21. Florence, benefaction to Taunton, iii 240; John, abbot of Cleeve, 1421, 512. Nicholas and Joan, inscriptions in Sutton-Bingham church, ii 350; William, owner of the manor and site of Glastonbury abbey, 259; Rev. William, memorial tablet in Babcary church, 62.

Stone memorial stone in Wedmore church, i 193.

Stone, hamlet in East-Pennard, iii 478.

Stone hundred, iii 203; granted to the burgesses of Ivelchester, 203, 299; afterwards held with the hundred of Catash by the earls of Huntingdon, 203; united to Yeovil, 203.

Stone manor, Mudford, iii 220; Domesday survey, 220, 221; held by the earl of Morton: thane-land in Glastonbury T.R.E. 221; subsequently granted to Bermondsey priory, 221; depopulated, 221.

Stone, tithing in Chew Magna, ii 95.

Stone-Allerton, hamlet in Chapel-Allerton, i 175.

Stone Easton: its situation, ii 153; Old Down inn, 153; owned by the bishop of Coutances, 153; Domesday survey, 154; held by Azelin de Percheval, 154; owned by the families of Easton, Clifton, Simon de Trewithose, Bartholomew Peytevyn, 154, 158; manors of Easton major and Easton minor, 154, 158; church and its monument, 155; bells (5), 155; yew tree, 155.

Stonehall, purchased by lady Elizabeth Luttrell, iii 500.

Stonen-Halle, Devon, lands in, held by lady Mary de Courtney, iii 567.

Stoner, Ida, of Loughton, wife of Sir Robert Wrothe, iii 68.

Stoner, Sir Francis, built a stone parapet round the King's bath, B 39.

Stoner, William, married Anne, eldest daughter of John, marquis of Montacute, ii 364; John, inherited the manor of Goathill, 364; William, 364; John, 364.

Stoneston, John [*sic* Collinson, but his name was *Sturton*, Som. A. & N. H. Society's *Proceedings*, vol. 38, pt. ii, p. 341], last abbot of Keynsham, ii 155, 402.

Stoney-Littleton, in Wellow, iii 326; Domesday survey, 327; owned by Roger de Curcelle: held by Norman: Almar, Osbern and Godric held it T.R.E. 327; subsequently held under the lords of Wellow by the Brook family, 327; John Smith, 327.

Stoney-Stoke, hamlet in Shepton-Montacute, iii 45.

Stoney-Stratton, Evercreech, iii 413; held under Glastonbury abbey by the Stawel family, 415, 250.

Stonhouse, Rev. Dr., governor of Bath hospital, B 49.

Stonor, Lucy, monument in Bath abbey, 1782, B 70.

Stony Easton (*see* Stone-Easton).

Stork family owned Trent, ii 381. William de, witness to a deed between Anastatia Croc and Sir Thomas Trivet, iii 101; John, holder of Corston, 346. Tristram, i *xl.* married Alice, daughter of Robert Bingham, ii 385; Joan, wife of Richard Compton, 385; Ann, wife of John Larder, 385; Isabel, wife of Alexander Seymour, 385; Mary, wife of William Gerard, 385; monument in Trent church, 385.

Stormont, viscount, J.P., i *xli.*

Storteforde, John de, owner of Alston, ii 393.

Storthwayt, John, chancellor of Wells, inscription on window in Kingsbury church, ii 469. tomb in Wells cathedral, iii 401; founded a chantry in Wells cathedral, 402.

Stortmanforde, granted to Cleeve abbey by William de Mohun, iii 511. [Sordemaneford in Domesday].

Story, Sir Edmund, married Silvestra Luttrell, daughter of — Capper, ii 12; Henry, benefaction to Wiveliscombe, 491. Sir Richard, knt., married Alice, widow of Sir Richard Stafford: she was daughter of Sir John Blunt and heiress to the manor of Ashington, iii 213.

Stote, Thomas, M.P. for Bath, 1361, B 20.

Stoughton, Upper and Lower, hamlets in Wedmore, i 188.

Stoughton, Leicester: lands in, bequeathed for the benefit of the poor of Shapwick, iii 428.

Stour, river, iii 42.

Stour-Cosin, Dorset: owned by the Wake family, iii 119.

Stourton, king Alfred's tower at, owned by Sir Richard Colt Hoare, ii 265.

Stourton family owned the hundred of Andersfield, i 71. Marston Magna, ii 374. Kingston-Pitney, iii 207; Vexford, 547; Charles, lord, caused John and William Hartgill to be murdered, 41. was attainted, 33. Edward, lord Stourton, sold Andersfield to Mr. Gore, i 71. Joan, wife of Richard Warre, iii 260. John, M.P., 1420, 1421, 1423, 1434, 1440, i *xxxi*; sheriff, 1428, 1431, *xxxv.* held land in Wellesleigh, iii 405; married Catherine Pain, 201; Alice, his daughter, owned Speckington and Yeovilton: married William Daubeney, 201; Sir John, built a new church at Stavordale priory, 34; held the bailiwick of Williton-Free-

Stourton family—*continued.*

manors, 485 ; John, lord, held also the hundreds of West-Perrot and Andersfield, 207. Margaret, wife of William Carent, ii 367. Margaret, daughter of John Chideock, part owner of Isle Brewers, i 54 ; Sir Reginald, sheriff, 1463, 1468, 1469, *xxxvi.* owned Ford, iii 613. William, M.P., 1399, 1402, 1403, i *xxxi.* married Elizabeth Moigne, ii 367; William, lord, owned Marston-Bigot, 214; Monks'-Ham, 216. lands in Barrow common, the manor of Roundhill, and rectory of Wincaunton, iii 33; Kingston Pitney, 207 ; Vexford, which he sold to John Sweeting, 547 ; a daughter of lord Stourton married Richard Brent, of Cossington, 436.

Stoweford, William (*see* William Sewey).

Stowel (*see* Stawel).

Stowell family (*see* Stawel).

Stowey, in Chew hundred, ii 110 ; petrifying spring, 110; Domesday survey, 110; held by Dodo: by Siwold T.R.E. 110 ; John Candell and Hamon Fitz-Richard, held half a knight's fee, 110 ; owned by Mrs. Jones, 110 ; church (St. Mary) and its monuments, 110, 111 ; bells (5), 110 ; birthplace of Parsons, the Jesuit, 111.

Stowey water, in Cutcombe, ii 6.

Strachey, Elizabeth, wife of William Jones, ii 111. Henry, J.P., i *xlv.* owner of Elm, ii 207 ; Henry, of Sutton court, 96 ; Hodges, married (1) Margaret Henley, (2) Ann Parkin, (3) Mary Smith, 99 ; monument in Chew Magna church, 99. Jane, wife of the Rev. William Dodd, monument in Charlton-Mackarell church, iii 194. John, owner of Sutton court, ii 96 ; Mr., observations on the strata in coal-mines, 145-148.

Stradling family owned Combe-Hay, iii 334, 335; descended from Sir Robert d'Esterling, of St. Donat's castle, Glamorgan, 335; dispute with the Hewish family as to the possession of Halsway, 546 ; Robert, wrote his name Stradling, married Hawise Brin, 335; Sir Gilbert, 335; Sir William, 335; Sir John, 335 ; Sir Peter, married Julian Hawey, and became possessed of Combe-Hay, 334, 335; Sir Edward, married Eleanor, daughter of Sir Gilbert Stradling, 335; Joan, wife of Alexander Popham, of Huntworth, 71. Sir Edward, M.P., 1342, i *xxx* ; sheriff, 1343, *xxxiv.* married Wentlian Berkrolls, iii 335; Sir William, knight of the Holy Sepulchre, married Julian St. Barbe, 335; Sir Edward, knight of the Holy Sepulchre, married Jane Beaufort, and became possessed of Halsway, 335, 546. sheriff, 1424, i *xxxv.* Sir Henry, knighted at Jerusalem, married Elizabeth Thomas, iii 335 ; Sir John, constable of Taunton, 228 ; Thomas, married Jennet

Stradling family—*continued.*

Mathew, 335; Henry, 335. Sir Edward, i *xl.* married Elizabeth Arundel, iii 335; Sir Thomas, married Catherine Gamage, 335 ; Sir Edward, author of a Welsh grammar, married Agnes Gage : left no issue, 335; Sir John, kinsman of Sir Edward, succeeded to the Combe-Hay estate, married Elizabeth Gage, 335; Rev. John, incumbent of Bawdrip, 92 ; William, John Jeanes, and Edward : monument in Chedzoy church, 95.

Strafford, Humphrey, earl of Devon (*see* Devon).

Stragelle (*see* Stretchill).

Strange, Eubulo, married Alice, widow of Thomas, earl of Lancaster, ii 357 ; George Stanley, summoned to parliament by title of lord Strange, 333. Lord, owner of Curry Rivel, i 26. John, curious entry respecting, in the register of bishop Oliver King, ii 35 ; Richard, Lord le, sold Cutcombe Mohun to Alexander Hody and others, 6.

Strangeways family owned Hardington, ii 348 ; Middle and West Chinnock, 328. Dunden, iii 447 ; monuments in Charlton-Adam church, 192 ; Hon. and Rev. Charles, incumbent of Brimpton-D'Evercy, 215 ; colonel, owner of Somerton, 185 ; Giles, sheriff, 1512, i *xxxvii* ; sheriff, 1517, 1524, 1533, 1541, *xxxvii* ; married Joan Wadham, ii 328. held Middle and West Chinnock, ii 328 ; Holwell, which he conveyed to Humphry Watkins, 369 ; Chisselborough, which he sold to John Wadham, 330. Sutton Mallet, iii 430 ; Chilton, 433. John, benefaction to Middle Chinnock, ii 329. Sir John, benefaction to Compton-Dunden, iii 448. Mrs., benefaction to Chisselborough parish, ii 330. Mrs., owner of the rectorial manor of Shapwick, iii 427. Mrs., owner of Wick-Champflower, i 219 ; Susannah, monument in Milton Clevedon church, 223. Susannah, wife of Thomas Horner, of Mells, ii 328, 463 ; monument in Mells church, 464 ; Thomas, who through his wife, Eleanor, became possessed of Middle and West Chinnock, 328 ; Thomas, whose estates passed to his daughter, Susannah, 328. Thomas and Maria, monument in Shapwick church, iii 428.

Stratford, John de, archdeacon of Lincoln : bishop of Winchester, 1323, iii 232.

Stratton, baron Berkeley of, title conferred on Sir John Berkeley, iii 281.

Stratton, Sir Matthew, whose daughter married Henry de Stawel, iii 250.

Stratton-on-the-Fosse : situation, ii 458 ; Roman fosse road, 458 ; granted by king Edgar to Glastonbury abbey, 458 ; held by Alwold T.R.E. 458 ; granted at the Conquest to

Stratton-on-the-Fosse—*continued*.
　　the bishop of Coutances, 458 ; Domesday
　　survey, 458 ; subsequently owned by the
　　Gournay family, 459 ; annexed to the duchy
　　of Cornwall, and held by the Prince of
　　Wales, 459 ; church (St. Vigor), 459 ; Pit-
　　cott manor, 459.
Stratton, Over, tithing in South Petherton,
　　iii 106.
Stream, hamlet in St. Decumans, iii 486 ; owned
　　by the Sydenham family, 215.
Strecche, Catherine, daughter of Sir John Beau-
　　mont, married Sir Hugh Luttrell, ii 10.
Streche, Sir John, knt., married Elizabeth Brad-
　　ston, and became possessed of Samford-
　　Arundel, iii 26 ; Sir John, married Mary
　　Molton, 26 ; Sir John, 26 ; held ten knights'
　　fees in Ashill and Sevington, 123. sheriff,
　　1383, i *xxxv*. Cecily, wife of Sir Thomas
　　Bonville, iii 26 ; Elizabeth, inherited Sam-
　　ford-Arundel : married Sir Thomas Beau-
　　champ, 26.
Street : situation, iii 423 ; Wearyall hill, 423 ;
　　derivation of name, 423 ; secluded by king
　　Ina from episcopal authority, 423, ii 241.
　　annexed to Glastonbury abbey, iii 423,
　　424 ; granted at the Dissolution to Edward,
　　duke of Somerset, 424 ; owned by the
　　Dyer family, 424 ; Joseph Brown, 424 ;
　　court-house called Street-farm, 424 ; ham-
　　lets of Upper, Middle and Lower Leigh,
　　424 ; Ivythorn-hill, 424 ; Ivythorn house,
　　424 ; Ivythorn manor, 424 ; church, 424 ;
　　bells (6), 424.
Street, East, hamlet in East Pennard, ii 275.
Street-farm, iii 424.
Street, hamlet in Pylle, iii 483.
Street, manor in Winsham, ii 478 ; mansion be-
　　longing to James Marwood, 478 ; given by
　　William the Conqueror to William de
　　Moion, 478 ; Domesday survey, 479 ; held
　　by Roger : Huscarl and Almar held it
　　T.R.E. 479 ; subsequently owned by
　　Henry Host Henley, 479 ; Roman fosse
　　road, 479 ; discovery of Roman coins, 479.
Street, William, mayor of Bath, 1784, B 27.
Streme, hamlet in Overweare, i 184.
Strengestone (*see* Stringston).
Strength, remarkable, of Sir John Hautville, ii 108
Stretchell or Stragelle manor, Pawlet, iii 101 ;
　　Domesday survey, 101 ; owned by Walter
　　de Dowai : held by Renewald : Leuegar
　　and Edwold held it T.R.E. 101 ; Anastatia
　　Croc granted lands here to Sir Thomas
　　Trivet, 101 ; William Baudrip released all
　　his rights here to John Wroughton, 91.
Stretchley, William, married Anne Gold, and
　　became part owner of Seaborough, ii 173.
Stringer, Anthony, owner of Freshford, i 125.
Stringston : situation, i 261 ; Douseborough
　　castle, 261 ; Domesday survey, 261 ; part

Stringston—*continued*.
　　owned by Alured de Ispania, and held by
　　Rannulf : by Alwi T.R.E. 261 ; another
　　part owned by Roger de Curcelle, and held
　　by William : by Siward T.R.E. 261 ;
　　owned by the families of Fichet, Cunte-
　　ville, Fourneaux, Blount, Stafford, Stury,
　　Roche, Strode and Oglander, 262, 263 ;
　　manor of Alfoxton, 263 ; hamlet of Ditch,
　　266 ; church and its monuments, 266, 267.
　　Taunton priory held lands here, iii 235 ;
　　Kilve chantry held lands here, 533.
Stringstone, Amelia de, wife of Adam de
　　Cunteville, i 262 ; Aubrea, wife of Hugh
　　Fichet, 262 ; conveyed the manor of Ditch
　　to John Fitz Gilbert on his marriage with
　　her daughter, Agnes, 266.
Strode family, owners of West-Cranmore, ii 209,
　　210 ; arms, 210 ; owned also Chilton-Can-
　　telo, 339 ; the manor of Glastonbury, 259,
　　Shurton, i 252 ; Stringston, 263. land in
　　Christon and Uphill, iii 578 ; members of,
　　buried in Barrington church, 114. Carew,
　　married Elizabeth Skinner, ii 210. Edward,
　　sheriff, 1688, *xxxviii*. Edward, ii 210 ;
　　Edward, married Alice Whiting, 210 ; Ed-
　　ward, married Alice Pore, 210 ; Edward,
　　210. Edward, married Joan Gunning :
　　monument in Shepton Mallet church,
　　iii 465 ; founded almshouse at Shepton
　　Mallet, 465 ; Elizabeth, daughter of Sir
　　Richard, of Newnham, second wife to John
　　Harbin, 209. Geffrey, of Shepton-Mallet,
　　married (1) Elizabeth Filiol, (2) Sarah Bar-
　　nard, ii 210 ; George, married Margery
　　Smith, 210 ; George, of London, married
　　Rebecca Crispe, 210 ; Sir George, of Parn-
　　ham : owner of Chilton - Cantelo, 339 ;
　　Henry, married Elizabeth Brent, 209 ;
　　Henry, married Maud Fichett Beaupre,
　　209. Henry, sheriff, 1721, i *xxxviii*. Hugh
　　de, ii 209 ; Sir Hugh de, 209 ; Hugh,
　　married Beatrice de Button, 209 ; James,
　　210 ; James, married Amy Pitt, 210 ;
　　James, married a daughter of — Head, of
　　Berkshire, 210 ; James, married Amy
　　Court, 210. John, J.P., i *xlv* ; John, trustee
　　of the Saxey charity, 212. John, ii 209 ;
　　Sir John, of Strode, 209 ; John, of Shepton-
　　Mallet, married Joan Okle, 209 ; John,
　　married Sophia Parker, 210 ; John, married
　　Mary Simpson, of Penrith, 210 ; John,
　　married a daughter of John Hippisley, 210 ;
　　John, married Margaret Luttrell, daughter
　　of Christopher Hadley, 12 ; John, owner
　　of land in Seaborough, 173. John and
　　Mary, monument in Stoke-under-Hamden
　　church, iii 321 ; Margaret, married George
　　Trevelyan, 539. Mary, wife of Henry
　　Bonner, monument in Combe-St.-Nicholas
　　church, ii 477 ; Richard, married Margaret

Strode family—*continued*.
Gerard, 209; Stephen married Mary Hodges, 210. Thomas, of Stringston, i 263. Thomas, ii 209; Thomas, of Batcomb, married a daughter of — Blanchard, 210; Thomas, of Shepton-Mallet, married (1) Alice Bulliford, (2) Anne Lane, 210; Walter, 209; Warine, came into England with the Conqueror: was lord of Strode, 209. William, sheriff, 1714, *xxxviii*. William, governor of Bath hospital, B 49. William, of Parnham, owner of Stringston, i 263. William, ii 109; Sir William de, of Strode, 209; William, of Chalmington, progenitor of the Strodes, of Parnham, 209; William, married Alice de Ledred, 209; William, married Elizabeth Upton, 210; William, of London, married Joan Barnard, 210. monuments in Shepton-Mallet church, iii 464, 465. William, owned the manor of Glastonbury, ii 259. William, of Bu[a]rrington, purchased the manor of Martock, iii 5; William, founder of a grammar school at Martock, 11.
Studley abbey, Oxfordshire, received a pension from Trent, ii 383. held Crowcombe-Studley, iii 515.
Stukely, Dr., on the origin of Hautville's Coit, ii 433; on the derivation of Pensford, 429. curious fact respecting a greyhound, iii 307. Elizabeth, wife of Sir John Wadham, i 48.
Sturges, —, married Mary Malet, i 91.
Sturidge, Edward, benefaction to Bath abbey, B 71.
Sturminster Marshall, Dorset: land in, held by Richard de Gorges and his descendants, iii 157.
Sturmy, captain Samuel, bequest to Easton-in-Gordano, iii 151; Sir William, owner of Bradney, 92.
Sturton (*see* Stourton).
Sturton, Mr., owner of Standerwick, ii 228.
Stury, Sir Richard, married Alice Stafford, daughter of Sir John Blount, i 262, 263.
Stylbond, Thomas, prior of Bath, who received pension, B 57.
Style, John, prior of Bath, who received pension, B 57.
Styward, abbot of Glastonbury, ii 249.
Suain, holder of Claverton, i 145. of part of Cucklington, iii 51.
Subchantership of Wells, iii 380.
Succedene (*see* Cheddon-Fitzpaine).
Sudbury, Thomas de, dean of Wells, 1381, i 190.
Sudcadeberie (*see* Cadbury-South).
Sudley, John, lord of Sudley, ii 419.
Suffolk, Charles, duke of, whose heirs had a claim to the manor of Curry Rivel, i 26. Henry, duke of, owned Norton under Hamden, which he forfeited on his attainder,

Suffolk family—*continued*.
1553, ii 334, owned Idstock, iii 90; Barrington, 113.
Suffolk, William de la Pole, marquis of, owned Chedzoy, iii 94.
Sugar (*alias* Norris), Hugh: chancellor of Wells and executor to bishop Beckington, iii 385; built a chapel in Wells cathedral, 399; arms, 399.
Suleny, Salignac, or de Saligniaco family, owned the manor and hundred of Kilmersdon, ii 445; branches of the family settled in Cornwall, Devon and Brittany, 445; arms, 445; John de, 445; Emma de, married Alexander de Arsick, who received a third of the manor, 446; Andrew de, 445; Geffrey de, 445; Ralph de, 445; released Mells and Leigh from all suit and service to the hundred of Kilmersdon, 461; Andrew de, 445; Andrew de, held lands in Babington, 445.
Sulesworth, lands in, granted by Alice de Ouvre to Woodspring priory, iii 594.
Sulfebrodacre, lands in, granted by Alice de Ouvre to Woodspring priory, iii 594.
Sullivan, George, bequest to Minehead, ii 31.
Sully, Elianor, daughter of Richard Sully, and wife of Henry Chester and Giles Dawberie: memorial tablet in Withycombe church, 1730, ii 48.
Sully, Sir Raymund de, holder of lands in Alston, ii 394. Sarah, wife of William Malet, of Enmore, iii 220.
Summers, Richard, purchased Chew-Magna from Edward Popham, ii 95.
Sumner, Humphry, prebendary of Wells, iii 396.
Surrage, John, benefaction to Chipstable, iii 508.
Surrey, Thomas Holand, duke of, married Joan de Woodstock, owned Somerton, iii 184.
Sussex, Robert, earl of, owned the manor of Old-Cleeve, the site of the abbey, and lands in London, Bilbrook, Washford, Goldsoncot, Roadwater, Leigh, and Langham, iii 512. Thomas, earl of, owned the site of the abbey at Glastonbury, Weary-all park, and other lands, ii 259.
Suthbruham bridge, boundary of Selwood forest, ii 195.
Suthstoke, John de, M.P. for Bath, 1312, B 19; 1338, 20.
Sutone (*see* Sutton-Montis).
Sutton, Alice, wife of Thomas Symcocks, iii 449; arms, 449. Basilia de, prioress of Minchin-Barrow, ii 311. Francis, against whom a law-suit was instituted, respecting the sale of lands belonging to Wobourne's almshouse, Yeovil, iii 212. John de, who released land in Stone-Easton to John de Chinereston, ii 154. Robert de, prior of Bath, 1332-1333, B 55; translated to Dunster, 1333, 55, ii 17. Robert, monument in

Sutton family—*continued.*
Bath abbey, 1775, B 70. Walter, holder of half a knight's fee in Sutton-North, ii 95 ; Walter de, holder of lands in Norton-Hautville, 107 ; William, holder of half a knight's fee in Sutton-North, 95 ; William de, holder of land in Norton-Hautville, 107.

Sutton, hamlet in Ditcheat, iii 471.

Sutton, hamlet in Wincaunton, iii 33. [Suddon].

Sutton-Bingham : situation, ii 349 ; river Parret, 349 ; Domesday survey, 349 ; owned by Roger Arundel, held by Roger Buissel : Ulward held it T.R.E. 349 ; subsequently held by the Bingham family, 350 ; Ralph, lord Bisset, and his descendants, 350 ; Wyndham Harbin, 350 ; church and its monuments, 350 ; bells (2), 350.

Sutton-Court, Chew Magna, ii 96.

Sutton-Crowthorne, Sutton Montis, ii 88.

Sutton-Damer, manor in Long-Sutton, iii 197 ; owned by — Williams, 197.

Sutton-Mallet : situation, iii 430 ; right of common on King's-Sedgmoor, 430 ; held under Glastonbury abbey by the Malet family, 430 ; held under Sir Giles Strangways, 430 ; owned by John, earl of Rochester, 430 ; viscount Lisburn, 430 ; Robert Knight, 430 ; Robert Knight, 430 ; Richard Reynolds, 430 ; church, 430 ; bells (3), 430.

Sutton-Militis (*see* Sutton-North).

Sutton-Montis : its situation, ii 88 ; Domesday survey, 88 ; owned by Robert, earl of Morton, and held by Drogo : by Bundi T.R.E. 88 ; owned by the families of Montagu, Blundell, Bevyn, Molyns, and Duport, 88 ; Crowthorne, 88 ; church (Holy Trinity) and brass plate, 89 ; bells (3), 89.

Sutton-North, hamlet in Chew Magna, ii 95 ; owned by the families of Sutton, St. Loe, Cavendish, Elizabeth Baber, Samuel Jep, and Strachey, 95, 96 ; the manor house, 96.

Sutton Wick, hamlet in Chew Magna, ii 95.

Swadling, Mr., owner of King-Weston, ii 81.

Swaine, Dulcibella, wife of Edmund Lambert, ii 479.

Swainswick : situation, i 153 ; probable derivation of name, 153 ; held by Matthew Gournay, Edmund Forde, Edmund Blunt, Roger Kemys, William Sewey, Richard Dudley, Oriel college, Oxford, 153 ; the mansion house, the residence of the Capells, in which is preserved an old military sword, 153 ; hamlet of Tatwick, 154 ; church (St. Mary) and its monuments, 154, 155 ; bells (5), 154 ; birthplace of William Prynne, 155. Philip Turney died seized of this manor, ii 225.

Swallow, William, gift to Castle Cary church, ii 58.

Swallow-cliff, Kew Stoke, iii 594.

Swan, John, memorial tablet in Weston church, i 161. Richard, provost of Wells, one of bishop Beckington's executors, iii 385 ; buried in Wells cathedral, 399 ; granted the manor of Shipham to the dean and chapter of Wells cathedral 601.

Swanmore, iii 197.

Swans kept by the abbot of Glastonbury, ii 272.

Swansey, Henry de, abbot of Glastonbury, 1186, obtained certain privileges ii 252 ; was promoted to Winchester, 252 ; he reinterred the relics of king Arthur, at Glastonbury, and wrote an inscription over them, 240.

Swanson, Jane, benefaction to Widcombe, i 174.

Swanton, Jane, monument in Bath abbey, 1697, B 70.

Swanwich, fee simple of manor purchased by trustees of Ilminster grammar school, i 4.

Swayn, Nicholas, M.P. for Bath, 1362, B 20.

Swayne, Rev. George, incumbent of East-Harptree, iii 589.

Swell : situation, i 65 ; ratable value, 65 ; fossils, 65 ; Domesday survey, 65 ; owned by Robert, earl of Morton, 65 ; held by Bretel : by Alwald T.R.E. 65 ; owned successively by Rivel family, L'Orti family, the Warres and the Grosvenor family, 65 ; the manor house, 65 ; church (St. Catherine), 66 ; bells (3), 66 ; chantry founded by Mabel Rivel, 66 ; rectory held by priory of Brewton, 214.

Sweetenham, Lawrence, married Anne Arthur, iii 178.

Sweeting family owned Thorncombe, iii 501. Henry, J.P., i *xlv.* owner of Kilve, iii 532 ; seat at Putsham, 532 ; John, owner of Vexford, 547 ; John, monument in Bicknoller church, 502.

Sweyn, earl of Somerset, i *xlvii.*

Swian, David, Margaret, owned Churchill, iii 580.

Swimming on horseback : traditional explanation of Trevelyan arms, iii 540.

Swinburne, Sir John, bart., monument in Bath abbey, 1744, B 70.

Swinford, hamlet in North Stoke, i 134.

Sword, ancient, in Swainswick manor house, i 153.

Swyft, Thomas, one of the jury to decide position of the city pillory, B 31.

Swymmer, William, owner of Rowberrow, iii 599.

Swynneshowe, John, received a pension from Witham priory, ii 234.

Sybbott, William, received a pension from Keynsham abbey, ii 403.

Syckedon, Devonshire, lands in, granted for the support of lights in Wotton chapel, ii 277.

Sydenham, in Bridgwater, iii 86 ; owned by Roger Arundel, 86 ; the Sydenham family, 86 ; the Caves, 87 ; the Percevals, 87 ; Mr. Bull, 87 ; George Bull Doddington, 87.

Sydenham family owned Sydenham, iii 86 ; Brimpton D'Evercy, 214 ; Orchard, 274, 489 ; Combe and Dulverton, 521—523 ; Combe-Sydenham, 547 ; owned also Ashbrittle, 21 ; Runnington, 25 ; Chilthorne Domer, 217 ; vault in St. Decuman's church, 493 ; arms, 86 ; Robert de, of Sydenham, 86, 521 ; John de, 86, 521 ; Walter de, of Sydenham, 86. landowner temp. Ed. I, i *xxviii*. John de, married the heiress of John de Kittisford, and became possessed of Kittisford, iii 24, 86, 521 ; Agnes, wife of Nicholas Blewet, 24. William de, landowner temp. Ed. I, i *xxviii*. married Joan de Gothayte, iii 22, 86, 521 ; Roger : Simon : William, his children, 521 ; Simon, married Marsilla Hillary, of Badialton, and founded a branch of the family there, 22, 86, 521 ; Simon : Margery : Christiana, 521 ; Margery, of Badialton, married John de Radyngton, 521 ; Roger de, was of Sydenham and Kittisford, 86, 521 ; John and Richard, 521. Richard, was of Combe-Sydenham (*see* Sydenham, of Combe-Sydenham). John, owned Sydenham and Dulverton, married Mary Peekstone, iii 86, 521 ; his daughter married John Carru, 86, 522 ; Hugh, second son of John, held an estate in Dulverton, married Joan Polleswelle, and was ancestor of the baronets of the Sydenham family, and of all the branches in the male line, 87, 522 ; Alice, Robert, 522 ; John of Sydenham, married Alice Redmere, 87 ; Joan, daughter of John, married (1) Richard Cave, to whom she conveyed Sydenham manor, 87 ; (2) Robert Bozun, 87 ; Alice, daughter of Hugh, married Roger Bolter, 522 ; Robert, married Alice Helyar, 522 ; Robert : John, 522 ; John, of Indecote, married Alice Choboroughe, 522. M.P., 1449, 1466, i *xxxi* ; sheriff, 1465, 1466, *xxxvi*. John, held an annuity out of Treborough manor, iii 522 ; John, married the heiress of Collyn, of Culmstock, and settled there, 522 ; Edward : Thomas : John, 522 ; John, rector of Brushford, 522 ; Edward, eldest son of John, married Joan Combe, of Combe, in which place he settled, 522 ; John : George, 522 ; Roger, son of George Sydenham, of Leigh, married a sister of Dr. Thomas Sydenham, 522 ; Roger, 522 ; Roger, married Anne Sydenham, of Chelworthy, 522 ; John Roger : Philip : Thomas, 522 ; Philip, married Sarah Whitlock, 522 ; John, of Combe, married Elizabeth Frank, 522 ; John : Thomas : Dorothy : Elizabeth, 522 ; Thomas, of Sterte, mar-

Sydenham family—*continued.*

ried Radigunde Glass, 522 ; Dorothy, wife of William Huysh, 522 ; Elizabeth, wife of Humphrey Cruse, 522 ; John, of Combe, married (1) Elizabeth Pollard, (2), Mary Ashford, 522 ; Nicholas : Humphrey : Amos : John : Thomas : George : Agnes : Jane : Margaret : Elizabeth : Joan : Anne : Ursula : Susan, 522 ; George, married Abignell Samford, 522 ; Margaret, wife of William Champneys, 522 ; Susan, wife of Martin Samford, 522 ; Humphrey, of Combe, married (1) Jane Champneys 522 ; (2) Jane Godolphin, 523 ; owned Stert and Heale, 524 ; John : Roger : Richard : William : Humphrey : Hugh : Mary, 522 ; Penelope : George : Gavregan : Nicholas, 523 ; Roger, married Joan Catford, 522 ; William, married Margaret Cudmore, 522 ; Penelope, wife of Henry Walrond, 523 ; John, of Combe, married Margery Poulet, 523 ; John : Henry : John : Anne : Margaret : Susan : Elizabeth, 523 ; Anne, wife of Thomas Tyllesley, 523 ; Margaret, wife of Thomas Slater, 523 ; Susan, wife of major George Sydenham, 523 ; Elizabeth, wife of Thomas Colford, 523 ; Humphrey, of Combe, styled " Silver Tongue Sydenham," married Mary Cox, 523 ; was rector of Ashbrittle, 22 ; Humphrey : Edward : Anne, 523 ; Anne, wife of Francis Thomas, 523 ; Humphrey, married Jane Pole, 523 ; William : Humphrey : John : Jane, 523 ; John, married (1) Margaret Butler, (2) Margaret Galard, 523 ; Jane, wife of John Williams, 523 ; Humphrey, of Combe, married (1) Elizabeth Peppin, (2) Katherine Floyer, 523 ; Humphrey : George : Philip : Elizabeth : Jane : Elizabeth : Floyer, 523 ; Elizabeth, wife of Laurence Jackson, 523 ; Humphrey, of Combe and Dulverton, married Grace Hill, 523 : was heir and executor to John St. Barbe, of Broadlands, 214. owned Marston Magna, the rectory, of which he conveyed to the Rev. John Rutherford, ii 375. monument in Dulverton church, 1757, iii 524 ; St. Barbe, of Combe and Dulverton, married Ellery Williams, 523 ; owned Ashington, 213 ; Draycott, 219 ; Catherine, daughter of St. Barbe, married Lewis Tregonwell, 523.

Sydenham family owned Ashbrittle, iii 21 ; John, 21 ; Walter, 21 ; Humphrey, rector of that parish, eminent preacher, 22.

Sydenham family, of Brimpton D'Evercy, iii 214 ; Joan, the wife of John, held the manors of Brimpton and Alvington, Combe-Sydenham, Stoke-Gomer, Preston, and Bossington : lands in Timberscombe, Kitnor, Quarum-Kitnor, Mountsey, Sydenham, Cothay, Smithay, Manworth, Novington,

Sydenham family—*continued*.

Thorn St. Margaret, and Langford-Budville: Ashbrittle: Chilthorne-Domer: Milverton: Streme: East and West Chescomb, 215; John, son of Walter, was heir to Joan, 215; Sir Philip, bart., 1739, last of this branch of the family, 215; Sir John, married Anne Hare, 216; Sir John Posthumus: Elizabeth (Pomfret), and lady Mary (daughter of the earl of Pembroke), his wives: monument in Brimpton D'Evercy church, erected by Philip, his son, 215, 216; arms, 215.

Sydenham family held Chilthorne-Domer, iii 217; Walter and Margaret, his wife, held it of Sir Humphry Stafford, knt., 217.

Sydenham family, of Combe-Sydenham, iii 547, 86; Richard, married Joan Delingrige, 547; Henry, 547; Simon, bishop of Chichester, 547; family owned also Stoke-Gomer and Preston, 548; Sir George and Sir John, monument in Stogumber church, 548; almshouse in Stogumber, founded by, 549.

Sydenham, John, of Badialton, married Joan Popham, i 264. became possessed of Orchard, iii 489; Joan, his widow, married John St. Albin, 489; John, married Elizabeth Gambon and became possessed of Merton, Columpton, Budley, and Gamberston, 489; John, married Catherine Hody, 489; John, married Catherine Paulet, 489; Jane, married Sir Thomas Bruges: Elizabeth, married Sir John Wyndham, 489.

Sydenham, Elizabeth, wife of Richard Baumfilde, ii 90. George, sheriff, 1577, i *xxxvii*. George, of Chilworthy, married Mary Warre, iii 262; major George, married Susan Sydenham, of Combe, 523. Henry and Elizabeth, monument in Combe-St.-Nicholas church, ii 477. Sir Philip,

Sydenham family—*continued*.

M.P., 1701, 1702, *xxxiii*; James, *xl*; Joan, wife of Robert Vernai, 254; Sir John, M.P., 1554, *xxxi*; Sir John, M.P., 1669, 1678, *xxxii*; John, sheriff, 1506, *xxxvi*, 1546, *xxxvii*; John, sheriff, 1573, *xxxvii*; Sir John, sheriff, 1554, *xxxvii*; John, *xxxix*; John, *xl*; John, trustee of Ilminster grammar school, 3. John, holder of Timberscombe, ii 44; John, who married Margaret Whyton, and purchased Walter Paunsfort's lands in Bossington, 38. John, married Anne Hoby, who after his death married Sir Francis Dodington, iii 519. Walter, of Timberscombe, ii 44.

Sydney, baron, J.P., i *xli*.

Sydney place, Bath, B 52.

Sylley, Sarah, wife of William Malet, i 90 (*see* Sully).

Symcocks (*see* Simcocks).

Symes family owned Berwick, ii 338; East-Coker, 341; monuments in Dundry church, 105, 106; Compton Martin church, 134. Edward, benefaction to South Brent, i 200; John, M.P., 1623, *xxxii*. Thomas, monument in Berwick church, ii 338; arms, 338; Rev. William, subscriber to the charity school at Chew Stoke, 102.

Symonds, Ann, the only pauper in Stocklinch St. Magdalen, i 64.

Symons, Thomas, owned East-Oldmixon, iii 591.

Symonsbath, in Exford, ii 20.

Syms, John, clerk of the castle, town and lordship of Taunton, surrendered that office, iii 228

Syms-Close, bequeathed by John Buckland to West-Harptree parish, ii 143.

Syndercombe, iii 510; Domesday survey, 510; owned by Turstin Fitz-Rolf: held by Hugh: Cerric held it T.R.E. 510; subsequently held by the Carews, 510.

T

Tabernacles, three, in Puckington church, i 57. Shepton Beauchamp church, iii 125.

Tablesford (*see* Telsford).

Tabuel, Margaret, held lands of the abbot of Muchelney, iii 135.

Tachfield, John, one of the first aldermen of Bath, B 23.

Tacle, Joan, first wife of Sir Baldwin Malet, i 92, iii 496.

Tadhill or Tothill house, Downhead, iii 475.

Tailleur, William le, received licence to enfeoff the commonalty of Dunster, 1363, ii 15.

Taklestone, iii 61.

Taland (*see* Tolland).

Talbot or Talebot family held Heathfield, iii 253; were descended from Talbot de Hethfield, 253. Anne, wife of Hugh

Talbot or Talebot family—*continued*.

Courtney, ii 161; Eleanor, of Butleigh, wife of John Moore: monument in West-Coker church, 345. Geffrey, a partisan of empress Maud, imprisoned at Bath, iii 379; Gilbert, of Heathfield, 253; received a grant of a fair at Lopen, 122. John, earl of Shrewsbury, married Margaret Beauchamp, ii 282. John, benefaction to Chipstaple, iii 508. lady Julian, i 262. Laurence, of Heathfield, iii 253. owned land temp. Ed. I, i *xxviii*. Philippa, second wife of Matthew de Gournay, ii 139; Sir William, married Eleanor Peverell, 49 (*see* Hethfield).

Tale, memorial stones in Creech St. Michael church, i 77.

Tan yards, Bickenhall, i 61.

Tancred, Ursula, memorial stone in Bath Weston church, i 166.

Tanfield, William, held Bagborough - West, Fydeok, Oldbury, Durborough - Quantock, iii 242; Francis, his son and heir, 242.

Tangle, Hampshire, owned by the Wake family, iii 119.

Tankerville, earl of, J.P., i *xli.*

Tanner, Bengemen, incumbent of Swainswick, i 154.

Tanner, memorial tablet in Swainswick church, i 155.

Tanner, Roger le, M.P. for Bath, 1312, B 19. Rev. Thomas, incumbent of Sandford-Bret, iii 544; William, owner of Lyde, 207.

Tantone, Geffery de, monk of Winchester, iii 239; Gilbert de, almoner of Glastonbury, 239; Walter de, abbot of Glastonbury, 239, ii 254. William de, prior of Winchester, iii 239.

Tap, Jyllyas, benefaction to Cannington, i 237.

Tarlton, John, minister of Ilminster, i 10.

Tarlton (*see* Orlton).

Tarnuc, in the tithing of Biddisham, i 176. but in the parish of Badgeworth, iii 565.

Tarr, hamlet in Lydiard - St. - Laurence, iii 265.

Tatchell, Rev. Christopher, J.P., i *xlv.* incumbent of Combe - St. - Nicholas, ii 476. of Long-Sutton, iii 198.

Tate, Catherine, wife of John Carew, iii 517.

Tatewiche (*see* Tatwick).

Tatwick, hamlet of Swainswick, i 154; Domesday survey, 154; held by William Hosed, Ralph de Bercheclai, 154; by Godric T.R.E. 154; subsequently owned by the monks of Bath, Sir Walter Dennis, and Elias de St. Alban, from whom lands were purchased for the maintenance of a chantry at Cold Ashton, 154.

Tatworth, tithing in Chard, ii 473.

Taunton, Hugh de, constable of Taunton castle, iii 227; held lands in Taunton, 227.

Taunton, John de, abbot of Glastonbury: buried at Glastonbury, 1274: epitaph, ii 253; built a grange at Mells, 463. owned lands and the capital messuage in Ashcot, iii 425; lands in Shapwick, where he built a grange, 427; built a grange at High Ham, 444.

Taunton, John de, prior of Barlinch, 1390, iii 503.

Taunton, Nicholas de, abbot of Keynsham, ii 402.

Taunton, Thomas, received a pension from Montacute priory, iii 313; Mr., of West-Lydford, owned Lotisham, 472. Rev. Dr., incumbent of North-Parret, ii 336.

Taunton : borough town, iii 226; ancient name, 226; situation, 226; river Tone, 226; town-hall, 226; market and fairs, 226; woollen

Taunton—*continued.*

and silk manufactures, 226; small-pox plagues, 226; town-government, 226, 227; "pot - wallers," 226; incorporated by Charles I, 226; corporation seal, 227; town, 227; the Bridewell, called the "Nook," 227; town bestowed by king Ethelard on the bishops of Winchester, 229; Domesday survey, 229, 230, 231; owned by the bishop of Winchester, held by Stigand T.R.E. 229; Goisfrid, Robert, Hugh, Goduin, Leveva, Alward, Aluric, Edmor, Lewi, earl Morton, Alured, and John, held lands here of the bishop, 230, 231; Wlward and Alward held lands in Lydiard and Leigh belonging to this manor, 231; list of bishops of Winchester, lords of the manor, 231, 232, 233; manor sold to Brampton Gurdon and John Hill, 1647, but recovered by the bishopric, 233; Holway, Hull, Poundisford, Staplegrove, and Nailsbourne, divisions of the manor, 233; recognition money, 233; Bondland and Overland, 233; custom of land-tenure, 233; Monmouth's Rebellion and the "Bloody Assize," 234; house of Carmelites founded by Walter de Meriet, 236; site owned by Henry Proctor Gale, 236; distinguished people born here, 239; benefactions, 240; lands here were held by the Bourchiers, lords Fitzwarren, 111, 271; by the hospital of White-hall, Ivelchester, 300; by Sir Michael Stanhope, 301.

Taunton almshouses : Richard Hewish's, in Mawdleyn lane, iii 237; Robert Gray's, at East-Gate, 238; lady Grace Portman's, 238; Dorothy Henley's, 239.

Taunton castle, iii 227; built by William Giffard, bishop of Winchester, 227; repaired and added to by bishop Langton, 227; by bishop Horn, 227; list of constables, 227, 228; besieged by Perkin Warbeck, 228, 109; by the Parliamentary army, 229; dismantled by Charles II, 229.

Taunton churches: St. Mary Magdalen, iii 236; appropriated to the priory, 236; bishop Haselshaw's ordination, 237; monuments, 237, 238; chantries, 238; Corfe church considered a chapelry, 249; St. James, 239; bells (5), 239.

Taunton hospitals, county, founded 1772, iii 240; lepers', founded by Lambright, 236.

Taunton priory : founded by bishop William Giffard, iii 234; endowments, 234, 235; list of priors, 235; granted at the dissolution to Sir Francis Brian and Matthew Colthurst, 236; library, 236; Stavordale priory united to Taunton, 1533, 34. the priors owned land temp. Ed. I, i *xxvi.* received benefactions from William de Mohun, ii 8; held a knight's fee from John de Mohun, 14; held Ash-Priors, where they

Thomas family—*continued.*
Sydenham, 523. Sir Noah, M.D., governor of Bath hospital, B 49. Rev. —, incumbent of Donyat, i 36. William, memorial stone in Ubley church, ii 157.
Thomas, prior of Bath, 1223-1261, B 55 ; 1300-1302, 55.
Thomas, prior of Montacute and abbot of Hyde, iii 312.
Thomas, prior of Woodspring, 1383, iii 595.
Thomas street, Bath, B 37.
Thomond, earl of : title conferred on Percy O'Brien Wyndham, iii 490.
Thompson, Archibald, benefaction to Taunton, iii 240. Lucy, monument in Bath abbey, 1765, B 70.
Thonodunum (*see* Taunton).
Thorlakeston family held Thurloxton, iii 102 ; granted lands there to Taunton priory, 102 ; Philip de, 102.
Thorn, holy, ii 265.
Thorn family gave lands in Thorn St. Margaret to the priory of Taunton, iii 27. William de, holder of two parts of a knight's fee from John de Mohun, ii 14 ; William de, holder of lands in Thorn-Falcon, 182.
Thorn-Fagon (*see* Thorn-Falcon).
Thorn-Falcon : its situation, ii 181 ; Domesday survey, 181 ; owned by Robert, earl of Morton, held by Ansger : by Algar T.R.E. 181 ; held by the families of Thorn, Richard de Acton, Roger de Mortimer, Sir Thomas Brook, the Chedders, the Capels, Burridge, of Lyme, and Nathaniel Butler Batten, 182 ; church and its monuments, 182 ; bells (3), 182.
Thorn-Coffin : situation, iii 322 ; Domesday survey : owned by Roger de Curcelle : held by Alric, 322 ; subsequently held of the barony of Montacute by the Coffin family, 322 ; the de Clevedons, 322 ; the Hogshaws, 322 ; the Bluets, 322 ; the priory of Stavordale held lands here, 33, 322 ; John Napier, of Tintinhull, 322 ; church (St. Andrew), 322 ; bells (2), 322.
Thorn-Parva (*see* Thorn-Falcon).
Thorn-St.-Margaret : situation, iii 27 ; natural products, 27 ; Domesday survey, 27 ; owned by the earl of Morton : held by Drogo and Ralph : Cheneve and two thanes held it T.R.E. 27 ; subsequently held by the Thorn family, who granted lands to Taunton priory, 27, 235 ; Edward Clarke, 27 ; church (St. Margaret), 27 ; bells (3), 27 ; manor forms a tithing with Samford-Arundel, 26 ; the Sydenham family held land here, 215.
Thornbury, Thomas, prior of Barlinch, 1456, iii 503.
Thorncombe, hamlet in Bicknoller, iii 501 ; owned by the Brets, 501 ; the Sweetings, 501.

Thorne, in Castle Cary, ii 56.
Thorney island, belonged at the Conquest to Muchelney abbey : partly in Kingsbury, ii 469. and partly in Muchelney, iii 134.
Thorngrove, hamlet in Middlezoy, iii 442.
Thornhill, William, married Barbara Speke, i 68.
Thorny cliff, a stratum of coal found at Clutton, ii 103.
Thorp, Catherine, owner of lands in Kingston-Seymour, ii 123.
Thorpshawe, lands in, granted to Richard Parker, ii 219.
Thredder, John, parson of Seaborough, received land from John Golde for the erection of a church, ii 174.
Threskwold, i 84.
Throckmorton, Anne, monument in Bath abbey, 1783, B 70 ; Francis, monument in Bath abbey, 1788, 70. Francis, of Woolavington, iii 437. George, monument in Bath abbey, 1762, B 70 ; Mary, monument in Bath abbey, 1763, B 70. Mr., leased the manor house of Stowey, iii 553 ; Michael, owner of Woolavington, 437. Robert, monument in Bath abbey, 1779, B 70 ; Sir Robert, governor of Bath hospital, 49.
Thrubwell manor, Butcombe, ii 314 ; owned by the Bretesche family, 314 ; the Percevals, 314, iii 173, 175. the Clevedon family held lands here, ii 315 ; Flaxley abbey held lands here, 315.
Thuri held Chelworth, ii 419.
Thurlbeer : its situation, ii 182 ; Domesday survey, 182 ; owned by the earl Morton, and held by Drogo : by Ulviet T.R.E. 182 ; owned by the families of Montacute, Cheyne, Bonville, lord Howard, and Portman, 182, 183 ; hamlet of Greenway, 183 ; church (St. Thomas), 183 ; bells (4), 183. living united with Stoke St. Mary, iii 291.
Thurlbury (*see* Thurlbeer).
Thurloe, Hugh (or Cunteville), i 262.
Thurlow, Right Hon. Edward Lord, lord high chancellor, J.P., i *xli.*
Thurloxton : situation, iii 102 ; seat of John Cross, 102 ; Leversdown, seat of William Harrison, 102 ; manor held by the Thorlakeston family, of the honour of Dunstercastle, 102 ; large territory here granted to the priory of Taunton, 102, 235 ; subsequently passed to William Babington, 103 ; the Portman family, 103 ; chapel given by William de Erleigh to the monks of Buckland, 103, 98 ; church (St. Giles), 103 ; bells (4), 103.
Thurstan (*see* Turstin).
Thurston, Alice, wife of Richard Wyatt : monument in Minehead church, iii 269 ; arms, 269. Malachi : inscription in West-Buckland church, ii 486. Walter : bishop Beckington's bequest to, iii 385.

Timsbury—*continued.*
sis and held by Gonuerd T.R.E. 112;
owned by the families of Waddone, William
de Paulton, St. Loe, Samborne, and Popham, 112; purchased out of chancery by
Jacob Mogg, Mr. Crang, Mr. Savage, and
Alexander Adams, 112; church and its
monuments, 112, 113; bells (6), 112.

Tincknel, Edward, benefaction to Wedmore,
i 193.

Tintinhill, eminence on which the hundred
courts were formerly held and from which
Tintinhull derived its name, iii 297.

Tintinhull hundred: situation, iii 297; given by
William, earl of Morton, to the monks of
Montacute, 297.

Tintinhull, iii 308; Domesday survey, 308;
owned by Wulfrick, 308; by Glastonbury
abbey, T.R.E. 308; by Robert, earl of
Morton, to whom it was given in exchange
for Camerton, 308, 329, 330; by Montacute
priory, 308; Sir Thomas Wyatt, 308; Sir
William Petre, 308; the Napiers, 308;
market and fair, 308; Bablew or Balhow,
cell to Montacute priory, 309; owned by
John Lyte, 309; church (St. Margaret) and
its monuments, 309; bells (5), 309; manor,
church, hundred, and fair formerly owned
by Montacute priory, 311.

Tipper and Dawe owned the fair at Lopen,
iii 122.

Tipping, Bartholomew, governor of Bath hospital, B 49.

Tipput, Benjamin, benefaction to Whitchurch,
ii 444.

Tiptop, Sir John, married Philippa, widow of
Sir Ralph de Ashton, iii 130; Sir John, inherited all the estates of the Wrothe family
lying in Middlesex, Surrey, Kent, Hants,
and Gloucester, 67; he was progenitor of
the earl of Worcester, 67. Sir John, lord
Powis, owned North Widcombe, ii 118;
Stawel, 379.

Tirhill park, West Bagborough, iii 243; seat of
Thomas Slocomb, 243.

Tithing, hamlet in Wincaunton, iii 33.

Tivington, manor in Selworthy, ii 41.

Toard, Mrs., benefaction to Blagdon, iii 570.

Tocheswelle (*see* Tuxwell).

Tochi, holder of Socke, iii 221.

Toclive, or More, Richard, bishop of Winchester, 1173: a native of Ivelchester,
iii 232.

Todbere, Dorset, lands in owned by the Carent
family, ii 367.

Todenei, Robert de (*see* Daubeney).

Tofts priory, Norfolk, annexed to Witham
priory, ii 233.

Tok, Roger le, holder of Greinton, iii 428.

Toke, John, governor of Bath hospital, B 49.

Toli, holder of Shepton-Montacute, iii 45.

Tolland: situation, iii 292; spring, 292; held of
the bishopric of Winchester by the families
of Gaunt and Luttrell, 292; owned by the
Warre family, 15, 261; William Lottisham,
261; the Clarkes, 261; lady Horner, of
Mells, 292; East - Tolland hamlet, 292;
Gorldon or Garmilden manor, 292; owned
by Francis Southwell, 292; church (St. John
Baptist), was granted by Ralph Briwere to
Buckland priory, 292, 98; bells (3), 292.

Tolland land: granted by Richard de Turberville to Taunton priory, iii 235.

Toller, John, last incumbent of the chantry of
the Virgin Mary, Bridgwater, iii 88.

Tone, the river: its course, i *xiii*, 74, 84, ii 177,
487, iii 19, 24, 225, 226, 243, 254, 267, 288,
289, 454, 509.

Tonk, William, M.P. for Bath, 1378, B 20.

Tooker family, owners of Stone-Easton manor,
ii 158; Jacob, memorial stone in Chicomp-
ton church, 131; Rev. James, married
Dorothy Trethewy, 130. James, J.P., i *xlvi*;
sheriff, 1766, *xxxix*. patron of Chilcompton, ii 129; holder of Norton Canonicorum,
151; Norton hall, 158; John and Bridget,
memorial stone in Chilcompton church, 130.
Rev. Trethewy, benefaction to Lamyat,
iii 477.

Toole, inscription in Swell church, i 66.

Toomer court, owned by the Toomer or Dummer family, ii 366; enlarged by William
Carent, 367; park, 366.

Toomer family, of Toomer park, in Henstridge,
ii 366; John de, held the hamlet of Dummer
of Elias de Aubeney, 18 Ed. II, 366; John
de, seal of, 20 Richard II, 366; Richard,
owned Toomer and lands in Henstridge and
Hinton St. George, 366; John, died without
issue, 366; Edith, 366; Alice, sister of
Richard, succeeded, married Sir William
Carent, 366; monument in Henstridge
church, 368.

Toomer, hamlet in Henstridge, ii 366; owned
by the Toomers, afterwards by the Carents,
366; William Carent added to the buildings,
367 [Toomer is called by Collinson, Dummer,
but incorrectly].

Toose, John, memorial stone in St. Mary Magdalen church, Taunton, iii 237.

Top, Edward, married Christiana Grey, and became possessed of Stowey, iii 553.

Torchil, holder of Chelvy, ii 316.

Torel, William, lord, of Isle-Brewers, fined for
neglecting to make proper enquiry respecting the death of Alured de Aneville, i 53.

Torlaberie (*see* Thurlbeer).

Tormenton, Roger, last prior of Woodspring,
iii 595.

Tornach, Reiner, holder of one-and-a-half
knight's fees from Sir William de Mohun,
ii 13.

Torne (*see* Thorn-Falcon or Thorn-Coffin).

Torney, John, i *xl.*

Tornie (*see* Twinney).

Torr hill, Glastonbury, ii 264; oratory dedicated to St. Michael, built by Saints Phaganus and Diruvianus, 240, 264; repaired by St. Patrick, 264; fair, 264; church and monastic buildings, 264; destroyed by earthquake, 1271, 265; church rebuilt: tower still remaining: the property of Richard Colt-Hoare, 265; this hill was the scene of the execution of abbot Whiting, 1539, 255, 256.

Torre (*see* Dunster).

Torrel family owned Torrel's Preston, iii 16; William, 16; Roger gave "Minster-land" to the church at Milverton, 16.

Torrel's-Preston (*see* Preston-Bowyer).

Tort family, owners of Langham manor, ii 25; John de, holder of knight's fees in Timberscombe, 44. James de, holder of lands in Elworthy and Willet, iii 525; Joan le, married Sir Simon de Raleigh, 537; Laurence de, levied a fine by which the whole estate of the Tort family passed to Simon de Raleigh, 537.

Tortes, Sire Rauf de, i *l.*

Tortesmains, Geffrey, holder of lands of the abbot of Glastonbury, ii 244.

Torweston or Torweston-castle, iii 544; Domesday survey, 544; owned by William de Moion: held by Hugh: Lefsin held it T.R.E. 544.

Tosti, earl of Northumberland, held Winsford, T.R.E. iii 555.

Toteyate, i 84.

Tothill or Tadhill house, Downhead, iii 475.

Tothill manor, Downhead, iii 476; owned by Richard Hippisley Coxe, 476; Mr. Bradley, 476.

Touchet, Sir John, married Joan, daughter of lord Audley, iii 552; Sir John, his grandson, inherited half the Audley estates, and took the title of lord Audley (*see* Audley), 552. Isabel, first wife of John Vernai, i 254, iii 552; Joan, wife of Sir John Luttrell, 552; lady Elizabeth, daughter of George, lord Audley, married Sir John Stawel, 251.

Toucker, Walter, incumbent of Weston-in-Gordano, against whom an injunction was issued, iii 174.

Toui held Berkley, ii 202.

Toulton, hamlet in Kingston, iii 258.

Tour, Eleanor de la, daughter and heir of John, was second wife of Theobald Russel, and ancestress of the dukes of Bedford, ii 372, iii 156.

Tours, Martin de, founded a Benedictine monastery, ii 131.

Toustoke, lands in, granted by the countess of Leicester to Buckland priory, iii 96.

Toute, Jane, benefaction to Brushford, iii 507.

Tovey, John, purchased an estate in Ashton-Theynes, ii 296.

Tovi held Dishcove, i 215. land in Belluton, ii 401, 434. land in Lopen, iii 122.

Tower-Head, hamlet in Banwell, iii 567.

Towers: King Alfred's, at Kilmington, iii 39. St. Michael's, at Glastonbury, ii 264, 265.

Towill, William, part owner of Broomfield, i 72; conveyed that manor to Hugh Halswell, 72; monuments in Broomfield church, 73; donation to Broomfield, 73.

Town gate, Bath, B 29.

Town hall, Bath, B 31.

Town tithing, Frome, ii 186.

Town tithing, Ilminster, i 4.

Town tithing, South-Petherton, iii 106.

Towneley, William, memorial stone in Weston church, i 165.

Townsend, Rev. Edward, D.D., monument in Bath abbey, 1765, B 70.

Townsend, viscount, J.P., i *xli*; Right Hon. Charles, J.P., *xlvi.*

Traberge (*see* Treborough).

Trace Bridge, hamlet in Stawley, iii 28.

Tracey, Henry de, attacked William de Percheval at Cary, 1153, ii 52. William, i 67; Oliver, 67.

Tracy, William, holder of a knight's fee in Emborow, ii 135; Henry, 135.

Trajectus, or passage over the Severn, B 38, i *xxiii*, 101, 131.

Trat, Elidni, vicar of Long Ashton, ii 299; buried, with Anna, his wife, in Long-Ashton church, 301; Henry, monument in Crewkerne church, 163.

Travel, Sir Thomas, purchased the manor of Ilminster, 1684, i 6. Sir Thomas erected, jointly with James Medlycott, the singers' gallery in Milborne Port church, ii 354.

Treberge (*see* Treborough).

Treborough: its situation, ii 45; Domesday survey, 45; owned by Ralph de Limesi and held by Edric T.R.E. 45; owned by the families of Basings, John Hamme, Luttrell, earl of Pembroke, Wyndham, and Sir John Trevelyan, 46; hamlet of Brown, 46; church (St. Peter), 46; bells (3), 46. John and Alianor de Sydenham had an annuity from this manor, iii 522.

Trees, subterranean, i 182, ii 272.

Tregarthin, Joan, wife of John Wadham, of Edge, i 48.

Treglaston, lands in, granted to Cleeve abbey by Richard, earl of Cornwall, iii 511.

Tregonwell, Jane, wife of Francis Luttrell, ii 13. Sir John, sheriff, 1553, i *xxxvii*. Lewis, married Catherine Sydenham, iii 523.

Tregory, John, M.P. for Bath, 1363, 1372, 1378, B 20.

Tregoz, Robert de, married Sibil de Ewyas and became possessed of Chelworth, ii 419; Robert, 419; Robert, slain at Evesham, 419; John, 420. owned also Burnham, i 180, ii 420; Clarice, married Roger de la Warre, to whom she conveyed part of the Tregoz estates, 411, 420; Sibyll, wife of William de Grandison, who received the remainder, 420.

Trelawney, John, married Florence Courtney, ii 161.

Tremayle, John, i *xl*; Thomas, *xxxix*. Thomas, one of the arbitrators in the dispute between the monks and parishioners of Dunster, ii 18.

Trenchammouth, ii 195.

Trenchard, Sir John, sheriff, 1509, i *xxxvii*; Sir Thomas, sheriff, 1523, *xxxvii*; Sir George, married Anne Speke, 68. Francis, married Elizabeth Gorges, iii 158; Henry, married Jane Rodney, 413, 604; John, married Jane Rodney, 605; William, of Cutteridge, married Ellen Norton, 154; John, his son, married Anne Blacket, and died without issue, 154; a daughter of William married Thomas Hippisley, who held in her right the manor of Abbot's-Leigh, 154; name assumed by Robert Hippisley, her son, 154; J. W. Hippisley, 154; arms, 154; inscriptions in Abbot's-Leigh church, 154.

Trendle castle, Roman encampment, Bicknoller, iii 501.

Trendle, hamlet in Pitminster, iii 284.

Trent, Mary, monument in Glastonbury church, ii 264.

Trent: situation, ii 380; river Ivel, 380; hamlets of Adbeer and Hummer, 380; Domesday survey, 380; owned by Robert, earl of Morton: held by Ansger: Brisnod held it T.R.E. 380; subsequently owned by the Mohun family, 381; the Briweres, 381; Walter le Bret, 381; a third held by the de Chastellains of Robert de Seford, 381; a third held by Robert Wyke of the honour of Farley-Monachorum, 381; a third owned by the Wests, 381; the whole manor owned by the Stork family, 381; divided between the families of Gerard, Wyndham and Young, 381; Henry Bromley, lord Montford, 381; Mr. Colliton, 381; the Seymour family, 381; house belonging to colonel Wyndham in which Charles II is said to have been sheltered, 381; schools, 381; chantry-house, 382; parsonage, 382; list of rectors, 383; church (St. Andrew) and its monuments, 383-388; bells (5), 384; benefactions, 388; yew-tree, 388; cross, 388; Adbeer hamlet, 382; formerly Over and Nether Adbeer, 382; Domesday survey, 382; owned by earl Morton: held by Drogo: Alwi held it T.R.E. 382; Siward held a manor, 382;

Trent—*continued.*

granted with Hummer to the priory of Montacute, 383; the Alneto family, 383; the Windsore family, 383; held by Thomas Huntlege of Sir Walter de Romesey, 383; the Carents, 383; George, duke of Clarence, 383; the Wadhams, 383.

Tretheke, Thomas, married Joan Horsey, daughter of John Brent, iii 435.

Tretherf, John, married Elizabeth Courtney, ii 161.

Trethery, John, part owner of Evercreech park, iii 414.

Trethewy, Dorothy, wife of Rev. James Tooker, ii 130; monument in Chilcompton church, 130; John, married Margaret Stocker, 130; monument in Chilcompton church, 130.

Trevanion, Elizabeth, wife of Malachi Malet, i 93; Charles, married Amice Malet, 92.

Trevilian, Trevillian or Trevelyan, Bartholomew, owner of East-Coker, ii 341. John, i *xxxix*; owned Drayton, 39; tombs in Drayton church, 39; in Curry Rivel church, 28; Sir John, sheriff, 1502, *xxxvi*.

Trevelyan, Elizabeth, of Minehead, monument in Crewkerne church, ii 164.

Trevelyan family owned Nettlecombe, iii 539; John, married Elizabeth Whalesborough, and became possessed of Nettlecombe, iii 539; John: Thomas: George: Humphrey, 539; George, chaplain to Henry VIII, 539; John, married Jane Hallywell, 539; John, 539; John, married Avice Cockworthy, 539; John, 539; John, married Maud Hill, 539; John, 539; John, married Wilmot Harris, 539; John, married Urith Chichester, 539; was high sheriff for Somersetshire, 539; monument in Nettlecombe church, 541. Elizabeth, wife of Nathaniel Holbeach, ii 442. John, married Margaret Luttrell, iii 539; George, 539; George, married Margaret Strode: sequestred and imprisoned for loyalty to Charles I, 539; George, 539; Sir George, bart., married Mary Willoughby, 539; John, 539; Mary, married Edmund Wyndham, 493; colonel Amos, married Anne Lacey: monument in Nettlecombe church, 541; Sir John, bart., married (1) Urith Pole, (2) Susanna Warren, 539. was M.P., 1695, i *xxii*, 1700, *xxxiii*; sheriff, 1705, 1715, *xxxviii*. Margaret, wife of Alexander Luttrell, ii 13. Sir George, bart., married Julia Calverley, iii 539; Julia, wife of William Yea, 290; Sir John, bart., 540; mansion at Nettlecombe, 540; arms, 540. M.P., 1780, 1784, 1790, i *xxxiii*; sheriff, 1777, *xxxix*; J.P., *xlii*. governor of Bath hospital, B 49. owner of Treborough, ii 46. of Huish Champflower, iii 530; of Wood-Advent, 540; of Rowden, 547. John, J.P., i *xlvi*.

Turberville, Henry de, warden of Nicholas Fitz-Martin, ii 132. William de, sheriff, 1256-1257, i *xxxiv*; Sir Richard de, sheriff, 1356, 1357, *xxxiv*; married Cecelia Seymour, sister of John Beauchamp, owned Merrifield manor, 45, 47, iii 125; arms, 125; granted Tolland and the church of Dulverton to Taunton priory, 235. William, part-owner of Moreton, ii 133. Sir John, sheriff, 1487, i *xxxvi*. Daubeny, M.D., benefaction to Wayford, 1723, ii 175.

Turchil, holder of Clewer, i 188. Clutton, ii 103; Backwell, 305.

Turf pits, Wedmore, i 194.

Turges, Robert, part owner of Moreton, ii 133.

Turgis held Nunney, ii 218. Brompton-Ralph, iii 505.

Turk's Castle, Roman encampment, Bicknoller, iii 501.

Turlick Mead, hamlet in Wookey, iii 421.

Turmund, holder of Stowel, ii 379.

Turner, Hester, benefaction to Yatton, iii 620; John, incumbent of Weston in Gordano, 174; John, incumbent of Bicknoller, 501. Rev. John, J.P., i *xlvi*. archdeacon of Taunton and canon of Wells, iii 239, 396; incumbent of Stogumber, 548. William, dean of Wells, 1550, i 190; William, J.P., *xlvi*. seat at Belmont, Wraxall, iii 155; Rev. William, incumbent of Loxton, 598.

Turney family owned Wolverton and Telsford, ii 224, 225, iii 363. arms, ii 225; Walter, held Wolverton of John Wadham, 224; Philip, 224; John, 225; Philip, 225; John, 225.

Turnham, hamlet in Chard, ii 473.

Turnock or Tarnick (*q.v.*), hamlet in Badgworth, iii 565; held of the barony of Worleston, successively by the families of Courtney, Zouch, Brook, Chedder, and Lisle, 565; granted to Edward, earl of Hertford, 565.

Turnor, Edmond, treasurer of the king's garrisons, 1645, i *xlvi*. John, monument in Bath Abbey, 1719, B 64, 70.

Turre, Sauvinus de, porter of Glastonbury abbey, ancester of the Brents, of Cossington, iii 435.

Turstin or Thurstan, abbot of Glastonbury, ii 250; rebellion of the monks against his rule, 250; his death, 1101, 250.

Turstin Fitz Rolf (*see* Fitz-Rolf).

Turstin, holder of Creech (Creech-St-Michael), i 75. Estham, ii 160. rents in Crewkerne, iii 107; land in Butleigh, 448.

Turveston (*see* Torweston).

Turville, Isabel, wife of Richard Arthur, of Clapton, iii 177.

Tuson, Rev. James, incumbent of Binegar, iii 412; of Westbury, 417.

Tutt, Elizabeth, wife of Robert Pierce, iii 336. James, received King-Weston manor from Henry VIII, ii 81.

Tuttebury, Thomas, dean of Wells, 1401, i 190.

Tutton, Samuel and Mary, monument in Bleadon church, iii 571.

Tuxwell manor, i 245; Domesday survey, 245; owned by Roger Arundel and held by Hugh and Brictric: by Estan and Goduin T.R.E. 245; owned by Sir Alexander Hody, George Sidenham, who alienated the premises to Humphry Blake, Henry Becher, 245; owned by Robert Blake, 245; earl of Egmont, 245.

Twerton (*see* Twiverton).

Twiney (*see* Twiniho).

Twiniho family, owners of Keyford, ii 189; curious petition to parliament, 189. owned also Twyniho, iii 328 (*see* Twynyho).

Twiverton or Twerton: situation, iii 347; river Avon, 347; Domesday survey, 347; owned by the bishop of Coutances, 347; held by Nigel and Goisfrid, 347; Alured held it of queen Eddid, 347; subsequently held by the Baiose or Bayeux family, 347, 348. the Rodneys, ii 306, iii 348, 603; manor divided and held in moieties by the duke of Chandos, 348; William Gibbs, 348; the Rev. Mr. England, 348; William Gore Langton, 348; John Walker Heneage, 348; church (St. Michael), 348; bells (6), 348; residence of Henry Fielding, 348.

Twyford family, holders of Kilmersdon, ii 446; monuments in Kilmersdon church, 448; arms, 448. Samuel, J.P., i *xlvi*. part owner of Kilmersdon, ii 446. owned part of the hundred of Wellow, iii 325. Sarah: Rev. Robert: Ann: Sarah, monuments in Kilmersdon church, ii 448.

Twyniho, or Twinney, in Wellow, iii 328; a member of Combe-Hay at the time of the conquest, 328; owned by the Twyniho family, 328; Hungerford family, 328; Muchelney abbey held lands here, 328.

Twynyho, Roger, petition to Parliament by, ii 189 (*see* Twiniho).

Tybauld, Peter, iii 66.

Tybone, Vincent, prior of Stoke-Courcy, about 1305, i 250.

Tyler, Thomas, abbot of Keynsham, 1463, ii 402.

Tyllesley, captain Thomas, married Anne Sydenham, iii 523.

Tylly family, owners of West-Harptree Tilly, ii 141. John de, landowner temp. Ed. I, i *xxvii*. John, gave lands in West-Harptree Tilly to the abbot and convent of Bruerne, ii 141; John, 141; John, 141; Richard, 141; William, benefaction to Glastonbury, abbey, 141.

Tymmeworth, Thomas de, holder of land in Brompton-Ralph, iii 505; land in Elworthy, 525.

Tynbury, John, owner of East-Ling, i 85; William, who conveyed it to Thomas Leigh and George Grenville, 85.

Tyndale, John, of Bristol, married Margaretta Warre, iii 263; Margaretta, wife of Charles Hill, 263; Charlotte, wife of Thomas Eagles, 263; Thomas Bampfylde, 263; John and Elizabeth, 263.

Tyndale monuments in Bathford church, i 113, 114.

Tyndall, John, J.P., i *xlvi.*

Tynte family owned Chelvy, ii 317. Goathurst, i 80. Whelpes place, Wraxall, iii 158; arms, 160; John, monument in Wraxall church, 1616, 160. Edward, married Anne Gorges, and purchased the manor of Chelvy, ii 317, iii 158. inscription in Chelvy church, 1629, ii 318; Robert, memorial inscription in Chelvy church, 1636, 318; John, married Jane Halswell, 317. and became possessed of Halswell, i 80. Sir Halswell, bart., married Grace Fortescue, ii 317; Grace: Halswell: Fortescue: John: Robert, 317; Sir John, bart., married Jane Kemeys, 317; Halswell: John: Charles Kemeys: Jane, 317; Sir Halswell, bart., M.P. for Bridgwater, 317; married Mary Walters, 317; received the manor of Regilbury from Edward Baber, 319; Sir John, bart., rector of Goat-

Tynte family—*continued.*
hurst, 317. Sir Charles Kemeys, M.P., 1747, 1754, 1761, 1767, 1768, i *xxxiii*; owner of Brent-cum-Wrington, 195; part owner of Durleigh, 78; of Goathurst, 80; owned Halswell, 80; married Anne Busby, to whom he bequeathed the manor of Goathurst, 80, ii 317; owned Chelvy, which on his death, 1785, became vested in John Johnson, who assumed the name of Tynte, 317; he was patron of Norton-Hautville, 108. lady Anne, widow of Sir Charles, owned Goathurst, i 80. West-Melcomb, iii 73; Ham, 84; Othery, 443; Chilton, 434. John Johnson Kemeys, J.P., i *xlvi*; married a niece of Sir Charles Kemeys Tynte, 80. became owner of Chelvy, and assumed the name of Tynte, ii 317.

Tynte, Hugh, held land in Dundry, ii 105.

Type, John, prior of St. John's hospital, Wells, 1409, iii 408.

Tyrel, Hugh, sheriff, 1341, 1342, i *xxxiv.*

Tyson, Richard, governor of Bath hospital, B 49.

Tytherington, hamlet in Frome, ii 186.

Tywe, Hugh de, owned a third of the manor of Kilmersdon, ii 446; Walter, married Emma de Whelton or Walton, 446; Emma, married as her second husband, Adam Nortoft, and sold this estate to bishop Burnel, 446.

U

Ubcedene (*see* Cheddon Fitzpaine).

Ubley: its situation, ii 156; owned by Ralph de Wake, Richard Damorie, Matthew Peche, Robert de Luccombe, Nicholas le Bole, Nicholas Huscarle, Sir Richard de Acton, John Stoke, the families of Brook, Chedder, Newton, Capel and Pulteney, 156; church (St. Bartholomew), 156; bells (4), 156; benefactions, 157.

Udecome (*see* Cutcombe).

Uffa gave Stoke to Glastonbury abbey, iii 484.

Ulf held land in Idstock, iii 90; Woolston, 501.

Ulgar held Whatley, ii 230. Downhead, iii 475.

Ulmar held land in Keynsham, ii 402.

Ulmer held Greinton, iii 428.

Ulmerstone (*see* Wolmersdon).

Ulnod held Isle-Brewers, i 53; Chapel Allerton, 175.

Ulster, William de Burgh, earl of, owned Easton-in-Gordano, iii 148; Lionel Plantagenet, duke of Clarence, earl of, held that title in right of his wife, Elizabeth, daughter and heir of William de Burgh, 148, 149.

Uluert held lands in Croscombe and Shepton-Mallet, iii 480.

Uluric held Almsford, ii 59; land in Chew-Magna, 94. Poleshill, iii 16; East-Harptree, 587.

Ulveva owned King-Weston, ii 80; Midsummer Norton, 150. Loxton, iii 597.

Ulviet held Thurlbeer, ii 182.

Ulward held Buckland St. Mary, i 20; Earnshill, 30; Bath-Easton, 106. Sutton-Bingham, ii 349; land in Keynsham, 401; Pisbury, 470. Aller, iii 188; lands in Mudford, 220.

Ulward, the wife of, held Chew, ii 415.

Ulwardestone (*see* Woolston).

Ulwen held Hinton-Charterhouse, iii 366.

Ulwi held Draycott, iii 219; land in Batcombe, 466.

Ulwin held Ashford, i 46. Browford, iii 527; land in Chedder, 575.

Ulwold held Hartrow, iii 546.

Umfraville, Alice de, wife of Simon de Fourneaux, i 262, iii 213, 533; Gilbert de, held the fourth part of a knight's fee in Northover, 306. Sir Henry, i 262; Isabel, 262. John de, held part of a knight's fee in Telsford, iii 363.

Umfray, prior of Barlinch, 1288, iii 503.

Undewiche (*see* Woodwick).

Unitarian chapel, Bath, B 74.

Upcot, hamlet in Ninehead-Flory, iii 267.

Upcott, hamlet in Hill-Bishops, iii 256.

V

Vaughan, Francis, owned Christon, iii 578 ; Francis, his son, sold it to lady Smyth, 578 ; memorial stone in Christon church, 578 ; Mr., owner of Winterhead, 602.

Vaughan, Richard Watkyn, owned Camely, ii 125 ; Polydore Watkyn, 125.

Vaughan, *alias* Watson, Richard, owned Marksbury and Hunstreet, ii 427.

Vault, subterranean, at Glastonbury, ii 263.

Vaus, Le Sieur de (*see* Vallibus).

Vaux or de Vallibus family, owned Sevington, iii 123 ; Hubert, 123 ; Maud de, married Thomas de Multon, to whom she conveyed that manor, 123.

Vavasour, Sir Thomas, purchased part of the manor of Frome, and sold the same to Sir Thomas Thynne, ii 188.

Veel, Peter de, M.P., 1337, 1358, i *xxx.*

Veel family held Norton-Veel, iii 272 ; Peter de la, 272 ; Sir Peter de, knt., granted this manor to Hugh Berd and John Gust, 272.

Veer, Margaret, held lands in Milverton, iii 15 ; Peter, married Anne Glamorgan, 214.

Veer family held Lympsham, i 203.

Veil, monastic, ii 251.

Vellow, in Stogumber, iii 546 ; called by the Normans Ailgi, 546 ; Domesday survey, 546 ; owned by William de Moion : held by Garmund : by Algar T.R.E. 546.

Venables, Alexander, married Joan Maltravers, daughter of Sir Laurence Sandford, iii 206.

Venn, lands in, held by William Carent, ii 367.

Venner, Gustavus, monument in Ninehead church, iii 269 ; arms, 269.

Venner, Tobias, M.D., monument in Bath abbey, 1660, B 70.

Ver, Gefferey de, held a knight's fee from Sir William de Mohun, ii 14.

Verderers of Mendip, iii 375.

Verdon, Elizabeth de, wife of Bartholomew, lord Burghesh, iii 352. Thomas de, married Eustachia Basset, ii 356.

Vere, Catherine, first wife of John Poulet, ii 167.

Vere, Sir John, married Elizabeth, daughter of Hugh Courtney, earl of Devon, iii 500 ; Elizabeth, his widow, married Sir Andrew Luttrell, 500.

Vere, Nicholas, prebendary of Wells, iii 396.

Vere, Roger de, prior of St. John's, of Jerusalem, in England, iii 97.

Vernai de family owned Durborough, i 252. Wellisford, iii 19 ; lands in Crandon, 92. Huntspill - Verney, Fairfield, and other manors, ii 393. Huish-Champflower, iii 530 ; Hill-Farence, 256 ; Allerford, 257 ; Ford, 244.

Vernai monuments in Stoke Courcy church, i 257, 258. in Hill-Farence, church, iii 257.

Vernai, Cecilia de, prioress of Cannington, 1504, 1533, i 233.

Vernai, Cecily de, wife of Philip de Columbers, i 253, iii 551 ; granted lands in Hill-Farence to her daughter, Maud de, 257.

Vernai, Elizabeth, married William Palmer, of Parham, i 254.

Vernai, Hugh, married Margaret Walsingham, of Scadbury, i 254.

Vernai, John, married Catherine Gambon, i 254.

Vernai, John, married (1) Isabel Touchet, iii 552 ; (2) Eleanor Brent, of Cossington, mother of William, 436. (3) Margaret Archer, mother of Alexander, i 254.

Vernai, John, married Amice de Wolmerston, i 253, iii 71. his son, John, married Alice Carey of Gotton, and retired into the priory of Stoke Courcy, i 254.

Vernai, John, married Joan Malet, of Enmore, i 91, 254.

Vernai, John, received land in trust for the Bicombes, i 266.

Vernai, Maud de, wife of Ernulph de Fulgeriis, i 253. settled her manor in Hill-Farence on her son, William, iii 257.

Vernai, Ralph, married Maud Trivet and left William, John, Ralph, Peter, and three daughters, i 253.

Vernai, Robert, married Joan Sydenham, i 254 ; owned the greatest estates the family ever possessed, and was the last who resided at Fairfield, 254 ; rebuilt Fairfield chapel, 256.

Vernai, Roger de, owned Ford, iii 244.

Vernai, William de, married (1) Denyse de Arundel, (2) Ancilla de Stokes, by whom he had two sons, Peter and Roger, (3) Agnes de Forde, i 253 ; built a chapel adjoining to the parish church of Hilfarence, and left several legacies for masses in the churches of Hilfarence and Stoke Courcy, 253, iii 257 ; William de, who witnessed the grant made by Anastatia Croc to Sir Francis Trivet, 101 ; William de, married Agnes Arthur, 178 ; William de, married Dionysia de Allarford, and became owner of Allarford, 257.

Vernai, William, procured a licence to build a wall and seven round towers at Fairfield, and to enclose two hundred acres for a park : married Joan Broughton and left John, George, rector of Witheridge, Cecily, prioress of Cannington priory, i 254 ; tomb in Stoke Courcy church, 254.

Vernai, William de, married Margaret Russell, i 253 ; knight of privy chamber to Edward I, died from wounds received in Scotland, and buried at Hilfarence, 253, iii 257. left three sons, William, Randulph, and Peter, and a daughter, Maud, married Robert de Staunton, i 253.

Vernai, William de, landowner temp. Ed. I, i *xxvii.*

Verney, earl of, J.P., i *xli.*

W

Walleys, Sire Jehan de, i *l.*

Wallis, Thomas, bequest to Lovington, ii 83.

Wallop, Sir John, owned Brompton - Bury, Warley, and the site of Barlinch priory, iii 503 ; Sir Henry, held Brompton-Regis, 504.

Wally, John, one of the first alderman of Bath, B 23 ; William, one of the first aldermen of Bath, 23.

Wally, John, monument in Bath abbey, 1615, B 70.

Wallys, John, of Worle, whose daughter married Robert de Coker, of Bower, ii 344.

Wallys family owned Worle, iii 615.

Walnut tree, Glastonbury, ii 265.

Walpulle or Walpille (*see* Walpole).

Walpole, iii 101 ; owned by Walter de Dowai, 101 ; Domesday survey, 101 ; held by Rademer : Edward held it T.R.E. 101 ; tenements here were held by Sir John Coumbe, 91 ; William Baudrip released his rights here to John Wroughton, 91.

Walpole, Maria, wife of James Waldegrave, ii 118.

Walrond family owned Isle-Brewers, i 54 ; Langridge, 132 ; monuments in Langridge church, 132, 133 ; arms, 9, 133 ; tomb in Ilminster church, 9 ; in Isle - Brewers church, 55 ; Humphry, founded Ilminster grammar school, 3 ; Henry, of Sea, 4 ; sheriff, 1594, *xxxviii.* owned also Alston, ii 393.

Walrond, Henry, of Bradfield, Devon, married Penelope Sydenham, iii 523.

Walscin held Over-Weare, i 185 (*see* Dowai).

Walshe or le Walesh family held Huish-Champflower, iii 530. tomb in Curry Rivel church, i 30 ; Agnes, wife of Nicholas Salisbury, 41. Catherine, wife of George Dodington, iii 518. John, M.P., 1557–9, i *xxxi* ; John, owned Cathanger, 41 ; married Jane Broke, took Holy Orders and retired to Muchelney abbey, 41 ; expelled and degraded, 42 ; married Mary Clause, 42 ; his eldest son, John, built the manor house at Cathanger, 42. John, iii 530. Lucy, wife of Thomas Cooke, i 41 ; Lucrece, 42. Laurence, chaplain of the chantry of St. John's Frome, ii 194. Nicholas, iii 530. Robert held a knight's fee from Sir William de Mohun, ii 14. Robert, last master of St. John's hospital, Bridgwater, iii 79. Robert, monument in Bath abbey, 1788, B 70. Susan, i 42 ; Thomas, *xl* ; Thomas, 42.

Walshawe, William, i *xl.*

Walsingham, baron, J.P., i *xlii.*

Walsingham, Sir Francis, knt., owned Charlton Adam, iii 191 ; sold it to Sir William Petre, 191. Margaret, wife of Hugh Vernai, i 254.

Walter, abbot of Muchelney, iii 135.

Walter, prior of Barlinch, 1175, iii 503.

Walter, prior of Bath, 1175, 1198, B 55.

Walter, prior of Bath, 1261—1300, B 55.

Walter, first prior of Montacute, iii 312.

Walter, prior of St. John's hospital, Southover, 1314—1323, iii 408.

Walter, prior of Witham, 1318, ii 234.

Walter family, memorial tablets in Wick Champflower chapel, i 219. in West-Pennard church, ii 276.

Walter held Goathurst, i 80 ; Bath Easton, 106 ; Combwich, 234. Whatley, ii 230 ; Aldwick, 315. Hill-Farence, iii 256 ; Tunley, 331 ; land in Ashcot and Pedwell, 425. Cosington, 434.

Walter, Rev. Dr. Alleyne, incumbent of Crowcombe, iii 516. Henry, sheriff, 1716, i *xxxviii.* Hubert, archbishop of Canterbury, granted lands at Wrotham to Geffery de Wrotham, iii 63. John, monument in Emborow church, ii 137 ; Nevill, incumbent of Chilcompton, 129.

Walter's hill, Batcombe, iii 466.

Walters, Henry, J.P., i *xlvi.* governor of Bath hospital, B 49. James, married Elizabeth Blanchard, i 138 ; monuments in Bath-Easton church, 109 ; Thomas, J.P., *xlvi.* Mary, wife of Sir Halswell Tynte, ii 317.

Walton, John, i *xl.* Juliana de, ii 152 ; Richard, Alice, Thomas, monument in Baltonsbury church, 270 ; Robert de, held the tenth part of a knight's fee in Beauchamstoke, 319. Thomas, owned Shapwick, iii 427.

Walton, name sometimes given to John de Perceval, iii 173.

Walton, situation, iii 424 ; Poldon hill, 424 ; Domesday survey, 424 ; Roger and Walter held lands of Glastonbury abbey, 425 ; granted at the dissolution to the duke of Somerset, 425 ; owned by Sir John Thynne, 425 ; the marquis of Bath, 425 ; the living is a chapelry to Street, 425 ; church (Holy Trinity) and monument, 425 ; bells (5), 425.

Walton castle, or lodge, iii 169, 170.

Walton hamlet, Kilmersdon, ii 446 ; Domesday survey, 447 ; owned by Edmund Fitzpaine : Elmar held it T.R.E., 447 : subsequently held by the Botreaux family, 447.

Walton-in-Gordano : situation, iii 169 ; moor, 169 ; ruins of old parish church, 169, 171 ; Walton castle, or lodge, 169 ; Domesday survey, 170 ; owned by Ralph de Mortimer : held by Richard : Gunni held it T.R.E., 170 ; owned by the Mortimer family, earls of March, until it passed to the house of York, 170 ; Andrew de Brompton held half a knight's fee, 170 ; the demesnes and other estates leased out to the Berkeley family, 170 ; mannor subsequently held by the Chedder family, 170 ; the Newtons, 170 ; Sir Thomas Griffin, 170 ; Sir Edward Seymour, 170 ; Sir John Thynne, 170 ; Chris-

Walton-in-Gordano—*continued.*
topher Ken, 170; the earls Poulett, 170; cross, 171; modern church, 171; bell(1), 171; mansion belonging to Sir John Durbin, 171.

Walyngford, John, held part of a knight's fee in Bower, iii 85; in Chilton, 89.

Walwyn, Giles, married Elizabeth Brook and became possessed of part of the estate of Ashton-Philips, ii 297; which he sold to Jane, widow of Matthew Smyth, 297.

Wampford, Joan, wife of John Keynes, iii 120.

Wandestrev (*see* Wanstraw).

Wandestrie family owned Marston-Bigot, ii 213; the chief manor in Wanstraw, 229; Odo de, 229.

Wansdike, i *xxii*, 170, ii 279, 423, 433, 438, 439, iii 140, 339.

Wanstraw: situation, ii 228; hamlet of Weston, or Weston-Town, 228; owned in part by canons of Wells, in part by Turstin Fitz-Rolph, 228; Domesday survey, 228; held of Turstin by Norman: Alwold held it T.R.E., 229; subsequently the principal manor was held by the de Wandestrie family, 229, 213; divided into East or Church Wanstraw, Wanstraw-Rogers, and Wanstraw-Bullers, 229; William de Isle held the chief manor of Lord Roger de Moels, 229; held by John de Acton and Elizabeth Clyvedon, 229; by Odo de Acton, John de Clyvedon and John de Berkeley, 229; Emmelina de Clyvedon, Idonea de Beauchamp, Odo de Acton, James de Wylton, and James Lovel held a knight's fee here of John de Moels, 229; Edmund de Clyvedon held a fourth part of Thomas Peverel, 229; Edmund Hogshaw, his heir, 229; estate divided between Thomas Lovel and John Bluet, 229; William de Beauchamp held a portion, 229; John Rogers held a fourth of Bartholomew Kylbeck, 229; manor granted to Newdigate and Founteyne, 229; another manor held by John Buller of the abbot of Muchelney, 229; passed at the dissolution to Hugh Sexey, and was by him granted, under the name of Buller's Wanstraw, to his hospital at Brewton, 229; another manor held by the Baynard family, 229; purchased by Messrs. Bethune and Spillowby, 229; passed to Rev. Mr. Bethune, 229; river and bridges, 228; church (St. Mary), 229; bells (5), 229; vault of the Baynard family, 229.

Wanstraw-Rogers (*see* Wanstraw).

Wanstraw-Bullers, manor in Wanstraw, ii 229; held by John Buller of the abbey of Muchelney, 229; by Hugh Sexey, 229; Brewton hospital, 229.

Wanton, Emma and Simon de, services of granted to Sir Thomas Trivet by Anastasia Croc, iii 101.

Warbeck, Perkin, attacked Taunton castle, but was repulsed and captured, iii 228; Walter, lord Hungerford assisted in the suppression of his rebellion, 356.

Warburton, George, dean of Wells, 1631, i 190; Gertrude, owner of Claverton manor, 146.

Ward family, monument in North Stoke church, i 135.

Ward, Edward, monument in Bath abbey, 1777, B 70.

Ware, John, benefaction to Wellington, ii 484.

Wark, a stratum of coal found at Clutton, ii 103.

Warknell monument in Midsummer Norton church, ii 151.

Warley manor, i 112; Domesday survey, 112; held by Hugoline and Azor, 112; owned by the Skrine family, 112.

Warmoor, i *xv*, ii 177.

Warmoor hamlet of Stoke Gregory, ii 180.

Warmund held land in Milborne, ii 353. in Mudford, iii 220; in Shapwick, 427.

Warmwell, Felicia, widow of Roger, held land in Preston Plucknet, iii 223; John, owned Newton-Sermonville, 206; Alice, inherited part of that manor, married (1) Richard Penny, (2) Simon Blyhe, 206; Agnes, sister and co-heir of Alice, married Ralph Brett, 206.

Warner, Mr., owned a moiety of the manor of Bratton-Seymour, iii 36.

Warnet, John, married Mary West, ii 413.

Warre family, of Brislington, ii 411; ultimately lords de la Warre, 412; built the chapel at Brislington, 413. owned also Goose Bradon, i 16. John, la, received the manor of Brislington from king John, ii 411; Jordan la, and Johanna, his wife, 411; Roger, married Clarice de Tregoz, 411. owned land temp. Ed I, i *xxviii*. John, held Brislington and a moiety of the lands of John de Tregoz, married Joan, sister and heir of Thomas, lord Grelle, ii 412; granted Chelworth to William and Joan de Beauchamp, 420; John, married Margaret Holland, 412; Roger held Brislington of Edward le Dispencer, fought at Poictiers, was buried at Swineshead abbey, 412. he lived at Goose Bradon, i 16. Thomas, rector of the church of Manchester, ii 412; Joan, sister of Thomas, married Thomas West, 412; Sir Reginald West, son of Joan Warre and Thomas West, created lord de la Warre: succeeded to the Warre estates: fought in France, 412; owned North-Parret, 335; Richard West, lord de la, received a pension from the manor of Old-Wutton, Wilts, for his services to the Lancastrian party, 412; Thomas West, lord de la, owned many estates in Sussex, 412; married (1) Eliza-

Warre family, of Brislington—*continued.*
beth Mortimer, 412 ; (2) Eleanor Copley, 413 ; Thomas, lord de la, Knight of the Garter, married Elizabeth Bonville, owned Brislington and Shepton-Mallet : died without issue, 413 ; his heirs were Joan Dudley, duchess of Northumberland, and Elizabeth Deering, Mary Warner and Anne Gage, 413.

Warre family, of Hestercombe, iii 259—263 ; a collateral branch of the barons de la Warre, 259 ; arms, 259 ; held also Wellisford, 19 ; Robert la, married a daughter of Kentisbere, of Huntworth, 259 ; Matthew, son of Robert, married Felicia Denbaud, with whom he received lands in Hinton-St.-George, thence called Crafte-Warre, 259 ; John, son of Robert, married Elizabeth Meriet, 259 ; and so brought Hestercombe to the Warre family, 259 ; Richard, son of John, married Joan Attwood, 260 ; Elizabeth : John, 260 ; Robert, 260 ; Elizabeth, daughter of Richard, married John Chisselden, of Holcombe, 260 ; John, son and heir of Richard, married Joan Combe, of Dalwood : was high-sheriff of Somerset and Dorset, 1414, 1429, 260, i *xxxv.* Robert, son of John, married Christian Hankford, of Annery : was sheriff of Somerset and Dorset : owned Hestercombe, Baghaye, Crafte Warre, Wellysforde, Bradford, and Grenevyleswyke : buried at Athelney abbey, iii 269 ; Richard, son of Robert, repaired the chapel at Hestercombe, 260, 261 ; succeeded by Richard Warre, of Chipleigh, 261. was sheriff, 1452, i *xxxvi.* Thomas, eldest son of Richard, inherited Hestercombe, Hinton-Crafte, Grenevyleswyke, Brushford, and Banwell, iii 261 ; and added Pulton to his estate, 262 ; married Joan Malet, of Enmore, 262, i 91. Richard, John, William, Henry, Thomas, Edward : Joanna, Mary, Alicia, iii 262 ; Joanna, daughter of Thomas, married Thomas Michell, of Cannington, 262 ; Mary, daughter of Thomas, married George Sydenham, of Chilworthy, 262 ; Richard, son and heir of Thomas, married Catharine Blewett, 262 ; Roger, son and heir of Richard, married Eleanor Popham, 262 ; he had twelve sons and two daughters, 262 ; Richard, son and heir of Roger, married the daughter of Thomas St. Barbe, 262 ; Roger : Thomas, 262 ; Thomas, second son of Richard, purchased Middlezoy and West-Monkton, 262, 442, 454 ; Roger, eldest son of Richard, married Anne Wyndham, 262 ; Sir John : knighted by Charles II : married Unton, daughter of Sir Francis Hawley, and widow of John Malet, 262. M.P., 1669, i *xxxii.* Sir Francis, bart., son of Sir John, married

Warre family, of Hestercombe—*continued.*
(1) Anne Cuffe, (2) Margaret Harbin, iii 262 ; held various offices, and represented Bridgwater and Taunton, 263 ; he was heir to Kentisbere, Meriet, Atwood, Percehaye, Clavile, Combe, Chipleigh, St. Barbe, and Cuffe, 263 ; his two sons died in his lifetime, 262 ; he was buried in Kingston church, 263. trustee of Rogers' charity, i 181. Margaret, daughter and heir to Sir Francis, second wife to John Bampfylde, by which means Hestercombe and many other estates came to that family, iii 263, ii 91.

Warre family, of Chipleigh, iii 261 ; owned also Milverton and Lovelinch, 15 ; Robert, second son to Richard and Joan Warre, of Hestercombe, married Thomasine Chipleigh and became possessed of the manor of Chipleigh, 15, 261 ; John, son of Robert, married Joan Mawbanck, 261. Sir Richard, i *xl.* son of John, was of Chipleigh, and succeeded to the estates of Richard Warre, of Hestercombe, iii 261 ; was one of the commissioners for the enquiry into cardinal Wolsey's lands in Somerset : sheriff and Knight of the Shire : married (1) Margaret Brockman, (2) Joan Hody : to his son by his second wife he gave Chipleigh, Tolland, Milverton, and Lovelinch : which were held by this branch of the family until by the marriage of an heiress they passed to that of Lottisham, 15, 261, 269.

Warre family, of Swell, i 65 ; Jane, wife of Sir Robert Grosvenor, 65 ; Joan, wife of Richard Malet, of St. Audries, 93.

Warren, James, J.P., i *xlvi* ; John, M.D., J.P., *xlvi.* John, received a pension from Taunton priory, iii 236 ; Robert, received pension from Montacute priory, 313 ; Rev. Mr., master of a school at Taunton, 239 ; Susanna, second wife to Sir John Trevelyan, 539.

Warry, Rev., incumbent of Berwick, ii 338. John, J.P., i *xlvi.*

Warton, Rev. Thomas, incumbent of Hill-Farence, iii 257.

Warwick, earls of, Henry de Bellomont, created earl by the Conqueror, ii 203 ; Richard Beauchamp owned Bedminster through his marriage with Elizabeth de Berkeley, 282 ; Richard Nevile, earl of Warwick and Salisbury (*see* Salisbury, earls of). George Grevile, owned Clutton, and patron of the living, ii 104.

Waryn, Thomas, M.P., 1355, i *xxx.* Thomas held a rent in Brook, iii 303.

Wasbrow, Richard, churchwarden of Easton-in-Gordano, iii 151.

Washford, iii 510 ; ruins of Cleeve abbey, 510 ; granted to Robert, earl of Sussex, 512 ; lands here were held of the abbot of Cleeve

Webber, Alexander, married Mary Colford, who at his decease married Oliver Galhampton, iii 273 ; Mary, his daughter, married Francis Prowde : inscription in Oake church, 274.

Webber, Mrs., owned Badialton, iii 22 ; Rev. Edward, incumbent of Badialton, 22. Alexander married Sarah Lucas, of Bampton : monument in Badialton church, 23.

Webber, colonel, mansion at Wellisford, iii 19.

Webber, Rev. Mr., incumbent of Pendomer, ii 349. Rev. David, of Combe-Florey, iii 248 ; mansion at Combe-Florey, 247.

Webber, William, married (1) Mary Haviland, (2) Elizabeth Brickley : monument in Langford-Budville church, iii 20 ; arms, 20.

Webber, memorial stone in Broomfield church, i 73.

Wedding monument in Stanton Drew, ii 433.

Wedmore : situation, i 187 ; largest parish in the county, 187 ; hamlets of Blackford, West Ham, Heath House, Sand, Oldwood, Mudgley, Bagley, Panborough, North Load, East Theal, West Theal, Cocklake, Latcham, Clewer, Perrow, Crickham, Upper and Lower Stoughton, 187, 188 ; tithings of Wedmore, the Borough, Churchland, Blackford, North Load, 188 ; portreeve government, 188 ; fair and revel, 188 ; remains of one of the Cangick giants, 189 ; owned by Berwald, abbot of Glastonbury, and Giso, bishop of Wells, 189, iii 392. Domesday survey, i 189 ; appropriated to the deanery of Wells, 189 ; conferred upon Edward Seymour, duke of Somerset, and upon his attainder reverted to the crown, 190 ; sold to Sir Henry Jernegan, 190 ; owned by the duke of Chandos, 191 ; prebend in the cathedral of Wells, 191 ; guild or fraternity of the Blessed Virgin Mary, 191 ; church (St. Mary), and its monuments, 191—193 ; bells (6), 191 ; benefactions, 193, 194.

Wedon, Walter de, held one-fourth of a knight's fee from John de Mohun, ii 15.

Week, hamlet in Drayton, i 38.

Week manor, Lydiard-Episcopi, ii 494 ; owned by Richard Cross, 494.

Week-Fitzpaine, hamlet in Stoke-Courcy, i 249 ; owned by the earl of Egmont, 252.

Week-St.-Laurence (*see* Wick).

Weekes family owned West-Chelworth, ii 420.

Weekes, John, benefaction to Milverton, iii 18.

Weeks, Charles, benefaction to Widcombe, i 174.

Weley castle, iii 280 ; passed from lord Botetourt to Sir Maurice Berkeley, of Stoke, 280.

Well, remarkable, at Weston - Super - Mare, iii 610.

Welle (*see* Wells).

Welle, land of the, owned by Montacute priory, iii 312.

Welles, Robert, received a pension from Brewton, i 214.

Welles, Hugh de, archdeacon of Wells and bishop of Lincoln, owned Chedder, iii 574 ; sold it to Joceline, bishop of Wells, 575 ; founded the priory of St. John, Southover, 408. benefaction to lepers' house, Selwood forest, ii 196.

Welles or Troteman, Joceline de, bishop of Wells, 1205—1242, iii 381 ; restored Glastonbury abbey, which had been annexed by his predecessors, to its former government, 381 ; reassumed the title of bishop of Bath and Wells, 381 ; banished, but restored, 381 ; he added to the possessions of the see : built two chapels and rebuilt the west end of the cathedral, 381 ; founded the hospital of St. John, Wells, 381 ; monument in Wells cathedral, 381, 400. his contest for East-Cranmore, ii 208 ; he broke down the mill at Baltonsbury, 269 ; decree endowing the provostship of Wells cathedral with the manor of Combe-St.-Nicholas, 475 ; granted the living of Bishop's Lydiard to the canons of Wells, 495. owned Milverton church, iii 16 ; confirmed the institution of the hospital of St. John, Bridgwater, 78 ; ordination respecting the rectory of Hinton-Charterhouse, 369 ; he augmented the priory of St. John, Wells, 408 ; appointed the vicarage at Evercreech, 415 ; received the manor of Blackford from the monks of Glastonbury, 452 ; purchased Chedder from Hugh de Welles, 575 ; owned the chief manor in Congresbury, 585 ; deed, granting Winscombe to the dean and chapter of Wells, 613.

Wellesleigh, hamlet in Wells, iii 405 ; held of the bishops of Bath by the de Wellesleigh family, 405 ; John Hill, of Spaxton, 405, 196 ; John Stourton held half a knight's fee here, 405.

Wellesleigh, William de, held land in Wellesleigh, iii 405 ; Philip de held also lands in Dulcot and the bailiwick of East-Perret, 405 ; owned Wheathill, 450 ; Lud-Huish, 541 ; Walrand de, 405.

Wellington : situation, ii 481 ; borough and market-town, 481 ; fairs, 481 ; owned by Asser, bishop of Sherborne, 481 ; the bishopric of Wells, 482 ; list of bishops up to the Conquest, 482 ; Domesday survey, 482 ; John held two hides of the bishops : Alveva held one hide T.R.E. 482. rated amongst the bishops temporalities, in 1293, iii 394 ; accompted for, in 1329, 394 ; granted by bishop Barlow to Edward, duke of Somerset, 395, ii 482 ; subsequently held by Sir James Fullerton and James Maxwell, 482 ; the Popham family, 482 ; manor held by Herbert Sawyer : borough held by Thomas Harrison, 482 ; church (St. John Baptist) [*sic* Collinson, but it is really dedicated to

Wells, dean and chapter—*continued.*
Chedder, iii 576. provostship endowed with Combe S. Nicholas, ii 475, 476; Winsham, 478; Chard, 472, 475; Wellington, 475, 476. treasurer received fifty marks from Martock church, iii 8; vicarschoral owned Newton-Placey, 70; and a manor in Chedder, 576.

Wells, bishop's palace at, iii 403; built by John de Vilula, 379; hall added by bishop Burnel, 382; fortified and surrounded by a moat by bishop Erghum, 383; damaged by a violent storm, 1703, in which bishop Kidder and his wife were killed, 390.

Wells cathedral: foundations laid by Wifeline, second bishop of Wells, iii 377; despoiled by Harold, earl of Wessex, 378; hall and dormitory for the canons, built by bishop Giso, who enlarged and beautified the grand choir, 379; bishop Giso's buildings demolished by bishop Villula, 379; bishop Robert's regulations, 380; rebuilt by bishop Robert, 380; west-end rebuilt by bishop Troteman, 381; vicar's close, begun by bishop Ralph de Salopia, 383; library, chapel and north-west tower, added by bishop Bubwith, 384; cloister, built by bishop Beckington, 385; vicar's close finished by bishop Beckington's executors, 385; chapel built by Robert Stillington, 386; destroyed by Sir John Gates, 386; cathedral repaired and beautified by bishop Montagu, 388; description and dimensions, 398; cloister, 398; chapter-house, 399; west window, 399; Peter Lightfoot's clock, 399; chapels, 399—401; monuments, 399, 400, 401; arms emblazoned on windows, 401.

Wells-Forum hundred, iii 373; includes part of the forest of Mendip, 373; bounds of the forest, 373; Mendip hills, Crook's peak and Blackdown, 374; lapis calaminaris, mangonesse and yellow ochre found here, 374; lead mines and miners' laws, 374; anciently four chief lords of Mendip: the king, whose part came to the bishop of Bath: Glastonbury abbey: lord Bonville: and afterwards the marquis of Dorset: Gournay, afterwards Newton, 375; value in the duke of Somerset's schedule, 375; the hundred granted to Edward, duke of Somerset, 395.

Wells, priory or hospital of St. John, iii 408.

Welman, Simon, J.P., i *xlvi*; Thomas, J.P., *xlvi.* owned Weston-Zoyland, iii 440; Norton-Veel, 272; Thomas, of Pitminster, 285; Mr. —, seat at Sherford, 294.

Welsteed, Elizabeth, monument in Whatley church, ii 231; arms, 231.

Welton, hamlet in Midsummer Norton, ii 149, 158; owned by the families of Vivonia,

Welton—*continued.*
Beauchamp, Fitz-Reginald, Fitzherbert, Gournay and prince of Wales, 150, 151.

Welwe, river, lands near, granted to the church of St. Andrew by king Kineulf, iii 377.

Welweton, John de, rector of Goose Bradon, i 16.

Welwoneton (*see* Welton).

Wembdon, iii 103; situation, 103; owned by the church of Bath, 103; Domesday survey, 103; held by Walter de Dowai, 103; subsequently alienated from the church, and held by the families of Testard, Hody and Mitchell, 103; church appropriated to the hospital of St. John, Bridgwater: bishop Haselshaw's ordination for a vicarage, 103, 104; church (St. George) and its monuments, 104; chantry, 104; St. John's well, 104; manors of Pury-Furneaux and Pury Fitchett, 103; land in Wembdon was held by Philip Cave, 87; also by Kilve chantry, 533.

Wemberham and Ham manor, Yatton, iii 618.

Wengham, Walter de, married Maud de Sancto Mauro, ii 122; Joan, wife of Richard de Ken, 122; Alice, wife of John de Wyke, 122; Maud, wife of Philip de Wyke, 123; Joan, wife of Sir John de Boudon, 123.

Wentworth, Frederick Thomas, owned Luckham, ii 23; Selworthy, 40; patron of Selworthy, 42. Sir William, bart., governor of Bath hospital, b 49.

Wentworth, Thomas, lord, owned North-Parret, ii 336. Chillington, iii 114. hon. lady, monument in Bath abbey, 1706, b 70.

Were (*see* Over Weare).

Were, John, one of the jury to decide position of city pillory, b 31. Robert de, who married Alice de Gaunt, i 247.

Were, Thomas, purchased Runnington manor, iii 25; Nicholas, 25.

Weremenesyre Wood, ii 195.

Werewell, John, preceptor of Buckland priory, iii 98.

Weritone (*see* Wrington).

Werocosale (*see* Wraxall).

Werre (*see* Over-Weare).

Werret family owned ancient house at Chilcompton, ii 129; Henry, benefaction to Chilcompton, 130.

Werrott, Henry, benefaction to Shepton-Beauchamp, iii 126.

Wesley's chapel, Bath, b 74.

Wesley, William, held Shipham, iii 601.

Wessex, Harold, earl of (*see* Harold).

West, Anne, wife of James Gage, ii 413. Eleanor owned land in Milverton, iii 18. Elizabeth, heiress of Robert Greyndor, the owner of Charlcombe, i 142. Elizabeth, wife of Nicholas Deering, ii 413; Mary, wife of John Warnet, 413; Sir Owen, who married

Whiteley, Elizabeth, held Lydiard-St.-Laurence, and land in Bridgwater, iii 266.

Whitelocke, Robert, last prior of Montacute, 1539, received a pension, iii 313.

Whitemore, George and Thomas, owned Yeovil, which they granted to the Phelips family, iii 205.

Whitemore, hamlet in Staplegrove, iii 289.

Whiteokesmede [Whittokesmede], John, de, M.P. for Bath, 1360, 1363, 1369, 1371—1373, B 20; John de, M.P. for Bath, 1399, 20; 1401, 1409, 1420, 1428, 1449, 21; Thomas de, M.P. for Bath, 1332, 19.

Whiteoxmead : Domesday survey, iii 327; owned by Roger de Curcelle : held by Robert, 327; John Att-Chambre held land here of Sir Elias de Cottel, 327; Richard de Rodney held land of Hugh le Despencer, 327; priors of Hinton held land here, 327, 328, 368; John Bisse held lands here, 328; the Wittokesmede family, 327.

Whitestaunton : situation, iii 126; formerly Stantune, 126; name derived from St. White, 126; Domesday survey : owned by Robert, earl of Morton : held by Ansger : Alward held it T.R.E. 126; subsequently owned by the Brett family, 127; held by the Stantones or Stauntons, 127; sold to the Elton family, 127; church (St. Andrew) and its monuments, 127, 128; bells (5), 127.

Whitewalls, i 100.

Whitfield, Sir William de, sheriff, 1327—1331, i *xxxiv*.

Whithear, Robert, monument in Nunney church, ii 220.

Whiting, Alice, married Edward Strode, ii 210.

Whiting family held West-Melcomb, iii 73.

Whiting, George, benefaction to Long-Ashton, ii 303.

Whiting, Richard, last abbot of Glastonbury, ii 255; finished Edgar's chapel and enlarged the buildings of the monastery, 255; lived there in great state, 256; refusing to give up the abbey to the king, he was seized, and hanged on the Torr hill, 1539, 255, 256.

Whitland, Brecknock, abbot of, held an estate in Bedminster, ii 283.

Whitley, Edward, incumbent of Stoke-under-Hamden, iii 321.

Whitley, hamlet in Staple-Fitzpaine, i 58.

Whitley hundred : situation, iii 423; Poldon-Hill, 423; Burtle - Moor, 423; King's Sedgmoor, 423; road from Glastonbury to Bridgwater, 423; abbots of Glastonbury, ancient lords of this hundred, 423.

Whitling street, hamlet in Nemnet, ii 318.

Whitlock, benefaction to Wedmore, i 193.

Whitlock, Mary and John, monument in Old-Cleeve church, iii 513; Sarah, wife of Philip Sydenham, 522.

Whitmarsh, Henry, J.P., i *xlvi*, iii 294; John, J.P., *xlvi*.

Whitmore, Anne, owned royalties in the manor and hundred of Keynsham, ii 405. Sir William and George owned the manor and castle of Bridgwater, the manor of Hay-grove and lands and tenements in Durleigh, Chilton, and North-Petherton : had many privileges and rights there, iii 81, 82; sold this property to Henry Harvey, 82.

Whitmore family owned East-Brent, i 196.

Whitnel, hamlet in Wells, iii 405.

Whitson, John, owned Burnet : granted it for the endowment of the Redmaids' Hospital, Bristol, ii 415.

Whitston, i 84.

Whitstone hundred, iii 459; Cannard's grave, 459; Whitstone-hill, 459; owned by the monks of Glastonbury, 459, ii 247. granted at the dissolution to Edward, duke of Somerset, iii 459.

Whittenhull manor, ii 158; owned by the families of Apharry, Walbeoff, Gunter, and Hippisley, 158.

Whittenton, Thomas, owned Combe-Monkton, i 151.

Whittington, John, owned Gowdies Farm, Weston, i 159.

Whitworth, Charles, owned Tivington or Black-ford, ii 41.

Whyton, John, held Bossington, ii 38; Elizabeth, wife of Walter Paunsfort : Margaret, wife of John Sydenham, 38.

Whytwell, John, incumbent of Trinity chantry, Aller, iii 188.

Wicha, Thomas de, ancestor of the Wyke or Wick family, iii 618.

Wichanger, ii 23. owned by Buckland priory, iii 98; lands in, held by Thomas Bratton, 555.

Wick, Court de, iii 617.

Wick family owned Norton Hautville, ii 107.

Wick family, monument in Yatton church, iii 619.

Wick, John de, whose widow Egelina married Robert Cheyne, ii 107. Maurice de, M.P., 1377, i *xxx*. Thomas de, held two knights' fees of the bishopric of Wells, iii 393; William de, abbot of Muchelney, 135.

Wick, hamlet in South Brent, i 199.

Wick or Estwick, Camerton, iii 331; Domesday survey, 332; owned by earl Morton : held by Alured : Alestan held it T.R.E., 332; lands here belonged to Hinton priory, 332.

Wick, in Curry Rivel, i 23.

Wick, tithing in Portbury, iii 142.

Wick or Week St. Laurence, iii 611; a member of Congresbury manor, and vested in the mayor and corporation of Bristol, 611; hamlets of Iceldown or Icinton, Cullum, and Ebdon, 612; Bourton : owned by the

Wick or Week St. Laurence—*continued.*
Percevals, the Vanhams, Mrs. Yate, Rev.
Mr. Somerville, 612 ; church (St. Lawrence), 612 ; bells (5), 612 ; cross, 612.
Wick-Champflower, situation and origin of its
name, i 218 ; owned by the family of de
Campo Florido (afterwards written Champ-
flour), 218, 219 ; Henry Southworth, who
erected a new chapel, 219 ; Mrs. Strangways, 219 ; the chapel and its monuments,
219, 220 ; bell (1), 219.
Wickham, Rev. Anthony, married (1) Jane
Brodripp, (2) Dorothy Lloyd : monument
in Horsington church, ii 373 ; Elizabeth
owned a moiety of Backwell manor, and
conveyed her right therein to Sir Walter
Rodney, 306 ; Elizabeth, memorial in Long-
Ashton church, 301. Rev. George, monument in Badgworth church, iii 566. James,
benefaction to Frome almshouse, ii 196 ;
James, principal trustee of Frome charity
schools : benefaction to the same, 197 ;
John, vicar of Long-Ashton, 299 ; monument in Long-Ashton, church, 301 ; John,
benefaction to Horsington, 373. Sarah,
monument in Over-Stowey church, i 260 ;
Theobold, sheriff, 1393, *xxxv.* Thomas,
vicar of Long-Ashton, ii 299 ; memorial in
Long-Ashton church, 301. William, bishop
of Winchester, 1595, iii 232 (*see* Wykham).
Wickham family, patrons of the living of Shepton-Mallet, iii 463.
Wicklond, in Norton-Fitzwarren, iii 272.
Wickmoor, hamlet in Milverton, iii 15.
Widcombe, North, hamlet in Chewton Mendip,
ii 118 ; owned by the families of Beauchamp,
of Hatch, Gournay, Tiptot, and Edmund,
duke of Somerset, 118.
Widcombe : situation, i 168 ; Lyncombe Spa,
169 ; king James' palace, 169 ; hanging
lands, 169 ; Beechen cliff, 169 ; Prior park
mansion built by Ralph Allen, 169, 170 ;
the Wansdike boundary and its supposed
origin, 170 ; the barracks, Berwick, 171 ;
Domesday survey, 171 ; held by the abbots
of Bath, 171 ; granted to John, lord Russel, who alienated them to the Bisse family,
afterwards conveyed by Hugh Saxey to
Brewton school, 171 ; the church (St.
Thomas, of Canterbury), built by William
Bird, prior. of Bath, 171 ; its monuments,
172 ; bells (5), 172 ; chapel founded by
prior Cantlow, 172 ; its monuments, 173,
174 ; lunatic hospital, 174 ; benefactions by
Charles Weeks, Jane Swanson, and William
Millard, 174 ; the poor house and burial
ground, 174 ; cross, 174 ; annual fair, 174.
Widcombe, South, hamlet in Hinton Blewett,
ii 145.
Widcombe, tithing in Montacute, iii 314 ; owned
by Montacute priory, 312.

Widepolle (*see* Withypool).
Widicumbe (*see* Withycombe).
Widney, hamlet in Donyat, i 35.
Wido held Halswell, i 80. land in Ashton,
ii 289.
Widows, ancient custom respecting, in Kilmers-
don, ii 446.
Widworthy, Hugh de, held half a knight's fee
in Hemington, ii 454.
Wielea (*see* Wells).
Wifeline, bishop of Wells, iii 377 ; laid the
foundations of the cathedral, 377.
Wigbere family (*see* Wiggeberre).
Wigborough manor, South-Petherton, iii 110 ;
Domesday survey, 110 ; held by John, the
porter : Alward held it T.R.E. 110 ; subse-
quently owned by the de Wiggeberre family,
110 ; the Cogans, 110 ; the Bourchiers,
lords Fitzwarren, 110, 272 ; Sir Richard
Hankford, 110 ; again by the Bourchiers,
111 ; John Selwood, 111 ; the Broome
family, 111 ; Robert Hilliard, 111 ; manor
house, 111 ; Roman remains, 107.
Wigborough family (*see* Wiggebere).
Wigden manor, Yeovil, iii 207 ; owned by the
de Wigetone family, 207 ; George Bragge
Prowse, 207.
Wigetone family owned Wigden and Kingston-
Pitney, iii 207 ; John de, 207.
Wigfruth owned land in Ham, iii 83.
Wiggeberre family owned Wigborough, iii 110 ;
Chilton and Hunstile, 89 ; and Idstock, 90 ;
John, the porter or doorkeeper to William
the Conqueror, owned Wigborough and
founded the family, 110 ; Richard owned
also land in Pegenes, 110 ; Sir William, knt.,
110. landowner temp. Ed. I, i *xxviii.* held
also land in East-Stratton, iii 108 ; Sir
Richard, 110 ; owned also Chilton and
Hunstile, 89 ; Maud, his widow, 89 ; Mary,
daughter of Richard, married Sir Richard
Cogan, of Huntspill, 110.
Wightwick, Rev. —, owned Barton - David,
ii 65 ; incumbent of Middle-Chinnock, 329 ;
of Chisselborough, 330.
Wigington, Henrietta, married (1) Sir Richard
Newdigate, (2) Sir Francis Wyndham,
ii 387.
Wildeland, granted by William Fitz-Odo to
Taunton priory, iii 235.
Wildemersh, Robert de, chaplain of the chantry
at Woolavington, iii 438.
Wileford, lands in, granted by Robert Ferun to
Symon de Locumbe, iii 256.
Wilege (*see* Wolley).
Wilfrid, saint, bishop of York, gave the island
of Wedmore to Berwald, abbot of Glaston-
bury, i 189.
Wilinton, Ralph de, governor of Bristol castle,
warden of the forest and chace of Keyns-
ham, ii 399.

Worle: situation, iii 614; Worle-hill, 614; Avon hamlet, 614; Domesday survey, 614; owned by Walter de Dowai: held by Esgar, T.R.E. 614; subsequently held of the barony of Oakhampton, 615; by the de Redvers or Rivers family, 615; the Courtneys, 615; the Engaine family, 615; the priors of Woodspring, 615, 594; William St. Loe, 615; Wallys family, 615; Coker family, 615; the Wyndhams, James Bishop, Arthur and Martha Peters, 615; Richard and Gregory Ash, 615; church (St. Martin), 615; bells (6), 615; land here was granted to the bishopric of Bath and Wells, 567; rating in 1293, 394.

Worle-Berry encampment, iii 610.

Worle-hill, i *xii*, iii 593, 610.

Worlestone (*see* East and West Rolston).

Worlestone barony: Tarnick held of, iii 565; Burton held of, 596.

Wormesly priory held lands in Chedder, iii 577.

Worminster, hamlet in Wells, iii 405. owned by the bishopric of Wells, ii 475, iii 378, 396.

Worminster-hill, ii 276.

Worral —, part owner of Kingston-Seymour, ii 124.

Worral, Jacob, benefaction to Wells, iii 410.

Worseley, Christopher, sheriff, 1460, 1465, 1470, i *xxxvi*.

Worsley, right hon. Sir Richard, J.P., i *xlii*.

Worspring priory (*see* Woodspring).

Worston (*see* Wroughton).

Worth, hamlet in Aller, iii 188; Domesday survey, 188; owned by Roger de Curcelle, 188.

Worthy, John, master of St. Catherine's hospital, Bedminster, ii 283.

Worthy manor house, Porlock, ii 37.

Wotton, North: situation, ii 276; Domesday survey, held by Adret, of the abbot of Glastonbury, 276; manor subsequently owned by William Gore Langton, 276; Lancelly and Worminster hills, 276; living annexed to Pilton, 277; church, 277; bells (3), 277; yew-tree, 277; lands at Syckedon, Devon, and in Pilton, granted for the support of lights in the chapel, were sold to Henry Portman, 277.

Wotton, Margaret, wife of Thomas Grey, i 56.

Wotton-Courtney: its situation, ii 48; Grabbist hill, 48; Dunkery hill, 48; hamlets of Ranscombe, Wotton-Ford, Huntsgate mill, Brockwell, and Burrow, 49; fair, 49; common rights, 49; Domesday survey, 49; owned by William de Faleise, held by Algar T.R.E., 49; owned by families of Courtney, Peverell, Hungerford, Hastings, Huntingdon, Hilsborough, and lord Stawel, 49; the living appropriated to Stoke Courcy priory and granted by Henry VI to Eton college,

Wotton-Courtney—*continued.*
49; the church (All Saints), 49; monuments, 50; bells (5), 49.

Wotton-Ford, hamlet in Wotton-Courtney, ii 49.

Wrangway, hamlet in Wellington, ii 485.

Wrantage, hamlet in North Curry, ii 178; granted to the bishopric of Bath and Wells, iii 380.

Wraxall, Richard de, monk of Athelney, 1516, i 87.

Wraxall: situation, iii 155; Naish-house, seat of Walter King, 155; Charlton-house, owned by the families of Berkeley, Gorges, Yates, Muggleworth and Henry Goodwin, 155; Fayland, owned by the families of de Fayland, Meade, Jubbe, and John Blagrave, 155; Belmont, seat of William Turner, 155; limestone rocks, 155, yew-trees, 155; Wraxall manor, 155; owned by Geffery, bishop of Coutances, 155; Domesday survey, 155; held by Aluric T.R.E., 155; subsequently owned by the de Wrokeshale family, 156; the de Morevilles, 156; the Gorges, 156, 157; John Codrington, 158; the Bampfyldes, 158; fair and market, 157; manor-house, called Wraxall lodge, 158; Whelpes place, 158; Crede-place, 158; church (All Saints) and its monuments, 158, 159, 160; bells (5), 158; benefactions, 160, 161; cross, 161; yew-tree, 161.

Wraxall-lodge, iii 158.

Wraxall-on-the-Fosse, or Wraxhill, Ditcheat, iii 471.

Wraxhill or Wraxall, Ditcheat, iii 471.

Wray, Henrietta, memorial stone in Bathwick church, i 123.

Wrech, Robert, whose services were granted to Wood-spring priory, iii 594.

Wrench, Elias, rector of Trent, ii 383; memorial stone in Trent church, 1680, 386. Robert, i 262.

Wrenchester-castle, Glamorgan: passed, by the marriage of Ela de Reigni, to the Raleigh family, iii 537.

Wrey, Sir Christopher, bart., married Anne Bourchier, ii 392; Sir Bourchier owned part of the manor of Huntspill Cogan, 392.

Wright, Henry, surgeon, B 46; governor of Bath hospital, 49; Henry, mayor of Bath, 1766, 1776, 26. Jenny, wife of the Rev. Baptist Isaac, ii 368; John, benefaction to Charleton Horethorne, 358; monument in Charelton Horethorne church, 358; arms, 358; John, benefaction to the poor of Keynsham, 409. Rev. John, incumbent of Ashcot, iii 426. of Shapwick, 427. Thomas, tomb in Staple-Fitzpaine churchyard, i 61.

Wrington: situation, i 206; market and fair, 206; hamlets of Lye and Havyat Green, 206; cultivation of teasels, 206; given by

Wrington—*continued.*

king Athelstan to duke Athelstan who conferred it upon the abbey of Glastonbury, 206; afterwards ratified and confirmed by Henry III, 207; Domesday survey, 206; held by Roger, 206; by Saulf, T.R.E. 206; owned by Sir Henry Capel and the Pulteney family, 207; survey of the manor from the roll of the Glastonbury estates, 207; tithings of Wrington, Broadfield, and Burrington, 207; the church, its tower, and its monuments, 208, 209; bells (6), 208; birthplace of John Locke, 209; free school, 209.

Wrington hundred (*see* Brent).

Writhlington: situation, ii 459; Domesday survey, 459; owned by Brictoward: Brictwold held it T.R.E. 459; subsequently owned by William Moore, of Charlton, 459; church (St. Mary Magdalen) and its monuments, 459, 460; bells (2), 460.

Wrockshall, Sir Geffery (*see* Wroxall).

Wrokeshall family owned Wraxall, Bourton and Nailsea, iii 156, 161; the heiress of Richard de, married Eudo de Moreville, 156.

Wroston (*see* Wroughton).

Wrotesleigh, John de, landowner temp. Ed. I, i *xxix*; one of the king's commissioners for the perambulation of forests, 1298, 16, ii 19, iii 57.

Wroth (*see* Wrothe).

Wrotham, Kent, lands in, owned by the Wrotham family, iii 63, 64; by Richard de Placetis, who took the name of Wrotham, 65.

Wrotham (afterwards Wrothe) family, of North-Petherton, owned great estates in Middlesex, Surrey, Essex, Kent, Hants, Glo'stershire, and Somerset, iii 63—69; owned Withypool, 558; Hawkridge, 529; Wellisford, 19; Geffery de and Muriel de Lyd, his wife, of Wrotham, in Kent, 63; William de, 55, 63, 64. baron in time of Henry II, i *xxvi*; forester of the county, 16; held Cathanger, 41; paid ten marks for the king's protection, 41. keeper of Selwood forest, ii 195. owned Wellisford, iii 19; Pitney, 131; Exton, 526; the bailiwick of the hundred of Williton freemanors, 485; was forester of all the king's forests in Dorset, Somerset, Devon, and Cornwall, 55, 64; sheriff of Kent, warden of the Cinque ports, and constable of Dover castle, 64; warden of the Stannaries, and founded the Stannery laws, 63; held North-Petherton and Newton, 55; and land in Ham, Creech, Monkton, Sutton, Hawkridge, and Exton, 64; married Maud de Cornhall, 64; William, Richard, his sons, 64; William, archdeacon of Taunton, succeeded to his father's estates, 64; received the cus-

Wrotham family—*continued.*

toms, trustee to Sutton hospital, 64; Richard, executed the office of forester for his brother William, 55; Richard: Muriel: Constance: Emma: Christian, his children, 55; Sir Richard succeeded to the estates of his uncle, William, 64; was justice of the court of common pleas: died without issue, and his sisters became his heirs, 64, i 41, ii 195, iii 444, 445, 485, 526. Muriel, wife of Hugh de Placetis, iii 55, 64. [Constance, i 41]. Susanna, wife of John le Blund, iii 64, i 41. [Constance, iii 55]. Emma, or Margaret, wife of Geffrey Scoland, iii 55, 64, i 41. Christian, wife of Thomas Picot, iii 55, 64, i 41. Richard de Placetis, son of Muriel de Wrotham and Hugh de Placetis, took the name of Wrotham, iii 65 (for possessions *see* "Placetis"); married Gladyna le Romeyn, 65; began the building of a church for the friars-preachers in London, 66; endowed the chaplaincy of Edelmetone, 66; Richard, of Shepperton: William: his sons, 65, 66; John, prior of the friar-preachers and confessor to Edward I, 66, i *xxviii*.

Wrothe, William, son of Richard Wrothe, of Sheperton, and grandson of Richard de Wrotham, succeeded to the estates, iii 66; was forester of Petherton park, 62; John, 66; was of Enfield and North-Petherton, owned also lands in Newton, North-Petherton, Creech, Monkton, and at Yeldam, in Kent, 66; arms, 66; John, his son, 66; collector of the king's duties in London, 66; purchased a rent-charge which had been paid out of his lands in Petherton and Sheerston, 66; lived at Wrothe-place, Enfield, 66; Sir John, knt., married (1) Alice —, (2) Maud Radington, daughter of Thomas Durant, 66, 67, 529; John: Agnes: William, 66, 67; John, married Margaret Willinton, 67; held no lands in Newton, 67; Elizabeth, 67; Elizabeth, married Sir John Paulton: left no issue, 67, 330; Agnes, daughter of Sir John, married Sir Pain Tibetot, by which marriage the Wrotham estates in Middlesex, Surrey, Essex, Kent, Hants and Gloucestershire, passed to the Tiptot family, 66; William, son of Sir John and Maud Durant, owned all his father's lands in Newton, North-Petherton, Monkton, and Michael-Creech, and his mother's estates in Newton, 67; arms, 67. sheriff, 1403, i *xxxv*. William, his son, iii 67; William, owned Newton-Wrothe: rebuilt the old court-house: was keeper of Petherton park: married a daughter of John Mortimer: buried at Bridgwater, 67; John, 67; John, married Elizabeth Lewknor, 67; John, 67; John, mar-

Y

Yeovilton family lived at Yeovilton, from which they took their name: were descended from Hugh Fitz - Richard, iii 199; Peter de, lived at Speckington, 200; Margery, his daughter and heir, married Thomas Pain, of Painshay, 200; arms, 200.

Yerbury, John, monument in Laverton church, ii 211; Ann, monument in Laverton church, 212; arms, 212; William, bequest to Beckington, 202; to Road, 224.

Yescomb, Rev., incumbent of Road and Wolverton, ii 225.

Yevelton, Peter de, granted land in Ashford, Ilton, and White Lackington to Athelney abbey, i 47.

Yew trees: Ashill, i 13; Broadway, 19; Buckland St. Mary, 21; Drayton, 39; Staple Fitzpaine, 61; Broomfield, 73; Creech St. Michael, 78; Enmore, 96; North Stoke, 136; Charlcombe, 143; Chapel Allerton, 176; Mark, 184; Burrington, 205; Stoke Courcy, 259. Wotton Courtney, ii 50; Chewton - Mendip, 119; Brockley, 120; Chilcompton, 131; West-Harptree, 144; Midsummer-Norton, 152; Stone-Easton, 155; Marston-Bigot, 216; West Pennard, 276; North-Wotton, 277; Sandford-Orcas, 378; Trent, 388; Fitzhead, 492; Priston, 431. Chillington, 114; Portbury, 143; Flax-Bourton, 161; Wraxall, 155, 161; Brimpton-D'Evercy, 216; Angers-Leigh, 241; West-Monkton, 456; Bicknoller, 502; Kilve, 533; Sandford-Bret, 544; Churchill, 582: Congresbury, 586; Stoke - Giffard, 607; Winscombe, 614.

Yhenele, John, one of the jury to decide position of city pillory, B 31.

Yhette, John, one of the jury to decide position of city pillory, B 31.

Yle, Thomas, prior of St. John's hospital, Southover, 1445—1462, iii 408.

Ynefford, granted by the countess of Leicester to Buckland priory, iii 96.

Ynge (*see* Inge).

Ynswystryn (*see* Glastonbury).

Yonge, Right Hon. Sir George, J.P., i *xlii*.

Yonge, Sir John, knt., owned Easton-in-Gordano: was lord mayor of London, iii 149; Thomas, 149; Thomas, 149; Alice, wife of William Malet, of Enmore, to whom she conveyed the manor of Easton-in-Gordano, 149.

Yonge, William, married Anne Carre and became heir to the manor of Woodspring, iii 595.

York, dukes of, owned Odcombe, ii 324. Walton-in-Gordano, iii 170; were foresters of Petherton, Exmoor, Neroche, Selwood, and Mendip, 61; held the bailiwick of Williton-Freemanors, 485; Richard Plantagenet, earl of Rutland and duke of York, succeeded to the honours and lands of Edmund Mortimer, earl of March: was slain at Wakefield and his estates confiscated, 149; he owned the castle and a third of the manor of Bridgwater, 80; owned Milverton, 14; Cecilia, his widow, held Milverton, 14, 15; Grenvilleswyke and Bickleigh, 261. Anne, daughter of Richard, duke of York, married Henry, duke of Exeter, ii 333.

York family, memorial inscription in Chewton-Mendip church, ii 119.

York, Right Rev. William, lord archbishop of, J.P., i *xli*.

York, William, canon of Brewton, elected prior of Taunton, 1523, iii 236.

Yorke family, monuments in Spaxton church, i 246.

Yorke, Rev., patron and incumbent of Fiddington, i 242. Walthera, widow of Thomas Dreloc and second wife of Hugh Luttrell, ii 11; William, benefaction to Winford, 322.

Young, Alice, wife of William Malet, i 91; Arthur, description of Halswell, 81, 82, 83. George owned Sewardswick, ii 423; John, of London, founded a free school at Trent, 381, 382.

Young family, part-owners of Trent, ii 381; vault in Trent church, 384.

Younge, Agatha, memorial stone in East Brent church, i 198.

Yow, the river: its course, i *xiv*, 206, ii 131, iii 584.

Yowwood, Ywood, or Highwood, hamlet in Congresbury, iii 584; owned by Mrs. Richardson, 585.

Yve, Thomas, last abbot of Muchelney, iii 136.

Yvery, name assumed by Waleran, son of William Lovel, iii 172; he owned large estates in Normandy, 172.

Yvethorne family owned Ivythorn and land in Compton-Dunden, iii 424; William de, 424; John de, 424; Richard de, 424.

Z

Zerde, Alicia de, prioress of Blaunchsale, iii 300.

Zerde or Yard, Combe Flory, iii 248.

Zerde or Yard-lane, Ivelchester, iii 298.

Zouche, lords, of Castle Cary and Harringworth, ii 55. held one knight's fee in Allerton, i 176; a moiety of Edingworth, 197; Pit-

Zouche family—*continued.*
combe, 224. Castle-Cary, ii 55; Barrow-North and South, 62, 63; Sparkford, 87; Road, 224; Odcombe, 324. Wincaunton, iii 32; Bratton-Seymour, 36; Bridgwater, 81; Sevington, 123; Charlton-Grey, 193.

Zouche family—*continued*.

lived in retirement at Marsh, near Brewton, ii 55. members buried in Stavordale priory church, iii 34 ; chantry founded by, 34 ; arms on priory buildings, 34. Alan, lord Zouche, of Ashby, ii 55 ; one of the witnesses to the charter for the fair at St. Michael de Torre, Glastonbury, 265 ; Ivo, or Eudo le, married Millicent de Montalt, daughter of William de Cantilupe, 337. and became possessed of the manor of Bridgwater, iii 81 ; Eve, wife of Maurice, lord Berkeley, 278. William, assumed the name of Harringworth, ii 55 ; William, lord, of Harringworth, married Alice St. Maur, 55. owned Bridgwater and lands in Haygrove and Odcombe, iii 81. John : Margaret : Elizabeth, ii 55 ; William, lord Zouche and St. Maur, obtained special livery of his lands,

Zouche family—*continued*.

55, iii 81. William : Elizabeth : Margaret, ii 55 ; John, lord, married (1) Dorothy Capel, (2) Joan or Jane Dynham, 55, 362 ; became possessed of part of the manor of Buckland-Dinham, 452 ; was attainted (after the battle of Bosworth), and his estates forfeited to the Crown, 55, iii 81. John, lord Zouche and Seymour, ii 452. Jane, wife of Sir Edward Hungerford, iii 356. Richard owned Barrow-North, 1552, ii 62. sold a moiety of the manor of Bratton-Seymour iii 36. Charles owned land in Barrow-North, ii 62. gave the other moiety of Bratton-Seymour to Jerome Dibben, iii 36. Elizabeth, a descendant of this family, married captain James Hopkins : monument in Stanton-Drew church, ii 437 ; arms, 437.

.

INDEX OF ARMORIAL BEARINGS.

EXPLANATORY NOTE.

THIS Heraldic Index consists of two parts, (1) "An Alphabet of Arms," in which the Coat of Arms can be found from the name; (2) "An Ordinary of Arms," in which the Coats are arranged in accordance with the heraldic similarity of the bearings, and the name to which any given Coat is to be attributed can be ascertained. The arrangement of the latter is, generally, that adopted by Papworth in his "British Armorials."

This is an Index only—not a Treatise on Heraldry. The possession of sufficient knowledge of the science to enable the reader to decipher the blazon, either with or without reference to a treatise, is necessarily assumed. A table of abbreviations used is given below.

No such index can be perfect. In the first place the shields were frequently incorrect from the first, whether from error or ignorance of the draughtsman or workman. (2)—The tinctures are frequently wanting, have faded or altered by decay, or have been "restored" in the wrong colours. (3)—An enormous number of Coats are practically the same—lions, for instance, are almost innumerable. (4)—Collinson was not a very accurate observer in this particular, and occasionally reads "a chief" as a distinct coat, or reverses that process; sometimes he transposes the husband's and wife's arms on an impaled shield. (5)—In stained glass, not always clean, small bearings—spindles and leaves for instance—are easily mistaken, and a discoloured azure readily becomes a sable.

In the identification the locality is not a safe guide, particularly in the impaled coats. Wives are frequently imported from other counties, and the enormous number of wealthy strangers in the residential locality of Bath necessarily introduced many Coats otherwise foreign to the district.

Collinson has frequently identified a shield in one place but has failed to recognise what are obviously the same bearings, and attributable to the same family, when they have been found elsewhere.

When the identification is not Collinson's the names are printed in *italics*. Any additions of tinctures, or otherwise, to the coat as blazoned by him, are also in *italics*. Occasionally an entirely substituted blazon is suggested in the same manner. It has not been thought necessary so to indicate the correction of *obvious* errors. In some cases where the same coat is blazoned in different words, *all having substantially the same meaning heraldically*, the best blazon has been selected. Where the differences are substantial they are set out. No distinction is made in the references to vol. and page, whether the identification is that of the author or of the compiler. Impaled and quartered Coats have been resolved and blazoned separately.

It should be noted that Vol. I (of Collinson) has eighty-four pages under the head of "Bath," after which the numbers begin afresh from page 1. These eighty-four pages are in this Index distinguished as "B" *ex. gra.* B 46. In Vol. II, pages 97 to 104 are numbered 89 to 96, those numbers being used twice over. This error should be corrected. In this Index it is assumed that the correction has been made.

In the case of surnames having the prefix of "St." they will be found under "S"; but the prefix "de" is ignored in the alphabetical sequence.

In the compilation of this Index I have had the invaluable assistance of the Heraldic MSS. (in my possession) of the late Mr. John Hanson Sperling, M.A., who visited the greater number of the Somerset churches, A.D. 1875 to 1880, and took very careful notes of the "Arms on Monuments and Painted Glass" therein. The bearings in most cases he afterwards drew in the proper Heraldic colours. These MSS. have provided an independent check upon our Author, the value of which it is almost impossible to overestimate; and it may be fairly stated that in their absence the amount of time necessary to verify and compile this Index would have been practically prohibitory. The original Note Book of the Visitation of Somerset by St. George, also in my possession, has afforded valuable information.

I have also to thank Mr. John Batten, F.S.A., for the loan of a MS. index which, as a check on my own independent work, has been of great value; also the Rev. Prebendary Coleman for careful notes and drawings of the Cheddar heraldry. Mr. F. Were has kindly presented to the Society a copy of his Heraldic Notes from Churches in North-East Somerset, which I have consulted with advantage.

The following printed works have been consulted :—Papworth's "British Armorials;" Burke's "General Armory;" Jewer's "Wells Cathedral, its inscriptions and heraldry;" Symonds's "Diary"—Camden Society; Jackson's "Farleigh Castle;" Batten's "South Somerset;" "Diary of Tristram Risdon," edited by Messrs. Dallas and Porter; "The Visitations of Somerset, 1531—1573," so carefully edited by my co-Secretary, the Rev. F. W. Weaver, M.A.; "The Visitation of Somerset, 1663, Harl. Society;" The *Proceedings* of the Somerset Arch. and Nat. Hist. Society; of the Wiltshire and other kindred Societies, *cum multis aliis*, etc., etc.

A good deal of the work of extraction and transcription has been done by my daughter.

JAMES R. BRAMBLE, *Fellow and Local Sec. S. A.; Pres. Clifton Antiq. Club; Hon. Gen. Sec. Som. Arch. and Nat. Hist. Soc.*

TABLE OF ABBREVIATIONS.

Arg.	.	Argent	Displ.	.	Displayed	Ind.	.	Indented
Az.	.	Azure	Embatt.	.	Embattled	Pass.	.	Passant
Betw.	.	Between	Eng.	.	Engrailed	Prop.	.	Proper
Bord.	.	Bordure	Erm.	.	Ermine	Purp.	.	Purpure
Cab.	.	Cabossed	Erms.	.	Ermines	Ramp.	.	Rampant
Chev.	.	Chevron	Gu.	.	Gules	Sa.	.	Sable
Counterch.		Counterchanged	Imp.	.	Impaling or	Salt.	.	Saltire
Cresc.	.	Crescent			Impaled			

INDEX OF ARMORIAL BEARINGS.

ALPHABET OF ARMS.

Bredwardine? Two lions couchant gardant.
ii 220.

Braunche (or Branch). A fleur-de-lis surmounted with a file of three points (antient). *Gu.* a leopard's head jessant de lis *or* (modern) (adopted by Leversedge).
ii 187, 192.

Brenne (or Brene). ( ) a bend betw. six balls on a chief two *(?).* i 179.

Brent (or de Brent). Gu. a wyvern disp. arg. (iii 160 charged on the breast with three erm. spots). i 256, 257, ii 212, iii 160, 435, 464.

Bretesche. Sa. a lion ramp. arg. double queued crowned or. ii 315.

Brett. Arg. a lion ramp. betw. five cross crosslets fitchée gu. iii 127.

Brewer. Gu. two bends wavy or. ii 473.

Brewer. Gu. two rams (*bends*) wavy erm. iii 290.
—— Gu. two bends wavy or a chief vaire. iii 290.

Brewton (or Bruton), **Monastery of.** Gu. in a maunch erm. a hand prop. holding erect a fleur-de-lis or. Or sometimes or a cross engr. sa. (Both derived from the de Mohuns). i 214, ii 9.

Brickdale (M.P. Bristol, of Gatcombe Court, Wraxall, granted by Ed. III to Jenkin Brickdale). Az. a chev. betw. three sheaves of five arrows or flighted arg. pheoned and banded gu. iii 454.

Brickley (or Bickley). Arg. a chev. engr. betw. three martlets sa. iii 20.

Bridges. Arg. on a cross sa. a leopard's head or. ii 405, 406.

Bridgwater, Town of. *Gu.* a castle surmounted by two others placed pyramidically and embattled standing on a gothic bridge with water (*all prop.*) underneath on each side the first castle a domed tower surmounted with a ball and the gate in the centre portcullised (*in ch. on the dexter side an estoile and on the sin. a fleur-de-lis both or*). iii 76.

Brightmore. Gu. a chev. voided (? *two chev.*) az. betw. three swans' heads erased prop. i 204.

Bristol, City of. *Gu.* on the sin. side on a mount a castle with two towers domed on each a pennon *all arg.* on the dexter base barry wavy of six *arg. and az.* a ship sailing from behind the castle *or* the fore and mainmast *sa.* with two sails on each in *sight of the second.* ii 416.

Bristow (or *Lister*). Arg. on a fesse cotised sa. three cresc. or. iii 359.

Brito. A fesse. iii 544.

Brokesby. Arg. on a bend az. three boars' heads of the first. iii 261.

Brome. Sa. on a chev. arg. three sprigs of broom prop. ii 339.

Brooke (of Lower Court, Long Ashton). Gu. on a chev. or three lions ramp. sa. ii 300.

Broughton (of Sandford). ( ) three stags' heads ( ). i 258.

Browne. Erm. an eagle disp. gu. i 105.

Browne (or *Brown*). Az. a chev. betw. three cranes or. i 119.
—— Gu. a chev. engr. erm. betw. three cranes' heads erased arg. i 161.
—— Arg. on a chev. sa. betw. three cranes az. as many escallops or. ii 77.

Brown. Gu. a chev. betw. three fleurs-de-lis or. i 135.

Brune. Az. a cross moline or. iii 256.

Bruton Priory (*see* Brewton).

Bryan (or *Rogers*). Two lions ramp. addorsed. ii 220.

Bubwith, Bp. *Arg.* a fesse engr. sa. betw. three bubbles (*twelve holly leaves vert four, four, and four arranged in quadrangles*). iii 399.

Buckland (of W. Harptree). *Gu.* three lions ramp. on a canton sa. a fret or. ii 142.

Bull. Or on a canton sa. a griffin's (*lion's?*) head erased of the first. i 149.

Bull. Or three bull's heads cab. gu. i 219, iii 428.

Bull (of Midsomer Norton). Or three bulls' heads sa. armed and langued gu. ii 151.

Bull. Gu. three bulls' heads cab. or. i 192.

Burnel. Arg. within a bord. az. a lion ramp. sa. crowned or. iii 359.

Burgess. Arg. a fesse lozengy or and az. in chief three mascles of the third a bord. of the last bezantee. i 162.

Burton. Az. a cres. arg. within an orle of mullets pierced or. i 165.

Byam. Arg. three boars' (*dragon's?*) heads erased vert. ii 24.

Byflet. Two swords in salt. iii 201.

de Bykele. *Arg.* a chev. engr. betw. three birds (*martlets sa.*) iii 15.

de Bytal. ( ) a chev. engr. betw. three birds ( ). iii 15.

Bythemore (or de la More). Barruly on a chev. three mullets. i 185.

Bytton. Erm. a fesse gu. iii 464.

Cabell. Sa. a horse erect arg. bridled or. ii 193.

Cabell. A text K and a bell or (*device*). ii 193.

Campbell. Gyronné of eight erm. and gu. i 161.

Camville. *Az.* three lions pass. *arg.* ii 358.
—— *Vert.* an eagle displ. or. ii 358.

Canning. Arg. three moors' heads wreathed sa. ii 103, iii 404.

Cannon or **Canon.** Arg. on a fesse gu. betw. three crosses patée sa. as many martlets of the first. ii 492, iii 269.

Cantelupe? Erm. three lions' heads jessant de lis az. iii 264.

Cantelow (or *Hart?*) Gu. a bend betw. three fleurs-de-lis arg. iii 360.

Cantlow, Prior? *Arg.* an eagle rising *or* (sic.)
B 58.

de Columbers (antient). A dove sitting on a bush. iii 551.
—— (modern) ( ) a bend ( ) with a label in chief. iii 551.
Comes. ( ) three lions passant in pale ( ) iii 406.
Compton. Arg. on a bend sa. three close helmets or. ii 443.
Compton. ( ) a lion pass. regard. betw. three helmets ( ). ii 455.
Coney. Sa. a fess cotised or betw. three conies sejant arg. iii 95.
Conway. Az. a chev. arg. betw. three gauntlets or. ii 344.
Coopey. Gu. a chev. erm. betw. three crosses calvary arg. iii 160.
de Coriwell. Three wells. iii 457.
Cornish. Sa. a chev. betw. three roses arg. iii 401.
Cornwall, Duchy of. Erm. a lion ramp. gu. within a bord. engr. sa. bezanty. iii 359.
Coterell. Sa. a bend nebulé arg. (arg. *a bend nebulé sa. ?*). iii 591.
Cottington. Az. on a fesse *arg.* betw. three roses *or* as many bugle-horns *sa.* ii 271.
Cotton. Az. a chev. betw. three bundles (*hanks*) of cotton yarn arg. i 164.
Cottrell. Arg. a bend betw. six escallops sa. ii 321
Court. Paly arg. (*or ?*) and az. on a chief of the first an eagle disp. with two necks sa. i 222, ii 470.
Courtenay. Or three torteaux in pile a label of three points az. ii 343, iii 359, 576 (arg.)
—— The same coat without the label. iii 333.
Courtney (or Hussey). Barry of six arg. (*sometimes or*) and gu. on each bar three roundels counterch. iii 360.
Coward. Or (*on*) two bars sa. three roses arg. *two and one.* iii 407.
—— Arg. on a chev. gu. three martlets of the field on a chief of the second a chamberpiece or. iii 468.
Cox. *Arg.* in chief three cocks' heads erased *gu.* in base a spur leathered *proper.* ii 303.
Cozens. Az. a lion ramp. or. iii 416.
Crofts. Quarterly per fesse *indented* arg. and az. in the chief dexter quarter a lion pass. or. iii 150, 606.
Crooke. Az. a fesse engr. erm. betw. three eagles disp. or. i 209.
Crosse. Az. three taus *two and one* or. ii 344.
Crowther. *Gu.* a bend wavy *vair.* ii 491.
Cudham ? Checquy or and gu. over all on a fesse az. three bezants. iii 620.
Cuffe. Arg. on a bend dauncettée sa. cotised az. bezantée three fleurs-de-lis of the field. i 77, iii 261, 269.
Cutts. Erm. on a bend sa. three plates. iii 406.
Dacre. Gu. three escallops arg. iii 589.
Damarel (*of Devonshire*). Gu. three cresc. or. iii 589.

Darknell. *The arms given are those of Compton, possibly the wife's.* ii 455.
Daubeny. Gu. a fesse lozengy arg. i 164, iii 94.
Dauney (*Rhys ap Tyder, or Rontons*). Arg. a dragon erect sa. i 236.
Davidge. Gu. on a bar (*fesse wavy*) betw. three lions pass. *arg.* as many crosses pattée *of the first.* ii 264.
Davis (Rice - Davis, of Tickenham). Gu. a griffin segreant or. ii 192, 308.
Dawe. Arg. on a pile gu. a chev. betw. three cross crosslets of the field. iii 472.
Deaudons (of Devon). Az. three escallops or. (Assumed by Malet). i 94.
De la Hay ? Or three escallops gu. iii 360.
Delamere (or Delamare). Gu. two lions pass. gard. or. i 220, ii 218, 220.
De la More (or Bythemore). Barruly on a chev. three mullets. i 185.
Desmond. Erm. a saltier engr. gu. iii 261, 263.
Devicke (or Deviocke ?) Per saltire sa. and arg. in (*each of*) the chief and base of the sa. part three trefoils or. ii 321.
Dickinson. Or a bend engr. betw. two lions ramp. gu. ii 81, 417.
Digby (Mansfield-Woodhouse, Notts.) Az. a fleur-de-lis arg. a canton of the last. i 165.
Dixon ? Quarterly first and fourth gu. second and third arg. a pale fusilly vert. iii 360.
Doble. Sa. a doe pass. betw. three bells arg. iii 291.
Dodington (antient). Sa. three bugle horns arg. ii 220, 373, iii 519, 593.
—— (modern). Sa. a bugle horn arg. iii 519.
Donne. Az. a lion ramp. and chief or. i 217.
Dormer. Az. ten billets or four, three, two, one, on a chief of the second a demi-lion (*ramp.*) issuant sa. iii 361.
Draper. Gu. three bends or *on* a chief per fesse erm. and arg. three mullets sa. ii 333.
Draycot. Arg. a cross engr. sa. on the first quarter an eagle displ. gu. i 225.
Drew (? Wickham). Arg. two chev. sa. betw. three roses gu. seeded or. ii 312.
Dundas. Arg. a lion ramp. guard. *and chief gu.* i 200.
Durston. Arg. a bull's head cab. sa. i 202.
Dyer. Arg. (? or) a chief dancettée *gu.* ii 264.
Dyer. Per fesse indented or and gu. (? *or a chief indented gu.*) iii 255.
Dymocke ? (or Kilpeck ?) A sword in pale. ii 286.
Dymock. Gu. a sword in pale sa. (*ppr.*) iii 476.
Dynham. Gu. a fesse lozengy arg. (*erm.*) iii 333.
Edgell. Arg. on a chev. embattled sa. betw. three cinquefoils gu. as many bezants. ii 202.
Edward the Confessor. Az. a cross patonce betw. five martlets or. iii 401.
Edwards. Per fesse sa. and arg. a lion ramp. counterch. i 220.

Glastonbury, Abbey of. A cross moline. iii 34.
—— Vert a cross flory arg. in the dexter chief a garb or over it a mitre. (*Virgin and Child ?*) iii 577.
Godolphin. Gu. an eagle displ. betw. three fleur-de-lis arg. CREST, a dolphin embowed sa. i 216.
Godolphin. Sa. an eagle displ. with two necks arg. i 220.
Godwin. A chev. betw. three blackamoors' (*leopard's ?*) heads. iii 406.
Godwyn. Sa. a chev. betw. three leopards' heads *or.* iii 84.
—— Sa. a chev. *erm.* betw. three leopards' heads *or.* iii 84.
Gold (*or Gould*). Az. a lion ramp. or betw. three scrolls arg. ii 264.
Goodden. Az. on a bend betw. two demi-lions ramp. erased or three lozenges vaire gu. and arg. iii 11.
Goodhind. Gu. a fesse betw. three fleurs-de-lis or. ii 443.
Goodman. Per pale sa. and erm. an eagle displ. or. ii 98, 448.
Gore (of Minchin Barrow). Gu. a fesse betw. three cross-crosslets fitchée or. ii 311, 312.
de Gorges (temp. Ed. III, assumed from More-ville). Lozengy or and az. *a chev. gu.* iii 156, 158, 159.
Gorges (of Wraxall, antient). *Arg.* a whirl-pool or gurges *as.* iii 157, 159.
Gould. Paly of six arg. and sa. six cross-crosslets or. iii 219.
de Gournay. Paly of six or and gu. (or or and az.) iii 320, 590.
Gracedieu. Or (*? arg.*) a fesse raguly gu. betw. three torteaux two and one. iii 620.
Greting ? (*or Secroft ?*) Arg. a chev. engr. betw. three pellets voided. iii 408.
Grevile (Earls of Warwick). Sa. on a cross engr. or five pellets *all within a bordure engr. of the second.* ii 104.
Greyndor. ( ) a chev. betw. ten cross-crosslets ( ). i 142.
Grosvenor. Az. a garb or in chief a bloody hand dexter. CREST, a talbot. i 65.
Gunning. Gu. three guns in pale arg. iii 465.
Gunter. Sa. three gauntlets arg. ii 312.
Hadeswell (*or Hyndfield*). Arg. a fesse betw. three pigs (*boars*) sa. iii 333.
Hadley ? ( ) on a chev. three crosses moline ( ). ii 193.
Hales. *Sa. a* chev. betw. three lions ramp. *arg.* CREST, a lion ramp. ii 130, 455.
Hales. Gu. three arrows *or birdbolts or feathered* arg. ii 70, iii 370.
Hall. Erm. in chief a lion pass (*? ramp.*) gu. i 164.
Hall. Arg. a chev. betw. three orles *or.* ii 345.
Hall. Sa. three pole-axes arg. iii 407.

Halliday (or Hollyday). Sa. *within a bord.* arg. three close helmets *of the last.* CREST, a demi-lion ramp. gard. or supporting an anchor prop. iii 359, 361.
Halswell. Az. three bars wavy arg. over all a bend gu. i 83.
Hampton. Az. a bend betw. six fleur-de-lis or. iii 589.
—— Gu. a bend az. betw. six fleurs-de-lis or. iii 620.
Harbin (of Newton). Az. a salt. voided betw. four spears erect or. iii 206, 261.
Harewel. Arg. on a fesse nebulée sa. three hares' heads couped or. iii 383.
Harptree. Arg. a cross flory gu. iii 590.
Harrington. Sa. a fret arg. CREST, on a torce or a talbot's head prop. i 129, 141, ii 130, iii 219, 347.
Hart (*of Hanham*). Sa. a hart pass. arg. ii 99.
—— (*or Cantelow ?*) Gu. a bend betw. three fleurs-de-lis arg. iii 360.
Hartgill. Arg. three bucks' heads cab. sa. iii 42, 176 (?).
Harvey. On a bend arg. three trefoils slipped vert. ii 59.
Harvey (of Brockley). Sa. a fesse or betw. three squirrels sejant arg. cracking nuts or. CREST, a squirrel sejant arg. tail or cracking a nut of the last. ii 121, 308.
Hassell. Vert three snakes coiled (*adders erect*) or. iii 333.
Hatton ? ( ) a chev. betw. three garbs or. ii 343.
Haviland. Arg. three towers triple-towered sa. ("*In chief*" *is an error. The shield is quartered*). iii 20.
Hawley. Vert a salt. engr. arg. i 115, iii 261.
Hayes. Or a sun radiated gu. iii 406.
Healy. Sa. on a chev. engr. arg. betw. three lions ramp. or as many crosses patée gu. iii 407.
Hele. Gu. a bend lozengy erm. iii 360.
Hendover. Gu. a lion ramp. betw. seven es-callops or. i 9.
Henley (of Leigh, Som.) Az. a lion ramp. arg. crowned or within a bord. of the second charged with eight torteaux. ii 171, 174, 479.
Henry VIII, Badge of. The rose and crown. ii 103.
Herbright ? Gu. three tigers' heads erased arg. ii 136.
Hewish. Arg. on a bend az. three whitings *of the field ?* iii 492.
Hext. Or a tower *triple-towered* betw. three battle-axes sa. iii 182.
de Heyron or Herun (of Long-Ashton. ( ) three herons ( ). ii 290.
Heytesbury. Per pale indented gu. and vert a chev. or. iii 358.
Heywood. Arg. on a bend within a bord. gu. three torteaux.
(*Arg. three torteaux in bend betw. two bend-lets gu. all within a bord. of the last*). i 148.

Knoyle. Gu. on a bend arg. three escallops sa. ii 378.

Lake, Bp. Sa. a bend betw. six cross-crosslets fitchée arg. i 220, iii 401.

Landawarnick (co. Cornwall). Sa. two bars arg. on a chief of the first (? *second*) a griffin or. iii 468.

Langham. Arg. three bears' heads erased sa. muzzled or. iii 512.

Langport, Town of. An embattled and crennellated tower (antient). Portcullis (modern). iii 132.

Langton, Bp. Or betw. four roses a cross *az.* (*per pale or quarterly az. and gu.*) charged with five roses *arg.* (*or*). iii 227.

Langton. *Quarterly* sa. and or a bend arg. (*In one case Collinson has blazoned two coats as one*). iii 344 (2).

Latch. Arg. on a fesse wavy az. betw. three escutcheons gu. as many lozenges or. iii 581.

Laud (Bp. of Bath and Wells). Sa. on a chev. or betw. three estoiles (*of the second*) as many crosses patée fitchée gu. iii 401.

Leeke. *Arg.* on a salt. engr. *sa.* nine annulets *or.* ii 130.

Legge. Az. a buck's head cab. arg. iii 252, 255.

Leigh (of Stoneleigh). Gu. a cross engr. arg. (? *or*). ii 97.

Leversege (or Leversedge). Sa. a chev. betw. three dolphins *arg.* ii 187.

——— (adopted from Branch). *Gu.* a leopard's head jessant de lis *or.* ii 192.

Leversedge. Sa. a chev. betw. three dolphins emb. arg. on a chief gu. a leopard's head jessant de lis or. ii 193.

Ley (Earl of Marlborough). Arg. a chev. betw. three bears' heads couped sa. i 129.

Lisle. Or *on a chief gu. three lions ramp. of the first.* iii 361.

Lisley. Or on a chev. az. three lions ramp. of the first. ii 443.

Lloyd (of Wycombe, co. Bucks). Quarterly *or and az.* four stags statant (*trippant ?*) counterch. ii 77.

Locke. Per fesse az. and or a pale counterch. three hawks with wings endorsed of the last. ii 193.

Lovel. Or semée of cross-crosslets a lion ramp. az. ii 54.

——— Or a lion ramp. *az.* iii 34.

Lovell. Barry nebulée of six or and gu. iii 93.

Luccombe. Arg. a chev. betw. three lions' heads erased gu. iii 491.

Luellin. Or a lion ramp. sa. iii 406.

Luther. Arg. two bars sa. in chief three round buckles az. i 164.

Luttrell. *Or* a bend betw. six martlets *sa.* ii 11.

——— (of East Quantockshead ?) ( ) four martlets ( ). iii 498.

——— Barry of four pieces ( ) and ( ) four martlets ( ). iii 498.

Lychefield. Two bends couped. B 66.

Lyde. Az. an eagle with two necks displ. or. ii 436 (2).

Lygon. *Arg.* two lions pass. *in pale gu.* iii 165.

Lyons (of Long Ashton). Arg. a chev. sa. betw. three lions dorm. coward gu. ii 299, 312.

——— (of Whitchurch). Arg. two lions ramp. respecting sa. ii 441, 443.

Lyte (of Lytes Cary). Gu. a chev. betw. three swans arg. iii 193.

Macie. Az. a chev. arg. in chief two mullets or in base a dexter gauntlet fesseways of the second holding in pale a mace or. CREST, a demi-lion or. i 162.

Malet (antient). Paly of six erm. and gu. over all a lion pass. or. i 94.

——— (modern). Az. three escallops or. (Adopted from Deaudon). ii 103, 277, iii 248, 260.

Malet. Arg. three escallops or. ii 343.

——— Arg. (*az.*) three mallets purp. (*arg.*) i 65.

Malet (of Sutton Mallet). *Gu.* (*or sa.*) a chev. between three roundels (*round buckles or*). iii 430.

Maleverer ? Arg. three greyhounds statant sa. ii 343.

Malherbe. Gu. a chev. erm. betw. three leaves vert. iii 576, 577.

Maltravers. Sa. a fret or. iii 207.

de Mansel (or Maunsel). A hand clenched (antient). Sa. three gambs az. (modern). iii 72.

Marchant (co. Devon). Or three anchors sa. ii 220.

Marshall. Arg. on a fesse betw. three chessrooks sa. as many mullets of the field. iii 424.

Martyn (or Martin). Arg. two bars gu. ii 42, iii 479.

Maude. *Arg.* three bars or charged with a lion ramp gu. i 119.

Maunsell (*see* Mansel).

Mawbank. Arg. four bars wavy gu. over all a salt. or. iii 260.

Medlycott. Quarterly gu. and az. per fesse indented three lions ramp. arg. ii 354, 378.

Meriet. Barry of six or and sa. a bend erm. ii 170, iii 260.

Methen. Arg. a chev. betw. a cross patée gu. in chief and a heart of the last in base. ii 193.

Methwin (or *Methuen*). Arg. three wolves' heads erased prop. two and one. ii 193.

de Middleney. ( ) three snails ( ). iii 445.

Middleton. Per fesse or and gu. within a bord. engr. a lion ramp. counterch. CREST, a stag's head or. MOTTO, Fortis in arduis. i 161.

Milborne Port, Borough of. ( ) a lion pass. gard. ( ) with the letter R in base. ii 353.

Mildmay. Arg. three lions ramp. az. two and one. ii 75.

Miller. Arg. a fesse gu. betw. three wolves' heads erased az. i 65, 105.

R R

de Perceval. Arg. on a chief indented gu. three crosses patée of the first. CREST, a man armed on horseback with one leg couped. iii 173.

Periam. Gu. a chev. engr. betw. three leopards' heads or. ii 495.

Perrot. *Gu.* three pears *arg. on a ch. of the second a demi-lion iss. sa.* iii 619.

Pever. Arg. on a chev. gu. three fleurs-de-lis or. i 9.

Peverel. Az. three garbs arg. *a chief or.* iii 359.

Pewtrell. Arg. a bar (*fesse*) erm. betw. three roses *gu.* ii 61.

Phelips (of Montacute). Arg. a chev. betw. three roses gu. seeded and barbed vert. MOTTO, Tout jours fidele. i 62, iii 314.

Phillips. Arg. a lion ramp. sa. within a bord. engr. of the same. i 114.

Pierce (*or Peirce*). Sa. a bend raguly betw. two unicorns' *heads erased or.* iii 336.

Pierce. Or two bars az. in chief three escallops gu. iii 401.

Pinney (of Bettiscombe). Gu. three cresc. each gripping a cross fitchée. ii 175.

Pinsent. Gu. a chev. arg. betw. three estoiles or. ii 42.

Pitt (Earl of Chatham). Sa. a fesse checqué or and az. betw. three bezants. CREST, a crane close prop. beaked and membered or holding his dexter foot on an anchor erect or. i 25.

Place. Per pale or and gu. a lion pass. counterch. iii 151.

Plantagenet (*of Court, in Braunch, Corn.*) Or within a bord. invected *sa.* bezanty a lion ramp. gu. i 9.

Pointz. Barry of eight gu. and or. iii 589.

Pokeswell. Or a buck's head cab. gu. betw. horns a cross patée of the second. iii 71.

Pontington. ( ) on a bend three roundels ( ). ii 375.

Poole. Az. a fesse betw. three leopards' heads or. i 267.

—— Az. semée of fleurs-de-lis or a lion ramp. arg. langued gu. ii 206.

Pope. Arg. two chev. gu. on a canton of the second an escallop or. ii 436.

—— *Arg.* a chev. *sa.* betw. two roses *gu.* in chief and a talbot *pass. of the last* in base. iii 404.

Popham. A stag's head on a chief three roundels (17 Rich. II). i 264.

—— Arg. on a chief gu. two bucks' heads cab. or. i 9, ii 428, 484, iii 243, 260, 328, 620.

Portman. Or three fleurs-de-lis *two and one* vert. ii 344.

Portman. Or a fleur-de-lis az. iii 274, 495.

Portnew ? Gu. a gate *or.* ii 220.

Poulet (Poulett or Pawlet). Sa. three swords in pile arg. *Pommels and hilts or.* i 258, ii 167, 220, iii 133, 170, 406, 593, 620.

Powel. Per pale *az. and gu.* three lions ramp. *two and one arg.* i 29.

Prater. In chief a lion couch. (*pass.*) in base three wolves' heads erased. ii 220.

Pratt ? On a fesse betw. three bezants sa. (? *ogresses*) three lozenges gu. i 65.

Pratt. Arg. on a chev. sa. betw. three ogresses each charged with a martlet of the first three mascles or. i 77.

Prideaux. Arg. a chev. sa. over all a file (*label*) with three lambeaux (*points*) gu. ii 307, iii 581

Proctor. Arg. a chev. gu. betw. nine crosscrosslets sa. ii 345.

Prowse. Sa. three lions ramp. arg. iii 562.

de Punchardon. *Arg.* a cross cercelée voided *gu.* ii 494.

Radcliffe. Arg. a bend engr. sa. iii 198.

Radington. Gu. three bezants in pale. ii 443.

Ragland. *Arg.* three unicorns pass. *sa.* ii 103.

de Raleigh (antient). ( ) six cross-crosslets ( ). iii 541.

—— (modern). Gu. a bend fusilly arg. iii 541 (2).

Raymond. Sa. a chev. betw. three eagles displ. arg. on a chief of the first three boars pass. sa. iii 222.

—— (of Oake). Arg. three bars sa. iii 274.

Reade. Gu. a bend lozengy erm. i 9.

de Reigni. Three grapple-hooks. i 237.

Reigni or Reyney (adopted by Paulet or Poulett). A pair of wings conjoined in lure arg. ii 166, iii 74.

Rice (*Rice-Davis, of Tickenham*). Sa. a chev. or betw. three spears' heads arg. ii 208.

Richmond (or *Colman*). *Per fesse arg. and* gu. a cross moline betw. four mullets counterch. ii 443.

Ridout. Per pale arg. and gu. a griffin segreant counterch. within a bord. engr. or. i 223.

Rigby. Barry of six arg. and az. on a chief of the second three cinquefoils or. i 135.

Riggs. Gu. a fesse erm. (*vaire*) betw. three water spaniels arg. B 65.

Risedon (or *Risdon*). *Arg.* three arrows (*birdbolts*) in fesse sa. i 257, iii 406, 421.

Rishton. Arg. a lion pass. sa. on a chief of the last a trefoil of the first. i 192.

Rivers. *Az.* two bars dauncettée *or.* ii 103.

Robinson. Sa. a chev. erm. betw. three gauntlets arg. iii 370.

Robyns. Quarterly or and az. four eagles erect counterch. i 236.

Rodbard. Or a chev. betw. three bulls *statant* sa. attired arg. ii 171, iii 415.

Rodney. CREST, an eagle displ. prop. charged on the breast with a cresc. or rising out of a coronet. ii 129.

Rodney. Or three eagles displ. gu. ii 129, 394, 407, iii 165, 306, 577, 606, 607.

Roe. Az. a roebuck lodged arg. iii 577.

Rogers (of Cannington). Arg. a chev. betw. three bucks trippant sa. i 236, ii 39.

Smythes (of Wrington). Arg. a chev. az. betw. three oak leaves vert each charged with an acorn or. iii 463.

Somerset. Or on a bend vert three mullets of the first. CREST, a dove prop. i 200.

Somerville. Az. betw. seven cross-crosslets fitchée three, one, two and one arg. three mullets two and one or. i 162, iii 413.

Somery. Or two lions pass. *in pale* az. i 217, 220.

Southby. Sa. a chev. betw. three cross-crosslets or. ii 492.

Southcott. Arg. a chev. gu. betw. three coots sa. iii 332.

Southey. Gu. a chev. betw. three cross-crosslets arg. ii 495.

Southwell. Arg. three cinquefoils gu. ii 407, iii 607.

Southworth. Arg. a chev. betw. three cross-crosslets sa. i 219, iii 428.

Sparrow (Flax Bourton). Arg. three roses gu. seeded or barbed vert a chief of the second. ii 302.

Specot. Or on a bend gu. three fer-de-molins pierced arg. i 129.

Speke. Arg. two bars sa. (or az.) (another barry of eight az. and arg.) over all an eagle displ. with two necks gu. CREST, a porcupine. i 9, 68, ii 406.

Spilsbury ? ( ) two escallops in chief ( ). ii 286.

Spurstow. Vert three mullets or pierced sa. i 149.

Stafford. *Or a* chev. *gu.* within a bord. *sa.* i 263.

Stafford, Bp. Or on a chev. arg. *(?)* a mitre of the first. ii 349.

Stalling (of Ken). Gu. three escallops in bend arg. on a ch. of the second a martlet sa. iii 593.

Stawel. Gu. a cross lozengy arg. iii 252, 253, 264, 568.

Staynings. Arg, a bat displ. sa. ii 42.

Stead. *Arg.* a chev. sa. betw. three boars' (*bears'*) heads sa. *muzzled or.* ii 59, 70 ?

Steerrs. *Az.* three lozenges (*cronels or spear heads*) arg. ii 110.

Stephens. Per chev. *az. and arg.* in chief two falcons volant *or.* ii 121.

Sterling. Az. a cross flory or betw. four estoiles gu. ii 343.

Stewart. Or a fesse checquy arg. and az. i 162.

Stiff. Arg. on a chev. engr. sa. betw. three estoiles gu. as many stags' heads cab. of the second (*first*). ii 71.

Stillingfleet (or *Thwaites ?*) Arg. on a fesse sa. betw. three pheons of the first two fleurs-de-lis gu. i 235, 236 ?

Arg. on a fesse sa. betw. three fleurs-de-lis gu. two pheons az. (Sper.)

Stillington. Gu. on a fesse betw. three leopards' heads or as many fusils (*fleurs-de-lis*) sa. (*See Lewer's Wells Cath.,* 274). iii 404.

Stocker. Gyronny of six az. and arg. three parrots vert. ii 443.

Stoke Courcy Priory. A scaling ladder. i 258.

Stourton. Sa. a bend or betw. six fountains prop. (or plates). ii 349 (2), 268, iii 260, 408.

Strachey (of Sutton Court). Arg. a cross betw. four eagles displ. gu. CREST, an eagle displ. of the second. ii 99.

Strange ? (*gu. ?*) two lions statant *arg ?* ii 220.

Strangways. Sa. two lions pass. in pale paly of six arg. and gu. i 223.

de Strode (or Strode). Erm. on a canton sa. an estoile of five points arg. (a crescent arg.) ii 209, 210, iii 35, 464.

Sugar. Sa. three sugar-loaves arg. in chief a doctor's cap. iii 399, 401, 404.

de Sulleny (or Salignac). Quarterly arg. and gu. ii 455.

de Sully. Barry of six ( ) and ( ). ii 394.

Sutton. Arg. a canton sa. iii 449.

Swan. Sa. a chev. or betw. three swans with wings erect arg. armed gu. i 161.

—— Vert a fesse or betw. three swans arg. iii 401, 404.

Sweeting. Sa. on a chev. betw. three horses pass. arg. three orles (*annulets*) sa. ii 42.

Sydenham. Arg. three rams pass. sa. iii 86, 215, 523.

—— (of Kittisford). Arg. a bend fusilly (or lozengy) sa. iii 86, 523.

Sydenham (*of Langford*). Arg. a chev. betw. three rams sa. iii 408.

Symes. Or two lions pass. langued sa. on a quarter of the last three bezants. ii 106.

—— Az. three escallops in pale or. ii 338.

Talbot ? Bendy arg. and gu. ii 343.

Taunton (original seal of borough). An eagle (*cherub*) standing on an imperial crown with wings displ. under the crown on a scroll "Defendamus." iii 227.

—— Borough of. A castle triple-towered crenellated and embattled. *In base a fleur-de-lis betw. two peacocks respecting each other.* DEVICE, the letter T passed through a tun lying fesse-ways. iii 227.

Taylor. Sa. a lion pass. arg. ii 193, 349.

—— Arg. a bar (*fesse*) counter-embattled betw. six fleurs-de-lis sa. *three and three.* ii 349.

Temple. Arg. two bars sa. on each three martlets arg. (or or). iii 581.

Thurston. Sa. three bugle-horns stringed or garnished az. iii 269.

Thwaites ? (or *Stillingfleet*). See Stillingfleet.

Thynne. Barry of ten or and sa. ii 188.

Tibbot. Barry gu. and arg. a fesse embatt. sa. ii 106.

Tilly (of West Harptree). ( ) a fesse bendy counter-bendy in chief three fleurs-de-lis ( ). ii 142.

—— (of Devon). Arg. a wivern sa. ii 377.

Tooker (Norton Hall). Five bars wavy (*barry wavy arg. and az.*) over all a chev. guttée raguly *or* betw. three sea-horses naiant *arg.*   ii 130.

—— Vert on a bend engr. arg. three body-hearts gu.   ii 312.

Toomer (or de Tomere). Gu. three bars wavy arg.   ii 366, 368.

Touchet (Lord Audley). Quarterly erm. and gu. a chev. fretty or.   i 256.

Tregarthin. Arg. a chev. betw. three escallops sa.   i 9.

Tremayne (or Botetourt). Or. a salt. engr. sa.   i 220.

Trent. Az. three chevronels or in chief two roses arg.   ii 264.

Trethewy (of Treneage, Corn., and Dicheat, Som.) Sa. a chev. engr. betw. three goats statant arg.   ii 130.

Trevelyan. Gu. a demi-horse arg. armed or issuing out of the sea in base prop. iii 540.

Tripp. Gu. a scaling ladder betw. six cross-crosslets arg.   iii 35.

Tristram. Arg. three torteaux a label of three points az.   ii 443.

Trivet. Arg. a trivet sa. i 256, 258, ii 344, iii 159.

Tryon. Sa. and az. parted per fesse embatt. (*az. a fesse embatt.*) betw. six mullets of eight points or.   i 147.

Tufton. Arg. on a pale sa. an eagle displ. of the first.   iii 359.

Turberville. Checky *or and gu.* iii 125, 127.

Turney. Arg. a chev. betw. three bulls pass. sa. attired or.   ii 225.

Turnor. Erm. on a cross quarter-pierced arg. four fers de moulins sa.   B 64.

Twyford. Arg. two bars sa. on a canton of the last a cinquefoil or.   ii 448.

Twyniho. *Arg.* a chev. betw. three lapwings sa.   ii 189, 193.

Tyder, Rhys ap (Dauney or Rontons). Arg. a dragon erect sa.   i 236.

Tyndale. Arg. a fesse gu. betw. three garbs sa. CREST, a plume of feathers prop. i 114.

Tynte. Gu. a lion couched betw. six cross-crosslets three in chief and as many in base arg.   i 83, iii 160.

Ufford. Gu. a cross moline arg.   ii 71.

Upton. Sa. a cross moline arg.   iii 464.

de Valletort. Vert on a bend arg. three mullets gu.   i 239.

Vansittart. Erm. an eagle displ. sa. armed gu. on a chief gu. a ducal coronet betw. two crosses patée arg.   i 163.

Venner. Gu. on a fesse or three escallops sa.   iii 269.

Verdon. Or fretty gu. *charged with fleurs-de-lis.*   iii 358.

Vernai (or Verney). Arg. a chev. betw. three bugle-horns sa.   i 236, 253, 258.

—— Arg. three fern leaves vert.   i 256.

Vernai (or Verney). Gu. three crosses recercelé or a chief vaire erm. and ermines.   ii 376.

Vowell. Three escutcheons charged with as many cinquefoils.   iii 576, 577, 606.

Wadham. Gu. a chev. betw. three roses arg. CREST, a rose arg. betw. two branches (*red deer horns*) prop.   i 8, iii 611.

Waldegrave. Per pale arg. and gu.   ii 118.

Wale. Or on a cross sa. five lions ramp. of the first.   i 139.

Waleys or Walsh (of Hutton). Erm. a bend sa.   i 235, iii 590.

Walrond. Arg. three bulls' heads cab. sa. attired or.   i 9, 55, ii 443 (?), iii 269.

Walrond. Barry of six or and az. over all an eagle displ. gu. CREST, on a wreath a demi-horse naiant.   i 9, 133.

Walsgrave ? or Fleet. Per pale az. and gu.   ii 263.

Walsh. Arg. a chev. gu. betw. three pheons sa.   i 220, 258.

Walshe. Az. seven (*six ?*) mullets or (*within a bord. gobonated arg. and gu.*)   i 42.

Walters. Az. two keys in salt. or a squirrel sejant prop. *Another* six keys and two squirrels.   i 109.

Walton. Arg. a fleur-de-lis *gu.*   ii 270.

—— Arg. a chev. betw. three fleurs-de-lis *az.*   ii 231, 271.

Warre. Gu. crusuly fitchée arg. a lion ramp. of the last.   iii 259, 260, 269.

Warre. Gu. a lion ramp. betw. eight cross-crosslets arg.   i 65.

—— Gu. a lion ramp. betw. five cross-crosslets or.   i 202.

Watts. Az. three broad arrows or on a chief of the second as many moors' heads side-faced couped prop.   ii 99, iii 52.

Way (or Kinge). ( ) a chev. betw. three fishes haurient arg.   i 65.

Wear. Arg. on a bend sa. betw. six cross-crosslets fitchée gu. three croziers or.   i 164.

Webb. Or a cross quarterly *counterch gu. and* sa. in the chief dexter quarter an eagle displ. *of the third.*   i 140.

Webb. Or on a bend engr. gu. three cross-crosslets fitchée arg.   ii 443.

Webber. Barry raguly (*nebulée ?*) or *and gu.* on a bend or two lions current regard. sa.   iii 20.

Wells, See of. Az. a St. Andrew's cross or and arg. (per saltire quarterly quartered or and arg.)   i 220, ii 300.

—— Chapter of. Az. a salt. or.   ii 343, 398.

—— City of. Per fesse arg. and vert a tree prop. issuant from the fesse line in base three wells two and one masoned gu. iii 376.

Welstead ? (or Walton). ( ) a chev. betw. three fleurs-de-lis.   ii 231.

Weston. Or an eagle displ. sa.   ii 368.

Weston. Sa. on a chev. betw. three leaves or a mullet of the field. iii 590.

Whalesborough. Arg. three bends gu. within a bord. sa. charged with ten bezants. iii 541.

Wharton. Sa. within a bord. or a maunch arg. i 165.

Wheeler. Arg. three Catherine-wheels *two and one* gu. ii 349.

Whitchurch. Gu. three talbots' heads erased or on a chief arg. guttée de sang a lion pass. sa. ii 221.

Whippie. Arg. three greyhounds current sa. ii 443.

Whiting. Arg. a bend nebulée cotised sa. iii 261.

Whitmore. Vert fretty or. ii 97.

Wickham. Arg. two chev. sa. betw. three roses gu. ii 98, 142, 300, 312, 373.

Widville. Per fesse gu. and arg. a canton sinister of the field. iii 590.

Wike (or Wyke). Arg. a chev. gu. betw. three crosses moline sa. iii 268.

Wilkins. Per pale or and arg. a wyvern ramp. vert. iii 151.

Willoughby ? Sa. a cross engr. or. в 60, ii 71.

Wittewronge. Bendy of six *arg. and gu.* on a chief *sa.* a bar indented *or.* ii 26.

Witty. Erm. on a chev. sa. three martlets arg. (*arg. on a chev. az. three mullets of the first*). iii 464.

Windham. Az. a chev. betw. three lions' heads erased or langued gu. i 258.

de Woky. ( ) a chev. ( ) betw. three bugle-horns ( ). iii 421.

Wolmerston. Vert a chev. betw. three lions ramp. or. i 256, ii 373, iii 71.

Wolmington (Dorset). Az. a chev. erm. betw. three lions ramp. arg. ii 284.

Wood. Or a tree vert supported by a greyhound sejant sa. collared and chained of the first. iii 611.

Worgan. Or in (*on a*) chief sa. three martlets of the first. i 168.

Wray ? Vert on a chief sa. three martlets or (*? sa. on a ch. az. three martlets or*). iii 407.

Wright. Az. two bars arg. in chief three leopards' heads or. CREST, out of a ducal coronet or a dragon's head prop. ii 358.

Wrothe (antient). A lion's head erased crowned. iii 67.

—— (modern). Arg. on a bend sa. three lions' heads erased of the field crowned or. i 256, iii 66, 67.

Wroughton. Arg. a chev. gu. betw. three boars' heads *couped sa.* ii 270.

Wyatt. Sa. a fesse dauncettée arg. betw. three eagles displ. or. iii 269.

Wyndham. Arg. a chev. betw. three leopards' (or lions') heads erased or langued gu. ii 235, iii 260, 264, 332, 455, 491, 495.

Yea. Vert a ram pass. arg. iii 290.

de Yeovilton. Two bars nebulée. iii 199.

Yerbury. Per fesse or and arg. over all a lion ramp. az. iii 212.

York. Arg. on a salt. az. an escallop or. iii 362.

Zouch. Gu. bezantee (or ten bezants) a canton erm. ii 437, iii 34, 361.

Zouch. Gu. ten bezants *in pile.* i 217, 220.

—— Arg. ten torteaux, four, three, two, one. ii 345.

—— Gu. a chev. betw. nine bezants. i 9.

ORDINARY OF ARMS.

Anchors. Or three anchors sa. Marchant, co. Devon.

Annulets. Az. six annulets or three, two, and one. Musgrave.

Arrows. Arg. three birdbolts in fesse sa. Risedon or Risdon.

Az. three arrows erect or. Chaldicote or Chalcot.

Az. three broad arrows or on a chief of the second as many moors' heads side-faced couped prop. Watts.

Gu. three arrows in pale or feathered arg. Hales.

Axes. Arg. three battle-axes in pile sa. Gibbs.

Sa. three pole-axes arg. Hall.

( ) three pole-axes ( ). Seaman ?

Bars. Two. Arg. two bars gu. Martyn or Martin.

Two bars conjoined in fesse wavy *(sic)* ?

Bars. Two—*continued.*

Az. two bars dauncettée or. Rivers.

Two bars nebulée. de Yeovilton.

Arg. two bars sa. over all a bend gu. de Ashton.

Arg. two bars az. over all an eagle displ. with two necks gu. Speke.

Arg. two bars az. an escarbuncle gu. Blount of Mangotsfield.

Bars. Two, betw. Arg. two bars engr. betw. nine martlets sa. Moore.

Bars. Two and in chief. Arg. two bars sa. in chief three round buckles az. Luther.

Az. two bars arg. in chief three leopards' heads or. Wright.

Or two bars az. in chief three escallops gu. Clarke.

Sa. two bars and in chief three mullets or. Freke.

Bars. Two and in chief—*continued*.

Sa. two bars arg. in chief three plates. Hungerford.

Sa. two bars arg. on a chief of the second a griffin or. Landawarnick, co. Cornwall.

On two Bars and in chief. Or two bars gu. on each three trefoils arg. in chief a greyhound courant sa. Palmer, of Cannington.

Or on two bars sa. three roses arg. two and one. Coward.

Arg. two bars sa. on each three martlets arg. (or or). Temple.

Arg. two bars sa. on a Canton of the last a Cinquefoil or. Twyford.

Gu. two bars or on a canton sa. a fer de mouline erm. Panton.

Bars. Two, within a bordure. Gu. within a bordure arg. two bars erm on a canton sa. a fer de mouline of the second. Panton.

Bars. Three. Arg. three bars sa. Raymond, of Oake.

Erm. three bars gu. Hussey.

Arg. three bars wavy az. Sandford.

Az. three bars wavy arg. Sanford.

Arg. three bars wavy gu. Bassett.

Gu. three bars wavy arg. Toomer or de Tomere

Az. three bars wavy arg. over all a bend gu. Halswell.

Arg. three bars or charged with a lion ramp. gu. Maude.

Bars. Four. Arg. four bars wavy gu. over all a salt. or. Mawbank.

Barry of four az. and or in the dexter chief an escallop of the first. Clarke.

Barry of four pieces ( ) and ( ) four martlets. Luttrell, of East Quantockshead.

Bars. Five. Five bars wavy arg. and az. over all a chev. gutteé raguly or betw. three seahorses naiant arg. Tooker, Norton Hall.

Barry of six. Barry of six ( ) and ( ). de Sully.

Barry nebulée of six or and gu. Lovell.

Barry nebulée of six or and sa. Blount.

Barry of six or and sa, a bend erm. Meriet.

Barry of six or and az. over all an eagle displ. gu. Walrond.

Barry of six arg. (or or) and gu. on each bar three roundels counterch. Courtney or Hussey.

Barry wavy of six arg. and gu. Bayouse.

Barry wavy of six arg. and az. a cresc. or. Seaman.

Barry of six and in chief. Barry wavy of six arg. and az. on a chief gu. three bezants. Astry.

Barry of six arg. and az. on a chief of the second third cinquefoils or. Rigby.

Barry of eight. Barry of eight gu and or. Pointz.

Barry of eight az. and arg. over all an eagle displ. with two necks gu. Speke.

Barry of ten. Barry of ten or and sa. Thynne.

Barry of ten embattled gu. and or.

Barry of ten arg. and gu. over all a bendlet az. Moncaster ?

Barry of ten arg. and az. over all six escutcheons sa. each charged with a lion ramp. arg. Cecil.

Barry (unnumbered). Barry nebulée or and gu. on a bend or two lions current regardant sa. Webber.

Barry gu. and arg. a fesse embatt. sa. Tibbot.

Barruly on a chev. three mullets. Bythemore or de la More.

Barnacles. Arg. three pair of barnacles open in pale gu. Orange or Orenge.

Bat. Arg. a bat displ. sa. Staynings.

A bat displ. surmounted by a label of three points. Cary, of Gotton.

Beast. Bear. Arg. a demi-bear erect sa. muzzled or. Barnard, of Downside.

Beast. Deer. Az. a roebuck lodged arg. Roe.

Sa. a doe pass. betw. three bells arg. Doble.

Sa. a hart pass. arg. Hart, of Hanham.

Sa. a buck statant arg. Jones, of Astall, co. Oxon.

Beast. Dog. Two talbots pass. de Montacute.

Arg. three greyhounds statant sa. Maleverer ?

Arg. three greyhounds current sa. Whippie.

Sa. three talbots pass. arg two and one. Horner.

Beast. Horse. Sa. a horse erect arg. bridled or. Cabell.

Gu. a demi-horse arg. armed or issuing out of the sea in base prop. Trevelyan.

( ) three horses current arg. Fry.

Beast. Lion. Arg a lion ramp. gu. Forward.

Arg. a lion ramp. gu. St. Cleer de Stapleton.

Arg. a lion ramp. sa. Mompesson ?

Az. a lion ramp. or. Cozens.

Or a lion ramp. az. Brabant.

Or a lion ramp. az. Lovel.

Or a lion ramp. sa. Luellin.

Sa. a lion ramp. arg. double queued crowned or. Bretesche.

Sa. a lion ramp. billety or. Nempnet.

Sa. a lion pass. arg. Taylor.

( ) a lion pass. gard. ( ) with the letter R in base. Borough of Milborne Port.

Gu. a lion ramp. or (later debruised with a bend erm. or arg. on the bend three escallops). Fitchet.

Sa. a lion ramp. bebruised with a bendlet gu. Churchill.

Beast. Lion and in chief. Arg. a lion ramp. guard. and chief gu. Dundas.

Arg. a lion pass. sa. on a chief of the last a trefoil of the first. Rishton.

Az. a lion ramp. and chief or. Donne.

Az. a lion ramp. arg. in chief three escallops of the second. Clutterbuck.

Beast. Lion within bordure. Arg. within a bord. az. a lion ramp. sa. crowned or. Burnet or Bradney.

Arg. a lion ramp. sa. within a bord. engr. of the same. Phillips.

Az. a lion ramp. arg. crowned or within a bord. of the second charged with eight torteaux. Henley, of Leigh, Som.

Erm. a lion ramp. gu. within a bord. engr. sa. bezanty. Cornwall.

Or within a bord. invected bezanty a lion ramp gu. Plantagenet, of Court in Braunch, Cornwall.

Beast. Lion between. Arg. a lion ramp. betw. three cross - crosslets fitchée gu. Bowyer.

Arg. a lion ramp. betw. five cross-crosslets fitchée gu. Brett.

Gu. a lion ramp. betw. five cross-crosslets or. Warre.

Gu. a lion couch. betw. six cross-crosslets three in chief and as many in base arg. Tynte.

Gu. a lion ramp. betw. eight cross-crosslets arg. Warre.

Gu. a lion ramp. betw. seven escallops or. Hendover.

Az. a lion pass. or betw. three fleurs-de-lis arg. North (Lord).

Sa. a lion pass. regard. or betw. three helmets arg. Compton.

Sa. a lion ramp. or betw. three mullets arg. Oliver.

Az. a lion ramp. or betw. three scrolls arg. Gold or Gould.

Beast. Demi-lion. A demi-lion ramp. gard. or supporting an anchor prop. Halliday (Crest).

Two Beasts. Lions. Arg. two lions pass. in pale gu. Lygon.

Arg. two lions ramp. respecting sa. Lyons, of Whitchurch.

Az. two lions pass. gard. arg. Barnes.

Gu. two lions pass. gard. or. Delamere or Delamare.

Gu? two lions statant arg? Strange?

Gu. two lions erect ramp. in pale arg. Ambridge.

Or two lions pass. in pale az. Somery.

Or two lions pass. langued sa. on a quarter of the last three bezants. Symes.

Sa. two lions pass. in pale paly of six arg. and gu. Strangways.

( ) two lions ramp. addorsed ( ). Rogers or Bryan.

( ) two lions couchant gard. ( ). Bredwardine ?

Three beasts. Lions. Arg. three lions ramp. az. two and one. Mildmay.

Arg. three lions pass. sa. two and one. Hutchins.

Three beasts. Lions—*continued.*

Az. three lions ramp. or. De Fieules (Flenes or Fiennes).

Az. three lions pass. arg. Camville.

Gu. three lions ramp. arg. on a canton sa. a fret or. Buckland, of West Harptree.

Gu. three lions arg. pass. in pale. England, of London.

Or three lions pass. in pale sa. armed and langued gu. Carew.

Sa. three lions ramp. arg. Prowse.

( ) three lions pass. in pale ( ) Comes.

( ) three lions pass. ( ). de la Ford.

( ) three lions pass. ( ). de Fauconbergh.

Six beasts. Lions. Sa. six lions ramp. three, two and one in pile or. St. Martyn.

( ) six lions ramp. ( ). Orescuilz, Normandy.

Beast. Ram. Vert a ram pass. arg. Yea.

Three beasts. Rams. Arg. three rams pass. sa. Sydenham.

Three beasts. Snails. ( ) three snails ( ). de Middleney.

Three beasts. Toads. Arg. three toads sa. Botreaux.

Bend. Arg. a bend gu. St. Lo.

Arg. a bend gu. cotised sa. Frampton.

Arg. a bend nebulée cotised sa. Whiting.

Arg. a bend fusilly (or lozengy) sa. Sydenham, of Kittisford.

Arg. a bend engr. sa. Radcliffe.

Or (Arg?) a bend sa. a label of three points gu. St. Lo, of Chideock.

Az. a bend engr. arg. cotised or. Fortescue.

Az. a bend or. Scrope.

Erm. a bend sa. Waleys or Walsh, of Hutton.

Gu. a bend lozengy arg. Ruddock.

Gu. a bend fussily arg. de Raleigh.

Gu. a bend. raguly arg. Penruddock.

Gu. a bend lozengy erm. Hele or Reade.

Gu. a bend wavy vair. Crowther.

Sa. a bend nebulée arg. (? Arg. a bend nebulée sa.) Coterell.

Per bend. Per bend crenellée arg. and gu. Boyle, Earl of Cork and Orrery.

Per bend erm and erms a lion ramp. or. Simpson.

Per bend or and gu. two lions' heads counterch. Fern.

Bend and in chief. ( ) a bend ( ) with a label in chief. de Columbers (modern).

Arg. a bend gu. on a chief of the second two mullets or. St. John.

Arg. a bend gu. on a chief az. three escallops of the first. Gamage.

Bend within a bordure. Az. within a bord. engr. erminois a bend fusilly of the last. Sainsbury.

Az. within a bord. erm. a bend between six cross-crosslets fitchée arg. Cheyne.

S 2

Bend within a bordure—*continued.*
A bend cotised (5 Ed. III). Bendy within a
bord. (46 Ed. III). De Bradney.

Bend between beasts. Or a bend engr.
betw. two lions ramp. gu. Dickinson.

Bend between birds. Or a bend between six
martlets sa. Luttrell.

Bend between crosses. Az. a bend cotised
between six crosses formée or. Bingham
or de Bingham.
Gu. a bend between six cross-crosslets or.
de Fourneaux or Ormsby.
Gu. a bend embatt. (raguly ?) betw. two cross-
crosslets arg. Pelsett.
Gu. a bend betw. six cross-crosslets fitchée
arg. Howard.
Sa. a bend betw. six cross-crosslets fitchée
arg. Lake (Bishop of Bath and Wells).

Bend between escallops. Arg. a bend betw.
six escallops sa. Cottrell.
Arg. a bend gobonated az. and arg. (or ?)
betw. three escallops gu.

Bend between fleurs-de-lis. Az. a bend
betw. six fleurs-de-lis or. Hampton, New-
ton, Mon., and East Harptree.
Gu. a bend. az. betw. six fleurs-de-lis or.
Hampton.
Gu. a bend betw. three fleurs-de-lis arg.
Cantelow or Hart.

Bend between heads. Arg. a bend gu. betw.
three dragons' heads erased sa. Pederton.
Sa. a bend raguly betw. two unicorns' heads
erased or. Pierce or Peirce.

Bend between fountains. Sa. a bend or
between six fountains prop. Stourton.

Bend between mullets. Sa a bend between
six mullets arg. Inckell.

Bend between plates. Sa. a bend or betw.
six plates. Stourton.

Bend between . . . and in chief. ( ) a
bend betw. six balls on a chief 2 . . . . .
Brenne or Brene.

Two bends. Two bend couped. Lychefield.
Gu. two bends wavy erm. Brewer ?
Gu. two bends wavy or. Brewer.
Or two bends engr. sa. Blathwaite, of Dyr-
ham.

Two bends and in chief. Gu. two bends
wavy or a chief vaire. Brewer.

Between two bends. Sa. between two bends
six leopards heads cab. or.

On a bend. Annulets. Arg. on a bend sa.
three annulets or. St. Lo. or St. Loe.

On a bend. Birds. Arg. on a bend sa. three
eagles displ. or. Ernele.
Gu. on a bend three martlets az. Collins.

On a bend. Crosses. Or on a bend engr. gu.
three cross-crosslets fitchée or. Webb.

On a bend. Escallops. Gu. on a bend arg.
three escallops sa. Knoyle.

On a bend. Fer-de-moulins. Or on a bend
gu. three fer-de-moulins pierced arg. Specot.

On a bend. Fish. Arg. on a bend az. three
whitings (of the field ?) Hewish.

On a bend. Flowers. Arg. on a bend sa three
fleurs-de-lis of the field. Bradford. Holt.
Arg. on a bend dauncettée sa cotised az. bezantée three fleurs-de-lis of the field. Cuffe.
Arg. on a bend engr. sa. three roses of the
field in sinister chief an anchor of the
second. Cary of Putney.
Gu. on a bend arg. three trefoils slipped vert.
Harvey.

On a bend. Heads. Arg. on a bend cotised
sa. three leopards faces or. Kingston.
Arg. on a bend, wavy cotised gu. within a
bord. bezantée three lions' heads erased of
the first. Coker.
Arg. on a bend sa. three lions' heads erased
of the field crowned or. Wrothe (modern).
Arg. on a bend az. three boars' heads of the
first. Brokesby.
Erm. on a bend (cotised ?) sa. three boars'
heads or. Bowerman.

On a bend. Hearts. Vert on a bend engr. arg.
three body-hearts gu. Tooker.

On a bend Helmets. Arg. on a bend sa.
three close helmets or. Compton.

On a bend. Horseshoe. Erm. on a bend sa.
two arms prop. wresting a horseshoe or.
Borlase.

On a bend. Mullets. Arg. on a bend gu.
three mullets or. Bampfield.
Or on a bend gu. three mullets arg. Bamp-
fylde.
Or on a bend vert three mullets of the first.
Somerset.
Vert on a bend arg. three mullets gu. de
Valletort.

On a bend. Roundels. Arg. on a bend
dauncettée or double cotised az. bezanty
three fleurs-de-lis or. Cuffe, of Ilchester.
Arg. on a bend gu. five plates. Chamberlain.
Erm. on a bend sa. three plates. Cutts.
Erm. on a bend sa. three bezants. St. Albon
or St. Albyn, of Alfoxdon.
Erm. on a bend gu. three bezants. Fulcher.
( ) on a bend three roundels ( ). Pontington.

On a bend between. Arg. on a bend betw.
two lions ramp. sa. three escallops of the
first. Clarke. Norton, of Abbot's Leigh.
Az. on a bend betw. two demi-lions ramp.
erased or three lozenges vaire gu. and arg.
Goodden.
Sa. on a bend arg. betw. six falcons three
Catherine wheels or.
Arg. on a bend sa. betw. six cross-crosslets
fitchée gu. three croziers or. Wear.
Arg. on a bend cotised betw. two lions ramp.
sa. three escallops or. Norton, of Abbot's
Leigh.

On a bend between—*continued.*
Arg. on a bend gu. betw. three pellets as many swans of the first. Clarke.

On a bend within a bordure. Arg. on a bend gu. three leopards' heads or within a bordure engr. sa. Coker.

Arg. three torteaux in bend betw. two bendlets gu. all within a bord. of the last. Heywood.

Three bends. Arg. three bends gu. within a bord. sa. charged with ten bezants. Whalesborough.

Az. (Arg?) three bends embatt. sa. de Castello (Bp. 1504-18.)

Gu. three bends or on a chief per fesse erm. and arg. three mullets sa. Draper.

Or three bends az. within a bord. engr. gu. Newborough.

Bendy. Bendy of six arg. and gu. on a chief sa a bar indented or. Wittewronge.

Bendy arg. and gu. Talbot.

Bendy az. and arg. Columbers.

Bezants. Gu. a bezant betw. three demi-lions ramp. arg. Bennett.

Gu. three bezants. Hydon.

Gu. three bezants in pale. Radington.

Gu. ten bezants in pile. Zouch.

Ten bezants a canton erm. Zouch.

Billets. Az. ten billets or four, three, two, one, on a chief of the second a demi-lion ramp. iss. sa. Dormer.

Sa. billety arg. a cross flory of the last. Norris.

Bird. A dove sitting on a bush. de Columbers (antient).

Arg. an eagle rising or. Cantlow (Prior).

Arg. an eagle displ. vert. Monthermer.

Az. an eagle with two necks displ. or. Lyde.

Erm. an eagle displ. gu. Browne.

Or an eagle displ. vert armed gu. Monthermer.

Or an eagle displ. sa. Weston.

Sa. an eagle displ. with two necks arg. Godolphin.

Vert an eagle displ. or. Camville.

A cherub standing on an imperial crown with wings displ. under the crown on a scroll "Defendamas." Taunton (original seal).

An eagle displ. prop. charged on the breast with a cresc. or. Rodney (crest).

Erm. an eagle displ. sa. armed gu. on a chief gu. a ducal coronet betw. two crosses pattée arg. Vansittart.

Gu. an eagle displ. betw. three fleurs-de-lis arg. Godolphin.

Three birds. Or three eagles displ. gu. Rodney.

( ) three herons ( ). de Heyron or Herun, of Long Ashton.

Per bend rompu arg. and sa. six martlets counterch. Allen.

Az. three swans arg. Cary, of Gotten.

Four birds. ( ) four martlets ( ). Luttrell, of East Quantockshead?

Six birds. Sa. six martlets arg. (an empaled coat on same tomb has five). Arundel.

Eight birds. Gu. eight martlets in an orle arg. Forest.

( ) parrots ( ). Fromund (Abbot of Glastonbury).

Candlestick. Arg. a pillar (candlestick?) betw. two human heads respecting or.

Canton. Arg. a Canton sa. Sutton.

Erm. on a canton dexter gu. a mullet sa. Bassett.

Erm. on a canton sa. an estoile of five points arg. (a cresc. arg.) de Strode or Strode.

Gu bezantée a canton erm. Zouch.

Or on a canton sa. a lion's head erased of the first. Bull.

Castle. Arg. three towers triple-towered sa. Haviland.

Or a tower triple-towered betw. three battle-axes sa. Hext.

Gu. on the sinister side on a mount a castle with two towers domed on each a pennon all arg. on the dexter base barry wavy of six arg. and az. a ship with three masts sailing from behind the castle or the fore and main-masts sa. with two sails on each in sight of the second. Bristol (City of).

Gu. a castle surmounted by two others placed pyramidically and embatt. standing on a gothic bridge with water all prop. underneath on each side the first castle a domed tower surmounted with a ball and the gate in the centre portcullised in chief on the dexter side an estoile and on the sin. a fleur-de-lis both or. Bridgwater, Borough of.

An embatt. and crenellated tower (antient) portcullis (modern). Langport, Borough of.

A castle triple-towered crenellated and embatt. in base a fleur-de-lis between two peococks respecting each other. Taunton, Borough of.

Gu. a portcullis crowned or. Newman, of N. and S. Cadbury.

Checky. Checky arg. and sa. St. Barbe.

Checky or and gu. Turberville.

Chevron. Arg. a chev. engr. sa. Holbeach.

Arg. a chev. sa. over all a label with three points gu. Prideaux.

Gu. a chev. arg. Berkeley, Earl (antient).

Lozengy or and az. a chev. gu. de Gorges, temp. Ed. III. (assumed from Moreville).

Chevron within a bordure. Or a chev. gu. within a bord. sa. Stafford.

Chevron and in chief. Arg. a chev. sa. on a chief gu. three mullets of the field. Towell.

Az. a chev. arg. in chief two mullets or in base a dexter gauntlet fesseways of the second holding in pale a mace or. Macie.

Chevron and in chief—*continued.*

Gu. a chev. or in chief two bezants in base a griffin's head erased of the second. Blanchard.

Chevron between anchors. Sa. a chev. betw. three anchors arg. Holder.

Chevron between annulets. Arg. a chev. sa. betw. three annulets gu. Secroft.

Arg. a chev. engr. sa. betw. three pellets voided. Greting or Secroft.

Vert a chev. or betw. three annulets arg. Minifie.

Chevron between arrows. Az. a chev. betw. three sheaves of five arrows or flighted arg. pheoned and banded gu. Brickdale.

Chevron between beasts. Arg. a chev. betw. three bucks trippant sa. Rogers, of Cannington.

Arg. a chev. betw. three bulls pass sa. attired or. Turney.

Arg. a chev. vert betw. three bulls pass. gu. Bragge.

Or a chev. betw. three bulls statant sa. attired arg. Rodbard.

Or a chev. betw. three bulls pass. sa. Bragge, of Hatfield-Peverel, Essex.

Sa. a chev. engr. betw. three goats statant arg. Trethewy, of Treneage, Cornwall, and Dicheat, Som.

Arg. a chev. sa. betw. three lions dorm. coward gu. Lyons, of Long Ashton.

Az. a chev. erm. betw. three lions ramp. arg. Wolmington, Dorset.

Sa. a chev. between three lions ramp arg. Hales of Mychurch, Som.

Vert a chev. betw. three lions ramp. or. Wolmerston.

Arg. a chev. betw. three rams sa. Sydenham, of Langford.

Chevron between billets. Arg. a chev. betw. three billets gu. Kelly.

Chevron between birds. Arg. a chev. engr. between three birds (martlets) sa. de Bykele.

A chev. engr. betw. three birds. de Bytal.

Arg. a chev. gu. betw. three coots sa. Southcott.

Az. a chev. between three cranes or. Browne.

Arg. a chev. betw. three ducks sa. collared gu. Hymerford.

Or a chev. vert betw. three eaglets ( ). de Inge.

Or a chev. betw. three eagles displ. vert. Blewet.

Sa. a chev. betw. three eagles displ. arg. on a chief of the first three boars pass. sa. Raymond.

A chev. betw. three eagles displ. on a chief a rose betw. two lozenges over all a mitre and crozier. Bird (Prior).

Chevron between birds—*continued.*

Az. a chev. betw. three falcons close arg. Jepp, of Sutton Court, Som.

Arg. a chev. betw. three lapwings sa. Twyniho.

Arg. a chev. betw. three martlets sa. Sanford.

Arg. a chev. engr. betw. three martlets sa. Brickley or Bickley, of Rendy Oak, Par.

Gu. a chev. betw. three swans arg. Mitchell or Michel, of Garmstreet, co. Som.

Gu. a chev. betw. three swans arg. Lyte, of Lytes-Cary.

Sa. a chev. or betw. three swans with wings erect arg armed gu. Swan.

Chevron between buckles. Arg. a chev. betw. three round buckles gu. Fitzwalter.

Gu. (or sa.) a chev. betw. three round buckles or. Malet, of Sutton Mallet.

Chevron between bugle horns. Arg. a chev. betw. three bugle horns sa. Russell, of Fairfield, adopted 23 Ed. III, by Ralph de Vernai.

Arg. a chev. vert betw. three bugle horns sa. Foster.

( ) a chev. betw. three bugle-horns ( ). de Woky.

Chevron between clarions. Gu. a chev. arg. betw. three clarions or horsemens' rest or. Arthur.

Chevron between crescents. Az. a chev. betw. three cres. or. Berkerolles.

Chevron between crosses. Arg a. chev. betw. a cross pattée gu. in chief and a heart of the last in base. Methen.

Arg. a chev. gu. betw. three crosses moline sa. Wike or Wyke.

Arg. a chev. engr. az betw. three crosses gu. Gilbert.

Arg. a chev. betw. three cross-crosslets sa. Southworth.

Az. a chev. betw. three crosses flory or. de Fluri.

Gu. a chev. betw. three cross-crosslets arg. Southey.

Gu. a chev. or betw. three crosses pattée arg. Barclay,

Gu. a chev. erm. betw. three crosses calvary arg. Coopey.

Sa. a chev. betw. three cross-crosslets or. Southby.

Arg. a chev. gu. betw. nine cross-crosslets sa. Proctor.

Gu. a chev. betw. ten crosses pattée or formée arg. Berkeley (from 1189).

Gu. a chev. erm. betw. ten crosses pattée arg. Berkeley, of Stratton.

( ) a chev. betw. ten cross-crosslets. Greyndor.

Chevron between ermine spots. Arg. a chev. betw. three ermine-spots sa. Jerard ?

Chevron between escallops. Arg. a chev. betw. three escallops sa. Tregarthin.

Sa. a chev. erm. betw. three escallops arg. Cheddar.

( ) a chev. erm. betw. three escallops the point charged with a cresc. Seward.

Sa. a chev. engr. betw. three escallops arg. Farewell.

Chevron between estoiles. Arg. a chev. betw. three estoiles sa. Mordaunt.

Gu. a chev. arg. betw. three estoiles or. Pinsent.

Chevron between fishes. Erm. a chev. betw. three fishes haurient arg. Way or Kinge.

( ) a chev. erm. betw. three fishes haurient az. (arg.) Cator or Ord.

Sa. a chev. betw. three dolphins arg. Leversege.

Sa. a chev. betw three dolphins embowed arg. on a chief gu. a leopard's head jessant de lis or. Leversedge.

Sa. a chev. betw. three dolphins embatt. naiant arg. a chief or. Cobbe.

Chevron between fleurs-de-lis. Arg. a chev. betw. three fleurs-de-lis az. Walton or Welsteed.

Gu a chev. betw. three fleurs-de-lis or. Brown.

Gu. a chev. betw. three fleurs-de-lis vert.

Chevron between flowers. Gu a chev. betw. ten cinquefoils arg. Berkeley, of Wymondham.

Arg. a chev. betw. three roses gu. seeded and barbed vert. Phelips, of Montacute.

Arg. a chev. sa. betw. two roses gu. in chief and a talbot pass. of the last in base. Pope.

Arg. a chev. the upper part engr. betw. three roses gu. Gilbert.

Gu. a chev. betw. three roses arg. Wadham.

Sa. a chev. betw. three roses arg. Cornish.

Arg. a chev. sa. betw. three sprigs vert. Baldwin.

Az. a chev. sa. betw. three trefoils vert. Beckford.

Chevron between fruit. Az. a chev. arg. betw. three pears or. Orchard.

Gu. a chev. or betw. three pears prop. Abbot (Archbp.)

Chevron between garbs. Arg. a chev. az. betw. three garbs or (or sa.) Blake.

( ) a chev. betw. three garbs or. Hatton ?

Chevron between gauntlets. Az. a chev. arg. betw. three gauntlets or. Conway.

Sa. a chev. erm. betw. three gauntlets arg. Robinson.

Chevron between hanks. Az. a chev. betw. three hanks of cotton yarn arg. Cotton.

Chevron between heads (beasts). Arg a chev. betw. three bears' heads couped sa. Ley (Earl of Marlborough).

Arg. a chev. betw. three bears' heads sa. muzzled or. Stead.

Chevron between heads (beasts)—*continued*

Arg. a chev. gu. betw. three boars' heads couped sa. Wroughton ?

Arg. a chev. betw. three bucks' heads cab. sa. Parker.

Az. a chev. betw. three stags' heads cab. or. Chipleigh.

Sa. a chev. per pale arg. and or betw. three bulls' heads cab. arg. armed or. Clavelshey.

Vert a chev. betw. three wolves' heads erased arg. Jones, of Langford Court.

Gu. a chev. engr. betw. three leopards' heads or. Periam.

Sa. a chev. erm. betw. three leopards' heads or. Godwyn.

Arg. a chev. betw. three lions' heads erased gu. Luccombe.

Az. a chev. betw. three lions' heads erased or. Wyndham.

Chevron between heads (birds). Gu. a chev. engr. erm. betw. three cranes' heads erased arg. Brown.

Az. a chev. betw. three kites' heads erased or. Keyt.

Gu. a chev. voided (? two chevs.) arg. betw. three swans' heads erased prop. Brightmore.

Arg. a chev. erm. betw. three moors' heads prop. Gilbert.

Arg. a chev. or betw. three griffins' heads erased sa. in chief a mullet for dist. Skinner.

Sa. a chev. or betw. three spears' heads arg. Rice.

Chevron between leaves. Arg. a chev. az. betw. three oak-leaves vert each charged with an acorn or. Smythes, of Wrington.

Gu. a chev. erm betw. three nettle leaves vert. Malherbe.

Chevron between mullets. Arg. a chev. sa. between three mullets gu. pierced or. Samborne.

Arg. a chev. betw. three mullets gu. Francis.

Arg. a chev. sa. betw. three mullets gu. a cresc. for dist. Sherwood.

Az. a chev. arg. betw. three mullets or. Hilliard.

Az. a chev. betw. three mullets or. Cely.

Chevron between orles. Arg. a chev. betw. three orles or. Hall.

Chevron between pheons. Arg. a chev. gu. betw. three pheons sa. Walsh.

Chevron between bezants. Arg. a chev. or betw. three bezants on a chief erm. three cinquefoils gu. Jennings.

Gu. a chev. arg. betw. nine bezants. Zouch.

On a chevron. Beasts. Gu. on a chev. or three lions ramp. sa. Cobham, of Kent; Brooke, of Lower Court, Long Ashton.

On a chevron. Birds. Arg. on a chev. gu. three martlets of the field on a chief of the second a chamber-piece or. Coward.

On a chevron. Birds—*continued.*

Erm. on a chev. sa. three martlets arg. Witty.

Or on a chev. gu. three martlets arg. Chesildon.

Gu. on a chev. or three eagles displ. sa. Cobham.

On a chevron. Crosses. ( ) on a chev. three crosses moline ( ). Hadley?

On a chevron. Escallops. Arg. on a chev. sa. three escallops of the first. Ballowe.

Arg. on a chev. gu. three escallops ( ). Jernyngham?

On a chevron. Estoiles. Gu. on a chev. arg. three estoiles sa. Carr, of Bristol.

On a chevron. Flowers. Arg. on a chev. gu. three fleurs-de-lis or. Pever.

Arg. on a chev. sa. three quatrefoils or. Eyre.

Gu. on a chev. sa. three roses az. Gilbert, of Corton Dinham.

On a chevron. Garbs. Arg. on a chev. az. three garbs or. Newton, of Harptree, Court de Wyck (Yatton), etc.

On a chevron. Heads. Erm. on a chev. az. three foxes' heads erased or on a canton of the second a fleur-de-lis of the last. Fox, Earl of Ilchester.

Erm. on a chev. az. three bucks heads cabossed or. Servington.

On a chevron. Mitre. Or on a chevron arg ? a mitre of the first. Stafford (Bishop).

On a chevron. Mullets. Arg. on a chev. az. three mullets of the first. Witty.

On a chevron. Sprigs. Sa. on a chev. arg. three sprigs of broom prop. Brome.

On a chevron between beasts. Sa. on a chev. betw. three horses pass. arg. three annulets sa. Sweeting.

Sa. on a chev. engr. arg. betw. three lions ramp. or as many crosses pattée gu. Healy.

On a chevron between birds. Arg. on a chev. sa. betw. three cranes az. as many escallops or. Brown or Browne.

( ) on a chev. betw. three martlets ( ) as many mullets ( ).

( ) on a chev. betw. three martlets five bezants. Collins?

On a chevron between crescents. Arg. on a chev. gu. betw. three cresc. or as many stags' heads of the same cab. Parker?

On a chevron between estoiles. Arg. on a chev. engr. sa. betw. three estoiles gu. as many stags' heads cab. of the second (first?) Stiff.

Sa. on a chev. or betw. three estoiles of the second as many crosses pattée fitchée gu. Laud, Bishop.

On a chevron between flowers. Arg. on a chev. embatt. sa. betw. three cinquefoils gu. as many bezants. Edgell.

Gu. on a chev. or betw. three cinquefoils (trefoils) arg. two (as many?) leopards' faces gu. (sa.) Smith.

On a chevron between flowers—*continued.*

Gu. on a chev. betw. three cinquefoils arg. as many leopards' faces sa. Smyth, of Long Ashton.

Sa. on a chev. betw. three leaves or a mullet of the field. Weston.

Arg. on a chev. sa. betw. three trefoils of the second three mullets or. Holsworthy.

On a chevron between mullets. Arg. on a chev. betw. three mullets gu. as many lions' paws erased or. Parham.

Arg. on a chev. sa. betw. three egresses each charged with a martlet of the first three mascles or. Pratt.

On a chevron between pistols. Sa. on a chev. betw. three pistols or as many roses gu. Hopkins.

Per chevron. Per chev. arg. and gu. a cresc. counterch. a canton of the second. Chapman.

Per chev. embatt. az. and arg. in chief three crosses fitchée or in base a lion currant sa crowned or. Smith, of Bristol.

Per chev. sa and or in chief two eagles displ. of the last. Shute.

Per chev. az. and arg. in chief two falcons volant or. Stephens.

Two chevrons. Arg. two chev. gu. on a canton of the second an escallop or. Pope.

Az. two chevronels betw. three martlets arg. Hunt.

Arg. two chev. gu a label of three points vert. St. Maur, of Castle Cary.

Arg. two chevronels gu. and sa. betw. three roses prop. Jeane.

Arg. two chev. sa. betw. three roses gu. Wickham.

Arg. two chev. sa. betw. three roses gu. seeded or. Drew (Wickham?)

Three chevrons. Az. three chev. or in chief two roses arg. Trent.

( ) three chev. ( ). de Elworthe.

Erm. three chev. gu. Selfe.

Four chevrons. Or four chev. gu. Every. Fewtrell.

Chief. Arg. a chief indented vert surmounted by a bend gu. Nevile.

Or a chief dauncettée gu. Dyer.

Checquy or and gu. a chief vaire. Chichester.

Arg. a chief indented three mullets pierced. (Arg. a fesse engr. gu. betw. three mullets sa.) de Brattone.

Arg. in chief three bucks' heads cab. sa. (prop?). de Bosco or Hartgill.

Arg. in chief three cocks' heads erased gu. in base a spur leathered prop. Cox.

Gu. (az.) in chief on the dexter side a castle arg. on the sinister a lion ramp. erm. in base the same counterch. Skrine.

Erm. in chief a lion pass. gu. Hall.

( ) in chief two mullets ( ). St. John.

Chief—*continued.*

In chief a lion couch. (pass.) in base three wolves' heads erased. Prater.

On a chief. Arg. on a chief gu. two bucks' heads cab. or. Popham.

Arg. on a chief or a fleur-de-lis sa. Rogers.

Arg. on a chief indented gu. three crosses pattée of the first. de Perceval.

Arg. on a chief indented gu. three cross-croslets or. Otterbourne.

Gu. on a chief arg. two mullets sa. Bacon.

Gutté de sang on a chief az. three ducal coronets or. Kingston.

Or on a chief sa. three martlets of the first. Worgan.

Or on a chief gu. three lions ramp. of the first. Lisle.

Or on a chief az. three lions ramp. of the first. Lisley.

Sa. on a chief or three lozenges gu. Moulins.

Vert on a chief sa. three martlets or. (Sa. on a chief az. three martlets or). Wray?

Cinquefoils. Arg. three cinquefoils gu. Southwell.

Arg. three cinquefoils per pale az. and gu. Choke, of Long Ashton.

Sa. a cinquefoil arg. in chief three talbots' heads erased or. Bower, of Wells.

Crescent. Az. a cresc. arg. within an orle of mullets pierced or. Burton.

In a cresc. an estoile of sixteen points. Ivelchester or Ilchester Borough.

Three crescents. Erm. three cresc. gu. Kenn.

Gu. three cresc. each griping a cross fichée or. Pinney, of Bettiscombe.

Gu. three cresc. or. Damarel, of Devon.

Three cresc. betw. nine billets (gu. billettée and three cresc. or). Colmer or Colmore.

Or three cresc. sa. on a canton of the second a ducal crown of the first. Hodges.

Cross. Arg. a cross moline gu. Percehaye.

Arg. a cross gu. St. George, of England.

Arg. a cross flory gu. Harptree.

Arg. a cross moline gu. in the dexter chief a chess-rook. Percehaye.

Arg. a cross of three spells of a sieve or riddle sa. Skirlaw?

Arg. a cross engr. sa. on the first quarter an eagle displ. gu. Draycot.

Arg. a cross cercelée voided gu. de Punchardon.

Arg. a cross az.

( ) a cross wavy ( ).

Az. a St. Andrew's cross or salt. per salt. quarterly quartered or and arg. Wells, See of.

Az. a cross moline or. Brune.

Arg. (or?) a cross vert. Hussey.

Gu a cross lozengy arg. Stawel.

Gu a cross engr. (or?) Leigh, of Stoneleigh.

Cross—*continued.*

Gu. a cross arg. St. John of Jerusalem.

Gu. a cross flory vaire. Aubemarle.

Gu. a cross moline arg. Ufford.

Or a cross engr. sa. Mohun and Brewton or Bruton Priory.

Or a cross quarterly counterch. gu. and sa. in the chief dexter quarter an eagle displ. of the third. Webb.

Sa. a cross engr. or. Willoughby.

Sa. a cross moline arg. Upton.

Vert a cross botonnée arg. on a canton of the last the Virgin and Child—*or* on the dexter chief quarter the Virgin Mary holding the Infant in her dexter arm and in the sinister a sceptre or in each of the other quarters a ducal crown of the last. Abbey of Glastonbury.

Cross between. A cross betw. two cups. Beer, Abbot. (Badge or device).

A cross coupee (or flory) betw. four martlets. Bird.

( ) a cross betw. four sheldrakes ( ). Baudrip.

Arg. a cross gu. betw. four choughs sa.

Arg. a cross betw. four eagles displ. gu. Strachey, of Sutton Court.

Arg. a cross betw. four mullets gu. Banbury.

Az. a cross flory or betw. four estoiles gu. Sterling.

Az. a cross patonce betw. five martlets or. Edward the Confessor.

Sa. a cross betw. four leopards' heads cab. or. Boulting.

On a cross. Arg. on a cross sa. a leopard's head or. Bridges.

Erm. on a cross quarter pierced arg. four fer de moulins sa. Turnor.

Or on a cross sa. five lions ramp. of the first. Wale.

Sa. on a cross engr. or five pellets all within a bord. engr. of the second. Grevile, Earl of Warwick.

Three crosses. Gu. three crosses bottonnée arg. on a chief az. two escallops or. Payne, of Hutton.

Gu. three crosses recercele or a chief vaire erm. and erms. Verney (borne by Lord Willoughby de Broke).

Az. three taus two and one or. Crosse.

Six crosses. ( ) six cross-croslets ( ) de Raleigh (Antient).

Seven or more crosses. Az. betw. seven cross-croslets fichée three, one, two, one arg. three mullets two and one or. Somerville.

Or semée of cross-croslets a lion ramp. az. Lovel.

Gu. semée of cross-croslets or. Ferneland or Fernland?

Gu. crusuly fichée arg. a lion ramp. of the last. Warre.

Crozier. Az. a crozier in bend dexter arg. betw. two keys endorsed and interlaced in bend sinister or. (For Wells Deanery, but incorrect).

Cups. ( ) three cups. Siderfin.

Escallops. Two escallops in chief. Spilsbury ?

( ) three escallops ( ). de Avenant.

Arg. (or az.) three escallops or. Malet. Deaudons, of Devon.

Az. three escallops in pale or. Symes.

Gu. three escallops arg. Dacre.

Gu. three escallops or ? de Erleigh or Erle. Antient). Gu. three escallops within a bord. engr. arg. (Modern).

Gu. three escallops in bend arg. on a chief of the second a martlet sa. Stalling, of Ken.

Or three escallops gu. De la Hay ?

Sa. three escallops in pale arg. Bisse, of Spargrove and Westcombe.

Escutcheons. Three escutcheons charged with as many cinquefoils. Vowell.

Fesse. Arg. a fesse cotised sa. Chetle.

Checky arg. and sa. a fesse gu. Acland, of Columb John, co. Devon.

Erm. a fesse gu. Bitton or Button.

Erm a fesse sa. Isley.

Gu. a fesse lozengy arg. (four fusils in fesse). Daubeny.

Gu. a fesse lozengy erm. Dynham.

Or a fesse checky arg. and az. Stewart.

( ) a fesse ( ) Brito.

Or a fesse az. over all a salt. gu. charged with five bezants. Ash.

Checky or and gu. over all on a fesse az. three bezants. Cudham ?

Gu. a fesse lozengy arg. each lozenge charged with an escallop sa. de Cheney.

Fess within bordure. Arg. a fesse indented paly vert. and sa. cotised of the first within a bord. engr. of the second in chief. a mullet sa. Hody.

Fesse and in chief. Gu. a fesse sa. in chief two eagles displ. Saxey.

( ) a fesse bendy counter-bendy in chief three fleurs-de-lis ( ). Tilly, of West Harptree.

Arg. a fesse lozengy or and az. in chief three mascles of the third a bordure of the last bezantée. Burgess.

Per fesse. Per fesse arg. and az. counterch. in the chief dexter quarter a lion pass. or. Crofts.

Per fesse or and arg. over all a lion ramp. az. Yerbury.

Per fesse sa. and arg. a lion ramp. counterch. Edwards.

Per fesse crenellée gu. and arg. a pale and three demi-lions ramp. counterch. crowned or. Bennet.

Per fesse arg. and gu. a cross moline betw. four mullets counterch. Richmond or Colman.

Per fesse—*continued.*

Per fesse emb. az. and gu. the base masoned crenellée sa. in chief of the first two bars wavy arg. over all in pale a sword of the last hilted and pomelled or on the blade a key. Bath, City of.

Per fesse or and gu. within a bord. engr. a lion ramp counterch. Middleton.

Per fesse or. and gu. a demi-rose and a demi-sun conjoined counterch. of the field issuant from the rose an eagle displ. with two heads sa. Knight.

Per fesse indented or and gu. (Or a chev. indented gu. ?) Dyer.

Per fesse gu. and arg. a canton sinister of the field. Widville.

Per fesse az. and or a pale counterch. three hawks with wings endorsed of the last. Locke.

Per fesse arg. and vert. a tree prop. issuant from the fesse line in base three wells two and one masoned gu. Wells, City of.

Quarterly per fesse indented arg. and az. Acton.

Quarterly per fesse indented arg. and az. in the first quarter a mullet gu. Acton.

On a fesse betw. beasts. Gu. on a fesse wavy betw. three lions pass. arg. as many crosses pattée of the first. Davidge.

On a fesse between billets. Or on a fesse dauncettée betw. three billets sa. (az.) each charged with a lion ramp. guard. of the first three bezants. Rolle.

On a fesse between birds. Or on a fesse sa. betw. as many ravens prop. three plates. Biggs, of Worcestershire.

On a fesse between chess-rooks. Arg. on a fesse between three chess-rooks sa. as many mullets of the field. Marshall.

On a fesse between chevrons. Arg. on a fesse gu. betw. two chev. erm. three roses (leopards' heads ?) of the first. Seward.

On a fesse between crosses. Arg. on a fesse gu. betw. three crosses pattée sa. as many martlets of the first. Cannon or Canon.

On a fesse between escallops. Or on a fesse sa. betw. three escallops az. five lozenges arg. Gay.

On a fesse between escutcheons. Arg. on a fesse wavy az. betw. three escutcheons gu. as many lozenges or. Latch.

On a fesse between flowers. Or on a fesse sa. betw. three cinquefoils vert a cross flory of the field. Moysey.

Az. on a fesse arg. betw. three roses or as many bugle-horns sa. Cottington.

On a fesse between heads. Arg. on a fesse az. a mitre with labels expanded or betw. three bucks' heads cab. gu. in chief and in base as many pheons sa. Beckington, Bishop.

On a fesse between heads—*continued.*

Arg. on a fesse engr. betw. three greyhounds' heads erased sa. collared or as many trefoils slipped of the last. Churchey or Churche.

Arg. on a fesse wavy betw. three talbots' heads erased az. three bezants. Houlton.

Or on a fesse engr. az. betwn. three horses' heads erased sa as many fleurs-de-lis of the first. Bayley.

Gu. on a fesse between three leopards' heads or as many fusils (fleur-de-lis) sa. Stillington.

On a fesse between pheons. Arg. on a fesse sa. betw. three pheons of the first two fleurs-de-lis gu. (? Arg. on a fesse sa. betw. three fleurs-de-lis gu. two pheons az.) Stillingfleet or Thwaites?

On a fesse between roundels. ( ) on a fesse sa. betw. three bezants three lozenges gu. Pratt.

On a fesse. Birds. Erm. on a fesse gu. three martlets or. Pavy.

On a fesse. Crescents. Arg. on a fess cotised sa. three cresc. or. Bristow.

On a fesse. Crosses. Arg. on a fesse sa. three cross-croslets fitches or.

On a fesse. Escallops. Gu. on a fesse or three escallops sa. Venner.

On a fesse. Heads. Arg. on a fesse nebulée sa. three hare's heads couped or. Harewell.

Arg. on a fesse gu. three hawks' head erased of the first. Baber.

On a fesse. Mascles. Checquy or and arg. (az.) on a fesse erm. (sa.) three mascles or. Capell.

On a fesse. Roundels. Arg. on a fesse gu. three bezants. Jenyngs.

Or on a fesse sa. three plates. Bramston, Essex.

Fesse between annulets. Arg. a fesse erm. betw. three annulets gu. Portman.

Fesse between beasts. Arg. a fesse betw. three boars sa. Hadeswell or Hyndfield.

Sa a fesse cotised or betw. three conies sejant arg. Coney.

Gu. a fesse erm. (vaire) betw. three water spaniels arg. Riggs.

Az. a fesse dauncettée arg. betw. three lions pass. gard. of the second. Fisher.

Sa. a fesse or betw. three squirrels sejant arg. cracking nuts or. Harvey, of Brockley.

Fesse between billets. Arg. a fesse betw. six billets gu. Allworth, Devon.

Fesse between birds. Az. a fesse engr. erm. betw. three eagles displ. or. Crooke.

Sa. a fesse dauncettée arg. betw. three eagles displ. or. Wyatt.

Arg. a fesse betw. three martlets sa. Berkeley, of Dursley and Eldresfield.

Fesse between birds—*continued.*

Gu. a fesse or betw. six martlets three, two, and one of the second. Beauchamp.

Sa. a fesse cotised betw. three martlets or. Smith, of Sidling, Dorset.

Vert a fesse or betw. three swans arg. Swan.

Fesse between buckles. Arg. a fesse betw. three round buckles gu. Bacon.

Fesse between crosses. Gu. a fesse betw. three cross-crosslets fitchée or. Gore, of Mynchin Barrow.

Fesse between escallops. Gu. a fesse or betw. three (six ?) escallops arg. Fitzwilliam.

Fesse between flowers. Arg. a fesse erm. betw. three roses gu. Pewtrell.

Arg. a fesse counter-embatt. betw. six fleurs-de-lis sa. three and three. Taylor.

Az. a fesse sa. betw. two fleurs-de-lis or. Ewens, of Wincanton.

Gu. a fesse betw. three fleurs-de-lis or. Goodhind.

Arg. a fesse engr. sa. betw. twelve holly leaves vert four, four, and four arranged in quadrangles. Bubwith, Bishop.

Fesse between garbs. Arg. a fesse gu. betw. three garbs sa. Tyndale.

Fesse between heads. Az. a fesse betw. three leopards' heads or. Poole.

Arg. a fesse gu. betw. three wolves' heads erased az. Miller.

Az. a fesse betw. three griffins' heads erased arg. Bradford.

( ) a fesse az. betw. four unicorns' heads three in chief and one in base. Inyn ?

Fesse between mullets. Arg. a fesse betw. two mullets in chief and a cresc. in base ( ). Carse, Scotland.

Az. a fesse emb. betw. six mullets of eight points or. Tryon.

Gu. a fesse betw. six mullets arg. Ashburnham.

Sa. a fesse checquy or and az. betw. three bezants. Pitt (Earl of Chatham).

Arg. a fesse betw. three torteaux. Eschallers ?

Or (arg ?) a fesse raguly gu. betw. three torteaux two and one. Gracedieu.

Fish. Az. a dolphin embowed arg. Fitz James.

Az. a dolphin naiant or on a chief of the second two salts. gu. Frankland.

Sa. a dolphin embowed betw. three crosses botonée or. James.

Six fishes. Sa. six fishes haur, three, two and one arg. Fishacre.

Fleur-de-lis. Arg. a fleur-de-lis gu. Walton.

Az. a fleur-de-lis arg. a canton of the last. Digby, Mansfield Woodhouse, Notts.

Or a fleur-de-lis az. Portman.

( ) a fleur-de-lis ( ). Flower.

Fleur-de-lis—*continued*.

( ) A fleur-de-lis surmounted with a file of three points ( ). Braunche or Branch (antient). Gu. a leopard's head jessant de lis or (modern). (Adopted by Leversedge).

Az. a fleur-de-lis or a chief gu. (per fess gu. and az. three fleurs-de-lis or). Pauncefoot.

Three fleur-de-lis. Arg. three fleurs-de-lis gu. a label of three points az. Scobell.

Az. three fleur-de-lis or. Giffard.

Az. a cresc. betw. three fleurs-de-lis or. de Fleuri.

Or three fleurs-de-lis two and one vert. Portman.

Six fleur-de-lis. Or six fleurs-de-lis az. or sa. Mortimer.

Az. semée of fleurs-de-lis a lion ramp. arg. Holland.

Az. semée of fleurs-de-lis or a lion ramp. arg. langued gu. Poole.

Flower . . . . a rose . . . . de Modiford or Modyford.

The Rose and Crown. Badge of Henry VIII.

Or a rose gu. on a chief az. a lion cour. arg. Bave.

Three flowers. Arg. three roses gu. seeded or barbed vert a chief of the second. Sparrow, Flax Bourton.

Az. three roses two and one or. Bardolf.

Four flowers. Or betw. four roses az. a cross per pale and quarterly az. and gu. charged with five roses arg. (or). Langton, Bishop.

Fret. Sa. a fret arg. Harrington.

Sa. a fret or. Maltravers.

Or fretty gu. charged with fleurs-de-lis. Verdon.

Vert fretty or. Whitmore.

Az. a fret or on a chief arg. three leopards' heads gu. Jefferson.

Az. fretty or on a chief gu. a plate. St. Leger.

Fruit. Az. an annulet betw. three pears or. Orchard.

Gu. three pears arg. on a chief of the second a demi-lion iss. sa. Perrot.

Fusils. ( ) two fusils in chief. Moleyns or Molyns.

Arg. three fusils in fesse gu. Montacute or Montague.

Erm. three fusils in fesse sa. Sherborne.

Gu. three fusils in fesse arg. each charged with an escallop sa. Cheney.

Arg. within a bord. sa. three fusils in fesse gu. Montague.

Or four fusils in fesse az. over all a bend gu. Pennington.

Gambs. Arg. three gambs. couped sa. Gambon, of Devon.

Sa. three gambs arg. Maunsell or Mansell (modern).

Garbs. Az? a wheat sheaf or. Hungerford, badge of.

Garbs—*continued*.

Out of a Ducal Cor. a wheat. garb or betw. two sickles erect prop. Hungerford, crest of.

Erm. a garb az. on a canton of the second an annulet or. Gatchell.

Az. a garb or in chief a bloody hand dexter. Grosvenor.

Az. three garbs arg. a chief or. Peverel.

Gu. three garbs within a bord. engr. or. Kempe, Archbishop.

Gu. three garbs or (also within a bord. arg. charged with eight torteaux). Clement.

Gate. Gu. a gate or. Portnew?

Gauntlets. Az. three gauntlets or. Fane.

Sa. three gauntlets arg. Gunter.

Sa. three gauntlets or.

Or five falconer's gloves pendant prop. (misdescription?)

Guns. Gu. three guns in pale arg. Gunning.

Grapple-hooks. ( ) three grapple hooks ( ). de Reigni.

Gyrons. Tierce in girons arondi arg., or and gu.

Gyronny of six az. and arg. three parrots vert. Stocker.

Gyronny of eight erm. and gu. Campbell.

Gyronny or and erm. over all a tower triple turreted sa. Hooper.

Hands and arms. ( ) a hand clenched ( ). de Mansel or Maunsel (antient).

Dexter hand in a chaplet. St. Loe (Crest)?

Gu. a dexter arm habited with a maunch erm. the hand holding a fleur-de-lis or. Mohun, also Priory of Bruton or Brewton.

Head. Arg. a bull's head erased sa. Carslake, of Devon.

Arg. a bull's head cab. sa. Durston.

Az. a buck's head cab. arg. Legge.

Or a buck's head cab. gu. betw. horns a cross pattée of the second. Pokeswell.

Gu. a leopard's head jessant de lis or. Leversedge. (Adopted from Branch).

( ) a lion's head erased ( ) crowned ( ). Wrothe (antient).

A moor's head in a chaplet wreathed. More. (crest).

Head and in chief. A stag's head on a chief three roundels. Popham (antient).

Arg. on a chief gu. two bucks' heads cab. or. Popham (modern).

Three heads. Arg. three bears' heads erased sa. muzzled or. Langham.

Erm. three bears' heads couped sa. muzzled or. Simcocks.

Arg. three boars' (dragons) heads erased vert. Byam.

Arg. three boars' heads erased sa. Booth, of Chester.

Arg. three bulls' heads cab. sa. Bole. (Walrond?)

Three heads—*continued.*

Arg. three bulls' heads cab. sa. attired or. Walrond.

Gu. three bulls' heads cab. or. Bull.

Or three bulls' heads cab. gu. Bull.

Or three bulls' heads sa. armed and langued gu. Bull, of Midsomer Norton.

Arg. three bucks' heads cab. sa. Hartgill.

( ) three stags' heads ( ). Broughton, of Sandford.

Az. three horses' heads couped or bridled gu. Horsey.

Az. three leopards' heads cab. or.

Erm. three lions' heads jessant-de-lis az. Cantelupe ?

Arg. three blackamoors' heads prop. Canning.

Arg. three blackamoors' heads sa. Murison.

Arg. three wolves' heads erased prop. two and one. Methwin or Methuen.

Arg. three griffins' heads erased sa. langued gu. (sa. on a chev. betw. three griffins' heads erased arg. three stars gu.) Beale.

Three heads and in chief. Gu. three talbots' heads erased or on a chief arg. guttée de sang. a lion pass. sa. Whitchurch.

Gu. three tigers' heads erased arg. on a chief of the second a talbot sa.

Helmets. Sa. within a bord. arg. three close helmets of the last. Hollyday or Halliday.

Horns. Sa. a bugle-horn arg. Dodington (modern).

Arg. in base a bugle-horn strung in chief three yew-trees prop. Morse.

Arg. three bugle-horns sa. garnished or. Bellingham.

Sa. three bugle-horns arg. Dodington (antient).

Sa. three bugle-horns two and one arg. strung or. Dodington, co. Soml.

Sa. three bugle-horns stringed or garnished az. Thurston.

( ) three bugle-horns ( ) Horn, Bishop.

Keys. Az. a St. Peter's key double warded or. St. Peter (emblem).

Gu. a key and sword in salt. or (or arg. and or). Bath Abbey (St. Peter and St. Paul.)

Az. two keys in salt. or a squirrel sejant prop. (another) six keys and two squirrels. Walters.

Az. two keys endorsed in bend sin. the upper or the lower arg. enfiled with a sword in bend dext. of the last. Bath Abbey.

Or three keys gu. Clavile.

Leaves. Arg. three fern leaves vert. Vernai or Verney, of Fairfield, Cannington.

Leg. Gu. an armed leg couped at the thigh spurred or betw. two broken spears arg. Gilbert of Derbyshire.

Letter. A text K and a bell or (device). Cabell.

Lozenges. Az. three lozenges (Cronels or spear heads) arg. Steers.

Or three lozenges gu. Montague, of Cathanger.

Mallets. Arg. (az.) three mallets purp. (arg.) Malet.

Maunch. Gu. in a Maunch erm. a hand prop. holding erect a fleur-de-lis or or sometimes or a cross engr. sa. Mohun, also Brewton or Bruton, Monastery of.

Sa. within a bord. or a maunch arg. Wharton.

Monster. Dragon. Arg. a dragon erect sa. Dauney, Rhys ap Tyder or Rontons.

Monster. Griffin. Arg. a griffin ramp. (segreant) gu. winged az. Bottreaux.

Gu. a griffin segreant or. Davis (Rice-Davis, of Tickenham).

Gu. a griffin (lion ?) ramp. or debruised with a bend erm. Fitchet.

A griffin segreant (or ramp.) de Montacute.

Monster. Wivern. Arg. a wivern sa. Tilly, of Devon.

Gu. a wivern displ. arg. (charged on the breast with three spots of erm). Brent.

Gu. a wivern pass. sejant arg. Brent.

Gu. a wivern pass. arg. de Brent.

Three monsters. Arg. three unicorns pass. sa. Ragland.

Checky arg. and sa. three wiverns of the first.

Three mullets. Vert three mullets or pierced sa. Spurstow.

Three mullets between. Sa. three mullets betw. two bendlets or. Hippisley, of Emborough.

Four mullets. (Az.?) four mullets (or?). Amery.

Six mullets. Sa. six mullets arg. three, two, and one. Bonville.

Sa. six mullets or. Bonville.

Seven mullets. Az. seven (six ?) mullets or (within a bord. gabonated arg. and gu.) Walshe.

Pale between. Vert a pale arg. betw. two griffins segreant or. Adams.

On a pale. Arg. on a pale sa. an eagle displ. of the first. Tufton.

Pale within a bordure. Arg. a pale fusilly gu. within a bord. az. crusilly fitchée or. Holloway.

Per pale. Per pale arg. and gu. Waldegrave.

Per pale arg. and gu. a bull pass. counterch. Coles.

Per pale arg. and gu. a griffin segreant counterch. within a bord. engr. or. Ridout.

Per pale arg. and sa. within a bord. of the same engr. and counterch. a lion ramp. or. Champneys, of Orchardley.

Per pale az. and gu. Fleet or Walsgrave.

Per pale az. and gu. a lion ramp. or. Oulton.

Per pale—*continued.*

Per pale az. and gu. three lions ramp. two and one arg. Powel.

Per pale az. and or a sun in splendour counterch. St. Clere.

Per pale indented gu. and arg. four lions ramp. counterch. Elsworth.

Per pale gu. and az. a lion ramp. arg. Rosewell.

Per pale gu. and az. three lions ramp. arg. Jones, of Stowey.

Per pale or and arg. a wyvern ramp. vert. Wilkins.

Per pale gu. and az. a chev. engr. or betw. three lions ramp. arg. Hoskyns.

Per pale indented gu. and vert a chev. or. Heytesbury.

Per pale indented or and vert a chev. gu. Hungerford.

Per pale or and gu. a lion pass. counterch. Place.

Per pale or and sa. a chev. betw. three griffins pass. counterch. Eveleigh.

Per pale sa. and erm. an eagle displ. or. Goodman.

Per pale vert and az.

Per pale on a chev. three escallops King (Bp).

Three Pales. Arg. three pales gu. on a canton sa. a spur or. Knight.

Or three pallets gu. within a bord. az. bezantée. Basset.

Paly of six. Paly of six arg. and az. over all a bend gu. Ansley or Annesley.

Paly of six arg. and sa. six cross-croslets or. Gould.

Paly of six erm. and gu. over all a lion pass. or. Malet (Antient).

Paly of six or and az. on a fesse gu. three mullets with six points of the first. Clambow.

Paly of six or and gu. (or or and az.). De Gournay.

Paly wavy of six or and gu. Moleyns.

Paly of six or and gu. over all on a bend sa. three mullets or. Elton.

Paly of eight. Paly of eight sa. and arg. per fesse counterch. St. Barbe.

Paly unnumbered. Paly arg. (or ?) and az. on a chief of the first an eagle displ. with two necks sa. Court.

Paly arg. and sa. two fleurs-de-lis counterch. Ayleward.

Paschal Lamb. The Paschal Lamb. Axbridge, borough of.

Pheon. Az. a pheon arg. within a bord. or charged with eight torteaux. Sharp.

Pile. Or a pile gu. Chandos.

On a pile. Arg. on a pile gu. a chev. betw. three cross-croslets of the field. Dawe.

Two piles. Erm. two piles sa. Holles.

Quarterly. Quarterly arg. and gu. de Sulleny or Salignac.

Quarterly arg. and sa. Bovyll.

Quarterly arg. and sa. (or gu.) on a bend gu. (or sa.) three fleurs-de-lis or. Ryall.

Quarterly erm. and gu. a chev. fretty or. Touchet, Lord Audley.

Quarterly gu. and arg. a pale fusilly vert. Dixon ?

Quarterly gu. and az. per fesse indented three lions ramp. arg. Medlycott.

Quarterly gu. and az. in pale three lionels couch. or in chief three fleurs-de-lis of the third.

Quarterly or and az. four stags statant (trippant ?) counterch. Lloyd, of Bradenham Ho, near Wycombe, co. Bucks.

Quarterly or and az. four eagles erect counterch. Robyns.

Quarterly or and gu. over all a bend arg. (sa.) Clavering.

Quarterly or and gu. a saltire fretty counterch. Essexe.

Quarterly sa. and or, a bend arg. Langton.

Quarterly per fesse indented arg. and az. (sometimes in first quarter a mullet gu.) Acton.

Reptiles. Vert three adders erect or. Hassell ?

Roundels. ( ) ten plates; another ten torteaux ; sometimes with the addition of a lion ramp. De Babington.

( ) three roundels ( ) Bradney ?

Arg. ten torteaux in pile. Gifford.

Arg. three torteaux a label of three points az. Tristram.

Or three torteaux. Courtenay.

Arg. ten torteaux, four, three, two, one. Zouch.

Roundels between. Az. three bezants betw. five cross-croslets or. Coffin.

On roundels. Arg. three torteaux having on each as many chevronels (or two chevronels) of the last. Carent.

Saltire. Arg. a salt gu. Neville ?

Az. a salt. or. Wells (See of)

Erm. a salt. engr. gu. Desmond.

Arg. a salt gu. St. Patrick.

Or a salt. engr. sa. Botetourt or Tremayne.

Or a salt. engr. sa. Botetourt

Vert. a salt. engr. arg. Hawley.

Per salt. arg. and gu. (Per pale erm. and gu. a salt. counterch.) Fitzstephen.

Saltire and in chief. Arg. a salt. sa. on a chief gu. three lions ramp. or. Baker.

Arg. a salt. sa. on a chief of the second five escallop shells erm. Baker.

Per salt. sa. and arg. in each of the chief and base of the sa. part three trefoils or. Devicke or Deviocke ?

Saltire between. Arg. a salt. engr. betw. four roses gu. seeded or. Napier.

Saltire between—*continued.*

    Az. a salt. or. betw. four cross-croslets fitchée arg. Russ.

    Az. a salt. voided betw. four spears erect or. Harbin, of Newton.

    Gu. a salt. betw. four leopards' faces. Ansell.

    Gu. a salt. vaire betw. four mullets arg. Hill.

On a saltire. Arg. on a salt. az. an escallop or. York.

    Arg. on a salt. engr. sa. nine annulets or. Leeke.

Scaling ladder. A scaling ladder. Stoke-Courcy priory.

    Gu. a scaling ladder betw. six cross-croslets arg. Tripp.

Shell. Vert. a nautilus or.

Spurs. Two spurs leathered.

Square. Gu. within a bord. erm. a square arg. (gu. a fesse couped and bord. erm). Chamberlain.

Stirrups. Az. three stirrups or within a bord. engr. arg. Gifford, of Wilts.

Sugar-loaves. Sa. three sugar-loaves arg. in chief a doctor's cap. Sugar.

Sun. Or a sun radiated gu. Hayes.

Sword. Gu. a sword in pale sa. (ppr.) Dymock.

Sword—*continued.*

    Two swords in salt. Byflet ?

    Sa. three swords in pile arg. pomels and hilts or. Poulet, Poulett or Pawlet.

    Sa. two swords in salt. arg. betw. four fleurs-de-lis or a bordure erm. Abarough or Barough, of Dicheat.

Tree. Or a tree vert supported by a greyhound sejant sa. collared and chained of the first. Wood.

Trivet. Arg. a trivet (or three trivets) sa. Trivet.

Vaire. Vaire arg. and az. Beauchamp.

Water bougets. Arg. three water bougets or. Boucher.

Wells. Three wells. de Coriwell.

Wheels. Arg. three Catherine-wheels two and one gu. Wheeler.

Whirlpool. Arg. a whirlpool or gurges az. Gorges, of Wraxall (antient).

Wings. Arg. a pair of wings conjoined gu. Fitzpayne.

    A pair of wings conjoined in lure arg. Reigni or Reyney. (Adopted by Paulet or Poulett.)

    Gu. a pair of wings conjoined arg. debruised by a bend az. Kentisbere.

    Gu. two wings conjoined. Seymour.

Lightning Source UK Ltd.
Milton Keynes UK
05 January 2011

165201UK00004B/19/P